D1427667

Freedom in the World

The findings of the *Comparative Survey of Freedom* and the Map of Freedom include events up to 1 January 1996.

Freedom in the World
The Annual Survey of Political Rights & Civil Liberties
1995-1996

Freedom House Survey Team

Adrian Karatnycky
Survey Coordinator

Jill Crawford
Charles Graybow
Christopher Kean
Thomas R. Lansner
Douglas W. Payne
Arch Puddington
Leonard R. Sussman
George Zarycky

Roger Kaplan
General Editor

Freedom House

First published in 1996.

Cover design and maps by Emerson Wajdowicz Studios, N.Y.C.

The Library of Congress has catalogued this serial title as follows:

Freedom in the world / —1978-
New York : Freedom House, 1978-
v. : map; 25 cm.—(Freedom House Book)
Annual.
ISSN 0732-6610=Freedom in the World.
1. Civil rights—Periodicals. I. R. Adrian Karatnycky, et al.   I. Series.
JC571.F66 323.4'05-dc 19   82-642048
AACR 2   MARC-S
Library of Congress   [84101]
ISBN   0-932088-86-4 (pbk.)
          0-932088-87-2 (cloth)

Distributed by arrangement with:

University Press of America, Inc.
4720 Boston Way
Lanham, MD 20706

3 Henrietta Street
London WC2E 8LU England

Contents

Foreword

Freedom in the World is an evaluation of political rights and civil liberties in the world's nations and related territories, now numbering 191 and 57 respectively, that Freedom House provides on an annual basis.

Freedom House is a nonprofit organization based in New York that monitors political rights and civil liberties around the world. Established in 1941, Freedom House believes the effective advocacy of human rights at home and abroad must be grounded in fundamental democratic values and principles.

Freedom House first began to evaluate political rights and civil liberties during the 1950s, when racial violence increased in the United States. The first year-end review of freedom was completed in 1955. During those early years, the project was called the Balance Sheet of Freedom, and later the Annual Survey of the Progress of Freedom. By the late 1960s, the Freedom House Board of Trustees felt there was a need to create a single standard by which to measure and record the development of freedom around the world.

When Freedom House's *Comparative Survey of Freedom* was established in the early 1970s, democracy was in a perilous condition in many states and on every continent: Spain, Portugal and Greece were under military rule; the world's largest democracy, India, was sliding toward martial law; an American president faced the possibility of impeachment; Africa was torn by both factional strife and racial conflict; and the prospects for liberalization—not to say democratization—in Eastern Europe, Latin America and Asia were dim. By the 1980s this dispiriting picture had changed and we witnessed a decade of unprecedented gains in democratization and freedom in much of the world. The years of 1993 and 1994, however, revealed the fragility of many of those gains, as they were undercut by corruption, interfactional feuding, ethnic rivalry, open conflict, economic stress and citizen dissatisfaction.

The *Survey* project has continued to develop over the years, being incorporated in the late 1970s into *Freedom in the World*, where it is now complemented by regional essays and country-by-country reports. In 1989 it became a year-long effort produced by our regional experts, consultants, and human rights specialists. As the resources listed at the back of this book attest, the *Survey* acquires its information from a wide range of diverse sources.

Freedom House has become known, over the years, as a dependable and fair advocate for those deprived of civil liberties and political rights. Because of that record, it has the privilege of being the recipient of information provided by many human rights activists, journalists, editors, and political leaders from around the world. The transmission of this information often exacts a high price from those who send it, as they frequently risk endangering their livelihoods, their health and lives, and sometimes the lives of their families. Much of the material in this book is, therefore, the contribution of heroic figures, many of whose names will go unremarked in the history of our times.

Western journalists have a long tradition of putting themselves in physical danger to obtain information, of finding ingenious ways to penetrate almost inaccessible places. They do this today in some places where there are few if any human rights advocates. We have benefited from their reports from areas such as Somalia, Bosnia, Rwanda, and Chechnya. They have brought back, or sent back, reports of horrendous human rights abuses, often humanizing gruesome reports that statistics seem to deaden by giving the names of particular families and individuals who have deprived of their basic rights.

We have been pleased to note and to benefit from the increasing number of human rights organizations forming in Africa and Asia. Operating under the most trying conditions, economic and political, these nongovernmental organizations (NGOs) face the same obstacles that other human rights organizations know so well. But in addition they must make the case for the protection of individual human rights in political cultures that would often subordinate them to the demands of the state, as those demands are interpreted by autocratic or dictatorial leaders. Even as they struggle to defend their fellow citizens, they must combat charges that they are operating under the sway of foreign influences, specifically those from the West.

Throughout the year Freedom House personnel regularly conduct fact-finding missions to gain more in-depth knowledge of the vast political transformations affecting our world. During these week-to month-long investigations, we make every effort to meet a cross-section of political parties and associations, human rights monitors, religious figures, representatives of both the private sector and trade union movement, academics and the appropriate security forces and insurgent movements where they exist.

During the past year, Freedom House staff traveled to Azerbaijan, Burkina Faso, Burma, Cameroon, Canada, Côte d'Ivoire, Cuba, East Timor, Egypt, Eritrea, France, Ghana, Indonesia, Japan, Mauritania, Nepal, Poland, Russia, Senegal, South Korea, Switzerland, Tanzania, Trinidad and Tobago, Uganda, Ukraine and the United Kingdom.

The *Survey* project team also consults a vast array of published source materials, ranging from the reports of other human rights organizations to often rare, regional newspapers and magazines.

This year's *Survey* team includes Adrian Karatnycky, the project coordinator, Jill Crawford, Charles Graybow, Christopher Kean, Thomas R. Lansner, Douglas W. Payne, Arch Puddington, Leonard R. Sussman and George Zarycky. The general editor of *Freedom in the World* is Roger Kaplan; the deputy editor and assistant editor are Mark Wolkenfeld and Pei C. Koay, respectively. This year's research assistants were Art Artman, Nelson DeSousa, Shahrzad Elghanayan, Harry Gamble and Sarah Gershman. Roger Kaplan is the editor of *Freedom Review*.

The *Survey* team gratefully acknowledges the expertise of specialists Anne Applebaum, Prof. Charles Gati, Kaku Kimura, Seth Lipsky, Richard Messick, Prof. John Micgiel, Dr. Alexander Motyl, Dr. Daniel Pipes and Prof. Arthur Waldron, as well as members of the *Survey* review team, Prof. Jeane Kirkpatrick, Dr. Joshua Muravchik, Dr. Francis Fukuyama and Prof. Seymour Martin Lipset.

Substantial support for the *Comparative Survey of Freedom* has been generously provided by The Pew Charitable Trusts, the Lynde & Harry Bradley Foundation, and the Smith Richardson Foundation.

The Comparative Survey of Freedom 1995-1996

Democracy and Despotism: Bipolarism Renewed? Adrian Karatnycky

After years of political volatility and strife that in several countries attained appalling levels of carnage, the world in 1995 cohered into radically divergent polities—generally free societies characterized by democratic governance and unfree societies characterized by arbitrary rule.

The good news is that many free societies are showing signs of increasing durability, as years of democratic rule and toleranfter years of political volatility and strife that in several countries attained appalling levels of carnage, the world in 1995 cohered into radically divergent polities—generally free societies characterized by democratic governance and unfree societies characterized by arbitrary rule.

The good news is that many free societies are showing signs of increasing durability, as years of democratic rule and tolerance are creating a stronger infrastructure of civil society, especially in the post-Communist countries of Central Europe and in Latin America.

But major obstacles to the expansion of freedom and democracy are emerging in the form of: a) ideologies that promote authoritarian market transitions—most prevalent in East Asia; b) "red-brown" alliances between Communists and the economic nomenklatura on the one hand and ultranationalist and neo-fascist groupings on the other—most prominently in Russia; c) radical Islamism.

As the year ends, there are 76 Free countries whose citizens enjoy a broad range of political rights and civil liberties (the same number as last year); 62 Partly Free countries (61 last year), in which there are some constraints on political rights and civil liberties, and 53 Not Free countries (54 last year), in which basic rights are denied. One country, Mali, joined the ranks of Free, becoming the only predominantly Muslim state to achieve that status.

Three countries saw their political and civil rights improve enough to go from Not Free to Partly Free in the Freedom House ranking: Eritrea, Ethiopia and Tanzania. However, Bolivia, which underwent six months of emergency presidential rule, lost its Free ranking and is now Partly Free. Cambodia went from Partly Free to Not Free, as political violence against political parties and the media intensified and there were signs of growing consolidation of power by forces linked to the Khmer Rouge. Lebanon, which saw an undemocratic and indefinite extension of presidential power, also became Not Free.

1,114.5 million people (19.5 percent of the world's population) live in Free societies and have a broad range of political rights and civil liberties; 2,365.8 million persons (41.5 percent) live in Partly Free societies in which there are some constraints on basic rights as a consequence of government practice and as a result of insurgencies, politi-

Freedom in the World—1996

The population of the world this year is estimated at 5,701.5 billion persons, who reside in 191 sovereign states and 57 related territories—a total of 248 entities. The level of political rights and civil liberties as shown comparatively by the Freedom House Survey is:

Free: 1,114.5 billion (19.55 percent of the world's population) live in 76 of the states and in 44 of the related territories.

Partly Free: 2,365.8 billion (41.49 percent of the world's population) live in 62 of the states and 6 of the related territories.

Not Free: 2,221.2 billion (38.96percent of the world's population) live in 53 of the states and 8 of the related territories.

A Record of the Survey
(population in millions)

SURVEY DATE	FREE		PARTLY FREE		NOT FREE		WORLD POPULATION
January '81	1,613.0	(35.90%)	970.9	(21.60%)	1,911.9	(42.50%)	4,495.8
January '82	1,631.9	(35.86%)	916.5	(20.14%)	2,002.7	(44.00%)	4,551.1
January '83	1,665.1	(36.32%)	918.8	(20.04%)	2,000.2	(43.64%)	4,584.1
January '84	1,670.7	(36.00%)	1,074.8	(23.00%)	1,917.5	(41.00%)	4,663.0
January '85	1,671.4	(34.85%)	1,117.4	(23.30%)	2,007.0	(41.85%)	4,795.8
January '86	1,747.2	(36.27%)	1,121.9	(23.29%)	1,947.6	(40.43%)	4,816.7
January '87	1,842.5	(37.10%)	1,171.5	(23.60%)	1,949.9	(39.30%)	4,963.9
January '88	1,924.6	(38.30%)	1,205.4	(24.00%)	1,896.0	(37.70%)	5,026.0
January '89	1,992.8	(38.86%)	1,027.9	(20.05%)	2,107.3	(41.09%)	5,128.0
January '90	2,034.4	(38.87%)	1,143.7	(21.85%)	2,055.9	(39.28%)	5,234.0
January '91	2,088.2	(39.23%)	1,485.7	(27.91%)	1,748.7	(32.86%)	5,322.6
January '92	1,359.3	(25.29%)	2,306.6	(42.92%)	1,708.2	(31.79%)	5,374.2
January '93	1,352.2	(24.83%)	2,403.3	(44.11%)	1,690.4	(31.06%)	5,446.0
January '94	1,046.2	(19.00%)	2,224.4	(40.41%)	2,234.6	(40.59%)	5,505.2
January '95	1,119.7	(19.97%)	2,243.4	(40.01%)	2,243.9	(40.02%)	5,607.0
January '96	1,114.5	(19.55%)	2,365.8	(41.49%)	2.221.2	(38.96)	5.701.5

cal terrorism and rampant corruption; and 2,221.2 million people (39 percent of the world's population) live in Not Free societies.

Twenty-five countries registered significant gains in freedom without changing broad rating categories, while eight registered declines. Nearly half of these significant changes were in Africa, which in 1995 was the most politically volatile region in the world.

The most repressive states

Eighteen states received Freedom House's lowest rating—7 for political rights and 7 for civil liberties. The worst rated of these repressive states were Iraq, North Korea and Sudan. In the same category were Afghanistan, Bhutan, Burma, China, Cuba, Equatorial Guinea, Libya, Saudi Arabia, Somalia, Syria, Tajikistan, Turkmenistan, Uzbekistan and Vietnam. Nigeria was the sole new entrant into the ranks of the least free. There, a military dictatorship that seized power in 1993 capriciously executed Ken Saro-Wiwa and eight other human rights advocates of the rights of the Ogoni nationality. The swiftness of the verdict and the rigged judicial process were evidence that political terror masquerading as the rule of law has become commonplace under the military dictatorship.

Democracies on the rise

The rise in the number of formal democracies continued in 1995. This year's survey shows that there are now 117 democracies, with Moldova and the Kyrgyz Republic new entrants and the Dominican Republic re-entering the ranks of the world's democracies. This represents just over 61 percent of the world's 191 countries. From the perspective of a decade ago the gain is all the more impressive. Ten years ago, less than 42 percent of the world's countries were formal democracies.

Today, 3.1 billion persons out of a world population of 5.7 billion live under democratically elected governments. While not yet a universal standard, democracy has deepening and widening roots in all parts of the world. Western Europe remains the most democratic region of the world, with 24 democracies representing 100 percent of the states in the region. Democracy predominates in

4 Gains in Freedom Changing Categories		
Countries	**1994**	**1995**
Eritrea	Not Free	Partly Free
Ethiopia	Not Free	Partly Free
Mali	Partly Free	Free
Tanzania	Not Free	Partly Free

3 Declines in Freedom Changing Categories		
Countries	**1994**	**1995**
Bolivia	Free	Partly Free
Cambodia	Partly Free	Not Free
Lebanon	Partly Free	No Free

the Americas, where there are 31 democratic polities among 35 countries (88.5 percent). Just six years after the collapse of the Berlin Wall and four years after the collapse of the USSR, there are now 19 democracies among the 27 countries of Central and Eastern Europe and the former Soviet Union (70 percent). There are 25 democracies among the 52 countries of the Asia/Pacific region (48 percent). The least deep roots for democracy are in Africa, where there are 18 democracies among the region's 53 countries (34 percent).

That 61 percent of all countries and nearly 55 percent of the world's population live under governments and legislatures elected in generally free and fair political processes represents a landmark shift. Today it is the expectation of the clear majority of citizens that their governments be accountable to them through regular elections. Such a broadening global consciousness does not guarantee full freedom, but it does create the basis for more free societies and for greater engagement by citizens in public affairs. Widening public democratic consciousness throughout the world, as well as growing expectations by the Western advanced industrial democracies that countries which receive significant aid should respect fundamental human rights and democratic procedures reinforces this trend.

Democracy and basic freedoms

Democracy is not synonymous with freedom. Of 117 democracies, 76 are Free, 40 democracies are Partly Free, and one democracy—war-ravaged Bosnia—is Not Free. Nevertheless it is significant that 34 of the democracies that are not rated Free are what Freedom House would call "high Partly Free countries," in which there is a substantial degree of freedom, as well as some measure of respect for basic human rights.

Many of the low-rated Partly Free democracies register an erosion of basic freedoms as a result of ethnically based insurgencies and terrorist movements, which destabilize free institutions. Still, even in war-torn and Not Free Bosnia, with over half its territory ethnically cleansed and ruled by indicted war criminals, the year-end prospect of peace holds open the possibility of a broad expansion of political rights and civil liberties.

Wars, insurgencies and the influence of military establishments in the political process are among the reasons why many democracies fail to observe or protect the basic rights of their citizens. Eight Partly Free democracies—and the sole Not Free Democracy, Bosnia—face insurgencies and military emergencies affecting parts of their territory. Ten Partly Free democracies are heavily influenced by a military that has intervened directly in taking state power. Other Partly Free democracies are dealing with past periods of dictatorship and totalitarian rule and do not have strong and vibrant nongovernmental structures of civil society and sufficiently strong private economic sectors, which are indicators of Free societies. With all their imperfections, democracies still represent the best terrain for the expansion of significant freedoms and so deserve to be the focus of Western aid and assistance efforts.

What accounts for the unprecedented phenomenon of democratic governance? In part, it is the growing power of the global communications revolution, which has strengthened international public awareness of global trends toward democracy. Another important factor has been the growing pressure of the international community, particularly donor nations from among the advanced industrial democracies, which increasingly are pressing governments to hold free and fair elections as a condition of eligibility for development assistance.

> ## The 18 Worst Rated Countries*
>
> Afghanistan
> Bhutan
> Burma
> China
> Cuba
> Equatorial Guinea
> Iraq
> Korea, North
> Libya
> Nigeria
> Saudi Arabia
> Somalia
> Sudan
> Syria
> Tajikistan
> Turkmenistan
> Uzbekistan
> Vietnam
>
> ## The 5 Worst Rated Related Territories
>
> East Timor (Indonesia)
> Kashmir (India)
> Kosovo (Yugoslavia)
> Tibet (China)
> West Papua (Indonesia)
>
> * For explanation of Survey Methodology see p. 531

Even in strife-torn Algeria, presidential elections in November 1995—though not completely open and free—offered voters a meaningful range of political options. No less important, a high voter turnout became a means for expressing public support for democratic solutions to political differences and represented a repudiation of Islamist-inspired mass terror, as well as military repression of non-violent opponents of the regime, which in the last four years has claimed as many as 50,000 lives.

The consequences of ethnic cleansing

The early 1990s were characterized by rising interethnic carnage that claimed hundreds of thousands of lives each year. Violence on such a scale appears to have abated in 1995. The phenomena of ethnocide and ethnic cleansing, fed by virulent forms of xenophobic nationalism, declined as 1995 drew to a close, in part because the proponents of the politics of group hatred had achieved their horrible goal and in part because of growing international pressures to stop such practices. In 1995, ethnic cleansing and ethnocide abated even as they left a horrible legacy in Bosnia and Rwanda.

In other settings which had seen recent massive atrocities, the death toll drastically declined as the year drew to an end. In Chechnya, a war prosecuted by Russia,

25 Gains in Freedom Without Changing Categories		8 Declines in Freedom Without Changing Categories
Algeria	Lithuania	Armenia
Angola	Mauritania	Bangladesh
Benin	Mozambique	Belarus
Botswana	Nicaragua	Cameroon
Brunei	Philippines	Columbia
Djibouti	Poland	Kenya
Dominica	Rwanda	Kyrgyz Republic
Estonia	St. Kitts and Nevis	Nigeria
Georgia	Seychelles	
Ghana	South Africa	
Ireland	Thailand	
Japan	Uganda	
Latvia		

which had claimed as many as 50,000 lives, most of them noncombatant Chechens, was winding down, leaving a legacy of destruction and hundreds of thousands of refugees. In 1995, ethnic strife and open warfare escaped the predominantly Russian Transdnister region of Moldova, where the indigenous population sought secession. Similarly, the conflicts between Georgia and separatist Abkhazia and South Ossetia and Georgia were kept in check this year, leaving in their wake thousands dead and over a quarter million refugees. A cease-fire between an ethnically cleansed Nagorno-Karabakh and Azerbaijan held as the year ended, but years of conflict between Armenians and Azeris had resulted in nearly a million refugees from both nationalities, who continued to live in uncertainty and poverty.

Despite an end to much ethnically based carnage, the new year holds out the prospect that the international community must now deal with the toll of ethnic conflicts— massive refugee populations and a legacy of fear, suspicion and hatred that can be a breeding ground of future conflicts.

In recent years, ethnic hatreds have not been simply spontaneous expressions of age-old atavistic hatreds. Most major interethnic civil wars and violent separatist movements have been aided and abetted by states and organized political movements. It is increasingly clear that when the volatile power of states merges with the passion of ethnic kinship and nationalism, conflict spins out of control. In 1995, it was international pressure against states engaged in such reckless and dangerous interventions that helped bring the promise of an end to some of the worst instances of ethnocide, most notably in Bosnia.

In 1995, a combination of international engagement and fatigue by warring parties had deepened progress toward peace and reconciliation in Northern Ireland. International pressure, internal opposition and war fatigue were likewise factors that pressured Russia to back off from the indiscriminate prosecution of a murderous war.

In part absorbed by an intense political struggle culminating with a 17 December parliamentary election and by the debilitating effects of the ill-conceived war in Chechnya, Russia—which had intervened actively in support of ethnic separatist forces in a number of new independent post-Soviet states—retreated from such overtly destabilizing interventions in 1995.

Russia also began to play a more responsible role in the Crimea, a peninsula that is part of Ukraine. There, despite occasional provocative statements by Russian parliamentary leaders, Russian Prime Minister Viktor Chernomyrdin and his Ukrainian counterpart, Prime Minister Yevhen Marchuk, sought to resolve differences over the disposition of the Black Sea Fleet. There was little evidence of the Russian state's efforts to foment separatism among Crimea's majority Russian population as Russia and Ukraine sought to rebuild economic links severed after the collapse of the USSR.

Yet, ominously, even as the Russian foreign and defense ministries were behaving with greater restraint in the border countries Russian officials call the Near Abroad, a chorus of voices in the Russian political establishment raised the issue of the reunification of the former Soviet states, and disparaged the fragile independence of many post-Soviet states. In the Russian parliamentary campaign of November-December 1995, calls for the restoration of a single state, the military-political unity of the peoples of the USSR and the legislative renunciation of the agreement that led to the USSR's demise were made by several major parties. A powerful political movement—the Congress of Russian Communities—campaigned on the basis of efforts to reunite the countries of historic Russian settlement into a single state.

While progress could be seen in ethnic conflict zones in Central Europe and the former USSR, there remained a number of

The Global Trend		
Free Countries	Partly Free Countries	Not Free Countries
1986 56	56	55
1993 75	73	38
1994 72	63	55
1995 76	61	54
1996 76	62	53

settings in which ethnic and other communal conflicts continued to rage. In Burundi, ethnically motivated killings were estimated to have claimed over 10,000 lives in 1995. In India (especially in the territory of Jammu and Kashmir) and in Pakistan interethnic and religious strife continued to destabilize democracies. The Kurdish struggle for independence—led in large measure by the terrorist Kurdish Workers Party (PKK)—coupled with the Turkish government's military and security measures to hold on to Turkish Kurdistan, continued to constrict the political rights and civil liberties of all Turkish citizens.

In Sri Lanka an ethnic separatist movement led by the guerrilla army of the Tamil Liberation Tigers as well as vigorous efforts at counter-insurgency by the island country's authorities, had resulted in thousands killed and nearly half a million refugees. Despite year-end successes by Sri Lankan authorities in capturing the former Tamil stronghold of Jaffna, the ethnically based struggle shows little sign of peaceful resolution. In Sudan, one of the world's most repressive governments continued to prosecute an ethnically based war that has displaced over a million people.

Regional variations

Democratic and Free societies can be found within societies at all levels of economic development, among different ethnic and racial groupings, all major world religions and in all parts of the world. It is, nevertheless, instructive to look at the state of freedom and democratic governance from a broader, regional perspective.

Asia/Pacific

The vast majority of the world's citizens (nearly three in five) live in the Asia/Pacific region, which extends from Turkey in the West to Japan and the Pacific Island countries in the East. Of the 52 countries in the Asia/Pacific region, there are 25 formal democracies. Out of a total Asia/Pacific population of 3.4 billion, 47 percent, or 1.6 billion, live in democracies. Of the 52 Asian states, 15 are Free, 16 are Partly Free, and 21 are Not Free. But only 6 percent of the population of the Asia/Pacific region lives in Free societies. Forty-three percent of the population lives in Partly Free regions, and 1.73 billion inhabitants of Asia (51 percent of the population) lives in Not Free societies.

In Asia, a combination of residual Marxist-Leninist one-party states—North Korea, Vietnam, Laos and China—as well as the resilience of the Marxist-Leninist Khmer Rouge in Cambodia contributed to the high proportion of Not Free countries. A reactionary trend in East Asia is represented by the effort of Singapore's leaders to justify authoritarian transitions to free markets. To some degree this approach can be termed Neo-Confucianism, but it has intellectual pretensions of relevance as a model for rapid economic development well beyond Asia.

By contrast, in the Philippines a democratic government led by Fidel Ramos, a hero of the democratic transition, is seeking to prove that democratic change can proceed and be a catalyst for free market reform and rapid growth. The outcome of this debate is important not only to the fate of democracy in Asia, but to the appeal of authoritarian paths to market reform in other parts of the world.

The Islamic world

Societies in which Islam is the traditional religion of more than 50 percent of the population span a vast expanse from Africa to Indonesia. They include the North African states, the Arab world, the Turkic peoples of Eurasia and some large countries of South Asia.

The relationship of Islam and democracy has been the subject of analytic research and keen debate. The Freedom House *Survey* offers an opportunity to assess this widely divergent group of societies, cultures and peoples.

While Islamist movements have failed to seize state power outside Iran and Sudan, their growing popularity and their willingness to engage in mass terrorism have destabilized many states—including several democracies. Islamism is on the march in a number of Asian countries, giving them a pretext to adopt increasingly tough police measures that enhance the power of the military and the security apparatus. States confronting Islamist mobilization frequently take steps to dampen Islamist appeal by adopting certain aspects of shariah, or Islamic law, in their political systems. The result is a contraction of political rights and civil liberties, notably for women.

Among states with a Muslim majority, there is one Free state—democratic Mali; 13 Partly Free states; and 29 Not Free states. There are seven predominantly Muslim democracies. In addition to Mali, these formal democracies are Albania, Bangladesh, the Kyrgyz Republic, Niger, Pakistan and Turkey. There are no democracies among the 16 majority Arab countries, four of which are rated as Partly Free—Jordan, Kuwait, Morocco and Lebanon.

Significantly, of the 18 states judged most repressive by Freedom House, 11 are states with a majority Muslim population.

The Americas

Among the 35 countries in the Americas there are 19 Free states (inhabited by 48 percent of the region's population of 773.7 million), 15 Partly Free States (51 percent of the population), and one Not Free state—Cuba (a little over 1 percent of the population). Democratic values are predominant in the region; of the 35 states, 31 are democracies, with a combined population of 639.6 million—83 percent of the regional total. There are two dominant party states—Antigua and Barubuda and Mexico; one—Peru—which is a civilian-military hybrid ruled by an authoritarian president; and one—Cuba—which is a Communist one-party state.

In the region, gains in freedom this year were registered by Dominica, Nicaragua and St. Kitts and Nevis. Colombia registered a decline in its level of freedom but the most marked decline was registered by Bolivia, which shifted from Free to Partly Free. Yet despite the decade's important gains for democracy and freedom, there are signs that some transitions remain very fragile.

Africa

Africa, which in recent years had been ravaged by waves of ethnocide, showed the highest degree of volatility of any region of the world. One country advanced from Partly Free to Free, and four others advanced in status from Not Free to Partly Free. A further twelve African countries showed significant gains in freedom and three registered significant declines. South Africa's and Namibia's democratic transitions continued on track. Mali's entry into the ranks of Free countries was an important signpost, as were significant advances that led Eritrea and Ethiopia to exit the ranks of the Not Free and to join the ranks of the Partly Free countries. On the negative side, the Nigerian government's brutal execution of ethnic rights advocates marked that military dictatorship's descent into the ranks of the most repressive states joining Equitorial Guinea, Libya, Somalia and Sudan as the continent's worst.

In North Africa, modest progress was also reflected in Algeria's flawed election, which was nevertheless important as a referendum on the willingness of the vast majority of that country's citizens to reject violent Islamist terrorism and military violence in favor of the ballot box.

Today there are 9 Free countries in Africa (representing approximately 10 percent of the continent's population of 721.8 million). There are 20 Partly Free countries (accounting for approximately 34 percent of the population). And there are 24 countries that are rated Not Free (with 55 percent of the region's population). Of the 53 countries in Africa, 18 are formal democracies inhabited by 18 percent of the continent's population.

Western Europe

All 24 countries in Western Europe are democracies and all of Western Europe's population of 387.6 million lives in freedom, except for the Partly Free related territory of Northern Ireland. In 1995, several of these European democracies confronted corrosive problems. Corruption wracked Italy's political system, enveloping successive waves of the country's most prominent political leaders. Xenophobia, and significant support for neo-fascist and ultra-nationalist movements exist, especially in France, where they have a strong base (15-20 percent) among voters, and to a diminishing degree in Germany and Austria. In France, terrorist acts linked to fundamentalist Muslims brought Algeria's civil strife across the Mediterranean. On the plus side, significant progress toward greater democratic stability was registered in the Anglo-Irish accord and negotiations between Sinn Fein and the British authorities.

Central and Eastern Europe and the Former Soviet Union

What is the legacy of post-Communist collapse, six years after the fall of the Berlin Wall and four years after the collapse of the Soviet Union? As 1995 drew to a close, the balance sheet showed that there are 9 Free countries (representing 20 percent of the region's population of 414.7 million). There were 13 states rated Partly Free and inhabited by 63 percent of the region's population. And there were seven states rated Not Free in which 17 percent of the region's population live. None of the countries in the Commonwealth of Independent States was rated Free.

The balance sheet of formal democracy was somewhat more encouraging in this post-Communist expanse. Of the region's 27 states, 19 were formal democracies, in which 80 percent of the region's population lived.

The year saw worrying trends represented by a deterioration of political rights in Armenia, the deterioration of human rights and political freedoms in Belarus, and by the consolidation of one-party strongman rule by Azerbaijan's Heidar Aliyev. Three states in the region—Tajikistan, Turkmenistan and Uzbekistan—were among the 18 most repressive countries.

While Russia remained a Partly Free democracy with a resilient press, an alarming trend has emerged within the structure of social and economic life. Increasingly, Russia's economic life was dominated by major energy and industrial corporations, which had been privatized by the nomenklatura that managed them and continued to enjoy powerful privileges.

By contrast, starved of available credit, a nascent private sector of small business and small scale entrepreneurs had limited success. It is uncertain whether this independent sector will be able to resist the attacks on the private sector in economics and on independent civic life that is likely to come from the increasingly popular political forces represented by resurgent Communists and hardline nationalists.

Certainly, both the private sector in business and independent civic groups are more powerful than they have been at any time in Russian history, holding out the hope that Russia's democratic transition may endure, despite the setbacks by democrats that are predicted at the polls.

Recent electoral victories by ex-Communists in Poland, as well as earlier victories by the ex-Communist left in Hungary, Slovakia, Bulgaria and Lithuania, mark an important comeback by forces that trace their roots to the Communist past. Communist parties did well in elections in Belarus and Kyrgyzstan, and the Communists and their allies won a majority of seats in Russia's recent parliamentary elections.

But while gains by forces associated with the old order were cause for concern, many of these parties—particularly in Central Europe—had embraced social democratic solutions and posed little threat to democracy. More worrying were regional trends that demonstrated growing links between ex-Communist parties and leaders with ultra-nationalists and fascists. In Russia the Communist party is building a solid alliance with ultra-nationalist groupings including the Congress of Russian Communities, whose leader, Gennady Zyuganov, embraces traditional fascist rhetoric, placing the interests of the nation above class differences or rights of citizens. A similar trend has emerged in a new political alliance between Romania's ruling party and three neo-fascist and ultra-nationalist parties. And in Slovakia, Prime Minister Vladimir Meciar exploits Slovak nationalism by attacking the rights of the Hungarian ethnic minority. Serbia's President Slobodan Milosevic initially made common cause with ultra-nationalist proponents of Greater Serbia, whom he has now discarded after having attained political dominance.

With the appeal of communism waning, Marxist-Leninist movements have abandoned their traditional calls for class struggle and are increasingly advocating extreme nationalism, often attached to xenophobic and anti-Western sentiments. These factors are contributing to long-term problems that promise to afflict transitions to democracy in many countries of the former Communist world.

U.S. policy and freedom in the world

This year's *Survey* shows that freedom's expansion has slowed even as democratic states increased in number. The *Survey* also shows that some forty formal democracies confront a broad range of problems that threaten their political rights and civil liberties.

How well have the U.S. and other advanced democracies responded to this democratic challenge of the 1990s?

Without question, in 1995 U.S. foreign policy helped contribute to a number of openings for the expansion and strengthening of freedom and democracy. In 1995, U.S. leadership was essential to the peace negotiated among the governments of Croatia, Serbia and Bosnia. U.S. diplomacy also played an important role in pressing for further advances in relations between Israel and the Palestine Liberation Organization and in the peaceful resolution to the conflict in Northern Ireland.

Yet while U.S. diplomacy was vigorous this year, U.S. efforts to strengthen democratic transitions around the world revealed a more mixed picture. One complicating factor in U.S. efforts to stabilize democratic gains were the growing constraints on foreign aid, public diplomacy and democracy-building programs.

At a time when worrying trends were emerging in Russia, Belarus, Central Asia, Azerbaijan and Slovakia, cutbacks in funding in such programs as the National Endowment for Democracy and efforts to gut an already drastically pared-down Radio Free Europe/Radio Liberty appeared short-sighted. There was little sign of momentum in NATO's expansion to embrace the democracies of East-Central Europe, a process the region's democratically elected leaders argue is essential to preserving and deepening democratic gains.

Also, growing Western economic engagement with the world's remaining one-party Communist dictatorships—especially China and Vietnam—coupled with a dampening of U.S. and Western efforts to promote democratic values and ideas in these closed societies, left the impression that the West has muted its moral condemnation of Marxist-Leninist regimes and their violations of fundamental human rights. In this regard, the administration's failure to live up to its promise to launch a vigorous Asian Democracy Radio was an important failure that is likely to have long-term consequences for the evolution of the closed societies of China, Burma, Laos and Vietnam.

At the same time, U.S. foreign aid continued to provide technical assistance to strengthen the economies of a number of tyrannies, most notably in Central Asia and Indonesia. In a period of diminishing foreign aid resources, such assistance could have been more constructively targeted to the many economically strapped countries that are playing by the democratic rules of the game.

Amid drastic cuts in funding for programs that strengthen democratic values abroad and provide objective information about closed societies and democratic values, democratic activists in unfree societies are increasingly going to be denied a lifeline of needed information, education and resources to pursue their struggles. One remedy to declining resources should be an effort to redirect foreign aid—including a vast array of developmental, environmental, economic reform, and democracy efforts—to transitional democracies, while demonstrably denying such assistance to countries that violate human rights and do not play by democratic rules.

One unfortunate consequence of the new inward turn, particularly within the Congress, is a weakening of America's democratic voice abroad because of a cutback at the Voice of America and drastically scaled-back public diplomacy programs of the U.S. Information Agency.

A U.S. foreign policy focused on the priority of promoting democracy that is mindful of key strategic goals should be the basis for a broad-based bipartisan foreign policy consensus. Such a consensus is above all necessary if the U.S.—as the world's sole global power—is to constructively project its influence internationally in an increasingly multipolar world. Yet there is little evidence as yet that such a consensus is emerging. And there is little sign that there is a good understanding by the broader public of the strategic importance to U.S. national security interests of such peaceful mechanisms as information, education and foreign aid to support market reforms and privatization. Instead, if one is to judge by congressional debates and the public mood, foreign aid and public diplomacy spending is on a downward trajectory for years to come.

It may take some major political setbacks in key countries to reverse this short-sighted and insular mood. China's increasingly menacing behavior and its growing economic and military strength—absent fundamental democratic reform—may serve as one catalyst. Russia's turn away from Western democratic values and toward an alliance of Communists and ultra-nationalists, which may culminate in the election of a new president in June 1996, may be another.

Adrian Karatnycky, president of Freedom House, is coordinator of the Comparative Survey of Freedom.

Central Europe:
Nice Guys Finish Last Anne Applebaum

In 1993, at the time of the last Polish parliamentary elections, I happened to be in Poland, staying near the small village of Wystep, in the western part of the country. In the middle of that village sits a shop: a new shop, a private shop, a shop which did not exist five years ago. Out of curiosity, I asked the shopkeeper, a classic small businesswoman, exactly the sort of the person who brought Mrs. Thatcher to power in Britain, for whom she was going to vote.

"The Communists, of course," she replied immediately. She meant, of course, the reformed Communists, now called the SLD, or the Union of the Left Democrats. "People don't have enough money, and the Communists have promised to make them rich. If they have more money, they will buy more things in my shop."

Given what is usually written in Western newspapers about the resurgence of former Communist parties all over the former Soviet bloc, this was certainly not what one would have expected to hear. The considered opinion of most Western analysts, and many Western diplomats, is that voters who choose to vote for parties which are direct heirs to former Communist parties in Central and Eastern Europe are doing so purely out of nostalgia for the past.

But the story of the Wystep shopkeeper illustrates, better than any piece of political theory could do, that this is not quite the case. People vote for former Communists for a wide variety of reasons, some, indeed, connected to nostalgia; no doubt the Russian pensioners who support the Communist Party of Gennady Zyuganov, for example, are doing so out of loyalty to the past. But what is more important, and more interesting, is that many people, especially in Central Europe, also vote for former Communists because they represent success: more than any other identifiable social group in Eastern Europe, they are seen to have achieved the most in the new regime.

In most of Central Europe the Communists are prosperous and they promise to make people prosperous. They have come to represent a rising social class in Central Europe; or perhaps it is better to say a rising ruling class. Marxist Leninism is dead: but the most characteristic feature of post-Communist societies is that the people who ran them ten years ago continue to exist and prosper in democracies just as they did before. While the causes of this change are well known, there has been less written about what this might mean—and obviously, the meaning is different in different countries. But although general speculation will not explain the politics of every country in the region, it may help outline patterns which will become more visible in years to come.

What's a former Communist?

What do I mean by "former Communists"? The Polish politician Jaroslaw Kaczynski has said, quite rightly, that most of the 2 million-odd members of the old Party never really mattered in politics. But the inner core, of about 100,000, do have, and have always had, a strong sense of identity, not unlike the class identity of, say, the British aristocracy. They have been to the same schools, the same universities, the same higher institutes of Marxist-Leninism. They have jobs in government, heavy industry, the army, the secret police and the media; they recognize one another, as does any ruling class in any country, through dress, accent, mutual friends and manner of speech.

Of course, not all former Communists are still involved directly in politics. Edward Wnuk-Lipinski, a Polish sociologist, recently carried out a study, tracking the careers of several hundred top nomenklatura—officials in the government and bureaucracy—from 1988 to 1993. He discovered that over half of the Poles had become top executives in the private sector; in Hungary the number was about 60 percent. Simple observation will suffice to confirm that high-ranking, former Communist government officials dominate the banks of Central and Eastern Europe; in many countries, they also dominate a large chunk of the media, especially regional media. They do not necessarily dominate retailing, small services or low-level trading; Poland, for example, has experienced a genuine small business boom, which has little or nothing to do with the influence of former Communists. It is also still possible, in many East European countries, including Russia, to start with very little money and, with very few connections, to build a small business out of nothing.

But the "inner core" of former Communist politicians still dominate the state bureaucracy, and much more importantly, they play a role in what might be called the "concessionary capitalist" economy: that part of the private sector, enormous in Central Europe, which still, in one way or another, lives off state subsidies, state contracts, state largesse. Former Communists who gained control of businesses through corrupt privatization deals—and there are many—are concessionary capitalists. Friends of the old regime who were able to start companies with soft loans, guaranteed by the government, are also concessionary capitalists. Those who have a quicker and easier access to licenses because their friends in the mayor's office are concessionary capitalists, too.

To explain this last point, a critical one, it is much better to use anecdotes than statistics. One of the best examples of the workings of "concessionary capitalism" emerged during the most recent Polish presidential election campaign. About halfway through the campaign, the Polish press uncovered the existence of an insurance company, Polisa S.A., which has a curious ownership structure. Formerly a so-called cooperative—effectively a state-owned company—it was privatized, and is now partly owned by various state institutions and agencies, which help give the company the credibility it needs to make profits. The rest of its shares were meant to have been publicly traded. However, it has also emerged that some of its shares were sold off privately—and illegally. About $65,000 worth of Polisa shares (quite a lot in Polish terms) turn out to be owned by the wife of Alexander Kwasniewski, the ex-Politburo candidate of the SLD, who eventually won the election (of whom more later). Another $100,000 worth are owned by the wife of Jozef Oleksy, the ex-Communist prime minister. Other shareholders include two former Communist deputy prime ministers, as well as a former Communist finance minister and a former Communist party first secretary. Because the "private" shares were sold illegally, the company's trading in shares was suspended by the Warsaw Stock Exchange;

curiously, Mr. Kwasniewski failed to declare his wife's interest in the company in his parliamentary register of interests, not that that prevented him from enjoying a surprising amount of support among the Polish public.

The story of Polisa is typical, in that it demonstrates how concessionary capitalism operates through the mechanism of nomenklatura privatization, which is the dominant form of privatization all across Eastern Europe. This, of course, is a form of privatization which gives, or sells for a nominal sum, state property to its current managers. While this can be a legitimate process—management buyouts happen in the West, too—in the former eastern bloc, where there is very little public accountability, these deals easily become corrupt. In the case of Polisa, it meant that shares were unethically acquired by the wives of politicians. Sometimes, nomenklatura privatization simply means that the state continues to subsidize the company and the newly enriched managers. I once came across an astonishing example of this process in Lviv, in western Ukraine, where an electronics company—really a conglomerate, including 39 subsidiaries, 22 daughter companies and 19 joint ventures—called Elektron was being privatized by "selling shares." Just like the West—except that the company was valued according to the cost of its buildings (under $18 million at the exchange rates of the time) and members of the management were using company profits to "buy" their own shares. Even after privatization, Elektron, one of the managers told me, would still have the same privileged access to raw materials—subsidized, that is—as other state companies.

Naturally, not all the corruption of the transition period could be ascribed to the former Communists. Early Solidarity governments in Poland talked about corruption as "the inevitable price to be paid for transition to capitalism," which made it sound natural; the Democratic Forum government in Hungary made no secret of the fact that it had its friends among the old business class. Nevertheless, it is the inner core of former Communists who have been the most successful, by fair means or foul, at turning their economic power back into political influence.

That, then, is who the former Communists now are: the most successful economic actors in Central and Eastern Europe. Which is also, of course, what they always were: in the past they dominated through the diktat of central planning; now they use their political power to control the semi-free markets which characterize Eastern Europe. And now, thanks to these semi-free markets, the amount of money they command is greater.

Wealthy and sleek

The election to power of former prominent Communists—whether as "social democrats" or as "nationalists"—in every Central European country with the exception of the Czech Republic and East Germany—is, I believe, a direct reflection of this economic success. With financial help from their friends in the business world (and sometimes with old Communist party money which was never confiscated) former Communists are able to run better election campaigns. They still have Party organizations, with lists of workers and prearranged cells. Their more experienced leaders often make more plausible candidates. They seem wealthier, sleeker, more experienced, and usually they are. In most countries, they have better contacts in the media. No wonder they had become a symbol of prosperity to the shopkeeper in Wystep: in many parts of Eastern Europe, they have also styled themselves, very professionally and very successfully, as the party of the future. Economic success and political success are feeding back into one another.

Of course, not all former Communists are even members of "reformed" Communist parties or ex-social democratic parties. Such parties do exist, in Poland, Hungary and Lithuania, for example. But in Slovakia, for example, many of the "inner core" have joined the Movement for Democratic Slovakia, a nationalist movement led by Vladimir Meciar, a former Communist and a former Slovak prime minister. Slobodan Milosevic, president of Serbia, also heads a former Communist party, one transformed into a particularly virulent nationalist movement. The "Russia Our Home" party, led by the current Russian prime minister, is clearly not a party filled with former dissidents either. Above all, it is a mistake, however, to refer to any former Communist parties as representatives of the "far left," in the older meaning of the term. What is important about parties in post-Communist democracies is not their ideology; in Poland, they are more inclined towards free markets; in Slovakia less so. What is important is how closely their leaders are tied into the economic elite: the closer they are tied, the more they reflect the views and interests of the "inner core" of former Communists in that particular country.

Kwasniewski's comeback

What is also important is how former Communists choose to portray themselves—the cleverest have chosen to portray themselves, quite plausibly, as harbingers of the new capitalism. Again, typical of this type of ex-Communist leader is Alexander Kwasniewski, the new president of Poland. Only six years have passed since the day that Kwasniewski was not chosen—much to his surprise—to join the new Solidarity government of Tadeusz Mazowiecki, but they have been six good years for Alexander Kwasniewski. In what must count as one of the great political comebacks in recent Polish history, Kwasniewski was recently elected president of Poland, defeating the incumbent, Lech Walesa—Solidarity hero, Nobel prize winner, household name—by a narrow, but decisive, 3 percent margin.

No doubt many will now describe Kwasniewski's victory purely as a rejection of "harsh" economic reform—and it is certainly true that some of his supporters are among the approximately one-quarter to one-third of Poles who have not managed to succeed in what is now, in fact, the fastest-growing economy in Europe. No doubt a few are pensioners, along with others who feel nostalgic for the past. No doubt a few of the unemployed long for the certainties of the past, and believe that Kwasniewski will bring them back.

Equally, it is certainly true that Kwasniewski's victory has quite a lot to do with the failure of his opponents. Lech Walesa, who surrounded himself with an absurd collection of fools, flattering courtiers and former chauffeurs, proved a bumbling, unpredictable, ineffective president; the former dissident intellectuals, who should have become the core members of the new democratic political system, spent the past six years squabbling with one another. They can also be blamed for failing to remove the privileges and perks of the former Communists when they could have done so. Girding themselves up to fight a "nationalist" right-wing threat which never emerged, many missed the resurgence of the left-wing threat happening under their noses.

But what is more important about Kwasniewski's victory is that it establishes in Poland what is true in most countries: in most countries, former Communists no longer represent the past. They represent the capitalist future. Poles voted for Kwasniewski because since 1989, he, like other former Communists in Central Europe, has come to represent success.

There is no mystery about how this change was affected. In the past six years, Alexander Kwasniewski has lost weight, stopped drinking and taught himself to speak good English. He has familiarized himself with the concepts of "NATO" and "European Community." He has even dutifully toured Western capitals, making appearances at the offices of the *Wall Street Journal* and the Royal Institute for International Affairs in London, impressing audiences in a way that Walesa, who is rumored never to have read a book, could not.

No wonder that Kwasniewski seemed the candidate more likely to build upon Poland's substantial economic achievements as well. When the former Communist party came back to power in Hungary last year, it emerged afterward that over 60 percent of people who described their occupation as "businessmen" had voted for it, which was not what one would expect if one still thought that the words "former Communist" and "capitalist" were somehow contradictory. The numbers are no doubt similar in Poland; the statistics show that Kwasniewski's electorate is certainly younger and wealthier than Walesa's in any case. Kwasniewski's triumph is the political reflection of his former comrade's economic success—and therefore of his country's economic success as well.

When the economic and political resurrection of former leading Communists first began to happen, many people, myself included, thought that it might be temporary: that the influence of former Communists would wane with time, along with other features of the Communist era. Obviously, this is no longer the case. Their children, brought up wealthy and well-connected, do no less well than they. Moreover, many of the people who vote for former Communist political candidates are young. In the first round of the Polish presidential elections, 42.3 percent of Poles over sixty years old voted for Lech Walesa, while only 28.9 percent of Poles between eighteen and twenty-nine voted for him. Kwasniewski received much firmer support among younger people. 32.6 percent of Poles between eighteen and twenty-nine voted for him, 32.8 percent of Poles between 30 and 39 voted for him, and 37.4 percent of Poles between forty and forty-nine voted for him. The phenomenon of the former Communists as a ruling class is here to stay.

"Democracy? We love democracy"

What then, will be the long term political effects of empowerment of one particular class of people in Central Europe? As I have said, a "return to totalitarianism" is probably not on the cards, at least not on the western borders of the old Soviet empire. "Democracy? We love democracy. Democracy brought us back to power," is what Josef Oleksy, the Polish prime minister once cheerfully told me when asked about his party's commitment to an open society. But that does not mean, however, that there will be no other long term effects.

To begin with, the economic domination of the former Communist elite will have a profound impact on the shape of the economies of the eastern bloc. Of course, it might be argued that the former Communists are now merely a nascent bourgeoisie, which is to be applauded; and that is what the best of them indeed are. But things are not quite that simple. The evolution of a bourgeoisie is a healthy phenomenon when it grows and prospers thanks to bourgeois values: hard work, honesty, personal responsibility. What happens when you have a corrupt business class which is intimately entwined with a corrupt political class? You might still have a bourgeoisie, and you might still have capitalism, but they won't necessarily take the form that everyone would applaud. For all the talk of liberalism and Thatcherism and free markets that took place in the region in 1989, there is no Eastern European country which remotely resembles an Anglo-Saxon economy, or even a German social market economy. Even the Czech republic, which has had the most honest privatization process, remains dominated by the corrupt new business class.

Markets and corruption

It may be, in fact, that the model which Central Europe will most closely resemble in the coming years is that of pre-Tangentopoli Italy. Whether northern or southern Italy depends upon the country (Poland might be the former, Romania is perhaps the latter) but the idea is the same: there will be some forms of robust private entrepreneurship, an enormous, untaxed, gray market, and large companies, some state-owned and some private, which enjoy deeply corrupt relationships with powerful politicians. Various forms of criminal mafia will dominate some parts of the region; politicians will come to "represent" various business interests, as they clearly do already, particularly in Russia. Some post-Soviet republics may, of course, slide further. Yegor Gaidar once said that Russia faced the choice between aspiring to be like America, or being forced to become like Africa. But Latin America is an option, too: huge gaps between the rich and poor, political violence, massive slums, perennially unstable fiscal and monetary policies.

In some countries, this sort of corruption will simply slow growth, and make economic transformation more difficult. It is worth noting that most of the time, when former Communist parties come to power in Central Europe they have tried to slow down privatization, presumably because it isn't happening in a manner which is good for their friends. This happened most notably in Hungary, but in Poland as well. Or perhaps privatization will be allowed to go just so far—far enough to enrich the ruling class—and then will be halted. As capitalism develops, there may be other problems. Small companies may find it difficult to get loans and to become bigger, for example, if they do not have good political connections. Circles will close.

The existence of those closed circles poisons public life in other ways. In Poland, the figure of Ireneusz Sekula, a deputy prime minister in the last Communist government, illustrates the potential size of this problem. Temporarily ejected from politics by the collapse of the last Communist government in 1989, Sekula used his connections to launch himself in business, among other things buying several East German airplanes only a few hours before the collapse of East Germany, or so he claimed. By 1993 he was back in politics—running the customs department—but allegations of fraudulent loans continued to follow. Eventually, even one of his party colleagues, a former Communist justice minister, ruled that there was indeed a case to answer. A prosecution was announced but the Communist-dominated parliament voted not to lift Sekula's immunity, presumably because his fellow former Communist members of parliament did not want to establish a dangerous precedent. That vote may well have represented Poland's rite of passage from an errant democracy to a nascent kleptocracy.

It is also possible that in some countries, some Communists returning to power will start to rig election rules and play games with the media to ensure that they stay there. This has already happened in Belarus, for example. When election time comes around, blank pages appear in newspapers, a protest against ongoing government censorship. It is also likely that Boris Yeltsin's presidential victory was helped along with some skullduggery at the ballot box. In much of the Caucuses, democratic opposition has been slowly crushed; prisoners are tortured in jails in Georgia.

While there is no evidence yet of anything like this occurring Central Europe, it is equally true that the concentration of political and economic power in the hands of a small group of people is unhealthy in any case. Even aside from the corruption it will engender, there will certainly be undemocratic temptations as well. In Slovakia there have been clumsy attempts to close down unfriendly newspapers, and in Romania life is sometimes made difficult for the outspoken. In Poland, the former Communist party will now effectively control state television (there is, as yet, no other television to speak of, an absence which can be laid firmly on the head of, among others, Lech Walesa, who failed to push for it). In Poland, the now total domination of former Communists may, eventually, force other opposition groups to finally reunite. Or it may not: without money, without access to power, Poland's myriad political parties may simply go on squabbling for years.

There is a final way, however, in which the resurgence of old elites will have a powerful impact on the politics of Eastern Europe in the future. Feelings about former Communists are different in different countries—Hungarian communities, for example, were not perceived the same way as Polish or Czech Communists—but in most countries the old Party is associated with a wide range of political crimes and a period of brutal totalitarianism. It is fairly safe to say that now, in most countries of the new post-post Communist Europe, there will never be an officially-sanctioned, symbolic break with the totalitarian past, the sort of symbolic break that Nazi Germany was forced to make after the Second World War during the Nuremberg trials. The one obvious exception is the Czech Republic, where a law has been passed, controversially enough, which prevents former high-ranking Party officials and former police informers, from holding public office. They have not been sent to Siberia, they have not been purged, merely prevented from being elected to anything. The existence of that "lustration" law probably does partly explain why no former Communist party has yet been returned to power in the Czech Republic.

But in most countries, lustration laws were defeated, either because none were proposed—in most of the republics of the former Soviet Union, for example, high-ranking communists never left power—or because former dissidents and "democrats" who came to power soon after 1989 were too closely linked, in the social and economic manner described above, to the old regime. They simply did not want it to happen—and now it never will. Scoundrels of the old regime shall go forever unpunished; good will in no way has been seen to triumph over evil. This may sound apocalyptic, but it is not politically irrelevant. People need morality tales to keep them good. The police do not need to catch all the criminals all the time for most people to submit to public order, but they need to catch a significant proportion. Nothing encourages lawlessness more than the sight of villains—even if they are merely corrupt villains, like Sekula, and not concentration camp guards—getting away with it, living off their spoils, and laughing in the public's face.

The lessons of nondecency

For millions of people, the Communists and their allies among the former dissidents have finally proven that it does not pay to be decent. Those people who had got ahead by collaborating with the Communist regime have kept their apartments, their dachas and control of the businesses which they bought up on the cheap. Millions of ordinary people, who were never seduced by the ideology, never joined the Party for the sake of a career, simply look foolish from today's perspective. The most basic concepts from which societies build their hierarchies of values have been debased. If you work hard you don't necessarily get ahead. If you have connections you do. The cycle of corruption will perpetuate itself.

Over time, it may well be that the sense of truths suppressed and spades not called spades will eventually develop into a form of Vichy syndrome: there will always be underlying secrets in Eastern Europe, hidden files, ways of blackmailing politicians. The past will continue to haunt the present. This does not mean that many good things are not happening in Eastern Europe: many people, in many countries, are better off than before in countless ways. Queues have disappeared; opportunities have appeared. Standards of living are rising, and it makes sense, at least in some small ways, to be ambitious again.

Nor, to put the region in perspective, is it unusual: as noted above, it is certainly true that the unpleasantness of public life the vitriolic rhetoric and the corruption exist in many regions—in Africa, in Asia, in Latin America, in parts of the United States. But again—and this is the third problem which the resurgence of Communist parties poses for the future of Central and Eastern Europe—these regions do not matter so much, for security reasons, to the Western alliance. For despite four years' worth of negotiating, the region remains in a security vacuum. Instability may not, in the end, be "their" problem alone. If there is a real economic crisis, refugees will come flowing West; if there is a real political crisis, either Russia, or Germany, or even NATO may feel it necessary to step into the breach. Again, this is apocalyptic language, and I hope it never proves to be anything more than that. But it is too early to stop watching the progress of Eastern Europe, to early to assume that everything there will simply turn out for the best. This is a region whose future is still far from assured.

Anne Applebaum, deputy editor of the Spectator, *is the author of*
Between East and West: Across the Borderlands of Europe (Pantheon,
1994). This article was adapted from a paper prepared for a Freedom
House conference on "Neocommunism and Democratic Change."

Russia: Soviet Remnants

Alexander Motyl

The Soviet political system is best envisioned as consisting of two analytically distinct parts: empire and totalitarianism. The USSR was an empire in which a Russian core exerted effective political control over non-Russian peripheries. Centralized Russian organizations ruled both Russia and the republics, while non-Russian organizations only administered them.

The USSR was also totalitarian. The Party-state exercised total control over public life. The state's reach extended into nearly all nooks and crannies; its penetration of formally nonstate organizations was also complete. As a result, there was no place in the Soviet Union for a market economy, civil society, rule of law or democracy.

The linchpin of the system was the Communist party. Its central organs in Moscow both ruled the empire and controlled the totalitarian state, while its non-Russian branches supervised the economy and polity at the level of the republics. Not surprisingly, the Party justified its dominance with an elaborate ideology that legitimated Russian rule and totalitarian centralization.

Although oppressive, the system was stable: opposition was minimal and actual threats to the ruling class were virtually nonexistent. But the system was also ineffective, inefficient and increasingly illegitimate. The pathologies of totalitarian over-centralization spurred Nikita Khrushchev to embark on de-Stalinization and Leonid Brezhnev to alight the "treadmill of reforms." Later they inspired Mikhail Gorbachev to adopt perestroika. Gorbachev's reforms undermined the totalitarian empire by subverting first the ideology and then the Party. Without effective Party dominance, the totalitarian system broke down. Without effective totalitarian control, the empire necessarily fell apart. In late 1991, fifteen new states replaced the Soviet Union.

Parts of the former system continued to exist in each of these states. All retained the Soviet-administrative structure; all entertained fundamentally Soviet beliefs and values; and all were politically ruled and economically managed—or mismanaged—by the former nomenklatura. As former colonies subject to centralized totalitarian control, however, the non-Russian states inherited only bits and pieces of the former system's ruling organizations. In contrast, Russia inherited fully functioning, if uncertainly related, components: the imperial-totalitarian central state; the lion's share of the military; and most of the former secret police. Although weakened by collapse, these organizations survived into the post-Soviet era and fundamentally distorted the misguided reform efforts of Russian political elites.

Obstacles to reform

The self-proclaimed task of the reformers was to introduce democracy, the rule of law, civil society and the market. Each of these goals represented a cluster of institutions absent from the imperial-totalitarian system. Democracy involves an effective division and balance of governmental powers, control of leadership through elections and the representation of popular interests in parties. Rule of law entails regularized and transparent procedures for running state agencies and their relations with society. Civil society refers to interconnected social institutions existing independently of the state. The market presupposes private property and a set of legal procedures for exchanging capital, land and labor.

Logically, there are two mutually exclusive ways of bringing about these four desired ends—rapidly and simultaneously or slowly and sequentially. Russia's reformers claimed to choose the first path, but their choice really was a direct consequence of, on the one hand, Boris Yeltsin's power struggle with Gorbachev and the intra-elite conflict that it engendered and, on the other, of the fact of collapse and the impetus it gave to the frenzied search for immediate and comprehensive solutions to Russia's post-imperial and post-totalitarian woes. In sum, it made great sense for the Yeltsin forces to adopt radical reform as a means both of pursuing and winning the power struggle and of responding to the perceived imperatives of systemic collapse.

The Yeltsin-Gaidar strategy of building democracy, rule of law, civil society and the market simultaneously and rapidly amounted to nothing less than a revolution. As transformations initiated and executed by state authorities, revolutions from above presuppose the support of a significant part of the government bureaucracy and the forces of coercion. Revolutions from below presuppose substantial popular support and a not insignificant degree of state weakness, conditions not present in Russia.

Yeltsin and his supporters proved incapable of pursuing either course of action. State authorities were either indifferent or hostile to a revolutionary transformation from above; and the state was too strong and the masses too confused to permit revolution from below. The minimal necessary conditions of successful revolution were absent in Russia. The Yeltsin-Gaidar strategy of revolution was, hence, doomed. Not surprisingly, it was abandoned by late 1993.

The attempt at revolution, however, did leave its mark on the desired ends of reform—democracy, rule of law, civil society and the market—and on the system Russia inherited from the USSR. On the one hand, attempted revolution actually undermined these ends; on the other hand, it ascribed greater systemic logic to the disparate components inherited from the Soviet past. In sum, attempted revolution did not just fail: it set Russia back. Democratic institutions were destroyed, nondemocratic procedures were institutionalized and the political spectrum was polarized; state bureaucracies were transformed into "states within the state"; society was profoundly fragmented; and the proto-market was captured by nomenklatura capitalists and organized crime.

Distortions after reform

Yeltsin's push for radical reform necessarily placed him on a collision course with the conservative, though hardly Stalinist, Parliament. The confrontation came to a head in the armed assault on the Parliament building in October 1993. The results were threefold. First, the emerging institutional balance between the presidency and the Parliament was destroyed and democratic deinstitutionalization actually ensued. Second, the president emerged, and was constitutionally enshrined, as the dominant, if not quite dictatorial, player in the political arena. Finally, the destruction of the conservative opposition effectively deprived Russia of a viable political center. Very quickly, Russia's emergent parties gravitated toward the extremes, while the collapsing center was eventually occupied by the failed revolutionaries-turned-moderates. The upshot was a significantly deinstitutionalized political arena within which a constitutionally powerful, but politically weak, president confronted a constitutionally weak, but politically powerful, opposition, inside and outside the parliament.

These developments had a direct impact on the feasibility of introducing rule of law. A law-governed state presupposes state coherence. Only if the agencies of the state inhabit a common political space can legal procedures regulate their relations. If no such space exists, there is little that legal procedures can do to create it.

The Communist party defined this space in Soviet times. With the demise of the USSR, however, Russia's state institutions were left adrift. It was up to Yeltsin to exercise a central function of all executive branches of government, regardless of the type of regime, and impose coordination and direction on disparate state agencies. Instead, by staging a revolutionary assault against the state and its institutions, Yeltsin achieved the opposite. He actually compelled them to retreat into their fortresses, accumulate resources, and consolidate their holdings. The failure of the revolutionaries to capture the state and force it to do their bidding, together with the presidency's war against the Parliament, had the unintended effect of driving state institutions still further apart.

Worse still, the fact that Yeltsin emerged from the struggle formally stronger, but politically weaker, deprived him of the ability to coordinate and direct at just the moment when presidential leadership would have been critical to maintaining some degree of state coherence. Instead, the weakened presidency proceeded to act in the manner of other state bureaucracies. It, too, built up its apparatus—so that the executive bureaucracy is significantly larger now than it was in Soviet times—and withdrew into the Kremlin.

Consequently, the state fragmented and individual state institutions consolidated. Under such conditions, with multiple sovereignties characterizing the state arena, rule of law became a chimera. Each organization might have regularized internal procedures, but inter-agency rules could not possibly take hold in a neo-feudal setting of competing duchies and princelings.

In search of civil society

The weakening of democracy and rule of law necessarily had a harmful impact on civil society. Inasmuch as civil society presupposes a minimally institutionalized political and legal environment within which autonomous social institutions can safely exist, democratic deinstitutionalization and state fragmentation deprived Russian social institutions of such a setting. Political polarization had an equally negative impact, for it drove people apart and fostered extremist attitudes and values.

To be sure, Russia's nonstate organizations are many and varied, and there is a good case to be made for their vitality as well. But the real question is not whether individual organizations can emerge and thrive, but whether some form of coherent civic space can take shape, one that represents more than mere clusters of like-minded individuals, and actually serves as an effective societal counterweight to the state. The answer seems to be no. Instead, just as Russia now has a fragmented state with consolidated state agencies, it seems also to have developed a fragmented proto-civil society with consolidated social organizations.

It was no surprise, therefore, for the incipient market to have been captured by the nomenklatura and gangsters. The privatization of state assets superficially resembled the piecemeal introduction of a capitalist economy, but the dominance of the former nomenklatura, the fragmentation of the state, the absence of rule of law and the weakness of civil society meant that strategically situated state elites could accumulate privatized resources, amass vast fortunes and form *de facto* alliances with organized crime.

Some analysts suggest that *prikhvatizatsiia* is an inevitable stage in Russia's transition to a market economy. But Russia's emerging system is far from transitional. Instead, it seems to have acquired a structure and a logic that may be relatively immune to elite dictates.

Toward a new system

In 1991, at the time of the Soviet system's collapse, Russia inherited fully functional state institutions, a revolutionary elite, and a nomenklatura-controlled economy. In 1995, after several years of revolutionary voluntarism and post-revolutionary retrenchment, Russia suffered defeats on each of the four fronts that the revolutionaries had opened. Democracy, rule of law, civil society and the market had all experienced setbacks. More important, a significant deformation of the state had taken place. Thus, virtually all state institutions had grown in size and strength; all had acquired greater autonomy; and all had seized control of significant parts of the economy. In effect, Russia's political and economic systems came to be dominated by elite cartels, each of which staked a claim to a defined space within which its interests and its authority were paramount.

So high a degree of cartelization, and so striking a trend toward bureaucratic empire-building, effectively means that the question of whether or not Russia can survive as a democracy is misguided. The kind of cartelized, corporatist, bureaucratic authoritarian system that has evolved in Russia is anything but democratic. Indeed, it is proto-fascist.

Fascist states, such as Mussolini's Italy and Franco's Spain, typically are ruled, and to a large degree owned, by powerful bureaucracies allied with the military and/or secret police, which patrol the public sphere and ensure popular compliance with bureaucratic rule. Fascist systems also require dictatorial figures, who balance bureaucratic interests, act as mediators in inter-agency disputes, and command the loyalty of the forces of coercion. Finally, such systems invariably adopt the language of national grandeur and neo-imperial destiny for legitimating bureaucratic rule, purporting to ground the state in the will of the people, and providing the cartels with a shared language of governance. In contrast to vigorous totalitarian states such as Nazi Germany, Maoist China and Stalinist USSR, fascist systems permit a fair amount of personal freedom—situated, as it were, in the cracks between and among bureaucratic empires—and they certainly tolerate, and to some degree thrive on personal entrepreneurship.

In addition to its corporatist-bureaucratic structure, Russia approximates this definition of fascism on several other counts. The military and secret police are central components of the Russian power structure. Budgetary shortfalls, loss of morale, and personnel cuts have affected both, but they continue to play an influential role in the constellation of bureaucratic forces dominating Russian politics. Moreover, while so far eschewing violence and coercion at home, they have been far less restrained on the peripheries or abroad. The presidency is potentially dictatorial and, if the elections of June 1996 either do not take place or do take place and produce virtually anyone but Yeltsin, may turn out to be dictatorial in practice as well.

Finally, the ideology of great power messianism and national pride has become common to virtually all segments of Russian society. Almost all members of the Russian elites speak in these terms, as do the media and much of the public. Such a language did not come from nowhere. It existed ready-made within Soviet ideology, which had, since the

1930s, emphasized the primacy of the Russian nation and the great-power aspirations of the Soviet state. The ideology survived collapse because it offered a simple diagnosis of what went wrong and an equally simple prescription for what should be done to set things right. And, finally, it could persist and survive within the cultural confusion of post-Soviet life because it could serve as the minimum program of all Russian elites and the most effective channel for communicating with the populace.

These considerations suggest that Russia may be headed toward some form of fascism. Supporters of democracy, rule of law and civil society may despair at the prospect, as cartelized proto-fascist systems are definitionally unsupportive of such ends. Supporters of capitalism, however, may actually take heart. Inasmuch as Russia's continued transition to capitalism would not have been smooth and social discontent would necessarily have been great, an exceedingly authoritarian regime could facilitate the country's ruthless transformation into a capitalist economy. Supporters of the market may also argue that, in the long run, the market is at least a facilitating condition, and perhaps even a necessary one, of democracy, rule of law and civil society.

Could an authoritarian outcome have been avoided had Yeltsin not embarked on a great leap forward? Counterfactuals are always a risky business, all the more so as we have no way of measuring the success of evolutionary policies in the short run. Nevertheless, it seems safe to suggest that such extreme cartelization and fragmentation would have been retarded, if not undercut, in the absence of a revolutionary push. Indeed, a very different proto-cartelized political system might have emerged, one somewhat more conducive to democratic institutions, political consensus and civil society. Of course, the price might have been slower economic reform, with the result that Russia, while more benign, could have turned out substantially poorer as well.

Implications for Russia

The historical experience of authoritarian and fascist regimes strongly suggests that even a full-blown fascist Russia will continue to evolve. Indeed, there is every reason to believe that fascist regimes are inherently unstable, especially if they prove successful in effecting a capitalist transformation and, thus, creating a possible precondition of democracy. In this sense, authoritarian systems may be doomed to long-term political failure by their own economic success.

More worrisome for Russia in the short run is the fact that a cartelized authoritarian system is likely to promote the decentralization and, possibly, disintegration of the country. It is at this point that Russia's inherited federal structure assumes critical importance. Its federal units not only serve as the administrative outposts of most non-Russian nationalities, but they also possess a fair degree of economic and political authority. Cartelization is likely to enhance their authority and, hence, the centrifugal tendencies within the system in one of two, or in both, ways. First, it is possible for cartels to coincide with regional administrations, thereby increasing their resources, augmenting their capacity to resist the dictates of the center and enhancing their chances of survival on their own. Second, and no less important, strong cartels amount to a weak, because more or less fragmented, state. The relative weakness of central authority, in combination with the growing strength of provincial authority, should therefore encourage regional power brokers to exploit centrifugal tendencies for their own ends. The fact that most of Russia's federal units have a non-Russian coloration and, thus, can also function as emotionally appealing ethnic homelands, only adds fuel to the potential fire.

These considerations seem to point to a relatively brittle, if outwardly imposing and inwardly illiberal, state. While democracy will not flourish under such conditions, democratic forces and autonomous social institutions should be able to find some space to maneuver. This would be grounds for guarded pessimism, were it not for the fact that a fascist Russia will almost certainly give pride of place to the forces of coercion and utilize the language of hypernational pride and neo-imperialism. The implications of fascism are, thus, especially worrisome for Russia's neighbors in the "near abroad."

Russia's neighbors

The military interventions in Moldova, Georgia, Tajikistan and Chechnya, the wrangling over the Black Sea Fleet and the unwillingness to fully recognize the political independence and national boundaries of its neighbors in general— and Ukraine and Kazakhstan in particular—all suggest that Russian policymakers may have already embarked, even if unwittingly, on the road to expansion and hegemony.

The consequences of intensified Russian expansionism will be twofold. On the one hand, neo-imperialist adventurism will complicate Russia's relations with its immediate neighbors. Some will follow Russia; but others, particularly Ukraine, the Baltics and possibly Uzbekistan and Kazakhstan, will seek either to balance or to increase their military potential. Their own security may or may not be enhanced as a result, but overall stability in the region will surely deteriorate, with obvious consequences for Eurasia.

The second dimension of the problem arguably is even more serious. Although Russia may embark on imperialism, its own fragmentation and brittleness will not permit it to engage in sustained and successful expansion in the medium to long term. That is, expansion will automatically result in overexpansion. This fact will hardly deter Russian policymakers from pursuing such foolhardy policies. After all, imperial blueprints rarely figure in the calculations of empire builders, while cost-benefit analyses can be made to support just about any course of action, especially one with glorious overtones. Thus, like interwar Italy, Russia will not be able to engage in successful military and political adventurism; like Italy, it may do so anyway. But, unlike Italy, Russia may not only experience enervation, but, in conjunction with the growth of internal centrifugal forces, it may actually implode.

Implications for the West

It may be the case that there is little, if anything, that the world community can do to prevent Russia's slide toward fascism. But, while the *domestic* irrelevance of the West may therefore be a fact, it is nonetheless true that the United States and its allies can influence the *international* behavior of states. Russia need be no exception.

Weimar Germany comes to mind as an instructive analogy. Although internal dynamics mostly account for its development into a fascist state, the international community contributed to Germany's expansionist probes. The lessons of Weimar suggest two policy rules. First, it makes sense to avoid gratuitous slights to Russian pride—while remembering, of course, that it is no less important to avoid equally gratuitous slights to the pride of Russia's non-Russian neighbors. As there is no point in isolating Russia for bad reasons, every effort should be made to include a responsible Russia in the international community and to assign to it a role commensurate with its status as an impoverished great power.

Equally important is the flip side of this injunction: it is imperative that the West indicate what the limits of Russian foreign policy behavior are, in the near abroad in general, and with respect to Ukraine and Kazakhstan, as the two largest and geopolitically most important non-Russian states, in particular. Russian policymakers should be made to understand that the sovereignty, independence and territorial integrity of their neighbors are non-negotiable. It is up to the West to insist that stable Russian-non-Russian relations are to Russia's benefit as well; and it is up to the West to support the non-Russian states and their independence. The continued existence and integrity of Ukraine and Kazakhstan is the best guarantee of Russia's nontransformation into a neo-imperial state. As a result, their continued existence is the best guarantee of stable Western relations with Russia. And, to complete this line of reasoning, their continued existence amounts to the best guarantee of no future Cold War. The choice before the West, therefore, is quite simple: Ukrainian and Kazakh independence *or* Cold War.

Consider NATO expansion in this light. First, even the possibility of expansion is perceived as humiliating and threatening by virtually all Russians. Second, expansion will therefore strengthen the forces of coercion, promote national-imperialist rhetoric and, thus, undermine democracy. Third, it will benefit those countries that have no immediate reason to fear Russia—the Czech Republic, Poland and Hungary—and strategically isolate those that do—the Baltic states, Ukraine and Kazakhstan. Ironically, NATO expansion therefore amounts to a gratuitously insulting, politically counterproductive and strategically unnecessary way of accelerating the very proto-fascist and expansionist tendencies that it is supposed to forestall. Naturally, should Russia obstinately pursue a policy of adventurism and expansion in the near abroad, despite all honest Western efforts at mediation and assistance, there may be no alternative to expanding NATO's security umbrella—not only to East-Central Europe but to the Baltic states and Ukraine as well.

Is there anything that Russian elites can realistically do to prevent the slide toward fascism? While it is possible to imagine any number of scenarios—diminishing neo-imperialist rhetoric, promoting democratic institutions and resisting opportunities for intervention—to put the matter in this way is merely to restate the problem. After all, which elites are supposed to embark on such a path if all of them are united in their commitment to a vision of a great-power, neo-imperial Russia? Even if such elites could be found, how exactly are they to come to power without compromising their principles? And even if they were to come to power, how could they stay there without resorting to the very authoritarian methods they supposedly decry? Finally, even if they were to square this particular circle, what exactly should they do to set the country on a democratic path? However gloomy, these questions suggest not that a fascist Russia is inevitable, but only that the task for would-be democrats is enormous.

The salvation of Russia, and of its neighbors, may ultimately lie in the possibility that brittle authoritarianism will accelerate the centrifugal forces already at work within the system and, perhaps, lead to its complete disintegration. Russia's implosion will be profoundly destabilizing, of course, but, by finally ridding the country of its troublesome Soviet legacy, it may be the only way for Russia to escape the grip of empire and totalitarianism and, as Russians put it, become a *normalnoe gosudarstvo.*

*Alexander J. Motyl is Associate Director of Columbia University's Harriman
Institute. This article was adapted from a paper prepared for a Freedom
House conference on "Neocommunism and Democratic Change."*

The Near Abroad: Along Russia's Rim: The Challenges of Statehood

George Zarycky

For Russia, December's parliamentary elections were an important benchmark. Ultra-nationalists and Communists capturing the lion's share of the vote meant that hardline, anti-reform forces—led by Vladimir Zhirinovsky's misnamed Liberal-Democrats and Communist leader Gennady Zyuganov—were poised to mount a formidable challenge to an ailing President Boris Yeltsin if he runs next June. It augured months of political infighting between parliament and the government and between reform and retrograde Duma factions, the denouement of which, though unlikely to wholly trammel increasingly entrenched market mechanisms or a resilient civil society, could steer the country in a more authoritarian direction.

For the already edgy fourteen states of the so-called "near abroad" the vote heightened concerns that an already intrusive Russia—with its economic infrastructure still enmeshed with transitional economies from Ukraine to Central Asia; destabilizing political intrigues in the Caucuses; and military bases and/or "peacekeeping forces" in nine former republics—would intensify neo-imperial ambitions never wholeheartedly abandoned. But while Russian meddling and a concomitant "psychology of servility" have indelibly colored the political discourse, economic and energy policies, internal ethnic relations and foreign affairs of the post-Soviet states, the complex processes of converting sudden sovereignty to statehood have moved, albeit in fits and starts, pretty much apace.

In the shadow of the Russian bear

Since the disintegration of the Soviet Union, Russia has continued to reassert its interests in the "near abroad." The strategic rationale for Russia's aggressive, xenophobic foreign policy antedates the Soviet Union; in part, it is a defensive reflex aimed at countervailing the political and economic influences of Turkey and Iran in the Caucasus and on the Turkic and Persian peoples of Central Asia, and the pull of the West on the Baltics, Ukraine, Moldova and, to an extent, Russia herself.

In the Transcaucasian countries, the proximity of the Chechen war served as a grim reminder of Russian power and their own internal conflicts. Moscow was widely believed to have masterminded two coups in oil-rich Azerbaijan, while claiming Soviet-era proprietary rights over Caspian Sea oil fields after Baku signed a deal with a consortium of Western petroleum companies. The Kremlin also was miffed by Azerbaijan's refusal, unlike its neighbors, to have Russian troops on its territory.

In neighboring Armenia, Russian troops patrol the county's border with Turkey and Iran. Moscow also foisted itself into a Organization for Security and Cooperation in Europe (OSCE) process to settle the war in Nagorno-Karabakh, the Armenian enclave in Azerbaijan. While agreeing in Budapest in late 1994 to work under the auspices of the OSCE, Moscow had been pressing for the use of Russian peacekeepers. Azeri and Western diplomats blame the continued impasse on Russian attempts to sabotage the Budapest agreement, which gave Russia less influence in the region.

In Georgia, Moscow in 1993 backed Abkhazian insurgents in breaking a Russian-brokered ceasefire that routed Georgian forces, which had abided by the pact and withdrawn. Though Georgian leader Eduard Shevardnadze accused the Russians of betrayal, he reluctantly agreed to the deployment of Russian peacekeepers to Abkhazia. In exchange for legalizing the presence of some 19,000 Russian troops in five Georgian bases, Moscow sent forces to help Shevardnadze quell an armed rebellion by former president Zviad Gamsakhurdia. Of late, Russia has reasserted its "broker role" in the Caucasus and tilted toward Georgia, blaming Abkhazian intransigence for the suspended negotiations. But under the proposed agreement Abkhazia, as well as South Ossetia and Adzharia, where Russia also plays a dominant role, would be granted widespread autonomy under Georgian federal control. Abkhazians hope that hard-line nationalists in the Russian parliament will back them, not Shevardnadze.

In Central Asia, Tajikistan has felt the destabilizing effects of Russian machinations. In December 1992, after months of ethnic and political conflict, the governing coalition of moderate Islamic activists, secular democrats and nationalists was overthrown by former Communist hardliners backed by the Russians. Today there are 25,000 Russian "peacekeeping" troops along the border of Afghanistan, a base for exiled Islamic, nationalist and ethnic guerrillas. Dushanbe paid a stiff price for Russia's military support. As collateral for loans, the Tajik government was forced to give a 50 percent share in the Nurek hydroelectric plant and a major allotment in industrial units to Russia, leading one local commentator to remark: "Moscow owns most of Tajikistan now, so it calls the shots."

Turkmenistan, with an estimated 700 million tons of oils reserves and 8,000 billion cubic meters of natural gas, has tried to balance relations with Iran and Russia, and cultivated trade with Turkey and Pakistan. But under the terms of a defense pact with Moscow, Russian troops patrol the Iran-Turkmenistan border.

Economic leverage

At times Russian pressure has been based on economic leverage. In Kazakhstan, the oil- and mineral-rich state the size of the Indian subcontinent but with only 17 million people (35 percent of them Russian), Moscow played hardball to get into the energy game. In June 1994, Almaty accused Russia of cutting off most of the country's oil exports as part of a campaign of political and economic intimidation. Moscow had demanded an equity share in the giant Karachagnak gas field and a stake in the rich Tengiz oil field. Moscow also sought veto rights over any resource development on the Caspian Sea. Ultimately, the Russian gas company, Gazprom, was able to muscle into the Karachagnak deal with the West, and the agreement opened the way for the field's production to be shipped through Russia's pipeline system.

Russian designs are not limited to the Caucasus and Central Asia. In November, the Duma proclaimed Moldova's separatist, mainly Slavic Transdniester region (Gen. Lebed's and the 14th Army's former stomping grounds) "of special strategic importance for the Russian Federation." Even the Baltics—Estonia, Latvia and Lithuania—have had a nettlesome time extricating themselves from the Russian sphere. All three, particularly Lithuania, are dependent on Russian energy to fuel their economies. Citizenship restrictions on the large Russian minorities in Latvia and Estonia have prompted tough talk from Moscow about protecting Russians in the near abroad, and the pitch will likely become more strident with the strong showing by ultra-nationalists and Communists in Russia's parliamentary vote. Estonia and Russia remain at loggerheads over a border region claimed by Tallinn under the 1920 Treaty of Tartu. And while Russian troops withdrew from the Baltics last year, in Latvia Russians retained control of the Skrunda early-warning antiballistic missile installation. In Lithuania there is great concern about Russian military transit through the country to Kaliningrad, the Russian Baltic enclave where some 150,000 troops are stationed.

But the most strategically vital target of Russia's covetous attention is Ukraine, which separates Russia from Poland, Romania, Hungary and the rest of Central Europe, making it the first line of defense against a neo-imperialist Russia. Russian Communist leader Zyuganov minces no words in his belief that Slavic Ukraine and Russia are part of an indivisible ethnic whole. The Communists and some nationalists have pledged to annul the 1991 treaty which was the legal basis for the dissolution of the Soviet Union. Since attaining independence in 1991, Ukraine has sparred with Russia over the Black Sea Fleet, the Crimea, the disposal of nuclear weapons, the Commonwealth of Independent States (CIS), membership in the Tashkent alliance (the fledgling Russian-led military bloc) and the 11-million-strong Russian minority. Ukraine's dependence on Russian oil and energy makes it vulnerable to economic blackmail.

The alarming prospect of a more esurient Russian irredentism has compelled the nations of the "near abroad" (with the exception of Belarus) to form regional bodies and develop economic and political ties beyond Russia. They have sought integration with the constellation of Western and Asian economic, financial and security structures—the EU, the EBRD, OECD, the IMF, World Bank, WTO, OSCE and others. The heads of the Baltic armed forces in late November supported establishing a defense union to support one another if attacked. They also hope to become permanent NATO members if and when it expands eastward. The six Muslim republics of the former Soviet Union have joined the Economic Cooperation Organization (ECO), reactivated by Iran, Turkey and Pakistan to develop Central Asian energy. Kazakhstan, Kyrgyz Republic and Uzbekistan signed an economic union. Turkmenistan and Iran recently agreed on regular exchanges of military delegations and considered joint military exercises. Many of the Asian states have unilateral trade agreements with China, South Korea and, to a lesser extend, Japan.

But reams of accords will not necessarily diminish Russian influence if they are not accompanied by a sense of statehood buttressed by meaningful economic reform, a strong civil society and the development of democratic institutions. And here, the nations of the "near abroad" diverge, ranging from the relatively stable democracies in the Baltics and, to a certain extent, Ukraine and Moldova, to the authoritarian democracies of the Caucasus, to the autocratic (benign or malignant) regimes in much of Central Asia.

The Baltics: making a go of it

Since breaking with the Soviet Union after fifty years of often brutal occupation, the three small Baltic states have made striking progress toward establishing market economies, multiparty democracies, a vibrant independent press and a healthy civil society. Yet, in 1995, all three faced growing public unease amid persistent unemployment, banking crises, high inflation and the perception that the old Communist nomenklatura was exploiting the privatization process.

In Lithuania, where the former Lithuanian Communist Party, renamed the Democratic Labor Party (LDDP), retook political control from the anti-Communist Lithuanian Reform Movement (Sajudis) in the 1992 parliamentary elections, the government of Prime Minister Adolfas Slezevicius faced the biggest demonstration since Soviet times when in October 7,000 protesters marched through Vilnius to protest the social pain that came with reform. July's failure of one of the country's largest banks, Aurabankas, as well as the collapse of several smaller banks, raised public anxiety. Nevertheless, the government remained committed to reforms, and pushed for a constitutional amendment to allow foreigners to own land, thus paving the way for membership in the European Union.

Estonia's second post-independence election for the 101-member parliament in March 1995 saw a shift to the left-of-center Coalition Party/Rural Union alliance, which won a major victory over conservatives in the Pro Patria/ENIP coalition. The results reflected popular dissatisfaction among the elderly and rural electorate, hardest hit by the previous Pro Patria led government's market reforms. The country was thrown into a political crisis in October when Prime Minister Tiit Vahi's center-left coalition collapsed because of a bugging scandal involving Interior Minister Edgar Savisaar. At the end of October, parliament approved a new coalition which included the Reform Party, an unabashedly pro-market group led by Siim Kallas, the former Central Bank president and darling of radical reformers. Vahi, a moderate never implicated in the scandal, was named prime minister. While the Reform Party pledged to steer the country back toward radical reform and away from government intervention in the economy, parliament remained badly fragmented over economic policy.

Estonia's leftward shift in the parliamentary vote came amid sustained economic growth. But the country remained politically divided along stark geographic and generational lines. Liberal business and trade policies have created an young entrepreneurial elite concentrated in Tallinn. Outside the cities, poverty persists. The country's large and impoverished pensioner population has been courted by ex-Communist politicians.

In Latvia, a quirky parliamentary election and shaky banks were key issues. In October's vote to the 100-seat legislature, Latvia's Way, the largely ex-Communist but strongly pro-market party which in 1993 took over 30 percent of the vote (and 36 seats), saw its percentage halved. The biggest surprise was the showing (over 15 percent) of the Movement for Latvia, formed in November 1994 and led by Joachim Siegerist, a German Latvian aristocrat who does not speak Latvian but whose consistently anti-Communist (and allegedly anti-Semitic) positions appealed to pensioners and rural voters. Also running strongly was Saimneks (roughly, Masters in Your Own Home), led by Ziedonis Cevers, a former leader of Latvia's Komsomol and one-time interior minister in the first post-Communist government. The party is run by smooth ex-Communist functionaries and businessmen who emerged from the old nomenklatura. Cevers message was a hybrid mixture of free-market rhetoric peppered with left-wing welfare assurances. By the end of November, Cevers was poised to become the new prime minister with the support of left and center-right parties.

Despite Latvia's populist surge, the economy is as robust as any in the former USSR. Nevertheless, the collapse of a third of the country's sixty-seven commercial banks, including the largest one, unnerved depositors and investors. Despite relatively low inflation, low unemployment and steady growth, pensioners and the poor have seen living standards fall. A persistent issue was also Russian-speakers, who make up half of the population. Only 40 percent of them have managed to pass Latvian language and history tests and prove the five-year-minimum length of residence needed for citizenship. So nearly one-third of Latvia's adult inhabitants could not vote.

Miraculous Moldova, uncertain Ukraine, baleful Belarus

In the rest of the European "near abroad," Moldova and Ukraine shored up statehood in the face of political, economic and ethnic-separatist tensions, while Belarus, under the leadership of an increasingly totalitarian President Alyaksandr Lukashenka, flouted democracy and a national identity and spun back into Russia's orbit.

To the surprise of many, Moldova, a landlocked Romanian-speaking country of 4.3 million with few traditions of independent government, has become a model of post-Communist reform under the leadership of President Mircea Snegur, who in June 1995 resigned from the ruling Democratic Agrarian Party (which won parliamentary elections in 1994 by promising to slow reforms), citing the party's pro-CIS stance. Even with the issue of separatist Transdniester and its 700,000 mainly Slavic population still unresolved, Moldova's old-guard ex-Communist politicians have overseen a painful economic stabilization program that since 1993 reduced inflation from 230 percent to 1 percent, included a "fast and clean" privatization program and the creation of well-regulated capital markets and opened opportunities to foreign investment. GDP is expected to grow by as much as 6 percent next year.

President Snegur, who prefers to look to the West than to Russia, hopes that continuing prosperity, rather than politics, will pull the Transdniester back into the fold (with limited autonomy). A healthy economy has also soured Moldovans on reunification with Romania. The pro-reunification Popular Front, in alliance with the Christian Democrats, only won nine seats in 1994. The only blight on an otherwise promising future scenario is the victory of ultra-nationalists and Communists in Russia and the soaring popularity of presidential hopeful Gen. Lebed, whose 14th Army sided with Transdniester Slavs before withdrawing.

But while Moldova is pressing forward, Ukraine's reformist President Leonid Kuchma is facing a society that in many ways is standing still. When Kuchma defeated Leonid Kravchuk in the 1994 presidential race, he announced an ambitious program of market reforms that won Western backing. However, his pursuit of consensus and moderation in working with an often obstreperous, factionalized 405-member parliament (elected in 1994, with 45 seats to have been filled in December 1995) dominated by a broad leftist coalition of Communists, Agrarians and

Socialists has slowed reform. While in mid-May, the president managed to wrest new political power from the legislature, which gave up its power to name Ukraine's cabinet and its claim to authority over provincial and local governments, he scaled back his reform program to dismantle a largely command economy, partly in light of polls showing declining confidence in his ability to manage the economy.

On 11 October, parliament approved the government's IMF-driven program of macroeconomic stabilization that emphasized evolutionary, not revolutionary, measures. It was the ninth such program since independence, none of which has panned out. Half measures, while assuring political stability, did not address Ukraine's critical economic problems—a drastic drop in production, the slow pace of privatization, an increase in money owed in balance of payments, stubborn inflation, declining purchasing power, "hidden unemployment," a dependence on Russian energy and concomitant external debt.

Nevertheless, Ukraine has made steady progress toward political and national stability. The Crimea crisis has been temporarily defused. It has managed to avoid ethnic strife and extremist violence. There is a vibrant independent media, established trade unions and other elements of a burgeoning civil society. But foot-dragging on reforms could undermine foreign assistance and prompt Russia to use economic means to provoke crisis and unrest. President Kuchma knows what's at stake. In late November he criticized Prime Minister Yevhen Marchuk's government for failing to act on economic reform programs, thus threatening international credit.

But if Ukraine has stagnated, Belarus is in full retreat. Non-party President Lukashenka has acted more like a Bolshevik than a Belarusian patriot. He has praised Hitler, reintroduced censorship, banned independent trade unions, ignored the Supreme Court when it overturned his decrees and barred candidates for parliament from putting up posters or appearing on state media. Last May, parliamentary elections produced only 120 deputies, well short of the two-thirds quorum for the 260-seat legislature, because the turnout in most constituencies was below the 50 percent minimum. In view of the president's threat to dissolve parliament, Belarusians turned out for the November rounds. And while the Communists and their Agrarian allies are likely to dominate parliament, the Popular Front and a block of economic liberals could provide a core of opposition. Thus far, the brazenly dictatorial Lukashenka has curbed foreign investment and private enterprise, and openly called for reunification with Russia.

The Caucasus: autocratic democracy in a turbulent region

In the four years since the fall of the USSR, the nations of the Caucasus, the historically turbulent crossroads between Europe, Russia, Asia and the Middle East, have been mired in ethnic conflict, civil war, coup attempts and war—some instigated or enflamed by Moscow—that has hampered economic development and the exploitation of the region's bountiful oil and mineral wealth. These factors undermined the early promise of a non-Communist democratic transition.

In Azerbaijan, Abulfaz Elchibey, the leader of the pro-independence, anti-Communist and anti-Russia Azerbaijan Popular Front (AzPF), was elected president in 1992, only to be overthrown a year later amid civil war and Azeri setbacks in Nagorno-Karabakh. He was replaced by Gaidar Aliyev, a former member of the Soviet Politburo and a sycophant of Leonid Brezhnev. In Georgia, nationalist leader and former dissident Zviad Gamsakhurdia was overwhelmingly elected president in 1991, only to be ousted after his erratic and authoritarian behavior alienated supporters and brought the country to the verge of civil war. Former Soviet Foreign Minister Eduard Shevardnadze was brought in, only to face armed rebellion by Gamsakhurdia loyalists (ultimately put down with Russian help) and a Russian-backed violent secession in Abkhazia, a strategic region bordering Russia and the Black Sea (still unresolved). In Armenia, popular human rights activist Levon Ter-Petrossian, whose democratic credentials and election as president in 1991 were touted by the West, has slowed the pace of reforms and banned a leading opposition party, thus undermining the institutionalization of a genuinely democratic system.

The shooting has stopped in Karabakh and Abkhazia, though internationally brokered mediation efforts have stalled. And while elections this year in all three countries were not entirely free and fair, voters opted for continuity and stability, suggesting that for many citizens regional and external factors were more to blame than governments for the lagging transition from communism to capitalism.

In Georgia, Shevardnadze survived an assassination attempt and won an overwhelming 74.3 percent of the vote in elections on November 5. His centrist Citizen's Union won 150 of 225 seats in parliament. Earlier, he had moved to break up the *Mkhedrioni* (Knights of Georgia), a paramilitary group and former allies in the 1992-93 civil war. Warlord Dzhaba Ioseliani, head of the Mkhedrioni, lost his parliamentary seat and was arrested in mid-November. A new constitution restoring Georgia as a presidential republic was adopted in August.

In September, Georgia's switch to a permanent currency marked the culmination of an austerity campaign that stamped out hyperinflation in less than a year. Prices were freed, state spending was frozen, and large-scale privatization was launched. Moreover, oil reserves were discovered in eastern and western regions by a British investor and, after much wrangling, Russia agreed to a pipeline carrying Azeri oil through Georgia.

A lot depends on Shevardnadze. But despite episodes of political violence, persistent corruption, Russian meddling, human rights abuses and Abkhazia, democratic elections, a new constitution and economic reform have set Georgia on the road to strengthening democracy.

Armenia, on the other hand, seems to be moving in the opposite direction. Once a leading reformer among ex-Soviet states, it has struggled to build and sustain a democracy. In January, President Ter-Petrossian banned the diaspora-based Dashnak, the largest opposition party, accusing it of terrorism. The party, along with eight others, was not allowed to compete in July's elections, which OSCE monitors described as "free but not fair," with the ruling Armenian National Movement controlling election commissions. Efforts have been made to muzzle the press. The new constitution, adopted concurrently with national elections, provided for a weak legislature and the strongest presidency among the OSCE nations. The president can dissolve parliament, appoint and dismiss the prime minister, appoint all judges and members of the Constitutional Court, and declare martial law. With the ANM controlling 160 of 190 parliamentary seats, Ter-Petrossian has virtual control of all three branches of government.

Yet, budget-tightening and other reforms have boosted the economy, as has a wealthy and vigorous diaspora. Inflation is minimal, as is foreign debt. Industrial production is rising strongly. Nevertheless, Armenia's authoritarian turn, and President Ter-Petrossian's increasingly testy and iron-clad grip on power, have caused consternation at home and in the West.

Authoritarianism is also a factor in neighboring Azerbaijan. While hoping to build a "new Kuwait" on the Caspian, President Aliyev has built a Soviet-style personality cult reinforced by a docile press. In October, four journalists were sentenced for up to five years in prison for "insulting the dignity of the president." The first-round of parliamentary elections in November were hardly "free and fair," with leading opposition parties and some 600 independent candidates excluded. The new constitution, allegedly supported by 91 percent of the vote, considerably strengthened the president's already wide-reaching powers over all branches of government.

The government has managed to slow inflation and launch privatization. Experts estimate that within fifteen years the country should be producing 700,000 barrels of oil a day, worth about $4.2 billion a year at today's prices. But with the war in Nagorno-Karabakh draining the treasury, average Azeris have not felt the benefits of oil wealth. Moreover, an alleged coup attempt against Aliyev served as a reminder that political stability—won at the expense of democracy—remains wafer-thin in this volatile region.

Central Asia: the men who would be king

If the history of the Caucasus demonstrates a proclivity for strong leaders and vibrant nations, the countries along the fabled "Silk road" in what was Soviet Central Asia reflect a past of Mongol absolutism. Tajikistan and Turkmenistan were carved out by Stalin from an amalgam of tribes and clans whose political influence persists to this day. Others, like the more nationally self-aware Uzbeks and Kyrgyz, were also rimmed by Stalin-era borders. Giant and sparsely inhabited Kazakhstan was populated by Russians and Ukrainians throughout the Soviet era, to the point where Slavs make up 41 percent of the population. The Muslim Turkic nations—the Kazakhs, Uzbeks, Turkmen and Kyrgyz—as well as the Persian-related Tajiks were, it can be argued, essentially formed under communism, although the intellectual elites of each were descendants of rich and ancient cultures. There was little in the historical experience of the Central Asians to prepare them for independent statehood.

Today, each country is ruled by a strong president, even if democratically elected as in the Kyrgyz Republic and, maybe, Kazakhstan. The parliaments are pliant; civil society weak; and the economies unsteady.

Tajikistan is the region's hard-scrabble case. Mineral-poor, the country is ruled by the repressive regime of President Emomali Rakhmanov, a former Communist, supported by the presence of 25,000 Russian troops along the Afghan border. Rakhmanov's ruling alliance, made up of the Leninabad and Kulyab tribes, launched an ethnic war against the Gharm and the Badakhshan who supported the democratic-Islamic coalition.

Parliamentary elections in February 1995 excluded the opposition. The constitution provides for a strong executive, who serves as head of parliament and has broad powers to appoint and dismiss officials. The government has total control of the media, and hundreds of journalists have fled the country. Talks with the expatriate opposition have been inconclusive.

Oil-rich Turkmenistan remains in the totalitarian grip of President Saparmurad Niyazov, a former first secretary of the Communist party who ran unopposed in 1991 and renamed himself Turkmenbashi, or head of the Turkmen, while building a cult of personality. Only Niyazov's Democratic Party of Turkmenistan was permitted to field candidates in the 1994 parliamentary elections. The legislature extended Niyazov's term to the year 2002. Political rights and civil liberties are severely curtailed.

Despite huge oil and gas reserves, the centralized economy is plagued by mismanagement and widespread corruption at the highest levels of government. Other obstacles to modernization are rooted in the country's tribal history. Niyazov's self-annointment as Turkmenbashi was intended to serve as an integrating force.

In Uzbekistan, President Islam Karimov, former first-secretary of the Communist Party, continues to consolidate his repressive hold on the country. Parliamentary elections in December 1994 were won overwhelmingly by the (former Communist) People's Democratic Party in a fraud-marred vote. The constitution and penal codes contain undemocratic restrictions on political activity, and activists of the opposition Birlik and Erk parties have been jailed. The oppressive political atmosphere and slow pace of reform has discouraged foreign investment despite the country's potential mineral and agricultural wealth.

In Kazakhstan, President Nursultan Nazarbayev continued to rule as a popular but authoritarian leader, seeking to maintain ethnic and political stability while attracting investment to exploit the country's tremendous mineral wealth, including large deposits of oil, natural gas, gold and uranium. He dissolved parliament in March 1995 and ruled by decree after dozens of candidates and parties charged that elections a year earlier were rife with fraud and irregularities. On 5 December, elections were held for the forty-member Senate, though most of the seats were uncontested.

The constitution nominally calls for a multiparty, presidential system and parties have been allowed to register and run, but de facto power is firmly centered in the hands of Nazarbayev. Opposition groups are closely monitored. While the press is economically hard-pressed and often practice self-censorship, there are independent newspapers and electronic media. Nazarbayev has tried to balance Kazakh nationalism with the concerns of ethnic minorities, particularly Russians in the industrial north (Russian is the language of "interethnic communication") and Germans, but Russians have been leaving in droves. Relations with Russia have been strained over oil and gas deposits.

Even the most "democratic" of the Central Asian states, the Kyrgyz Republic, has followed the regional trend of one-man rule. A non-Communist physicist and intellectual, President Askar Akayev ran unopposed and was elected in 1991. His rule was subsequently reaffirmed by a national plebiscite in January 1994. That same year Akayev sought and got popular approval by referenda to change a cumbersome, 350-member Soviet-era parliament dominated by conservative-Communist deputies. The president's decision was condemned by the opposition and some in the West as an authoritarian move to circumvent the legislature. Elections to the streamlined, 105-member parliament in February and April 1995 were plagued by irregularities, including ballot-stuffing, inflation of voter turnout, media restrictions and intimidation. While political parties exist, the largest being the umbrella Democratic Movement of Kyrgyzstan, party affiliation is weak. Most candidates ran as independents or were nominated by more than one party.

In the run-up to presidential elections slated for 24 December, there were persistent charges that regional political elites were refusing to verify signatures in support of other presidential candidates. The 3 December registration deadline narrowed the field from thirteen candidates to three opponents, but President Akayev enjoyed a commanding 76 percent support in pre-election polls and would surely be re-elected.

While Akayev has displayed some authoritarian tendencies, Kyrgyz society is relatively open. The press is among the freest in Central Asia (though some papers have been temporarily banned in the past), interest and business groups function without government intimidation, unions have been critical of government policies. The national currency has stabilized and inflation has dropped to single digits. Privatization has progressed slowly, though the World Bank estimates that some 20 percent of GDP is in private hands, probably the highest in Central Asia.

In many ways the most autocratic of the former Soviet republics, the nations of Central Asia, with the exception of Tajikistan, have achieved a degree of nation-building despite their history. Post-independence ethnic tensions with Meshketian Turks have diminished in Uzbekistan, border have remained fixed and serious efforts have been made at regional cooperation. Radical Islam has thus far been a nonfactor. But as in other regions of the "near abroad," it is Russia and its intentions that remain a wild card, and the miasma of the recent hard-line shift and the prospects of an empire-restoring president hang over the region.

Time may be on the side of the post-Soviet states. The longer they have to solidify their states and national identity, to build solid and effective economies, to integrate into international organizations, to abandon mistrust and build regional alliances, to resolve their internal ethnic problems, the greater the chances that their run of independence won't be cut short. But if Russia is a key part of their immediate political calculus, long-term stability will depend on economic equity, democratic institutions, the elimination of corruption, an active civil society and the habits of genuine pluralism and rule of law. The shifting tectonics of power and influence are often slow and gradual. But if these processes are too long delayed, from Ukraine to Uzbekistan, national cohesion could unravel not from without, but from within. The kind of Russia that develops in 1996 will tell a lot; but it will only be a part of the whole story.

George Zarycky is Central and Eastern Europe Area Specialist for Freedom House.

European Union: The Besieged Welfare State
Roger Kaplan

West Europeans were ending a dull and peaceful year, marked by modest signs of economic improvement (notably on the job-creation front) when French public-sector workers, spearheaded by railwaymen, went on strike, bringing on a "social movement" (as the French say) as extensive as anything seen since the events of May 1968. Though there was little chance of the French crisis spreading to neighboring countries—Italy had experienced a comparable "explosion" at the end of 1994—the body blow to the French economy was bound to affect the European Union's overall health and, in particular, it raised doubts as to the possibility of achieving Economic and Monetary Union in the 1990s, which is the major objective of the movement for European unity.

As in Italy, the social movement was brought on by a right-of-center government's attempt to fix, not undo, an extensive and expensive social security system. The plan, designed to reduce a deficit in the public finances that acts as lead on job-growth, was not "liberal" in the European sense, that is to say, libertarian. It was welfare-statist, although the "European" requirements (stable currency, low inflation, reduced public deficits) made it necessary to be more rigorous than anyone really wanted. Some top trade union leaders initially welcomed the plan, while intellectuals and social commentators by no means associated with the French right, approved it as a basis for dialogue toward restructuring—in view of saving—France's welfare state.

Resolving the "social question"
Until the "social question" is resolved, and Europeans decide what sort of balance they want between what the French call "solidarity" and the urge to fend only for oneself, other questions will be secondary, difficult to focus on. There is no reason to believe a balance can be struck that will lead to an original political model. The French government, instead of stating this obvious truth and patiently working toward it, attempted to move by fiat. The people felt their welfare benefits were threatened. The striking public service workers enjoyed wide support despite weeks of inconvenience as trains stopped running, public utilities were curtailed and so forth. Instead of reforms, France was faced with a political crisis and economic misery.

Europeans often give the impression they do not know what they want, and in the process they frustrate themselves and others, and then argue about whether the shortcomings are due to "Europe" or "not enough Europe." While this goes on, voices in the U.S. complain the Europeans are not pulling their weight in Bosnia. Voices in Africa complain the Europeans, after exploiting the continent, are abandoning it. European voices bemoan the irrelevance in world affairs of their nations and their Union. Civil libertarians worry about restrictive immigration policies and new hurdles for obtaining citizenship, which the Union is putting in place partly due to real population pressure from points east and south but also to establish Union-wide uniformities where in the past there were highly characteristic national approaches to these kinds of issues. (In fact, the uniformization of immigration and naturalization policies will have a generally liberalizing effect on some countries, Germany in particular.)

These issues matter, but Europeans will not have a clear sense of themselves and their place in the world until the social question is resolved. In 1995, it appeared the framework for resolving it would be, not individual nation states, but the European Union; but the last word on this federalist project, which began in the early 50s with the European Coal and Steel Community, has by no means been written.

Though it does not follow logically, part of the social contract has consisted of broadening the civil liberties enjoyed by Europeans. Over the years, the rights of defendants have, in general, been enhanced. Ironically enough, England in certain respects has lagged behind, even though both in principle and in tradition it has a legal system designed to protect individual liberties, which on the Continent, by tradition, are subordinate to the state's interests and prerogatives. At the same time, the rights of plaintiffs have been enlarged, to the point where some observers fear a U.S.-style litigation disease.

The European welfare states evolved in the same years as the modern European movement developed. At times the two were complementary; for example, human rights jurisprudence, which among other things has touched on women's rights, work regulations and defendant rights, has brought individual countries' penal codes to more liberal standards, in keeping with the welfare-statists' programs. However, since Europe-building has been a movement for free trade, it has not infrequently been criticized as undercutting some of the benefits that the welfare states have provided. This is, again, not strictly logical, but in general the welfare state has coexisted with a regulated market economy, rather than the loosely regulated free market that free traders, in practice, usually favor. Thus, it is not an accident that John Major's Conservative government in Great Britain "opted out" of the "social" provisions of the European Union (provisions that strongly encourage members to guarantee high levels of social insurance, labor rights and so on), while the opposition Labour party has promised to opt in. On the other hand, it is worth noting the Danes also "opted out" of the social chapter of the famous Maastricht Treaty, but mainly out of concern their welfare state would be diluted by the lower norms that prevail (on average) in the Union.

Defining Union

What has not been resolved is what kind of Europe the European Union will be. Perhaps it should not be. The Europeans are divided over fundamental questions of political orientation. Should Union be a form of enlarged, deeper and more comprehensive welfare state? Should it have a powerful central bank and a common currency? Should it be a land of immigration or a protective demographic enclave marked by carefully regulated additions to a population with a birthrate that is falling below replacement levels?

Paternalistic, dirigiste, nanny-state: call it what you will, European welfarism has this singularity: compared with other social policies inspired by nineteenth century socialist thought, it did not constrict individual liberties; on the contrary. Certainly there has been regulatory statism in some countries, confiscatory taxation in others. But this is democracy, not despotism. Criminalizing parental discipline is silly, even perverse, but it is reversible. Wrong headed policies, regarding drugs for example, have been reversed, when citizens, say, in Switzerland and Holland, saw they had gone down a well-intentioned road to hell. European welfare statism, for all its perverse consequences, has been sometimes a creation of elitist reformers, but it has a popular base, in the trade union movement and other free and voluntary associations of citizens, and it has evolved in response to the pressures from this base. This is why it was ill-considered of the French government to propose reforms without first seeking a consensus.

The European movement, in contrast, has been entirely an elite affair, run by technocrats almost invariably drawn from the ranks of the upper middle classes and operating with only indirect democratic controls, in that they are ultimately responsible to the ministers of elected governments. Until Maastricht, the European Commission, made up of appointed commissioners and professional staff, reported to the Council of Ministers, which in effect is the collegial presidency of Europe. After Maastricht, the Commission also is subjected to some control by the European Parliament. In this sense, one might argue by comparison with the United States, the operating departments of the executive branch of Europe are controlled both by the elected president and the elected legislature. However, the Europarliament is a lap poodle by the standards of the U.S. Congress.

With its elitist history and its "democratic deficit," the EU has been easy to blame for unpopular measures taken in its name. The wave of social protests in France at the end of the year, though due to budget deficits the French must deal with regardless of "Europe," underscored the contradiction between the European movement and the European social contract. To the committed Europeanists, European Union is the only way to remain politically and economically competitive in the world. To committed social democrats, reneging on the social contract is unthinkable. Many Europeans, including French President Jacques Chirac and German Chancellor Helmut Kohl, are convinced they can be true to both ambitions. They insist pain in the short term is only that. Those who feel the pain do not share their optimism.

Budgetary adjustments

To achieve certain economic and fiscal harmonies at the European level, which (supposedly) are needed to bring about conditions for stable growth, governments have had to make adjustments in budgetary policies, mainly to lower deficits that, in recent years, have attained levels that would be apocalyptic by American standards. The French government decided to raise social security taxes, simultaneously suggesting gradual cutbacks in consumer service and employee benefits in some of the state-run agencies like electricity and the heavily subsidized railway system. French payroll deductions and payroll taxes are already among the highest in the world (amounting to about half of gross pay). They are needed, however, to finance France's extraordinarily generous social welfare. Because having someone on payroll is so expensive, job creation is sluggish and unemployment is high.

In late 1994 Italy went through a similar shock between the needs of Europe and the maintenance of a social welfare system people were reluctant to tamper with. The result was the disintegration of the center-right reforming coalition led by Silvio Berlusconni, which had replaced the ruling coalition of parties known as the *partitocracia* that finally had attained corruption levels even Italians, who seemed to have a high tolerance level for the crooks who governed them, could no longer live with. There were other factors as well, to be sure, including questions about Mr. Berlusconni's probity; a case was developed against him during 1995 and at year's end he faced indictments for "occult financing" (kickbacks) of the notoriously corrupt PSI (Socialists), whose leader, Bettino Craxi, sentenced to eighteen years in absentia, remained in Tunisian exile.

The stream of scandals involving political corruption in Italy—with hundreds of politicians and businessmen facing indictments and one of the most prestigious representatives of the post-war regime, former Prime Minister Giulio Andreotti, on trial in Palermo for collusion with the Mafia, including in the murder of a journalist—has revealed the breathtaking rot permeating widespread sectors in the country. Corruption has become painfully apparent because the system, whose political immobility was the price paid for keeping the Communists out of power, had to be shaken up to make way for Europe-building. And as Italy "Europeanizes," it must, like France, make reforms in its public finances and, therefore, its social welfare structures. This stated reform of Berlusconni's center-right coalition was obscured by the fact that it, too—even its leader—could be, and was, targeted by the *mani pulli*, or clean hands, investigating attorneys, notably the avenging angel of Milan, Judge Antonio Di Pietro.

Germany and unity

There are at least three reasons why Germany has not been as troubled by the requirements of European unity. Post-World War II Germany was built alongside Europe, in a certain sense as the designated, self-conscious pillar of Europe. This does not mean the German national sentiment was extinguished, on the contrary. But it means the slogan, "a European Germany, not a German Europe," became almost as second nature to the German political mind as the American motto, "One country under God, with liberty and justice for all": often honored more in the breach, but unquestioned and, in a sense, unquestionable. Second, the German welfare state was built not so much on the foundation of some exceptional German gift for fiscal responsibility and managerial efficiency (as is often imagined), but on the basis of a tradition of management-labor union-state cooperation that flourished only in the Germanic and Nordic countries. The system was more adaptable, and probably more democratic, than the Italian or French systems, certainly than the British. Finally, Germany's federal structure prepared it for the give and take of a federal Europe that began to emerge, moreover, at a time when the Germans were preoccupied with their own unification. While the unification of Germany never threatened to displace the Germans' European loyalties—indeed, Chancellor Helmut Kohl insisted on accelerating the pace of Europe-building even as he was rebuilding the (albeit reduced) *"grosse Deutschland"* of pre-World War II—it certainly absorbed their attention. But even the Germans worried about Europe's "perverse" effects: not on their social welfare system so much as on their currency.

The Germans, who have benefited from a strong currency, the *Deutschmark*, and have been well-served by an independent and efficient central monetary authority comparable in its function and mandate to the U.S. Fed, the *Bundesbank*, have sound reasons to worry about the advent of the new money.

Monetary union pros and cons

There are advantages and disadvantages to monetary union, and it is because they are proceeding cautiously that the architects of the European movement have suggested that this may be a union within the Union. They do not want to risk the soundness of the German economy, and the German currency, by getting weak economies and currencies into it before they are ready. That is the logic behind the "Maastricht criteria" that have brought grief to France and Italy. There can only be a unified economy, with a single monetary authority and a single currency, if all the economies are in line, with approximately the same levels of inflation, public debt and deficit. It was on this basis that Germany's Europeanists, who come from both major parties, assured their compatriots there was nothing to fear from EMU. But in late 1995, they began to say there was indeed cause for worry. Moreover, it has been the conventional wisdom that EMU will be limited at first to a "hard core," usually understood to be France, Germany, the Benelux countries (though Belgium's public finances are among the worst in the EU) and Austria.

French Europeanists want to be included because they have always thought of European Union as the vehicle for French grandeur, and they broadened their appeal by insisting it was the way to preserve and indeed expand the welfare state. This is why both the British Labour Party and the French Socialists, at first skeptical of European-construction, were converted. Now that there is an eastward frontier for Europe, however, and the EU is officially, if reluctantly, on record as favoring eastern enlargement, there is an added reason. Should the French balk at EMU, or fail to meet its criteria, the Germans, in practice or in fact, will create a DM-zone, and Europe's center of gravity will move east. Helmut Kohl said in December that Poland, Hungary and the Czech Republic should be brought in soon.

In the U.K., the stated reason for fearing monetary union is that it will diminish sovereignty, more precious than the efficiencies that would be achieved. If Great Britain wants to conduct a reflationary policy, for example, but monetary policy for all of Europe is controlled by an agency in Frankfurt that is determined to follow a deflationary line, tough luck. EMU supporters argue that the control of national monetary policy is already largely outside the control of national governments, because the economies of the EU countries are so interwoven that being the odd man out in Europe just does not work.

In the meantime

In a sense, therefore, the Europeans are contemplating something resembling a marriage of convenience, and for quite some time now they have been having a hard time making up their minds. This does not mean life does not go on. France lost its long-serving president, Francois Mitterrand, in 1995, who retired after two seven-year terms in a sad way. Seriously ill, and beset by ugly and true stories about his past, Mitterrand did not leave on a high note or in a triumph of lonesome glory, like Charles de Gaulle. Mitterrand's popularity remained fairly high to the end, perhaps because the French recognized much of themselves in him, and surely, too, because of the dignity and courage with which he bore his illness. But there was something a little shamefaced about it all. And there has been so much that is shamefaced about the period of French history that Mitterrand so deeply incarnated. One wants to think the French people made the necessary connection, turned the page, got on with it.

The new men do not carry Mitterrand's baggage from the 1930s, '40s, '50s. Jacques Chirac served in the Algerian war as a young officer, as a minister of successive Fourth Republic governments, condoned torture and repression; Chirac's nearly successful Socialist opponent, Lionel Jospin, represents the generation of the left that opposed that awful mistake (the older generation of Socialists was largely responsible for it); for his voters, as indeed for Chirac's, it is ancient history (Chirac did better among very young voters.) Chirac is not, by his age could not be, a "historic" Gaullist, and Jospin had evolved from extreme leftism (gauchisme) to what he himself labels a pragmatic social democratic stance. Just as Alain Juppé's ministers are mainly in their forties, even thirties, so the coming men of the Socialist Party are still early in their careers. This reflects the changes that one finds throughout French society.

After letting a very young political leader, Rudolf Scharping, take the helm for a while, Germany's SPD returned to a still-young Oskar Lafontaine, minister-president of the Saar, who distinguished himself in the past by his leftist, somewhat anti-American, pacifist stances. Today few people remember the furious debates that raged around issues like the installation in Germany of U.S. Pershing-II missiles putatively to protect the Germans from Soviet monsters called the SS-20s. Lafontaine lost the penultimate general elections to the irresistible Helmut Kohl (Scharping lost the last one), in good part because of his doubts about the pace of German re-unification. The discontents of this expensive and, for many in the east, painful process have cost Kohl's CDU support, but it is not at all clear yet whether Lafontaine will know how to take advantage of this better than Scharping.

The wear and tear of power marked Spain's long-ruling socialist party, PSOE. It lost ground in local elections and was beset by financial scandals. There were nasty allegations regarding the role of the government of Felipe Gonzalez in sponsoring death-squads used to fight the terrorist ETA, the Basque extremist organization, in the 80s, measures that apparently led to the murder of individuals mistakenly identified as ETA activists. But at year's end, the PSOE was able to block a parliamentary inquiry into this affair. And with Felipe Gonzalez's loyal lieutenant, Javier Solana, winning NATO's top civilian job, things are looking up for the PSOE, who must go to the country no later than March 1996, with Gonzalez as leader.

Italy caught its breath, as it were, after two tumultuous years that demonstrated the deep strengths of Italian democracy and the civic sense of this country that so often is accused of having no civic sense. Led by a courageous band of judges (prosecuting attorneys), Italians hacked away at the tentacles of what they call the "octopus," which strictly speaking refers to the Mafia, but which in its broader connotation is the network encompassing organized crime and the bosses of Italy's political parties. With the Christian Democracy and the Socialist Party demolished, the question was how to rebuild the Italian Republic. While the government of Lamberto Dini runs the country steadily and calmly, the new generations choose their camps, with the main centers forming around the PDS (Party of the Democratic Left), the AN (National Alliance) and the federalists of the northern leagues. The bulk of the PDS comes from the old, dissolved PCI, whose democratic credentials were considered pretty solid by most observers even before the collapse of communism. The NA is made up largely of the old, dissolved MSI, which carries the fascist tradition. Their democratic credentials are generally accepted, though unlike their rivals on the left, they have not had the opportunity to show their stuff through municipal governance, as the left has done in many cities. (It was Socialist management of Milan that brought out the prosecuting attorneys; Communist management of such cities as Bologna and Naples has been, evidently, much cleaner.)

Great Britain's Labour Party found a new centrist leader in Tony Blair and Prime Minister John Major survived a challenge from his "Eurosceptic" right-wing. Sweden went from "right" to "left" in late 1994 but could not find a replacement in 1995 for retiring Inguar Carlsson. Norway, despite the entreaties of Prime Minister Gro Harlem Brundlandt (Social Democrat), turned down EU membership in a referendum. Denmark's government is Social Democratic. The truth is that everybody is in the center. Germany's CDU has a more activist, "social," line than many other European parties of the "right." There is no recognizable threat from the revolutionary anti-democratic left in Europe. The only country with a "dangerous" right is France, and even if it is pretty clear the National Front is racist, xenophobic and even fascist, it is not proven. They will not play by the democratic rules. There is a similar party in Austria whose leader, Joerg Haider, made a strong run for the chancellorship, but was beaten in December by Franz Uranitzky, a Social Democrat.

An Austrian human rights activist, seventy-one-year-old Maria Loley, was injured by a letter-bomb sent by terrorists opposed to her work resettling Bosnian refugees. The then mayor of Vienna, Helmut Zilk, was wounded in a similar attack in December 1993. Haider has been accused of encouraging Austrian xenophobia. Ugly as these incidents are, it is difficult to see extremists taking over in any European country.

But history is nothing if not surprising. Europe is indeed run by centrists with overwhelmingly sensible, tolerant, law-abiding constituencies, but the unresolved tensions between a social contract that has worked, and the demands of a new European system in a new global environment, are real and deep. The new Europeans, born in the 1940s, '50s and '60s, have inherited strong democratic institutions for dealing with social tensions. It is up to them to find the audacity and imagination to use their assets to fix their frayed economies and adapt their social contract to the new European realities.

Roger Kaplan is editor of Freedom Review.

The Middle East: Between Peaceand Jihad

Daniel Pipes

Much happens in a region of 300 million over twelve months. But in an era of American introspection, only four major Middle East stories reached the United States in 1995: the challenge of fundamentalist Islam, the potential of a New Middle East, the Arab-Israeli peace process, and the assassination in November of Israel's Prime Minister Yitzhak Rabin. Despite the shock of the last event, the first three had far more importance for the region's prospects to evolve toward freedom and democracy.

The fundamentalist threat

Fundamentalist Islam, or more exactly, the political ideology of Islamism, represents a very serious threat to the existing order. The Middle East has reached a fork in the road, posed between two paths, one marked "business as usual," the other "fundamentalist Islam." Business as usual means the continued rule of nonfundamentalists heading tired and corrupt regimes. Fundamentalist Islam represents an intellectually alive and politically dynamic movement. The former rule almost everywhere; the latter controls just a few countries, notably Iran and the Sudan. Will fundamentalists expand from their current bases to take over regimes throughout the region, or will existing leaders beat them back? Might their battle permit yet others come to power? This issue overrides the region's many other problems—including the Arab-Israeli conflict and the threat posed by Saddam Hussein in Iraq—because it has such wide consequences. Nonfundamentalist politicians in the Middle East understand the threat facing them, for they are personally targeted. In the words of Israel's Prime Minister Shimon Peres, "There is currently a clash not only between Jews and Arabs, as was previously the case, but between peace and those who want to murder it."

The battle for the future of the Middle East is taking place in virtually every country, but four have particular importance. Egypt serves as pivot of the Arabic-speaking countries and its fate will greatly affect the whole region, as well as the Arab-Israeli conflict. In 1995, Husni Mubarak changed policy, no longer tolerating ostensibly peaceful fundamentalists (such as the Muslim Brethren) who profess to work within the political system. Instead, he cracked down on all fundamentalists in an effort to save his weakened regime.

Turkey is the only Muslim state of the Middle East with an avowedly secular constitution; the collapse of Kemal Ataturk's legacy would spell a defeat for the great experiment to show the compatibility of Islam and modernity. Also, Turkey would be the one country where fundamentalists could attain power through democratic means, much boosting their legitimacy and perhaps their influence.

In contrast, the collapse of the Islamic Republic of Iran would be a major setback for fundamentalists throughout the Muslim world. A myriad of signs suggest that the population (and the youth especially) feels disaffected from the ruling ideology. So widespread is this alienation that many of the country's religious leaders have disassociated themselves from the regime in the hopes of thereby retaining their status. In certain ways, the situation in Iran resembles that of Poland during the 1980s: just as the rise of Solidarity indicated that workers had rejected the Workers' State, so in Iran are the mullahs turning away from the Islamic Republic.

The most intense, violent and important battle of all is being waged in Algeria, where already tens of thousands have lost their lives. The viciousness of this battle, fought without mercy on both sides, makes the Iranian revolution look like a tea party: "The most bunkered Iranian *pasdaran* [revolutionary guard] would seem moderate beside these obtuse militants" observes a well-traveled Iranian. Similarly, if the Shah of Iran went out of his way not to hurt his enemies (on finally deciding to form a military government, he gave instructions, "Begin applying the martial law tomorrow, but I do not want anybody's nose to bleed!"), Algeria's rulers use all means at their disposal to repress.

Iran, in other words, is of little help in understanding the second battle of Algiers. But Cambodia is. Just as the Khmer Rouge sought to purify their country by exterminating a quarter of the population, especially those with an education, so too in Algeria does an arch-fanatical group seek to rid the country of its Western-oriented citizens. If things go seriously wrong, Algeria could be the site of the last great human tragedy of the twentieth century.

Fortunately, the prospects in Algeria are better than conventional wisdom in Washington—which has virtually given up on the regime—would have it. The regime is ready to fight for its survival; it has resources (especially the hydrocarbon fields in the remote Sahara); and it seems to be gaining in popular support as the full extent of fundamentalist barbarism becomes evident. Algerians themselves expect the regime will survive, as an early 1995 Louis Harris survey of Algerians living in France revealed: 80 percent think the crisis will be settled through talks; 11 percent think the military will win; and a mere 1 percent expect a fundamentalist victory.

Indeed, the prospect of a fundamentalist takeover receded in November 1995, as the regime gained legitimacy in the Arab world's first ever pluralistic presidential election. In it, Liamine Zeroual won 61 percent of the vote, to some 25 percent for a fundamentalist candidate. As the army pressed its offensive, hundreds of fundamentalist fighters turned themselves in. The presidential vote was widely interpreted as a powerful statement calling for peace and democracy, one that the government apparently understood as such, and Zeroual promised legislative elections in 1996.

A new Middle East?

The visionary notion of a "New Middle East" has become a centerpiece of hopes for the region. While many leaders subscribe to this notion, Israel's Shimon Peres originated it and most articulately explains it. The "New Middle East" is premised on the belief that if the Middle East prospers economically, political passions will wither away. Decent wages, a good house and a car will temper the flames of irredentism and defang terrorism. This transformation inspires Peres. "Markets are more important than borders," he declares; his "great dream" is "the computerization of the Middle East." Those skeptical of this vision he dismisses as out of touch and out of date. "It's a changed world and...you are thinking in the past."

He sees Israel, the region's great economic success story, having a major role in the Middle East's turn to economics. If Israel could grow by 5 percent a year since 1985, the fastest rate in the industrial world, why not the Arabs, too? Peres has grand ambitions for his country: "Our real aim is to change the Middle East" by convincing the Arabs that economic growth is possible. To help accomplish this, he looks forward to Israel cooperating with Jordan and the Palestinian Authority on economic issues in a "Benelux-style arrangement."

For confirmation that the New Middle East is materializing, Peres looks at the bright side of things. In Gaza, seen by most as the region's worst slum, he finds that a "dynamic reconstruction has started." How so? By grasping at whatever wisps come to hand. "Women are throwing away their veils and are going swimming in the sea," he says, while "Coffee houses are opening."

Peres's message has won wide support internationally, for it exactly fits the common assumption of international financial institutions that prosperity solves political problems; the World Bank's Caio Koch-Weser states that "If the peace process has any hope of success, the Palestinians need to see improvements in their living conditions very quickly." The Western European and Japanese concur, of course, in this belief, as do such figures as President Clinton, King Hussein of Jordan and Husni Mubarak.

Interestingly, this message resonates far less well among the Israeli and Arab populations. Israelis are deeply torn by this vision, some uplifted by its strength and optimism, others wary that it lacks realism. Further, Peres has abandoned the long-standing Israeli position on the solution to the Arab-Israeli conflict, which stresses the need for the Arabs to recognize Israel's borders and accept the Jewish state politically. Instead, he advocates working to increase Arab wealth, on the assumption that this inevitably will lead to normalization. Arabs (and Muslims more generally) also divide on this vision, between those willing to switch emphasis to getting wealthy and those who see it as a new form of Israeli imperialism. The former camp includes leading politicians and a fair number of businessmen—elements aware of how their peoples are falling behind and eager to get ahead. But those who still see Israel as an enemy remain more numerous, and they now twist the benign vision of a New Middle East into a fearsome specter of Israeli economic dominion. An Egyptian newspaper explains this fear: "What it [Israel] has failed to achieve by war it will achieve by peace. A Zionist empire will spring up between the Nile and the Euphrates, one in which the mighty Zionists will be masters and the inept, misguided, and dysfunctional Arabs the underdogs." More alarming yet, an Arabic translation of Peres's book, *The New Middle East,* contains an introduction claiming his text provides "irrefutable proof" confirming *The Protocols of the Elders of Zion*—a century-old Russian forgery claiming that Jews seek to take control of the world; the introduction claims that Peres's plan confirms that Jews plan to start the process by dominating the Middle East.

Attractive as it is, Peres's approach has other problems. To begin, deep religious and nationalist issues predominate in the Middle East, perhaps more than in any other region, and prosperity is unlikely to cause them to subside. Indeed, readiness for peace appears to have little to do with standard of living. Survey research shows that Hamas is more popular in the (richer) villages of the West Bank than in (poorer) refugee camps of Gaza. On a larger scale, the richer countries of Iran, Iraq and Libya have compiled a far more anti-Israel record than have the poorer countries of Oman, Yemen and Tunisia.

Further, with the exception of Saddam Hussein's imperialistic venture into Kuwait, the Middle East's internal conflicts have had little to do with economics. Rather, they concern religion, ethnicity and ideology. This applies to the civil wars in Lebanon, Yemen, Sudan and Algeria, as well as the Iraq-Iran war. It also applies to the Arab-Israeli conflict, a hundred-years' war that has never primarily concerned material issues. Zionists did not move from northern Europe to the wastes of Palestine in search of economic gain. Affluent Palestinians in Amman today dream of Palestine not for material reasons. Rather, the conflict on both sides is intensely political. For two millennia, Jews longed for "next year in Jerusalem," and Palestinians now evince a similar longing for a "return." Speaking as a Palestinian, Fawaz Turki observes: "We plunge headlong into politics. There is no respite from this when you're with Palestinians. That's all they do." It is hard to see a computerized, Benelux-style solution overcoming such intense feelings. Yet Peres openly admits that he wishes to ignore those feelings: "In recent years, I have become totally tired of history, because I feel history is a long misunderstanding. The problem with the experts is there is a status quo on their mind. Well, the world is changing." Changing for sure, but to the point that history is rendered irrelevant?

Peace process developments

To explain Arab diplomatic failures vis-à-vis Israel, Abba Eban famously quipped in 1967 that "our Arab neighbors never lost a chance of missing an opportunity." True then, perhaps, but no longer. The Egyptian government signed a peace treaty with Israel in 1979, the Jordanians followed suit in 1994 and the Palestine Liberation Organization signed a series of interim agreements in 1993-95. The latter are much the most complex. The PLO won a Palestinian Authority that exercises autonomous control (not sovereignty) over Gaza and, by the end of 1995, nearly all the Arab towns on the West Bank; in return, Yasir Arafat accepted co-existence with Israel, an obligation he has only reluctantly fulfilled. The PLO finds itself in a shaky position between Israeli demands and the still-fervent anti-Zionism of so many Palestinians. Faysal al-Husseini, one of Arafat's leading supporters, acknowledged this weakness in 1994, referring to the accords with Israel: "After a twenty-seven-year pregnancy, we have given birth to a premature son, in weak health and who may not survive."

Israelis gained little on the ground from their several agreements with the Palestinians; the killing of citizens continued and even accelerated. Rather, the peace process brought gains to Israel in the international sphere. Thirty previously reluctant states established formal diplomatic relations with Israel in the year after the first Palestinian agreement had been signed, increasing their number from 116 to 146. This led to so many dignitaries seeking to visit Jerusalem, the Foreign Ministry began to discourage all but the highest-ranking guests. Israel's enhanced position could be seen in other ways, too. The prime minister, foreign minister and defense minister of Russia (population: 150 million) all pleaded in September 1995 with the prime minister of Israel (population: 5 million), "Do not underestimate us; Russia is still a superpower," implying that Israel's opinion was critical to its superpower status. The Russian prime minister then several times asked his Israel counterpart: "Why do you not call me? Why do you not keep in touch? Why should we not speak on the phone at least once a month?" Israel finally shed its pariah status and gained not only new popularity but real influence.

Borders or existence?

Beyond the many intricacies of the peace process, Arab intentions toward Israel remain yet unclear. Have Muslim peoples truly accepted the Jewish state, or do they still hope to eliminate it? Much evidence exists on both sides.

Optimists argue that the Arab-Israeli conflict has become a conventional diplomatic problem. As Fouad Ajami of Johns Hopkins University wrote in 1978, it "is no longer about Israel's existence, but about its boundaries." The State Department's "peace team" operates on this assumption; Aaron David Miller, one of its key members, wrote in 1988 that "for most Arabs the debate has ceased to focus on the patronizing and pointless question of whether Israel should exist; it turns instead on the more practical and promising matter of boundaries." These days, this body of opinion holds, as David Lamb of the *Los Angeles Times* writes, that "the Arab world has crossed a psychological barrier and come to accept what few Arabs would have dared say ten years ago: Peace with Israel is inevitable." Thomas L. Friedman of the *New York Times* goes so far as to claim that Israel's "war with the Arabs is over." A myriad of nonbellicose relations with Israel, from Muslims sitting in Israel's parliament to Qatar signing energy pacts, would seem to bear out this view.

To which the pessimists reply that the Arabs are biding their time in an era of weakness, but have not given up the dream of destroying Israel. The "Arab-Israeli conflict is no more about borders," argues Douglas Feith, a former White House official dealing with the Middle East, "than the U.S.-Soviet conflict was about missiles." In this view, Arabs recognize that their choices are limited: with the Soviet Union gone, Arab unity diminished and the oil bonanza over, they accept an end to open military belligerency with Israel, but only temporarily, and will renew the hot war when circumstances favor them again.

Treaties without normalization

These days, many Arabs appear to accept treaties and other agreements as a bitter necessity, without experiencing a change of heart. It appears that while Arabs have resigned themselves to formal agreements with Israel, they remain personally deeply reluctant to interact with Israelis. Strong antagonism toward Israelis remains in place, even as peace negotiations and treaties take place.

In two polls, Hilal Khashan of the American University of Beirut found that Levantine Arabs acknowledge the need to come to terms with Israel even as they refuse to accept it for the long term. Similarly, the Center for Palestine Research and Studies, an independent Palestinian research center located in Nablus, on the West Bank, discovered that 39 percent of Palestinians still wish to eliminate Israel. Hizbullah's leading intellectual, Muhammad Hussein Fadlallah, makes this same distinction when he states there is no "peace between Israel and the Arab and Muslim peoples. It is only a peace between Israel and these unelected Arab and Muslim regimes that do not represent their people." So long as a majority of Arabs are unwilling to legitimize their leaders' actions and accept the implications and potential rewards of peace with Israel, the warm peace that Israelis so desperately crave will remain beyond their grasp.

Two models of Arab-Israeli peacemaking

From the Israeli viewpoint, two distinct models of Arab peacemaking have emerged, one sincere and the other duplicitous. Egypt's Anwar al-Sadat and Jordan's King Hussein embody the first, Syria's Hafez al-Assad and the PLO's Yasir Arafat the second.

Sadat and Hussein came to the table with Israel with poor records. Sadat's anti-Semitism included writing an admiring eulogy of Hitler ("You many be proud of having become the immortal leader of Germany"). King Hussein went to war with Israel in 1967 and sided with Saddam Hussein's barbaric conquest of Kuwait in 1990-91. But they put these unpleasantries aside when making peace with Israel. At treaty-signing ceremonies with Israel, for example, both men showed pleasure to be making peace and they subsequently kept their word with sincerity and consistency. At the same time, both agreements had their limits. Israelis expected peace with Egypt and got an enhanced form of nonbelligerency. King Hussein tried to enthuse the Jordanian body politic for the peace treaty but failed. The two treaties' fragility has renewed Israeli wariness.

Some observers profess to find the same sincerity in Assad and Arafat. Two writers for the *New York Times* exemplify this thinking: Serge Schmemann writes of Assad that "the question is not whether Syria will make peace with Israel, but when and how," while Thomas Friedman tells of "the change of heart" he has seen "come over" Arafat. Stephen P. Cohen of the Center for Middle East Peace and Economic Cooperation flatly states that both Assad and Arafat "have decided to make peace." But this is hard to believe, for the two leaders engage in persistent pattern of double games, by which they say or do one thing today and quite the contrary tomorrow. Arafat sometimes calls for jihad, praises those Palestinians who killed Jews, and promises unending bloodshed ("The Palestinian people is willing to sacrifice its last boy and girl so that the Palestinian flag will fly over the churches and mosques of Jerusalem"). At other times he declares his readiness to "achieve coexistence" with Israel and says "we are neighbors, we can coordinate, cooperate, in all fields by all means for the sake of our new children." Assad has not signed an agreement with Israel, but since agreeing to negotiate with Israel in July 1991, he has taken a flurry of contradictory steps, moving both toward and away from Israel. As Yitzhak Rabin put it, "One [Syrian] hand is as if extended in peace. The other hand opens fire on you." For example, Syrian media coverage of Israel no longer exudes hostility. The regime has taken modest but real steps to prepare Syrians for accord with Israel: "peace" and its synonyms have replaced "steadfastness" and "confrontation" as the leitmotifs of public discourse about Israel. At the same time, Syria officials and media continue to bristle with hostility on the subject of Israel, using such terms as "the enemy," "the Zionist enemy," "occupied Palestine," "occupied Jerusalem" and "the Zionist entity."

This pattern of contradictions causes many Israelis to lose faith in the peace process. Back in July 1991, when Assad agreed to enter negotiations with Israel, it was possible to hope that the longtime Syrian dictator had decided on a basic change in policy. Likewise, in September 1993, when Rabin shook hands with Yasir Arafat on the White House lawn, one could hope that Arafat had shed his ways of old. At the end of 1995, these hopes are difficult to sustain.

Human rights improving?

In an era when democracy, the rule of law and private property have become globally powerful forces, the Middle East (along with most of Africa) severely lags behind.

Take democracy: the region has only two fully democratic states, Israel and Turkey. The rest are all, to one degree or other, autocracies. Nor is there much sign of change; with the possible exception of Kuwait, Arabs and Iranians indicate few strong impulses for self-rule. Rulers and peoples alike seem to have other priorities and so agree, implicitly, on its unimportance. This is particularly clear among the Palestinians. A 1993 study of Palestinian public opinion asked for "the main attribute you would like to see in a future Palestinian state." Fully 60 percent choose Islam, 10 percent Arabism, and just 20 percent opted for democracy. Confirming this conclusion, Said K. Aburish reports from extensive discussions on the West Bank a few years back that, "Not one interviewee had any attachment to the idea of freedom: they all thought freedom through democratic systems wasn't possible."

Middle Eastern leaders either have no idea what democracy is or pretend they don't. Jonathan Raban explains that the Arab political world remains "a domain of totalitarian metaphor in which satanic evil and godly heroism clash in an unending orgy of blood and guts." If these are the terms, what do civil society and the ballot box have to offer? Reflecting on his years of reporting from the Middle East, Thomas Friedman observes: "When push comes to shove, when the modern veneer of nation-statehood is stripped away, it all still comes down to Hamas Rules: Rule or die. One man triumphs, the others weep. The rest is just commentary."

Many "elections" degenerate into exercises in adulation. In Syria, voting takes place under the watchful eyes of policemen and ballots contain just one name: Hafez al-Assad. In the last such referendum, the ayes carried, 6,726,843 to 396, giving Assad a 99.994 percent approval. Not content with this landslide, a government spokesman hailed the results as proof of "the establishment of a solid democratic system" in Syria. For his part, Saddam Hussein won a mere 99.96 percent of the vote in an October 1995 referendum. Mu'ammar al-Qadhafi, a deeper thinker than his colleagues in Damascus and Baghdad, claims that democracy has already been instituted in Libya and explains what this means: "When authority becomes the people's, it will not be attacked or seen as an enemy. Only the enemies of the people will then conspire against that authority. They should be annihilated without any discussion...crushed under the feet of the masses even without trial." In short, as other parts of the world democratize, the authoritarian nature of Middle Eastern politics is becoming ever more conspicuous. This said, some glimmerings of progress having to do with democracy are slowly reaching the Middle East. The presidential elections in Algeria may have broken a taboo. And while nearly all governments remain in the hands of tyrants, decades of dictatorship have made at least some elements aware of the costs. As a result, human rights groups are gaining in strength, advocates of the rule of law and economic freedom are speaking up, the market and private property are making advances. Real change, however, probably lies many years in the future.

Daniel Pipes is editor of the Middle East Quarterly *and author of the forthcoming* Syria Beyond the Peace Process, *to be published by the Washington Institute for Near East Policy.*

Africa:
Recasting a Continent Thomas R. Lansner

Africa-watchers both optimistic and pessimistic could each in 1995 find ample material to argue their corners. The year's events in sub-Saharan Africa ranged from democratic consolidation in South Africa and tentative peace pacts in Angola, Liberia, Mali and Niger to continued conflict in Burundi, Rwanda and Sudan and the specter of national disintegration in Sierra Leone and Zaire. In countries such as Benin, Botswana and Namibia, the democratic process took deeper root. In others like Nigeria and Kenya, authoritarian rulers wrapped themselves in further infamy by exercising increasingly naked and brutal repression.

In the Maghreb, increasingly nervous authoritarian regimes tested combinations of openness and repression in efforts to contain growing Islamic militancy. Algerians responded to another year of terror and counter-terror by Islamic fundamentalists and the military by defying intimidation to vote in large numbers in a November presidential. The election gave President Lamine Zeroual victory but appeared more a plea for an end to violence than endorsement of any candidate.

Such contradictory developments encourage prudence in forecasting trends in Africa. Could anyone predict that the political rehabilitation of Zairian strongman Marshal Mobutu Sese Seko would be one consequence of the Rwandan slaughter? Would anyone have guessed that Uganda, after enduring fifteen years of brutal misrule by two of Africa's worst dictators, would today be viewed as a model for economic development on the continent?

Some indicators, however, point to positive long-term changes in Africa. One is that respect for fundamental freedoms shows signs of becoming a norm demanded by African leaders of each other, whereas until recently it was decried as an externally-imposed alien value. Another is growing awareness that close economic cooperation is a prerequisite for growth. Also, the information revolution that has so far largely bypassed Africa may finally get jumped-started by new and cheaper technologies in tandem with economic and political liberalization.

A combination of good leadership and good luck will be necessary to meld these elements into a package that helps spread peace and prosperity. But even slow progress will be obstructed so long as authoritarian regimes contemptuous of the rule of law continue to dominate vast areas of the continent.

Saro-Wiwa: Not in vain?

Nowhere is that contempt more blatantly displayed than in Nigeria. Human rights campaigner and eco-activist Ken Saro-Wiwa's murder at the hands of Nigeria's dictator-generals in November was yet another debasement of the Nigerian peoples' rights and that junta's latest slap at international opinion.

General Sani Abacha apparently feels strong enough to defy not only his own people, but the world. Yet international revulsion at the hanging of Saro-Wiwa—and eight other Ogoni activists—may mean that his death was not in vain.

Especially important was the response of South Africa's new leadership. Over three-plus decades of independence, most African leaders have been loathe to criticize any other African regime for human rights violations. Years of repression, massacres and genocidal ethnic cleansing have passed in various African states with barely a whisper of public consternation, much less condemnation, from their continental neighbors or the Organization of African Unity (OAU). But Saro-Wiwa's execution after a mock-trial evoked an angry reaction from President Nelson Mandela and his African National Congress colleagues, who had vigorously lobbied the Nigerian generals to grant clemency. The South Africans demanded stiff international sanctions against Nigeria to force the generals there to hand power to an elected government.

Despite Mandela's moral authority, the campaign to isolate the Nigerian junta will likely be long and difficult. Many industrialized countries and multi-national corporations are comfortable with corrupt and dictatorial regimes with whom they can do business. And most Africans leaders are wary of criticizing their counterparts. But there is new pressure on authoritarian African states to loosen repression and allow democratic development. Respect for fundamental freedoms and human rights might become as important as continental solidarity in assessing bilateral relations.

Other orthodoxies

The demise of the African custom against criticizing African political practices should lead to the questioning of other orthodoxies of the independence era. Most important is the allegedly sacrosanct premise that Africa's inherited colonial boundaries must remain forever inviolable. Eritrea's independence in 1992 and the de facto sovereignty of Somaliland already challenge that notion. Other intractable ethnic conflicts may never be resolved without some redrawing of borders. But however political entities are reconstructed, the idea that African states can exist separately as viable economic entities must be banished. Africa must move toward broad economic integration if the continent is ever to escape the instability inherent in grafting the superstructure of modern states on weak economies.

The industrialized world played a large role in creating the political and economic map of modern Africa. International bodies should encourage African regional cooperation that can promote larger sustainable markets across borders. This will certainly involve the surrender of some sovereign rights by individual states, but not more than already relinquished by members of the European Union or even signatories to the North American Free Trade Association treaty. New multi-lateral lending and aid from individual donors should focus on regional initiatives that help break down the artificial borders that currently severely constrain Africa's economic growth. A prime example of such irrationality can be seen in West Africa, where Ghana, once a British colony, functions as a virtual economic island in the midst of its Francophone neighbors.

Several African economic blocs intended to promote more open trade are still hindered by national rivalries and external ties far stronger than regional affiliations. The West African Economic and Monetary Union is the most concrete actor, providing a common currency and central banking facilities for seven Francophone states.

Its reliance on France severely limits its scope for action, however, and inhibits the emergence of the larger, sixteen-member Economic Community of West African States.

The Common Market for Eastern and Southern Africa comprises twenty-two states, but does not include South Africa, which was not considered for membership during the apartheid era. South Africa is in little hurry to join, since it already dominates the Southern Africa Development Community, and is busy forging its own bilateral economic links with numerous other countries across the continent.

Regional cooperation is only one step in resolving Africa's lack of economic development. The concentration of external loans and investment in extractive industries must be shifted to more productive enterprises for long-term gains. It is also important is for African governments to speed up reforms that reduce state involvement in the economy and promote freer markets. There is, in many countries, an urgent need to rebuild an agricultural sector debilitated by subsidized food prices and environmental neglect. But for these strategies to be pursued, more open governance with leadership accountability is required. The affliction of authoritarianism, particularly in its more corrupt forms, stunts economic growth as surely as it stifles political expression.

Information: Playing catch-up

Recasting the continent also requires efforts in the area of information access, the oxygen of modern economies. Sub-Saharan Africa's telecommunications infrastructure is severely lacking, with only about 4 million telephones serving over 500 million people—less than one line per 100 people, compared to an average of about sixty lines per 100 people in the industrialized world. Excluding South Africa from the calculation produces an even bleaker picture. Further, costs for equipment and international calling are very high, often prohibitively so in terms of local income levels, as well as a serious drain on scarce foreign exchange.

At present, only a dozen African countries are even on e-mail networks, and only a few are fully connected to the Internet. But new technologies may help bring Africa on-line. The traditional linkage between a country's wealth and its level of information access is being eroded. Cellular and optic-fiber technology are lowering the huge capital expense once needed to "hardwire" communications points. Also, ever-lower prices for computers and modems are reducing individual turnkey costs. Intra-African communications would also be greatly enhanced if an ambitious project proposed by AT&T goes ahead. The company is seeking U.S. government backing for a $2 billion project to lay 21,000-miles of fiber-optical cable around the entire African continent.

Internet access will certainly help open Africa's economies. It will also provide interactive communication that can as run easily from South to North instead of being dominated by flows from the opposite direction, as is the case today. Further, Internet access can provide low-cost intra-African communication that will engender greater information exchanges and encourage the regional integration essential for eventual widespread prosperity.

Other changes are necessary to bring the information revolution to Africa. Many countries retain laws that seriously restrict foreign investment. Few projects can move ahead without substantial external funding, and investors are often wary of entering long-term joint ventures with potentially unreliable state-run enterprises. But telecommunications monopolies, even if poorly-administered, produce a stream of guaranteed revenue into state coffers that officials are loathe to forego.

The security self-interest of authoritarian regimes—to which unrestricted information flows are anathema—is another choke-point. The state still controls most broadcasting in Africa, an especially important factor in lands with low literacy rates where radio is a prime means of disseminating information. Broad access to unrestricted information inevitably produces greater diversity of opinion that is ever-harder to quash. Such ideological and political barriers only impede introduction of cheaper and more accessible communications that fuel both economic growth and the growth of civil society. It is also a reminder that there is much work still to be done promoting and protecting the most basic of human rights in many African countries.

Democratization—mixed returns

While the array of daunting challenges facing Africa is not cause for total despair, prognostication over Africa's vast potential must not allow these problems to be glossed over. Severe human rights abuses continued in many countries during 1995 and intensified in some. Peace pacts brought a tenuous quiet to several states as other wars raged on. And it was a year of mixed returns for African democratization.

Further consolidation of the democratic process in South Africa is a most positive sign, not only for that country but the region overall. The Constitutional Court demonstrated its independence in overruling President Mandela's decree on apportioning voting districts, and the new constitution will include strong provisions protecting human rights and civil liberties. Local elections completed the transition to majority rule down to the community level. Violence and political infighting delayed voting in some areas not dominated by the ruling African National Congress, however, and ethnic and racial tensions remain a potential tinderbox. Continued institutionalization of the rule of law is an urgent priority for such a diverse society, especially one facing considerable uncertainties when Nelson Mandela's moderating influence no longer looms over the political landscape.

Reports elsewhere run the gamut from genuine openness to cynical manipulation of electoral systems. Several countries are successfully strengthening democratic institutions. In Benin, Botswana, Mali and Namibia, multiparty systems seem to be taking firm hold. Other transitions, as in the Central African Republic, Malawi, Mozambique and Niger are more tenuous, with hangovers of war or authoritarianism still clouding long-term prospects. In Zimbabwe, a strong patronage system and media restrictions are creating conditions for the de facto one-party state for which President Robert Mugabe has clearly expressed his preference. Elections in Ethiopia produced the country's first-ever popularly-elected government, though an opposition boycott and continual government harassment of media and political activists seriously devalued that achievement.

Côte d'Ivoire's October presidential race was even more of a non-contest. The regime simply barred the opposition's strongest potential candidate from standing. Incumbent Henri Bédié was returned with an overwhelming majority of the few voters who bothered to endorse the pre-ordained result. The same month saw elections in Tanzania marred by both fraud and utter disorganization. Many international observers believe the ruling party simply stole the elections on the island of Zanzibar, while those on the mainland were so poorly-run that it is difficult to judge the validity of the results.

In Eritrea and Uganda, non-elected leaders who led successful guerrilla struggles continue to rule, evidently with more popular support than many nominally elected governments. Both countries have undertaken broad constitutional consultations that included extensive public participation. And each boasts a president, Issayas Afwerki in Eritrea and Yoweri Museveni in Uganda, with a personal reputation for honesty and integrity. Uganda's open market economic revival has won international plaudits, as has Eritrea's single-minded pursuit of reconstruction after its thirty-year war for independence. But pressure against the independent media and ruling party dominance raises questions regarding even slow transitions to truly open societies in both countries.

Dictatorships—digging in

Manipulation of elections or maneuvering among competing political parties usually indicates that at least lip service is being paid to notions of pluralism and popular representation. In two of Africa's largest countries, Nigeria and Sudan, even such pretense is dropped.

Nigeria is one of the most closely-watched countries in Africa. With over 100 million people, it is the continent's most populous nation, and its immense oil wealth makes it a potential engine of regional economic growth. General Abacha announced in October that any return to civilian rule is at least three years away. The elected president, Moshood Abiola, languishes in detention, as do hundreds of opposition activists, human rights campaigners, journalists and trade union officials.

The November execution of Ken-Saro Wiwa and eight colleagues marked a further low point in the junta's brutality. Saro-Wiwa was charged with planning the death of four regime supporters. The regime's real need to silence him was his tireless and eloquent advocacy for rights for his minority Ogoni ethnic group. The Ogoni homeland is impoverished despite the vast quantities of oil that has been pumped from beneath it. Saro-Wiwa represented not only a challenge to the military's political dominance, but a movement that could threaten the regime's lifeblood of oil exports.

Other death sentences were handed down against alleged coup plotters convicted by secret military tribunals earlier in the year, but were commuted after heavy international pressure. Among those jailed is the widely-respected former Nigerian leader Olusegun Obasanjo, who headed a military government that returned Nigeria to civilian rule in 1979. Few observers believe Abacha's pledges to restore genuine civilian government. The continued denial of any avenues of political expression is building to dangerous levels of frustration, and might explode into terrible political violence along ethnic, religious and regional lines that could match Rwanda's 1994 carnage for intensity and dwarf it in scale.

Africa's other most thorough dictatorship, Sudan, is already engulfed by such a war. The Islamic fundamentalist regime that seized power in 1989 continues to struggle to impose its vision on diverse peoples across the vast land. Political opposition and free expression is almost entirely circumscribed. This year, even fax machines were confiscated to limit contact with the outside world. Any gathering of more than five people is illegal. The repression and economic collapse led to an outbreak of rioting that spread from university campuses in the capital, Khartoum, and several other cities in September, and was put down by a massive use of force that reportedly included the summary execution of several student leaders.

Sudan has been at war for twenty of its thirty years as an independent state, and since the conflict flared again in 1983 more than a million people have died in combat, massacres and war-related famine. The racial and religious divide between the Arab north and the black African animists and Christians of Sudan's south would be reconcilable only with the best of good will on both sides. The fundamentalist regime's efforts to impose a harsh version of Islamic shari'a law on the entire country precludes compromise. Intent to totally crush the rebel movements extends to genocidal attacks on black African ethnic groups and enslavement of women and children, especially among the Nuba people whose land covers potentially rich oil deposits. In November, a United Nations special representative to Sudan reported there has been "an alarming increase in...cases of slavery, servitude, slave trade and forced labor" in 1994-95. Many young boys are sold off as farm laborers. Women and girls are taken as servants or as concubines for soldiers.

The war's resolution is complicated by internecine struggles among southern rebels, who are also accused of egregious human rights violations. No end to the killing is in sight, and the conflict is becoming even more intractable as the war becomes entangled in cross-border guerrilla conflicts along Sudan's frontiers with Eritrea and Uganda.

Mobutu resurrected, Moi lingering

Africans in several other countries also continued to suffer under harshly authoritarian regimes. Zaire's descent into anarchy continued. But even as his country teetered closer to collapse, President Marshal Mobutu made good use of Rwanda's misfortunes to help reverse his own. Shrewdly manipulating more than a million Hutu refugees on Zairian soil and conflicting agendas of Western countries in Central Africa, Mobutu cast himself as a key actor able to spark or stay a new round or ethnic war. His reward for so far maintaining a relative peace has been official redemption among Western governments that in 1994 were ostracizing him as a corrupt and dangerous despot.

Mobutu maintains his leverage by allowing extremist Hutu factions—among them many of the planners and perpetrators of the 1994 Rwandan genocide—to regroup and re-arm on Zairian soil. According to reports by human rights investigators, these groups have received weapons and training from France, yet another manifestation of the highly questionable role the French government, military and secret services have played in the ongoing Central African tragedy.

The architects of genocide are also afforded refuge in Kenya, where President Daniel arap Moi steadily pulls further back from any tendencies towards liberalization conceded under heavy donor pressure in the early 90s. A combination of harassment, politically-motivated judicial actions and physical attacks are being used to intimidate the opposition. Moi's reaction to domestic and international criticism—and a crime wave that has many people calling the Kenyan capital of Nairobi "Nairobbery"—is to accuse local opponents and foreign governments of ever more byzantine plots to unseat him.

On Africa's western coastal region, Presidents Paul Biya of Cameroon, Omar Bongo of Gabon and Gnassingbe Eyadéma of Togo cling to office. Each is about midway through a term of office "won" in an election neither free nor fair. Each has the strong support of the army. And equally important, each enjoys the strong political, economic and military support of France, which has extensive commercial interests in all three countries and long and close ties to their authoritarian leaders. Also in West Africa, The Gambia's young army coup-makers still talk of a return to the civilian rule they overthrew in 1994. There is little sign, however, that they feel in any hurry to do so. Mauritania shows signs of a vigorous civil society, but serious discrimination against the country's black minority continues, and the democratic constitution of 1991 has not been subjected yet to the acid test of truly competitive election.

Some wars...

Until the end of the Cold War, Africa's post-independence wars were most often explained in the ideological context of superpower rivalry. In fact, communism and capitalism rarely had anything to do with the real roots of conflict, and merely amplified the level of violence by turning local rivalries into proxy wars.

Fighting is going on in several parts of Africa, mostly along ethnic lines among people casually mixed within colonial boundaries. A bush war in Sierra Leone is dragging through its fifth year. Large tracts of that country are given over to roving bands of soldiers and rebels, and distinguishing between the two is so problematical that local reports speak of violence by "sobels." The military regime promises to hold elections next year, and is relying on South African mercenaries to help quell rebel fighters.

Elsewhere, sporadic attacks by ethnic-based guerrilla forces are reported in Casamance in southern Senegal and in Oromia in southern Ethiopia. More serious unrest spread across southern Chad, where the military-backed interim government claims it cannot control deadly rampages by its army. Clashes among various clans continue to wreak havoc in Somalia, which in its lawlessness has lost nearly all the attributes of a modern state. The northern part of the country, once British Somaliland, has proclaimed its independence as the Somaliland Republic, although it, too, has been riven by clan clashes.

Occasional violence also erupted in Rwanda as the new government fought infiltrators from among the Hutu refugees in Zaire and undisciplined troops killed civilians. In Burundi, the "early warning" many observers believe is essential to averting serious conflict has been clearly and loudly sounded. Nonetheless, the country threatens to slip over the edge from intermittent killing to total conflagration as the world watches anxiously but seems able to offer little more than pious advice.

Some peace...

Resort to arms did not pay off everywhere. Elected governments in a pair of island-states were toppled in coups, but in both instances the coup-makers held power but briefly. Junior army officers in Sao Tome & Principe ousted the elected government to protest deteriorating economic conditions, but were persuaded to return to barracks by donor threats to cut off all aid coupled with a promise of amnesty. In the Comoros, French troops landed to roust a mercenary gang led by Bob Denard, who has defended his previous African military adventures by proclaiming he always acted in the interests of France. The deposed president, in this case, was not returned to office.

Peace agreements also brought to at least a temporary end to several bitter and bloody struggles. In Angola, demobilization of government and UNITA rebel troops began for a second time, and by year's end seemed to be proceeding smoothly in what might be the last act of a war that has lasted for two decades. Liberia's twelfth peace plan over the last three years seems to be its most viable, and an interim administration is preparing for 1996 elections. And in both Mali and Niger, a desert uprising by Tuareg nomads, complicated by the rise of non-government militias and marked by savagery on all sides, was settled with new recognition for local language rights and promises of local development. The halts in hostilities, however, might have been born more out of exhaustion than reconciliation. And in each instance, the ethnic roots of rebellion mean that problems in implementation of the peace could easily spark renewed violence.

Maghreb: Islamists and authoritarians

Across the Maghreb, new political alliances and tactics evolved to face Islamist radicals who demand strict theocratic rule. In Algeria, nearly four years of savage and shadowy civil conflict has killed about 50,000 people. The strong turnout in November's presidential polls could convince leaders of the banned Islamic Salvation Front (FIS) to accept a compromise with the military. Yet both camps are divided: extremists of the Armed Islamic Group (GIA) want nothing less than a strict theocracy; army hardliners seek a total military victory. Guerrilla attacks on civil society and government repression of civil rights continue. And the killing goes on.

Libya faced greater internal tensions in 1995 than at any time since Colonel Mu'ammar al-Qadhafi came to power in a 1969 coup, as armed Islamist groups clashed with security forces in a growing challenge to Qadhafi's dictatorial but secular regime. Libya's long-frayed relations with its neighbors improved in 1995 as they saw a common Islamist threat to their respective regimes. In Tunisia, continued economic growth and secular moderation has won President Zine el-Abidine Ben Ali some genuine support at home and abroad. But mounting repression makes sure that any real opposition and most criticism is kept under wraps, quite literally in the case of thousands of alleged Islamic fundamentalists or their suspected supporters now in detention. And in Morocco, King Hassan II's long-term program of controlled democratization proceeded through 1995 with a continued mix of greater openness spiked with occasional repression.

Rules and reality: Watching Ghana

A microcosm of Africa's potential for progress and for peril can be seen in Ghana, where political and economic liberalization is taking tenuous hold. Ghanaians go to the polls in 1996 to elect their president, and incumbent Jerry Rawlings, once a socialist military dictator and now an apostle of free markets, will seek another term in office. International technical experts are helping register voters. Media openness is increasing. For the first time since independence in 1957 governmental transparency and accountability is a concept that has a chance of being transformed into reality.

The conduct of the elections will be a test of Ghana's political maturity. Rawlings may, like Moi, Bongo or other strongmen, manipulate the voting to produce a victory positive for few beyond his immediate circle. He or his supporters may churn ethnic rivalries to gain votes. Or he may honor his promises to promote a genuine election, and thus, in victory or defeat, pave the way for long-term stability and growth. Ghana's voters will make rational choices to enhance their own futures if given the chance.

In Ghana, like anywhere else, respect for fundamental freedoms and access to information would help make that choice meaningful. Today, democracy is clearly working in some African countries. And in most others, leaders at least acknowledge, by signing human rights treaties, holding some sort of elections and paying at least lip service to respect for basic freedoms, that there are rules of governance and rules for humanity that should be obeyed. Only as Africa begins to call itself to account to respect these rules can peace and stability under the rule of law encourage the economic cooperation and growth that is a threshold requirement for any positive assessment of the continent's future.

Thomas R. Lansner is a contributing editor to Freedom Review.

China:
A Regime Against
its People
Arthur Waldron

Nineteen-ninety-five might have appeared in many respects to be the year that China finally returned to normal after the crisis of the democracy movement six years earlier. Economic growth continued its upward surge: indeed, by 2030, according to projections of the ninth five year plan, China's would be the largest economy in the world. Furthermore, the political situation in Beijing appeared remarkably stable: as Premier Li Peng told an international group on 12 April, "The core of political leadership has already been transferred from Deng Xiaoping, the second-generation leader, to President Jiang Zemin, who represents the third generation."

As foreign leaders streamed steadily through the capital they seemed far more concerned with trade and market access than with the once-paramount questions of human rights and democracy. The United States had made a humiliating back-down a year earlier over its attempt to link trade to freedoms, and now tiptoed around the issues. More generally, the conviction seemed to be growing that, as Helmut Kohl put it on 13 July, China was entitled to "its own concept of human rights."

Such an assessment reflected increasing worldwide acceptance of China's insistence that its "Asian values" saw social virtue in ways very different from those of Westerners: Instead of human rights and democracy alone, the argument goes, Asians value order, consensus and wise leadership. In keeping with this, the Chinese leadership of Jiang Zemin and Li Peng no longer pays even much lip service to liberal values and instead explicitly prepares world public opinion for an autocratic, if increasingly affluent, Chinese future. The shortcomings of democratization in the former Soviet Union are pointed out regularly; elections in Hong Kong and Taiwan are denounced as corrupt; the virtues of what has been (misleadingly) termed the "Singapore model" are acclaimed. The message is that the world will simply have to learn to let China do things its own way.

Harsh repression
This increasingly obdurate attitude toward the outside world has been matched, inside China, by decisive steps to reinforce the party dictatorship. If "Asian values" are promoted abroad, inside China the new watchword is "patriotism." The once-ubiquitous invocations of revolution and socialism have disappeared almost completely, replaced by the slogans of an officially-sponsored campaign of "patriotic education" which extolls traditional Chinese culture and recites the wrongs inflicted on China by imperialism. With its flag-raisings, military reviews, theatricals and pageants, the campaign seeks to restore various pillars of traditional Chinese culture, from Confucius to the Great Wall, that earlier generations

of Communist iconoclasts had anathematized. Officials have been rather candid about their purpose, which is to bolster the third-generation dictatorship by wrapping it in the flag of nationalism, and to support an increasingly assertive international campaign, which also aims to strengthen internal legitimacy, for the "recovery" of Chinese-claimed territories such as Taiwan and various islets in the South China Sea.

But just how effective the new Chinese hard line will prove to be, at home or abroad, and how well the patriotic campaign will serve to support it, are open to doubt. Indeed, the evident stability of 1995 is almost certainly illusory, as deeper forces continued to stir. For one thing, Chinese values, with their powerful stress on the role of virtue in legitimating rule, by no means provide ideological support for the government's ambitions. Furthermore, basic institutional changes in China since Mao Zedong's death in 1976 unleashed far-reaching and potentially uncontrollable economic, demographic and social changes which have not run their course. The observer has to wonder how long it will be before those began to produce political effects.

The words of Jiang Zemin

Jiang Zemin made clear what his government was trying to accomplish when he spoke to the United Nations in October. Talk of human rights is an assault on China's national dignity: "Certain big powers," he said, "often under the cover of 'freedom,' 'democracy' and 'human rights' set out to encroach upon the sovereignty of other countries, interfere in their internal affairs, and undermine their national unity and ethnic harmony."

On the democracy movement and legacy of Tiananmen the official line is equally unyielding. The Chinese president insisted that his meeting with President Clinton, much sought by Washington, be shifted from the New York Public Library, because of an exhibit there, entitled "What Price Freedom?," that included handbills and photographs from Tiananmen, as well as an early version of the American Declaration of Independence, a book by Galileo, and a tape of a speech by Mohandas K. Gandhi.

When, after long illegal detention, China's leading dissident Wei Jingsheng was finally charged formally on 21 November, commentators in Hong Kong summed up the recent trend of Beijing's policies. As Lau Yui-sui put it, "The action against the well known dissident shows Beijing's increasing confidence in dealing with criticism of its human rights by the outside world, following recent diplomatic successes." Luo Fu characterized the approach as dual tactics: "keeping tough in politics while relaxing its grip in economics." Wei was sentenced to fourteen years.

The dual approach—economic liberalization plus repression—to the domestic situation is reminiscent of the policies attempted by Eastern European Communist states in the 1970s and 1980s, as they searched for some way to liberalize the economy while keeping the lid on politics. As for the stress on international connections—it was a rare front page of the official *People's Daily* during the year that did not report at least one high-level visit or foreign trip, and sometimes several—that was in keeping with a diplomatic strategy Chinese governments have followed consistently in this century: to buttress weak political prestige at home by eliciting affirmations of their legitimacy from foreign leaders.

Missing entirely from the official picture was any acknowledgment of a need for institutional political reform. Yet there is good reason to think that this liberalizing agenda—perennial in China since the first drafts of a democratic constitution were produced by the Qing dynasty early in this century—could not be evaded indefinitely.

Hong Kong, 1997

The return of Hong Kong to Beijing's sovereignty in 1997 requires that the Chinese government confront constitutional issues, at least in connection with that small but crucial territory. As the deadline approached, however, the encouraging words of the Sino-British Joint Declaration of 1984 about democracy and a "high degree of autonomy" for Hong Kong are evaporating. Issue after difficult issue has come up: the personal status of Hong Kong residents (Beijing is unwilling to recognize the foreign citizenships of people of Chinese ethnicity); the stationing of troops (China is set to send perhaps 15,000 men as well as a several warships); the court of final appeal (which would have no jurisdiction over "matters of state"—an enormous loophole).

China tries to manage these problems by invoking patriotism and thus polarizing them along lines of nationality: Chinese versus British, and with some success, as in their attacks on governor Chris Patten. But the card is difficult to play. Legislative elections in September delivered a humiliating setback to the pro-China candidates and Beijing responded with pique—calling the vote "unfair and unreasonable"—and renewed statements of their intention to dissolve the elected assembly come 1997. Creating a nominated assembly to take its place, however, is a headache, as even reliably "pro-China" personalities in Hong Kong object to Beijing's initiatives. A furor arose when China declared that it would abolish the territory's Bill of Rights. As 1995 drew to a close, concrete measures for the transfer were not yet in place, and morale in Hong Kong was falling.

Taiwan...

In Taiwan, which China also claims, the process of democratization has produced personal attacks in Beijing media on President Lee Teng-hui of a crudity rarely seen since the Cultural Revolution of the 1960s, as well as a to series of military intimidation exercises, including missile firings, that continued to build as the year came to an end, with rumors of possible direct military action as early as March 1996. Again, Beijing has attempted to define the issues in nationalistic terms: national unity, patriotism, and so forth. But as in Hong Kong, the real threat comes from the emergence of a culturally-Chinese democracy. And as in China proper, the ultimate response of the Beijing authorities to such developments is not compromise or discussion, but the threat or use of force.

...and Xinjiang and Tibet

Unrest also plagues Beijing in the two large territories it controls that are not ethnically Chinese in population: Xinjiang, which is Muslim, and Tibet, which is Buddhist. A hard line on religion was signalled earlier in the year when Ye Xiaowen, well-known as a dogmatic atheist, was appointed head of the Religious Affairs Bureau of State Council, despite letters of objection from at least eight of his colleagues. Arrests of Muslim clerics and some violent incidents have been reported in Xinjiang, where resentment of Chinese rule runs deep, and where the revival of traditional cultural connections to Inner Asian states of the former Soviet Union has changed perspectives. Israeli experts on Islamic fundamentalism have been welcome visitors in China. In Tibet the resistance of the people continues. Clearance projects destroy traditional Tibetan buildings; foreign tourists are admitted into monuments off-limits to Tibetans, and floods of Chinese immigrants dilute the population. Arrests of monks and nuns continue, and—in an unprecedented action—Beijing is promoting its own candidate as Panchen Lama against the one recognized by the Dalai Lama. A possible omen of things to come was an explosion that damaged a plaque in Lhasa commemorating the Chinese "liberation" of the territory. Arrests were also reported in Chinese-controlled Inner Mongolia.

But the most important arena for the officially invisible issues of human rights and democracy is China itself. The precariousness of the leadership's actual grip on power was revealed by a series of humiliating votes in the normally rubber-stamp National People's Congress. Margins on education and banking laws in March votes were rather narrow, and the officially designated candidate for deputy prime minister received only 63 percent of the vote. Such results suggest that the Congress, under the leadership of the ambitious Qiao Shi, might be looking to take on real responsibility, as nominal parliaments did during democratic transitions in Eastern Europe and the USSR. Leaked comments by Qiao, late in 1995, in which he compares the political situation to the transitional era immediately after Mao Zedong's death in 1976, strengthen this possibility.

The power of resistance

Popular dissent has also continued, and labor and strike activity has been reported: seven demonstrations involving more than 1,000 people each in a six month period. When fifteen dissidents were sentenced to terms as long as twenty years in Beijing on 14 June, they shouted "Long live democracy," "Long live free trade unions" and "We are innocent," relatives said. A Nanjing group called "United Front" issued a three-page statement that China had no alternative but to overthrow its "feudal system" and become a "truly democratic" society. "The governing class does very little good for our country's development but enjoys most benefits."

Corruption is as strong an issue as human rights. The appointed mayor of Beijing, Chen Xitong, was removed amid accusations of flagrant corruption, but investigation proved half-hearted, no doubt because the entire party was implicated. A dissident biography, published abroad, estimated the Deng family fortune, mostly accumulated since 1989, at $500 million. Dai Qing, a well-connected activist and dissident, argues that Jiang Zemin faces an unpalatable choice. "He can either save the country or save the party. He could save the country by pushing the [anti-corruption] campaign through to its conclusion, but that would mean the end of the Communist Party." Such opinions are widely shared, even in official circles. As the important book by X. L. Ding, *The Decline of Communism in China: Legitimacy Crisis, 1977-1989* (Cambridge, England: Cambridge University Press, 1994) shows, liberal and dissenting views pervade not only Chinese society but the government itself, constituting effectively a currently-hidden but real counter-establishment.

The government's reaction to this range of challenges has been quite simple: stronger repression, including numerous executions. Sentences on dissidents have been harsh. The punitive labor system—the American Harry Wu has names of more than 1,000 separate camps—continues to operate, and the People's Armed Police—a force designed specifically to deal with domestic unrest—is being steadily expanded and equipped with everything up to and including tanks and aircraft.

The strategy is highly reminiscent of that followed by the USSR in its final decades—but with one difference. The USSR had maintained its border controls and tight internal policing till the end. In China, the imperatives of economic growth have rendered such an approach impossible in practice. Surveillance and arrests may have an effect, but total control is a thing of the past.

Radio broadcasts, Chinese-language materials from abroad, and a flood of sporadically-regulated publications within China itself have opened up information. Private conversation is remarkably free, and China's recent intellectual tradition is of course one of boldness and radical criticism. Known dissidents are detained and isolated, and their families cruelly penalized. Charges are regularly trumped up: thus Jiang Peikun and Ding Zilin, academics whose only son was killed at Tiananmen Square, were detained in August 1995 charged with "economic irregularities"—evidently a reference to their work in relief and support of other victims of the massacre.

But for significant numbers of Chinese, communications with the outside world are as easy as a long-distance telephone call or a fax or even an airline ticket, while the Internet has thousands of Chinese users. Sometimes the Internet is used simply to communicate with family abroad. But it can also deliver other sorts of messages: an image of "the goddess of democracy"—created by Chinese overseas—with message "It is painful to recall, but it is never to be forgotten" was available all over PRC last Spring on the Internet. (At Tiananmen Square in Beijing, persons unknown released hundreds of yellow paper slips into the air on 4 June, honoring the tradition of offering money to the dead). The government is attempting to create a controlled system of Internet access, but this looks to be difficult.

Limits of repression

China is simply too large to police and attempts to do so inevitably bring authorities up against economic imperatives, foreign public opinion, or other Chinese authorities. At root, however, they run up against Chinese culture. Attempts to portray the Chinese tradition as somehow heedless of individual rights and favorable to autocracy have a certain degree of truth—although that fact no more condemns China today to dictatorship than does the historical doctrine of divine right mean that France today needs a king. The question in both cases is whether cultural foundations exist for modern institutions of freedom and democracy, and in each the answer is yes.

If by Asian values we mean real philosophical theories from the Chinese past, then it should be noted that traditional Chinese theories of rule, elaborated by Confucius and Mencius, insisted that civil authority was grounded in virtue. A wicked man could not be a true sovereign, for to be corrupt personally was to forfeit the mandate of heaven. This view is far less favorable to the power-holder than is divine right. Under the Western scheme, legitimate rule passes through blood inheritance, regardless of individual merit. In China, inheritance came to be accepted (although the classics accorded higher praise to Yao and Shun, the legendary sage-rulers who gave the throne to chosen successors of great merit instead of their own sons) but with the possibility that a single individual's misconduct could forfeit the entitlement.

And what was the test of merit? In practice, it was whether people came to a sovereign's territory or left it. The virtue of the sage kings was made clear because ordinary people flocked to them, while fleeing oppressors. By the same token today, high emigration rates from Hong Kong, or prolonged residence abroad by Chinese students, reflect back culturally not simply on conditions of life, but on legitimacy of rule at home. Such concepts of course do not amount to "democracy." But they are certainly a cultural legacy far more favorable to freedom than to the sort of dictatorship that currently exists in Beijing.

One foreign visitor tells the story of meeting a top Chinese general shortly after the Tiananmen massacre. The general took him to task for the alien and destabilizing ideas of democracy which he blamed foreigners for introducing. In reply the visitor asked the general to forget about Western ideas, and say simply what the great

Confucius or the great Mencius would have said about the bloodshed. The general instantly changed the subject.

To this cultural foundation should be added the long tradition of constitutional thought in twentieth century China. Many people, both foreign and Chinese, are unaware of how thoroughly the issues of constitutionalism—far more than the now-fading concepts of revolution—have dominated Chinese political debate in this century. Chinese governments before 1949 promulgated twelve constitutions, while the People's Republic has produced one organic law and four constitutions. Representative bodies—unicameral or bicameral, elected or nominated, independent or controlled—have been in existence almost continuously since the early years of this century. Certainly they have not functioned effectively or sometimes even at all. The point, however, is that their existence has been considered indispensable by a variety of regimes, for the reason that "democracy" [*minzhu*] is the basic legitimating concept even of the People's Republic.

A liberal China?

What then are the actual prospects for liberalization in the People's Republic of China today? Probably as good as they were in the USSR in 1980 or so—which is to say rather mixed. In both states dissent had established itself as ineradicable whatever measures the government might take. In the Chinese case, further changes have also occurred: the economy has opened up and social control has greatly diminished. True believers in communism are far rarer than they were in the USSR. Cultural norms in China increasingly reflect international Chinese-language media—the styles and ideas of Hong Kong and Taiwan rather than of Beijing. The erosion of the dictatorship is far more advanced than it was in the USSR, and the economic and other institutions of the next regime are already more clearly visible.

On the other hand, the political challenges of transition are at least as formidable as in the former USSR. China in this century has been beset by internal strife and regionalism, often precipitated by attempts—not unlike those being made by Jiang Zemin and Li Peng today—to tighten central control. We can expect harsher administrative measures against dissenters and ethnic minorities as well as more arrests and trials, but these measures seem unlikely to create genuine stability. Externally, the regime looks set to continue raising tension over Hong Kong and Taiwan. But such measures are less likely to stabilize the situation than they are to elicit political opposition inside the ruling establishment.

China today is the last great dictatorship in the Soviet mold. It is one of the few countries where high officials will argue directly against democracy in principle. Its current leaders—many of whom were schooled in the USSR in the 1950s—have autocratic instincts and seem still to believe that communism can be made to work. But that is only part of the picture. The country is immense and more dynamic and uncontrollable now than at any time in memory. Cultural inclinations and the influence of the contemporary world combine to push for liberalization. Many within China, and in the Party, hope for such developments. While one may hope for a soft democratic landing in China, the potential for crisis and strife, particularly in the short term, remains very real. Even so, there are also many reasons for longer range optimism.

Arthur Waldron is Professor of Strategy at the Naval War College and author, most recently, of From War to Nationalism: China's Turning Point, 1924-1925 *(Cambridge University). The views expressed here are his own.*

South and East Asia: A Raw Deal for the Masses

Charles Graybow

Throughout Asia millions of ordinary citizens are trying to play by democratic rules, but in too many countries their leaders are blocking the way. The combination of corruption, bad governance, attacks on dissidents and the independent media, and the callous behavior of political elites may reduce democracy in several countries into little more than going through the motions of elections every few years.

This is in countries claiming to be democratic. North Korea remains the most tightly controlled country in the world. Burma's ruling military junta released Nobel Laureate Aung San Suu Kyi after six years of house arrest, but continues to run the country like a garrison state. Free trade has not made China's leaders less brazen in repression.

Nearly all Asian governments have, to a large extent, embraced the concept of free-market economics, but acceptance of democracy varies greatly. China, Vietnam, Laos and North Korea remain anachronistic, one-party states where all dissent is severely punished. The Burmese junta has decimated the opposition by banning several political parties, jailing dissidents, co-opting ethnic-based rebel armies by sharing the lucrative trade in opium and other illicit goods and instilling fear in society through torture, extrajudicial executions and the pervasive use of informers. Bhutan, with its record of severe ethnic persecution, and Brunei are among the world's last absolute monarchies.

At the other end is a core of countries—among them Thailand, South Korea, Taiwan and certainly Japan—in which pluralistic politics appears to be firmly entrenched. The mantra in the foreign investment community is that trade and economic development will do for democracy in China and Vietnam what they did for South Korea and Taiwan. But this ignores the absolute power of Communist parties in China and Vietnam and the institutions they control or are allied with, including the military. China's People's Liberation Army is deeply entrenched in business operations and is unlikely to submit to civilian authority while its officers are making money hand over fist.

China and Vietnam, having shed their Marxist dogma, are more likely to emulate the market authoritarianism of Indonesia, Singapore and Malaysia. In these three countries opposition groups face nearly insurmountable institutional barriers to taking power. Indonesia's ruling Golkar party allows two other parties to exist, but neither group dares to publicly refer to itself as the opposition. The government uses the country's *Pancasila* philosophy, which emphasizes social cohesion, to justify its tight political control and civil liberties restrictions.

Singapore and Malaysia have maintained the superficial trappings of parliamentary democracy bequeathed to them by the British. But both countries use tough internal security laws and controls on the media to severely limit opposition activity. Singapore has used judicial action or threats of judicial action to bankrupt and harass J.B. Jayaretnam, Chee Soon Juan and other dissident politicians.

Asian values?

Singapore's Senior Minister Lee Kuan Yew and Malaysian Prime Minister Mahathir Mohamad are the most influential proponents of the cultural relativist model of democracy that is allegedly based on "Asian values." Invoking Confucius, they claim to favor consensus, group-oriented politics over the pluralistic, individualistic, "Western" version of democracy.

But Lee and Mahathir manipulate the values argument to justify substantial restrictions on political rights and civil liberties that contravene the 1948 Universal Declaration of Human Rights, the document that forms the framework for democratic advocacy and practice throughout the world. In reality, the concept of an Asian, as opposed to universal, brand of democracy has become a euphemism for maintaining political power through repression.

Lee and Mahathir claim that the stability created by authoritarian government accounts for the spectacular economic growth rates achieved by many Asian countries over the past two decades. But East and Southeast Asian success owes more to hard work than to the political climate.

Authoritarian leaders point to the Philippines and India as places where free-wheeling politics have undermined economic growth. Again, this argument distorts the situation on the ground. The Philippines economy was stunted by the Marcos dictatorship, and is still slowed by the concentration of power in a handful of wealthy families. Economic growth in India is undermined not by political pluralism but by corruption, opportunistic politicians, a stifling bureaucracy, and money-losing state-enterprises, as well as a caste system that blocks opportunity.

Colonial legacies

While the concept of an "Asian," as opposed to universal model of democracy, is used as a smokescreen to legitimize political repression, in some countries it reflects post-colonial sensitivities. Author Ian Buruma recently wrote in the *New York Review of Books* that behind Singapore's authoritarianism is a "sensitivity to any suggestion that the institutions left behind by the British Empire may now be in less than perfect order." Thus the government is particularly defensive about the integrity of the judiciary, even as it uses the judiciary to weaken its opponents.

Buruma adds that "It is in new, insecure, racially-mixed states, such as Malaysia and Singapore, that you most often hear officials talk about Asia, or Asian values, or the Asian Way...Asia, as a cultural concept, is an official invention to bridge vastly different ethnic populations living in former Western European colonies."

In Singapore, with a Chinese majority and Malay and Indian minorities, and in Malaysia, where the Malays predominate and the Chinese and Indians are in the minority, authoritarian government rather than political pluralism is used to keep the social peace. The 1969 race riots in Malaysia over the Chinese minority's dominant business holdings no doubt have left a strong emotional scar. But as the middle classes in these countries continue to grow, they will no doubt call for greater freedom. This will confront political leaders with a choice between liberalization or increased repression.

Where dissent equals disloyalty

The authoritarian politics promoted under the cover of Asian values is particularly dangerous from the standpoint of civil liberties, because it ultimately equates political dissent with disloyalty to the state.

In Singapore Chee Soon Juan, secretary general of the opposition Democratic Party, challenged Premier Goh Chok Tong last July to a debate on the nature of the country's political system. At the time the Singaporean government had recently been criticized by the Philippines for executing a Filipina maid in the murder of another Filipina domestic worker despite contradictory evidence. Following the debate challenge, the ruling People's Action Party released a statement praising another opposition leader who had supported the government in the Filipina maid case as one who "closes rank as a loyal Singaporean when Singapore is unjustly attacked." It meanwhile ripped Dr. Chee as "unprincipled, disloyal and opportunistic."

In a similar vein, the specter of communism is haunting Indonesia—or so the government claims. President Suharto has ruled unopposed since seizing power in 1966, a year after the army suppressed a left-wing coup attempt, and the regime's historical legitimacy is based on its anti-Communist record. The government continues to justify its suppression of basic civil liberties on the grounds of an imminent Communist threat.

The Indonesian government frequently smears legitimate political dissent or labor advocacy by associating it with Communist activity. In 1995 Suharto warned that danger lurked in "formless organizations," the phrase leftists themselves used in the late 1960s when trying to regroup after the failed coup. In October army chief of staff General Soeyono named three of the country's leading dissidents as the alleged leaders behind the formless organizations without offering any evidence.

Targeting the media

Asian governments continue to be particularly sensitive to critical reporting and analysis by the independent media. In September an Indonesian court jailed two journalists for thirty-two months each for "sowing hatred" against the government by distributing a publication from an independent journalists' group. In Cambodia at least four editors or publishers of Khmer-language newspapers have been jailed or fined since 1994 on defamation or similar charges, and the government has filed criminal charges against five more Khmer-language newspapers and the English language *Phnom Penh Post*.

In January a court in Singapore found Christopher Lingle, an American academic, and the *International Herald Tribune* guilty of contempt of court over an October 1994 column critical of "intolerant regimes" in Asia that use a "compliant judiciary" to bankrupt opposition politicians. In November the IHT, which had already published an apology for the piece, agreed to pay Lee $210,000 for alleged defamation.

Even in freer countries the relationship between the government and media is tense. In Taiwan, the government's restrictions on private access to the airwaves has spawned numerous pirate radio stations, many of which are backed by opposition groups.

The Sri Lankan government has ordered domestic reporters to submit articles on the civil war in the Jaffna Peninsula to a censor, and the offices of several newspapers have been raided. In May the Pakistani government slapped a sixty-day ban on six Karachi-based publications for allegedly "sensationalizing" news about the violence in this port city. A Lahore-based journalist who has reported extensively on child-labor issues is being charged with sedition, while popular columnist Ardeshir Cowasjee is facing contempt of court charges for articles critical of the judiciary.

The bane of democracy

In the more pluralistic Asian countries democracy is undermined by corruption and bad governance. At the most basic level the cause of corruption is obviously sheer greed. But one type of corruption—spending huge sums of money to win votes—is also caused by the lack of real philosophical or ideological distinction between political parties in many countries. The decline of the left in many Asian countries means that even parties nominally committed to redistributive economic policies are little different in practice from their conservative counterparts. An extreme example is the Marxist government in the Indian state of West Bengal, which is actively courting foreign investment and has rejected the militant unionism of its past.

Political campaigns focus on vague pledges of "clean" government and unrealistic, populist promises that hold little chance of being implemented. Rarely is there debate on critical issues including widening income gaps between rich and poor, the need for tighter campaign finance and political ethics laws and civil service reform. Absent a substantive message to take to the voters, politicians often resort to vote buying and money politics, particularly in rural areas.

Widely publicized corruption scandals in many of the region's more developed countries have indicated the depth of the illicit links between big business and politics. Former South Korean President Roh Tae Woo was jailed in November after admitting he accumulated a $654 million slush fund through illegal business contributions while in office between 1988-93. President Kim Young Sam can help bury the old system of money politics if he reduces incentives for corruption by moving to deregulate the economy.

Thai Prime Minister Chuan Leekpai's democratically elected government fell in May after it emerged that several wealthy families had benefited from a land redistribution scheme designed to help poor farmers. Prior to the ensuing elections in July the going rate for attracting party-hopping MPs was about $400,000 per head. The forty-five day political campaign cost an estimated $680 million, most of it for buying votes. The resulting elections yielded a seven-party coalition headed by the Chart Thai's (Thai Nation) Banharn Silpa-archa. There are growing calls for an overhaul of the political system, including the power to impeach politicians, tighter electoral laws, and possibly a separation of legislative and political powers. Meanwhile, in neighboring Malaysia a program of redistributing corporate equity to *bumiputras* (native Malays, literally "sons of the soil") has been roiled by accusations of nepotism and favoritism.

A culture of incompetence

The Philippines's economy loses an estimated $3.6 billion a year to corruption. This translates into lost investment in public infrastructure, private enterprise and social welfare. In May former Foreign Minister Roberto Romulo, speaking before the Manila business community, described a government culture characterized by "The inability to deal with corruption, the non-existence of standards by which to measure performance and the lack of it—indeed a culture that rewards incompetence and discourages talent."

But the Filipino electorate has another reason for cynicism—the current debate over term limits and polity. President Fidel Ramos has said he will step down after his term expires in 1998, in line with constitutionally mandated term limits. However, Ramos's allies in Congress are floating the idea of amending the constitution to establish a parliamentary system and scrap term limits, allowing the president to remain in power beyond 1998.

Ramos has reached unprecedented popularity for his pragmatic policies, which have transformed a stagnant economy into one growing at nearly 5 percent per year. But more importantly, he has brought a rare measure of integrity to a country of feudal-style landlords with private armies and rent-seeking bureaucrats. A graceful exit by Ramos in 1998, even if his allies do rig the system to enable him to stay on, would set a worthy precedent for his successors.

Japan's frustrated electorate

Democracy is more firmly entrenched in Japan than anywhere else in East or Southeast Asia. Yet voter disillusionment runs high here. The July 1993 elections ended thirty-eight years of rule by the conservative Liberal Democratic Party (LDP) and brought a reformist coalition to power. Until then Japan's post-War political order had been characterized by the LDP's corrupt links to big business, an electoral system that favored the LDP's rural strongholds over the urban areas, and a powerful bureaucracy whose economic regulations jacked up prices for ordinary goods.

Yet two years on, there is a sense that little has changed. In June 1994 the LDP joined with its longtime rival, the Socialist Party, and a minor third party to regain power through a parliamentary vote of no confidence. This alliance of convenience between right and left increased popular cynicism with politics. The LDP holds the largest number of seats in parliament, but keeps Prime Minister Tomiichi Murayama, a Socialist, in power to avoid the internally divisive process of choosing one of its members for the top post.

Turnout for the July 1995 elections for the upper house of parliament fell below 50 percent for the first time since World War II. The New Frontier Party (NFP), a new center-right opposition coalition, handed the LDP its first loss in national proportional balloting in forty years. With the Socialists in decline, Japan's future political system may well be dominated by two strong conservative parties. The old-guard LDP would compete against a reform-oriented NFP (or a successor), which would promote economic deregulation, a more open political system and a more assertive Japanese role in foreign affairs.

Subcontinental blues

While five out of seven South Asian countries are nominally committed to democracy, the rule of law is weak throughout the subcontinent. Indian security forces continue to act with impunity in Kashmir and Punjab, as well as in Assam and other northeastern states. Meanwhile, in the northeast rebel armies, representing Khasis,

Bodos and other groups seeking greater autonomy, operate outside the democratic pale. In Sri Lanka civilians have been indiscriminately targeted during the country's civil war. In Pakistan police and paramilitary units are responsible for widespread rights violations, and in Bangladesh in 1995 at least twenty politicians were killed. In Bhutan, where there is no democratic accountability, the army and police are responsible for grave human rights violations against ethnic Nepalese citizens.

Politics in India, Bangladesh and Pakistan too often resembles a zero-sum game over the redistribution of scarce resources. Rather than pursue genuine but painful economic reforms, political leaders frequently resort to populist measures that will ultimately erode the public's confidence in democracy.

In India, parties representing lower castes and *dalits* (untouchables) have taken power in several states and are trying to increase the percentage of university and civil service slots reserved for their followers. The upshot is that politics is increasingly being fragmented along caste lines. An opposition party came to power in a southern state by promising subsidized rice at wildly unrealistic prices. Meanwhile the Hindu nationalist Bharatiya Janata Party (BJP) has revived 1970s-era economic nationalism in highly publicized measures including forcing the U.S.-based Enron corporation to renegotiate terms of a $2.8 billion power plant in Maharashtra, and closing a Kentucky Fried Chicken outlet in Delhi after investigators found two flies in the kitchen. In Bangladesh, Prime Minister Khaleda Zia and Sheik Hasina of the opposition Awami League shamelessly allowed their personal rivalry to lead to prolonged, nationwide strikes and a dissolution of parliament.

India heads into national elections in the spring of 1996 with the ruling Congress Party having lost eleven of sixteen state elections since 1993. The 110-year-old party has alienated voters with its pervasive corruption, and is accused of neglecting the downtrodden Hindus and disaffected Muslims who form the party's traditional support base.

Since taking office in May 1991 Prime Minister P.V. Narasimha Rao's economic reform program has helped reverse more than four decades of centralized socialist planning and hostility to foreign investment. But the restructuring has hurt poor Indians, who comprise perhaps 400 million of the country's 850 million citizens. Critics also charge Rao with abandoning the party's secular ideals by failing to prevent the destruction of a sixteenth-century mosque at Ayodhya in December 1992, and by not doing enough to protect Muslims during the subsequent Bombay riots in early 1993.

Opposition parties ranging from Hindu nationalists to groups championing the rights of lower caste and "untouchable" Hindus have taken power at the state level by tapping into a backlash against the economic reforms. The biggest beneficiary has been the right-wing BJP, which rules two states and Delhi and shares power in a fourth.

But the BJP is still seen as a party representing upper-caste Hindus, an image that was underscored after a coalition it formed with a lower-caste party in Uttar Pradesh quickly collapsed. This matters greatly in a country where poor voters have the highest turnout at elections. In both Uttar Pradesh and Bihar, another poor, populous state, lower castes and "untouchables" are translating their numerical superiority into political power via regional and leftist parties.

Pakistani Premier Benazir Bhutto admitted in mid-October that her government had arrested ten army officers and twenty-six enlisted men suspected of plotting a coup and subsequent Islamic revolution. Islamic militias bombed the Egyptian Embassy in Islamabad in November, further heightening fears of a radical Islamic threat to this secular society. During the year the commercial capital of Karachi continued to be torn by sectarian, civil and factional violence, which caused more than 1,500 deaths through October.

Bhutan: Himalayan bleakness

Since 1985 King Jigme Singye Wangchuk's government in Bhutan, dominated by the Tibetan-descended Ngalong Drukpas in the north, has systematically persecuted the ethnic Nepalese population in the south. In the early 1990s the Bhutanese army forcibly evicted some 100,000 Nepali-speaking citizens though rape, torture and burning of homes, giving the kingdom the distinction of having the highest per capita refugee population in the world.

The Bhutanese government has tried to portray the largely Hindu southern Bhutanese as a threat to the Drukpa's cultural survival. But the formation in June 1994 of the Druk National Congress (DNC), an exile-based group drawn largely from the Buddhist Sarchop community in eastern Bhutan, showed that the real issue is the suppression of fundamental freedoms under the absolute monarchy. In August 1995 a court sentenced Tandin Dorji, Bhutan's chief of police and the brother-in-law of the DNC chairman, to three years in prison on trumped-up charges of negligence over a jail break.

Keeping the bad guys in business

Many Asian countries have shown a chilling willingness to prop up repressive regimes through trade and investment. Vietnam's entry into the Association of South East Asian Nations (ASEAN) in July came with no strings attached, despite Hanoi's record of political repression and religious persecution. Malaysian Prime Minister Mahathir Mohamad characterized ASEAN's indifference to democracy and human rights when he said at the time, "We welcome Vietnam's entry into ASEAN because we are of the opinion that we do not need to question their system of government so long as they accept a free-market system."

ASEAN's policy of "constructive engagement" with Burma, designed to foster improvements in the regime's human rights record, has been a failure. Despite Suu Kyi's release, the State Law and Order Restoration Council (SLORC) continues to arrest lesser-known dissidents. The army is responsible for grave human rights violations, including forced labor, torture and beating of civilians, forced relocations and persecution of ethnic minority groups.

In late November the junta reconvened a sham constitutional convention designed to formalize the military's leading role in politics by making the president a military figure and giving the army a fixed number of seats in parliament. Suu Kyi's National League for Democracy, after earlier participating in the process, refused to rejoin the convention. Having justly chosen not to sanction a fraudulent process, Suu Kyi and her party must now find an effective way to promote democracy while avoiding a bloody military crackdown.

Cambodia plunges toward despair

In 1995 Cambodia's human rights situation was in a free fall. Besides cracking down on the free press, the government expelled ex-Finance Minister Sam Rainsy from

Parliament following his outspoken criticism of official corruption, detained six citizens for distributing pro-democracy pamphlets, and was apparently behind grenade attacks and other violence against journalists and opposition figures.

In November police arrested Prince Norodom Sirivudh, King Norodom Sihanouk's stepbrother and a critic of the government, for allegedly plotting to kill Second Prime Minister Hun Sen. Diplomats dismissed the charges as an apparent political frame-up. and viewed the arrest as a further sign that Hun Sen was consolidating his power at the expense of First Prime Minister Norodom Ranariddh.

The country has also become a regional center for money laundering and the heroin trade, as well as a haven for international fugitives. Sizing up the situation, one diplomat told the *Far Eastern Economic Review* that "The future of Cambodia is to be a colony of Asian countries."

Warfare then and now

Twenty-five years ago Southeast Asia was wracked by war and Communist insurgencies, and India and Pakistan were headed for the conflict that would give birth to Bangladesh. Today the situation overall is far more peaceful, but pockets of fighting remain.

The most serious, the civil war in Sri Lanka pitting the government against Tamil rebels in the north, has claimed an estimated 39,000 lives since 1983. In the summer of 1995 the Sri Lankan army began its strongest offensive yet in its campaign to recapture the rebel stronghold on the Jaffna Peninsula, and by the fall had largely reached its objective. But the rebels are likely to prolong the conflict by fighting from the jungles. Prime Minister Kumaratunga recognizes the need ultimately for a political solution that offers the Tamil community autonomy in a federal system. She may now have gained the negotiating leverage necessary to sell a plan to both the skeptical Tamil minority and to nationalists within the majority Sinhalese community.

Indian Prime Minister P.V. Narasimha Rao had hoped that elections in Kashmir would end federal rule and provide space for a political solution granting the country's only Muslim majority state greater autonomy. Since 1989 separatist violence and atrocities committed by army and paramilitary units have killed some 12,000 people. The Indian Election Commission rejected the proposed elections, citing the planned boycott by Muslim parties and the possibility of violence during the vote. A recent poll showed that 77 percent of residents in the Muslim-dominated Kashmir Valley doubted the possibility of a peaceful resolution of Kashmir's status within the Indian constitution. Many if not most Muslim Kashmiris favor holding the plebiscite on the territory's future that was promised under a 1948 United Nations agreement but never carried out.

The Burmese army has cease-fire agreements with fourteen ethnic-based rebel groups, but in 1995 fighting on three additional fronts caused thousands of villagers to flee to the Thai border. Meanwhile, the government of Papua New Guinea held peace talks with rebels from Bougainville Island in an attempt at ending a six-year old seccessionist movement.

Grassroots heroes

There are true heroes in the struggle to improve daily living conditions throughout the region. These are the men, and far more often, women, who work for the thousands of grassroots nongovernmental organizations (NGOs) that are bringing increased health and sanitation to rural villages, helping street children and victims of prostitution, providing counseling to female victims of violence and monitoring respect for basic civil rights. Most of these groups are apolitical, but in their efforts to empower women, educate often illiterate citizens as to their rights, smash prostitution rings and fight for worker's rights, they are shaking up entrenched interests and working to solidify the rule of law.

Pragmatic and dedicated, these organizations are finding innovative solutions to social welfare problems while operating on minuscule budgets. The leading role played by women in these conservative societies is remarkable. But this often comes at a price. In Bangladesh, Islamic fundamentalists vandalized some 1,400 girls' schools in 1994 to protest the spread of female-based NGOs.

A related development is the growth of microlending institutions that extend credit to poor and often uneducated borrowers who would be rejected by traditional banks. Women have proved to be the most responsible borrowers. In the 1970s the Grameen (rural) Bank in Bangladesh pioneered microlending of $100-$300 to female entrepreneurs, and similar institutions have formed in other Asian countries. According to one study cited by the Washington-based Women's World Banking, for every 100 rupees earned by an Indian women, 92 rupees gets put back into children, education and health. On-time repayment rates average around 95 percent.

While Asia's social problems will not be solved solely by the NGO sector, these grassroots groups are showing what can be done. Policy makers should take note. In a region of high-flying economies, the most significant developments of all may be taking place down on the ground.

Charles Graybow is Asian/Pacific Affairs Area Specialist at Freedom House.

Latin America and the Caribbean: Storm Warnings

Douglas W. Payne

In this century attempts to establish democratic rule in Latin America have come in roughly twenty-year intervals. The latest cycle may now to be drawing to an end, the casualty of both a political culture suffused with corruption and alien to the rule of law, and a global economy that cares little about the nature of governments as long as they comply with its rules.

Previous democratic cycles have ended in a wave of military takeovers. The threat from the barracks for the moment, however, is limited mostly to pockets of younger, nationalistic officers like those who led the attempted coups in Venezuela in 1992. Military high commands appear reluctant to shoulder the responsibility of governing. They probably would not consider stepping in unless their institutions and privileges were directly threatened by wholesale disorder. The specter of governmental breakdown does loom today in Colombia, Ecuador and Venezuela and it is in those countries where coup rumors are the most prevalent.

But what is happening in Latin America today generally is that the democratic cycle that began in the 1980s is slowly devolving into an intermediate stage of hybrid authoritarianism. In this stage, the trappings of formal democracy are retained and the tenets of market economics as prescribed by the international financial community are generally followed. But in response to mounting social unrest rule is more by decree than consent, media critical of government is bullied and power is maintained through corruption, intimidation and, ultimately, by force.

Market authoritarianism

Call it market authoritarianism. One version is already established in Peru, where President Alberto Fujimori has connived with the military to erect a Singapore-style dynasty. Fujimori is a favorite of foreign investors and for now remains popular at home. In 1995 he easily had himself reelected in what can be best described as a state-controlled plebiscite. In an interview after the vote, Fujimori spoke about his philosophy of "direct government," stating, "This is a democracy in which the intermediaries, the political parties, are eliminated." In other words, I am the state.

The shadow of market authoritarianism is now creeping across a number of Latin American countries. For example, when Bolivian President Gonzalo Sánchez de Losada met resistance from labor unions to his privatization program in early 1995, he simply declared a six-month state of emergency that allowed police to arrest hundreds of labor activists.

Worker rights are anathema to market authoritarianism. Latin America is the most dangerous region in the world to be a trade unionist, with thousands arrested and hundreds killed every year. Throughout the region's burgeoning export-processing zones workers are systematically denied the fundamental right to organize.

In Argentina President Carlos Menem has implemented economic reforms mostly by fiat. In 1995 he became the first Argentine leader to engineer his own reelection since Juan Perón. By the end of the year Menem was attempting to steamroll the legislature into declaring a state of economic emergency so that he could abide by the terms of Argentina's latest stand-by loan from the International Monetary Fund (IMF) unhindered.

In Brazil, barely a year after the 1994 election of President Fernando Enrique Cardoso, Cardoso's minions were already floating the idea of changing the constitution to make him eligible for a second term. During Cardoso's first year in office, five Brazilian journalists were murdered "with particular savagery," according to the Inter-American Press Association. Cardoso, like Fujimori and Menem, has won accolades from Washington and the international financial community for the improvement in his country's macroeconomic indicators and investment climate.

In today's Latin America such praise seems to encourage the autocratic impulse, an entrenched feature of Latin political culture since the days of Spanish and Portuguese colonialism. Moreover, there is little penalty for acting upon authoritarian aspirations or violating human rights as long as free-trade and market policies, known in Latin America as "neo-liberalism," are part of the package.

Fujimori, for example, got off with not much more than a wrist-slap from the international community when in 1992 he dissolved the Peruvian congress and tossed out the constitution so that he could build his presidential-military regime from scratch. Peru's jails now rival Cuba's for the number of political prisoners they hold.

But when Venezuelan President Rafael Caldera imposed exchange and other economic controls in 1994, Venezuela was left hung out to dry by international creditors. In 1995 a chastened Caldera began easing the controls, a prerequisite for Venezuela's readmission to the IMF emergency ward. If mounting social unrest and rumblings in the military don't reach flash-point first, the global economy may yet transform this aged, old-school populist into a market caudillo. It happened in the Dominican Republic, where the eighty-nine-year-old Joaquín Balaguer now presides over one of the largest export-processing operations in the region. In this vast network of foreign-owned plants a quarter million people, a majority of them women, labor in sweatshop conditions, stitching apparel and assembling other goods for first-world markets.

In Central America, meanwhile, militaries are happy to back the market reforms of civilian governments as long as they are allowed to retain their status as armed corporations above the law and feasting on the dividends. The exception is Costa Rica, which dissolved its military decades ago and remains an island of democratic governance.

But Costa Rica is practically broke and the demands of the international financial community for structural adjustment have placed increasing stress on its society and its institutions. And as Costa Rica attempts to compete with its Central American neighbors and Mexico in providing foreign investors with the cheapest labor, abuses are mounting in its own export-processing zones.

It is not unrealistic to ask whether Costa Rican democracy can withstand the competitive pressures of the global economy. But what continues to work in Costa Rica's favor is a profound, historically-rooted tradition of respect for the rule of law. The only other Latin American countries in which such a tradition exists are Chile and, to a lesser extent, Uruguay. Part of the reason is that Costa Rica and Chile, as outposts during the period of Spanish and Portuguese colonialism, were less susceptible to the lawless, anti-democratic legacy of the Conquest.

In Chile the tradition of democratic rule of law was strong enough to survive seventeen years of military rule. The Pinochet dictatorship, in fact, was market authoritarianism at its most brutal. The problem is that when Gen. Pinochet finally moved aside he left behind a constitution that endows the military with inordinate power and allows him to stay in charge of the army until 1998. Civilian authority in Chile ends at the barracks gate and Gen. Pinochet remains quick to rattle sabers whenever the military's autonomy and privileges are threatened.

The Mexican wild card

Market authoritarianism has been a relatively stable enterprise in a number of Asian countries, Malaysia and Singapore being prime examples. But is it sustainable in Latin America? The Mexican prototype, a state-party system retooled for free trade by former president Carlos Salinas and refinanced through foreign capital flows, seems now on the verge of unraveling.

The captains of the global economy hailed Mexico under Salinas as a model for the Third World. In response to nettlesome questions about Mexico's lack of democracy, Salinas supporters concocted a world-class oxymoron to deflect the criticism. Mexico's a democracy, they said, it's just an "authoritarian democracy." In April 1994 the Organization for Economic Cooperation and Development (OECD), the first-world club, embraced Mexico as its twenty-fifth member, evidently unconcerned that Mexico under Salinas had become one of the most unequal societies in the world.

Less than a year later Salinas bequeathed to his hapless successor, Ernesto Zedillo, an economic house of cards and a political powder keg. When the Mexican peso finally collapsed, Washington and the IMF bailed Zedillo out. They now publicly praise his stated commitment to democracy. Yet in keeping with bailout canon they lean on him to impose ever harsher austerity on a traumatized, desperate population and privately pray that he can just keep the lid on.

If Mexico were to blow, it could spell the end of market authoritarianism because there might not be any Latin American market left. Most of Latin America is, like Mexico, highly dependent on the flow of foreign capital, particularly "hot money," security and bond investments that account for more than two-thirds of all foreign investment in the region.

When a few thousand Indians took up arms in the southern Mexican state of Chiapas, arguably the first guerrilla uprising against a globalized economy, it was enough to spook skittish foreign investors in every Latin market. A Chase Manhattan Bank analyst, writing in a Chase Emerging Markets Group memorandum, concluded that the Mexican government "will need to eliminate the Zapatistas." When the Mexican peso went under a year later capital streamed out of Latin America and left banks tottering in many countries, a fiscal bomb that is still ticking.

The ripple effect of economic collapse or political turmoil in Mexico—the wholesale flight of foreign investment from the rest of the region—would leave Latin American economies running on empty and lead to widespread social and political upheaval. It would then be time to look for tanks in the streets.

Those who think such a scenario is implausible or alarmist did not hear the audible sigh of relief from every Latin capital after Washington and the IMF came to the Zedillo government's rescue. Nor have they considered why, aside from saving U.S. investors, the Clinton administration would be so compelled to go against U.S. public opinion and a majority of the U.S. Congress to put together a $50 billion package for Mexico, the largest bailout of a country ever.

Summits and Fidel

The Mexican bailout was understood among the Latin American political castes as a renewed endorsement by Washington of market authoritarianism. The primacy of commercial interests in U.S. foreign policy since the end of the Cold War is no secret. In the pursuit of those interests Washington embraced Salinas as the first step toward establishing a hemispheric free-trade bloc. The implicit message was that authoritarian behavior in the service of that goal was acceptable.

Washington still stands by a stated commitment to democracy in Latin America. But its criteria for judging democracy have been so diluted that market authoritarianism fits in easily. At the 1994 hemispheric summit in Miami, advertised as a gathering of "democracies," U.S. Vice President Al Gore stated that all the nations of Latin America but Cuba "have elected governments, a development unprecedented in this hemisphere's history." Yes, but he could not say governments that were elected freely and fairly, for that would have eliminated Zedillo, Fujimori and Balaguer, as well as Paraguayan President Juan Carlos Wasmosy and Prime Minister Lester Bird of Antigua and Barbuda.

The bottom line, apparently, is that anything short of a military dictatorship can be tolerated, and anything else can be called democracy. Cesar Gaviria, for example, secretary general of the thirty-five-member Organization of American States (OAS), stated before the Miami summit that in Latin America, "Democracy, once the exception, has become the rule." Gaviria was president of Colombia from 1990 to 1994 and was supported by Washington to head the OAS because of his free-trade credentials. During Gaviria's administration Colombia was given an investment-grade rating by Moody's Investors Service, while Colombian trade unionists were being killed with impunity at a rate of nearly three per week.

The killings have not abated under Gaviria's successor, Ernesto Samper. In fact, political violence involving guerrilla groups, paramilitary death squads and the army takes more lives in Colombia than in any other Latin American country, with more than ten killings and disappearances per day. Samper's imposition of a state of emergency in 1995 changed nothing, but brought allegations that he was trying divert attention from massive evidence that his 1994 presidential campaign was awash in drug money. As coup rumors and demands for Samper's resignation mounted amid a flurry of high-level political assassinations, Colombians braced themselves for the worst.

Fidel Castro has opened Cuba to foreign investment, but that was not enough to earn him an invitation to Miami. For Castro is not a market authoritarian but an aspiring market Leninist, a term that U.S. journalist Nicholas D. Kristof has used to describe China and Vietnam. In 1995 Castro stated that those two countries provided a model for Cuba and late in the year he even paid a visit to Beijing to see for himself how a Communist dictatorship can sustain itself through capitalism.

What galls Castro is that, unlike China and Vietnam, Cuba has to contend with a U.S. economic embargo. Castro noted Washington's decision on China to separate human rights and democracy from trade issues, as well as the recent restoration of U.S.-Vietnamese relations. Since then he has invited captains of U.S. industry and the editors of *Time* magazine to Havana to complain that Cuba is being treated unfairly and to say that potential U.S. investors are losing out. In 1995 he took advantage of his appearance at the United Nations in New York to lobby U.S. business further, hoping it would apply enough pressure in Washington that the embargo would be lifted.

Meanwhile, Castro gets invited to any Latin American regional meeting where the U.S. is not in attendance. He has attended each of the five annual Ibero-American summits, which also feature the leaders of Spain and Portugal. At the end of these gatherings everyone signs a declaration in support of "democracy and human rights" and against trade embargos. Castro claims victory and goes home to his police state and another reading of the IMF handbook. His Latin American counterparts claim credit for getting him to sign on to principles they know he holds in contempt. And Castro lets them have their play because he knows that a majority of them do not abide much by those principles either.

The ticking social bomb

Ordinary Latin Americans suffer through two annual summits. One with Castro, the Ibero-American gathering, the other without him, the OAS general assembly. They hear their leaders offering the same platitudes and making the same promises every year, and every year their lives become worse.

They hear that free trade and market reforms will lead to growth and prosperity. But the human costs of structural adjustment keep mounting. Unemployment grows every year, the gap between rich and poor, already bigger than in any other region of the world, continues to widen and the Latin American middle class, a narrow slice of the population to begin with, continues to waste away. U.S. trade advocates point to Latin America as a potential market of nearly a half billion people. One wonders how lucrative such a market can be when its configuration is that of a penthouse built on a slum.

Latin Americans also keep hearing that something will be done about corruption. Yet every year there are more mammoth scandals that confirm that in most Latin countries the problem is not corruption in the system, but rather that corruption *is* the system. In Ecuador, for example, where allegations of corruption have become the principal weaponry of political vendettas, scandals have made the country practically ungovernable.

Presidents, congressmen and judges may get caught gulping from the streams of foreign capital that flow into the region, but virtually no one is ever punished. There is no better word to describe the state of play in Latin American politics than impunity, and impunity perpetuates the system.

And they hear, too, about renewed commitments to fight the drug trade. The fact is that Latin America today offers optimum conditions to drug traffickers—

corrupt politics and low trade barriers. In this landscape traffickers are the ultimate market caudillos, and as long as these conditions and foreign drug markets exist, no matter how many kingpins are arrested there will be others to step in.

Meanwhile, drugs and crime permeate the layers of the urban poor—more than 50 percent of the population in most Latin cities—educational systems rot away and the toll on young people mounts daily. There are now an estimated 40 million street children in Latin America, 5 million in Brazil alone.

In Colombia they are called *chinches,* or bed bugs, in Bolivia, *polillas*, or moths, and in Peru, *pirañitas*, or little piranhas. They subsist as beggars, petty thieves and prostitutes. In Mexico City the street children who fill their mouths with diesel fuel, turn themselves into human torches and ask money for their feats are called *dragoncitos*, or little dragons. To deaden the pain of their lives, more and more street kids are inhaling cheap, easily acquired industrial solvents and glue. Those who survive graduate to drug-trafficking and other criminal enterprises like extortion rackets and kidnapping rings. Latin America is now the world's top region for ransom kidnapping. In Colombia, there is a kidnapping every seven hours.

Rampant crime and homelessness have spawned a phenomenon known in Latin America as "social cleansing," killings of street people and alleged criminals by vigilante groups. These outfits are usually paid by merchants and private sector companies and are often made up of off-duty police. Former military regimes sponsored anti-Communist death squads. Social cleansing gangs are the business-sponsored death squads of the market authoritarian era.

Another component of this ticking social bomb is the collapse of health-care systems. Cholera erupted in Latin America in 1991 after a three-decade absence and has swept the region. Dengue fever, once virtually eradicated, has re-emerged. It has reached epidemic proportions in Central America and in 1995 was plowing through Mexico toward the United States.

No market, no respect

As the fiscal bomb and the social bomb tick away in Latin America, and as eyes stay trained on Mexico waiting for the next shoe to drop, the twelve nations of the English-speaking Caribbean are left to fend for themselves. They account for nearly a third of the nations in the hemisphere. But their populations collectively constitute a market of only 5 million people, which makes them of little account given today's global priorities.

A review of Freedom House's survey for the last two decades shows that democracy in the English-speaking Caribbean has proved to be more effective and durable than in any other subregion in the Third World. The exceptions have been Guyana, where in 1992 free and fair elections were held for the first time in over two decades; Grenada, which endured nearly five years of Marxist rule before returning to democratic government in 1984; and Antigua and Barbuda, where the Bird family has reigned for decades.

What makes the English-speaking Caribbean different, especially from its Latin neighbors, is that rule is based on law, not power and the use of force. Constitutions mean something and the rule of law, while imperfect, is recognized by elites and ordinary citizens alike and actually functions as the basis for governance.

However, the parliamentary systems of the Caribbean are now buffeted by the whirlwind of global economic competition, whipsawed between the giant trading blocs of Europe and North America and prey to Latin American drug and money-laundering cartels. Structural adjustment, economic uncertainty and rising crime are putting enormous stress on democratic institutions in every country. A particularly destructive hurricane season in 1995 has not helped matters.

Thus far, the Caribbean democracies are maintaining. Between fall 1994 and fall 1995 opposition parties came to power in free and fair elections in five countries—Barbados, Dominica, St. Kitts and Nevis, Grenada and Trinidad and Tobago. The people of the region are searching for new types of leadership to address the new challenges of the post-Cold War world.

While Caribbean leaders are severely tested, they get little sympathy from outside the region. These nations are important voices on behalf of democracy and human rights at the Organization of American States and the United Nations. But in 1995 Washington seemed more interested in going to the World Trade Organization (WTO) to contest their preferential banana agreement with the European Union. A number of these small island nations are highly dependent on banana sales. Will Dominica or St. Vincent and the Grenadines be the first democracy to be put out of business by a WTO ruling?

Finally, there is Haiti. The U.S. intervention halted that country's slide into absolute hell. But despite the restoration of President Jean-Bertrand Aristide, Haiti's prospects remain uncertain at best. Aristide has had trouble resisting the temptation to exceed his constitutional powers. His elected successor, René Préval, is a question mark. And what role will the still overwhelmingly popular Aristide play after Préval takes office? Haitians are a remarkably resilient people, but they have no democratic traditions to draw on. If political violence spins out of control, as it has so many times in the past, their endurance will be tested yet again.

The United States: Deep Currents Fresh Challenges

Seth Lipsky

One of the most intriguing political remarks I've heard in recent years was attributed to the man who at the time was president of the Amalgamated Clothing and Textile Workers Union, Jack Sheinkman. The gist of it was that he didn't believe that it would have been possible to achieve in the United States the feat of labor union organizing that Solidarity had been able to achieve in Communist Poland. I first heard about the remark in the late 1980s. It sounded absurd to me at the time. Some years later, when I finally had the opportunity to make Sheinkman's acquaintance, I asked him about the remark. He told me that he didn't mean it literally—Solidarity, after all, had to be organized underground. He meant, rather, to emphasize the obstacles in law and economics that bedevil the labor movement in the United States. Today, with the share of America's private sector work force that is organized now down to about 10 percent, a new generation of labor leaders is coming into power and vowing to reverse the trends under the nose of a resurgent Republican Party that has won control of the Congress. The transition of labor is one of the major issues lurking in American politics at the close of 1995.

Labor's transition

Labor's transition came into focus with astonishing rapidity in 1995. There were mergers announced, proposed or consummated between the Communications Workers of America and the Newspaper Guild, between the United Rubber Workers and the United Steel Workers of America, between the Amalgamated Clothing and Textile Workers Union and the International Ladies' Garment Workers Union, between the National Education Association and the American Federation of Teachers, and among the United Auto Workers, the United Steelworkers, and the International Association of Machinists. Such combinations were capped in 1995 by the insurgency within the American Federation of Labor-Congress of Industrial Organizations that ended the reign of Lane Kirkland and Thomas Donahue. Kirkland and Donahue will go down in history for their vision in leading labor during its heroic participation in the Cold War in which the Soviet Union was defeated. Their successors at the AFL-CIO, John Sweeney, Richard Trumka and Linda Chavez-Thompson, turned to the domestic front, announcing plans to spend $20 million to put 1,000 new organizers in the field. The new team was more visibly active, from the aircraft plants of Seattle to the sweatshops of New York.

At one level it's easy to dismiss what is happening in labor. As the transition was under way at the AFL-CIO, the *Wall Street Journal* published an editorial called "Uncle Sam Gompers," arguing that what was really happening in organized labor was the evolution "from a movement that represented working folk of all stripes into one that is more and more a spokesman for government employees." The *Jour-*

nal pointed out that while the share of private sector workers that was organized had shrunk to 10.9 percent in 1994 from 16.8 percent in 1983, the share of public sector workers that was organized had risen during the same period to 38.7 percent from 36.7 percent. The overriding political goal for public unions, the *Journal* argued, is an ever-growing government that hires evermore workers, a trend that puts unions "increasingly at odds with those private-sector workers whose taxes have to finance ever-larger government." These trends don't diminish the prospect, however, that as the organizing drive in labor expands, the country is likely to see a new push at the bargaining table for higher wages, and that may well produce some strange ideological bedfellows.

One place this could happen is over the question of whether wage increases are inflationary, a cry that is raised whenever labor pushes for pay increases. Yet there are those—*Wall Street Journal* editorialists among them—who believe the ability of labor to combine, much as capital is able to combine, is essential to the working of a large market system and that a market system is essential to freedom. The *Journal*'s editorials, disputing the notion that wage increases are in and of themselves inflationary—inflation being a monetary phenomenon—have been faxed around for years by, among others, Gus Tyler, in-house intellectual of the International Ladies' Garment Workers Union.

The dollar

If there is a campaign for wage increases we may yet get a serious debate in the U.S. over the second big issue lurking in American politics: the dollar. The fundamental unsoundness of the dollar casts a shadow over the U.S. economy, keeping interest rates high, at least by historical measure, and making it more difficult for workers (and everyone else) to buy houses, cars and other goods, despite the startling rise in wages and incomes, in nominal terms, in the last generation.

The unsoundness of the dollar, by which I mean its lack of a legal definition in terms of gold, is one of the most serious medium term problems confronting America. It is also one of the few major agenda items of what has been called the "Reagan Revolution" still unaddressed by either the executive or legislative branches. And, incidentally, it is one of the major reforms that can be potentially claimed by either the Democratic or Republican party. Presidents Kennedy and Johnson, the last two Democrats to serve before the great inflation of the 1970s, both pledged their administrations to the gold standard; under American law at the time, the dollar was defined in terms of gold. Some will argue the seeds of destruction of the dollar were laid during the "guns and butter" policies of the Johnson administration. It was, though, under President Nixon, a Republican, that America closed the gold window and allowed the dollar to float, bowing to chaos and opening the way not only to inflation but to the embargo of the Organization of Arab Oil Exporting Countries and to the false wealth transfers of the Third World debt crisis. The problem of the dollar has become identified with the Democrats only because of their manifest lack of interest in fixing it.

The Republicans recognized the problem officially, which is to say in their campaign platform, as far back as 1980, when the party called for the restoration of a link between the dollar and a commodity of value. After James Baker moved to the Treasury from his post as chief of staff in the White House, there was talk of advancing this agenda. The Reagan administration, however, soon became enveloped in the Iran-Contra controversy, and the idea lay fallow during the Bush administration. Nothing much has been done since then. It is, therefore, significant that publisher Steve Forbes is mounting a campaign for the Republican nomination for the presidency, for it holds out the prospect of placing the question of the gold standard and sound money at the center of the political debate. Forbes is being widely derided for it, but his advocacy of the gold standard makes him unlikely to join the camp that is going to be using the fear of inflation to argue against wage settlements. He will be the only candidate raising at least the idea that ordinary families might once again contemplate obtaining a 4-5 percent mortgage in America.

Immigration

Another area where strange bedfellows may well emerge is on the issue—one of the biggest on the horizon of American politics—of immigration. What some regard as the greatest speech ever given on immigration was delivered on the floor of the Congress in 1917 by the first socialist ever to serve in the American legislature, Meyer London of the Lower East Side (his portrait still hangs in the offices of the *Jewish Forward* newspaper). The speech is remarkable not only for the eloquence with which he spoke against racial and cultural chauvinists and the radicalism of his view—he advocated essentially unregulated immigration—but also for the clarity with which he rebuked those in the labor movement who were tempted by the argument that restrictions on immigration might protect jobs for Americans. London said he would countenance a restriction on immigration only for an organized effort to break a strike. Other than that, he recognized that immigration is a contributor to growth, and ultimately, to jobs. More radically still, he said that immigration is, in effect, self-regulating; if there isn't work, job seekers won't come.

It is striking, three generations after London delivered his speech, to discover where his words are echoing in the American political debate—namely in such free market precincts as the *Wall Street Journal* and from such writers on the right as George Gilder. A number of politicians have sought in 1995 to raise a campaign on the immigration issue. Governor Pete Wilson of California went so far as to launch his bid for the presidency with an anti-immigration diatribe delivered in front of the Statue of Liberty. He was run out of the race within weeks, claiming an inability to raise funds. The leading anti-immigration agitator left standing on the stump is the right-wing columnist, Pat Buchanan, while in the Senate the outgoing Senator from Wyoming, Alan Simpson, makes opposition to immigration his last hurrah and is finding a certain amount of support within the Democratic Party, from, for example, Senator Dianne Feinstein of California.

Congressional/Executive clash

A fourth big issue in the background of the American political scene as 1995 drew to a close is the clash between the Congress and the Executive branch, and it couldn't be more dramatic. The struggle was begun in the 1970s by the House Judiciary Committee in its pursuit of evidence against President Nixon. The executive branch was shaken by the Supreme Court in a now famous ruling that would have been unanimous but for the fact that one justice did not vote. The fight has been waged on and off in the generation since then, with the Congress usually in the role of the aggressor, using such shenanigans as, say, the War Powers Act, in which it sought to curb the president's authority to carry out the constitutional oath. The battle has crossed party lines, with the Democrats attempting to circumscribe President Reagan's powers through the use of the Iran-Contra scandal special prosecutors. Currently, a Republican Congress is moving against the presidency with the Whitewater hearings, no small irony because one of the young lawyers assisting in the impeachment proceedings against President Nixon is today the first lady, Mrs. Clinton, at the center of the Whitewater controversy.

Some may argue that Whitewater does not present the kinds of constitutional questions that arose in, say, Iran Contra. In Iran-Contra, after all, partisans of the presidency were able—and did, in fact—assert that Mr. Reagan had a constitutional obligation to support the Nicaraguan contras, if he sensed, as he did, that Communist-backed operations in El Salvador represented a security threat to the United States. No one is suggesting that in Whitewater Mr. Clinton was acting under a constitutional obligation. The damage done to the presidency, though, is going to be on the same scale in both cases. If the Republicans are successful in gaining the presidency in 1996, it may be that we will enter a period in history where both the White House and the Congress are held by the same party and these issues may fall to the background. If, however, American voters decide, as they have done for much of the post-war period, to give executive power to one party and legislative power to another, the stage may be set for one of the most destructive periods in the war between Congress and the Executive, one that will leave the country weaker and less capable of dealing with its problems and its enemies, foreign and domestic.

Foreign affairs

That foreign enemies are active remained abundantly clear in 1995, despite the end of the Cold War in its classical sense, with the bombing of an American installation at Saudi Arabia. The bombing was obscured only by the fact that it occurred between the assassination of Yitzhak Rabin and the dispatch of U.S. troops to Bosnia. But challenges are brewing in the Middle East. An Islamic fundamentalist party is gaining ground in the legislature of a NATO member, Turkey, while Iran is advancing it its quest to assemble nuclear weapons, and it is far from certain the Israel-Palestinian accord will hold up, let along lead to a viable Israel-Syria peace.

These challenges ought to be made to order for a newly active CIA capable of mounting covert operations. But under two directors during the Clinton administration the Agency, preoccupied by internal treachery in the form of Aldrich Ames and oversight by the Senate, has hung back from a pro-active effort to take the terror war to the ground of our enemies. The Clinton administration did begin moving what will be 20,000 American troops into Bosnia as part of a peace-keeping effort that is arguably the first out-of-area military campaign of the North Atlantic Treaty Organization.

The most significant foreign policy development of the year, however, may well prove to be the Russian parliamentary elections of December, which raised at least the possibility of a classical red-brown coalition emerging in the Russian Duma. The Communists, along with their Agrarian allies and the neo-fascist Liberal Democrats of Vladimir Zhirinovsky emerged with more than 50 percent of the legislature. The danger was not only internal, where the effect could be the beginning of the crimping of the freedom Russians have been enjoying since the fall of the Communist dictators. It could well be external, for it takes place in the context of a period during which the American government has been vacillating over whether and how fast to expand NATO membership on behalf of the newly democratic countries of Central Europe. The leader of the resurgent Communists, Gennady Zyuganov, lost no time in speaking to the issue in the wake of the election. He was quoted by the *Washington Post* as warning the Baltic states not to rush into new military alliances, a suggestion that can only be seen as an early challenge to the expansion of NATO that is a central ambition of American foreign policy as the century draws to a close.

Seth Lipsky is editor of the Forward.

Press Freedom: Media Controls

Leonard R. Sussman

At year-end, the armistice halted bloodletting but could not yet heal wounds in Bosnia, Serbia or Croatia. From Slovenia, now the more peaceful outback of the former Yugoslavia, came a warning by 140 journalists from all the warring regions: News media have been weapons of war. If peace is to come, independent media must "become a major force in the establishment and development of democratic societies."

The journalists meeting in Ljubljana in November told the international community it must support "free, independent and pluralistic media which are essential to the creation of democratic societies."

Across the former Yugoslavia in 1995, there were no fully free news media. There were more than seventy graves of journalists killed during four years of bloodshed. Among living journalists there was a truce, broken and renewed from day to day, between government controllers and independent newspersons. State-run Serbian radio and television dominated the flow of news. Belgrade, initial stimulant of this war by adroit manipulation of the media, conducted year-long harassment of small broadcast and print media which were allowed some independence. These news outlets were kept on the brink of closure, hardly press freedom.

Yet Belgrade's Radio B-92 performed heroically, with its weak FM signal unable to reach beyond the city. For years, the Serb government wooed away its staff and denied B-29 adequate licensing, forcing it to perform as a pirate radio. Yet, on occasion B-92 stimulated demonstrations that brought tens of thousands into the streets to call for peace. The popular newspaper *Borba*, denied a license to publish, was reorganized as *Nasa Borba*, and allowed some latitude. In Sarajevo, the martyred but defiant capital of Bosnia, guns were quiet at year-end. The once-cosmopolitan city still had its heroic newspaper *Oslobodjenje* which published even during the worst days of terror.

A small sign of hope for the region: Starting in October, a weekly ten minute exchange of news by satellite began among three independent channels—NTV99 in Sarajevo, Studio B in Belgrade, and Kanal A1 in Skopje. The broadcasts are supported by UNESCO.

Following the Dayton peace plan, no small challenge faces the peacemakers, as the 140 journalists in Slovenia declared: What role for truly independent news media?

Free and independent media the exception

Looking for models beyond their ravaged country, journalists of ex-Yugoslavia have a gloomy picture. Worldwide, at mid-year, only 63 of 187 countries (34 percent) had *free* print and broadcast media. Some 63 nations (34 percent) permit *partly free* media and 61 countries (32 percent) are *not free*. In 1994, 36 percent were free, 33 percent partly free and 31 percent not free. The number of journalists killed in 1995—59 in 21 countries—was down from the 126 killed in 1994 when 72 died in Rwanda, Algeria and Russia alone. There were 1,418 reported cases of press-freedom violations in 1995, compared to1,499 in 1994.

Press freedom is gauged by the degree of legal bars to independent journalism, actual political or economic influence on the content of the news flow, and the diversity of both content and ownership. Journalists' access to varied official and unofficial information, and their abilty to criticize the government without penalty is also assessed.

The worst killing ground for journalists is, as in 1994, Algeria. Extremists murdered 26 journalists in 1995, 24 in 1994. News men and women were killed on the job, outside homes and offices, and even visiting a murdered mother in a cemetary. Just prior to the election in November, terrorists murdered 10 journalists. The government arrested and harassed some news persons, including editors-in-chief, and temporarily shut down at least one newspaper.

Four journalists died in Brazil because of their writing. Three were reporting on corruption. Four Russian journalists died on the job: one killed by a Chechen soldier, another by a Russian soldier during a hostage crisis, and two after death threats for their coverage. The war in Bosnia claimed three deaths, one from a grenade attack and two who died in prison.

Two ethnic Kurds died in Turkish prisons. One had been accused of "belittling" the president of Turkey. The government campaign against journalists reporting on the Kurds continued all year. There were thirty recorded cases of arrests, raids, beatings, censorship, suspension of publications, confiscation of press materials, and torture.

Rwanda, scene in 1994 of horrendous massacres, which included the killing of thirty-seven journalists, was relatively quiet for the news persons who were there in 1995.

Argentina moved from the free category into the partly free. Leaving the partly free for the not free group were Albania, Cambodia, Cameroon and Zimbabwe.

Improvements were noted in Cape Verde which went from partly free to free; and the Central African Republic, Mozambique, Niger and Serbia-Montenegro which moved into the partly-free category from the not-free.

Another bright spot: In May, the Supreme Court of Costa Rica ruled that the obligatory licensing of journalists was unconstitutional. For twenty-six years, the government had accredited only journalists who had certificates from the designated *colegio*, or journalism school. To work as a journalist without this license was illlegal, and subjected the individual to stiff penalties, including imprisonment. The ruling was a substantial victory for press freedom. A dozen other countries in the hemisphere, and many elsewhere, require licensing of journalists.

Soft censorship

Worldwide in 1995, a more pervasive though "silent" form of government domination of news media evolved in the form of new "press laws" that are under study in Western Europe as well as Eastern/Central Europe and the states of the former Soviet Union.

Abid Hussain, the United Nation's special rapporteur of the U.N. Human Rights Commission's committee on press freedom gave his approval to "permissible restrictions" to press freedom. The key term in the U.N. report is "press responsibility." There are no opponents of press responsibility, certainly not among journalists. But how does one define responsible journalism? And who does the defining?

The debate over press responsibility

Censorious governments, whether mildly or harshly so, increasingly employ the pattern codified by the U.N. rapporteur, which has also been set as a legislative model by the Council of Europe. They maintain, as did the Hussain report, that "any permissible limitation to the right to freedom of expreession must not only be provided by law, it must also be necessary to attain one of the following purposes: to respect the rights or reputations of others, to protect national security...public order...public health...public morals."

In free countries, such protections are covered in fair laws of libel, and other rarely invoked statutes. The likelihood now, however, is that debate over press responsibility will influence new press laws in Eastern and even Western Europe, Eurasia, Asia and Africa where governments are examining the role of news media with unprecedented intensity.

The words "libel" and "defamation" in American law are narrowly defined mainly to protect a private individual's good name. In the U.S., a public person, whether an official or celebrity, cannot successfully sue for libel unless it can be shown that the journalist knew of the falsity and published it out of malice. Elsewhere, increasingly, heads of state and governments cry "libel" when a journalist criticizes an official or his policies. The consequences for the journalist: arrest, heavy fines, imprisonment, loss of employment and even a career; or banning, confiscation or closure of the publication.

In December, Indonesia sentenced to two years in prison two journalists already behind bars for criticizing the Suharto regime. They had discussed in print the succession to President Suharto, and the comfortable incomes of the national leaders. This was translated—in the language of "responsible journalism"—to mean the writers had generated "feelings of hostility, hatred or contempt toward the government"—in brief, defamation. Truth would not be a defense against such charges of libel, nor is truth regarded as an established right of the citizenry which should know such basic facts of political life. Not in Indonesia or in many other countries, where new laws of the press invoke "permissible limitation" of expression immediately after bald assurance that press freedom exists, and censorship has ended.

Such press-controls were projected at the U.N. Fourth World Conference on Women in Beijing in September. The 150-page concluding document urged using news media as a "tool" of government to press for women's rights. Regimes, moreover, were asked to promote women's participation in both private- and public-run journalism. The participants at such meetings are all governmentally appointed delegates. They usually blur the distinction between public and private sectors, and imply that governments have the prerogative to control content and procedures of independent news media.

The U.N. last year briefly debated the moribund "new world information and communicaton order" which wreaked havoc at UNESCO for a decade. The U.N. stopped short of fully reopening that discussion. The concluding resolution, however, continued the brief reference to NWICO "seen as an evolving and continuous pro-

Press Freedom Violations—1995

(and cumulative figures since 1982)

	[ ] countries	Total 1982-1995
A. Killed	63 [22]	722
B. Kidnapped; Disappeared, Abducted	32 [17]	295
C. Arrested; Detained	310 [58]	3065
D. Expelled	10 [6]	415

A. Algeria-26; Angola-2; Azerbaijan-1; Bosnia-3; Brazil-4; Burundi-2; Canada-1; Chechnya-2; Colombia-2; Croatia-1; Dominican Republic-1; England-1; Guatemala-1; India-1; Mexico-1;   Russia-5; Somalia-1; Sri Lanka-3; Tajikistan-1; Turkey-2; Uganda-1; Ukraine-1.

B. Algeria-7; Bolivia-1; Bosnia-2; Chad-2; Chechnya-4; Colombia-3; Guatemala-1; Haiti-2; India-4; Latvia-1; Mexico-1; Pakistan-1; Russia-2; Rwanda-1; Tajikistan-1; Turkey-1; Zaire-2.

C. Afghanistan-4; Albania-15; Algeria-8; Azerbaijan-4; Bahrain-2; Bolivia-16; Bosnia-7; Burma-1; Burundi-1; Cameroon-4; Canada-1; China-4; Congo-1; Cuba-29; Ecuador-2; Egypt-2; Ethiopia-13; Gambia-12; Germany-4; Guinea-1; Guinea Bissau-1; Indonesia-11; Iran-1; Israel-9; Ivory Coast-8; Jordan-1; Kenya-4; Lebanon-4; Malawi-1; Malaysia-2; Maldives-1; Mali-1; Namibia-1; Nigeria-18; Pakistan-8; Palestinian Terr. 19; Peru-7; Russia-1; Sao Tome and Principe-2; Serbia-3; Sierra Leone-6; Somalia-1; South Korea-1; Sri Lanka-1; Swaziland-6; Tanzania-3; Thailand-1; Togo-2; Tunisia-1; Turkey-28; Turkmenistan-2; Uganda-3; United Kingdom-1; Venezuela-2; Yemen-6; Zaire-6; Zambia-3; Zimbabwe-3.

D. China-4; Cuba-1; The Gambia-2; Peru-1; South Korea-1; United Kingdom-1

		Total 1987-1995
E. Charge, Sentenced, Fined	123 [42]	461
F. Beaten, Assaulted, Tortured	170+ [51]	1141
G. Wounded in Attack	4 [3]	338
H. Threatened	93+ [37]	611
I. Robbery, Confiscation of Materials or Credentials	159 [41]	581
J. Barred from Entry or Travel	128+ [21]	362
K. Harassed	125+ [33]	1037
L. Publication or Program Shut Down	47 [21]	309
M. Publication or Program Banned, Censored or Suspended	101+ [40]	652
N. Home Bombed, Burned, Raided or Occupied	16 [9]	84
O. Publication or Program Bombed, Burned, Raided or Occupied.	82 [32]	218

Total Violations		1463 [116]

—Compiled by Kristen Guida, research assistant

cess," a formulation this writer negotiated in 1983 as a member of the last United States delegation to the UNESCO general conference.

In November, UNESCO's general conference without controversy approved communications programs for two years. News media issues that inflamed Western delegates and journalists in the 1970s and 1980s were gone. But the absence from UNESCO of the United States and United Kingdom, partly as a consequence of past press-control debates in the organizaton, still worries UNESCO. The fiftieth anniversary of the organization was noted in November by a warm letter from President Bill Clinton to Federico Mayor, director-general who had reformed UNESCO since 1987.

The president applauded UNESCO's "unique contribution" to the "free flow information across boundaries, natural and political." The president said that such effort is "integral to the success of global democratization." He particularly noted UNESCO's "critical role in breaking down obstacles to information sharing, enabling citizens an equal opportunity to take on the responsibilities and reap the rewards of international citizenship." He assured Dr. Mayor that "U.S. membership in UNESCO remains on my list of priorities for the future." He said he seeks funds to meet America's annual dues. They would be about $60 million, much of which is returned in some form or buys services the U.S. and its citizens receive.

What Mr. Clinton termed "breaking down obstacles to information sharing" is an increasingly controversial subject in both academic and official debates at international forums. The issue is routinely described at these forums as the "right to communicate." Today, UNESCO helps provide communication technology and training to developing countries and their private or public news and information media. In the divisive debates a decade ago, the "right to communicate" meant mainly assuring governments and others the right of access to the news flow of private and public media whose content, in the view of critical governments, was flawed.

The demand for the "right to communicate" has a complex history. It was raised initially by a French scholar with unquestioned libertarian credentials. The idea was adopted by authoritarian press-controllers, and pressed by academics in democratic societies. In real life, this means denying editors the right fully to determine what they publish and broadcast. In 1973, the U.S. Supreme Court took up this issue. In *Miami Herald v. Tornillo* the court ruled that the content of a newspaper must be chosen by the editor, and not regulated by goverment. Since neither the First Amendment nor the U.S. courts have jurisdiction anywhere else in the world, the "right to communicate" remains in play.

Clearly, among American and other news media, big-ticket corporate mergers and growing conglomerates concentrate not only ownership but editorial control as well. The phenominally expanding electronic networks have the capacity both to centralize linkage-control still further or break out the networks into limitless varieties of message-carriers. So limitless, and moving so instantaneously, that even the owners or managers of the electronic switches may not be able to influence the content.

Proponents of the "right to communicate" argue, however, that some institutional command should assure access, denying editors full control over word and picture. The dilemma: should the concentration of ownership deny anyone access to a communcation channel; or should a "right to communicate" limit the editorial prerogative of editors or owners?

In the early days of radio, the Federal Communication Commission required a percentage of public-service broadcasting for all licensees. Cable editors in the U.S., moreover, are required to provide public-access channels. But radio and cable were already regulated under a premise now considered archaic: the scarcity of the broadcast spectrum. New technology increasingly removes that limitation. The equivalent of public-access in newspapers is the editor's voluntary set-aside: the letters column. Such opportunities for access by the public depend on the ethical commitment of editors and publishers—an example, like many others, of a democratic state's tension between rights and privileges, to be mediated by the journalist's commitment to high professional standards—sometimes called social responsibility.

There can be no standard cure. Clashes of rights are increasingly common in a free society. The very tension between the citizen's right of access and the editors' right to choose, is one price of freedom. The cost could be far higher if public support for an independent press is undermined by failure to accomodate diverse views.

Leonard R. Sussman, senior scholar in international communications of Freedom House, is also adjunct professor of journalism and mass communication at New York University.

The Map of Freedom—1996

(Numbers refer to the map, pages 96-97)

FREE STATES

6 Andorra	60 Cyprus (G)	110 Italy	153 Mongolia	198 Sao Tome & Principe
10 Argentina	62 Czech Republic	112 Jamaica	158 Namibia	204 Slovakia
13 Australia	63 Denmark	113 Japan	159 Nauru	205 Slovenia
14 Austria	65 Dominica	118 Kiribati	161 Netherlands	206 Solomon Isls.
17 Bahamas	68 Ecuador	120 Korea (S)	164 New Zealand	208 South Africa
20 Barbados	73 Estonia	126 Latvia	172 Norway	209 Spain
22 Belgium	78 Finland	131 Liechtenstein	176 Palau	215 Sweden
23 Belize	79 France	132 Lithuania	177 Panama	216 Switzerland
24 Benin	85 Germany	133 Luxembourg	183 Poland	227 Trinidad & Tobago
30 Botswana	88 Greece	139 Malawi	184 Portugal	232 Tuvalu
34 Bulgaria	90 Grenada	142 Mali	193 St. Kitts-Nevis	236 United Kingdom
40 Canada	96 Guyana	143 Malta	194 St. Lucia	237 United States
42 Cape Verde	100 Hungary	144 Marshall Islands	196 St. Vincent and the	238 Uruguay
48 Chile	101 Iceland	147 Mauritius	Grenadines	240 Vanuatu
57 Costa Rica	106 Ireland	150 Micronesia	197 San Marino	248 Western Samoa
	109 Israel	152 Monaco		

FREE RELATED TERRITORIES

2 Aland Isls. (Fin.)	43 Cayman Isls. (UK)	81 French Polynesia (Fr)	154 Montserrat (UK)	188 Reunion (Fr)
5 Amer. Samoa (US)	45 Ceuta (Sp)	87 Gibraltar (UK)	162 Ne. Antilles (Ne)	192 St. Helena and
8 Anguilla (UK)	47 Channel Isls. (UK)	89 Greenland (Den)	163 New Caledonia (Fr)	Dependencies (UK)
12 Aruba (Ne)	50 Christmas Is. (Austral.)	91 Guadeloupe (Fr)	168 Niue (NZ)	195 St. Pierre-Mq. (Fr)
16 Azores (Port)	52 Cocos (Keeling Isls.)	92 Guam (US)	169 Norfolk Is. (Austral.)	213 Svalbard (Norway)
25 Bermuda (UK)	(Austral.)	108 Isle of Man (UK)	171 No. Marianas (US)	224 Tokelau (NZ)
32 Br. Vir. Is. (UK)	56 Cook Isls. (NZ)	137 Madeira (Port)	182 Pitcairn Islands (UK)	231 Turks & Caicos Isls. (UK)
41 Canary Isls. (Sp)	75 Faeroe Isls. (Den)	138 Mayotte (Mahore) (Fr)	185 Puerto Rico (US)	244 Virgin Isls. (US)
	76 Falkland Is. (UK)	145 Martinique (Fr)	187 Rapanui (Easter Is.)	246 Wallis & Futuna Isls. (Fr)
	80 French Guiana (Fr)	148 Melilla (Sp)	(Chile)	

PARTLY FREE STATES

3 Albania	58 Croatia	123 Kuwait	179 Paraguay	233 Uganda
9 Antigua & Barbuda	66 Dominican Republic	124 Kyrgyz Republic	180 Peru	234 Ukraine
11 Armenia	70 El Salvador	128 Lesotho	181 Philippines	242 Venezuela
19 Bangladesh	72 Eritrea	135 Macedonia	189 Romania	252 Zambia
21 Belarus	74 Ethiopia	136 Madagascar	190 Russia	253 Zimbabwe
27 Bolivia	77 Fiji	140 Malaysia	200 Senegal	
31 Brazil	82 Gabon	149 Mexico	201 Seychelles	
35 Burkina Faso	84 Georgia	151 Moldova	203 Singapore	**PARTLY FREE RELATED TERRITORIES**
44 Central African	86 Ghana	155 Morocco	210 Sri Lanka	
Republic	93 Guatemala	156 Mozambique	212 Suriname	61 Cyprus (T)
53 Colombia	95 Guinea-Bissau	160 Nicaragua	218 Taiwan (ROC)	99 Hong Kong (UK)
54 Comoros	97 Haiti	165 Nicaragua	220 Tanzania	122 Kurdistan (Iraq)
55 Congo	98 Honduras	166 Niger	221 Thailand	134 Macao (Port)
	102 India	175 Pakistan	225 Tonga	170 Northern Ireland (UK)
	114 Jordan	178 Papua New Guinea	229 Turkey	

NOT FREE STATES

1 Afghanistan	46 Chad	119 Korea (N)	211 Sudan	**NOT FREE RELATED TERRITORIES**
4 Algeria	49 China (PRC)	125 Laos	214 Swaziland	
7 Angola	111 Côte d'Ivoire	127 Lebanon	217 Syria	67 East Timor (Indo.)
15 Azerbaijan	59 Cuba	129 Liberia	219 Tajikistan	107 Irian Jaya (Indo.)
18 Bahrain	64 Djibouti	130 Libya	223 Togo	115 Kashmir (India)
26 Bhutan	69 Egypt	141 Maldives	228 Tunisia	121 Kosovo (Yugo.)
29 Bosnia-Herzegovina	71 Equatorial Guinea	146 Mauritania	230 Turkmenistan	157 Nagorno-Karabakh
33 Brunei	83 The Gambia	167 Nigeria	235 United Arab	(Armenia/Azerbaijan)
36 Burma	94 Guinea	174 Oman	Emirates	173 Occupied Territories
37 Burundi	103 Indonesia	186 Qatar	239 Uzbekistan	and Palestinian
38 Cambodia	104 Iran	191 Rwanda	243 Vietnam	Autonomous Areas (Isr.)
39 Cameroon	105 Iraq	199 Saudi Arabia	249 Yemen	222 Tibet (China)
	116 Kazakhstan	202 Sierra Leone	250 Yugoslavia	247 Western Sahara (Mor.)
	117 Kenya	207 Somalia	251 Zaire	

89

101

237

40

195

16

PACIFIC OCEAN

25

ATLANTIC OCEAN

137

170
106
108

84

17

185
244
32

8
193
9
54
63
91
145
94
96
227

15

41

247

146

42

83
209
95

202
129

59

231

43

97
66

112

162
12

90

76

149

237

123
95
165
93 70

57
177

53

242

96

212 80

68

180

31

5
168
56

81

182

187

48

27

170

10

238

76

FREEDOM

HOUSE

FREE   PARTLY FREE   NOT FREE

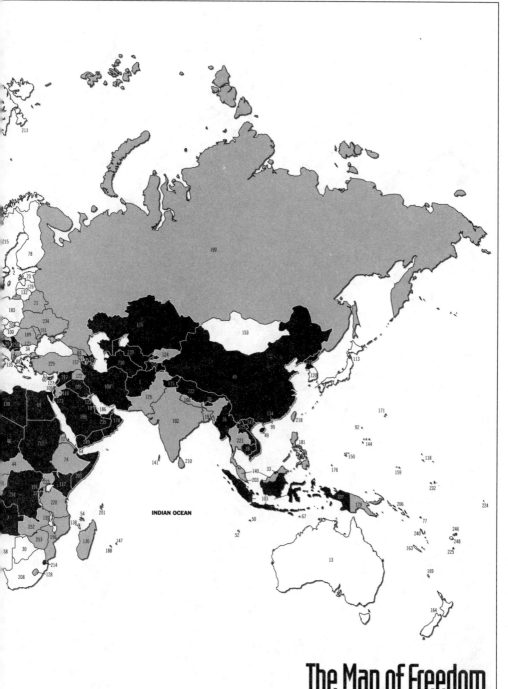

INDIAN OCEAN

The Map of Freedom

JANUARY 1996 ©FREEDOM HOUSE

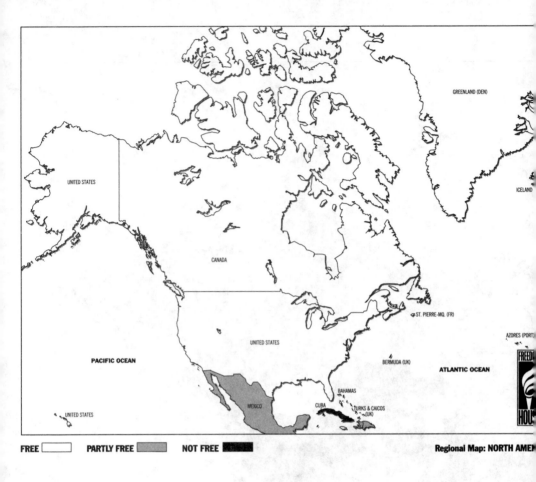

FREE ☐   PARTLY FREE ▒   NOT FREE ■   Regional Map: NORTH AME

MEXICO

CUBA

TURKS & CAICOS
(UK)

CAYMAN
ISLANDS
(UK)

JAMAICA

HAITI

BELIZE

HONDURAS

GUATEMALA

EL SALVADOR

NICARAGUA

COSTA RICA

PANAMA

NE. ANTILLES (NE)

ARUBA (NE)

DOM. REP.

PUERTO RICO

VIRGIN ISLANDS (US)

BRITISH VIRGIN ISLANDS (UK)

ANGUILLA (UK)

ST. KITTS-NEVIS

ANTIGUA & BARBUDA

MONTSERRAT (UK)

GUADELOUPE (FR)

DOMINICA

MARTINIQUE (FR)

ST. LUCIA

ST. VINCENT & THE GRENADINES

GRENADA

BARBADOS

TRINIDAD & TOBAGO

VENEZUELA

GUYANA

SURINAME

FRENCH GUIANA
(FR)

COLOMBIA

ECUADOR

PERU

BRAZIL

RAPANUI/
EASTER ISLAND
(CHILE)

BOLIVIA

PARAGUAY

CHILE

URUGUAY

ARGENTINA

FALKLAND ISLANDS (UK)

PARTLY FREE   NOT FREE

Regional Map: SOUTH AMERICA

FREEDOM HOUSE

SVALBARD (NORWAY)

ICELAND

FAEROE ISLANDS
(DEN)

SWEDEN

FINLAND

NORWAY

ALAND
ISLANDS
(FIN)

ESTONIA

RUSSIA

LATVIA

DEN.

LITHUANIA

NORTHERN IRELAND (UK)

NETHERLANDS

BELARUS

IRE.

UNITED
KINGDOM

POLAND

ISLE OF MAN (UK)

BEL.

GERMANY

UKRAINE

CHANNEL ISLANDS (UK)

LUXEMBOURG

CZECH

SLOVAKIA

LIECH.

MOLDOVA

FRANCE

SWITZ.

AUSTRIA

HUNGARY

ROMANIA

SLOV.

MONACO

CROATIA

YUGO.

KOSOVO (YUGO)

SAN
MARINO

BOSNIA-
HERZ.

BULGARIA

ANDORRA (FR-SP)

MACEDONIA

PORTUGAL

ITALY

ALBANIA

SPAIN

GREECE

TURKEY

GIBRALTAR (UK)

CEUTA (SP)

MELILLA (SP)

MALTA

CYPRUS (T)
CYPRUS (G)

MADEIRA (PORT)

FREEDOM
HOUSE

FREE   PARTLY FREE   NOT FREE

Regional Map: EUR

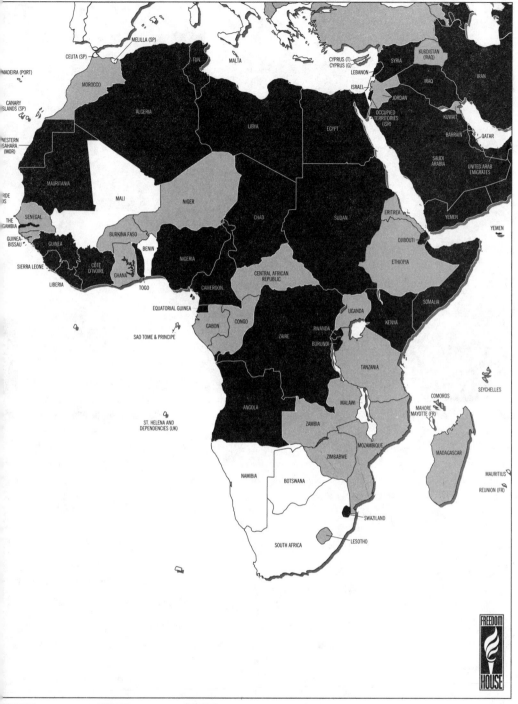

PARTLY FREE   NOT FREE

Regional Map: AFRICA

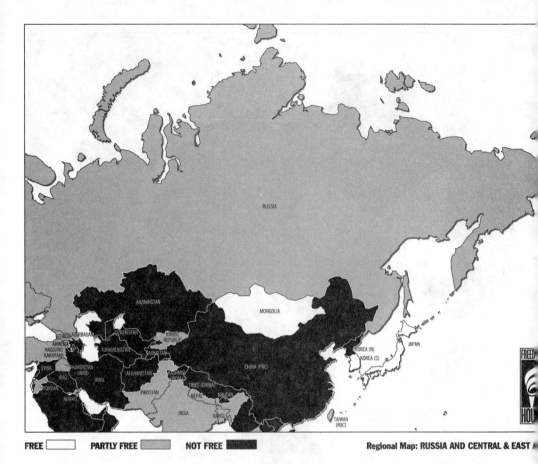

FREE ☐ PARTLY FREE ▨ NOT FREE ▰ Regional Map: **RUSSIA AND CENTRAL & EAST**

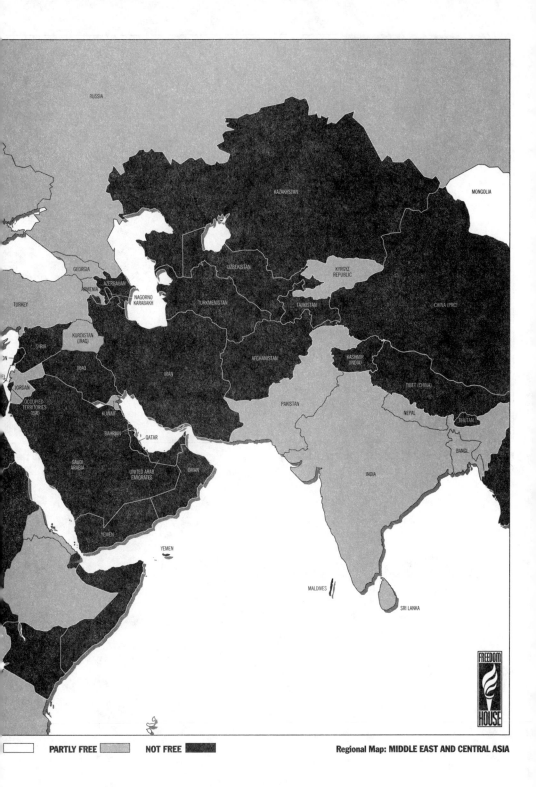

RUSSIA

KAZAKHSTAN

MONGOLIA

GEORGIA

ARMENIA

AZERBAIJAN

NAGORNO
KARABAKH

TURKEY

UZBEKISTAN

KYRGYZ
REPUBLIC

TURKMENISTAN

TAJIKISTAN

CHINA (PRC)

KURDISTAN
(IRAQ)

SYRIA

ON

IRAQ

EL

JORDAN

OCCUPIED
TERRITORIES
(ISR)

IRAN

AFGHANISTAN

KASHMIR
(INDIA)

TIBET (CHINA)

KUWAIT

BAHRAIN

QATAR

PAKISTAN

NEPAL

BHUTAN

BANGL.

SAUDI
ARABIA

UNITED ARAB
EMIRATES

OMAN

INDIA

YEMEN

YEMEN

MALDIVES

SRI LANKA

FREEDOM
HOUSE

PARTLY FREE   NOT FREE   Regional Map: **MIDDLE EAST AND CENTRAL ASIA**

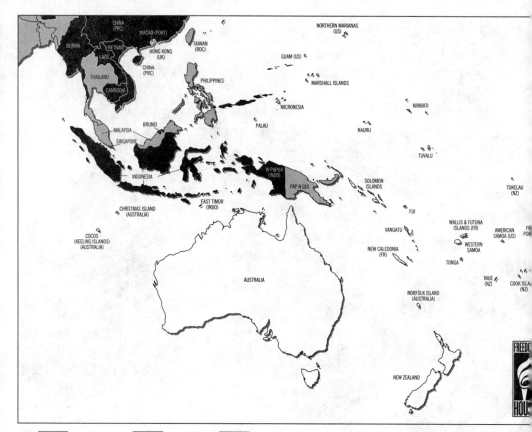

FREE ☐   PARTLY FREE ▨   NOT FREE ■   **Regional Map: SOUTHEAST ASIA AND THE PAC**

Introduction to Country and Related Territory Reports

The *Survey* team at Freedom House wrote reports on 191 countries and 14 related territories.

Each report begins with brief political, economic, and social data. This information is arranged under the following headings: **polity, economy, political rights, civil liberties, status, population, purchasing power parities (PPP), life expectancy,** and **ethnic groups.** There is also a brief explanation of **ratings changes and trends** since the last yearbook. When actual events changed the rating or trend, a succinct explanation follows. Readers interested in understanding the derivation of the ratings in this *Survey* should consult the chapter on methodology.

More detailed information follows in an **overview** and in an essay on the **political rights** and **civil liberties** of each country.

Under **polity**, there is an encapsulated description of the dominant centers of freely chosen or unelected political power in each country. Most of the descriptions are self-explanatory, such as Communist one-party for China or parliamentary democracy for Ireland. Such non-parliamentary democracies as the United States of America are designated presidential-legislative democracies. European democratic countries with constitutional monarchs are designated parliamentary democracies, because the elected body is the locus of most real political power. Only countries with powerful monarchs (e.g. the Sultan of Brunei) warrant a reference to the monarchy in the brief description of the polity. Dominant-party polities are systems in which the ruling party (or front) dominates government, but allows other parties to organize or compete short of taking control of government. There are other types of polities listed as well. Among them are various military and military-influenced or -dominated regimes, transitional systems, and several unique polities, such as Iran's clergy-dominated parliamentary system. Countries with genuine federalism have the word "federal" in the polity description.

The reports label the **economy** of each country. Non-industrial economies are called traditional or pre-industrial. Developed market economies and Third World economies with a modern market sector have the designation capitalist. Mixed capitalist countries combine private enterprise with substantial government involvement in the economy for social welfare purposes. Capitalist-statist economies have both large market sectors and government-owned productive enterprises, due either to elitist economic policies or state dependence on key natural resource industries. Mixed capitalist-statist economies have the characteristics of capitalist-statist economies plus major social welfare programs. Statist systems have the goal of placing the entire economy under direct or indirect government control. Mixed statist economies are primarily government-controlled, but also have significant private enterprise. Developing Third World economies with a government-directed modern sector belong in the statist category. Economies in transition between statist and capitalist forms may have the word "transitional" in the economy description.

Each country report mentions the category of **political rights** and **civil liberties** in which Freedom House classified the country. Category 1 is the most free and category 7 is the least free in each case. **Status** refers to the designations "free," "partly free," and "not free," which Freedom House uses as an overall summary of the general state of freedom in the country.

The ratings of countries and territories that are different from those of the previous year are marked with an asterisk (*). The reasons for the change precede the "Overview" of the country or territory.

Each entry includes a **population** figure that is sometimes the best approximation that is available. For all cases in which the information is available, the *Survey* provides **life expectancy** statistics.

Freedom House obtained the **Purchasing Power Parities (PPP)** from the U.N. Development Program. These figures show per capita gross domestic product (GDP) in terms of international dollars. The PPP statistic adjusts GDP to account for real buying power. For some countries, especially for newly independent countries, tiny island states, and those with statist economies, these statistics were unavailable.

The *Survey* provides a listing of countries' **ethnic groups**, because this information may help the reader understand such questions as minority rights which the *Survey* takes into account.

Each country summary has an **overview** that describes such matters as the most important events of 1995 and current political issues. Finally, the country reports contain a section on **political rights** and **civil liberties**. This section summarizes each country's degree of respect for the rights and liberties that Freedom House uses to evaluate freedom in the world. These summaries include instances of human rights violations by both governmental and nongovernmental entities.

Reports on related territories follow the country summaries. In most cases, these reports are comparatively brief and contain fewer categories of information than one finds in the country summaries.

Beginning in 1995-96, we are including reports only for thirteen related territories rated "Partly Free" and "Not Free," and for the U.S. territory of Puerto Rico, which has a civil liberties situation of particular concern. However, ratings are provided for all fifty-seven related territories.

Afghanistan

Polity: Competing war-
lords, traditional rulers,
and local councils
Economy: Mixed-statist
Population: 18,410,000
PPP: $819
Life Expectancy: 43.5

Political Rights: 7
Civil Liberties: 7
Status: Not Free

Ethnic Groups: Pashtun (38 percent), Tajik (25 percent), Hazara
(19 percent), Uzbek (6 percent)
Capital: Kabul

Overview: A new militia swept across southern and western Afghanistan in 1995, organized around radical theology students
fed up with the fighting among the rival Islamic factions
that overthrew the Communist government in 1992. However, the *Taliban* (seekers) failed to wrest control of Kabul, the capital, from President Burhanuddin
Rabbani's nominal government.

King Zahir Shah ruled Afghanistan from 1933 until his cousin deposed him in
a 1973 coup. An April 1978 coup brought the Khalq faction of the Communist
People's Democratic Party of Afghanistan (PDPA) to power. In late December
1979 the Soviet Union began airlifting tens of thousands of troops into Afghanistan
and installed the PDPA's Parcham faction in power. Over the next several years the
Soviet army could not overcome fierce resistance from foreign-backed *mujahideen*
rebel fighters, and withdrew its last troops in February 1989. In April 1992
Mohammad Najibullah's Communist government fell to the mujahideen.

A power-sharing process quickly collapsed as fighting broke out among nine
major mujahideen militias. Battles between two of the most powerful factions, the
ethnic-Pashtun forces of Gulbuddin Hekmatyar's Hizb-i-Islami (Islamic Party) and
the Tajik-dominated Jamiat-i-Islami (Islamic Society) headed by Burhanuddin
Rabbani and military commander Ahmed Shah Masood, reflected longstanding
rivalries between Afghanistan's two largest ethnic groups.

In December 1992 a Grand Council of tribal elders, religious leaders and
militia commanders elected Rabbani to a two-year presidential term. However,
Hekmatyar and several other mujahideen factions boycotted the vote, refusing to
accept Rabbani's authority.

In 1993 some 18,000 civilians were killed or wounded in fighting. In March a
Pakistani-backed peace process led to a nine-party transitional government with
Hekmatyar as prime minister. Nevertheless, in early 1994 Hekmatyar and Abdul
Rashid Dostam, the powerful ex-Communist warlord whose Uzbek-based militia
controls much of northern Afghanistan, joined forces for an assault on the capital.
The two armies failed to overrun Kabul in heavy fighting in January and June. In
November a new militia, the Taliban, composed largely of radical theology
students angered by the rape, banditry and extortion committed by rival factions,
gained control of the key southern city of Kandahar.

By early 1995 the predominantly ethnic-Pashtun Taliban had captured a string of cities on the 300-mile road from Kandahar to Kabul, ultimately routing Hekmatyar's mujahideen near the capital in mid-February. Along the way the Taliban disarmed local militia commanders, cleared road checkpoints that had been used to hijack vehicles and extort money from travelers, and cracked down on opium traders. However, in mid-March government offensives drove the Taliban from Kabul and a nearby base at Charasyab.

The Taliban overran much of western Afghanistan in late August, capturing the strategic city of Herat in early September. On 16 November Rabbani agreed to transfer power to a council representing eleven factions, but by year's end neither the Taliban nor Dostam had accepted the plan.

In another development, in April Russian jets and helicopters targeting Tajik rebels operating inside Afghanistan attacked the northern villages of Maymay and Taloqan.

Political Rights and Civil Liberties: Afghanistan, nominally led by President Burhanuddin Rabbani, lacks an effective national administration. Roughly half the country is controlled by the Taliban militia, which seeks to establish a theocratic Islamic republic. The government controls Kabul and surrounding areas; warlord Abdul Rashid Dostam's Uzbek-dominated army controls the northern third of the country; and smaller militias hold scattered territory.

Over 25,000 people, mainly civilians, have been killed in clashes between rival groups since the Communist regime fell in April 1992. Militias have indiscriminately shelled populated areas, particularly Kabul, and deliberately targeted civilians. Between three and four million citizens are either refugees or internally displaced. Looting by soldiers routinely follows military victories. Rape is widespread.

There are credible reports of torture and extrajudicial killings carried out by rival groups against opponents. In the absence of the rule of law, small tribal feuds and disputes over drug turf frequently turn deadly. Armed gunmen roam Kabul at night, and banditry, kidnapping for ransom, and extortion are commonplace in many areas.

Freedoms of speech, press and association are sharply restricted throughout Afghanistan. There are few independent publications. The state radio and television stations rarely if ever air opposition views, and mujahideen factions that own broadcast facilities similarly control news content. Journalists are routinely harassed.

Justice is administered according to *shari'a* (Islamic law) or, in some areas, tribal customs. Due process rights are nonexistent and there are reports of summary executions after trials. In Taliban-held areas the punishment for theft is amputation of a hand. Torture of detainees is common throughout Afghanistan.

In January 1993 a Grand Council of religious and tribal leaders declared that only Muslims could work for the government, banned all non-Muslim organizations and ordered television and print media to conform to Islamic principles. According to the U.N. Special Rapporteur, the nominal High Court has issued twenty-one ordinances regulating the activities, dress and behavior of women on religious grounds. Fundamentalists occasionally throw acid in women's faces as punishment for wearing makeup, and routinely harass women for wearing Western clothes or not wearing the veil.

In Taliban-held areas, women are barred from occupations other than women's healthcare and teaching in girls' schools, kept out of market areas and other public places and forced to wear the *burqa*, a garment covering nearly the entire body. Some U.N. offices have reportedly kept female staff at home to comply with these directives. The Taliban also frequently orders men to have short haircuts, bars soccer games and smashes television sets.

Sikhs and Hindus often are attacked, and thousands have fled the country. There are several thousand Tajik refugees in northern Afghanistan.

Freedom of movement is hampered by continued factional fighting and by the millions of uncleared landmines strewn across Afghanistan. No known independent trade unions exist.

⬇ Albania

Polity: Presidential-parliamentary democracy
Economy: Transitional
Population: 3,451,000
PPP: $3,500
Life Expectancy: 72.0
Ethnic Groups: Albanians (two main ethnic/linguistic groups: Ghegs, Tosks, 95 percent), Greeks (3 percent)
Capital: Tirana

Political Rights: 3
Civil Liberties: 4
Status: Partly Free

Trend Arrow: A new law would effectively ban a number of opposition deputies from running for parliament. The independence of the Supreme Court was undermined with the dismissal of its chairman.

Overview: In 1995, President Sali Berisha faced discord in the ruling Democratic Party (PD), as well as an opposition boycott of parliament following the dismissal of the Supreme Court chairman, who had questioned the independence of Albania's judiciary. The government launched a massive privatization effort, as emigrant remittances fueled a burgeoning private sector. In June, the Council of Europe approved Albania's membership application.

Albania gained independence in 1912 after 450 years of Ottoman rule. Annexed by Italy in 1939, Albania saw a one-party Communist regime established in 1946 under World War II partisan Enver Hoxha, who died in office in 1985. In 1990, Ramiz Alia, Hoxha's successor as first secretary of the Albanian Party of Labor (Communist), was elected president as head of the Socialist Party (PS), (renamed Communists). In 1992 elections for the 140-member People's Assembly, Berisha's DP captured 92 seats; the PS, 38; the Social Democratic Party, 7; the Union for Human Rights of the Greek Minority, 2; and the Republican Party, 1. Lawmakers elected Berisha president. Alexander Meksi was named prime minister.

The rejection of a new constitution in a November 1994 referendum influenced politics in 1995. The Social Democrats and the Democratic Alliance, which split with the PD, had criticized the draft for giving the president power to appoint and dismiss the prime minister, ministers and judges, and preside over the Supreme Court. In February, opposition parties presented a draft curtailing some presidential powers. In March, Berisha orchestrated the ouster of PD chairman Eduard Selami, who backed reducing executive authority. Later purges of PD dissidents suggested Berisha was becoming more authoritarian.

A year-long conflict between the government and Supreme Court Chairman Zef Brozi over judicial independence culminated with the latter's dismissal. Brozi had clashed with the government over the continued imprisonment of former prime minister and PS leader Fatos Nano, sentenced to nine years in 1993 for corruption (but widely regarded as a political prisoner), and his release of four ethnic-Greek Albanians charged with "espionage."

In September, parliament adopted a controversial "law against Communist genocide." It banned political activity by former Politburo and central committee members, and by people in parliament prior to May 1991. Some dozen PS parliamentarians could be barred from the April 1996 election under the new law.

Political Rights and Civil Liberties: Albanians can change their government democratically. The 1992 parliamentary elections were judged free and fair, despite some irregularities. Voters' rejection of a new constitution leaves in force the 1991 Law on Majority Constitutional Provisions. Political parties are allowed to organize. In February 1995, six right-wing organizations created the Albanian Rightist League.

There is a multiparty parliamentary opposition, but the "genocide law" bars former high-ranking Communists from running in the 1996 elections, including leading opposition figures. The opposition Socialists have won numerous local elections. While the 1993 Law on Fundamental Freedoms and Human Rights codifies equality under the law and cultural and linguistic rights for minorities, ethnic Greeks in southern Albania (70,000-80,000) have reported the closing of Greek-language schools, the expulsion of Greeks from the military and discrimination in privatization auctions. Ethnic Greeks do hold positions in local government, the national parliament and various ministries.

Provisions of the 1993 press law susceptible to abuse include poorly defined guidelines for publications' confiscation and removal from circulation. The Association of Professional Journalists has protested high tariffs on the independent and opposition press and a rate increase by the main government-owned printer. In June, Filip Cakuli, editor of the satirical magazine *Hosteni 2000*, was detained by secret police but released after agreeing to change a cover lampooning the president. Radio and television are state monopolies. Two journalists were targets of bombings by unknown assailants.

Persons can face imprisonment for three months to five years for denigrating the president or the Albanian nation and its symbols. In June, Ilir Hoxha, son of the former Communist strongman, received one year in jail for "inciting national hatred by endangering public peace," a charge he denied. Arbitrary restrictions on freedom of assembly exist. Police banned May Day celebrations by labor unions in Tirana, ostensibly because they endangered public order. Religious activity is unrestricted in this predominantly Muslim country with Orthodox and Catholic minorities. A special religious affairs office monitors proselytizing by foreign Christian groups.

In 1995 a new penal code enhanced defendants' rights and reduced sentences, but the executive branch has interfered with the judiciary. The Association of Judges of Albania criticized government organs that "directly affect the independence of the judicial powers." Supreme Court chief Zef Brozi was ousted for protesting executive interference.

The Independent Confederation of Trade Unions of Albania is an umbrella organization for a number of smaller unions. The Confederation of Unions, a successor to the "official" Communist-era federation with links to the Socialist Party, has few members.

Algeria

Polity: Civilian-military **Political Rights:** 6*
Economy: Statist   **Civil Liberties:** 6*
Population: 28,400,000 **Status:** Not Free
PPP: $4,870
Life Expectancy: 67.1
Ethnic Groups: Arabs (75 percent), Berbers (25 percent)
Capital: Algiers
Ratings Change: *Algeria's political rights rating changed from
7 to 6, as did its civil liberties rating, because of elections that drew wide participation.

Overview: Algerians responded to another year of terror and counterterror by Islamic fundamentalists and the military by defying intimidation to vote in large numbers in a November presidential election. The election gave President Lamine Zeroual victory, but appeared more a plea for an end to violence than an endorsement of any candidate. The strong turnout could convince leaders of the banned Islamic Salvation Front (FIS) to negotiate a compromise with the military. Yet there are divisions in both camps, with extremists of the Armed Islamic Group (GIA) seeking a strict theocracy while army hardliners desire total military victory. Guerrilla attacks on civil society, government repression of civil rights and killings continue.

About 50,000 people have been killed in nearly four years of savage and shadowy civil conflict, sparked in January 1992 when Algeria's army canceled the second round of parliamentary elections in which the FIS had already taken a commanding lead. The vote for FIS was democratic; their avowed objectives to create a theocratic state under *shari'a* law clearly would have destroyed many of the constitutional protections Algerians have formally enjoyed since winning independence from France in 1962 after a bloody liberation struggle. The National Liberation Front (FLN) led that fight, and still held power three decades later in 1992. By then, over two-thirds of Algerians had been born since independence, and the FLN's claim to legitimacy had faded. Economic stagnation, widespread housing shortages, unemployment and other social ills blamed on FLN corruption and indifference prompted broad support for opposition parties.

After the elections were voided, a state of emergency was declared and thousands of FIS supporters detained. The army forced President Chaldi Benjedid from office and installed NLF veteran Mohammed Boudiaf as head of a military-dominated junta. He was assassinated just six months later, and after a period of collective rule Major-General Zeroual was appointed president. Zeroual pursued a two-track strategy, seeking talks with moderate Islamic leaders while pursuing a ruthless campaign to crush the fundamentalists' guerrilla organization. Army officers, police and government officials are among the Islamists' favorite targets, but the entire range of civil society is under assault. Anyone considered uncommitted to an Islamist state is considered fair game. Islamist death squads have slaughtered unveiled women, foreigners from French nuns to Latvian sailors, people reading French newspapers and, particularly, journalists, often in a calculatedly cruel manner intended to maximize the slayings' terrorist effect. The government has responded with repression and brutality as well. Thousands of militants and suspected militants have died in clashes and in extrajudicial killings by security forces. Many more are detained and some reportedly tortured. And the regime respects journalists' freedom to write little more than the fundamentalists respect their lives.

Zeroual gained some popular legitimacy through the 75 percent turnout in November, and has worked to present himself as a voice of moderation. It is far from certain whether he can structure a compromise that will bring enough calm to allow a genuine government to be elected in promised 1996 parliamentary elections.

Political Rights and Civil Liberties: Algerians are unable to change their government in open democratic elections. The revised 1989 constitution marked the start of Algeria's transition to a multiparty system after decades of the FLN's one-party rule. The process was abruptly halted in January 1992 as the FIS was poised for a resounding electoral victory, and a narrowly based military junta has ruled since. The November 1994 presidential election included no credible challenger to President Zeroual, and the leading opposition party, the FIS, remains banned with its most prominent leaders under arrest.

Algeria's media have suffered terribly in the civil war. The tally of journalists murdered by fundamentalist terrorists is nearing fifty. Employees of state broadcasting services are particular targets, but many journalists have been killed simply for not supporting the Islamist line. While not as brutal, the regime is equally unrelenting in its efforts to bend the press to its point of view. Beyond directly controlling broadcast media and some newspapers, the regime has threatened and arrested reporters and editors, and closed some newspapers. The regime has almost unlimited power under the declared emergency and an antiterrorist decree. Reports on the security situation must be vetted before publication.

Reporting during the period before November's presidential election was especially constrained. Newspapers were told not to report on calls for a boycott or any other unfavorable information. Three issues of a weekly newspaper critical of the proposed polls were confiscated. In December, Algeria's independent newspapers closed for three days to protest the two-week suspension of the French-language daily *La Liberte* and the arrest of two of its top editors. *La Liberte*'s closure is the latest in a string of actions against the independent media. Government control of newsprint and presses is also an effective weapon, especially against financially weaker publications. Combined with Islamist killings, the threat of arrests and closures has caused extensive self-censorship among journalists. Many have fled into exile. Those who remain and continue to report openly are under no illusions that they are, in effect, under sentence of death.

Islamist terror and government strictures limit public debate. Strict security measures prohibit nearly all public assemblies except those backing the government, but legal opposition parties need no permits to hold meetings. Nongovernmental organizations must be licensed; among active human rights groups are the

Algerian League of Human Rights and the Algerian League for the Defense of Human Rights.

Government response to guerrilla action and terror attacks has been draconian. The Antiterrorist Decree of 1992 created special courts and increased powers of detention. Security forces routinely go far beyond even these expanded limits, and torture and killing of suspected Islamists is reportedly widespread. In what appeared to be a goodwill gesture by newly elected President Zeroual, the last of a number of desert detention camps holding fundamentalist prisoners was closed in November, but about 17,000 other suspected or convicted Islamists remain in government jails. The International Committee of the Red Cross has no access to these prisoners.

Few rights are safe. Anyone associated with the government is a target. Members of the Berber minority, who predominate in the northeastern Kabylie region, are also targeted by extreme fundamentalists because of their generally looser interpretations of Islamic practice. Religious freedom guaranteed by the constitution is clearly under threat by the fundamentalists. People accused of not following shari'a law have become special targets. Women who work outside the home or who go unveiled in public have been assassinated. Women also suffer discrimination under some laws, as well as traditional practice. The shari'a-based family code relegates women to inferior legal status

Trade union rights are protected, and over 60 percent of the labor force is unionized. The government banned a union aligned with the FIS, but has not interfered with strikes and other union activity under emergency regulations, beyond existing requirements for notice and conciliation.

Algeria's economy is still strongly dominated by state enterprises. Privatization will likely become a priority when and if a functioning civil government can be restored.

Andorra

Polity: Parliamentary democracy
Economy: Capitalist
Population: 65,000
PPP: na
Life Expectancy: na
Ethnic Groups: Spanish (61 percent), Andorran (30 percent), French (6 percent)
Capital: Andorra la Vella

Political Rights: 1
Civil Liberties: 1
Status: Free

Overview:
In 1993 Andorra became a sovereign nation with a new constitution and U.N. membership. Since 1278 the six parishes of Andorra, held under the joint control of France and the bishop of Urgel in Spain, had existed in an unwritten democracy without official borders. The General Council (parliament) functioned in numerous legislative and executive capacities under the supervision of the co-princes since 1868. In 1990 the General Council sent a statement to both co-princes declaring

that the time had come for Andorra to join the modern world. After extensive negotiations, French President Francois Mitterand and Bishop Joan Marti i Alanis agreed to grant full sovereignty to Andorra.

When Andorra joined the European Community customs union in 1991, its neighbors began to push for measures to modernize and liberalize the economy. As the country has no currency of its own, circulating francs and pesetas instead, inflationary pressures are felt from prices in Spain and France. Still, low-priced luxury items draw large shopping crowds that complement the booming tourism industry. The vibrant economy also attracts many foreign workers and immigrants, driving up the public debt for education, health care and infrastructure maintenance. Increasing debt and the status of native Andorrans as a minority of the population are among the reasons why citizenship requirements remain stringent and immigrants do not enjoy equal rights.

Political Rights and Civil Liberties: Andorrans are able to change their government by democratic means. The new constitution equalized representation in parliament considerably, with half of the representatives now elected by parish and half according to the population as a whole. Political parties and workers' organizations tend to be centered on political personalities rather than ideology.

Although there are no legal barriers to their participation, women have played a minor role in Andorran politics. Women were granted full suffrage in 1970 and since that time only two cabinet-level posts have been occupied by female politicians. Social conservatism adds to the already difficult task of gaining access to a tightly knit political world.

The constitution prohibits discrimination based on birth, race, sex, origin, religion, disability, opinion, language or any other "personal or social condition," with the exception that many rights and privileges are granted exclusively to Andorran citizens. Citizenship is attained through lineage, marriage, birth or after thirty years of living and working in the country; however, dual citizenship is prohibited. Immigrant workers are not entitled to social benefits, but noncitizens have been granted the right to own businesses.

The constitution proclaims respect for the promotion of liberty, equality, justice, tolerance and defense of human rights and human dignity. The right to "physical and moral integrity" is guaranteed, and cruel, inhuman or degrading treatment as well as torture and the death penalty are outlawed. There have been no documented cases of police brutality. Data are not available concerning the incidence or handling of domestic violence cases.

Citizens enjoy the right to due process, the presumption of innocence and the right to legal counsel, including free counsel for the indigent. There are an independent judiciary, a separate supreme court for deciding constitutional issues and appeals and a public prosecution system to enforce the law and supervise the police. Andorra has only a small internal police force and no defense force.

Freedom of association and assembly are guaranteed. Organizers of demonstrations must give authorities advance notice and take care not to "prevent the free movement of goods and people." The right to strike is absent from the constitution, although Article 19 states that workers and employers both have the right to "defend their own economic and social interests." The fact that workers may be dismissed without notice, receive social security and health benefits for only twenty-five days and have no unemployment insurance may act as powerful deterrents to protest.

The Roman Catholic Church is guaranteed the "preservation of the relations of special cooperation with the State in accordance with the Andorran tradition." The Church is not, however, subsidized by the government. Other religions are respected but subject to limitations "in the interests of public safety, order, health or morals or for the protection of the fundamental rights and freedoms of others."

There are no restrictions on domestic or foreign travel, emigration or repatriation. Andorra has a tradition of providing asylum for refugees although there is no formal asylum policy. Asylum requests are considered on an individual basis.

The constitution guarantees freedoms of expression, communication and information, but allows for laws regulating rights of reply, correction and professional confidentiality. The domestic press consists of two daily papers and one weekly. There is local public radio and television service as well as easy access to print and broadcast media neighboring countries.

Angola

Polity: Presidential-legislative (transitional)
Economy: Statist
Population: 11,524,000
PPP: $751
Life Expectancy: 46.5
Ethnic Groups: Ovimbundu (37 percent), Kimbundu (25 percent), Bakongo (13 percent), others
Capital: Luanda
Ratings Change: *Angola's political rights rating changed from 7 to 6, as did its civil liberties rating, because of a slow implementation of peace accords.

Political Rights: 6*
Civil Liberties: 6*
Status: Not Free

Overview: Angola's prospects for peace appeared better at the end of 1995 than at any time in the preceding three decades. A ceasefire prevailed over most of the country and elements of the rebel National Union for the Total Independence of Angola (UNITA) began to assemble for integration into the national army. UNITA leader Jonas Savimbi appeared ready to return to the Angolan capital, Luanda, to take up a newly-created post as vice-president, but a flare-up of fighting in December could delay or even sabotage lasting peace.

Fourteen years of anti-colonial bush war ended with Portugal's withdrawal from Angola on 11 November 1975. Fifteen more years of fighting followed as ethnic-based rivals were armed by East and West as Cold War proxies. South Africans and Cubans each intervened and eventually withdrew. A large-scale covert American aid program bolstered UNITA's fortunes, but produced no clear victor.

The end of the Cold War allowed the United Nations to become deeply involved in the Angola peace process, but did not end the fighting. A U.N.-supervised election in September 1992 was to bring an end to the long-running war. Despite many irregularities, international observers described the election as generally free and fair, and President Jose Eduardo dos Santos, leader of the leftist Popular Movement for the Liberation of Angola (MPLA), led by a wide margin in the first round. UNITA leader and presidential candidate Savimbi rejected this defeat and refused to enter a second-round runoff, and war resumed in October.

Hundreds of thousands of people died in combat and of starvation and disease before a new peace accord was reached in November 1994. Seven thousand U.N. peacekeepers are now in Angola, and although 1995 has been described as a year of "no war, no peace," it was a vast improvement over the country's recent past.

Some reconstruction has begun in the countryside and the rudiments of civil administration are being reintroduced. But genuine peace and rule of law remain relatively distant goals. It is likely that only both parties' realization that a decisive and comprehensive military victory was unattainable opened the door to reconciliation. In the oil-rich northern enclave of Cabinda, at least two of the various rebel factions fighting a secessionist war have agreed to ceasefires. The pressure on Cabindan rebels to settle will intensify if there is a general settlement in the rest of the country.

International donors met in September to pledge a billion-dollar development fund, but competition for command of economic resources continued inside Angola. A prime flashpoint is the struggle for control over northeastern diamond mining areas.

Political Rights and Civil Liberties: The 1992 presidential and legislative elections, although seriously constrained by wartime conditions, allowed Angolans to freely elect their own representatives for the first time. It remains uncertain, however, whether the Angolan people will be free to change their government through the ballot box in the future. UNITA's return to war precluded the second round runoff required when neither presidential candidate won an outright majority. President Jose Eduardo dos Santos was the clear leader in the first round, but the constitutional requirements for his proper election were never consummated. The MPLA dominates the 220-member national assembly. Opposition deputies of eleven other parties attend and participate in debate, although incidents of harassment have been reported, and the assembly remains largely a rubber-stamp to the MPLA executive. Local elections were planned but then postponed as the war resumed in 1992.

The political process has been largely a contest of military strength between the MPLA and UNITA. Other parties have participated and are represented in the national assembly, but until the basic issue of war and peace is resolved, broader popular participation, especially from the rural areas, will be problematic.

Nascent free media operate in Luanda, but are under constant threat. Ricardo de Mello, the well-regarded editor of a fax news sheet, was killed in January. Other journalists have been threatened and harassed, and the government maintains tight control over broadcast media. In UNITA-controlled areas, there is even less opportunity for media access.

Economic problems are also raising tensions in urban areas. Foreign-owned retail shops in Luanda were attacked in September, and clashes broke out as handicapped war veterans tried to loot military foodstuffs. The situation in the countryside is also very difficult. A particular problem is the great number of land mines, many sown haphazardly, in many areas. The enormous number of weapons that have poured into Angola—and continue to do so—has encouraged armed banditry. Reinstituting civil authority will be difficult even if there is a genuine peace. While local courts adjudicate civil matters and petty crime in many areas, an overall lack of training and infrastructure inhibits judicial proceedings.

Women's rights are protected legally, but societal discrimination remains strong, particularly in rural areas. Religious freedom is generally respected. Constitutional guarantees protect freedom of assembly and labor rights, but implementing legislation and administrative procedures to allow free trade union activities are lacking. Some independent unions are operating, however, and several strikes have resulted in negotiated settlements. Nearly all organized labor activities occur in Angola's cities, and the vast majority of agricultural workers remain outside the modern economic sector.

The state remains deeply involved in the country's limited economic activity, which is largely confined to extractive industries, and corruption and black marketeering are serious problems. Diamonds and immense oil deposits are sources of vast potential wealth, but their full-scale development must await a lasting peace.

Antigua and Barbuda

Polity: Dominant party
Economy: Capitalist-statist
Population: 100,000
PPP: $4,436
Life Expectancy: 74.0
Ethnic Groups: Black (89 percent), other (11 percent)
Capital: St. John's

Political Rights: 4
Civil Liberties: 3
Status: Partly Free

Overview: **P**rime Minister Lester Bird's structural adjustment program sparked labor strikes and anti-tax demonstrations. The economy was set back years when Hurricane Luis inflicted severe damage in the fall.

Antigua and Barbuda is a member of the British Commonwealth. The British monarchy is represented by a governor-general. The islands gained independence in 1981. Under the 1981 constitution, the political system is a parliamentary democracy with a bicameral parliament consisting of a seventeen-member House of Representatives elected for five years and an appointed Senate. In the House there are sixteen seats for Antigua and one for Barbuda. Eleven senators are appointed by the prime minister, four by the parliamentary opposition leader, one by the Barbuda Council and one by the governor-general.

Antigua and Barbuda has been dominated by the Bird family and the Antigua Labour Party (ALP) for decades. Rule has been based more on power and the abuse of authority than on law. The constitution has consistently been disregarded and the Bird tenure has been marked by corruption scandals. A commission headed by prominent British jurist Louis Blom-Cooper concluded in 1990 that the country faced "being engulfed in corruption."

In 1994 Vere Bird, the family patriarch and prime minister, stepped down in favor of his son Lester. In the run-up to the 1994 elections three opposition parties united to form the United Progressive Party (UPP). Labor activist Baldwin Spencer became UPP leader and Tim Hector, editor of the outspoken weekly *Outlet*, deputy leader. The UPP campaigned on a social democratic platform emphasizing rule of law and good governance.

In the election the ALP won eleven of seventeen parliamentary seats, down from fifteen in 1989. The UPP won five, up from one in 1989. The Barbuda People's Movement (BPM) retained the Barbuda seat, giving the opposition a total of six seats. Despite unfair conditions, the UPP opted to accept the outcome because it believed that political momentum was now on its side.

After taking office as prime minister, Lester Bird promised cleaner, more efficient government. But his administration continued to be dogged by scandals. In 1995 Bird's brother, Ivor, was convicted of smuggling cocaine into the country, but was let off with a fine.

With the nation facing a huge per capita foreign debt, Bird imposed a structural adjustment program in 1995. Tax hikes and fiscal tightening sparked labor strikes and demonstrations. In late summer Hurricane Luis slammed the islands. While Bird looked for international aid, the UPP claimed the storm had set development back a decade.

Political Rights and Civil Liberties: Constitutionally, citizens are able to change their government by democratic means. But the 1994 elections were neither free nor fair because 1) the balloting system did not guarantee a secret vote; 2) the ruling party dominated the broadcast media to the exclusion of the opposition; 3) the voter registration system was deficient; 4) the voter registry was inflated by possibly up to 30 percent with names of people who had died or left the country, and; 5) the electoral law allows the ruling party to abuse the power of incumbency with impunity.

Political parties, labor unions and civic organizations are free to organize. There is an Industrial Court to mediate labor disputes, but public sector unions tend to be under the sway of the ruling party. Demonstrators are occasionally subject to harassment by the police, who are politically tied to the ruling party. Freedom of religion is respected.

The judiciary is nominally independent but weak and subject to political manipulation by the ruling party. It has been nearly powerless to address corruption in the executive branch. There is an inter-island court of appeals for Antigua and five other former British colonies in the Lesser Antilles.

The ALP government and the Bird family control the country's television, cable and radio outlets. During the 1994 elections, the opposition was allowed to purchase broadcast time only to announce its campaign events. The government barred the UPP from the broadcast media through a strict interpretation of the country's archaic electoral law, which prohibits broadcast of any item "for the purpose of promoting or procuring the election of any candidate or of any political party." Meanwhile, the ALP rode roughshod over the law with a concerted political campaign thinly disguised as news about the government.

The government, the ruling party and the Bird family also control four newspapers, including *Antigua Today*, an expensively produced weekly established in 1993 as an election vehicle for Lester Bird. The opposition counts solely on the *Daily Observer*, a small but vocal twelve-page publication, and the weekly *Outlet*, which the government is continually trying to throttle, albeit unsuccessfully, through intimidation and libel suits.

⬇ Argentina

Polity: Federal presiden-   **Politic Rights:** 2
tial-legislative democracy   **Civil Liberties:** 3
Economy: Capitalist   **Status:** Free
Population: 34,587,000
PPP: $8,860
Life Expectancy: 72.1
Ethnic Groups: European (mostly Spanish and Italian, 85 percent), mestizo, Indian, Arab
Capital: Buenos Aires
Trend Arrow: The down trend arrow reflects concern about mounting evidence of systemic government corruption and authoritarian behavior by the country's president.

Overview: **P**resident Carlos Menem's authoritarian impulse remained evident after his May 1995 re-election, when he pressed Congress for the right to implement economic policy by decree.

The Argentine Republic was established after independence from Spain in 1816. Democratic governance was often interrupted by military takeovers. The end of authoritarian rule under Juan Peron (1946-55) led to left-wing violence and repressive military regimes. Argentina returned to elected civilian rule in 1983.

Most of the 1853 federal constitution was restored in 1983. As amended in 1994 it provides for a president elected for four years with the option of re-election for one consecutive term. Presidential candidates must win 45 percent of the vote to avoid a runoff. The legislature consists of a 257-member Chamber of Deputies elected for six years, with half the seats renewable every three years, and a 72-member Senate nominated by elected provincial legislatures for nine-year terms, with one-third of the seats renewable every three years. Two senators are directly elected in the Buenos Aires federal district.

Peronist party leader Menem won a six-year presidential term in 1989, defeating Eduardo Angeloz of the incumbent, moderate-left Radical party. Menem discarded Peronist traditions by implementing, mostly by decree, an economic liberalization program.

In 1993 Menem cut a back-room deal with Radical leader Raul Alfonsin for a series of constitutional amendments, including an end to the prohibition on presidential re-election—Menem's main aim—a four-year presidential term and measures to limit the inordinate power of the presidency.

The 1995 election was contested by Menem, Sen. Jose Octavio Bordon, a

Peronist defector at the head of the new center-left Front for a Country in Solidarity (FREPASO), and Radical Horacio Massaccesi, a lackluster provincial governor. Bordon hammered Menem on corruption and his authoritarian tendencies. Menem, struggling with an economic crisis sparked by the Mexican peso meltdown, effectively played the fear card, declaring the choice was between "me or chaos."

Menem captured nearly 50 percent of the vote against about 30 percent for Bordon and 17 percent for Massaccesi. The Peronists gained a narrow majority in both houses of Congress.

Menem later confronted renewed social unrest as unemployment rose to 18 percent, infighting among Peronists and a major government bribery scandal involving IBM's Argentine subsidiary. Needing to impose further economic austerity to comply with the terms of an IMF loan, Menem at the end of the year was trying to steamroll the Congress into declaring an "economic state of emergency" to allow him to implement policy by decree.

Political Rights and Civil Liberties:

Citizens can change their government through elections. Constitutional guarantees regarding freedom of religion and the right to organize political parties, civic organizations and labor unions are generally respected.

However, the separation of powers and the rule of law have been undermined by President Menem's authoritarian ways and his manipulation of the judiciary. Legislative attempts to challenge Menem in court have been blocked since 1990, when Menem pushed a bill increasing the number of Supreme Court justices from five to nine through the Peronist-controlled Senate and stacked the court with politically loyal judges. In December 1995 Menem used the Peronist-controlled Senate to put yet another crony on the Supreme Court.

Menem has used the Supreme Court to uphold decrees removing the comptroller general, whose main function is to investigate executive wrongdoing, and other officials mandated to probe government corruption. Overall, the judicial system is politicized and riddled with the corruption endemic to all branches of the government, creating what Argentines call "juridical insecurity."

Despite nearly two dozen major corruption scandals and the resignations of at least that many senior government officials since 1989, no investigation has ended in a trial. Polls show that more than 80 percent of Argentines do not trust the judicial system.

Since condemning Menem's 1990 pardon of military officers convicted for human rights violations committed in the "dirty war," human rights groups have been subject to anonymous threats and various forms of intimidation. In 1993 the Inter-American Commission on Human Rights of the Organization of American States determined that the 1990 pardons were incompatible with Argentina's treaty obligations under the American Convention on Human Rights.

Newspapers and magazines are privately owned, vocal and reflect a wide variety of viewpoints. Television and radio are both private and public. But Menem's authoritarian style has been particularly evident in his antagonism toward the media, which has created a climate in which journalists have come under increasing attack. Journalists and publications investigating official corruption are the principal targets. They have also been subjected to a libel-suit campaign and cuts in government advertising.

In 1995 international pressure kept the government from passing a series of restrictive press laws. But intimidation, including death threats and illegal searches, continued with impunity. Prominent journalist Guillermo Cherashny was shot and wounded in June, the latest among dozens of attacks against reporters investigating government corruption in recent years.

There continue to be frequent reports of arbitrary arrests and ill-treatment by police during confinement. Police brutality cases rarely go anywhere in civil courts due to intimidation of witnesses and judges. Criminal court judges are frequent targets of anonymous threats.

The 1994 car-bombing of a Jewish organization in Buenos Aires provided Menem with an excuse to establish by decree a security super-secretariat encompassing the foreign, interior, intelligence and defense ministries, and answerable directly to the president. Critics charged that Menem was less concerned about terrorism than about being able to confront chronic social unrest in the provinces.

The Catholic majority enjoys freedom of religious expression. The Jewish community, numbering up to 250,000, is often the target of anti-Semitic vandalism. Neo-Nazi organizations and other anti-Semitic groups remain active.

Labor is dominated by Peronist unions. But union influence has diminished because of corruption scandals, internal divisions, and restrictions on public-sector strikes decreed by Menem to pave the way for his privatization program.

Armenia

Polity: Dominant party   **Political Rights:** 4*
Economy: Mixed-statist   **Civil Liberties:** 4
(transitional)   **Status:** Partly Free
Population: 3,749,000
PPP: $2,420
Life Expectancy: 72.6
Ethnic Groups: Armenian (93 percent), Azeri (3 percent)
Capital: Yerevan
Ratings Change: *Armenia's political rights rating changed from 3 to 4 because of the banning of several political parties, violations of electoral laws, and unequal access to state-run media for the opposition.

Overview: In 1995, President Lev Ter-Petrossian tightened his grip on power amid indications the country was becoming more authoritarian. Nine parties, including the largest opposition group, the Armenian Revolutionary Federation (ARF-Dashnak), were banned from participating in 5 July parliamentary elections, which were dominated by the president's ruling Armenian National Movement (ANM) and labeled "free but not fair" by international observers. Voters also adopted a new constitution giving the president virtual control of all government branches.

Russia obtained this landlocked, predominantly Christian Transcaucasus republic from Persia in 1828. Ottoman Turks controlled a western region prior to their World War I defeat, and between 1894 and 1915 engaged in a genocidal campaign. The Russian component became a Soviet Socialist republic in 1922, western Armenia having been returned to Turkey. Armenia officially declared independence from the USSR on 23 September 1991. About one month later, former human rights activist Ter-Petrossian was elected president.

The 1995 elections occurred amid deepening polarization between authorities and the opposition, and Western concerns about setbacks in democratization. In 1994, after several massive opposition rallies; government intimidation of opposition newspapers; a Ter-Petrossian ally's assassination; and an opposition boycott of parliament, the president announced to a national TV audience the suspension of the diaspora-based ARF-Dashnak, which he labeled terrorist. The Supreme Court banned the organization in January 1995.

As the 1995 campaign began, the government-controlled Central Election Commission arbitrarily excluded certain parties and candidates, leading to violent demonstrations late in June. Though over forty registered parties existed, by election day only thirteen parties/blocs had emerged and/or survived the registration process to contest the forty seats allocated for proportional voting.

In the proportional voting, the ANM-led Republican Bloc won twenty seats; the two-month-old Shamiram party, led by wives of government officials, won eight; the Communist Party won six; and the National Democratic Union, among the president's severest critics, and the Union for Self-Determination, led by Soviet-era political prisoner Paruir Hairikian, who opposed the president's constitutional draft, won three each. In the majoritarian races, runoff and repeat elections were held on 29 July. All but ten of the legislature's 190 seats were filled, with the president's Republican Bloc controlling an estimated two-thirds. About 54 percent of eligible voters reportedly took part, but about 25 percent of ballots were declared invalid. The opposition charged unequal access to state-run broadcasting, in violation of electoral laws. After the vote, the president renamed Hrant Bagratian prime minister.

In the concurrent vote on the constitution, 68 percent voted for and 28.7 percent against. The charter provides for a weak legislature and the strongest presidency among the Organization on Security and Cooperation in Europe (OSCE) states. The president can dissolve parliament, appoint and dismiss the prime minister, appoint all judges and members of the Constitutional Court, and declare martial law.

The new parliament's priorities include promoting the president's economic reforms, specifically, broadening privatization to include larger enterprises and attracting foreign investment. To address crippling energy shortages caused by Azerbaijan's blockade (spurred by the war in the Armenian enclave of Nagorno-Karabakh), Armenia restarted a nuclear reactor and is pursuing a natural gas deal with Iran. Budgetary and other reforms have boosted the economy, as has a wealthy, vigorous diaspora. Inflation and foreign debt are minimal, and industrial production is burgeoning. In the Nagorno-Karabakh conflict, a May 1994 ceasefire held through 1995, with few exceptions. OSCE and Russian-brokered negotiations have stalled.

On 16 March, Ter-Petrossian and Russian President Boris Yeltsin signed a treaty allowing Russia to have bases in Armenia for twenty-five years. Russian troops patrol the country's borders with Iran and Turkey.

Political Rights and Civil Liberties: Armenians can change their government, though the 1995 parliamentary elections excluded nine parties, and fraud and tampering with voting lists were charged.

The media also came under pressure in 1995. During February and March, journalists protested the closing and/or suspension of about a dozen opposition publications, a printing house, TV programs and a documentary center. The government moved to evict the strongly oppositionist *Golos Armenii* and closed the independent *Laragir*, allegedly for outstanding debt. Interior Ministry officers searched the offices of *Aragast,* confiscating equipment, books and documents. State television and radio gave the opposition limited access, particularly during the elections.

Freedoms of movement and assembly are generally unrestricted, and 1995 saw several public demonstrations. In April the government launched a campaign against Protestant sects and the Bahai that saw premises raided, members assaulted and property destroyed. In April, Beirut-based Karekin II was elected Catholicos of All the Armenians. Ter-Petrossian's strong support of Karekin raised charges of interference in church affairs.

While the Soviet-era criminal code has largely been preserved, the new constitution enshrines the presumption of innocence and ensures people against self-incrimination or testifying against spouses or close relatives. Oppositionists say thirty-two opponents of the government, including twenty-two Dashnak members, are imprisoned and cases are pending against another sixty. Forty-year-old ARF-Dashnak activist Artavazd Manuktyan died suspiciously in prison. Nine oppositionists were arrested in late July, including leading Dashnak member Vahan Hovanessia. Generally, defendants' access to attorneys has been restricted, and lawyers themselves reported harassment, intimidation and beatings.

Nearly 80 percent of Armenian workers are unionized. Almost all unions are Soviet-era successors, but several small, independent unions exist. The 1992 employment law guarantees workers' right to form unions. A January 1993 presidential decree permits strikes, as does the new constitution. Employers are prohibited by law from discriminating against women, but the law is frequently violated in this male-dominated, traditional society, and women face obstacles to advancement. Unemployment among women is several times higher than among men. A women's party placed second in the parliamentary elections.

Australia

Polity: Federal parliamentary democracy
Economy: Capitalist
Population: 18,031,000
PPP: $18,220
Life Expectancy: 77.6
Ethnic Groups: European (95 percent), Asian (4 percent), Aboriginal (1 percent)
Capital: Sydney

Political Rights: 1
Civil Liberties: 1
Status: Free

Overview: The opposition Liberal/National coalition won a key by-election in March 1995 and topped the opinion polls as Australia headed into federal elections due by May 1996.

The British claimed Australia in 1770. In January 1901 six states formed the Commonwealth of Australia, adding the Northern Territory and capital city of Canberra as territorial units in 1911. The Queen of England is the nominal head of state in this parliamentary democracy. The directly elected bicameral parliament consists of a seventy-six-member Senate, drawing twelve members from each state plus two each from the capital and the Northern Territory, and a 147-member House of Representatives.

Since World War II political power has alternated between the center-left Labor Party and the conservative coalition of the Liberal Party and the smaller National Party. Prime Minister Bob Hawke led Labor to four consecutive election victories between 1983 and March 1990, and introduced measures to liberalize the economy. In December 1991, during a deep recession, then-Treasurer Paul Keating unseated Hawke in a confidence vote among Labor MPs.

Despite a severe recession, at the March 1993 elections Labor achieved the greatest electoral upset in post-War Australian history, taking eighty seats. The Liberal Party took forty-nine; the National Party, sixteen; and independents, two. Elections for forty of seventy-six Senate seats gave Labor thirty-two seats; the Liberals, twenty-nine; the center-left Democrats, eight; the National Party, five; and the Greens, two.

In January 1995 John Howard replaced Alexander Downer as head of the Liberal Party. At a 25 March by-election in Canberra Labor lost a seat it had held for fifteen years. Opinion polls showed the opposition coalition leading Labor by 53 percent to 34 percent, largely due to continuing concerns over the economy. Industrial relations will also be a key issue in the 1996 campaign.

In another development, in June Premier Keating outlined a plan for a constitutional referendum in 1998 or 1999 on replacing the British monarch as head of state with a ceremonial president.

Political Rights and Civil Liberties: Australians have the democratic means to change their government. Fundamental freedoms are respected in practice. The judiciary is fully independent of the government.

Australia's major rights issue is the treatment of its indigenous population of approximately 230,000 Aborigines and 28,000 Torres Straits Islanders. A 1991 Royal Commission Report found Aborigines are incarcerated at a rate twenty-nine times higher than the rate for whites, often because they could not afford a fine or were denied bail for minor offenses. Gaps in nutrition, life expectancy and child mortality rates between the indigenous and white populations are the highest in the Western world. The government has taken positive measures, including a national Aboriginal health program and the opening of "bail hostels" so that Aborigines suspected of minor crimes are not denied bail for lack of a fixed address. The Australian Institute of Criminology reported in June 1994 that the rate of deaths in custody has dropped and is now on a par with or lower than the rate for whites. However, mistreatment in custody continues.

Native land rights are also a key issue. In June 1992 the High Court formally overturned the concept of *terra nullius* (no man's land), which from a legal standpoint had considered Australia to have been vacant when the British settlers arrived. The Mabo Decision (after claimant Eddie Mabo) formally recognized that

Aboriginal groups inhabited the land prior to the British arrival, and that native titles to the land would still be valid in government-owned areas, provided the indigenous people had maintained a "close and continuing" connection to the land.

The December 1993 Native Title Act requires the government to compensate Aboriginal groups with valid claims to state-held land. The Act also subjects mining leases, upon expiration, to native land claims and negotiation over future use. However, since many groups have been pushed off their traditional land, in practice only about 10 percent of Aborigenes would be able to take direct advantage of the law. Parliament is setting up a land procurement fund for groups not benefiting directly from the Mabo Decision.

Refugees are kept in detention until their asylum applications have been decided, a legal process that can take several years. Domestic violence is common. The Law Reform Commission reports that women face discrimination in the judicial system.

Australian trade unions are independent and vigorous. The government establishes centralized minimum wage awards as a backup to the regular collective bargaining process. However, the controversial 1994 Industrial Relations Reform Act encourages the use of individual contracts at the workplace rather than collective bargaining. In November 1995 Australia's coal miners began a strike to protest the CRA corporation's use of individual contracts in Weipa, Queensland.

Austria

Polity: Federal parliamentary democracy
Economy: Mixed capitalist
Population: 8,095,000
PPP: $18,710
Life Expectancy: 76.2
Ethnic Groups: German (99 percent), Slovene, Croat
Capital: Vienna

Political Rights: 1
Civil Liberties: 1
Status: Free

Overview: After the governing coalition collapsed in early October due to disagreement over the 1996 budget, a sporadic letter-bombing campaign believed to be the work of anti-immigrant extremists underscored fears of the far-right populist opposition gaining significant ground. In the worst incident of racial terrorism in post-war Austria, four gypsies were killed by a bomb encased in a placard reading "Gypsies go back to India" in Oberwart, a settlement 120 kilometers south of Vienna. The following day, an explosion in the ethnically mixed town of Stinatz mangled the hand of a municipal worker. In December's general election voters clearly heeded the government's warning, denying Jorg Haider's anti-immigrant Freedom party even a slight gain in the legislature.

The republic of Austria was established in 1918 after the defeat of the Austro-

Hungarian Empire and reborn in 1945 after seven years of annexation under Nazi Germany. Occupation by the allied forces and the Soviet Union ended in 1955 under the Austrian State Treaty, which guaranteed Austrian neutrality and restored national sovereignty.

The two leading parties, the Christian Democratic Austrian People's Party (OVP) and the Social Democratic Party (SPO), have governed the country for nine years. The recently dissolved parliament formed in the October 1994 federal elections had Social Democrat Franz Vranitzky as chancellor and OVP members Thomas Klestil and Wolfgang Schussel as president and vice-chancellor respectively. After threatening to overtake the OVP with a gain of nine seats in the 1994 elections, the anti-immigrant Freedom Party led by Haider has garnered the support of an estimated 25-30 percent of the electorate. The xenophobic hate crimes at Oberwart and Stinatz, and a sporadic campaign of letter bombs directed at minorities and those assisting foreigners, prompted urgent appeals to Austrian voters from the chancellor and other politicians to avoid "political experimentation" with the far right. Election results showed a 3.4 percent gain for the Social Democrats, who are expected to renew the broken partnership with the OVP.

Seeking to redefine its international role, Austria has tilted away from its forty-year tradition of neutrality. In addition to membership in the European Union, Austria became the twenty-fifth member of NATO's Partnership for Peace while maintaining its desire to concentrate on peacekeeping, humanitarian and environmental missions.

Political Rights and Civil Liberties: Austrians have the right to change their government democratically. The country's provinces possess considerable latitude in local administration and can check federal power through electing members of the upper house of parliament. Voting is compulsory in some provinces. The independent judiciary is headed by a Supreme Judicial Court and includes both Constitutional and Administrative courts. In recent years, women have held about 10 percent of Federal Assembly seats and more than twice that number serve in provincial government.

A 1955 State treaty prohibits Nazis from exercising freedom of assembly or association. All Nazi organizations are illegal, although Nazis have enjoyed sympathy and membership in the Freedom Party. Parliamentary legislation passed in 1992 officially outlawed both denying the Holocaust and approving or justifying Nazi crimes against humanity in public, including in the media. At the same time, penalties were weakened to discourage acquittals on the grounds that the punishments were too harsh. Regardless, the Austrian police tend to enforce anti-Nazi statutes more when extremists attract international attention.

In other aspects, the media are generally free. The Austrian Broadcasting Company (ORF), which controls both radio and television, is state owned but protected from political interference by a broadcasting law. Despite a 1989 government decision to end the ORF's monopoly by licensing private broadcasting, the launching of the first commercial radio station scheduled for September 1995 was derailed by a constitutional court decision to review the regulations. The two ORF television stations are straining under increased competition from German satellite cable. The few restrictions on press freedom concerning public morality and security are rarely put to use.

Religious faiths judged consistent with public order and morality are guaranteed freedom of worship in this predominantly Catholic country. This freedom, generous welfare provisions, and a historical open-door policy for refugees fleeing Eastern Europe have contributed to an enormous influx of immigrants and refugees.

Since 1990, prospective newcomers have been required to apply for visas, restrictions have been tightened on entry, particularly from Bosnia-Herzegovina, and ex-Yugoslav refugees are no longer accepted from third countries. A 1992 Asylum Law has been sharply criticized as failing to meet international protection standards; not guaranteeing access to asylum procedures; not granting the right to remain in Austria pending final decisions on asylum; and arbitrarily granting asylum irrespective of existing legal procedures. Additionally, there have been reports of ill-treatment in pre-expulsion detention, where refugees and undesired foreigners may be held for as long as six months.

Azerbaijan

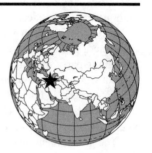

Polity: Dominant party **Political Rights:** 6
Economy: Statist **Civil Liberties:** 6
transitional **Status:** Not Free
Population: 7,275,000
PPP: $2,550
Life Expectancy: 70.6
Ethnic Groups: Azeri (82 percent), Russian (7 percent), Armenian (5 percent)
Capital: Baku

Overview: Azerbaijan's first post-Soviet parliamentary elections were neither free nor fair, as five leading opposition parties and some 600 independent candidates were excluded. A new constitution strengthened the already broad powers of President Gaidar Aliyev, a Soviet-era politburo member who has built a personality cult since assuming power amid civil strife in 1993. Faud Guliyev, acting prime minister since early 1994, was confirmed by parliament on 5 May.

Azerbaijan's northern sector, which Persia ceded to Russia in the early 1800s, briefly joined Armenia and Georgia in a Transcaucasia Federation after the 1917 Bolshevik Revolution. It declared independence the following year, but Red Army forces subdued it in 1920. In 1922 it entered the USSR, becoming a separate SSR in 1936.

Azeris voted for independence in a 1991 referendum. Hardline Communist Ayaz Mutalibov was elected president. The 360-member Supreme Soviet, elected in fraudulent 1990 elections, was Communist-dominated, with the nationalist Azerbaijan Popular Front (AzPF) under Abulfaz Elchibey holding some forty seats. After months of turmoil, the Supreme Soviet created a fifty-seat National Council, with the president and opposition each filling half the seats. Elchibey was elected president in June 1992, but ousted after battlefield setbacks in the Armenian enclave of Nagorno-Karabakh and Russian support of a military renegade sparked violent instability. Aliyev replaced him, and was elected president in an October 1993 vote boycotted by the AzPF and declared "undemocratic" by Western observers.

In 1994 the government cut an $8 billion exploration deal with several Western and one Russian oil companies.

Aliyev, who survived several allegedly Russian-backed coup attempts, sought to consolidate his authority in 1995 and transform oil-rich Azerbaijan into "Kuwait on the Caspian." The government banned five of twelve parties from the 125-member parliament (100 seats directly elected and twenty-five parceled out among the top parties), including the AzPF and the moderate Musavat, a decision publicly criticized by U.N. and Organization for Security and Cooperation in Europe (OSCE) observers. Two days before the 13 November first-round vote, authorities detained Neymat Panakhov and banned a rally by his National Statehood Party. Of eight parties in the race, the state election commission disqualified eighty-seven of 111 AzPF candidates, undermining the only influential opposition group among eight parties in the race.

Aliyev's Yeni Azerbaijan (New Azerbaijan) won 78 percent of the vote to take eighteen of twenty-five seats reserved for parties; the "banned" AzPF won two. The ruling party won most seats in the 27 November second round. As a 50 percent turnout was required for the elections to be valid, the government claimed an 80 percent turnout and that 90 percent approved the constitution. Oppositionists challenged both figures. The OSCE deemed the balloting neither free nor fair, while the Council of Europe cited "irregularities and clear cases of fraud."

The government managed to slow inflation and launch privatization. Azerbaijan's estimated 68 billion barrels of oil and the economy were key issues. A yearlong argument was settled in October when Russia agreed to two oil pipelines, one each through Russia and Turkey.

But the Nagorno-Karabakh war has drained the treasury, and ordinary Azeris felt no benefits from newfound oil wealth. Aliyev, who foiled a police mutiny in March and another in August by supporters of former-President Mutalibov (who lives in Moscow), maintained that political stability and economic improvement necessitated stronger control. A ceasefire in Karabakh held through 1995, but internationally mediated negotiations stalled.

Political Rights and Civil Liberties: Azerbaijan's citizens have the means to change their government, but the November 1995 elections were exclusionary and rife with irregularities. The new constitution gives Aliyev control over all government branches, powers he said allow him to "prevent provocation from our external and internal enemies."

Some forty-three political parties, though legal, face restrictions, harassment and arbitrary state election commission decisions. Several were banned, including the AzPF congress, and their leaders arrested. The Justice Ministry openly monitors some opposition activities. The government limits the press to "constructive criticism," and censorship is common. In early 1995, the opposition newspapers *Azadlyg* and *Cheshma* were raided by police and harassed, allegedly for libeling officials. Over 500 Azeri- and Russian-language publications are registered, and some criticize government policies without sanction. On 29 March, fourteen newspapers suspended publication to protest censorship. Most broadcasting is government-controlled. The government leases time to semi-private outlets like the Azerbaijan News Service. Radio Liberty broadcasts have been periodically blocked.

Freedom of assembly and association have been periodically curtailed, and police brutally dispersed several demonstrations.

There is no state religion, though most Azeris are Shiite Muslims. Significant Russian and Jewish minorities worship freely. There are reports of continued persecution of the small Kurdish and Lezghin minorities.

In March, officials arrested over 400 people, including pro-Elchibey opposition deputy and former interior minister Iskander Gamidov, head of the Gray Wolves nationalist party, after violence left forty dead. The government dubbed the action a coup attempt, but oppositionists and outside analysts called the rebellion a power struggle, a natural outgrowth of organized crime, corruption and clan strife. On 1 April, the government extended emergency rule, imposed in October 1994, for two months. In September Gamidov was sentenced to fourteen years and leading opposition lawmaker Tofik Gasymov was arrested, allegedly for involvement in the March unrest.

The judiciary is not independent and maintains a Soviet structure. The president appoints judges and has substantial influence over the judiciary.

The only significant labor organization remains the post-Communist Azerbaijan Labor Federation, which depends on government support. The largest independent union, the reform Communist-dominated oil workers' union, represents about 85,000 people, or about 80 percent of oil workers. Cultural norms and the Karabakh war have led to discrimination and violence against women.

Bahamas

Polity: Parliamentary democracy
Economy: Capitalist-statist
Population: 276,000
PPP: $17,360
Life Expectancy: 73.1
Ethnic Groups: Black (85 percent), European (15 percent)
Capital: Nassau

Political Rights: 1
Civil Liberties: 2
Status: Free

Overview: As Prime Minister Hubert Ingraham proceeded with a major privatization program, the political focus remained on the official inquiry into corruption in the former government of Lynden O. Pindling.

The Commonwealth of the Bahamas, a 700-island nation in the Caribbean, is a member of the British Commonwealth. It was granted independence in 1973. The British monarchy is represented by a governor-general.

Under the 1973 constitution, a bicameral parliament consists of a forty-nine-member House of Assembly directly elected for five years, and a sixteen-member Senate with nine members appointed by the prime minister, four by the leader of the parliamentary opposition and three by the governor-general. The prime minister is the leader of the party that commands a majority in the House.

After twenty-five years in office, Pindling's Progressive Liberal Party (PLP) was ousted by Ingraham and the Free National Movement (FNM) in the 1992 elections. The PLP had been dogged for years by allegations of corruption and high official involvement in narcotics trafficking. Ingraham, a lawyer and former cabinet official expelled by the PLP in 1986 for his outspoken criticism regarding corruption, had become the FNM leader in 1990.

Ingraham vowed to bring honesty, efficiency and accountability to government. Pindling, at the time the Western hemisphere's longest-serving elected head of government, relied on his image as the father of the nation's independence.

But many voters were born after independence and many workers had been left unemployed as a result of a protracted economic downturn. The PLP and the FNM are both centrist parties, but the FNM is more oriented toward free enterprise and a "less government is better" philosophy.

With 90 percent of the electorate voting, the FNM won thirty-two seats in the House of Assembly to the PLP's seventeen. Pindling held his own seat and became the official opposition leader.

Upon taking office, Ingraham appointed a Commission of Inquiry to investigate the Pindling government. In 1995 the commission detailed widespread mismanagement and malpractice in the national telephone and airline companies under Pindling. Prosecution of former cabinet officials was expected and the commission was to continue its investigations.

The commission recommended the telephone and airline companies be privatized. That fit in with Ingraham's restructuring program. By mid-1995 the government had already sold off seven of ten tourist hotels.

Political Rights and Civil Liberties: Citizens are able to change their government through democratic elections. Unlike previous balloting, the 1992 vote was relatively free of irregularities and fraud allegations. In 1992 indelible ink was used for the first time to identify people who had voted.

Constitutional guarantees regarding the right to organize political parties, civic organizations and labor unions are generally respected, as is the free exercise of religion. Labor, business and professional organizations are generally free. Unions have the right to strike and collective bargaining is prevalent.

There are a number of independent rights groups, who have documented the increase in recent years of violent crime and the problem of police brutality during arrests and interrogations. Rights groups also criticize the "subhuman conditions" and overcrowding in the nation's prisons. The Fox Hill prison remains filled to more than twice its intended capacity.

There are an estimated 25,000 to 40,000 Haitians living illegally in the Bahamas. Tight citizenship laws and a strict work permit system leave Haitians in limbo and with few rights. The influx has created social tension because of the strain on government services. In early 1995 the Bahamas reached an agreement with Haiti on a program of repatriation of illegal Haitian immigrants. But a resurgence of Haitian boat people in the second half of 1995 threatened to undermine the effort.

Full freedom of expression is constrained by strict libel laws. These laws were used by the Pindling government against independent newspapers, but the Ingraham government has refrained from the practice. The Ingraham government has amended media laws to allow for private ownership of broadcasting outlets. At least two newspaper companies have been awarded the first-ever licenses to operate private radio stations and many applications have been submitted to start cable television stations.

The judicial system is headed by a Supreme Court and a Court of Appeal, with the right of appeal under certain circumstances to the Privy Council in London. There are local courts, and on the outer islands the local commissioners have magisterial powers. Despite anti-drug legislation and a formal agreement with the United States in 1987 to suppress the drug trade, there is evidence that drug-related corruption and money-laundering remain a problem, although to a far lesser extent than during the Pindling years. In late 1995 the government finally introduced anti-money-laundering legislation.

Bahrain

Polity: Traditional monarchy
Economy: Capitalist-statist
Population: 603,000
PPP: $14,590
Life Expectancy: 71.6
Ethnic Groups: Bahraini (63 percent), Asian (13 percent), other Arab (10 percent), Iranian (8 percent)
Capital: Manama

Political Rights: 6
Civil Liberties: 6
Status: Not Free

Overview: This Persian Gulf archipelago off Saudi Arabia achieved independence from the United Kingdom in August 1971. The Al Khalifa family has ruled since 1782. Current emir Sheik 'Isa ibn Salman Al Khalifa assumed power in 1961, and rules with his brother, Prime Minister Khalifa ibn Salman Al Khalifa, and his son, Crown Prince Hamad ibn 'Isa Al Khalifa. Although Shiites represent 65 percent or more of the native population, the ruling family and top officials are from the Sunni minority. The 1973 constitution provides for a National Assembly consisting of a cabinet and thirty popularly elected members. The emir dissolved the Assembly in August 1975 and has not reconvened it.

In December 1992 the government created a thirty-member, appointed *majlis al-shura*, essentially a consultative council with little legislative power that consists of business and religious leaders. On 5 December 1994 police arrested Shiite cleric Sheik 'Ali Salman, who had called for the restoration of the National Assembly, and several followers. This sparked some of the worst unrest in Bahrain's history, as Shiites clashed with police in Manama, the capital, and several villages. Police fired on demonstrators on 17 December, killing two, and during the month arrested several hundred protesters.

On 15 January 1995 police forcibly exiled Sheik 'Ali Salman and two other Shiite clerics to Dubai. In predominantly Shiite areas unrest continued through May, with frequent demonstrations, clashes between protesters and police, and arson attacks on various targets. The authorities, backed by Saudi riot police, dispersed several demonstrations and arrested hundreds more Shiites, including veteran opposition leader Sheik 'Abd al-Amir al-Jamri in April. The six months of disturbances left at least a dozen protesters and police dead.

Political Rights and Civil Liberties: Bahrain's citizens cannot change their government democratically. Political parties are prohibited. The emir rules by decree and appoints all government officials, the urban municipal councils and the rural *mukhtars* (local councils). Citizens may submit written petitions to the government, and can appeal to the emir and other officials at audiences called *majlises*.

The Interior Ministry monitors some communications, and maintains informal control over most activities through pervasive informant networks. Agents can search homes without warrants, and frequently searched Shiite homes during the 1994-95 civil disturbances.

The 1974 State Security Act permits the government to detain individuals accused of "anti-government activity" for up to three years without trial. "Anti-government activity" can include peaceful demonstrations and membership in outlawed organizations. Between December 1994 and May 1995 police arrested several hundred mostly Shiite demonstrators; Amnesty International documented 700 arrests through March, and believed more were being held. Many have since been released. Police reportedly use force to coerce confessions.

Ordinary trials feature due process safeguards, but defendants tried in security courts do not enjoy such guarantees. According to Agence France-Presse, several individuals arrested in the 1994-95 disturbances were tried in absentia. Convictions in security courts are often based on coerced confessions.

Freedom of public speech is sharply restricted, although private political discussion is tolerated. The government restricted press reporting on the 1994-95 disturbances, and expelled a BBC journalist in December 1994. Private newspapers do not criticize the government or report on sensitive issues. All radio and television is government-owned and presents official views only. Public political meetings and demonstrations are forbidden. On 11 February police disbanded a demonstration by dozens of women in front of a court trying Shiite protesters. The few legal private associations are closely monitored.

Women face fewer restrictions than in most Islamic countries, but wage and job discrimination continue. Islamic *shari'a* courts rule on matters of divorce and inheritance, occasionally rejecting divorce requests. Domestic violence is reportedly common. Foreign domestic workers are occasionally beaten and sexually abused.

The government occasionally exiles dissidents, including the January 1995 deportation of Sheik 'Ali Salman and two other clerics. The 1963 Citizenship Law denies full citizenship to some 3,000-5,000 Persian-origin Shiites, known as *bidoon* (those without). Bidoon are restricted in business activities, and have difficulty obtaining passports and government loans. Islam is the state religion, but other faiths worship freely. The majority Shiites face discrimination in employment and social services, and are largely barred from the army and police. In January 1995 police reportedly raided two Shiite mosques during a crackdown on activists. Shiite demonstrators vandalized several Asian businesses during the 1994-95 unrest.

No independent labor unions exist. The government has instead created Joint Labor-Management Consultative Committees (JCC), composed of worker and employer representatives. Foreign laborers and non-industrial workers are underrepresented in the sixteen JCCs. The 1974 Security Law restricts strikes deemed damaging to worker-employer relations or to the national economic interest, and few strikes occur. In the absence of unions, effective collective bargaining is impossible. Employers frequently exploit foreign workers.

Bangladesh

Polity: Parliamentary democracy
Economy: Capitalist-statist
Population: 119,184,000
PPP: $1,230
Life Expectancy: 55.6

Political Rights: 3*
Civil Liberties: 4
Status: Partly Free

Ethnic Groups: Bengali (98 percent), Bihari (1 percent), various tribal groups (1 percent)
Capital: Dhaka
Ratings Change: *Bangladesh's political rights rating changed from 2 to 3 because of increasing political violence and usage of detention to limit freedom of association.

Overview:
Following more than a year of violent nationwide strikes and demonstrations against her government, Bangladeshi premier Khaleda Zia dissolved parliament in November 1995 in advance of elections called for January 1996.

Bangladesh won independence in December 1971 after India invaded then-East Pakistan. There have been some nineteen coup attempts or successful takeovers since. The last, in March 1982, brought General H.M. Ershad to power. The country's democratic transition began with Ershad's resignation in December 1990 following weeks of pro-democracy demonstrations.

Bangladesh's cleanest elections were held on 27 February 1991 for the 300 directly-elected seats in the 330-member National Assembly. (Thirty seats are reserved for women). The Bangladesh National Party (BNP), led by Khaleda Zia, took 138 seats; the center-left Awami League, led by Sheikh Hasina, 89; the jailed Ershad's Jatiya (National) Party, 35; the fundamentalist Islamic League, 19; smaller parties and independents, 19. In March Zia became the country's first female prime minister.

In a September 1991 referendum, voters overwhelmingly approved scrapping the presidential system in favor of a parliamentary democracy. Zia became head of government with executive powers, and parliament approved the BNP's Abdur Rahman Biswas for the new, largely ceremonial presidency.

In March 1994 the Awami League accused the BNP of rigging a by-election in Magura in western Bangladesh. The League, joined by the Islamic League and the Jatiya Party, began a parliamentary boycott to force Zia to appoint a neutral, caretaker government to preside over fresh parliamentary elections. The standoff reflected the intense, personal rivalry between Zia and Sheikh Hasina. Throughout the summer and fall, politics degenerated into street clashes between the opposition and police. On 28 December, 147 of 154 opposition lawmakers resigned.

On 25 November 1995, following months of violent nationwide strikes, Zia dissolved parliament. The Supreme Court subsequently ordered fresh elections on 18 January 1996.

Zia's government is also facing an upsurge in Islamic fundamentalism. Militants angered by feminist author Taslima Nasreen—now in exile in Sweden— and by the proliferation of female-led nongovernmental organizations, burned some 1,400 girls' schools in 1994. In 1995 fundamentalists attacked several rural carnivals and rioted in the city of Sylhet to prevent a poet from appearing.

In the southeastern Chittagong Hill Tracts (CHT) the government continued peace talks with the Shanti Bahini tribal group, which since 1973 has been fighting for greater autonomy for the Chakmas and other Buddhist hill tribes. Power in the CHT has been decentralized somewhat through local district councils, but a heavy military presence remains, and law and order and control over land tenure are not under local authority.

Political Rights and Civil Liberties: Citizens of Bangladesh have the democratic means to change their government. Political rallies, elections and strikes are frequently marred by violence. At least twenty political figures were killed in 1995, and numerous demonstrators were killed in clashes with police, including twelve people during protests in March against fertilizer shortages.

The rule of law is weak and police, army and paramilitary units are routinely responsible for rights violations. Police frequently torture suspects during interrogations, leading to several deaths each year. Abuse of prisoners in the lowly Class "C" cells is widespread. In the Chittagong Hill Tracts the indigenous Chakmas accuse security forces of rape, torture and illegal detention of villagers, and violence between Chakmas and Muslim settlers is common.

The Zia government has detained hundreds under the 1974 Special Powers Act, often on political grounds, although courts have ordered the release of many detainees. The judiciary is independent of the government. However, the system is weakened by a severe backlog of cases and rampant corruption. Due process rights are occasionally ignored in rural areas.

Women face discrimination in health care, education and employment. Domestic violence is common. In 1994 an estimated 300 women were killed over dowry disputes. In rural areas women accused of moral offenses are sometimes brought before a *shalish*, an informal council of fundamentalist leaders that imposes floggings and other sanctions. In November parliament approved special tribunals to try and execute individuals accused of certain crimes against women and children, although shalish rulings are not covered. Fundamentalists have physically attacked nongovernmental activists, particularly women, claiming their work is "anti-Islamic."

Most publications depend heavily on the government for advertising revenues, and advertising apportionment is politically slanted. Journalists and newspaper offices are occasionally attacked by police, fundamentalists and party militants. Broadcast media are state-owned and coverage favors the government.

Political protests frequently degenerate into violence between activists and police. Officials occasionally ban opposition rallies on narrow legal grounds. Dozens of students have been killed in the past several years in politically-related campus violence.

Islam is the official religion, but Buddhist, Hindu and Christian minorities can worship freely. However, Hindus are subject to random violence, and reportedly receive less police protection than their Muslim counterparts. Sexual exploitation of children is rampant in urban areas, and throughout the country children are occasionally kidnapped and sold into bondage.

Some 238,000 Bihari Muslim refugees, who opted for Pakistani citizenship after independence, live in Bangladesh pending resettlement. In the southeast, the U.N. has repatriated 192,000 of the 270,000 Rohingya Muslim refugees who fled from abuses by the Burmese army only to face subsequent harassment by Bangladeshi troops.

Unions are heavily politicized and generally do not act as true advocates of labor rights. Most civil servants are forbidden from joining unions and cannot engage in collective bargaining. The labor code allows workers suspected of union activities to be transferred, and in practice union organizers in the garment industry face often violent harassment. Formation of a new union requires signatures of 30 percent of the workers in an establishment; collecting these is nearly impossible due to legal restrictions on activity by unregistered unions. Child labor is a serious problem and relevant laws are rarely enforced.

Barbados

Polity: Parliamentary democracy
Economy: Capitalist
Population: 262,000
PPP: $9,667
Life Expectancy: 75.6
Ethnic Groups: Black (80 percent), European (4 percent), mixed (16 percent)
Capital: Bridgetown

Political Rights: 1
Civil Liberties: 1
Status: Free

Overview: The government of Prime Minister Owen Arthur completed its first year amid hopes that it had ended years of economic drift and put the economy on a stronger footing through enhanced trade and service-oriented exports.

Barbados, a member of the British Commonwealth, achieved independence in 1966. The British monarchy is represented by a governor-general.

The system of government is a parliamentary democracy. The bicameral parliament consists of a twenty-eight-member House of Assembly elected for five years, and a twenty-one-member Senate, with twelve senators appointed by the prime minister, two by the leader of the parliamentary opposition, and seven by various civic interests. Executive authority is invested in the prime minister, who is the leader of the political party commanding a majority in the House.

Since independence, power has alternated between two centrist parties, the Democratic Labour Party (DLP) under Errol Barrow, and the Barbados Labour Party (BLP) under Tom Adams from 1976 until Adams' death in 1985. Adams was succeeded by Bernard St. John, but the BLP was defeated in the 1986 elections and Barrow returned as prime minister. Barrow died in 1987 and was succeeded by Erskine Sandiford who led the DLP to victory in the 1991 elections.

Under Sandiford Barbados suffered through a prolonged economic recession as revenues from the twin pillars of sugar and tourism declined. By 1994 the economy appeared to be improving, but unemployment was still nearly 25 percent. Sandiford's popularity continued to plunge and he was increasingly criticized for his authoritarian style of rule. Sandiford lost a no-confidence vote in parliament, fourteen to twelve, when the nine BLP legislators were joined by four DLP backbenchers and one independent legislator who had quit the DLP.

Sandiford called for new elections and gave up the leadership of the DLP, which elected David Thompson, the young finance minister, to replace him.

In the 1994 election campaign Owen Arthur, the forty-four-year-old economist elected in 1993 to head the BLP, promised to build "a modern, technologically dynamic economy," create jobs and restore investor confidence. Thompson argued the economy had already turned the corner. The BLP won nineteen seats, the DLP eight and the New Democratic Party (NDP), a disaffected offshoot of the DLP formed in 1989, one.

Voter participation dipped to 60.6 percent, down from 62 percent in 1991 and 76 percent in 1986. According to one local analyst the trend reflected "a growing disenchantment with voting, particularly among the youth where the scourge of unemployment is the greatest."

In his first year Arthur seemed able to combine a technocratic approach to revitalizing the economy with savvy politics. He also appointed a number of promising, young cabinet officials. By mid-1995 unemployment was down to 20.5 percent, the lowest level since 1990. Renewed confidence in government, however, seemed threatened late in the year when Arthur was criticized for a series of high-salaried appointments to the state-owned tourist company.

Political Rights and Civil Liberties:

Citizens are able to change their government through democratic elections. Constitutional guarantees regarding freedom of religion and the right to organize political parties, labor unions and civic organization are respected.

Apart from the parties holding parliamentary seats, there are other political organizations including the small left-wing Workers' Party of Barbados. There are two major labor unions and various smaller ones, and all are politically active and free to strike. Human rights organizations operate freely.

Freedom of expression is fully respected. Public opinion expressed through the news media, which are free of censorship and government control, has a powerful influence on policy. Newspapers are privately owned, and there are two major dailies. There are both private and government radio stations. The single television station, operated by the government-owned Caribbean Broadcasting Corporation (CBC), presents a wide range of political viewpoints. The highlight of the 1994 election campaign was a first-ever televised debate between the major candidates.

The judicial system is independent and includes a Supreme Court that encompasses a High Court and a Court of Appeal. Lower court officials are appointed on the advice of the Judicial and Legal Service Commission. The government provides free legal aid to the indigent.

In 1995 human rights concerns continued to center on the high crime rate, much of it fueled by an increase in drug abuse and trafficking, and occasional allegations of police brutality during detention to extract confessions and excessive use of force during arrests. In 1992 the Court of Appeal outlawed the practice of public flogging of criminals. Also in 1992, a Domestic Violence law was passed to give police and judges greater powers to protect women against battering in the home.

Belarus

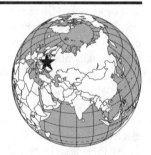

Polity: Presidential-parliamentary (presidential-dominated)
Economy: Statist transitional
Population: 10,340,000
PPP: $6,850
Life Expectancy: 71.0

Political Rights: 5*
Civil Liberties: 5*
Status: Partly Free

Ethnic Groups: Belarusian (78 percent), Russian (13 percent), Polish (4 percent), Ukrainian (2 percent), Jewish (1 percent)
Capital: Minsk
Ratings Change: *Belarus's political rights rating changed from 4 to 5, as did its civil liberties rating, because the president ignored Supreme Court decisions, banned independent unions, reintroduced censorship, and violated the constitution. Elections were neither free nor fair.

Overview: Populist, nonparty President Alyaksandr Lukashenka strengthened his grip on power in 1995 by reintroducing censorship, banning independent trade unions, reimposing the use of Soviet-era textbooks, ignoring the Supreme Court when it overturned his decrees and limiting the rights of candidates for the year's parliamentary elections. In a May referendum, over 80 percent of voters backed a presidential proposal to tighten economic ties with Russia, restore Russian as the official language and restore Soviet-era symbols.

Present-day Belarus was part of the tenth-century Kievan realm. After a lengthy period of Lithuanian rule, it merged with Poland in the sixteenth century and became part of the Russian Empire after Poland was partitioned in the eighteenth century. It became a constituent republic of the USSR in 1922. With the collapse of the Soviet Union, nationalist-minded centrist Stanislaw Shushkevich eschewed the post of president and became head of state as well as chairman of the Communist-dominated 360-member Supreme Council, in which the democratic Belarusian Popular Front controlled 37 seats. Throughout 1993, Shushkevich clashed with conservative, pro-Russian Prime Minister Vyacheslav Kebich and parliament over economic reform, relations with Russia and the constitution. After parliament ousted Shushkevich in 1994 and created the post of president, elections saw a surprising victory by Lukashenka, a poorly educated populist, former state farm director and chairman of parliament's anti-corruption committee.

Two rounds of elections in May 1995 failed to elect a parliament, a complex voting scheme producing only 108 deputies in the second round for a new, 260-member parliament, well short of the two-thirds quorum (174 seats) required by the constitution. The Council of Europe deemed the elections neither free nor fair, citing restrictions on media access, the barring of posters and limited campaign financing, all of which curtailed debate and left most voters in the dark about candidates and platforms. Over half the precincts failed to meet the 50 percent turnout required to validate the vote. Communists and Agrarians captured most of the seats. The Soviet-era parliament was supposed to fill the vacuum until fall elections, but did not meet until September. Ignoring the constitution, the president did not recognize its legitimacy and essentially ruled by decree. He stripped deputies from the holdover parliament of their parliamentary immunity and threatened to impose presidential rule.

Turnout for 29 November parliamentary elections was higher, and brought the total to 139 deputies, still short of a quorum. In a 10 December runoff, fifty-nine additional deputies were elected, bringing the total to 198. Of the seats elected, the Communist Party of Belarus won forty-two; the Agrarian Party, thirty-three; the Party of Popular Accord, eight; the United Civic Party, seven; the Social Democratic Hramada, two; and the Party for All Belarusian Unity and Accord, two. No Popular Front candidates were elected.

During the year, Belarus signed a customs agreement with Russia, virtually opening up the border between the two countries. Lukashenka granted Russia, with 40,000 troops in Belarus, a twenty-five-year lease for two military facilities. A proponent of "market socialism," Lukashenka oversaw an economy plagued by high inflation and plummeting industrial production. His decision to roll back food prices unleashed an inflationary spiral.

Political Rights and Civil Liberties: Belarus citizens can change their government democratically, but President Lukashenka has instituted de facto presidential rule. A parliamentary quorum was not reached until 10 December after several election rounds.

Although legal, opposition parties face harassment and restrictions such as limited access to state media and bans on posters and literature. The media law facilitates government closure or suspension of publications. The press faces censorship. At least eight newspapers were effectively banned by being denied access to the central printing plant. Some papers ran blank spaces to protest censorship. Several editors were dismissed by presidential decrees, and the paper *Svaboda* was prosecuted for allegedly insulting the president. Many editors from numerous state newspapers, radio and television stations, which dominate the media, were removed in favor of the president's cronies.

Increased authoritarianism has put limits on freedoms of speech and assembly. Freedom of religion is guaranteed by law and usually respected in practice. Catholics (with strong links to Poland) and Jews have complained of government foot-dragging in returning church property and synagogues.

The judiciary is not independent and remains a remnant of the Soviet era subject to executive influence.

In August, the president banned the activity of the independent free Trade Union of Belarus, which led to a transport workers' strike. Several strike leaders were arrested and sentenced to brief terms of forced labor. Women's organizations have been established to document discrimination and abuses. There are no legal restrictions on the participation of women in politics and government, though social barriers to women in the public arena exist.

Belgium

Polity: Federal parliamentary democracy
Economy: Capitalist
Population: 10,151,000
PPP: $18,630
Life Expectancy: 76.4
Ethnic Groups: Fleming (55 percent), Walloon (33 percent), mixed and others, including Moroccan, Turkish and other immigrant groups (12 percent)
Capital: Brussels

Political Rights: 1
Civil Liberties: 1
Status: Free

Overview: **D**espite investigation of a national bribery scandal and predictions of significant gains for the extreme right, general elections in May left the ruling coalition virtually unchanged. With elections out of the way, Christian Democratic Prime Minister Jean-Luc Dehaene and his center-left coalition focused once again on the country's huge national debt, nearly 14 percent unemployment and the costly social security system.

Belgium declared its independence from the Netherlands in 1830 and elected Prince Leopold of Saxe-Coburg as king early the following year. The monarch symbolizes Belgian unity in this diverse country with linguistic and cultural divisions among Dutch-speaking Flanders, French-speaking Wallonia and a primarily German-speaking minority along the eastern border.

Ethnic and linguistic antagonism in the 1960s, primarily between the Dutch and French-speaking regions prompted a series of constitutional amendments in 1970-1971 conferring a considerable degree of power to regional councils at the expense of central government. In 1993 a constitutional amendment formally transformed Belgium into a federation of linguistic communities including Flanders, Wallonia and bilingual Brussels, with the German-speaking area also accorded cultural autonomy. The same year, parliament adopted an amendment establishing three directly elected regional assemblies with primary responsibility for housing, transportation, public works, education, culture and the environment as well as partial responsibility for the economy. The federal parliament continues to oversee foreign policy, defense, justice, monetary policy, taxation and the management of the budget deficit.

Political parties are split along linguistic lines, with both Walloon and Flemish parties ranging across the political spectrum. The dominance of three major groupings— Social Democrats, Christian Democrats and Liberals—has declined somewhat with the emergence of numerous small ethnic parties and special interest groups. Governments come and go rapidly, with many of the same politicians and parties reappearing in various coalitions.

Politicians, academics, bishops and even the king urged the electorate to vote "positively" after the extremist Flemish Bloc, whose militant supporters had engaged in violence against foreigners, and two right-wing Walloon parties made substantial gains in 1994 local elections. Even as allegations of political corruption pointed to senior Socialist politicians of both ethnic groups and implicated Flemish and Walloon Christian Democrats, the ruling coalition retained a slim majority. During pre-election budget talks that focused in part on reforming the generous social security system, Flemish liberals supported by the Belgian employers' federation called for cuts in employers' costs, pension reform and other spending cuts to promote competitiveness. Socialists were able to portray themselves as defenders of the welfare state. With Dehaene and his coalition secure, attention returned to those same austerity measures, particularly reducing unemployment, bringing the deficit down to 3 percent of GDP, and reducing the public debt to 60 percent of GDP by 1997 to meet eligibility requirements for the EU monetary union.

Political Rights and Civil Liberties:

Belgians can change their government democratically. Nonvoters are subject to fines. Political parties generally organize along ethnic lines, with different factions of the leading parties subscribing to a common platform for general elections. Each language group has autonomy within its own region. However, tensions and constitutional disputes arise when members of one group get elected to office in the other's territory and refuse to take competency tests in the regionally-dominant language.

In general, freedom of speech and of the press are guaranteed. Under the Basic Law of 18 May 1960, information transmission (including news and current events) cannot be censored by the government. Some forms of pornography and all incitements to violence are prohibited. Libel laws have some minor restraining effects on the press, and restrictions on civil servants' criticism of the government may constitute a slight reduction of freedom of speech. Autonomous public boards govern the state television and radio networks and ensure that public broadcasting is linguistically pluralistic. The state has permitted and licensed independent radio stations since 1985.

Immigrants and linguistic minorities argue that linguistic zoning restricts opportunity and freedom of movement. The municipalities around Brussels have the right to refuse to register new residents from countries outside the European Community.

Freedom of association is respected. Although Belgian workers are among the most unionized in Europe, trade unions are witnessing the rapid decline of their bargaining power. A one-day general strike in 1994 to protest a government austerity package effectively paralyzed the country. In the end, the austerity measures passed with most controversial points intact.

Christian, Jewish and Muslim institutions are state-subsidized in this overwhelmingly Roman Catholic country, and other faiths are respected. According to tradition, the seventh son or seventh daughter born to any Belgian family is the godchild of the monarch or his consort.

Belize

Polity: Parliamentary democracy
Economy: Capitalist
Population: 214,000
PPP: $5,619
Life Expectancy: 73.6
Ethnic Groups: Mestizo (44 percent), Creole (30 percent), Maya (11 percent), Garifuna (7 percent)
Capital: Belmopan

Political Rights: 1
Civil Liberties: 1
Status: Free

Overview: The government of Prime Minister Manuel Esquivel was concerned about a slowing economy but upbeat about a decline in crime.

Belize is a member of the British Commonwealth. The British monarchy is represented by a governor-general. Formerly British Honduras, the name was changed to Belize in 1973 and independence was granted in 1981.

Because neighboring Guatemala refused to recognize the new state, Britain agreed to provide for Belize's defense. In 1991 Guatemala recognized Belize and diplomatic relations were established. However, Guatemala reaffirmed its territorial claim in 1994.

Belize is a parliamentary democracy with a bicameral National Assembly. The twenty-nine-seat House of Representatives is elected for a five-year term. Members of the Senate are appointed, five by the governor-general on the advice of the prime minister, two by the leader of the parliamentary opposition and one by the Belize Advisory Council.

In the 1984 election the center-right United Democratic Party (UDP) overturned thirty years of rule by George Price and the center-left People's United Party (PUP). Businessman Manuel Esquivel became prime minister. Price returned to power in the 1989 elections.

Price called snap elections in 1993, compelled to renew his mandate in the wake of political instability in neighboring Guatemala and the announcement that Great Britain would withdraw most of its troops in 1994.

In a tumultuous campaign the UDP assailed Price for being soft on the Guatemala threat. It accused the PUP government of corruption, and charged that it was awarding citizenship to Central American immigrants to bolster the PUP vote.

The UDP won, taking sixteen seats to the PUP's thirteen. Five seats were won by margins of five votes or less, and the PUP actually won the popular vote with 51.2 percent. The determining factor in the election may have been the support of the National Alliance for Belizean Rights (NABR) for the UDP. The NABR, which split from the UDP in 1992, takes a hard line on the Guatemala issue.

In response to Guatemala's renewed claim to Belize, Esquivel made a futile attempt to get London to reverse its decision on withdrawing troops, but did win a commitment for joint British training with the 900-member Belizean Defense Force.

While Belizeans kept a wary eye on Guatemala, a principal concern in 1995 was an economic slowdown after years of sustained growth. The government announced spending cuts and a plan to streamline the public sector, prompting criticism from the PUP and labor demonstrations. Meanwhile, the government took credit for what it claimed was a 28 percent decline in crime in the first half of the year.

Political Rights and Civil Liberties: Citizens are able to change their government through free and fair elections. There are no restrictions on the right to organize political parties. Civic society is well established, with a large number of nongovernmental organizations working in the social, economic and environmental areas. There is freedom of religion.

Labor unions are independent, well organized and have the right to strike, but the percentage of the work-force that is organized has declined to less than 20 percent. Disputes are adjudicated by official boards of inquiry. Businesses are penalized for failing to abide by the labor code. In 1995, however, banana growers were still refusing to recognize a newly formed banana workers union.

The judiciary is independent and nondiscriminatory, and the rule of law is generally respected. The Belize Human Rights Commission is independent and effective.

Human rights concerns include the plight of migrant workers and refugees from neighboring Central American countries and charges of labor abuses by Belizean employers. Most of the estimated 40,000 Spanish-speakers who have immigrated since the 1980s do not have legal status. Some have registered under an amnesty program implemented in cooperation with the United Nations High Commissioner for Refugees. But reports continue of detention and mistreatment of migrant workers.

The small community of Maya Indians in the Toledo district has few rights of ownership to ancestral lands, which have been targeted by foreign agricultural investors.

In recent years Belizeans have suffered from an increase in violent crime, much of it related to drug trafficking and gang conflict. Tough anti-crime measures, including a quick-trial plan, were introduced in 1995 and a gang truce was brokered by the government. But rights groups insisted that anti-crime measures impinged on civil liberties and reported a number of incidents of unlawful use of force in making arrests.

There are five independent newspapers representing various political viewpoints. Belize has a literacy rate of over 90 percent. Radio and television play a prominent role during elections, when they are saturated with political ads. There are fourteen private television stations, including four cable systems. There is an independent board to oversee operations of government-owned outlets.

Benin

Polity: Presidential-   **Political Rights:** 2
parliamentary democracy   **Civil Liberties:** 2*
Economy: Statist-   **Status:** Free
transitional
Population: 5,409,000
PPP: $1,630
Life Expectancy: 47.6
Ethnic Groups: Aja, Barriba, Fon, Yoruba (99 percent)
Capital: Porto-Novo
Ratings Change: *Benin's civil liberties rating changed from 3 to 2 because of continued consolidation of democratic processes and civil society.

Overview:

Benin continued a democratic transition in 1995 that saw power divided between President Nicephore Soglo and a National Assembly controlled by an opposition coalition led by the Democratic Renewal Party (PRD). PRD leader Adrien Houngbedji is expected to be Soglo's principal challenger in presidential elections set for March 1996. While Soglo's economic policies have won him increasing international support, there remain concerns that Benin's army, dominated by northern ethnic groups, is not yet fully committed to the democratic process.

The modern state of Benin was once the center of the ancient kingdom of Dahomey, and took that name upon independence in 1960 after over six decades of French rule. The country experienced a succession of coups over its first dozen years, until Mathieu Kerekou seized power in 1972. Instituting strongly nationalistic policies, Kerekou changed the country's name to Benin in 1975 and pursued Marxist-Leninist economics through one-party rule under the Benin People's Revolutionary Party. By 1989 the country was essentially bankrupt and facing mounting internal unrest. Kerekou accepted democratization, which led eventually to his defeat by Soglo in March 1991 presidential elections. Benin's human rights record has improved dramatically since, and civil society and free institutions are generally flourishing.

Legislative elections held on 28 March 1995 returned an opposition majority of forty-nine seats in the eighty-nine-seat National Assembly. The PRD won nineteen seats. A more moderate opposition leader replaced PRD leader Houngbedji as National Assembly president, allowing smoother presidential-parliamentary relations. The president's Benin Renaissance Party is the largest parliamentary party, with twenty seats. Fard-Alafia, a northern-based opposition party made up of supporters of former dictator Kerekou, took twelve seats and may offer a presidential candidate in 1996. Seventeen parties are represented in the National Assembly.

The legislative results do not guarantee that Benin's democratization process is permanent. The country's historical north-south ethnic divisions are reflected in the current political parties. The army remains dominated by ethnic northerners recruited during Kerekou's eighteen-year rule. Recent restiveness has been ascribed to poor pay and living conditions for soldiers, hit hard like everyone in

Benin by rising prices and 1994's 100 percent devaluation of the CFA currency. In an effort to control over 50 percent inflation, the government in May tightened price controls first imposed in 1994. Isolated violence believed to involve renegade military elements, and arrests in October related to an alleged assassination and coup plot against Soglo, increased apprehension.

Soglo visited the United States in July, meeting with President Clinton. Increased U.S.-Benin security cooperation was discussed, and could bolster Benin's fragile democracy, which has strained relations with French-backed authoritarian regimes in neighboring Togo and Burkina Faso.

Political Rights and Civil Liberties: Benin's citizens freely elected their government in the country's first genuine multiparty elections in 1991. March 1995 legislative polls generally went smoothly and returned an opposition majority. The president is limited to two five-year terms, and legislators may serve an unlimited number of four-year terms. There is universal adult suffrage and voting is by secret ballot.

Freedom of expression guaranteed by the constitution is respected in practice. Broadcast media are state-owned and -operated, but opposition voices have access and reports critical of the government are aired. There is an independent and pluralistic press that includes party-affiliated newspapers and publishes highly critical articles. Foreign periodicals are freely available and uncensored.

Freedom of assembly and association are respected, with permits and registration requirements treated as routine formalities. Numerous nongovernmental organizations are active and suffer no governmental interference. Several focus on human rights work, among them the League for the Defense of Human Rights in Benin and the Study and Research Group on Democracy and Economic and Social Development. Religious freedom guaranteed by the constitution is respected.

The judiciary is generally considered independent, though lacking in staff and training. Prisons conditions are harsh, with severe overcrowding and lack of medical care and proper nutrition causing unnecessary deaths among prisoners.

Legal rights for women are often not enforced, especially in rural areas and in family matters where traditional practices prevail. Women generally have fewer educational and employment opportunities.

The constitution guarantees the right to organize and join unions. Strikes are legal and collective bargaining widely used in labor negations. There are several labor federations, some of which are affiliated to political parties. The formal sector of Benin's economy is small, however, and about 80 percent of the workforce is rural, working subsistence farm holdings.

Soglo, a former World Bank official, is aggressively pursuing privatization programs and civil service reforms under structural adjustment policies that emphasize raising agricultural production. His austerity budgets have won international loans but led to an effective reduction in living standards and rising disgruntlement among urban workers.

Bhutan

Polity: Traditional monarchy
Economy: Pre-industrial
Population: 823,000
PPP: $750
Life Expectancy: 50.7
Ethnic Groups: Ngalung, Sarchop, Nepalese, others
Capital: Thimphu

Political Rights: 7
Civil Liberties: 7
Status: Not Free

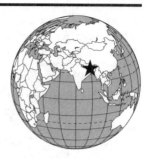

Overview: The continued exile of over 100,000 southern Bhutanese refugees who have fled persecution in recent years, and a May 1995 underground, pro-democracy wall poster campaign highlighted the need for political reform in this absolute monarchy.

The Wangchuk dynasty has ruled this Himalayan land as an absolute monarchy since Britain, then guiding Bhutan's affairs, installed it in 1907. In 1972 the current monarch, Jigme Singye Wangchuk, succeeded his father to the throne.

The 150-member National Assembly meets irregularly and has little power. Every three years village headmen choose 105 legislators, while religious groups fill twelve seats and the king appoints thirty-three.

Since the late 1980s the government, dominated by the minority Ngalung Drukpa ethnic group, has systematically persecuted ethnic Nepalese citizens, also known as southern Bhutanese. A 1988 census showed southern Bhutanese formed majorities in five southern districts. The government began applying a discriminatory 1985 Citizenship Act to arbitrarily strip thousands of southern Bhutanese of their citizenship.

The Citizenship Act confirmed the primary basis for citizenship to be residence in Bhutan in 1958, the year the kingdom extended citizenship to most southern Bhutanese. But to prove citizenship, southern Bhutanese had to show a land tax receipt for 1958, which amounted to asking a largely illiterate population to produce a document that had been of little importance when issued three decades earlier. The Act also tightened the requirements for transmitting citizenship to persons born after 1958 by requiring that both parents be citizens, whereas previously only the father needed to be a Bhutanese national.

From 1989-92 the government arrested thousands of southern Bhutanese as "anti-nationals," and soldiers randomly raped and beat villagers and forcibly expelled tens of thousands. Many were forced to sign "voluntary migration forms," forfeiting their land and property. The refugee flow decreased sharply after 1993 but there are currently over 100,000, including some 87,000 in camps in eastern Nepal. Bhutan claims it acted to avoid being swamped by illegal immigrants, but according to Nepalese authorities 97 percent of the refugees possess some form of Bhutanese citizenship documentation.

In June 1994 a group of exiled dissidents from the eastern Sarchop community launched the Druk National Congress (DNC) to press for democratic reforms. In late May 1995 the DNC organized an underground campaign of pro-democracy wall posters calling for basic rights. In August a court sentenced Col. Tandin Dorji, the chief of police and brother-in-law of DNC Chairman Rongthong Kunley Dorji, to three years for alleged negligence concerning a jailbreak. The action was widely deemed politically motivated.

Political Rights and Civil Liberties:

Bhutanese cannot change their government democratically. The king rules absolutely, and policymaking centers around him and a small Buddhist aristocratic elite. The National Assembly has become a forum for diatribes against southern Bhutanese, who hold a disproportionately small number of seats. Political parties are *de facto* prohibited and none exists. The Bhutanese Coalition for Democratic Reforms, formed in June 1995, is an umbrella group for some twenty-six exile-based nongovernmental organizations and parties.

The rule of law is nonexistent. From 1989-92 the army and police committed grave rights violations against southern Bhutanese, including arbitrary arrests, beatings, rape, robbery and destruction of homes. While the number of such incidents appears to have decreased in the past two years, there is little indication that the government has punished those responsible. Security forces continue to conduct arbitrary searches of homes in the south.

Semi-official village vigilante groups in southern Bhutan harass residents and reportedly have conducted extrajudicial executions. The government charges southern Bhutanese with terrorist actions, but according to the U.S. State Department most attacks in the south appear to be the random work of bandits.

The king appoints and can dismiss judges, and the judiciary is not independent. Several detainees and prisoners have reportedly died in custody in recent years due to torture and poor conditions. The government has released over 1,600 southern Bhutanese arrested between 1989-92, but several hundred may remain in detention. The country's most famous dissident, Tek Nath Rizal, was sentenced in November 1993 to life imprisonment under a 1992 National Security Act legislated three years after his imprisonment.

Southern Bhutanese are required to obtain "No Objection Certificates" (NOC) from the government to enter schools, take government jobs and sell farm products. NOCs are frequently denied. Many southern schools and hospitals closed by the authorities in 1990 remain closed or have been turned into army barracks.

Freedom of speech is restricted and criticism of the king is forbidden, except indirectly during National Assembly discussions. The state-owned weekly *Kuensel*, the country's only regular publication, is a government mouthpiece and frequently runs articles biased against the southern Bhutanese. Editions of foreign publications carrying articles critical of the king or government are censored. Since 1989 Bhutan has banned satellite dishes to prevent reception of foreign broadcasts. There is no freedom of association for political purposes, although some business and civic organizations are permitted.

The sixth Five Year Plan (1987-92) introduced a program of "One Nation, One People" that included the promotion of *Driglam Namzha*, the national dress and customs of the ruling Ngalungs. A January 1989 Royal Decree made Driglam Namzha mandatory for all Bhutanese. The government also banned teaching in the Nepali language. In 1995 the government ordered conversion of signboards into Dzongkha, the Ngalung language.

The Druk Kargue sect of Mahayana Buddhism is the state religion. Buddhist lamas wield considerable political influence. The largely Hindu southern Bhutanese cannot worship freely, and also face difficulty in traveling freely throughout the country. Trade unions and strikes are forbidden. In the summer of 1995 twenty people from central Wangdiphodrang District were reportedly sentenced to two to three years for not meeting compulsory government labor quotas. According to the United Nations Children's Fund, pre-teens are sometimes put on road-building teams.

Bolivia

Polity: Presidential-
legislative democracy
Economy: Capitalist
Population: 7,428,000
PPP: $2,410
Life Expectancy: 59.4

Political Rights: 2
Civil Liberties: 4*
Status: Partly Free

Ethnic Groups: Quechua (30 percent), Aymara (25 percent), other Indian (15 percent), mestizo and other Indian (25-30 percent), European (5-15 percent)
Capital: La Paz (administrative), Sucre (judicial)
Ratings Change: *Bolivia's civil liberties rating changed from 3 to 4, moving Bolivia into the Partly Free category, principally because of the imposition of a six-month state of emergency in response to labor protests against government economic policy.

Overview:

In response to widespread protests against his economic reforms and a U.S.-sponsored coca-eradication program, President Gonzalo Sanchez de Lozada imposed a six-month state of siege during which hundreds, possibly thousands, of labor activists and coca growers were arrested.

After achieving independence from Spain in 1825, the Republic of Bolivia endured recurrent instability and military rule. The armed forces, responsible for over 180 coups in 157 years, returned to the barracks in 1982 and the 1967 constitution was restored. Since then, Bolivia has had elected civilian governments.

The constitution provides for the election every four years (five years beginning in 1997) of a president and a Congress consisting of a 130-member House of Representatives and a twenty-seven-member Senate. If no candidate receives an absolute majority of votes, Congress chooses the president from among the three leading vote-getters. Starting in 1997, the outcome will be decided by a runoff between the top two candidates.

Bolivia's principal parties are Sanchez de Lozada's center-right Nationalist Revolutionary Movement (MNR), the conservative National Democratic Action (ADN) and the social-democratic Movement of the Revolutionary Left (MIR). The MIR's Jaime Paz Zamora became president in 1989 at the head of a MIR-ADN coalition. His term was marked by corruption scandals and social unrest.

In 1993 the MIR-ADN candidate was former dictator and retired Gen. Hugo Banzer. Sanchez de Lozada, the planning minister in a former MNR administration

(1985-89), was the MNR candidate. His reputation as a successful and honest businessman gave him the edge. He took 33.8 percent of the vote to Banzer's 20 percent. Two populists, talk-show host Carlos Palenque and beer magnate Max Fernandez, won 13.6 and 13.1 percent respectively. Antonio Aranibar of the leftist Free Bolivia Movement (MBL) took 5.1 percent.

The MNR won sixty-nine seats in the bicameral legislature. Sanchez de Lozada secured the backing of Fernandez, whose Civic and Solidarity Union (UCS) took twenty-one seats, and Aranibar, whose MBL took seven, by offering cabinet posts. The three-party coalition elected Sanchez de Lozada president. Running mate Hugo Cardenas, an Aymara Indian, became vice president, the first indigenous leader in Latin America to hold such high office.

In his first two years Sanchez de Lozada initiated a sweeping privatization program and, under U.S. pressure, stepped up coca eradication. These measures were assailed by labor unions and coca growers. Early 1995 saw a series of labor strikes and mass protests. Sanchez de Lozada imposed a six-month state of siege that allowed him to repress protests and implement his policies by decree. Strikes resumed after the state of siege was lifted and in November Sanchez de Lozada put troops onto the streets of major cities. The MNR fared poorly in local elections in December.

Political Rights and Civil Liberties: Citizens are able to change their government through elections. In 1991 a new electoral court consisting of five relatively independent magistrates was created, and a new voter registration system was implemented.

The political landscape features political parties ranging from fascist to radical left. There are also a number of indigenous-based peasant movements, including the Tupac Katari Revolutionary Liberation Movement headed by Victor Hugo Cardenas, the nation's vice-president. The languages of the indigenous population are officially recognized, but the 40 percent Spanish-speaking minority still dominates the political process.

The constitution guarantees free expression, freedom of religion and the right to organize political parties, civic groups and labor unions. Unions have the right to strike.

In 1995, however, labor rights and many civil liberties were suspended during a six-month state of siege imposed by the government to quell protests against its economic and coca-eradication policies. Strikes and demonstrations were violently repressed and hundreds of labor activists were arrested. After the state of siege was lifted the government put troops in the streets in response to renewed protests and a number of people, including two children, were killed in violent clashes.

There is strong evidence that drug money has penetrated the political process through corrupt government officials, police and military personnel, and through electoral campaign financing. The drug trade has also spawned private security forces that operate with relative impunity in the coca-growing regions. Bolivia is the world's second largest producer of cocaine after Peru.

A U.S.-sponsored coca-eradication program has angered peasant unions representing Bolivia's 50,000 coca farmers. In 1995 their peaceful protests and demonstrations were violently repressed by security forces and hundreds, possibly thousands, were arrested in the course of the year. Inhabitants of coca-growing regions were subject to arbitrary searches and beatings.

The emergence of small indigenous-based guerrilla groups has caused an overreaction by security forces against legitimate government opponents.

The judiciary, headed by a Supreme Court, is the weakest branch of government. Despite recent reforms it remains riddled with corruption, over-politicized and subject to the compromising power of drug traffickers. The creation of a Constitutional Tribunal and a "people's defender" branch have not yet led to any marked improvement.

Human rights organizations are both government-sponsored and independent. Their reports indicate an increase in recent years in police brutality and torture during confinement. There is occasional intimidation against independent rights activists. Prison conditions are poor and nearly three-quarters of prisoners have not been formally sentenced.

The press, radio and television are mostly private. Journalists covering corruption stories are occasionally subject to verbal intimidation by government officials, arbitrary detention by police and violent attacks. There are a number of daily newspapers including one sponsored by the influential Catholic church. Opinion polling is a growth industry. Eight years ago there was no television, but now there are more than sixty channels. The impact has been evident in the media-based election campaigns.

Bosnia-Herzegovina

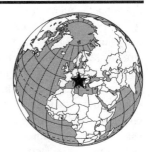

Polity: Presidential-parliamentary democracy (transitional)
Political Rights: 6
Civil Liberties: 6
Status: Not Free
Economy: Mixed-statist (severely war-damaged)
Population: 3,459,000
PPP: na
Life Expectancy: 70.0
Ethnic Groups: Pre-war—Slavic Muslim (44 percent), Serb (33 percent), Croat (17 percent)
Capital: Sarajevo
Trend Arrow: The Dayton Accords and an October ceasefire brought an end to forty-four months of war.

Overview: In 1995, the leaders of Bosnia-Herzegovina, Serbia and Croatia signed the U.S.-brokered Dayton Accords, bringing an end to almost four years of war. The complex agreement established a constitutional framework for the creation of a federative state with two republics (one Serbian and the other under the Bosnian-Croat federation), free and fair elections, and repatriation of refugees. It also opened the way for the deployment of a NATO-led international peace force (IFOR), which was to include some 20,000 American troops to be stationed around Tuzla.

Bosnia-Herzegovina became one of six constituent republics of Yugoslavia in November 1945. During World War II, brutal internecine conflict had left 700,000 dead, mostly Serbs.

As Yugoslavia began to unravel, Bosnia-Herzegovina held multiparty elections in September 1990, with the three nationalist parties representing Muslim, Serb and Croat constituencies winning a majority in the 240-member Assembly. In a February 1992 referendum boycotted by Serbs, 99 percent favored secession from Yugoslavia. President Alija Izetbegovic issued a declaration of independence on 3 March. Two weeks later, Muslim, Croat and Serb leaders agreed to divide Bosnia into three autonomous units based on the "national absolute or relative majority" in each area. The agreement, however, fell apart.

The U.S. recognized Bosnia on 7 April. As fighting intensified, outgunned Muslims and their Croat allies faced an estimated 100,000 Serbs supplied by the Serbian government of Slobodan Milosevic. Serbs controlled over 70 percent of the country by year's end, and a systematic policy of "ethnic cleansing" had killed or displaced hundreds of thousands of Muslim, Croat and Serb civilians. In 1993, Bosnian Croats and renegade Muslims in Bihac fought government forces. The Vance-Owen plan—named for former U.S. Secretary of State and U.N. mediator Cyrus Vance and European Community negotiator Lord David Owen—which called for the partition of Bosnia into ten autonomous provinces, was widely criticized and never implemented. The presence of over 20,000 U.N. peacekeepers did not deter aggression.

In 1994, the U.S brokered a ceasefire between Bosnian Croats and Muslims and established a Bosnian-Croat federation with loose ties to Croatia. U.S., French, British and Russian foreign ministers formed a Contact Group, which backed a solution that would award the new Bosnian-Croat federation 51 percent of Bosnian territory, with the Serbs taking 49 percent. Though Serb President Milosevic suggested he would support the plan in exchange for lifting the economic embargo on Yugoslavia, it was rejected by Bosnian-Serb leader Radovan Karadzic and the Bosnian-Serb parliament. Serb aggression and "ethnic cleansing" continued around Banja Luka and eastern Bosnia, and the Bosnian capital of Sarajevo remained under siege and subject to Serb shelling.

In May 1995, retaliatory NATO air strikes against Serbs for confiscating U.N. heavy weapons and blocking aid convoys to Sarajevo led the Serbs to take 350 U.N. peacekeepers hostage. Serbs also seized the "safe haven" of Srebrenica and massacred 6,000 men before moving on and taking Zepa, another "safe haven." NATO warned that any attacks on safe areas would incur massive air strikes.

The tide of war shifted against the Serbs. In May, Croatia recaptured West Slavonia, which had been occupied by the Serbs. In August, a Croat offensive routed Serbs in Croatia's Krajina region. Bosnian Serbs authorized President Milosevic to negotiate for them after the U.S. proposed a new series of talks. In September, after a Sarajevo mortar attack by Serbs, NATO launched a series of air strikes on Serb forces. Meanwhile, a joint Muslim-Croat offensive seized control of much of northwest Bosnia, reducing Serb control from 70 percent to 50 percent of Bosnian territory. Abandoned by their Serb benefactors and facing further battle losses, the Serbs agreed to a ceasefire on 12 October. Negotiations got under way in Dayton, Ohio, on 1 November. The Serbs agreed to return Eastern Slavonia to Croatia. On 21 November, the presidents of Bosnia, Croatia and Serbia initialed the Dayton Accords, which were formally accepted in December. Bosnian President Izetbegovic said the agreement "was not just, but it is more just than continuing the war..." By year's end the ceasefire was holding, and NATO had begun deploying its forces.

The key provisions of the complex agreement—containing ten articles, eleven annexes, and over 100 maps—included: a united Sarajevo; internationally supervised elections; a constitution calling for a loose federative state with semi-autonomous Muslim-Croatian (51 percent) and Serb (49 percent) territories; a rotating presidency and the assignment of posts by nationality; U.N.-supervised disarmament; and the introduction of 60,000 IFOR troops. Indicted war criminals, including Bosnian-Serb President Karadzic and Gen. Ratko Mladic, would be barred from public office. Provisions for the return of refugees were less certain in light of "ethnic cleansing" and the destruction of homes and villages.

Political Rights and Civil Liberties: The provisions of the Dayton Accords dealing with a new constitution, federal and subnational structures, and elections were not implemented by the end of 1995.

Izetbegovic, leader of the Party of Democratic Action (PDA) and president of a ten-member, multi-ethnic collective presidency, heads a government that was legally constituted following multiparty elections to the 240-member Assembly in late 1990. Other parties represented in that parliament were the Serbian Democratic Party, the Croatian Democratic Community, the League of Communists-Social Democratic Party of Bosnia-Herzegovina, and the Alliance of Reformist Forces. After the outbreak of war in 1992, de facto partition and "ethnic cleansing" seriously undermined the ability of the democratic national leadership to govern. The self-styled Serb Republic elected its own regional and local leaders, as did Croats in areas they controlled.

Political parties exist, but have no national scope or influence given the partitions caused by war.

While most Bosnian newspapers stopped printing in 1993, the Sarajevo daily *Oslobodjneje* continued publication, as did local papers in government- and Serb-held areas. Bosnia Radio and Television broadcast government views, while in Serb-held areas local radio and television broadcasting had a decidedly pro-Serbian bias. Some papers in Serb-held areas freely criticized the Karadzic regime, Milosevic and the conduct of the war.

Freedoms of association and assembly have been circumscribed by war. Muslims, Catholic Croats and Orthodox Serbs practiced their religion in areas they controlled. Mosques, churches and cemeteries were intentionally targeted in war zones.

The rupture of the federal state also led to the fragmenting of a functioning national judiciary. The federal system maintained a judiciary relatively free of government interference, but lack of judges and infrastructure seriously hampered its operation. In Serb-held areas, the self-styled authorities set up local structures to deal with criminal cases.

Human rights violations were rampant throughout 1995. Civilians faced deportation, execution, torture and unlawful imprisonment in labor camps. Thousands of non-Serbs were expelled from areas around Sarajevo, Banja Luka, Bihac and Bijeljina. Serbs massacred thousands of civilians when they overran Srebrenica and Zepa.

Trade unions exist, but their functions have been limited by economic and social dislocation. Women have borne a terrible burden in this war-torn country, victimized by rape, poverty and dislocation, particularly in rural areas. In Sarajevo, the government, as much as it could, guaranteed equal rights for women in terms of education and employment. Nongovernmental organizations existed in the larger cities, including humanitarian, charity and cultural associations.

Botswana

Polity: Parliamentary democracy and traditional chiefs
Political Rights: 2
Civil Liberties: 2*
Status: Free
Economy: Capitalist
Population: 1,487,000
PPP: $4,690
Life Expectancy: 60.3
Ethnic Groups: Tswana and Baswara (95 percent), Kalanga, Kgagaladi, European
Capital: Gaborone
Ratings Change: *Botswana's civil liberties rating changed from 3 to 2 because of deepening respect for individual rights and a stronger civil society.

Overview: **B**otswana marked another year of steady economic growth, with the formation of an independent election commission and the lowering of the voting age from twenty-one to eighteen pointing toward greater democratization in what is already one of Africa's freest countries. But the country's usual calm was marred by riots in February that revealed underlying tensions regarding wealth distribution and police conduct.

Botswana gained independence from Britain in 1966, and for thirty years has been ruled by elected governments. Elections are seen as increasingly free and fair, and in October 1994, the opposition Botswana National Front made a strong showing in national assembly elections, winning thirteen of thirty-five seats contested. The new independent election commission could finally end lingering suspicions that the Botswana Democratic Party (BDP)—which has ruled without interruption since independence—has manipulated elections in its favor. The next elections are set for October 1999. The national assembly elects the president to serve a concurrent term with the legislature.

Despite the entrenchment of democratic rule, serious rioting shattered the peace in the capital, Gaberone, in February. What began as a student protest over perceived police inaction in investigating the ritual murder of a schoolgirl late in

1994 flared into larger confrontations. Unemployed youth joined the protests, and public anger was fanned by a heavy police reaction that reportedly included the beating of innocent bystanders. Other instances of police brutality are occasionally reported but rarely properly investigated.

The riots ended quickly, but point to a growing disparity in incomes among Botswana's people. Opposition parties have increased calls for greater social development programs that would expand opportunities in rural areas. National debate is possible through free media, though the government retains control of broadcasting.

Political Rights and Civil Liberties:

Botswana's citizens choose their government through open elections that are considered generally free and fair. The ruling BDP's long tenure in power raises concern over its dominant influence over the political system, but recent opposition electoral gains indicate a more open system is taking hold. Botswana's human rights record is one of the best in Africa, and its strong bill of rights is generally respected by the government. There remain, however, some areas of concern. Several potentially repressive laws regarding sedition and detention without trial (under the National Security Act) remain on the books. Though they are rarely used, they are a lingering threat to freedom of expression and political activity.

Treatment of the country's Baswara, or N/oakwe ("red people") is coming under increasing scrutiny. A 1992 report by a religious coalition, the Botswana Christian Group, found widespread discrimination and abuse of N/oakwe people, and reported forcible evictions from their traditional lands. Only about 3,000 N/oakwe still live traditional nomadic lives as "bushmen" in the central Kalahari desert. About 45,000 others have been resettled in villages or work as farm laborers, often under difficult conditions that border on servitude. N/oakwe activists are demanding land rights and permission to hunt on traditional land, much of which is now farms or game preserves.

Inequality in women's rights is another point that is criticized, particularly the citizenship law that withholds citizenship from children of female citizens married to foreigners. Offspring of male citizens automatically receive citizenship regardless of whether their spouse is a Botswana national. Married women must receive their husbands' permission to receive a bank loan. Gay rights also came under scrutiny when a rarely enforced statute forbidding homosexuality was used to charge two men in February.

In May, the formation of a new labor union to represent domestic workers was announced. While other unions exist, the right to strike and to bargain for wages is restricted. Concentration of economic power has hindered labor organizing. The government has begun to address widespread public perception of corruption and administrative malpractice by setting up an ombudsmen's office in April. However, while widely reported in the independent media, investigations into corrupt practices often are not made public, reinforcing a persistent image of a lack of accountability.

Brazil

Polity: Federal presidential-legislative democracy
Economy: Capitalist-statist
Population: 157,800,000
PPP: $5,240
Life Expectancy: 66.3
Ethnic Groups: European (53 percent), black mixed (46 percent), Indian (less than 1 percent)
Capital: Brasilia

Political Rights: 2
Civil Liberties: 4
Status: Partly Free

Overview: Business applauded President Fernando Henrique Cardoso's economic reform efforts, but his first year in office saw new corruption scandals and a series of unresolved murders of Brazilian journalists.

After gaining independence from Portugal in 1822, Brazil retained a monarchical system until a republic was established in 1889. Democratic rule has been interrupted by long periods of authoritarian rule, most recently under military regimes from 1964 to 1985.

Elected civilian rule was reestablished in 1985 and a new constitution implemented in 1988. It provides for a president elected for four years and a bicameral Congress consisting of an eighty-one-member Senate elected for eight years and a 503-member Chamber of Deputies elected for four years.

Civilian rule has been marked by constant corruption scandals, one of which led to the impeachment by Congress of President Fernando Collor de Mello (1989-92). Collor resigned and was replaced by his vice-president, Itamar Franco, whose weak, feckless administration prompted rumors of a military coup.

In early 1994 the fiery Luis Ignacio "Lula" da Silva of the leftist Workers' Party (PT) was the frontrunner in a field of eight presidential candidates. Cardoso, Franco's finance minister and a market-oriented centrist, was the author of an anti-inflation plan linked to a new currency. He cobbled together a center-right, three-party coalition centered around his own Social Democratic Party (PSDB). His plan went into effect in July and within months inflation had plummeted from 50 percent to less than 2 percent. The campaign turned around as Cardoso, backed by big media and big business, jumped into the lead.

In October 1994 Cardoso won the presidency with 54 percent of the vote, against 27 percent for Lula. The Senate was left divided among eleven parties and the Chamber of Deputies among eighteen. Cardoso's three-party coalition did not win a majority in either branch.

Cardoso spent 1995 cajoling and horse-trading for the congressional votes needed to carry out his economic liberalization program. Progress was slow as the Congress remained a gridlock-prone labyrinth of overlapping special interests and corrupt patronage machines. In the fall Cardoso's government was rocked by a bribery and phone-tapping scandal involving U.S.-based Raytheon's bid to install a radar system in the Amazon. There were a number of high-level resignations and suspicions that the scandal might reach Cardoso himself.

Political Rights and Civil Liberties:

Citizens can change governments through elections. The 1994 elections were relatively free, but there were irregularities in northeastern states and in Rio de Janeiro, and evidence that candidate Cardoso benefited from government support.

The constitution guarantees freedoms of religion and expression and the right to organize political and civic organizations. However, a national breakdown in police discipline and escalating criminal violence—much of it fueled by the burgeoning drug trade—have created a climate of lawlessness and generalized insecurity in which human rights are violated on a massive scale with impunity.

Brazil's police are among the world's most violent and corrupt. Although nominally commanded by elected officials, police in each state get military training and are under the jurisdiction of military courts, in which they are rarely held accountable. Military police use the inefficiency and corruption of local civil police as an excuse to justify their tactics of simply eliminating suspected criminals.

Brazil's numerous independent rights organizations have documented killings by military police and systematic abuse and torture in police detention centers. Conditions in Brazil's packed, violence-plagued penal system are wretched, and the military police are charged with quelling disorder.

Vigilante "extermination squads," linked to the police and financed by local merchants, are responsible for thousands of extrajudicial killings yearly. Violence, including disappearances, against the 35 million children living in poverty—at least 20 percent of whom live on the streets of burgeoning urban centers—is systematic. Two former "street kids" who had gained prominence for campaigning against violence were murdered in December 1995. Up to five street kids a day are murdered in Brazil according to researchers at the University of Sao Paulo, yet very rarely are their killers caught. About 80 percent of the victims are of African descent.

The climate of lawlessness is reinforced by a weak judiciary. Brazil's Supreme Court is granted substantial autonomy by the constitution. However, the judicial system is overwhelmed (with only 7,000 judges for a population of more than 150 million) and vulnerable to the chronic corruption that undermines the entire political system. It has been virtually powerless in the face of organized crime, much of it drug-related.

Since 1994 the federal government has occasionally deployed the army in Rio de Janeiro's 400 slums, most of which had been taken over by drug gangs in league or in competition with corrupt police and local politicians.

Because there is little public confidence in the judiciary, poorer citizens have resorted to lynchings, with hundreds of mob executions reported in the last three years. The middle class, unable to afford costly private security measures, is targeted by kidnappers-for-ransom who often operate in league with police.

Violence associated with land disputes continues unabated. Brazil's large landowners control nearly 60 percent of arable land, while the poorest 30 percent share less than 2 percent. Every year dozens of activists, Catholic church workers and rural unionists are killed by paramilitary groups and hired killers in the pay of large landowners, with very few cases brought to court. In August 1995 eleven "land squatters" were massacred in the Amazonian state of Rondonia. A local leader of the left-wing Workers' Party who demanded justice in this case was murdered in December.

There are continued reports of forced labor of thousands of landless workers by ranchers in the Amazon and other rural regions, often with the complicity of local police. Forced labor is against Brazilian law, but the judicial response remains indifferent at best.

Rubber tappers and Indians remain targets of violence, including killings, associated with Amazon development projects initiated under military rule and with the gold rush in the far north. The constitution grants land rights to Brazil's quarter million Indians, but the government has only reluctantly tried to stop incursions by settlers and miners into Indian reserves.

Violence against women and children is endemic, much of it occurring in the home. Protective laws are rarely enforced. In 1991 the Supreme Court ruled that a man could no longer kill his wife and win acquittal on the ground of "legitimate defense of honor," but juries tend to ignore the ruling. Forced prostitution of children is widespread.

Industrial labor unions are well-organized, politically connected and prone to corruption. The right to strike is recognized and there are special labor courts. There have been hundreds of strikes in recent years against attempts to privatize state industries. Child labor is prevalent and laws against it are rarely enforced.

The press is privately owned. There are dozens of daily newspapers and numerous other publications throughout the country. The print media have played a central role in exposing official corruption, which has led to intimidation and violent attacks. Five journalists were murdered in 1995, the most in any Latin American country, with no arrests in any of the cases.

Radio is mostly commercial. Television is independent and a powerful political instrument. Roughly two-thirds of the population is illiterate, while 85 percent of households have television sets. The huge TV Globo is a near-monopoly and has enormous political clout. There are three much smaller networks, plus educational channels.

Brunei

Polity: Traditional monarchy
Economy: Capitalist-statist
Population: 295,000
PPP: $20,589
Life Expectancy: 74.2
Ethnic Groups: Malay (64 percent), Chinese (20 percent), others (15 percent)
Capital: Bandar Seri Begawan

Political Rights: 7
Civil Liberties: 5*
Status: Not Free

Ratings Change: *Brunei's civil liberties rating changed from 6 to 5 because of an increasingly open climate for political discussion.

Overview: Located on the northern coast of the Southeast Asian island of Borneo, Brunei became a British protectorate in 1888.

The 1959 constitution provided for five advisory councils: the Privy Council, the Religious Council, the Council of Succession, the Council of Ministers and a Legislative Council. In 1962 the leftist Brunei People's Party (PRB) took all ten of the elected seats in the twenty-one member Legislative Council; late in the year British troops crushed a PRB-backed rebellion. The sultan then assumed constitutionally-authorized emergency powers for a stipulated two-year period. These powers have been renewed every two years since then, and elections have not been held since 1965. Sultan Haji Hasanal Bolkiah Mu'izzadin Waddaulah ascended the throne in October 1967.

The country achieved independence in January 1984. The sultan serves as prime minister and has nearly complete authority over the country. Currently only the Council of Ministers, composed largely of the sultan's relatives, and the Legislative Council, with all members appointed by the sultan, are convened. In 1985 the government recognized the moderate Brunei National Democratic Party (PKDB), followed a year later by the offshoot Brunei National United Party (PPKB). However, in 1988 the sultan ordered the PKDB dissolved and detained two of its leaders for two years, reportedly after the party called on the sultan to hold elections. The PPKB currently has fewer than 100 members and wields no influence.

In February 1995 Abdul Latief Chuchu, one of the two ex-leaders of the PKDB who had been detained from 1988-90, formed the Brunei National Solidarity Party.

Political Rights and Civil Liberties: Citizens of Brunei, a hereditary sultanate, lack the democratic means to change their government. Nearly all political power is wielded by the sultan and his inner circle of relatives. Since 1992 there have been local elections for village chiefs, who serve life terms. All candidates must have a knowledge of Islam (although they may be non-Muslims) and cannot have past or current links with a political party. The only other means of popular political participation is through petitions to the sultan. The constitution does not protect freedoms of speech, press, assembly or association, and these rights are restricted in practice. Criticism of the government is rare due to the threat of sanction. A government commission is in the process of reviewing the 1959 constitution, although its exact mandate is unclear.

A 1988 law mandates corporal punishment for forty-two criminal offenses, including drug-related crimes. Police have broad powers to make arrests without obtaining warrants. The Internal Security Act (ISA) allows the government to detain suspects without trial for renewable two-year periods. There have been no new detentions under the ISA since 1988, but there are several political prisoners still in jail for their role in the 1962 rebellion.

The judiciary is independent of the government. Hong Kong provides judges for the High Court and the Court of Appeals. Defendants enjoy adequate procedural safeguards, with the notable exception of the right to trial by jury. The only private newspaper practices self-censorship by avoiding discussion of religious issues and of the sultan's paramount political role. Sensitive articles and photographs in foreign periodicals are often censored. The one television station is state-owned and does not offer pluralistic views.

Since 1991 the government has been asserting the primacy of Islam through a national ideology of Malay Muslim Monarchy (MIB), which it says dates back more than 500 years. The government frequently refuses non-Muslims permission to build new places of worship, and has closed some existing ones. Other restrictions on non-Muslims include bans on proselytizing and on the importation of religious books or educational materials, restrictions on religious education in non-Muslim schools and a requirement that Islamic education and MIB be taught at all schools.

The ethnic Malay majority enjoys advantages in university admission and employment. Most Chinese were not granted citizenship when the country became independent, and the rigorous Malay-language citizenship test makes it difficult for them to be naturalized. Women face discrimination in divorce and inheritance matters, and in obtaining equal pay and benefits. Muslim women are strongly encouraged to wear the *tudong*, a traditional head covering, although there is no formal sanction against those who do not. Foreign servants are occasionally beaten or otherwise treated poorly.

Citizens can travel freely within the country and abroad. The government must approve of all trade unions, but does not interfere in their affairs. Three exist, but they cover just 5 percent of the workforce and have little influence. The constitution neither recognizes nor denies the right to strike, and in practice none occurs.

Bulgaria

Polity: Parliamentary democracy
Economy: Mixed statist transitional
Population: 8,454,000
PPP: $4,250
Life Expectancy: 71.2
Ethnic Groups: Bulgarian (86 percent), Turkish (9 percent), Roma (4 percent), Macedonian
Capital: Sofia

Political Rights: 2
Civil Liberties: 2
Status: Free

Overview: In 1995 Bulgaria witnessed tension between Prime Minister Zhan Videnov's ex-Communist government and President Zhelyu Zhelev, former leader of the opposition Union of Democratic Forces (UDF), over issues including privatization, land ownership and NATO membership.

Occupied by Ottoman Turks from 1396 to 1878, Bulgaria only achieved complete independence in 1908. Communists seized power after Bulgaria's 1944 "liberation" by the Soviet Army. Communist Party strongman Todor Zhivkov, who ruled from 1954-1989, was forced to resign one day after the fall of the Berlin Wall in November 1989.

Parliamentary elections were called in December 1994 after Prime Minster Lyuben Berov's nonparty government, in power since 1992, collapsed amid widespread criticism of the slowness of economic reform and unpopular price and tax increases. The vote saw the former-Communist Bulgarian Socialist Party (BSP) win a clear majority with 125 of 240 seats. The fragmented UDF won 69; the Popular Union, 18; the Turkish-based Movement for Rights and Freedoms (MRF), 15; and the pro-market Bulgarian Business Block, 13. After the 1991 elections, the UDF had controlled 110 seats, with the BSP holding 106 and the MRF a crucial 24-seat swing vote.

In 1995, the key issue facing the Videnov government—the country's sixth since 1990—was improving the economy, which trailed others in East-Central Europe. The BSP, elected by pensioners and the poor, had promised to ease the pain of reform (including 20 percent unemployment, triple-digit inflation and lagging productivity) without abandoning the goals of a market economy and integration with Europe.

Obstacles included the old Communist elite's entrenchment in private business, weak or nonexistent business laws that allowed these elites to abuse their new power and slow privatization (only thirty-four medium- or large-sized enterprises had been privatized by early 1995). In August, the government launched a plan including cash and mass privatization, in which citizens could buy vouchers to be exchanged for shares in 1,300 state enterprises. President Zhelev and oppositionists criticized the plan because it did not allow foreign ownership of land and provided favorable state credits for Bulgarian business, thereby favoring former Communists who have disproportionate control over the private economy—all of Bulgaria's 1,000 millionaires and five billionaires are BSP members.

In other issues, a Joint Bulgarian-European Union Parliamentary Commission was established to facilitate Bulgarian integration into European structures. The government has delayed any decisions on NATO membership in deference to Bulgaria's traditionally strong ties with Russia. The Constitutional Court rejected government amendments to a restitution law returning property confiscated under communism; the amendments sought to protect current tenants who faced eviction if properties were restored to previous owners.

The BSP won an overwhelming number of posts in municipal elections.

Political Rights and Civil Liberties:

Bulgarians can change their government democratically. The 1994 elections were free and fair. Over 160 parties exist, though many are inactive (only fifty-one signatures are needed to register a party).

Bulgaria's press freely criticizes officials despite proscriptions against acting "to the detriment of the rights and reputations of others." Virtually all Bulgaria's estimated 1,400 publications are private. Over sixty private radio stations broadcast, and three private national television broadcasters have been licensed. Censorship allegations persist. Thirty-four journalists of the Khorizont national radio program issued a declaration protesting "administrative interference in the preparation and airing of programs," including dictating topics for broadcast. A parliamentary commission was established to investigate the allegations.

Freedoms of public discussion, association, assembly and religion are generally respected, although the government regulates churches and religious institutions through a Directorate of Religious Beliefs. A 1994 registration law caused thirty-nine mostly Protestant associations to lose their status as "juridical entities," thus preventing their re-registration. Rights groups charged the law violated Articles 12 and 13 of the constitution, which guarantee religious freedom and separation of church and state. Discrimination against Turks, Roma (Gypsies) and Pomaks (ethnic Bulgarian Muslims) reportedly continued.

The judiciary is constitutionally guaranteed independence and equal status. A 1994 law stipulating that judges have at least fifteen years' experience, hindering de-communization of judicial organs, was declared unconstitutional. The Constitutional Court has rejected several government measures. Judges and prosecutors have discriminated against minorities in criminal procedures.

Workers can strike, and have done so. Bulgaria has two large union confederations, the Confederation of Independent Trade Unions, a successor to the Communist-era union, and Podkrepa, an independent federation founded in 1989.

Corruption remains a problem. Renata Indzhova, a former caretaker prime minister, said, "No breakthrough has been made on organized crime and the merging of the state apparatus and the mafia." A U.N.-sponsored report ranked Bulgaria twentieth among 116 countries surveyed regarding women's opportunity to exercise power. The high rating is largely due to the substantial share of educated women holding administrative and managerial positions.

Burkina Faso

Polity: Dominant party
Economy: Mixed statist
Population: 10,423,000
PPP: $810
Life Expectancy: 47.4
Ethnic Groups: Mossi, Gurunsi, Senufo, Lobi, Bobo, Mande, Fulani
Capital: Ouagadougou

Political Rights: 5
Civil Liberties: 4
Status: Partly Free

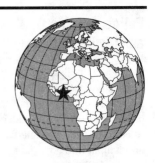

Overview:

President Blaise Compaore and his ruling Organization for Popular Democracy/Labor Movement (ODP/MT) continued to dominate Burkina Faso's politics in 1995, despite a burgeoning civil society. The government was faced with social unrest and strikes, spurred by economic difficulties compounded by a poor harvest and popular perceptions of official corruption.

Compaore is the latest military ruler since the country's independence from France in 1960 as Upper Volta. Compaore's vicious 1987 coup, resulting from rivalries within a junta that had ruled since 1983, included the murder of populist and charismatic President Thomas Sankara and thirteen of his closest associates. More Sankara supporters were executed two years later. The regime has since moderated itself, adopting a new 1991 constitution enshrining pluralism. December 1991 presidential polls saw widespread violence and an opposition boycott. Only a quarter of registered voters cast ballots, and Compaore won with a reported 85 percent of votes. Turnout remained low for May 1992 legislative elections despite opposition participation, and the ODP/MT took seventy-eight of 107 seats in the Assembly of People's Deputies. Repression has gradually eased in spite of the ruling party's dominance, though security forces sometimes remain unaccountable to the law.

February 1995 local elections made only a small dent in ODP/MT control, as the opposition won five of thirty-three municipalities. Opposition parties continued to seek a united front to mobilize for 1997 legislative and 1998 presidential elections, but remained weak and divided. The head of a small party supporting the late President Sankara's policies was sentenced to six months in August for libel after his allegations of presidential corruption were published. The widespread perception of corruption prompted the ruling party to pass legislation in May that effectively provided only nominal reassurance of government probity. Senior officials must disclose their assets, but only in confidential documents filed with the Supreme Court. Lingering economic repercussions from the 1994 CFA franc devaluation and an austerity and structural adjustment program prompted several serious railway workers' and teachers' strikes. Student demonstrations against school closings turned violent in May, and security forces killed two students.

Poor rains aggravated the government's economic dilemma. A meager 1996 harvest is predicted, and international donors have been asked to supply 24,000 metric tons of grain to avert a shortfall and possible hunger.

Political Rights and Civil Liberties: Burkinabes' constitutional right to change their government through periodic multiparty elections has not yet been realized in practice. The opposition boycotted 1991 presidential polls, which were marked by irregularities and considerable violence. Legislative polls in 1992 were conducted in a calmer atmosphere with opposition participation, but were not truly open. Compaore and his ODP/MT still hold most power. Top ODP/MT leaders were prominent in the military-dominated juntas that ruled from 1983-91. There are over sixty other political parties, but these have little direct input into governance.

Gradual democratic gains in recent years are reflected in vigorous independent media. While some self-censorship remains, the trend toward harsher libel and defamation legislation seen in several other authoritarian states is absent in Burkina Faso. Independent radio stations and newspapers operate with little overt interference, and there is broad public debate, including publication of material highly critical of the government.

Freedom of assembly is constitutionally protected and generally respected, with required permits usually issued routinely. Many nongovernmental organizations operate freely, including the Burkinabe Movement for Human Rights and Peoples (MBDHP) and several other human rights groups. Religious freedom is respected.

The Burkinabe judiciary lacks resources and training, but is considered generally independent in civil and criminal matters. Political cases are more susceptible to government influence. Police routinely ignore legal limits on detention, search and seizure, and national security laws allow a variety of special arrest and surveillance powers. Prison conditions are very harsh, with overcrowding, poor diets and scant medial attention.

Traditional courts, widely used in rural areas to resolve civil and family disputes, often invoke customary law that discriminates against women. Legal and constitutional protections for women's rights are lacking. Educational and wage employment opportunities for women are most limited in the countryside, and women hold few well paid positions in the formal sector. Female genital mutilation remains common despite a government campaign against the practice.

Workers in essential services may not join unions, but most others enjoy a broad range of legally protected labor rights, including the right to strike. Several labor confederations and independent unions bargain with employers and conduct various job actions.

The government's extensive privatization program continued in 1995, seeking to attract increased international investment. This could be deterred by persistent allegations of corruption, which are engendered by the flamboyant lifestyles of many senior officials.

Burma (Myanmar)

Polity: Military   **Political Rights:** 7
Economy: Mixed statist   **Civil Liberties:** 7
Population: 44,759,000   **Status:** Not Free
PPP: $751
Life Expectancy: 57.6
Ethnic Groups: Burmese (68 percent), Karen (7 percent),
Shan (9 percent), Rakhine (4 percent), others
Capital: Rangoon

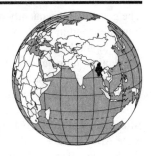

Overview: **T**he Burmese junta's July 1995 release after six years of house arrest of Aung San Suu Kyi, the country's most famous dissident, underscored the regime's confidence in its near-absolute hold on power. The overall human rights situation remained bleak, and during the year the junta continued a sham constitutional convention process aimed at formalizing the army's leading political role.

Following the Japanese occupation in World War II, Burma achieved independence from the United Kingdom in 1948. The army overthrew the elected government of Prime Minister U Nu in 1962 amid an economic crisis and threats from ethnic-based rebel groups.

During the next twenty-six years, General Ne Win's Burmese Socialist Program Party (BSPP) turned one of Southeast Asia's richest countries into an impoverished backwater. In September 1988 the army cracked down on massive, peaceful pro-democracy demonstrations, killing some 3,000 people. Army leaders General Saw Maung and Brigadier General Khin Nyunt instituted military rule under the State Law and Order Restoration Council (SLORC). In July 1989 the SLORC placed Aung San Suu Kyi, secretary general of the National League for Democracy and the country's foremost pro-democracy campaigner, under house arrest.

The SLORC organized the country's first free elections in three decades on 27 May 1990. The NLD won 392 of the 485 parliamentary seats, while the SLORC-sponsored National Unity Party, the successor to the BSPP, won just ten. The junta refused to recognize the results and jailed hundreds of NLD members, including several elected MPs.

In 1992 the SLORC carried out superficial liberalization measures and began a limited dialogue with opposition parties. General Than Shwe replaced hardliner Saw Maung as prime minister and junta leader.

The SLORC convened a constitutional convention in January 1993 with the goal of formalizing the military's leading role in politics. From the beginning the junta controlled the affair and warned the 702 delegates, of whom only 106 were elected MPs, against dissent. By June the SLORC had drafted guidelines for an Indonesian-style polity in which the president would be a military figure and hold broad executive powers, and the military would have one-quarter of the parliamentary seats. The junta convened the convention several times in 1994.

On 10 July 1995 the SLORC released Suu Kyi after six years of house arrest.

The generals subsequently rejected her calls for a dialogue on a democratic transition, and in late November reconvened the constitutional convention after a seven-month hiatus. The NLD, which had participated in earlier rounds of the convention, now pulled out of the process. Yet the NLD appeared to face a dilemma on how to advocate democracy effectively without the army carrying out another bloody crackdown.

The SLORC has strengthened its position by signing ceasefire deals with fifteen ethnic-based rebel armies in the border areas, the latest with the New Mon State Army in June—although a pact reached in March with the Karenni Nationalities People's Party (KNPP) subsequently collapsed. For decades these rebel armies have fought the central government, dominated by ethnic Burmans, for greater autonomy. The deals allow the armies to keep their weapons and territory. Many have entered the drug trade, helping to make Burma the largest opium producer in the world.

On 27 January 1995 the army captured the headquarters of the Karen National Union, the strongest of the insurgent groups still fighting, at the eastern village of Manerplaw. The military operation, and the subsequent capture of a secondary base at Kawmoora, sent more than 8,000 Karen refugees into Thailand. Through May Burmese army troops launched several raids on Karen refugee camps in Thailand, burning hundreds of homes and forcibly repatriating some refugees. By October aid workers in Karen state reported that tens of thousands of ethnic Karens faced starvation because fighting had forced them from their fields. Meanwhile heavy fighting occurred in July between the army and the KNPP in neighboring Karenni State. On another front, in March the Burmese army, joined at times by the ethnic-based United Wa State Army, began offensives against drug-lord Khun Sa's Maung Tai army in northeastern Shan state, sending several thousand villagers fleeing to the Thai border.

Political Rights and Civil Liberties: Burmese citizens cannot change their government democratically. The rule of law is nonexistent. Freedoms of speech, press and association and other fundamental rights are severely restricted. Trade unions, collective bargaining and strikes are illegal. Sixteen elected MPs are among an estimated several thousand political prisoners. The most serious rights violations frequently occur in areas where the government is conducting counterinsurgency operations against active ethnic-based rebel groups.

In November 1995 U.N. Special Rapporteur Yozo Yokota reported continuing rights violations including: arbitrary beatings and killings of civilians by the army; the use of civilians as porters and human minesweepers by the army under brutal conditions, with soldiers sometimes killing porters who are too weak to work, or executing those who refuse to become porters; summary executions of civilians who refuse to provide food or money to army units; the arrest of civilians as alleged insurgents or insurgent sympathizers; and sexual abuse of women by soldiers.

The judiciary is wracked by corruption and is not independent of the government. Political trials do not meet minimum international standards of due process. Prison conditions are abysmal and torture of both criminals and political prisoners is routine. In June the International Committee of the Red Cross withdrew from

Burma following the government's refusal to allow it regular and unimpeded access to prisons. In September Amnesty International listed nine previously unknown labor camps across the country, each with about 500 prisoners.

The use of forced labor is widespread, particularly for building roads and other infrastructure, including public works and beautification projects related to the official "Visit Myanmar Year" in 1996. The laborers toil under harsh conditions, receive no compensation and must pay for their transportation, bring their own food and tools and rent bulldozers. In some areas workers are forced to provide up to sixty days of labor per year. Major forced labor projects include a six-lane highway from Rangoon to Mandalay, and a road and railway line from Ye to Tavoy in conjunction with a foreign-financed natural gas pipeline.

In eastern Kayah and Karen states and northeastern Shan state, the army has forcibly relocated thousands of villagers in or near rebel-held areas into government-controlled towns. Forced relocations also continue against Muslims in western Arakan state. Nearly one million residents of Rangoon have been forcibly relocated to seven squalid satellite "new towns," and residents of Pagan, a tourist site, have been forced to build new homes and relocate to a newly created village

In August the BBC reported that the government had begun jamming its Burmese-language broadcasts for the first time in their fifty-five-year history. Outdoor gatherings of five or more people are prohibited, although the SLORC has permitted crowds to gather outside the home of Aung San Suu Kyi to listen to her addresses. The 1975 State Protection Law permits detention without trial for up to five years (as amended in 1992) and was used to detain Suu Kyi for six years.

Since April 1992 the SLORC has released more than 2,000 "political prisoners"; however, many are believed to be common criminals, while the true political prisoners among them had in any case been sentenced following unfair trials. Meanwhile arrests and imprisonment of dissidents continues. In May a court sentenced nine students to seven years' imprisonment each under the 1950 Emergency Provisions Act for delivering a eulogy at the funeral of former premier U Nu.

The Directorate of Defense Services Intelligence (DDSI) routinely searches homes, intercepts mail and monitors telephone conversations. Diplomats estimate that one in seven Burmese either works for the DDSI or is an informant. Universities in particular are closely monitored.

Some 300 monks were arrested during a violent October 1990 crackdown on monasteries suspected of supporting pro-democracy activities, and most remain in detention. Religious centers are closely monitored. Christians and Muslims have trouble openly practicing their religion, and the government occasionally confiscates their land and orders their places of worship demolished.

The government is dominated by the majority Burman ethnic group and discriminates against minority groups through a strict citizenship law and through language and other cultural restrictions. Thousands of Burmese women and young girls have been trafficked across the Thai border by criminal gangs to work in brothels.

By November 1995 the government had repatriated 192,000 of the 270,000 Rohingya Muslim refugees from Arakan state who fled to Bangladesh in 1991 and 1992 to escape forced labor and beatings by the Burmese army. Fighting in 1995 caused 8,000 Karens to join some 70,000 Karen and Mon refugees already in Thailand.

⬇ Burundi

Polity: Civilian-military
Economy: Statist
Population: 6,393,000
PPP: $720
Life Expectancy: 50.2
Ethnic Groups: Hutu (85 percent), Tutsi (14 percent),
Twa (pygmy) (1 percent)
Capital: Bujumbura
Trend Arrow: Burundi's downward trend arrow is due to
increased ethnic and tribal tensions.

Political Rights: 6
Civil Liberties: 7
Status: Not Free

Overview: Diplomats, human rights activists, journalists and others sounded repeated "early warnings" over increasing carnage in Burundi during 1995, but as violence intensified late in the year action to avert impending catastrophe was mainly limited to mediation missions with only slight hopes of healing the country's deep ethnic divide.

Burundi gained independence from Belgium in 1962 under a system that left political and military power mostly in the hands of the country's 15 percent Tutsi minority. Sporadic waves of killings both by and against the country's Hutu majority have wracked the country since, and simmering tensions were sometimes sparked by similar ethnic confrontations in neighboring Rwanda. In June 1992, leaders of the long-ruling Tutsi army-dominated Unity for National Progress (UPRONA) party agreed to legalize other parties. The African trend toward multiparty elections came to Burundi in June 1993, when Melchior Ndadaye, leading the Burundi Front for Democracy (FRODEBU) became the country's first Hutu president with 60 percent of the vote and led his party to a large victory in legislative elections.

Burundi's democratic transition was aborted in October 1993 when President Ndadaye and several other senior officials were murdered by Tutsi soldiers. Ethnic violence since has left over 100,000 dead and forced 600,000 of Burundi's 5.6 million people to flee their country. In April 1994, Ndadaye's successor, Cyprien Ntaryamira, was killed in a still-unexplained plane crash with Rwandan President Juvenal Habyarimana. The event marked the start of the anti-Tutsi genocide in Rwanda, and provoked more killings in Burundi. In October 1994, a forum of political and civic leaders chose Hutu politician Sylvestre Ntibantunganya as Burundi's new president under a power-sharing arrangement among the main political parties. He has presided over a deteriorating situation in which he has little control over the Tutsi-led army—and even less over various Hutu guerrilla forces (the most active being the Front for National Liberation, National Council for the Defense of Democracy and Hutu People's Liberation Party) and local militias and death squads from both ethnic groups.

Efforts at power-sharing and reconciliation continue, but face sabotage by extremists in a spiraling cycle of murder and revenge. North Korean weapons and advisors are reportedly aiding the Tutsi military, and Hutu irregulars appear to have easy access to cash and guns. In the words of ex-President Jean-Baptiste Bagaza, a radical Tutsi leader, "Everyone here is sharpening their knives."

Political Rights and Civil Liberties: In June 1993, Burundi citizens freely elected their president and legislative representatives to five-year terms by secret ballot in the country's first open multiparty elections. The murder of President Ndadaye together with his constitutional successors in October 1993 eventually led to the creation of a coalition government, and security conditions have left the elected parliament barely functioning. The army is largely independent of civilian political control, as are numerous other armed groups. The negotiated power-sharing arrangement between the UPRONA and FRODEBU parties has managed to maintain no more than an increasingly strained semblance of civilian administration.

A variety of newspapers is published in Burundi's capital, Bujumbura. Many are little more than mouthpieces bankrolled by extremist parties and filled with ethnic diatribes and crude incitements to violence. A 1992 press law allows many restrictions of publications, but in practice is not enforced. Self-censorship is practiced by journalists who fear attacks or reprisals. Several journalists have fled Burundi after receiving death threats. Radio broadcasts are far more effective at reaching people, especially in the countryside, and have been a favorite mobilizing tool for Hutu radicals. Burundian officials have asked for international pressure on Zaire to shut down an extremist Hutu radio station operating from its territory. International nongovernmental organizations have helped set up independent local radio stations to broadcast nonpartisan programming. The state-run radio and television have provided access to major political parties, and according to some reports have become more impartial since the coalition government's formation in March 1995.

There is little government interference in religious practice, formation of political parties or associations, although private militias have been known to target even nonviolent activists. The arrival on 5 November of a U.N.-appointed five-member commission to investigate the murder of President Ndadaye and subsequent human rights violations was welcomed by the Burundi Human Rights Association (ITEKA), which says the human rights abuses are encouraged by impunity of perpetrators. The judicial system, barely functioning as the country slides towards civil war, is widely distrusted by the Hutu majority because of Tutsi predominance.

Legal and customary discrimination affects Burundian women. Inheritance laws allow women to be dispossessed, and women find it very difficult to find credit. Women's educational opportunities are fewer than men's, especially in the countryside, and even with laws providing for equal pay for equal work, few opportunities exist for women to advance in the formal sector. Violence against women is reported, but there are only anecdotal accounts of its prevalence.

Workers' right to form unions is guaranteed by the constitution, and the labor code provides the right to strike. The sole labor confederation, the Organization of Free Unions of Burundi, has been independent since the rise of multipartyism in 1992. Most union members are civil servants and have bargained collectively with the government.

Cambodia

Polity: Monarchy, con-
stituent assembly, and
Khmer Rouge occupation
Economy: Statist
Population: 10,561,000
PPP: $1,250
Life Expectancy: 51.6

Political Rights: 6*
Civil Liberties: 6*
Status: Not Free

Ethnic Groups: Khmer (90 percent), Vietnamese (5 percent), Chinese (1 percent)
Capital: Phnom Penh
Ratings Change: *Cambodia's political rights rating changed from 4 to 6 and its
civil liberties rating from 5 to 6, moving Cambodia into the Not Free category,
because of crackdowns on opposition politicians and independent media.

Overview: Cambodia's two-year-old democratic transition appeared to
end in 1995 as an increasingly authoritarian government
cracked down on the opposition and independent media.

Cambodia achieved independence from France in 1953 under King Norodom
Sihanouk. In 1970 Premier Lon Nol ousted Sihanouk in a bloodless coup. In April 1975
the Maoist Khmer Rouge, led by Pol Pot, took power and began a genocidal effort to
create a classless agrarian society. Over one million Cambodians died through torture or
starvation. Vietnam invaded in December 1978 and installed the Communist Khmer
People's Revolutionary Party (KPRP), led largely by Khmer Rouge defectors.

In 1982 Sihanouk, the Khmer Rouge and former premier Son Sann joined their
armies against the KPRP. Several rounds of internationally supervised talks yielded
a peace accord in Paris in October 1991.

The Khmer Rouge subsequently refused to participate in the electoral process
and demobilization program stipulated in the Paris Accords. In May 1993 the
country held elections under the protection of 22,000 United Nations troops. Final
results for the 120-seat National Assembly gave fifty-eight seats to the royalist
opposition United Front for an Independent, Neutral and Free Cambodia
(FUNCINPEC), headed by Sihanouk's son Prince Norodom Ranariddh. Prime
Minister Hun Sen's governing Cambodian People's Party (CPP), the successor to
the KPRP, won fifty-one; Son Sann's Buddhist Liberal Democratic Party (BLDP),
ten; and Moulinaka, a FUNCINPEC offshoot, one.

In June 1993 a brief secessionist movement in seven eastern provinces, led by a
CPP official, served notice to FUNCINPEC that it would have to share power with
the ex-Communists. A compromise reached in September made Ranariddh First
Prime Minister and Hun Sen Second Prime Minister. Under a new constitution
stipulating that the king "reigns but does not rule," Sihanouk formally reassumed
the throne he had abdicated in 1955.

In October 1994 the government sacked outspoken Finance Minister Sam
Rainsy, who had criticized rampant official corruption. In May 1995 Rainsy was
expelled from FUNCINPEC, and in June the National Assembly removed him
from his seat. On 9 November Rainsy, despite having received death threats during

the year, formed the opposition Khmer Nation party. The government immediately ruled it illegal. On 22 November police arrested (and later exiled) Prince Norodom Sirivudh, a reformist-oriented FUNCINPEC leader, on trumped-up charges of plotting to kill Hun Sen. The move reaffirmed the ex-Communists' dominant role in the government.

In another development, early in the year Khmer Rouge troops attacked dozens of villages in western Battambang Province, burning homes and crops, destroying schools and hospitals, and killing at least 100 people, including local officials. However, the defection of some 7,000 soldiers in the past two years has weakened the group.

Political Rights and Civil Liberties:

Cambodians elected a new government in May 1993 in the freest vote in the country's history. Since then, the political and human rights situation has sharply deteriorated.

The Cambodian People's Party, nominally the junior member of the coalition government, effectively runs the country due to its control of the army, police, bureaucracy and provincial posts. Politically related murders occur fairly frequently. Official corruption is widespread and the country is becoming a regional center for money laundering and the drug trade, as well as a haven for international fugitives. The Khmer Rouge controls 10-15 percent of the country, and the roughly 6 percent of the population living in these areas is denied all basic rights.

The rule of law is especially weak in the countryside. Both army and Khmer Rouge soldiers are responsible for rape, extortion and banditry. A U.N. report leaked in August 1994 described a reign of terror by the army in northwestern Cambodia, including a detention center where soldiers reportedly executed thirty-five civilians. Extrajudicial killings and other army abuses reportedly continue. Authorities rarely prosecute rogue members of the security forces. Khmer Rouge guerrillas routinely kidnap and murder civilians, force villagers to serve as porters and attack trains. Civilians are frequently killed by indiscriminate shelling by both the government and the Khmer Rouge.

The judiciary is not independent. Due process rights fall short of international norms. Prisons are dangerously overcrowded and unsanitary, and detainees and inmates are frequently abused.

The government has initiated a broad campaign against free expression. In 1995 courts sentenced or fined at least three independent newspaper editors for "disinformation" or similar charges, and the government announced it would press charges against six other papers. The government suspended publication of several critical newspapers in 1995. A press law approved in July permits the government to shut papers without going through the courts, provides fines for several broadly-defined offenses, and permits courts to invoke criminal sanctions against the press.

In February police confiscated materials for a booklet calling for King Sihanouk to play a more active role in politics. In August authorities arrested six people for launching balloons with pro-democracy messages, detaining them for six weeks. Authorities are believed to be behind a pair of grenade attacks in September, one against the offices of an independent newspaper, and another against a pagoda where BLDP leader Son Sann had called a party meeting. The government outlawed the Khmer Rouge in July 1994, and rights groups are concerned that the law may be applied against legitimate opposition figures.

The constitution refers only to the rights of the ethnic Khmer majority, leaving in limbo the legal status of the estimated 200,000-500,000 Vietnamese in Cambodia. In recent years the Khmer Rouge has massacred scores of Vietnamese villagers.

Domestic violence is reportedly common. According to the United Nations Children's Fund there are 5,000-10,000 street children in the capital, Phnom Penh. Child prostitution is also increasing. Travel throughout much of the country is restricted by land mines and banditry. The right to form trade unions and bargain collectively is guaranteed by the constitution but not widely practiced.

Cameroon

Polity: Dominant party (military-dominated)
Economy: Capitalist
Population: 13,521,000
PPP: $2,390
Life Expectancy: 56.0
Ethnic Groups: Adamawa, Bamileke, Beti, Dzem, Fulani, Mandari, Shouwa, other—over 100 tribes and 24 languages
Capital: Yaounde

Political Rights: 7*
Civil Liberties: 5
Status: Not Free

Ratings Change: *Cameroon's political rights rating changed from 6 to 7 because of increasing government repression against the media and political activists.

Overview: President Paul Biya further consolidated power in 1995 and pressed constitutional amendments to strengthen the presidency. Media harassment intensified, and official intimidation weakened an already divided opposition.

Containing nearly 200 ethnic groups, Cameroon is also divided between users of English or French as a second language. A German colony from 1884 until 1916, Cameroon was seized during World War I and divided between Britain and France. Cameroon was reunited at independence in 1961, but the linguistic distinction remains its sharpest political division—about a quarter of the population is Anglophone.

Cameroon suffered unbridled authoritarian rule until 1992, when Biya held multiparty elections. His Cameroon People's Democratic Movement (CPDM) won a plurality of legislative seats after a truncated campaign boycotted by the main opposition, the Social Democratic Front (SDF), whose leader, John Fru Ndi, charged serious irregularities in election preparations. Fraudulent presidential polls returned Biya to office in October 1992. In response to widespread protests, he imposed a state of emergency in some areas and placed opposition candidate Fru Ndi under house arrest for three months.

In December, Cameroon's parliament passed constitutional revisions, ostensibly resulting from a four-year consultative process among the government, opposition and civic activists. Yet the revisions, granting the presidency almost unchecked power, were essentially a CPDM reworking of the inadequate 1972 constitution. They became law despite strenuous rejection by oppositionists and even rare criticism from CPDM members.

The SDF split into three factions, weakening an already fragmented opposition that includes about 100 mostly small parties. The split bolstered Biya's position, as did Cameroon's admission to the Commonwealth despite its authoritarian regime. New legislation allowing the seizure and banning of publications endangering "public order" or violating undefined "accepted standards of good behavior/values" further institutionalized repression. "Democracy shall be built...at our own pace," Biya told a CPDM congress in October. "We have no lessons to learn from outside."

Political Rights and Civil Liberties:

Cameroonians cannot change their government democratically. Marked by serious irregularities and fraud, 1992 legislative and presidential elections did not reflect the popular will. The legislature meets for two months annually. At other times Biya rules by decree, rendering the legislative opposition impotent. Biya's decree powers and executive control of the judiciary offer little recourse to Cameroonians seeking justice.

Biya holds nearly all power with a small CPDM coterie drawn mostly from his own Beti ethnic group. The judiciary is executive-dominated, and subnational administrators are appointed. Opposition and independent observers fear that twice-delayed municipal elections now set for 21 January 1996 will be manipulated, if held at all. The elections fall within the annual voter registration period, when polls are proscribed, but this should not deter balloting because elections are conducted by the Ministry of Territorial Administration and dominated by the CPDM. Oppositionists have already complained of registration irregularities and lack of access to state-run broadcast media.

The regime maintains a broadcasting monopoly and censors, suspends and closes independent publications. A 1990 press law formalized pre-publication censorship, and 1995 legislation encumbered licensing of publications, and expanded government's power to seize and ban publications conflicting with "the principles of public policy." Editions of some newspapers are sometimes withheld, or contain blank spaces where censors ordered cuts. Authorities closed at least three newspapers in 1995, and charged journalists with insulting the president.

Despite increased intimidation and some reported arrests, numerous nongovernmental organizations are active, including the Organization for Freedom of the Press in Cameroon, the National League for Human Rights, the Organization for Human Rights and Freedoms, the Human Rights Clinic and Education Center and the Association of Women against Violence. Religious freedom is generally respected.

Indefinite pretrial detention is permitted after a warrant is issued or to "combat banditry." Courts are often corrupt and subject to extreme political influence.

The Beti ethnic group enjoys preference in employment and economic opportunity, and Anglophones complain that systematic discrimination affords them no real voice in government. Indigenous pygmy peoples often work in de facto slave labor conditions, and reports persist of slavery in Cameroon's northern areas.

Customary law commonly discriminates against women, usually denying them inheritance rights and land ownership even where these have been codified. Violence against women, especially wife-beating, is reportedly widespread, and many laws contain sex-biased provisions and penalties.

The 1992 labor code permits unions, but many government workers are not covered and some of the code's provisions remain unimplemented. The Confederation of Cameroonian Trade Unions, Cameroon's only labor confederation, is technically independent, but authorities intervened to oust its leader in 1994 when he attempted to pursue policies counter to CPDM edicts.

Corruption and a lack of independent courts limit business development. Government delays in beginning the promised 1995 privatization of over thirty state-run enterprises have deterred new investors and slowed release of international financial support.

Canada

Polity: Federal parliamentary democracy
Economy: Capitalist
Population: 29,600,000
PPP: $20,520
Life Expectancy: 77.4

Political Rights: 1
Civil Liberties: 1
Status: Free

Ethnic Groups: British (40 percent), French (27 percent), other European (20 percent), Asian, aboriginal or native (Indian and Inuit) (1.5 percent), Caribbean black, others
Capital: Ottawa

Overview:
Quebec's sovereignty referendum in October left Canada uneasy but intact by a margin of less than 1 percent of the vote. Elsewhere in the country, several territorial disputes led to armed standoffs between police and native Indians occupying private land they claimed was never ceded to Canada.

Originally colonized by both France and Britain in the seventeenth and eighteenth centuries, Canada came under the control of Britain with the Treaty of Paris in 1763. After granting home rule in 1867, Britain retained a theoretical right to overrule the Canadian Parliament until 1982, when Canadians established complete control over their own constitution. The British monarch remains nominal head of state, represented by a ceremonial governor-general appointed by the prime minister.

In recent months Canadian politics have taken a slow but steady turn to the right, as illustrated by Ontario's sudden shift from a Socialist to a conservative government. Many attributed the trend to anger over high taxes, unemployment and the former New Democratic Party government's reluctance to cut spending from the generous social safety net the party had helped to create. However, Ontario's new premier, Michael Harris, has been confronted with boisterous protests from citizens feeling the effects of sharp budgetary cuts. In September, roughly 5,000 protesters rushed the provincial parliament and were met with pepper spray and police billy clubs.

As Quebec's referendum approached, separatists gained support by posing the independence question within the context of economic and political union with Canada, despite Prime Minister Jean Chretien's insistence that no such union would be guaranteed. Wary of growing separatist support, federalists reconsidered an effort to placate Quebec with constitutional recognition as a "distinct society" and increased authority over its own affairs. Although the "no" vote prevailed with 50.6 percent support, those accommodations are still seen as a means of avoiding a future breakup. Shortly after blaming the defeat on "money and the ethnic vote," Quebec Premier Jacques Parizeau announced his resignation. In November, charismatic and popular *Bloc Quebecois* leader Lucien Bouchard made the widely expected announcement that he intended to replace Parizeau, and indicated that a new referendum would be held within two years.

Political Rights and Civil Liberties:

Canadians can change their government democratically. Due to government canvassing, Canada has nearly 100 percent effective voter registration. Prisoners have the right to vote in federal elections, as do citizens who have lived abroad for less than five years. In the 1993 elections, the government held three days of advance voting for people unable to vote on election day.

A federal law prohibiting the broadcasting of public opinion poll results two days prior to and during federal elections was upheld this year. However, a 1988 Tobacco Products Control Act limiting all forms of cigarette advertisement was struck down as a violation of free speech. Other limitations on expression range from unevenly enforced "hate laws" and restrictions on pornography to rules on reporting. The media are generally free, although they exercise self-censorship in areas such as violence on television. The Canadian Broadcasting Company, an autonomous government broadcaster, is scheduled to cease international shortwave radio broadcasts in March after more than half a century on the air.

Civil liberties are protected by the federal Charter of Rights and Freedoms, limited by the constitutional "notwithstanding clause," which permits provincial governments to exempt themselves from applying individual provisions within their jurisdictions. Quebec has used the clause to retain its provincial language law, which restricts the use of English on outdoor commercial signs. The provincial governments, with their own constitutions and legislative assemblies, exercise significant autonomy. Each has its own judicial system as well, with the right of appeal to the Supreme Court of Canada.

A generous welfare system supplements the largely open, competitive economy. Property rights for current occupants are generally strong, but increasing Indian land claims have led to litigation and strained relations between the government and Canadian Indians. In 1995, land claimed as sacred sites was occupied by Indian rebels unaffiliated with any tribal governments, but highly representative of widespread frustration over unresolved land issues and lack of self-determination. One conflict ended in the first shooting death of an Indian by Canadian authorities in nearly a century.

Trade unions and business associations are free and well-organized. A national rail strike in March stopped services on both state-operated and privately owned railway systems. Only weeks after issuing a decree to end disruptive strikes on the docks of Vancouver, parliament passed a bill to force rail workers back on the job and end lockouts. The economy suffered an estimated $2.1 billion in losses in addition to layoffs and delays in transportation-dependent industries, particularly automobile manufacturing.

Religious expression is free and diverse, but there has been some controversy in recent years concerning religious education. Many provinces have state-supported religious school systems that do not represent all denominations. Legislation in Newfoundland to reform the system, creating nondenominational schools and eliminating religious affiliation as a criterion for hiring teachers, has met resistance from religious groups who fear precedents will be set making all church-run school systems vulnerable to court challenges. Other controversies center on government recognition of holy days, particularly in regard to closing schools and government offices for Muslim observances.

Despite restrictions announced in 1994, the flow of immigrants into the country remains strong. Although paramilitary groups and the willful promotion of racial hatred are against the criminal code, incidents of harassment and vandalism against minorities have increased. At the site of a bomb attack that leveled five houses in the suburbs of Toronto, hate graffiti and a swastika were found among the debris. Canada has expanded the opportunities for political asylum to include refuge on the grounds of spousal abuse and sexual orientation.

Cape Verde

Polity: Presidential-par-
liamentary democracy
Economy: Mixed statist
Population: 392,000
PPP: $1,750
Life Expectancy: 64.7
Ethnic Groups: Creole (71 percent), black (28 percent),
European (1 percent)
Capital: Praia

Political Rights: 1
Civil Liberties: 2
Status: Free

Overview: Despite accusations of corruption and recent high-level defections, the ruling Movement for Democracy (MPD) was returned to power in December's parliamentary elections, with 59 percent of the vote and fifty seats. Ballot shortages and long delays did not keep Cape Verde's 200,000-strong electorate from the polls in the country's second multiparty legislative elections since independence. Prime Minister Carlos Veiga pledged his party would continue with economic reforms aimed at relieving the widespread poverty and over 30 percent unemployment that have plagued the tiny nation.

The MPD won a landslide victory in 1991 in the first democratic legislative elections after sixteen years of Marxist, single-party rule under the African Party for the Independence of Cape Verde (PAICV). As the first former Portuguese colony in Africa to abandon Marxist political and economic systems, Cape Verde has enjoyed relative economic success with growth in exports and tourism, and has attracted foreign investment through a program of tax incentives. Extensive plans for infrastructure improvements have recently been implemented to assist in private-sector development. The country has few exploitable natural resources, however, and even when producing at optimum capacity the agricultural sector can only supply food for a quarter of the population. These obstacles—coupled with a growing cholera epidemic and falling revenues from earnings sent back by emigrants working abroad in Portugal and the U.S., traditionally a large portion of the country's GDP—have worked strongly against the alleviation of poverty.

Political Rights and Civil Liberties:

Cape Verdeans have the means to change their government democratically. The president and members of the National People's Assembly (parliament), including six representatives chosen by citizens living abroad, are elected through universal suffrage in free and fair voting. The new constitution adopted in 1992 effectively transformed the presidency to a figurehead position with only the authority to delay ratification of legislation, propose amendments and dissolve parliament after a vote of no confidence. Popular referenda are permitted in some circumstances, provided they do not challenge individual liberties or the rights of opposition parties to exist and operate freely.

The independent judiciary includes a Supreme Court and regional courts that generally adjudicate criminal and civil cases fairly and expeditiously. Trials are public, with free legal counsel provided to indigents and all defendants presumed innocent until proven guilty. The law requires that judges present charges within twenty-four hours of arrests. The police force, in existence as a separate entity from the military for over a year, is controlled by and responsible to a civilian government authority.

The freedoms of peaceful assembly and association are guaranteed and respected. All workers are free to form and join independent unions without restriction. Union members possess the constitutional right to strike and the freedom to affiliate with international organizations.

Although the vast majority of the population belongs to the Roman Catholic Church, the constitution requires the separation of church and state. The PAICV remains politically haunted by certain unpopular policies instituted in this conservative and religious society, including legalizing abortion. Despite the predominance of Roman Catholics in government, there are no restrictions on minority religious groups within the population.

Freedoms of expression and of the press are guaranteed and respected in practice. Newspapers and other publications may be established without authorization. Although the most widely read newspaper, along with radio and television broadcasting, are controlled by the government, coverage is generally fair and balanced. National Assembly sessions are broadcast live via radio in their entirety.

Despite legal prohibitions against gender discrimination as well as provisions for social and economic equality, discrimination against women persists. The most overt forms include less pay for equal work, exclusion from traditionally male professions and domestic violence, which is consistently under-reported. The government has not publicly addressed violence against women; however, the Ministry of Health and Social Affairs has recently undertaken campaigns to promote women's civil and human rights along with awareness about child abuse.

↑ Central African Republic

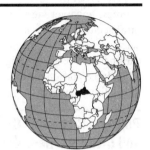

Polity: Presidential-parliamentary democracy
Economy: Capitalist-statist
Population: 3,210,000
PPP: $1,130
Life Expectancy: 49.4
Ethnic Groups: Baya (34 percent), Banda (27 percent), Mandja (21 percent), Sara (10 percent)
Capital: Bangui
Trend Arrow: The Central African Republic's up trend arrow is due to increased efforts to combat corruption.

Political Rights: 3
Civil Liberties: 4
Status: Partly Free

Overview: Despite two years since democratic rule returned to the Central African Republic (CAR), democracy may not yet be consolidated. President Ange-Felix Patasse endorsed a populist agenda including an anti-corruption drive and decentralization to improve the standing of the parliamentary coalition supporting his Central African People's Liberation Movement (MLPC). Economic problems and ethnic divisions weakened Patasse politically, however, and there are signs his government may revert to authoritarianism and French support to bolster its rule.

The CAR gained independence from France in 1960 after a particularly exploitative colonial period. Colonel Jean-Bedel Bokassa seized power, renaming the country the Central African Empire and imposing an increasingly bizarre dictatorship, with himself on the throne. French support waned only after Bokassa began murdering schoolchildren, and French troops helped oust him in 1979. His French-installed successor lost favor in the metropole, and General Andre Kolingba deposed him in 1981. Kolingba introduced the facade of civilian rule and eventually accepted a transition to multipartyism, leading to democratic elections in 1993. The autocratic legacy still lingers, however, and the country's media, judiciary and civil service are still struggling for real independence.

The crackdown on corruption Patasse announced in August included the arrest of a former health minister, and could help revive domestic support even as official tolerance of criticism dwindles. It might also reassure international lenders, whose aid is crucial to the impoverished CAR. Relations with France, which garrisons intervention forces in the country, improved in 1995. The CAR reportedly served as a base for retraining and rearming French-supported Hutu extremists ousted from Rwanda after committing genocide there in 1994.

Political Rights and Civil Liberties: Citizens of the Central African Republic chose their government in open and democratic elections under the 1986 constitution for the first time in 1993. Patasse's victory was not matched by a clear triumph for his MLPC in the eighty-five-seat national assembly. The party now rules in a coalition with several smaller parties.

A new constitution was adopted via referendum in December 1994 after a year of broad discussion and debate. The constitution increases judicial and legislative autonomy and enshrines a multiparty system. August 1998 legislative elections and the 1999 presidential contest will test the strength of the new institutions. Ethnic divisions may potentially divert attention from issues, and could provoke armed intervention in the political process.

The state dominates broadcast media; opposition activities are sometimes reported but rarely given prominence. The only private radio stations are music or religion-oriented. The new government has interfered little in private media, although self-censorship may be encouraged after an August court decision sentenced opposition editor Geneyo Repago to two years on charges of insulting Patasse. Repago, editor of *Le Rassemblement*, the newspaper of former president Andre Kolingba's Central African Democratic Rally, was also fined $1,000. Other newspapers, some blatantly partisan, publish various parties' political statements and critiques. But independent publications are generally read only in the capital, Bangui, and have no sound financial base to guarantee independence.

There is open public discussion, and the new constitution guarantees freedom of assembly. However, public meetings must be registered forty-eight hours in advance, and the government banned an opposition May-Day rally. At least twenty-three registered political parties are active to varying degrees. Many nongovernmental organizations operate without interference, including the Central African Human Rights League and the Movement for the Defense of Human Rights and Humanitarian Action. Religious freedom is respected, though religious groups must register with authorities.

CAR judicial institutions continue to lag behind the pace of democratic transition. Legal requirements regarding searches and detention are often ignored. Police brutality remains a serious problem, and prison conditions are harsh. Political interference and a lack of training and resources also hinder judicial efficiency and impartiality.

Constitutional guarantees regarding women's rights are not reflected in reality. Women's educational, employment and other economic opportunities are far inferior to men's, especially in rural areas. Societal discrimination reduces women to second-class status in many areas.

The CAR's formal economic sector is small, as is reflected in the level of union activity. The labor code protects workers' right to form or join unions of their choice. Five labor federations compete for affiliates. Unions may call strikes, but only after a conciliation process. Although collective bargaining is not specifically protected, unions have negotiated wage agreements. However, the government still sets wage guidelines in consultation with employers and unions.

Economic opportunity is limited by the country's low level of development. Coffee and a few other commodities produce most export earnings, and the state bureaucracy provides most wage-paying jobs. The World Bank and other lenders and donors are pressing the government to implement civil service reforms and reduce political interference in development decisions in order to qualify for new aid.

⬇ Chad

Polity: Interim legisla-
ture (military-dominated)
(transitional)
Economy: Capitalist
Population: 6,361,000
PPP: $760
Life Expectancy: 47.5

Political Rights: 6
Civil Liberties: 5
Status: Not Free

Ethnic Groups: Arab, Bagirmi, Sara,Wadai, Zaghawa, Bideyat Gorane,
200 distinct groups
Capital: N'Djamena
Trend Arrow: Chad's down trend arrow is due to increased uncertainty
regarding its democratic transition.

Overview:
Chad's transition toward a multiparty system remained tenuous through 1995, as elections were delayed in an atmosphere that oscillated between repression and openness. Continuing guerrilla conflicts and army brutality threatened stability, and the military-dominated government's ability and even willingness to oversee free and fair elections were increasingly questioned.

Chad has been almost perpetually at war since achieving its independence from France in 1960. Ethnic and religious differences, exacerbated by clan rivalries and external interference, have kept the country in turmoil. The country is roughly split between Christian farmers who inhabit the country's south, and Arab and Saharan peoples who occupy vast areas across the north.

Although over 200 ethnic groups are found among the country's 6.5 million people, the Zaghawa and the Bideyat, two small groups from the northeastern region, dominate Chad's army and consequently its political life. Thus far Chadians have had little experience with the rule of law by a constitutional and accountable authority.

**Political Rights
and Civil Liberties:**
Chadians have not been permitted to choose their government through free and fair elections. There is no tradition of peaceful and orderly transfer of political power. President Idriss Deby was the latest ruler to reach power through the gun, overthrowing Hissein Habre in December 1990. Deby lifted the ban on political parties and in 1993 convened a national conference attended by a broad array of civic and political groups, including his own Patriotic Salvation Movement (MPS), which controls the transitional parliament. Dozens of opposition parties now operate, though many are little more than one-person talking shops with no popular base.

A 19 November 1995 referendum approved a new constitution to replace the one thrown out by Deby when he seized power. Adoption of the new charter clears the way for presidential polls scheduled for February and legislative elections in April and May 1996, respectively. Formal transfer of power to an elected government is set for August 1996. It is unclear whether this process, already delayed, can be kept on track. Voter registration planned for February-March 1995 was halted by the Court of Appeals after oppositionists charged the process was fraught with irregularities. Particularly worrisome was that the process was supervised by the Interior Ministry rather than the newly formed National Electoral Commission. In June, the government and opposition agreed that a new round of registration would be overseen by a new National Election Registration Commission that included political party representation.

Beyond the issue of political will to hold a free and fair election are also formidable financial, logistical and security obstacles. The registration process alone could cost $10 million, and infrastructure for voting in a country as vast as Chad will be costly. Conducting elections could be problematic in many areas of the countryside, where two dozen or more armed factions are in varying states of rebellion against the Deby government, and where plain banditry also contributes to pervasive security problems.

Chad's long and porous borders are not easily policed, and trade in weapons is rife among nomadic Sahelian peoples. A contributing factor is that Chad was a major recipient of Western arms shipments during its 1980s conflicts with Libya. The Movement for Democracy and Development has been staging raids in the eastern Lake Chad area, and the Armed Forces for a Federal Republic remains active in the south, although another rebel leader, Moïse Kette, laid down arms and joined the transitional government in April.

It is in the southern districts that the worst human rights abuses are reported. Tens of thousands of Chadians have fled the country. The worst violations are blamed on Deby's elite presidential guard. In a May 1995 report, Amnesty International charged that over 1,500 civilians have been murdered by government forces "continuing to act with complete impunity" over the past five years. The report went on to point out mounting reports of torture.

A reconstituted political police, the National Security Agency (ANS), began operating after the former unit was dissolved under pressure from the 1993 national conference. The brief detention of a leading opposition figure, Saleh Kebzabo, leader of the National Union for Development and Renewal (UNDR), sparked riots that left five people dead in September.

ANS agents ransacked the offices of a leading opposition newspaper in June, and is accused of intimidating other opponents of Deby. However, the government apologized for the attack on the newspaper, and numerous independent publications are highly critical of the government. But there is no sign that the state-controlled broadcast media will be opened anytime soon, a crucial factor in a country as vast and with as low a literacy rate as Chad.

The record on labor rights is also mixed. The government has banned several demonstrations, but has been responsive to union demands for negotiations on wages and working conditions since it signed a "social pact" with labor leaders after a general strike in 1994.

Freedom of religion is generally respected in Chad, though religion remains one of the markers dividing the society. Women's rights, however, are protected neither by traditional law or in the penal code. Female genital mutilation is commonplace. The literacy rate for women is very low, and few educational opportunities are available, especially in rural areas.

Chile

Polity: Presidential-
legislative democracy
Economy: Capitalist
Population: 14,251,000
PPP: $8,410
Life Expectancy: 73.8
Ethnic Groups: Mestizo, Spanish, other European, Indian
Capital: Santiago

Political Rights: 2
Civil Liberties: 2
Status: Free

Overview: **A**n extended confrontation between President Eduardo
Frei's government and the military under former dictator
Gen. Augusto Pinochet made clear the limitations on
elected civilian rule in Chile.

The Republic of Chile was founded after independence from Spain in 1818.
Democratic governance predominated in this century until the 1973 overthrow of
Salvador Allende by the military under Pinochet.

The 1980 constitution Pinochet installed provided for a plebiscite in which
voters could reject another presidential term for Pinochet. In 1988, 55 percent of
voters said "no" to eight more years of military rule, and competitive presidential
and legislative elections were scheduled for 1989.

Following 1989 and 1994 constitutional reform, presidents are elected for six
years. There is a bicameral Congress with a 120-member Chamber of Deputies
elected for four years and a Senate with thirty-eight senators elected for eight years,
and eight appointed by the government for eight years.

In 1989 Patricio Aylwin, the candidate of the center-left Concertacion for
Democracy, was elected president over two right-wing candidates and the
Concertacion won a majority in the Chamber. But with eight senators appointed by
the outgoing military government, it fell short of a Senate majority.

Aylwin oversaw a broadly representative, remarkably clean government that
was responsive to a wide social base. But efforts to reform the constitution, which
allows Pinochet and other military chiefs to remain until 1997, were stopped by the
right-wing Senate bloc.

Frei, a fifty-two-year-old businessman, was the Concertacion candidate in
December 1993 elections and won easily over right-wing candidate Arturo
Alessandri. Frei vowed to establish full civilian control over the military, but like
Aylwin he did not have the numbers in Congress. In 1993 the Concertacion lost a
Senate seat and two Chamber seats, leaving it even farther from the two-thirds
majority needed for constitutional reform.

The military defied a June 1995 Supreme Court ruling that Gen. Manuel
Contreras, Pinochet's former secret police chief, go to jail for the 1976 murder in
Washington, D.C., of opposition leader Orlando Letelier. Contreras was finally
jailed in October, but only after much saber rattling by Pinochet and Frei's subsequent
retreat from demanding full accountability for rights violations under military rule.

Frei eventually proposed a reform package that was soft on resolving rights issues but would have enhanced civilian authority over the military. But the proposals, which led to divisions on the right and within the Concertacion, languished.

Political Rights and Civil Liberties:

Citizens can change their government democratically. Democratic institutions are better established than in any other Latin American country outside of Costa Rica.

However, while reformed in some aspects, the 1980 constitution installed under Pinochet still limits civilian authority over the armed forces. The president cannot change armed forces commanders until 1997 or reduce the military budget. The constitution also allowed the former Pinochet regime to appoint eight senators to eight-year terms in 1989.

In 1990 a Truth and Reconciliation Commission was formed to investigate rights violations committed under military rule. The Commission's report implicated the military and secret police at the highest levels in the deaths or disappearances of 2,279 people between September 1973 and March 1990. However, in 1978 the Pinochet regime had issued an amnesty for all political crimes, and the Supreme Court, packed by Pinochet before leaving office, has blocked all government efforts to lift it.

The amnesty has not stopped civilian governments from investigating rights cases. Hundreds of cases involving incidents after 1978 have been brought to civilian courts, resulting in a handful of convictions. In late 1995, however, the Supreme Court, possibly under pressure from the military, began dismissing dozens of cases with increasing speed and without the depth of investigation it had exhibited previously.

In 1991 the Court made a dramatic turnaround in the special case of the 1976 murder in Washington of former Chilean ambassador to the U.S., Orlando Letelier. The Court ruled that the alleged authors of the crime—former secret police chief and retired Gen. Manuel Contreras and Col. Pedro Espinosa—be tried in civilian courts. Both were convicted in November 1993, the first time a civil court had convicted ranking officers for crimes committed under military rule. They were sentenced to seven and six years in prison, respectively, and were jailed in 1995 as described in the Overview.

Most laws limiting political expression and civil liberties were eliminated by constitutional reforms in 1989. Media freedom was almost fully restored. Scores of publications represent all points of view. Radio is both private and public. The national television network is state-run, but open to all political voices. Universities run three noncommercial television stations.

However, a journalists' licensing law remains in place, and a number of restrictive laws remain in effect, including one granting military courts power to convict journalists or others for sedition or libeling members of the military.

The draconian 1978 labor code has undergone significant reform. Strikes are legal, but organizational and collective bargaining provisions remain weak. The Frei administration has proposed reforms to strengthen labor rights guarantees, but in 1995 the right-wing bloc in Congress was still able to block legislation.

Sporadic actions by remnants of the Manuel Rodriguez Patriotic Front (FPMR), the former armed wing of the Communist Party, continue. Human rights groups remain concerned about anti-terrorist legislation that broadened police powers. There are still frequent reports of police abuses, including torture and use of excessive force against political demonstrators, but there are also signs of greater accountability.

Implementation of a 1993 indigenous rights law has been slow because of a lack of resources, according to the government.

China

Polity: Communist one-party
Economy: Mixed statist
Population: 1,214,233
PPP: $1,950
Life Expectancy: 68.5
Ethnic Groups: Han Chinese (93 percent), Azhuang, Hui, Uygur, Yi, Miao, Manchu, Tibetan, Mongolian, others
Capital: Beijing

Political Rights: 7
Civil Liberties: 7
Status: Not Free

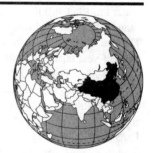

Overview:

The fourteen-year sentence handed down to China's most famous dissident in December 1995 on the outlandish charge of trying "overthrow the government" underscored the regime's anxiety that economic and demographic changes could combine with political dissent to undermine its absolute authority.

Chinese Communist Party (CCP) Chairman Mao Zedong proclaimed the People's Republic of China on 1 October 1949 following victory over the Nationalist Kuomintang. From 1958-1960 Mao attempted to accelerate industrialization and agricultural collectivization through the disastrous Great Leap Forward, creating a rural famine that killed over 30 million peasants. In 1966 Mao encouraged an infamous mass movement, the Cultural Revolution, in a bid to regain control of a fractious CCP. By 1976 up to one million had died and millions more had been disgraced, including party secretary Deng Xiaoping. Following Mao's death in September 1976, Deng assumed several top-level posts, and in December 1978 began introducing free market reforms.

In April 1989 several thousand students gathered at Beijing's Tiananmen Square to mourn the death of moderate ex-CCP secretary general Hu Yaobang. The students later boycotted classes, demanding democratic reforms and protesting rising prices. By mid-May the protests had spread to other cities. The Beijing demonstrations ended with a bloody army assault on Tiananmen Square on 3-4 June in which hundreds, perhaps thousands, were killed. Hardliner Jiang Zemin replaced the relatively moderate Zhao Ziyang as CCP secretary general.

Since Tiananmen the government has continued modest free market reform while suppressing all political dissent. Policies are ultimately shaped by a core of aged revolutionary veterans, whose ranks have dropped from eight at the time of Mao's death to five following the April 1995 death of Chen Yun, a staunch advocate of central planning. Deng, who turned ninety-one in August 1995 and is in poor health, no longer holds any official title but remains China's highest authority by virtue of his leading role in the Communist rise to power in the 1930s and 1940s.

In 1992 Deng made his strongest effort to root economic reforms deeply enough to make them irreversible after his death. In January Deng made a highly symbolic visit to the booming Shenzhen Special Economic Zone in southern Guangdong Province. At its Fourteenth Party Congress in October 1992, the CCP formally adopted the goal of a "socialist market economy," a seemingly innocuous phrase that in fact all but buried the 1949 revolution's orthodox Marxist ideology.

In March 1993 the rubber-stamp National People's Congress (NPC) elected CCP secretary general Jiang as state president. Deng's handpicked successor as paramount leader, Jiang holds a third title as chairman of the Central Military Commission but is viewed as a weak figure who will have to struggle to keep power after Deng's death. The NPC also elected premier Li Peng to a second five-year term, and named as its chairman Qiao Shi, the CCP's former internal security chief and a likely key political figure in coming years.

In April 1995 an ongoing investigation into corruption in Beijing's municipal government culminated in the suicide of a deputy mayor and the sacking of Beijing party chief Chen Xitong. Observers viewed the corruption probe as an attempt by Jiang to weaken Chen, a potential rival.

Meanwhile, dissidents sent at least half a dozen petitions to political leaders between March and May calling for a reversal of the official verdict branding participants in the 1989 pro-democracy demonstrations "counterrevolutionaries," as well as for political reforms and checks on official corruption. Police arrested several signatories and by year's end roughly twenty remained in detention. In a key development, in December a court sentenced Wei Jingsheng, China's most prominent dissident, to fourteen years in prison on trumped-up charges of trying to "overthrow the government."

In recent years there have been hundreds of peasant riots protesting illegal land seizures and arbitrary taxes levied by rogue provincial officials. The growing income disparity between coastal areas and interior provinces has contributed to a "floating population" of over 100 million people seeking work in urban areas.

Political Rights and Civil Liberties:

Citizens cannot change their government democratically. The Chinese Communist Party (CCP) wields ultimate authority. Although economic reforms have somewhat reduced government intrusion in the daily lives of many ordinary Chinese, the regime remains among the worst human rights violators in the world and the rule of law is nonexistent.

Under the 1987 Village Committees Organic Law, approximately 90 percent of China's village bodies are now chosen through local elections. However, only CCP candidates—and independents in some places—can compete. The conduct and fairness of these elections varies. In many villages independents have won seats, but balloting throughout China is characterized by irregularities and unfair procedures.

The lack of accountability at all levels is most evident in the judicial and penal systems. The judiciary is subservient to the government and ignores due process rights. Defendants are presumed guilty and over 99 percent are convicted. Suspects are frequently tortured to extract confessions. Abuse of prisoners, particularly ordinary workers, is routine and widespread. In January 1995 the government reiterated its refusal to allow the International Committee of the Red Cross unsupervised access to any of China's 1.285 million prisoners.

Two special types of punishment exist: the *laojiao*, or "re-education through labor" camps, and the *laogai*, or "reform through labor" camps. The laojiao system allows administrative detention for up to four years without a hearing, completely bypassing the formal judicial process. In late 1993 Chinese authorities reported that 153,000 prisoners were undergoing "re-education through labor," although the actual number may be higher. A third process, "shelter for investigation," permits detention without charge or trial for up to three months, and this period is frequently extended. By official accounts over one million people are detained through "shelter for investigation" each year.

In May 1995 a former police official testified before the U.S. Senate that authorities sometimes sell executed prisoners' organs for transplant purposes, and that executions have been scheduled to meet transplant demand. In recent years there has been a chilling rise in executions during mass crackdowns on corruption and drug trafficking, often immediately following summary trials. Individuals have been executed for offenses as minor as forging tax invoices.

It is impossible to estimate accurately the number of political prisoners in China. In January 1995 the government said 2,679 "counterrevolutionaries" were being held. However, the government is increasingly charging dissidents with ordinary crimes rather than "counterrevolutionary" offenses. The June 1994 "Detailed Implementation Regulations" for the 1993 State Security Law criminalized peaceful acts, including working with foreign human rights organizations and any writings or speech that "endangers state security." In addition, many dissidents are held without trial in laojiao camps.

China frequently uses political prisoners as bargaining chips in international affairs. Most recently, Beijing released several in the months prior to the U.S. government's May 1994 decision to "de-link" human rights considerations from renewal of China's Most Favored Nation (MFN) trade status. Since the MFN decision, China has largely ceased releasing political prisoners. Dissidents are frequently detained for questioning, and many former political prisoners and families of current prisoners face surveillance and other forms of harassment.

In June border police arrested Harry Wu, an American citizen who had documented Chinese prison abuses, and in August a court sentenced him to fifteen years for espionage and ordered him expelled. In September a Shenzhen court sentenced Jimmy Peng, an Australian businessman, to eighteen years in prison on charges of embezzling company funds. Peng had challenged Shenzhen authorities over ownership rights to his company before Chinese police abducted him in Macao in October 1993.

Freedoms of expression and association are nonexistent. At least a dozen journalists are believed to be in prison, some merely for meeting with Western journalists. All media are state-controlled and coverage must conform to the CCP Propaganda Department's strict guidelines. Foreign journalists are occasionally detained for questioning.

In August 1995 the official *People's Daily* reported that more than ten people in Beijing had been executed to ensure "public order" during the Fourth World

Conference on Women in September. The Chinese government also shunted a parallel nongovernmental organization (NGO) forum to Huairou, some thirty miles outside of Beijing; denied visas to numerous NGO activists, including representatives of Tibetan groups; monitored NGO gatherings in Huairou; ordered translators not to interpret references to Tibet during speeches at the main Conference; and forced several dissidents to leave Beijing during the Conference.

Religious practice is tightly controlled and officially limited to government-sanctioned "patriotic" churches. Students attending seminaries run by state-approved churches must pass exams on political as well as theological knowledge. The government regulates the publication and distribution of religious books and other materials. Small, unofficial Catholic and Protestant churches are sometimes tolerated, provided they maintain a low profile. However, scores of unofficial churches have been closed, and hundreds of bishops, priests and worshipers have been detained for months and even years. In January 1994 the government codified a long-standing ban against proselytizing by foreigners. In Muslim-majority areas, officials have placed restrictions on building mosques and providing Islamic education to youths under eighteen.

China's harsh one-child family-planning policy is applied inconsistently from region to region. Some local officials zealously enforce it through sanctions and even forced abortion and sterilization. Couples adhering to the policy receive preferential education, food and medical benefits, while those failing to comply face a loss of benefits and fines. Failure to pay fines can result in seizure of livestock and other goods and destruction of homes. Expecting mothers often use ultrasound machines to determine a baby's sex. A Chinese newspaper reported in January 1995 that 97.5 percent of all abortions are performed on female fetuses. Infanticide is practiced in a small fraction of births. The ratio of male to female births in 1992 reached 118.5:100; a normal ratio is roughly 105:100. Female babies and young girls are occasionally abandoned.

Women face discrimination and sexual harassment in the workplace. In rural areas tens of thousands of women annually are reportedly abducted or otherwise sold into prostitution or marriage. Recruitment and kidnapping of children for prostitution or other work are also increasing. Authorities recognize fifty-five ethnic minorities, although few minority representatives hold key positions in the CCP or state hierarchies.

Independent trade unions are illegal. All unions must belong to the CCP-controlled All-China Federation of Trade Unions. The 1982 constitution does not recognize the right to strike. In practice strikes are permitted to protest dangerous or inadequate conditions and low wages, and occur most often in foreign-owned factories. Most prisoners are required to work, receiving little if any compensation.

The successes of both the Special Economic Zones in the south and the small-scale township and village enterprises in the countryside have helped remove millions from dependence on the *danwei*, or state work unit. But for most urban dwellers the danwei controls key choices, from the right to change residence to permission to have a child. The system of *hakou*, or residence permit, has also been loosened to give workers more flexibility in filling jobs in areas of fast economic growth. Over one million residents will be relocated during construction of the Three Gorges Dam on the Yangtze River.

Colombia

Polity: Presidential-
legislative democracy
(insurgencies)
Economy: Capitalist-
statist
Population: 37,707,000
PPP: $5,480
Life Expectancy: 69.3

Political Rights: 4*
Civil Liberties: 4
Status: Partly Free

Ethnic Groups: Mestizo (58 percent), European (20 percent), Mulatto (14 percent), Black, (4 percent), Indian (1 percent)
Capital: Bogota
Ratings Change: *Colombia's political rights rating changed from 3 to 4 because of evidence that narco-corruption has deeply penetrated the executive branch.

Overview:

Massive evidence that President Ernesto Samper's 1994 election campaign had been awash in drug money confirmed ever-violent Colombia's status as the capital of narco-corruption.

Following independence from Spain in 1819, the Republic of Colombia was established in 1886. Politics has since been dominated by the Liberal and Conservative parties. Under Liberal President Cesar Gaviria (1990-94) a new constitution was implemented that limits presidents to single four-year terms and provides for an elected bicameral Congress, with a 102-member Senate and a 161-member Chamber of Representatives.

Modern Colombia has been marked by the corrupt machine politics of the Liberals and Conservatives, left-wing guerrilla insurgencies, right-wing paramilitary violence, the emergence of giant drug cartels and the gross violation of human rights with impunity.

Little changed under Gaviria, whose free-trade policies were applauded abroad while about three Colombian trade unionists were being killed per week. Medellin cartel chief Pablo Escobar was hunted down and killed, but the Cali cartel emerged as the largest, most efficient cocaine- and heroin-trafficking operation in the hemisphere.

In the 1994 legislative elections the Liberals retained a majority in both houses of Congress. Samper, a forty-three-year-old former economic development minister, won the Liberal presidential primary. The Conservatives backed Andres Pastrana, a thirty-nine-year-old former mayor of Bogota, the capital. Both candidates vowed to continue Gaviria's free-market, free-trade reforms.

Samper won in a June 1994 runoff election, taking 50.4 percent of the vote to Pastrana's 48.6 percent. He took office under a cloud of suspicion after four tape recordings surfaced in which the top Cali cartel leaders discussed million-dollar contributions to Samper's campaign.

Under U.S. pressure Samper went after the Cali cartel, and most of its top figures were captured in 1995. But the arrests netted overwhelming evidence of drug ties to Samper's campaign. The campaign finance chief was arrested and told investigators that the cartel had given $6 million to the campaign and that Samper signed off on it. His testimony was corroborated by a former top cartel accountant who had surrendered to U.S. investigators.

Samper defied opposition pressure to resign and vowed to complete his term. In the second half of 1995 he twice imposed states of emergency that allowed him to govern virtually by decree. Meanwhile, criminal and left-wing guerrilla violence escalated, the business community and the military grew increasingly anxious and new traffickers stepped in to fill the shoes of the arrested Cali chiefs. In December a congressional commission dominated by Liberals cleared Samper of charges he authorized cartel contributions to his campaign. Opposition politicians and much of the media called it a whitewash.

Political Rights and Civil Liberties:

Citizens can change their government through elections. The 1991 constitution provides for broader participation in the system, including two reserved seats in the Congress for the country's small Indian minority.

But voter participation rarely exceeds 40 percent because of fear of political violence and a widespread belief that corruption renders elections meaningless.

During elections candidates campaign under heavy security and tend to limit themselves to indoor appearances. In 1994 dozens of congressional and local candidates were killed, kidnapped or injured. There were indications that left-wing guerrillas controlled up to 15 percent of the nation's 1,000-plus municipalities.

The scandal described in the Overview involving drug contributions to President Samper's 1994 campaign underscored Colombia's status as the capital of narco-corruption. There is strong evidence that the Cali cartel, through its lawyers, virtually dictated the 1993 penal-code reform to Congress. It allows traffickers who turn themselves in as much as a two-thirds sentence reduction, and the dismissal of any pending charges they do not plea to. In 1991 traffickers also influenced the constituent assembly through bribery to ensure that it banned extradition in the new constitution.

Constitutional rights regarding free expression and the freedom to organize political parties, civic groups and labor unions are severely restricted by political and drug-related violence and the government's inability to guarantee the security of citizens, institutions and the media.

Political violence in Colombia continues to take more lives than in any other country in the hemisphere, with about ten killings and disappearances per day in 1995. The military and security forces are most responsible, followed by right-wing paramilitary groups, left-wing guerrillas, drug-traffickers and hundreds, possibly thousands, of paid assassins. All perpetrators of political violence operate with a high degree of impunity.

Another category of killings is "social cleansing"—the elimination of drug addicts, street children and other marginal citizens by vigilante groups often linked with the police. Overall, criminal violence results in dozens of murders per day. Homicide is the number-one cause of death in Colombia. Kidnappings occurred in 1995 at a rate of three per day, about half by left-wing guerrillas.

There are numerous human rights organizations, but activists, as well as labor, peasant and student organizations, are consistently the targets of violence and intimidation. In 1995 at least three human rights activists were murdered. More than a dozen trade unionists were killed per month as Colombia remained the most dangerous country in the world for organized labor.

Over the last decade the entire judicial system has been severely weakened by the onslaught of the drug cartels and generalized political violence. Much of the system has been compromised through corruption and extortion.

Under the 1991 constitution, the judiciary, headed by a Supreme Court, was revamped. A U.S.-style adversarial system was adopted and government prosecutors are able to use government security services to investigate crimes. Previously, judges had investigated crimes without the help of major law enforcement agencies.

But the judicial system remains overloaded and ill-equipped to handle high-profile drug and corruption cases. To protect the judiciary from drug traffickers, the Gaviria government instituted a system of eighty-four "faceless judges." But it is a system in which defendants are denied due process and traffickers are able to penetrate the veil of anonymity.

The 1991 constitution created an independent public prosecutor, in whose beleaguered office resides the only hope that powerful Colombians may some day have to answer for their crimes.

The military was untouched by constitutional reform. No demands were made on spending accountability, and mandatory military service was left intact. Cases involving police and military personnel accused of human rights violations are tried in military rather than civilian courts. In effect, the military and police remain accountable only to themselves, reinforcing the atmosphere of impunity that pervades the entire country. The sense of impunity and climate of fear were enhanced during the states of emergency imposed by President Samper in the second half of 1995.

Radio is both public and private. Television remains mostly a government monopoly and news programs tend to be slanted. Moreover, the "right to reply" provision of the new constitution has resulted in harsh judicial tutelage over all media. In 1995 the government pressed for passage of a law that would prohibit the media from reporting on official corruption cases.

The press, including dozens of daily newspapers and weekly magazines, is privately owned. Dozens of journalists have been murdered in the last decade and numerous others kidnapped. While fewer journalists have been murdered in recent years, impunity and the states of emergency in 1995 ensured that reporters continued to work in a climate of intimidation.

The new constitution expanded religious freedom by ending the privileges of the Catholic church, which had long enjoyed the advantages of an official religion.

Comoros

Polity: Dominant party **Political Rights:** 4
Economy: Capitalist **Civil Liberties:** 4
Population: 549,000 **Status:** Partly Free
PPP: $1,350
Life Expectancy: 56.0
Ethnic Groups: Majority of mixed African-Arab descent,
East Indian minority
Capital: Moroni

Overview: **A** failed coup attempt orchestrated with the assistance of foreign
mercenaries resulted in the ousting of President Mohamad Said
Djohar and the formation of a new unity government by former
prime minister and self-declared president Caabi El Yachourtou. Late in October the
National Reconciliation Conference, which includes all major political parties, decided
Yachourtou should remain in power until elections scheduled for March 1996.

The Federal Islamic Republic of Comoros, a tiny three-island Indian Ocean
archipelago formerly governed by France, gained independence in 1975 with the
exception of Mayotte island, which opted to remain under French administration.
Having been overthrown after serving only briefly, Comoros' first president,
Ahmed Abdallah Abderrahman, reclaimed power in 1978 with the help of Col. Bob
Denard, a French mercenary. Abdallah stood for election unopposed in 1978 and
1984, with Denard supporting his one-party regime as head of the army and
presidential guard. Abdallah was assassinated in 1989, allegedly by his own troops
on the orders of Col. Denard. After succeeding Abdallah on an interim basis,
Supreme Court Justice Djohar won a six-year term as president the following year
in the country's first contested, though fraudulent, elections since independence.
Denard and his mercenaries were deported to South Africa and his presidential
guard was replaced with a contingent of French paratroopers.

On 28 September 1995, rebels stormed the presidential palace, seized the state
radio station and freed all prisoners at Moroni jail, including former army officers
implicated in a failed 1992 coup attempt. Coup leader Captain Ayouba Combo
claimed the rebels' mission was to ensure public order until free elections could be
organized, and charged the president and "his corrupt entourage" with jeopardizing
the conditions for democracy. Citing an article of the constitution allowing the
premier to exercise presidential powers in case of the head of state's absence or
temporary inability to carry out his functions, Prime Minister Yachourtou declared
himself interim president from his refuge at the French embassy at Moroni. Six days
after the coup began, French troops stormed the island. Having secured amnesty for
the rebels, Denard and his mercenaries surrendered, released the president and left
the island. After his release, President Djohar was flown to Reunion Island to
receive medical attention and has remained there under de facto house arrest while
accusations of corruption pile up against his former government. Yachourtou and
his new unity government have in effect banned Djohar from returning to
Comoros, saying his return might ignite further political and civil unrest.

Political Rights and Civil Liberties: Comorans have a theoretical right to change their government democratically, but electoral fraud and irregularities, constant coup attempts and elite intrigues are what has changed the government in practice. Numerous political parties exist, but in the past President Djohar attempted to restrict them with imprisonment and alleged gerrymandering. In November, acting head of state Yachourtou formed a fifteen-member government of national unity that included ministers from both the Comoros Union for Progress (UDZIMA) and Comoros National Union for Democracy, two parties that openly supported the coup. In an apparent indication of a changing political climate, justice minister Sali Hassan ordered an investigation into a financial scandal in which the president and the speaker of the National Assembly were allegedly involved.

The legal system is based on both Islamic law and remnants of the French legal code. The judiciary is largely independent and headed by a Supreme Court. Most disputes are settled by village elders or by a civilian court of first instance.

With the exception of security measures imposed in the context of coup attempts, free expression is generally permitted. There are two weekly newspapers, one state-owned and one independent. The government operates *Radio-Comores* and news bulletins are available via satellite from *Radio France Internationale*.

The government occasionally bans assemblies. Frequent civilian riots and army mutinies have left civilian-military relations strained and protection from political terror inconsistent. Trade unions and strikes are permitted, but collective bargaining is weak. Although Islam is the state religion, other religions may practice without proselytizing. Despite the influence of Islamic law, women are denied neither political nor property rights.

The population is among the poorest and the fastest growing in the world. With only 10 percent of the population engaged in salaried work, economic opportunity remains quite limited. The government is highly dependent on foreign aid for its administrative and development costs and to lower its trade deficit.

↑ Congo

Polity: Presidential-parliamentary democracy
Economy: Mixed statist
Population: 2,505,000
PPP: $2,870
Life Expectancy: 51.3
Ethnic Groups: Kongo (48 percent), Sangha (20 percent), Teke (17 percent), others
Capital: Brazzaville

Political Rights: 4
Civil Liberties: 4
Status: Partly Free

Trend Arrow: Congo's up trend arrow is due to signs of waning violence and increased political pluralism.

Overview: In 1995 efforts proceeded to integrate into the national army various party militias that had battled in the capital, Brazzaville, in late 1993 and early 1994. There also was intense political maneuvering among several regional/ethnic-based parties that make up the ruling and opposition coalitions. In a major political gamble, President Pascal Lissouba imposed an austerity budget and privatization program with deep job cuts in order to increase foreign investment and international loans.

A 1970 coup established a socialist state in Congo a decade after its independence from France. In 1979, General Denis Sassou-Nguesso seized power and maintained one-party rule as head of the Congolese Workers' Party (PCT) until domestic and international pressure forced a transition to multipartyism and open elections in 1992. Pascal Lissouba of the Pan-African Union for Social Democracy (Upads) won a clear victory in the second round of presidential voting. Legislative elections produced no clear majority, and after an anti-Lissouba coalition formed, the president dissolved the assembly and called new elections. The 1993 polls were marked by numerous irregularities, and several parties boycotted the second round. By the end of 1993, serious violence among militias recruited from ethnic-based political parties—with such names as Ninjas, Zulus and Cobra—wracked the capital. A January 1994 peace accord helped reduce tensions by providing for a new degree of power-sharing and decentralization. Lawlessness declined through 1995, and the government asserted increased control over both militias and the national army, which has long been dominated by Sassou-Nguesso loyalists. In November, troops were deployed throughout the capital after almost eighty army and police officers were purged, but no violence was reported.

Economic reforms have cost the government some support and provoked labor unrest. There are also reports that poor security at Brazzaville airport and along the Zairian frontier are allowing large amounts of drugs to transit the Congo.

Political Rights and Civil Liberties:

Congolese have the constitutional right to elect their president and National Assembly deputies to five-year terms of office through competitive multiparty elections. Local councils elect members of the less important Senate to six-year terms. Although President Lissouba's 1992 victory was widely considered free and fair, 1993 legislative elections were disputed by the opposition. An international commission rejected most of these claims, but armed clashes and intense political infighting quieted only after negotiations that produced a power-sharing arrangement. Congolese politics are marked by shifting alliances of ethnic-based parties; while Lissouba has sought balance by including members of different groups in his cabinet, those of his own ethnicity hold the most important posts. The 1997 presidential and 1998 legislative contests will measure the multiparty system's maturity.

Numerous independent newspapers are published and circulate freely in Brazzaville. State-run media have shown increasing autonomy in recent years, including allowing some access to the opposition. However, the government tightened its control over the state-monopoly broadcast media in 1995, and some print journalists were briefly jailed on defamation charges. A new press law passed in August provides stronger penalties for defamation of senior officials. It also requires media to "show loyalty to the government" and permits seizure of private printing works during emergencies.

Freedom of assembly and association are constitutionally guaranteed, but the Interior Ministry must approve public gatherings and occasionally denies permission. Religious freedom is respected in law and practice. Many nongovernmental organizations operate freely, including several human rights groups that publish reports highly critical of official practices and/or societal discrimination.

The formal judiciary consists of a three-tier system including local courts, courts of appeal and a Supreme Court, and is generally considered politically independent. However, understaffing and a lack of resources produce a backlog of cases often resulting in long periods of pretrial detention. Outside the cities, traditional courts retain broad jurisdiction, especially in civil matters.

Discrimination against women is extensive despite constitutional protections. Limited access to education and employment opportunities, especially in the countryside, are de facto forms of societal discrimination, while civil codes regarding family and marriage formalize women's inferior status. Violence against women is a commonplace but little-discussed occurrence.

Workers' rights to join trade unions and to strike are legally protected, and there are a half dozen labor confederations with various linkages to the government or political parties. Unions are legally required to accept nonbinding arbitration before striking, but many strikes have gone forward without respecting this process.

The government's ambitious privatization plan is increasing both foreign investment and local business opportunities. Civil service positions and jobs in state enterprises have been slashed in the process, however, in a political gamble by Lissouba that the pain of structural adjustment will be erased by economic growth before his expected 1997 re-election bid.

Costa Rica

Polity: Presidential-
legislative democracy
Economy: Capitalist-
statist
Population: 3,347,000
PPP: $5,480
Life Expectancy: 76.3
Ethnic Groups: Spanish, large mestizo minority
Capital: San Jose

Political Rights: 1
Civil Liberties: 2
Status: Free

Overview:
Economic belt-tightening led to a political backlash and mass anti-government demonstrations during President Jose Maria Figueres's second year in office.

The Republic of Costa Rica achieved independence from Spain in 1821 and became a republic in 1848. Democratic government was instituted in 1899 and briefly interrupted in 1917 and 1948. The 1949 constitution, which bans the formation of a national army, provides the framework for democratic governance.

The constitution provides for three independent branches of government—executive, legislative and judicial. The president and the fifty-seven-member Legislative Assembly are elected for four years and are prohibited from succeeding themselves. The Assembly has co-equal power, including the ability to override presidential vetoes.

Figueres's party, the social democratic National Liberation Party (PLN), has held power for eighteen of the last twenty-six years. In the 1994 elections, Figueres defeated Miguel Angel Rodriguez of the Social Christian Unity Party (PUSC), the country's other principal political organization.

The forty-five-year-old Figueres, son of former President Jose "Pepe" Figueres, a national hero for leading the fight to preserve democracy in the 1948 civil war, campaigned against the neoliberal economic policies of outgoing President Rafael A. Calderon, Jr. of the PUSC. Rodriguez proposed to deepen structural reforms. The campaign was marked mostly by acrimonious personal attacks.

Figueres won with 49.7 percent of the vote, 2.2 points ahead of Rodriguez. The PLN won twenty-eight seats in the Assembly, one short of a majority, and the PUSC twenty-five. A handful of small parties divided the remaining four seats.

In 1995 PLN supporters felt betrayed when Figueres reversed his campaign pledge and pushed through a structural adjustment package to secure international loans. The measure, which Figueres claimed was necessary in the face of a gaping budget deficit, prompted a teachers' strike in midyear that led to the largest protests in nearly five decades. But Figueres seemed determined to keep whittling away at the generous welfare state his father had helped create.

Political Rights and Civil Liberties:

Citizens are able to change their government through free and fair elections. The political landscape is dominated by the PLN and the PUSC, but numerous other parties run candidates in elections.

Allegations implicating both major parties in drug-tainted campaign contributions have been made during recent elections. New campaign laws have been instituted to make party financing more transparent. But Costa Rica, with no army, navy, or air force, remains an easy target for drug traffickers, and there is great concern about increasing drug-related corruption and money laundering.

Constitutional guarantees regarding freedom of religion and the right to organize political parties and civic organizations are respected. However, in recent years there has been a reluctance to address restrictions on labor rights.

Solidarity, an employer-employee organization that private business uses as an instrument to prevent independent unions from organizing, remains strong and has generally been tolerated by successive governments. Solidarity organizations are entrenched in Costa Rica's free-trade zones, where labor abuses by multinational corporations are prevalent. Minimum wage and social security laws are often ignored and fines for noncompliance are minuscule. Women workers are often sexually harassed, made to work overtime without pay and fired when they become pregnant.

The judicial branch is independent, its members elected by the legislature. There is a Supreme Court with power to rule on the constitutionality of laws, as well as four courts of appeal and a network of district courts. The members of the independent national election commission are elected by the Supreme Court.

The judicial system is marked by delays, creating a volatile situation in overcrowded, violence-prone prisons. The problem is linked to budget cuts affecting the judiciary and to the nation's economic difficulties, which have led to a rise in violent crime and clashes in the countryside between squatters and landowners.

There continue to be numerous charges of human rights violations by police. Independent Costa Rican rights monitors report increases in allegations of arbitrary arrests and brutality, and there have been a few reports of torture in secret jails.

An official ombudsman provides recourse for citizens or foreigners with human rights complaints. The ombudsman has the authority to issue recommendations for rectification, including sanctions against government bodies, for failure to respect rights.

The press, radio and television are generally free. There are a number of independent dailies serving a society that is 90 percent literate. Television and radio stations are both public and commercial, with at least six private television stations providing an influential forum for public debate. In 1995 the Supreme Court ruled that a decades-old law requiring the licensing of journalists was unconstitutional. However, inordinately restrictive libel laws remain in place.

⬇ Côte D'Ivoire

Polity: Dominant Party **Political Rights:** 6
Economy: Capitalist **Civil Liberties:** 5
Population: 14,253,000 **Status:** Not Free
PPP: $1,710
Life Expectancy: 51.0
Ethnic Groups: Baule (23 percent), Bete (18 percent),
Senoufou (15 percent), Malinke (11 percent), others
Capital: Yamoussoukro (official); Abidjan (de facto)
Trend Arrow: Côte D'Ivoire's down trend arrow is due to blatantly
fraudulent elections and increased ethnic violence.

Overview: Henri Konan Bedie was declared president of Côte d'Ivoire with 95 percent of the vote in an October victory so thoroughly devalued by government manipulation that it was meaningless as a measure of the popular will. The gravely flawed election barred the most viable challenger, Alassane Dramane Ouattara, from candidacy and was boycotted by the major opposition parties. It also raised religious tensions and sparked the first large-scale ethnic violence in the country in many years, leaving at least twenty-three dead. National Assembly elections in November produced another big victory for Bedie. His ruling Democratic Party of the Ivory Coast-African Democratic Rally (PDCI-RDA) took 147 of 175 National Assembly seats in elections conducted in relative calm but marred by irregularities involving voter lists and bans on opposition demonstrations.

Many observers believe Bedie could have won both sets of elections fairly, built a stronger base for democracy in the country and enhanced his personal stature. His unwillingness to risk such a course reflects both his country's authoritarian history and the strong backing he received from France as he prepared the mock-elections. Felix Houphouet-Boigny was the country's undisputed ruler from independence until his death in 1993. During most of this time he made a show of popular participation through the only legal party, the PDCI. In 1990 domestic unrest combined with Africa-wide and then French-supported demands for democratization, and multipartyism was legalized. The first multiparty presidential and legislative elections in 1990-91 were no-contests that maintained the status quo. Only after Houphouet-Boigny's death and Bedie's appointment to complete his term did a real political opening seem possible.

This year's elections have dashed those hopes, at least temporarily. Bedie's government has sought to muzzle the media and restrict public debate. He has also received formidable international backing. As security forces fired on demonstrators protesting the one-sided presidential election, the visiting French Minister for Cooperation, Jacques Godfrain, said: "France will be by your side, Mr. President, for the long period that lies ahead of you."

Political Rights and Civil Liberties: The right of Ivorians to change their government was not honored in the 1995 presidential and legislative elections. The presidential poll was manifestly unfair. The leading potential opposition candidate, Alassane Ouattara, was prohibited from running by a new electoral code tailored to exclude him by demanding that both parents of a candidate be born within the country's borders. The vote-count was accurate according to some international observers, but a ban on demonstrations and intimidation of the media prevented the creation of the "level playing field" necessary for a fair election. Irregularities in voter lists added to opposition handicaps in the legislative elections.

The electoral manipulation kept most power in the hands of politicians from the country's south and east, fanning ethnic unrest. Ouattara's exclusion could also become a serious grievance for the 40 percent of Ivorians who share his Muslim faith.

Increasing intolerance of free media marked the 1995 campaigns. Several journalists were fined and sentenced to prison on various charges. Crimes including "insulting the president," "threatening public order" or "defaming or undermining the reputation of the state" are loosely defined prohibitions interpreted by the regime to silence unwanted criticism. State broadcasting services are unabashedly pro-government, and state-owned newspapers only slightly less so. Still, a vigorous private press sought to fulfill its role as watchdog and advocate, but at increasing risk. In June, Security Minister Gaston Ouassenan Kone called Abou Drahamane Sangare, a politician and publisher of an opposition newspaper, to his office, where Sangare was stripped and beaten by policemen.

There are forty-three registered political parties and perhaps an equal number of unrecognized parties. Their ability to organize was limited by a three-month ban on demonstrations imposed on 20 September that followed rallies violently dispersed by security forces. The government requires all private associations to register, although it is unclear whether this is constitutional or has simply been used to ban groups. Several rights organizations are active, notable among them the Ivorian Human Rights League. While there is no systematic or official discrimination, Muslims complain of bias. Two journalists who reported on the sensitive issue of Muslim grievances were sentenced to one year's imprisonment in March.

The judiciary is not independent. Judges are political appointees without assured tenure and thus highly susceptible to external interference. Legal provisions regarding search warrants, rules of evidence and pretrial detention are often ignored. Traditional courts still prevail in many rural areas, especially in handling minor matters and family law.

Prison conditions are reportedly extremely harsh, and only ameliorated for prisoners with money to buy special treatment. The death rate from disease, aggravated by a poor diet and inadequate or nonexistent medical attention, is high.

Protection of women's rights is constitutionally enshrined and officially encouraged, but societal discrimination is prevalent. Equal pay for equal work is the standard in the small formal sector, but women's chances of obtaining or advancing in wage employment are limited. Education and job opportunities for women are scarcer in rural areas relying on subsistence agriculture.

Trade unions are permitted, but were for three decades dominated by the government-controlled the General Union of Workers of Côte d'Ivoire (UGTCI). The Federation of Autonomous Trade Unions of Côte d'Ivoire (FESCACI) represents several independent unions formed since 1991. The right to strike exists, but only after notification and conciliation requirements. Collective bargaining agreements are often reached with the participation of government negotiators who influence wage settlements. Plans for privatizing many Ivorian state corporations have been announced in hopes of attracting renewed foreign investment and international loans, but business opportunities often come from political connections rather than financial acumen.

↑ Croatia

Polity: Presidential-parliamentary democracy
Economy: Mixed statist
Population: 4,495,000
PPP: na
Life Expectancy: 70.0
Ethnic Groups: Pre-1995: Croat (77 percent), Serb (12 percent), Muslim (1 percent), Hungarian, Slovene, Czech, Albanian, Montenegrin, Ukrainian, others
Capital: Zagreb
Trend Arrow: The reunification of Croatian land (Krajina, Western and Eastern Slavonia) and the Dayton Accords were positive developments, though political problems remain.

Political Rights: 4
Civil Liberties: 4
Status: Partly Free

Overview: In 1995, Croatian forces recaptured the Serb-controlled Krajina region, boosting President Franjo Tudjman's ruling Croatian Democratic Union (HDZ) to a strong victory in parliamentary elections. Tudjman also was a signatory of the U.S.-brokered Dayton Accords, which ended forty-four months of war in Bosnia.

Hungary ruled most of what is Croatia from the 1100s until after World War I. In 1918, it became part of the Kingdom of Serbs, Croats and Slovenes, renamed Yugoslavia in 1929. A short-lived independent state was proclaimed in 1941 by the pro-fascist *Ustasa* movement. In 1945, Croatia joined the People's Republic of Yugoslavia under Communist leader Josip Broz (Tito). On 25 June 1991, Croatia and Slovenia declared independence. The Serb-dominated Yugoslav People's Army and Serb militias seized parts of Croatia, ultimately controlling one-third of the country and establishing the Krajina Serbian Republic (RSK). In December, all sides agreed to the deployment of U.N. peacekeepers. Croatia accused the 12,000-strong U.N. force of failing to disarm Serb paramilitary forces, confiscate heavy weapons, and repatriate refugees. In 1993-94, Croatia supported the Croatian Defense Council in Bosnia in a war with Muslims. But in March 1994, President Tudjman endorsed a Washington-engineered peace accord signed by Bosnia's Muslims and Croats, leading to the formation of a federated entity in loose confederation with Croatia.

After negotiations broke down, 1995 opened with threats of renewed fighting in Krajina. Tudjman threatened not to renew the U.N. mandate when it expired 31 March. However, on 12 March he allowed a reduced force to remain.

Croat forces launched a May-June campaign to recapture Western Slavonia, and in August Croatian forces took three days to rout Serbs from Krajina. Hundreds of thousands of Serbs fled the Croatian assault, and there were verifiable reports of Croat abuses against Serbs, including burning homes and executing civilians. After a September campaign by Bosnian Croat and Muslim forces recaptured 20 percent Serb-held Bosnia, a ceasefire took effect on 12 October prior to November negotiations in Dayton.

Elections to the 138-member House of Representatives, the lower house of parliament, were held on 29 October after parliament dissolved itself on 20 September. Critics charged that the plan to reapportion seats before parliament's term ended in 1996 unfairly favored the HDZ, which already held an overwhelming majority. Authorities argued parliament's dissolution was necessary to provide representation to recaptured lands. International observers criticized the government for allowing 300,000 Bosnian Croats to vote. The decision also raised questions about the Bosnian Muslim-Croat federation, a key element in the peace process.

The HDZ won 44.8 percent of the vote. The joint list of the Croatian Peasants' Party, Istrian Democratic Assembly, Croatian People's Party, Christian Democratic Union, and Croatian Party of Slavonia and Baranja won 18.2 percent. The opposition Croatian Social-Liberal Party won 11.5 percent and the Social Democratic Party of Croatia 8.9 percent. On 4 November, Tudjman appointed Zlatko Matesa prime minister, replacing Nikica Valentic.

During the Dayton negotiations, Tudjman won Serb agreement to return eastern Slavonia, but was criticized for promoting an officer charged with war crimes by an international tribunal.

Political Rights and Civil Liberties: Citizens can change their government democratically, but a constitutionally strong presidency has led to charges of authoritarianism. Critical decisions are made by the National Security Council, whose sixteen members are presidential supporters.

Irregularities in the 1995 parliamentary elections included lack of guarantees for secret balloting. Candidates in some districts were declared winners based on incomplete results, and the opposition petitioned to nullify results in several districts. Changes in the election law gave more seats to the Croatian diaspora at the Serb minority's expense. Each party was allowed just one hour of free time on state-owned television, and could not criticize the HDZ—a restriction on freedom of expression.

While several political parties exist, the HDZ has become dominant due to the election law and to intimidation. The government maintains strict control of radio and television, effectively denying the opposition equal access. Its ownership interest in print media and near monopoly of the distribution system limit media independence. On 22 March, parliament canceled live coverage of its proceedings after opposition members criticized the speaker. Economic measures have pressured the opposition press. In March, the Constitutional Court exempted the satirical weekly *Feral Tribune* from the 50 percent tax levied on pornographic publications, imposed in 1994. The tax had forced the paper, which regularly criticizes and satirizes Tudjman, to the brink of bankruptcy. Tudjman has arranged for friendly banks to buy out independent papers, then dismiss independent-minded editors.

Religious freedom is nominally assured but during Orthodox Serb control of Krajina and Western Slavonia, Roman Catholic Croats were expelled or persecuted and churches destroyed. When the Croats returned, hundreds of thousands of Serbs fled.

The judiciary is not wholly free from government interference. The power of judicial appointments and dismissals is firmly in the hands of an influential parliamentary committee dominated by a hardline HDZ faction. Minority rights have been trampled. In retaking Krajina, Croats massacred civilians and left others, mainly the elderly, to freeze or starve. Laws also threatened Italian schools and cultural institutions in Istria, home to 30,000 ethnic Italians.

There are several independent union federations, among them the Croatian Unified Trade Union, the Coordinating Committee of Croatian White-Collar Trade Unions and a coalition patched together from the Federation of Independent Trade Unions of Croatia and the Union of Trade Unions of Public Employees. Private business and nongovernmental organizations are allowed to function. Women are guaranteed equal rights under the law and women are involved in politics, government and business.

Cuba

Polity: Communist
one-party
Economy: Statist
Population: 11,168,000
PPP: $3,412
Life Expectancy: 75.3
Ethnic Groups: Creole (51 percent), European (37 percent),
black (11 percent)
Capital: Havana

Political Rights: 7
Civil Liberties: 7
Status: Not Free

Overview: Fidel Castro traveled to Beijing, Tokyo and Wall Street in a less-than-successful effort to secure investments needed to refinance the Cuban police state.

Cuba achieved independence from Spain in 1898 as a result of the Spanish-American War. The Republic of Cuba was established in 1902, remaining subject to U.S. tutelage under the Platt Amendment until 1934. In 1959 Castro's guerrillas overthrew the dictatorship of Fulgencio Batista, who had ruled for eighteen of the previous twenty-five years.

Since then Castro has dominated the Cuban political system, transforming it into a one-party Communist state. Communist structures were institutionalized by the 1976 constitution installed at the first congress of the Cuban Communist Party (PCC). The constitution provides for a National Assembly which, in theory, designates a Council of State which, in turn, appoints a Council of Ministers in consultation with its president, who serves as head of state and chief of government.

In reality, Castro is responsible for every appointment. As president of the Council of Ministers, chairman of the Council of State, commander-in-chief of the Revolutionary Armed Forces (FAR) and first secretary of the PCC, Castro controls every lever of power in Cuba. The PCC is the only authorized political party and it controls all governmental entities from the national to the municipal level.

Since the collapse of the Soviet Union, Castro has desperately sought Western foreign investment. With the U.S. embargo still in place, most investment has come from Europe and Latin America, but it has been a mere fraction of the former $5 billion in annual Soviet subsidies. The government claimed a return to economic growth in 1995, but Cuba officially remained in a "special period," meaning a drastic austerity program involving severe cutbacks in energy consumption and tight rationing of food and consumer items.

Castro continued to state in 1995 that he would not retreat from one-party rule. Economic reforms, including the legalization of the dollar, since 1993 indicate he has opted for the market Leninism of China. On his trip to Beijing in 1995 he voiced his approval of the Chinese model.

Dollarization has heightened social tensions as the minority with access to dollars from abroad or through the tourist industry have emerged as a new moneyed class, and the majority without have become increasingly desperate as state-paid salaries dwindled to four dollars or less per month.

Since Castro began making economic reforms that threaten to unleash social forces he might not be able to control, cycles of repression have become more frequent. Nonetheless, independent rights activists, who in late 1995 united to form the Concilio Cubano (Cuban Council), and independent journalists and economists continued to defy arrests, attacks and confiscations in a valiant attempt to establish the seeds of a civil opposition.

Political Rights and Civil Liberties: Cubans are unable to change their government through democratic means. All political and civic organization outside the PCC is illegal. Political dissent, spoken or written, is a punishable offense.

With the possible exceptions of South Africa, Indonesia and China, Cuba under Castro has had more political prisoners per capita for longer periods than any other country. In 1995 there were an estimated 600-plus political prisoners, most locked in with common criminals, about half convicted on vague charges of "disseminating enemy propaganda" or "dangerousness." In 1995 a number of high-profile political prisoners were released in an effort to gain greater economic cooperation with the European Union.

Since 1991, the U.N. has voted annually to assign a special investigator on human rights in Cuba, but the Cuban government has refused to cooperate.

Although there has been a slight thaw in cultural life, the educational system, the judicial system, labor unions, professional organizations and all media remain state-controlled. Outside of the Catholic church, whose scope remains limited by the government, and small, courageous groups of rights activists and dissident journalists, there is little semblance of independent civil society.

Those groups struggling to exist apart from the state are labeled "counterrevolutionary criminals" and remain subject to cyclical and systematic repression, including arrests, beatings while in custody, confiscations and intimidation by uniformed or plainclothes state security. Members of four small labor groups that have tried to organize independently remain subject to blacklisting and arbitrary arrest.

There is continued evidence of torture and killings in prisons and in psychiatric institutions, where a number of dissidents arrested in recent years have been incarcerated. Since 1990 the International Committee of the Red Cross has been denied access to prisoners. According to Cuban rights activists, more than one hundred prisons and prison camps hold between 60,000 and 100,000 prisoners of all categories. In 1993 vandalism was decreed to be a form of sabotage, punishable by eight years in prison.

Freedom of movement and freedom to choose one's residence, education or job are restricted. Attempting to leave the island without permission is a punishable offense.

Official discrimination against religious believers was lifted by constitutional revision in 1992. The measure was welcomed by the Catholic Church, which has seen an increase in membership in recent years.

As has been evident during the trials of human rights activists and other dissidents, due process is alien to the Cuban judicial system. The job of defense attorneys registered by the courts is to guide defendants in their confessions.

The government has continued restricting the ability of foreign media to operate in Cuba. Journalist visas are required, and reporters whom the government considers hostile are not allowed entry.

Cyprus (Greek)

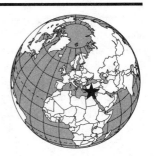

Polity: Presidential- **Political Rights:** 1
legislative democracy **Civil Liberties:** 1
Economy: Capitalist **Status:** Free
Population: Entire island: 805,000 Greeks: 602,000
PPP: $15,050 (sector not specified)
Life Expectancy: 77.0 (sector not specified)
Ethnic Groups: Greek majority, Turkish minority, and
small Maronite, Armenian, and Latin communities
Capital: Nicosia

Overview: One month after vetoing European Union (EU) aid to Turkey and Turkey's inclusion in an EU customs union, Greece reversed its stance in return for securing entry into the EU for both parts of Cyprus by the year 2000. Turkey agreed in turn not to sabotage the reunification of the island should that occur, nor bar its entry into the EU. In May the British foreign office reported that delegates from both Greek and Turkish Cyprus had entered into secret talks in London sponsored by the United States and Britain. Although no details were released the talks may represent a step forward, as Turkish Cypriot leader Rauf Denktash previously had won three elections on a nationalist platform, and Greek Cypriots had consistently refused to negotiate with his "illegitimate" government.

Since gaining its independence from Britain in 1960, Cyprus has been plagued by tensions and intermittent violence between the Greek and Turkish populations. The U.N. established a 2,000-member peacekeeping force on the island after the outbreak of civil war in 1963. Following an unsuccessful 1974 coup attempt aimed at unifying the island with Greece, Turkey invaded the northern portion, installed 35,000 troops and displaced approximately 200,000 Greek Cypriots, who were forced to settle in the South. For the twenty-one years since, a buffer zone called the "Green Line" has partitioned the island. The capital, Nicosia, remains the world's only divided city. In 1983 Turkish Cyprus made a unilateral declaration of independence that was subsequently condemned by the U.N. and remains unrecognized internationally with the exception of Turkey.

The U.N. and officials on both sides of the Green Line agree it would take very little to re-ignite the conflict. Younger Cypriots remain quite unfamiliar to their island neighbors, apart from propaganda in schools and the media and the obvious economic differences between the prosperous South and stagnating North. Greek Cypriot President Clerides has said, "For over twenty years, our young men have been trained in the art of war...They are trained not to fight an external foe, but an internal enemy. This has had a devastating effect on the younger generation."

Although the last serious clash took place over two years ago, Cyprus remains one of the most heavily militarized places in the world.

Political Rights and Civil Liberties: Greek Cypriots can change their government democratically. Suffrage is universal and compulsory, and elections are free and fair. An ethnically representative system designed to protect the interests of both Greek and Turkish Cypriots was provided by the 1960 constitution. Under that system, a Greek president and a Turkish vice-president would name a balanced cabinet, and a unicameral legislative body of thirty-five Greek and fifteen Turkish members would be elected by their respective communities. After the Turkish Cypriot withdrawal from the government in 1963, adaptations were made including amendment of the electoral law and changes in the judicial structure.

The independent judiciary operates according to the tradition of the British legal system, upholding the presumption of innocence and the right to due process. Trial before a judge is standard, although requests for trial by jury are regularly granted.

Freedom of speech is respected and a vibrant independent press frequently criticizes authorities. In addition to those owned by the government, several independently owned radio stations have been allowed to operate since 1990. The first independent television station began operating in 1992, followed more recently by international cable stations.

Freedom of assembly and association and the right to strike are all respected. More than 90 percent of the labor force is unionized. High economic growth rates and a shortage of labor pushed the government to relax regulations on the issuance of work permits to foreigners, who often work at lower wage levels than the domestic labor force. Although women are legally entitled to equal pay for equal work, many women's rights groups argue that they are overrepresented in lower-income-level jobs.

Greek Cypriots enjoy freedom of movement with the exception of travel to the North, which is discouraged when the traveler must fill out an entry card with the Turkish Republic of Northern Cyprus inscription. Freedom of worship is respected. The Greek Orthodox Church has the character of a state institution, with all of its property and activities tax exempt. Although the church wields considerable influence in public policy, it does not inhibit other religious groups from operating freely.

Czech Republic

Polity: Parliamentary democracy
Economy: Mixed capitalist
Population: 10,357,000
PPP: 7,690
Life Expectancy: 71.3
Ethnic Groups: Czech (94 percent), Slovak (3 percent), Roma (2 percent)
Capital: Prague

Political Rights: 1
Civil Liberties: 2
Status: Free

Overview: In 1995, Premier Vaclav Klaus's government continued fine-tuning the market reforms that have given the Czech Republic the strongest economy in East-Central Europe. In November, it became the first post-Communist country to be admitted to the Organization for Economic Cooperation and Development.

Economic measures taken in 1995 included abolishing wage regulations, making the koruna fully convertible, changing bankruptcy laws to expedite liquidation proceedings, and tightening conflict-of-interest laws. Low inflation, little foreign debt, a 3 percent growth in output, 3 percent unemployment and record hard currency reserves contributed to political stability and relative prosperity.

The Czech Republic emerged in 1993 after the peaceful dissolution of Czechoslovakia, which had been created in 1918 after the Austro-Hungarian empire's collapse. Former dissident playwright and Czechoslovak president Vaclav Havel was elected Czech President in January 1993. Premier Klaus and his aggressively pro-market Civic Democratic Party (ODS) led a four-party coalition that had won control of the Czech parliament in 1992.

While the ODS continued to lead in opinion surveys throughout 1995, the Social Democrats, which held some twenty-one seats in the 200-member parliament, gained support partly because of growing opposition to foreign involvement in privatization, particularly in telecommunications, oil and other strategic areas. The controversy arose after the 1 March end of a second round of voucher privatization, which allowed citizens to purchase inexpensive vouchers representing shares of state assets. The government moved to sell a foreign company a stake in the state telephone company, excluding Czech companies from bidding. Opposition also grew to ceding control of the oil refining industry to foreign investors. The prospect of revaluation of the koruna and the new bankruptcy laws also raised fears of unemployment. There was also growing concern regarding rising crime rates and organized crime, particularly from Russia.

In September 1995 legislators approved the establishment of a constitutionally mandated Senate. Elections are to take place in eighty-one electoral districts in a two-round majority system. Parties may nominate candidates, but independents must gather at least 1,000 signatures. At the outset, one-third each of the senators will be elected for two, four and six years. Havel opposed holding the elections concurrent with next year's parliamentary vote sometime in June. By late November, leaders of the four parties in the governing coalition failed to agree on a date for Senate elections.

In September, parliament extended the "lustration laws," which ban former police agents and high-level Communist officials from office, to the year 2000. Havel vetoed the bill, arguing that an extension was premature since the law did not expire until the end of 1996. Parliament overrode the veto on 18 October.

In late July, five former Czechoslovak Communist Party (KSC) leaders were charged with treason over the 1968 Warsaw Pact invasion of Czechoslovakia, including former KSC general-secretary, Milos Jakes.

In December, parliament agreed to send a Czech military unit to join the NATO peace implementation force in Bosnia.

Political Rights and Civil Liberties: Czech Republic citizens can change their government democratically. Over fifty political parties exist. In December, the extra-parliamentary Free Democrats merged with the Liberal National Social Party, which has five seats in parliament.

There are scores of independent newspapers, an independent news agency, and private local and national radio stations. The national broadcaster NOVA, run by CET 21, is private. In 1995, Premiera, a local television station financed largely by Italian interests, joined NOVA. In December, an American investor bought 15 percent of Premiera. On 18 October, the government approved a controversial draft press law that would deprive journalists of the right to protect sources.

Though free public discussion is allowed, a man was sentenced in March to four months in jail (suspended) after being found guilty of defaming Havel.

Religious freedom is respected, and there is no official church. Restitution of Roman Catholic Church property nationalized by the Communists, including a church in Prague Castle—a series of buildings that house government—remained largely unresolved.

The constitutional definition of judicial power corresponds to the European concept of a state based on the rule of law. There is a lack of fully qualified lawyers in public administration. The lustration laws, extended to the year 2000 by parliament, remain controversial. Although ethnic and minority rights are protected under law, there have been problems, particularly for the Roma (Gypsy) population, who number anywhere from 150,000-300,000, many of them from Slovakia. They have faced discrimination in housing, education, employment and public services, and violence at the hands of skinheads. There were several attacks in 1995, including one in October that sent three girls to the hospital. In one locality, Roma were banned from a public swimming pool after being told they presented a health hazard. In November, the extreme right-wing Assembly for the Republic-Czechoslovak Republican Party called the Roma "black racists who are acting as parasites," and called for a law banning non-Czech "parasites." In June, the Constitutional Court overturned local and district court decisions refusing a Sudeten German the right to reclaim his family's house (some 2.5 million Sudeten Germans were expelled between 1945 and 1947).

Workers exercise freely the right to organize and join trade unions, the major one being the CKOS (the Czech Confederation of Trade Unions). Unions work closely with government and business on such issues as wages, prices and rent controls. In 1995, both teachers and doctors held job actions protesting inadequate wages.

There are several women's organizations, and there are no legal obstacles based on gender. Women have held key government and public posts. Political parties, professional organizations, cultural groups and other nongovernmental organizations can organize freely. In September, parliament approved a law to encourage the development of nonprofit organizations in social services, sports, culture, health care and education.

Denmark

Polity: Parliamentary democracy
Economy: Mixed capitalist
Population: 5,210,000
PPP: $19,080
Life Expectancy: 75.3
Ethnic Groups: Overwhelmingly Danish, small German and immigrant groups
Capital: Copenhagen

Political Rights: 1
Civil Liberties: 1
Status: Free

Overview:

Tensions heightened during 1995 in the already strained relations between Denmark and its primarily self-governing territory the Faeroe Islands over an island banking crisis, in which mainland institutions played an unclear role. Denmark's Social Democratic minority government had economic worries of its own, with unemployment at about 10 percent and anticipated financial penalties from the referendum decision to opt out of European Monetary Union (EMU) participation. A national distraction came in November with the first royal wedding since 1967, as Prince Joachim, second in line for the throne, married Alexandra Manley, an economist from Hong Kong.

As the oldest monarchy in Europe, with a constitution dating from 1849 and a unicameral parliament established in 1953, Denmark has a long history as a model of political democracy. Due to the country's multiparty system, single parties rarely secure more than a plurality of the popular vote, and most post-War governments have been minority governments or coalitions.

Though executive power is nominally vested in the monarch, it is in actuality exercised by a cabinet responsible to the *Folketing* (parliament). In addition to two representatives from both of the autonomous regions, the Faeroe Islands and Greenland, 135 of the 179 Folketing members are elected in seventeen mainland districts. The remaining seats are allocated on a proportional basis to parties receiving over 2 percent of the vote. An extensive system of local representation includes both regional and local councils, with mayors presiding over each.

Prime Minister Poul Nyrup Rasmussen's center-left governing coalition slipped into the minority in September 1994 legislative elections. Since assuming power the previous year, Rasmussen's government has pursued EMU-tailored economic policies in an effort to minimize the financial impact of opting out of formal EMU participation. Voters rejected the Maastricht Treaty in a 1992 referendum, forcing negotiations with the European Union (EU) to allow Denmark to opt out of certain key provisions, including joining EMU. Many voters believed that increased European integration would result in a loss of Danish national identity. Today, with construction underway of the Oresund Bridge between the Swedish city of Malmo and the capital, Copenhagen, Danish citizens look forward to Copenhagen developing into the hub of Northern Europe.

Political Rights and Civil Liberties:

Danes are able to change their government through democratic means. At least once every four years, representatives are elected to the Folketing through universal suffrage and a modified system of proportional representation. The independent judiciary includes local courts, two high courts and a fifteen-member Supreme Court with judges appointed by the sovereign. The Folketing appoints an ombudsman to investigate government cases and specialized courts oversee labor and maritime affairs.

Press freedom is guaranteed and several privately owned newspapers and magazines publish freely. Although only one newspaper is directly party-owned, several reflect established party viewpoints and are frequently critical of the government. The state finances radio and television broadcasting; however, the state-owned television companies have independent editorial boards. Private radio stations are heavily regulated and occasionally prohibited from broadcasting. For example, the Danish National Socialist Movement was banned from opening a radio station in Southern Copenhagen this year because it planned to broadcast

"Nazi music" and campaign for a "racially clean" country. Spreading racist propaganda is not against the law in Denmark, but the group's intention was considered incitement to racial hatred, which is illegal.

More than 90 percent of the population belongs to the established and state-funded Church of Denmark, which is Evangelical Lutheran in denomination. Freedom of worship, however, is guaranteed to all. Freedoms of assembly and association are also guaranteed, as are rights of workers to organize and strike. The vast majority of wage earners are affiliated with free trade unions and their umbrella organization, the Danish Federation of Trade Unions, which is linked to the Social Democratic Party. Scattered multi-industry antiprivatization strikes took place in April of this year, with 3,000 workers converging outside the Folketing during debates over privatization.

Roughly 45 percent of the wage labor force is made up of women, 40 percent of whom are concentrated in service and textile jobs. Women generally hold between 20 and 30 percent of national legislature seats, but enjoy significantly less representation at the local level. Gender, racial and language-related discrimination have all been outlawed, and the media in particular have implemented measures to prevent the rise of racism by educating the public about incoming non-Nordic immigrants and refugees. Denmark has also taken steps toward ensuring the civil rights of gays and lesbians, including becoming the first country to officially sanction same-sex marriages outside of the church.

Djibouti

Polity: Dominant party   **Political Rights:** 5*
Economy: Capitalist   **Civil Liberties:** 6
Population: 577,000   **Status:** Not Free
PPP: $1,547
Life Expectancy: 48.3
Ethnic Groups: Somali (60 percent), Afar (35 percent), Arab
Capital: Djibouti

Ratings Change: *Djibouti's political rights rating changed from 6 to 5 because the opposition gained representation in the government and peace has been sustained.

Overview:

In mid-1995, six months after the government and rebel Front for the Restoration of Unity and Democracy (FRUD) signed an agreement to end the armed insurgency, include opposition members in government, and reform electoral lists before the next general election, President Hassan Gouled Aptidon appointed two FRUD leaders to the Cabinet. This reshuffled government is expected to focus on the ailing economy, which has been badly damaged by three years of civil war.

This small East African nation gained independence from France in 1977. Gouled has governed since independence, despite a new constitution adopted by referendum in 1992 establishing a multiparty system. In 1993 Hassan Gouled Aptidon took 60 percent of the popular vote and won a fourth six-year term in

Djibouti's first contested presidential elections, which were considered fraudulent by both the opposition and international observers. In part because the election was boycotted by ethnic Afar-dominated FRUD, all of the opposition candidates were members of the Issa ethnic group.

Djibouti is divided between the ethnically Somalian Issa group, which comprises about half of the population and is concentrated in the south, and the Afar, who make up about 35 percent of the population and occupy the northern and western regions. The remainder of the population is composed of Somalis from Somalia and Yemeni Arabs. FRUD was formed in 1991 on a platform calling for the overthrow of the "tribal dictatorship" and installation of a democratic, multiparty system, and has waged a violent campaign against the government since November of that year. Amnesty International has indicated that in response to the armed insurgency, Djibouti security forces have committed gross violations of human rights against Afars including rape, torture and extrajudicial executions.

The FRUD/government agreement called for a coalition government; power-sharing in politics, the military and administration based on a quota arrangement; decentralization of power; the legalization of FRUD as a political party; and the integration of hundreds of FRUD fighters into the national army. In return for these concessions and others, FRUD pledged to abandon armed struggle. It remains unclear to what extent these resolutions have translated into concrete changes.

Political Rights and Civil Liberties:

Djiboutians are unable to change their government democratically. Elections in both 1992 and 1993 were reportedly fraudulent. Though each post-independence cabinet has allegedly sought to strike a balance in ethnic representation and all three prime ministers named by the president have been Afars, many claim that political power remains concentrated in the hands of the Issa majority. The president has appointed the FRUD leader, Ali Mohammed Daoud, and its chairman and secretary general, Ougoureh Kifleh, as ministers of health and agriculture, respectively. The real effect of these appointments is not yet apparent. The new constitution provides for universal suffrage in presidential elections.

Freedoms of assembly and association are protected under the constitution; however, the government has effectively banned political protest. Twice in 1994, demonstrators in the Afar district of Arhiba protesting the demolition of temporary shelters for internal refugees were dispersed by police using tear gas and rubber bullets. At least six deaths resulted, as well as numerous injuries and arrests.

Formation of opposition parties is also permitted by the constitution, but the ruling party determines which groups can be legalized. Due to routine government interference, the judiciary is not independent. Although the constitution stipulates that arrests may not occur without a decree presented by a judicial magistrate, security forces commonly arrest political demonstrators without proper authority. Despite a constitutional provision for freedom of speech, that privilege is severely curtailed. Freedom of worship, however, is respected.

Workers may join unions and strike, but the government routinely obstructs the free operation of unions. A general strike movement launched in September protesting austerity measures, which lowered civil servants' wages by 15 percent and severely cut benefits, was effectively weakened in two days as security forces were deployed in large numbers and union leaders were placed under arrest. In a joint communiqué, the Djibouti General Workers' Union and the Djibouti Labor Union denounced the "non-respect by the government of workers' union rights, fallacious promises and the brutality of the security forces."

Among the human rights violations cited in a March 1994 Amnesty international report was the rape of women and girls in the Oueima and Mabla regions by government soldiers. FRUD alleged that the incidents were frequent and directed at Afar women in retaliation for attacks on army troops. Injuries from these attacks are compounded by both ethnic groups' common practice of female genital mutilation and the lack of public recognition of the "taboo" crime of rape.

Dominica

Polity: Parliamentary democracy
Economy: Capitalist
Population: 71,000
PPP: $3,526
Life Expectancy: 72.0
Ethnic Groups: Black and mulatto with a minority Carib enclave
Capital: Roseau
Ratings Change: *Dominica's political rights rating changed from 2 to 1 because it held a free and fair election in which an opposition party came to power.

Political Rights: 1*
Civil Liberties: 1
Status: Free

Overview: The opposition United Workers' Party (UWP) won a narrow victory in elections held in June. UWP leader Edison James became prime minister. He replaced Eugenia Charles, who had earlier decided to retire after fifteen years in power.

Dominica has been an independent republic within the British Commonwealth since 1978. Internally self-governing since 1967, Dominica is a parliamentary democracy headed by a prime minister and a House of Assembly with twenty-one members elected to five-year terms. Nine senators are appointed, five by the prime minister and four by the opposition leader. Over half the island's population depends directly or indirectly on banana production.

Charles narrowly won a third term in 1990 as the DFP (Democratic Freedom Party) won eleven of twenty-one seats. The newly formed UWP, led by James, took second with six seats and displaced the leftist Dominica Labor Party (DLP), with four seats, as the official opposition. James is a former head of the Banana Growers' Association

In 1993 the septuagenarian Charles announced she would retire at the next general election in 1995. External Affairs Minister Brian Alleyne defeated three other candidates in a vote of DFP delegates to become the new party leader.

In fall 1994 the DFP lost a by-election to the UWP, prompting local observers to give the UWP the edge in the upcoming 1995 vote. The campaign heated up when the UWP alleged the DFP had plotted to spy on the opposition through a bugging operation. But a commission of inquiry concluded the key witness was lying. As the vote approached, a rejuvenated DLP led by Rosie Douglas appeared to make it a three-way race.

On 12 June 1995 the UWP won a narrow majority, taking eleven seats. The DFP and the DLP won five seats each. James became prime minister. The UWP victory marked a significant shift in power from the traditional establishment to a new and younger business class.

The DFP's Alleyne and the DLP's Douglas reached an agreement to share the official opposition post, with each holding it for a year at a time. Alleyne assumed the post first. But a High Court ruled that one of the winning DFP candidates was not qualified to sit in parliament because he still held a public service post. The ruling reduced the DFP's representation in parliament to four seats pending appeal, and Douglas became opposition leader.

Problems in the crucial banana industry under Charles had worked in the UWP's favor during the campaign. But those problems paled in comparison to the damage wrought by Hurricane Marilyn in September. The James government claimed nearly 90 percent of the crop was destroyed.

Political Rights and Civil Liberties:

Citizens are able to change their government through free and fair elections. There are no restrictions on political, civic or labor organization. Several civic groups have emerged in recent years calling for more accountability and transparency in government.

There is an independent judiciary and the rule of law is enhanced by the court system's embrace of the inter-island Eastern Caribbean Supreme Court. But the judicial system is understaffed, which has led to a large backlog of cases.

The Dominica Defense Force (DDF) was disbanded in 1981 after it was implicated in attempts by supporters of former prime minister Patrick John to overthrow the government. John was convicted in 1986 for his involvement and given a twelve-year prison sentence. He was released by executive order in 1990, became active in the trade union movement and lost as a DLP candidate in the 1995 election.

The press is generally free, varied and critical. Television and radio, both public and private, are open to pluralistic views. Since 1990 television has been used as an effective campaign tool by all parties.

Freedom of religion is generally recognized. However, the small Rastafarian community has charged that their religious rights are violated by a policy of cutting off the "dread locks" of those who are imprisoned, and that Rastafarian women are harassed by immigration officials who single them out for drug searches.

Since 1990 the 3,000 indigenous Carib Indians, many of whom live on a 3,700-acre reserve on the northeast coast, have been represented in the House of Assembly by an elected Carib parliamentarian. In 1994 Hilary Frederick was elected chief of the Carib people for a five-year term, defeating Irvince Auguiste, the incumbent. A policeman was charged with the murder of a young man during the ensuing celebration.

Government welfare officials have expressed concern over the growing number of cases of child abuse.

Dominican Republic

Polity: Presidential-
legislative democracy
Economy: Capitalist-
statist
Population: 7,823,000
PPP: $3,280
Life Expectancy: 69.6
Ethnic Groups: Mestizo and Creole (73 percent),
European (16 percent), black (11 percent)
Capital: Santo Domingo

Political Rights: 4
Civil Liberties: 3
Status: Partly Free

Overview: **D**espite President Joaquin Balaguer's pledge to finally step
down, the aged caudillo cast a long shadow over the
campaign for the May 1996 election.

After achieving independence from Spain in 1821 and Haiti in 1844, the
Dominican Republic endured recurrent domestic conflict. The assassination of
Gen. Rafael Trujillo in 1961 ended thirty years of dictatorship, but a 1963 military
coup led to civil war and U.S. intervention. In 1966, under a new constitution,
civilian rule was restored with the election of the conservative Balaguer.

The constitution provides for a president and Congress elected for four years. The
Congress consists of a 120-member Chamber of Deputies and a thirty-member Senate.

Balaguer was re-elected in 1970 and 1974 but defeated in 1978 by Silvestre
Antonio Guzman of the social democratic Dominican Revolutionary Party (PRD).
The PRD repeated in 1982 with the election of Salvador Jorge Blanco, but
Balaguer, heading the right-wing Social Christian Reformist Party (PRSC), won
again in 1986 and 1990 in elections marred by fraud.

In the May 1994 election the main contenders were Balaguer, fellow octoge-
narian Juan Bosch of the Dominican Liberation Party (PLD) and the PRD's Jose
Francisco Pena Gomez. Polls showed Pena Gomez, a charismatic black, with a
significant lead. The Balaguer machine then unleashed a campaign of race-based
attacks that branded Pena Gomez a Haitian who secretly planned to unite the
neighboring countries. The attacks, ugly even by Dominican standards, appeared to
narrow the gap.

Despite clear evidence of widespread fraud, Balaguer was declared the winner
by a few thousand votes. Amid street protests and international pressure Balaguer
agreed to new presidential elections in eighteen months. The legislative results
stood. The PRD and allies took fifty-seven seats in the Chamber and fifteen in the
Senate, the PRSC fifty and fourteen, and the PLD thirteen and one.

When Congress convened, the PLD backed a PRSC subterfuge to lengthen
Balaguer's shortened term from eighteen months to two years, with elections in
May 1996. In exchange, Balaguer made a PLD legislator president of the Chamber.
The PRD protested, but tacitly conceded by announcing that Pena Gomez would
again be its candidate in 1996.

In 1995 Vice President Jacinto Peynado, head of a wealthy business family, won the

PRSC primary. His grandfather was, like Balaguer, one of dictator Trujillo's puppet presidents. The PLD nominated the young Leonel Fernandez in place of the ailing Bosch.

The campaign got underway amid daily twelve-hour electricity blackouts and mounting social unrest and violent crime. Polls showed Fernandez with a slim lead over Pena Gomez, with Peynado trailing. The cagey Balaguer received Fernandez in the national palace and did not endorse Peynado.

When the PLD began spending lavishly, there were suspicions the money came from Balaguer. It was alleged that Balaguer, thinking Peynado would lose, wanted to co-opt Fernandez and ensure his victory to avoid corruption investigations by a potential Pena Gomez government. Meanwhile, the PLD took a page from Balaguer and started playing the race card, as placards appeared at Fernandez rallies showing him as a lion eating Pena Gomez, portrayed as a monkey.

Political Rights and Civil Liberties:

Citizens cannot change their government through democratic elections. The 1994 election was steeped in fraud as hundreds of thousands of opposition voters were disenfranchised through manipulation of the electoral rolls. President Balaguer controlled the police, the armed forces, the bureaucracy and the national electoral board, and clearly used all of them to remain in power.

In 1995 a new, nominally more independent electoral board was established and a revision of the electoral rolls was begun in preparation for the May 1996 vote.

Constitutional guarantees regarding free expression, freedom of religion and the right to organize political parties and civic groups are generally respected. But political and civic expression is restricted by the violent climate surrounding political campaigns and frequent government-labor clashes, and by the repressive measures taken by police and the military. Dozens died during interparty clashes in the 1994 campaign, and violence marked the beginning of the 1995 campaign.

The judiciary, headed by a Supreme Court, is politicized and, like other government institutions, riddled with corruption. The courts offer little recourse to those without money or influence. Prisons are abysmal and violence routine. Nearly nine of ten prisoners have not been convicted of a crime.

Independent rights groups continue to report widespread police brutality, including torture, and arbitrary arrests by the security forces. Criminal violence, much of it drug-related, and police corruption threaten citizen security. Poor women are vulnerable to criminal rings who promise jobs in Europe for a fee, then press the indebted women into prostitution in Spain and Germany.

Labor unions are well-organized. Although legally permitted to strike, they are often subject to government crackdowns. Peasant unions are occasionally targeted by armed groups working for large landowners. A new 1992 labor code established standards for workplace conditions and strengthened the right to bargain collectively. But companies in the twenty-seven industrial free zones, employing almost 10 percent of the nation's workforce, remain reluctant to comply. Worker conditions in the zones remain below international standards, and discriminatory practices against women are prevalent.

Haitians, including children, continue working on state-run sugar plantations in slave-like conditions. The new labor code recognizes sugar workers' right to organize, but reports of abuses continue.

The media are mostly private. Newspapers are independent and diverse but subject to government pressure through denial of advertising revenues and taxes on imported newsprint. There are dozens of radio stations and at least six commercial television stations. Journalists critical of the government are occasionally threatened. Narciso Gonzalez, a journalist and government critic, disappeared in May 1994, apparently after being arrested by state security forces. In 1995 the government continued to deny knowledge of his arrest or whereabouts.

⬇ Ecuador

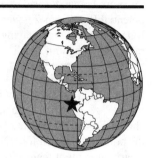

Polity: Presidential-legislative democracy
Economy: Capitalist-statist
Population: 11,460,000
PPP: $4,140
Life Expectancy: 66.2
Ethnic Groups: Mestizo (55 percent), Indian (25 percent), European (10 percent), black (10 percent)
Capital: Quito
Trend Arrow: The down arrow reflects concerns about mounting evidence of systemic corruption in all branches of government.

Political Rights: 2
Civil Liberties: 3
Status: Free

Overview:

President Sixto Duran Ballen's scandal-scarred government limped into its last year. With corruption allegations the principal weaponry of political vendettas, Ecuador was verging on ungovernability.

Established in 1830 after achieving independence from Spain in 1822, the Republic of Ecuador has endured many interrupted presidencies and military governments. The last military regime gave way to civilian rule when a new constitution was approved by referendum in 1978.

The constitution provides for a president elected for four years, with a runoff between the two frontrunners if no candidate wins a majority in the first round. There is a seventy-seven-member unicameral National Chamber of Deputies with sixty-five members elected on a provincial basis every two years and twelve elected nationally every four years.

The main candidates in the 1992 election were Duran Ballen, who left the right-wing Social Christian Party (PSC) to form the Republican Union Party (PUR), the PSC's Jaime Nebot, Abdala Bucaram of the populist Ecuadorian Roldosist Party (PRE), and Raul Baca of the incumbent Democratic Left (ID). Duran Ballen won the first round with 31.9 percent of the vote. Nebot came second to make the runoff.

Both candidates espoused market economics. But the septuagenarian Duran Ballen offered the patrician style of the elite of Quito, the nation's highland capital, while the forty-five-year-old Nebot, a lawyer and businessman, displayed the fiery demeanor characteristic of coastal Guayaquil, the nation's business hub.

Duran won with 57 percent of the vote but took office with a weak hand as his PUR had won only thirteen of seventy-seven legislative seats. Nebot, backed by the PSC's twenty-one seats, opted to stake out opposition turf, highlighting the fact that personal rivalries count more than ideology in Ecuadorian politics.

Duran Ballen's term has been marked by general strikes against his economic austerity measures, indigenous protests against business-backed land reform and the impeachment of numerous cabinet ministers by an opposition-controlled legislature. Impeaching government officials on corruption charges has been a staple of the country's fragmented, gridlocked politics since the return to civilian rule.

In 1995, Vice President Alberto Dahik was charged with corruption and fled into exile in Costa Rica. Duran Ballen himself was implicated and came under attack by the legislature and the Supreme Court. In November, his proposals for constitutional reform were soundly rejected in a national referendum and opposition demands for his resignation mounted. As Ecuador descended into gloom, some questioned whether Duran Ballen could hold on until the end of his term in mid-1996.

Political Rights and Civil Liberties:

Citizens can change their government through elections. Competition is fierce and violence usually mars election campaigns. Constitutional guarantees regarding freedom of expression, religion, and the right to organize political parties, labor unions and civic organizations are generally respected.

The near-constant gridlock among executive, legislative and judicial branches has made the country practically ungovernable. Opinion polls and rising voter abstention indicate that the credibility of political institutions is in deep decline.

There is evidence that drug traffickers have penetrated the political system through campaign funding, and sectors of the police and military through bribery. Ecuador is a transshipment point for cocaine passing from neighboring Colombia to the U.S. and a money-laundering haven.

The judiciary is headed by a legislatively appointed Supreme Court. The Court is frequently caught in political tugs-of-war between the executive and the legislature, and its impartiality is often in doubt. The judiciary is generally undermined by the corruption afflicting the entire political system.

There are numerous human rights organizations. Although activists are occasionally targets of intimidation, they continue to report frequent allegations of arbitrary arrest and police brutality, including torture and rape of female detainees. Prisons are overcrowded and conditions poor.

The military is responsible for a significant percentage of abuses, particularly when it is deployed under states of emergency during labor strikes, demonstrations and land disputes. Abuses are committed with relative impunity because police and military personnel are tried in military rather than civil courts.

The government and military have generally sided with landowners and multinational oil companies as they continue to infringe upon land rights granted to Indians in the eastern Amazon region by former administrations. Paramilitary units employed by landowners against indigenous organizations operate with a high level of impunity.

Labor unions are well-organized and permitted to strike. Strikes are often marked by violent clashes with police and several labor activists have been killed.

Unions have protested amendments to the labor code limiting public-sector strikes.

Newspapers are mostly private and outspoken. Radio and television stations are privately owned, but the government controls radio frequencies. Broadcast media are supervised by two independent associations. Ecuador's numerous, mostly commercial television stations play a major role during political campaigns.

Egypt

Polity: Dominant party (military-influenced)
Economy: Mixed statist
Population: 61,948,000
PPP: $3,540
Life Expectancy: 63.6
Ethnic Groups: Eastern Hamitic (90 percent), Greek, Syro-Lebanese
Capital: Cairo

Political Rights: 6
Civil Liberties: 6
Status: Not Free

Overview:　The ruling National Democratic Party (NDP) took over two-thirds of parliamentary seats in November 1995 elections marred by widespread irregularities.

The British granted Egypt independence in 1922. In July 1952 military leaders overthrew the monarchy, establishing a republic one year later. Coup leader Colonel Gamel Abdel Nasser ruled until his death in 1970.

The 1971 constitution adopted under Nasser's successor, President Anwar al-Sadat, grants full executive powers to the president, who is nominated by the 454-member People's Assembly and elected for a six-year term in a national referendum. In 1978 President Sadat established the governing NDP, and subsequently cleared the way for additional parties. In October 1981 Islamic militants, angered by Egypt's recognition of Israeli sovereignty in a peace treaty two years earlier, assassinated Sadat.

Under Sadat's successor, Hosni Mubarak, the military-backed NDP continues to dominate politics. In October 1993 Mubarak won a third presidential term with 96.3 percent approval as the sole candidate in a national referendum. However, there is widespread frustration with official corruption, high unemployment and pervasive poverty. Islamic fundamentalist groups, including the nonviolent Muslim Brotherhood and the militant Islamic Group, have built support by tapping into this discontent.

In the spring of 1992 the Islamic Group sharply escalated its drive to topple the government and set up a fundamentalist state, killing police, Coptic Christians and tourists. The government responded with broad security crackdowns. In early 1994 the authorities began arresting members of the Muslim Brotherhood, which is technically outlawed but had been allowed to operate openly.

In 1995 the government detained scores of Muslim Brotherhood members. In the 27 November People's Assembly elections, and subsequent runoffs in early December, the government won 317 seats; independents, many allied with the government, 114; and small opposition groups, 13; with 10 seats by law appointed by the president.

Political Rights and Civil Liberties: NDP domination of the media, the large state sector and labor unions, as well as official restrictions on political organizing, effectively prevent Egyptians from having the democratic means to change their government. The 1995 parliamentary elections were characterized by considerable irregularities. The Muslim Brotherhood, despite having widespread support, cannot participate in the electoral process due to a ban on religious-based parties, although its members can compete as independents.

There are almost daily clashes in upper Egypt between police and Islamic fundamentalist militants. Over 800 security officers, militants, civilians and tourists have been killed since 1992. Security forces are accused of killing some militants through excessive use of lethal force.

Since Sadat's assassination in 1981 the country has been under a State of Emergency, which parliament renews periodically. Authorities can detain suspects without charge for up to ninety days, and often prolong this period by re-arresting those released. By some estimates there are 10,000-20,000 Islamic fundamentalists detained for security reasons at any one time, many without charge.

The authorities arrested dozens of Muslim Brotherhood activists in 1995, including several who planned to compete in the November parliamentary elections. In November a military court sentenced fifty-four Muslim Brotherhood members to jail terms of up to five years for nonviolent activities.

The Interior Ministry's General Directorate for State Security Investigations has been accused of repeated, systematic human rights violations, including torturing and in some cases killing suspects to extract information and coerce confessions, and detaining and torturing women and children related to suspects who are at large. Local police routinely abuse suspects in ordinary criminal offenses.

In recent years the judiciary has shown increasing independence. However, since December 1992 the government has tried civilians accused of terrorist acts in military courts, where due process rights are inadequate. The Muslim Brotherhood trials described above marked the first time civilians accused of nonviolent crimes were tried in military courts.

In late May the government rammed the controversial Press Law 93 through parliament, increasing minimum penalties for libel and slander to five years in prison, raising the maximum fine to $6,000 and rescinding a previous prohibition against detaining journalists. The government promised to review the law following pressure from journalists. The government regulates the press through licensing and other legal means, and occasionally confiscates editions of newspapers. Most major newspapers are state-owned and offer some pluralistic views, but the state-owned broadcast media rarely air opposition views. Extremists have physically attacked journalists and intellectuals.

Under the Emergency Law the Interior Ministry must grant approval for public meetings. During the 1995 parliamentary election campaign, police broke up several rallies by the Muslim Brotherhood but permitted those organized by the NDP and small opposition groups. The Ministry of Social Affairs can merge and dissolve nongovernmental organizations. The government refuses to license the Egyptian Organization for Human Rights, and its members are frequently harassed.

Women face official and informal discrimination in many legal and social matters. According to the London *Observer*, female genital mutilation is practiced on an estimated 3,000 girls per day. Islam is the state religion. In November 1992 the government placed all mosques under the control of the Ministry of Religious Affairs, but many unlicensed mosques still operate.

Fundamentalist militants have murdered dozens of members of the Coptic Christian minority in recent years, and Copt houses, shops and churches have been burned and vandalized. Copts also face official discrimination, including difficulty in obtaining permission to build or repair places of worship required under an 1856 Ottoman Empire-era law. The authorities occasionally close Copt places of worship.

The government-backed Egyptian Trade Union Federation is the only legal labor union federation. The 1976 law on labor unions sets numerous regulations on the establishment and operation of unions, including the conduct of elections. There is no implicit right to strike, but strikes do occur. Child labor remains a serious problem.

El Salvador

Polity: Presidential-legislative democracy (military-influenced)
Economy: Capitalist-statist
Population: 5,870,000
PPP: $2,250
Life Expectancy: 66.4
Ethnic Groups: Mestizo (94 percent), with small Indian and European minorities
Capital: San Salvador

Political Rights: 3
Civil Liberties: 3
Status: Partly Free

Overview: Labor strife, social unrest, police abuses and the government's failure to fully implement the 1992 peace accords underscored the continued weakness of the country's democratic process.

Independence from the Captaincy General of Guatemala was declared in 1841 and the Republic of El Salvador was established in 1859. Over a century of civil strife and military rule followed.

Elected civilian rule was established in 1984. The 1983 constitution provides for a president elected for a five-year term and an eighty-four-member, unicameral National Assembly elected for three years. Over a decade of civil war ended with the United Nations-mediated peace accords signed in 1992 by the Farabundo Marti

National Liberation Front (FMLN) and the conservative government of President Alfredo Cristiani.

The FMLN participated in the 1994 elections, backing former ally Ruben Zamora of the Democratic Convergence (CD) for president and running a slate of legislative candidates. The incumbent Nationalist Republican Alliance (ARENA) nominated San Salvador Mayor Armando Calderon Sol. The Christian Democrats (PDC) nominated Fidel Chavez Mena. The PDC had previously held power under President Jose Napoleon Duarte (1984-89).

ARENA, a well-oiled political machine, sounded populist themes and attacked the FMLN as Communists and terrorists. The FMLN-CD coalition offered a progressive but moderate platform and called for compliance with the peace accords.

In the March 1994 vote Calderon Sol won just under 50 percent, setting up a runoff against Zamora, who came in second with 25 percent. In the legislature ARENA won thirty-nine seats, the FMLN twenty-one, the PDC eighteen, the CD one, and the Unity Movement (MU), a small evangelical party, one. The right-wing National Conciliation Party (PCN) won four seats, giving ARENA an effective right-wing majority. In the runoff Calderon Sol defeated Zamora by 68 percent to 32 percent.

President Calderon Sol promised full compliance with the peace accords. But as of December 1995, two months after implementation of the accords was to have been completed, the U.N. noted that major problems remained regarding the program to transfer land to former FMLN and army combatants, and mounting human rights and corruption problems within the new National Civilian Police

These conditions, coupled with Calderon Sol's structural adjustment of the economy, including thousands of public-sector layoffs, led to widespread protests in late 1995. In the wake of harsh government crackdowns, there were fears El Salvador might revert to chronic disorder and even rumors of a military coup.

Political Rights **C**itizens can change their government democratically. Still, **and Civil Liberties:** the 1994 election was marred by right-wing violence, the ruling ARENA party's inordinate financial advantage, and registration irregularities that disenfranchised tens of thousands of eligible voters.

The opposition accepted the outcome of the election, having recognized that the results reflected the competing parties' relative electoral strength. The former FMLN guerrillas won a significant bloc of seats in the legislature, although the FMLN subsequently split, with one group leaving to form the social-democratic Democratic Party (PD).

The constitution guarantees free expression, freedom of religion and the right to organize political parties, civic groups and labor unions. Although the 1992 peace accords have led to a significant reduction in human rights violations, political expression and civil liberties are still circumscribed by sporadic political violence, repressive police measures, a mounting crime wave and still-existing right-wing death squads, including "social-cleansing" vigilante groups. With the sharp increase in criminal violence it remains difficult to discern motive in many murder, robbery and kidnapping cases.

The underlying problem remains an ineffectual judicial system and a climate of impunity. A first step toward judicial reform came in 1994 with the naming by the new legislature of a more politically representative fifteen-member Supreme Court, which controls the entire Salvadoran judiciary. In late 1995 fourteen judicial officials were removed and a number of judges placed under investigation. But much remained to be done toward establishing a rule of law in a country where traditionally it has been nonexistent.

Two amnesty laws have added to the sense of impunity. In 1992 the FMLN and the government agreed to the first, which covered most rights violations by both sides during the war. In 1993 the Cristiani government pushed a blanket amnesty through the legislature that immunized the military from charges subsequently recommended by a U.N.-sponsored Truth Commission.

The peace accords mandated creation of a new National Civilian Police (PNC) incorporating former FMLN guerrillas. But up to 500 former members of disbanded security forces were apparently integrated into the new force, and the PNC as a whole appeared in 1995 to be falling into corrupt practices and increasing rights violations. The U.N. and local rights groups were investigating reports of a tangled web of criminal operations within the new police.

Prisons are overcrowded, conditions are wretched and up to three-quarters of prisoners have not been sentenced. Dozens of inmates have been killed during prison riots in the last two years.

Most media are privately owned. Election campaigns feature televised interviews and debates among candidates from across the political spectrum. The FMLN's formerly clandestine Radio Venceremos operates from San Salvador and competes with nearly seventy other stations. Left-wing journalists and publications are occasionally targets of intimidation. At the end of 1995 the government was trying to push through a constitutional amendment that would severely restrict the media's access and ability to report on judicial matters.

Labor, peasant and university organizations are well-organized. The archaic labor code was reformed in 1994, but the new code was enacted without the approval of most unions because it significantly limits the right to organize, including in the export-processing zones known as *maquiladoras*. Unions that strike remain subject to intimidation and violent police crackdowns. In 1995 hundreds of maquiladora workers were fired for organizing.

Equatorial Guinea

Polity: Dominant party (military-dominated)
Economy: Capitalist-statist
Population: 420,000
PPP: $700
Life Expectancy: 48.0
Ethnic Groups: Fang (75-80 percent), Bubi (15 percent), Puku, Seke and others (5-10 percent)
Capital: Malabo

Political Rights: 7
Civil Liberties: 7
Status: Not Free

Overview: In 1995, the government arrested several opposition party members, including Severo Moto Nsa, president of the Progressive Party of Equatorial Guinea (PPGE), and a number of military officers accused of plotting a coup. More arrests occurred in October after opposition party members and international observers accused the government of falsifying municipal election results.

Equatorial Guinea gained independence from Spain in 1968. The country's first president, Macie Nguema, was overthrown by his nephew, Teodoro Obiang Nguema Mbasogo, in 1979 and subsequently executed for his genocidal policies against the population. Obiang assumed power and soon created a similar atmosphere of repression, albeit to a lesser degree. In the last four years, pressured by donor countries eager to see democratic reform, Obiang has tried to present himself as a moderate leader willing to accommodate political opposition.

After announcing an "era of pluralism" in January 1992, Obiang agreed to legalize political parties. Since that time, opposition parties have been subject to sporadic crackdowns featuring unlawful arrests, intimidation and torture. On 27 January 1995 Severo Moto Nsa and Tomas Elo, two leading members of PPGE, were arrested in connection with an alleged coup attempt. According to Amnesty International, both men were convicted of corruption without evidence and subsequently held incommunicado at Blackbeach prison, described as the most inhumane in the country. A second trial for Moto and two former army officers accused of treason and other offenses ended in a thirty-year sentence for Moto and death sentences for the two other men. In response to an international call for leniency, Moto was pardoned in August.

Both the opposition and Obiang's Democratic Party of Equatorial Guinea claimed victory in the country's first contested democratic elections since 1968. Parties of the Joint Opposition Platform argued that numerous irregularities, intimidation and arrests of activists at voting centers, and the lack of international observers to the vote-count allowed the ruling party to claim victory falsely. In a radio address on the anniversary of independence, Obiang accused international skeptics and Spain in particular of meddling in the country's internal affairs and warned that the circulation of "fake" election results would prompt him to take measures to guarantee law and order.

Political Rights and Civil Liberties: Citizens of Equatorial Guinea lack the means to change their government democratically. President Obiang's repressive regime prevents most citizens from influencing public policy in any meaningful way. The basic law of November 1991 prohibits the impeachment of the head of state. Although opposition parties are permitted they may not be organized on a tribal, regional or provincial basis, and each recognized party must pay a deposit of CFA30,000,000 (approximately $110,000). Opposition parties face harassment, intimidation, arrest and torture, particularly outside the capital.

The judiciary cannot act independently of the executive, and the government has allegedly employed false charges and unjust and summary trials to eliminate political opponents. Police have reportedly tortured detainees to extract confessions.

Freedom of association, with the partial exception of members of legalized political parties, is illegal and repressed, as is freedom of assembly. Opposition demonstrations without prior authorization were banned in 1993. Any gathering of ten or more people for purposes the government considers political is illegal. There are no free trade unions. Freedom of movement is also restricted in that citizens and residents must obtain permission for travel both within the country and abroad, and political activists are often stopped by security guards and forced to pay bribes. There is one opposition newspaper.

Approximately 80 percent of the population is Roman Catholic. The Catholic Church has been persecuted in an effort to rid the country of "foreign influence," and in a 1995 radio address Obiang warned the clergy against interfering in political affairs.

Eritrea

Polity: One-party (transitional)
Economy: Mixed statist
Population: 3,531,000
PPP: na
Life Expectancy: na
Ethnic Groups: Afar, Arab, Beja, Bilin, Jabarti, Kunama, Saho, Tigrawi
Capital: Asmara

Political Rights: 6
Civil Liberties: 4*
Status: Partly Free

Ratings Change: *Eritrea's civil liberties rating changed from 5 to 4, moving it into the Partly Free category, because of broad constitutional consultations that included significant public discussion of basic issues.

Overview: Eritrea's transition following a three-decade independence struggle continued in 1995, with broad public consultations on a new constitution that is expected to be adopted in 1996, prior to the country's first elections scheduled for 1997. The Provisional

Government of Eritrea and the country's political life remain dominated, however, by President Isaias Afwerki's Popular Front for Democracy and Justice (PFDJ), created in February 1994 as a mass-based successor to the wartime Eritrean Peoples Liberation Front (EPLF).

Ethiopia gained control over Eritrea in 1950 after nearly a half-century of Italian occupation was ended with the Axis defeat in World War II. The Eritrean war began in 1962 as a Marxist and nationalist guerrilla war against the Ethiopian government of Emperor Haile Selassie. The ideological logic of the struggle disappeared when a Marxist regime seized power in Ethiopia in 1974, and the EPLF adapted to radically changed international circumstances by the time it finally defeated Ethiopia's northern armies in 1991. Independent Eritrea was recognized in May 1993 after a U.N.-supervised independence referendum was approved overwhelmingly.

An austere, single-minded commitment to rebuilding Eritrea has won the PFDJ administration many admirers. Its occasional intolerance of criticism on religious or political grounds raised worries that the broad consensus and popularity inherited from wartime might not translate to a pluralistic system. An independent judiciary was formed by decree in 1993, but its autonomy has not yet been seriously tested.

The government strives to maintain a balance between roughly equally divided Christian and Muslim populations. This aim could be tested as radical Islamist guerrillas of the Eritrean Islamic Jihad, believed to be financed by Sudan's fundamentalist regime, increase activities along the two countries' frontier. Eritrea can ill afford the distraction from crucial development tasks posed by its increasingly tense relations with Sudan, with which it has broken diplomatic ties. In December, Eritrean forces clashed with Yemeni troops over control of several disputed red sea islands, further raising regional tensions.

Political Rights and Civil Liberties:

Eritreans' ability to change their leadership democratically has yet to be tested. Under Ethiopian rule, legislative representatives were elected within the Ethiopian system, but this was a hollow exercise in the context of closed dictatorships and open war. The PFDJ has essentially evolved from the wartime EPLF, a military-dominated organization most concerned with winning the independence war. The current legislature is comprised of the seventy-five PFDJ central committee members plus three appointed representatives from each of Eritrea's administrative regions, which were reduced from ten to six in 1995.

Presidential and legislative elections under the new constitution are planned by May 1997. The new charter is expected to allow the operation of independent parties, although parties based on ethnicity or religion will be prohibited. The government's desire to reduce ethnic identification has extended to the naming of the country's new regions; all are now named based on geography rather than ethnic composition. The government's administrative competence will probably result in well-run elections, and the PFDJ's popularity likely ensures it a strong victory. However, it remains unclear whether other conditions for a genuinely fair election, such as access to media and impartial allocation of state resources, will exist.

The process of creating Eritrea's new constitution highlights the country's transitional situation. The fifty-member drafting committee is composed of PFDJ appointees, yet the government has taken elaborate measures to encourage broad public debate on the shape of the new document. Through early 1995 over 500,000 people attended more than a thousand seminars, which have been followed by an education campaign and further public debate.

Public participation is constrained, however, by government control of broadcasting and pressure on the small independent print media. In November, a Catholic-supported newspaper was closed after criticizing the government. While open discussion in public fora is tolerated, disseminating dissenting views is not. The government says new legislation will allow for varied media, but no timetable has been announced. The opposition Eritrean Liberation Front-Revolutionary Council (ELF-RC) complains it is excluded from any official role in government meetings, although its members participate in their individual capacities.

Religious freedom is generally respected, although activities of Islamist fundamentalist groups, most believed to be externally-sponsored either by Sudan or Iran, could strain ties between religious communities. The government has denounced what it described as political activities by the Roman Catholic Church, and a number of Jehovah's witnesses were stripped of their citizenship and had property seized after refusing to serve in the armed forces or take a national oath of allegiance.

There are reports of minor armed dissident activity among Danakil people along Eritrea's eastern frontier. Ex-EPLF fighters, tens of thousands of whom have been demobilized and face an uncertain future, could pose a more serious challenge to the government. The PFDJ government is actively involved in the economy, but claims to intercede only in areas where private capital is unavailable. The country faces severe environmental problems, especially as hundreds of thousands of Eritrean refugees return home.

A small civil society is taking root. The PFDJ has effectively spun off several of the components of the EPLF, and newly-independent youth, labor and women's organizations are struggling to find a new role. It remains to be seen whether these groups will develop genuine autonomy.

Women formed at least a third of the EPLF combat forces during the independence struggle, and the government has strongly supported improvements in women's status. Equal educational opportunities, equal pay for equal work and penalties for domestic violence have been codified, yet traditional societal norms prevail for many women in this largely rural, agricultural country. Female genital mutilation is still widely practiced, though it is discouraged by official education campaigns.

The next year will be a crucial test of the leadership's commitment to an open and democratic society. Pluralistic media and rights to political organization must soon emerge if the 1997 elections are to be free and fair.

Estonia

Polity: Presidential-   **Political Rights:** 2*
parliamentary democracy   **Civil Liberties:** 2
Economy: Mixed   **Status:** Free
Capitalist
Population: 1,477,000
PPP: $6,690
Life Expectancy: 69.3
Ethnic Groups: Estonian (62 percent), Russian (30 percent),
Ukrainian, German, others
Capital: Tallinn
Ratings Change: *Estonia's political rights rating changed from 3 to 2
because of clarifications in citizenship, alien and naturalization laws.

Overview: **P**arliamentary elections in March and the collapse of Prime
Minister Tiit Vahi's center-left coalition after a bugging
scandal involving Interior Minister Edgar Savisaar
highlighted political events in Estonia in 1995. Vahi, never implicated in the
scandal, was reappointed.

Dominated by Sweden in the sixteenth and seventeenth centuries and annexed
by Russia in 1704, Estonia became independent with the collapse of the Russian
Empire in 1918. Soviet troops occupied the country during World War II as a result
of the 1939 Hitler-Stalin pact, which forcibly incorporated Estonia, Latvia and
Lithuania into the Soviet Union. Under Soviet rule, over 100,000 Estonians were
deported. Russian immigration substantially changed the country's ethnic composition; ethnic Estonians made up 88 percent of the population before Soviet rule and
just over 61 percent in 1989. Estonia regained independence with the disintegration
of the Soviet Union in 1991.

Estonia's second post-independence election for the 101-member parliament in
March 1995 saw a shift to the left-of-center Coalition Party/Rural Union alliance,
which won a major victory over ruling conservatives in the Pro Patria/Estonia
National Independence ruling coalition, gaining forty-one seats to the latter's eight.
The Reform Party, a pro-market group led by Siim Kallas, a former president of the
Central Bank, came in second in coalition with the Liberals, winning nineteen
seats. Vahi, a moderate, was elected prime minister. The election results reflected
popular dissatisfaction among the elderly and rural electorate, hardest hit by the
Pro-Patria-led government's market reforms.

The government collapsed in early October when Interior Minister Savisaar
was implicated in the bugging of leading politicians. His Center Party, with sixteen
seats in parliament, left the ruling coalition, leading to Vahi's resignation. Parliament subsequently approved a new coalition that included the Reform Party, the
Coalition Party and the Rural Union, an alliance of leftists backed by pensioners
and farmers opposed to land reform. The delicate left-right coalition commanded
fifty-five seats.

Estonia's political crisis came amid sustained economic growth. But the country remained politically divided along stark geographic and generational lines. Liberal business and trade policies created a young entrepreneurial elite concentrated in Tallinn, the capital. Poverty persists outside the cities, and the country's large and impoverished pensioner population and large Russian-speaking minority were courted by ex-Communist politicians. While the Reform Party pledged to steer the country back toward radical reforms, parliament remained fragmented over economic policy.

Political Rights and Civil Liberties: Estonians are able to change their government democratically, although restrictive citizenship and alien laws have disenfranchised some non-Estonians, particularly Russians.

Political parties and groupings are allowed to organize freely, including several organizations representing the Russian minority. While the issue of citizenship for Soviet-era immigrants remains controversial, several steps were taken in 1995 to clarify their legal status and naturalization requirements. The Law on Citizenship introduced a longer residency requirement (five years), than the previous one-year waiting period. This new requirement applies only to new immigrants, as Soviet-era immigrants will continue to fall under the two-plus-one requirement. The citizenship law also adds a civics exam to the naturalization process. The exam's parameters have yet to be finalized.

Amendments were made to the 1993 Law on Aliens. Of special concern was the need to resolve the issue of residency permits and citizenship for the country's 400,000 mostly Russian noncitizens. Under citizenship legislation, all Soviet-era immigrants were required to undergo naturalization procedures to obtain citizenship. Until then they were granted temporary residence permits, valid until July 1996, and were required to apply at least for permanent residence permits by July 1995. After complaints about the slow and unfair procedures involved in applying for residence and work permits, the government took steps to accommodate a rush of applications before the 12 July 1995 deadline. Almost 320,000 applications had been received by then, an estimated 80 percent of the possible total (in predominantly Russian-speaking Narva, 98 percent applied). Resisting pressure to extend the deadline formally, parliament authorized the government to develop a plan within four months for receiving late permit applications. Those who did not apply by 12 July 1995 will have three additional years before their rights and obligations as legal residents will be withdrawn, effectively extending temporary residence permits beyond July 1996. The government has so far granted temporary residence (no more than five years) to sixty-eight ex-Soviet military officers and their families, as part of the troop pullout deal concluded in 1994. More than 10,000 ex-military and their families have applied for the permits. Permanent residents in Estonia have the right to vote in local elections.

The new Law on Language marked a shift from the 1989 law in more clearly defining the role of Estonian as the state language, especially in state and local agencies. It included provisions allowing another language such as Russian to be an additional language of administration where its speakers compose a majority. However, requests must be made by municipalities individually to the government.

Estonians can freely express their views and there is a lively independent, private press, including English- and Russian-language publications. There are private television and radio stations, and an independent news agency.

Freedom of religion is guaranteed by law and honored in practice. The judiciary is independent and free from government pressure. The Central Organization of Estonian Trade Unions was created in 1990 to replace the Soviet federation. There are some thirty unions in the country and the right to strike is legal and utilized. Private, nongovernmental organizations are permitted. Women possess the same legal rights as men and are legally entitled to equal pay for equal work.

Ethiopia

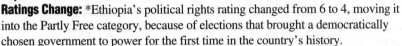

Polity: Dominant party   **Political Rights:** 4*
Economy: Statist   **Civil Liberties:** 5
Population: 55,979,000   **Status:** Partly Free
PPP: $330
Life Expectancy: 47.5
Ethnic Groups: Afar, Amhara, Harari, Oromo, Somali, Tigrean, others
Capital: Addis Ababa
Ratings Change: *Ethiopia's political rights rating changed from 6 to 4, moving it into the Partly Free category, because of elections that brought a democratically chosen government to power for the first time in the country's history.

Overview:
    Ethiopia took a great stride forward in achieving at least the form of democratic governance in the first national elections since the 1991 overthrow of Marxist dictator Colonel Mengistu Haile Mariam. However, inadequate protection of basic rights and the substance of the May 1995 polls, in which the ruling Ethiopian People's Revolutionary Democratic Front (EPRDF) scored overwhelming victories in national and regional contests as opposition parties boycotted the vote, raised concerns over future progress.

The transitional government was formed by the EPRDF after its military victory over the Marxist Mengistu regime in 1991, which in turn had overthrown Emperor Haile Selassie in 1974. It is estimated that at least 100,000 people were killed in anti-rebel drives and waves of political terror during that period. Extrajudicial executions, torture and detention without trial were common. The downfall of Mengistu saw the disappearance of these practices on any broad or organized scale. However, the EPRDF's record in honoring fundamental freedoms remains mixed.

The parliamentary elections took place under a constitution promulgated in December 1994 by a constituent assembly elected six months earlier. Opposition parties had also boycotted that election, claiming the government was giving unfair advantage to the ruling party. The boycott of the May 1995 vote allowed the EPRDF easily to take 483 of 548 seats in the new parliament, known as the Council of People's Representatives.

The transitional government handed power to the new parliament in August. The head of the outgoing government, President Meles Zenawi, was elected prime minister, and under the new constitutional arrangement in fact retains much of the power he held before. Prime Minister Meles's Tigray Peoples Liberation Front

(TPLF), which led the military drive that toppled the Mengistu regime, remains the most important political grouping and at the heart of the EPRDF. A largely symbolic president was also appointed.

Political Rights and Civil Liberties: The May 1995 elections allowed the people of Ethiopia to choose their government through a relatively free and fair electoral process for the first time. Most international observers declared the election to be largely free and fair, despite the opposition's charges of government manipulation. But more critical assessments pointed to the absence of the opposition and a crackdown on the independent media in the months before the vote as warning signs that a genuine democratic process might not be taking firm hold in the country.

The new government faces a host of problems in seeking to develop what remains one of the world's very poorest nations. Eritrea's successful secession has convinced the government to promote devolution of power to regional and local governments. The constitution adopted in December 1994 allows far greater regional autonomy and even the possibility of secession from the federation. In practice the EPRDF now controls all regional governments directly or through coalition partners, and the likelihood of any region soon invoking its right to secede is slight.

Serious opposition to the government in Addis Ababa remains, however. Most persistent and perhaps most dangerous is the armed rebellion being mounted in the south by the banned Oromo Liberation Front (OLF) and Islamic Front for the Liberation of Oromia. The Oromo ethnic group is Ethiopia's single largest, comprising roughly 40 percent of the country's 58 million people. Fighting in the countryside has produced many casualties and reports of human rights abuses. Numerous OLF supporters have been imprisoned. Oromo grievances include long periods of neglect of their region by the central government, which was dominated by the Amhara ethnic group until the TPLF, with its power base in northern Ethiopia, seized power. The potential for unrest remains high in the northeastern Ogaden and Afar areas.

Nonviolent democratic oppositionists have also suffered. Some have been intimidated and jailed or harassed by security officials, and some of their offices have been closed, international rights groups have reported.

The independent print media have been a particular target, since broadcast media remain firmly under government control. One independent journalist was "disappeared" in 1994. Several others were detained for extended periods without charge between 1993 and mid-1995, and five were sentenced to prison for periods of six months to two years. Over 100 more journalists were detained, most for about a month before being released on bail, but there is no guarantee that they will not be re-arrested. About 100 publications were closed during the same period.

The government has promised to establish a new commission for human rights, but remains highly sensitive of any criticism. Nevertheless, it is acting to punish human rights abuses committed by members of the previous regime. Citing the Nuremberg trials and Ethiopian law, a special prosecutor appointed in 1992 has begun presenting evidence to a court in Addis Ababa. Forty-five defendants, including eight members of the former ruling junta, have appeared in court. Twenty-four defendants are being tried in absentia, including the exiled Mengistu.

Mengistu survived a November 1995 assassination attempt in Zimbabwe, which has refused requests for his extradition.

There are some other signs of the potential for a more open society. The government is starting to sell off numerous assets, including hotels, factories and retail businesses. Trade unions are operating, though their freedom to bargain and to strike has not been fully tested. Religious freedom is respected. Yet, as European election observers commented, the "near-monopoly" enjoyed by the ruling party raises fears that Ethiopia's "democratic evolution is not assured."

Fiji

Polity: Parliamentary democracy and native chieftains (ethnic limits)
Economy: Capitalist
Population: 773,000
PPP: $5,410
Life Expectancy: 71.5
Ethnic Groups: Fijian (49 percent), Indian (46 percent), other Pacific islander, Chinese
Capital: Suva

Political Rights: 4
Civil Liberties: 3
Status: Partly Free

Overview: Fiji's paramount chiefs ceded sovereignty over these South Pacific islands to the British in 1874 to end frequent territorial conquests among rival kingdoms. In 1879 the British began bringing Indian laborers to the islands to work on sugar cane and cotton plantations. At independence in 1970 the size of the country's ethnic Fijian and Indian communities was roughly equal.

April 1987 elections brought to power a coalition of two Indian-based parties, the National Federation Party (NFP) and the Fiji Labor Party (FLP), breaking the seventeen-year rule of the ethnic Fijian Alliance Party. Alarmed by the Indian community's emerging political influence, then-Lieutenant Colonel Sitiveni Rabuka took power in a pair of bloodless coups in May and September 1987.

In January 1990 Fiji returned to full civilian rule. In July an interim government promulgated a controversial new constitution guaranteeing ethnic Fijians a perpetual majority in parliament. The constitution reserves thirty-seven of seventy seats in the House of Representatives for ethnic Fijians, with twenty-seven for Indians, five for "other races," mostly Chinese and Europeans, and one to the island dependency of Rotuma. Twenty-four of thirty-four seats in the unelected Senate are reserved for ethnic Fijians. Further, the prime minister must be an ethnic Fijian. The Great Council of Chiefs, a group of unelected, traditional rulers, selects the largely ceremonial president and appoints the ethnic Fijian senators.

May 1992 elections, though held under the racially biased constitution, restored partial democracy. Rabuka took office as prime minister after his Fijian Political

Party (SVT) took thirty seats and formed a coalition government. In November 1993 parliament rejected the government's 1994 budget proposal, leading to a dissolution of parliament and early elections in February 1994.

The key campaign issue was the Indian community's concerns over the constitution, which Rabuka promised would be reviewed. In the 18-25 February 1994 vote, results of the ethnic Fijian polling gave the SVT thirty-one seats; the Fijian Association Party, led by Joseveta Kamikamica, a Rabuka rival, five; independents, one. The militant Fijian National United Front lost all five of its seats. In the Indian voting the NFP took twenty seats and the FLP seven. The General Voters' Party (GVP) took four of the seats reserved for "other races" and an independent, one. On 28 February Rabuka began a five-year term as head of a coalition government consisting of his SVT, the GVP and the two independents.

Political Rights and Civil Liberties:

Fijians have voted twice under a constitution that ensures ethnic Fijians a parliamentary majority, and that was promulgated by an unelected, interim government without a referendum. The parliament's ethnic Fijian seats are heavily weighted toward rural areas, where more voters tend to support Fijian nationalist parties and traditional leaders. In addition, under specified emergency situations the constitution allows parliament to pass acts that can effectively override its civil liberties protections. A multiparty commission reviewing the constitution is due to report by the end of 1996.

Police abuse of detainees is a persistent problem. The judiciary is independent of the government. Of concern are the magistrates' courts, which deal with 95 percent of the cases handled by police. Some magistrates have handed down highly questionable judgments in criminal cases.

Fijians speak freely on all issues, although the Public Order Act, which prohibits speech or actions likely to incite racial antagonism, remains on the books. The Press Correction Act (PCA) allows the Minister of Information to order a paper to print a "correcting statement" to an article, with a fine and/or imprisonment possible if the paper refuses and is found guilty by a court. Under the PCA authorities can also arrest individuals for publishing "malicious" material, including false news that can result in "detriment to the public." These laws are rarely applied but reportedly lead to some self-censorship. The Rabuka government has occasionally pressured publications not to run articles on sensitive topics. The government-produced Nightly News Focus does not grant equal time to opposition viewpoints.

Rape and domestic violence are serious problems. *Pacific Islands Monthly* (PMI) columnist 'Atu Emberson-Bain has noted that in some rape cases the practice of *Bulubulu* (traditional reconciliation) is applied, allowing the offender to apologize to the victim's father or family (although not the victim herself). If the apology is accepted the felony charge is dropped. Women are generally paid less than men for equal work. Child abuse is also a growing problem. Ethnic Indians are occasionally subject to racially motivated harassment.

Freedom of religion is respected. Workers have the right to join independent unions and strike. The May 1994 *PMI* exposed grim working conditions at the state-owned Pacific Fishing Company cannery in Lekuva. Women on the production line face stifling heat, dangerous conditions and low wages.

Finland

Polity: Presidential-
parliamentary democracy
Economy: Mixed
capitalist
Population: 5,084,000
PPP: $16,270
Life Expectancy: 75.7
Ethnic Groups: Finn (94 percent), Swede, Lapp (Saami)
Capital: Helsinki

Political Rights: 1
Civil Liberties: 1
Status: Free

Overview: The Social Democratic Party dominated the March 1995
general elections, ending the reign of Prime Minister Esko
Aho's Center-Right coalition, which had set Finland on
course to economic recovery through strict austerity measures. Paavo Lipponen,
Social Democratic party leader and the new prime minister, set out to build a
broad-based and strong government by forming a coalition with the Conservatives,
the Swedish People's Party, the Left Alliance and the Environmentalists.

After eight centuries of foreign domination, Finland declared independence at
the end of 1917 and issued its present constitution in July of 1919. That document
provides for a 200-seat Parliament elected by universal suffrage and headed by a
presidentially appointed premier. The directly elected president holds considerable
power, particularly in light of a multiparty, proportionally representative system
that prevents any single party from gaining a parliamentary majority. The president
can initiate and veto legislation, dissolve parliament at any time and call for
elections. Eleven mainland provinces are headed by presidentially appointed
governors, while the Swedish-speaking island province of Aland enjoys autonomy.

This year's general elections produced results that were very close to projections.
Former Prime Minister Aho of the rural-based Center Party employed rather unpopular
austerity measures to pull the nation out of its deepest recession this century. With the
collapse of the Soviet Union in 1990, so went an enormous portion of Finland's export
market. The first three years of the decade saw a 15 percent drop in GDP, a teetering
banking system and unemployment as high as 20 percent. Aho's program assisted in
producing an 18.5 percent increase in export volume in 1993, and 12.5 percent in
1994. Under his care, the deficit shrank rapidly and Finland took a step toward
aligning itself to Western Europe by joining the European Union.

Although the new ruling party won the election in part because of the center-right's
unpopular spending cuts, prior to taking office, the new coalition outlined further cuts in
welfare and unemployment benefits, state transfers to local governments and
housing and agriculture subsidies. According to Prime Minister Lipponen, this
government will focus on the nation's rising debt and unemployment as well as
meeting the Maastricht Treaty requirements for economic and monetary union.

Political Rights   Finns are able to change their government democratically.
and Civil Liberties: In 1994, the country held its first direct presidential

election since independence. Legislation passed in 1992 provides all Finnish citizens with the right to their own culture and equal protection under the law. However, gypsies who outnumber the Saamis (or Lapps) several times over, often report being treated as outsiders by the largely homogeneous population despite the fact that they have lived in Finland since the 1500s. Discrimination on the basis of race, religion, sex, language or social status is illegal, and a recently adopted law mandates that newspapers cannot identify people by race.

Until the fall of the Soviet Union, newspapers censored themselves on issues considered sensitive to Finland's eastern neighbor. Traditionally, many political parties owned or controlled newspapers, but in recent years several dailies have folded. A wide selection of publications is presently available to the Finnish public, including private newspapers. The Finnish Broadcasting Company controls most radio and television programming, although limited private broadcasting is available.

Women comprise over 45 percent of the labor force and an average of 30 percent in the elective bodies of the last few years. There are seven women in the present cabinet as well as the first Green Party minister in Europe.

Finnish workers have the right to organize, bargain and strike and an overwhelming majority belong to free trade unions. The Central Organization of Finnish Trade Unions (SAK) dominates the labor movement.

The population is highly homogeneous with only 60, 000 foreign residents and a strict refugee quota of 500 persons per year. For those refugees who are granted admission, free housing, medical care, monthly stipends and language lessons are provided. In an effort to prevent "ethnic ghettos" from forming, some refugees are placed in small villages, many of whose residents have never seen foreigners. In many instances, the government has instituted educational programs to teach children about their new neighbors. Adding to the homogeneity is the predominance of the Lutheran church. Both Lutheran and Orthodox established churches are financed through a special tax from which citizens may exempt themselves. Other faiths are permitted the freedom to worship.

France

Polity: Presidential-parliamentary democracy
Economy: Mixed capitalist
Population: 58,109,000
PPP: $19,510
Life Expectancy: 76.9
Ethnic Groups: French, regional minorities (Corsican, Alsatian, Basque, Breton), various Arab and African immigrant groups
Capital: Paris

Political Rights: 1
Civil Liberties: 2
Status: Free

Overview: Former premier Jacques Chirac of the conservative Rally for the Republic (RPR) became president with 52.6 percent of the vote, overcoming obstacles including demands he withdraw in favor of RPR Prime Minister Edouard Balladur's candidacy. The far right made alarming gains, but the Socialist Party, which had been stagnating after fourteen years in power, regained vitality and unity. The fall saw widespread labor protests against proposed economic reforms.

Early in presidential campaigning Balladur was considered the frontrunner, as the only potentially significant Socialist challenger, outgoing European Commission President Jacques Delors, had declined to run. However, Balladur's popularity began to suffer, partly because his government backed down after a decree tightening university admissions prompted student demonstrations. Balladur was also hurt by charges he had personally authorized an illegal wiretap on the father-in-law of a judge investigating bribery within the RPR.

Relatively unknown Socialist Lionel Jospin unexpectedly won the 23 April first round with 23.3 percent of votes, but Chirac outpolled Balladur by 20.8 percent to 18.6 percent. Fringe candidates received nearly 40 percent, notably the extreme-right National Front leader Jean-Marie Le Pen, who took a record 15.1 percent. A 7 May runoff was called as no candidate had received a majority.

Chirac's runoff victory over Jospin gave the RPR and its allies control over the presidency and both legislative chambers. Chirac took power on 17 May from the terminally ill Francois Mitterand, who had been president since 1981. New premier Alain Juppe immediately confronted France's 12 percent unemployment, planning to provide various employer subsidies and tax exemptions to encourage job creation. However, the languid pace of change fueled criticism and workers took to the streets protesting budget revisions and public-sector pension reforms.

Widespread strikes began in October as France's seven traditionally divided unions formed a common front, organizing millions of civil servants against Juppe's proposed pay freezes, job cuts and privatization. Paris was left with virtually no public services amid sporadic violence between demonstrators and police. Juppe relented after over three weeks without services, virtually abandoning his plans for pension reform and layoffs in the state railroad, France's most indebted and subsidized company. Manufacturing, retail and tourism lost millions of dollars as sporadic labor actions continued into December.

Further unrest, particularly in French Polynesia's capital of Papeete, Tahiti, followed the first of several proposed nuclear tests, resumed despite a 1992 international moratorium. French officers were sent to Papeete after rioters firebombed the territorial assembly and airport.

Several violent incidents between youths and police occurred in French suburbs, disproportionately affected by unemployment and social disadvantages. The Ministry for Integration and the Fight Against Exclusion plans to encourage business development by converting the worst areas to tax-exempt "free zones." Inner-city police will also be reinforced and issued flak jackets, faster cars and possibly guns firing rubber bullets.

Political Rights and Civil Liberties: The French can change their government democratically. The constitution grants the president significant emergency powers, including rule by decree under certain circumstances. The president can call referenda and dissolve a hostile parliament, but may not veto its acts or routinely issue decrees.

Fifteen years of decentralization has given mayors considerable power over housing, transportation, schools, culture, welfare and some aspects of law enforcement. In June, the National Front took over 1,000 new city council seats and competed in runoff voting in 116 of 231 cities, pledging to institute a "national preference" policy favoring French people over foreigners whenever possible. Despite left-right coalitions formed to defeat them, National Front candidates won three mayoralties. The Front has been charged with inciting racial hatred and violence against minorities, including the death of a Moroccan man during a rally and the shooting death of a seventeen-year-old student of Comoran descent by Le Pen supporters.

France has repeatedly been charged with treating immigrants poorly. Children of immigrants are not granted citizenship at birth, but must apply between sixteen and twenty-one years of age or else forfeit the right. Despite legal provisions authorizing those seeking refugee status to cross the border without visas or identity papers, border guards have occasionally used excessive force to discourage "illegal" crossings. In August, an officer accidentally shot and killed an eight-year-old Bosnian child as a convoy of trucks fled, mistaking a roadblock of unmarked police cars for armed bandits.

The threat of terrorism spilling over from Algeria has led to restrictions on freedom of expression. Three publications concerning Islam were banned this year for threatening public order. Most publications banned in recent years have been neofascist or anti-Semitic tracts.

In 1995, seven people were killed and 180 wounded in various bombings allegedly connected to Islamic fundamentalists protesting French financial and diplomatic support for Algeria's military-backed government. Nationwide police sweeps produced hundreds of arrests, and thousands suspected to be of "North African origin" were routinely stopped by police checking identity and residence papers. A paratrooper killed one bombing suspect, Khaled Kelkal, after an extensive manhunt. Critics of the government crackdown called the shooting an execution to avert further terrorist acts to secure Kelkal's release had he been jailed.

Despite open suspicion toward Muslims and prohibitions against wearing religious garb or symbols in state schools, religious freedom is guaranteed. Labor rights are respected in practice, and strikes are permitted (see Overview).

The press is largely free, although the government partially subsidizes journalism and registers journalists. Publication of opinion poll results is prohibited in the week preceding any voting. In December, the Senate overwhelmingly rejected a controversial law that would have sharply curtailed media coverage of corruption scandals involving politicians. Although the Constitutional Court overturned legislation requiring the use of French on all products and public announcements, there are French-language quotas on national television channels.

Gabon

Polity: Dominant party
Economy: Capitalist
Population: 1,320,000
PPP: $3,913
Life Expectancy: 53.5
Ethnic Groups: Duma, Fang (25 percent), Mpongwe, Shogo, others
Capital: Libreville

Political Rights: 5
Civil Liberties: 4
Status: Partly Free

Overview:

Gabon experienced relative social and political calm in 1995, as even its first national constitutional referendum failed to arouse much passion among the electorate. International objections surfaced, however, when the government issued an ultimatum to illegal residents that they either regularize their immigrant status or face mass expulsion.

Situated on the west coast of central Africa, this heavily forested, tropical nation gained independence from France in 1960. After ascending to the presidency in 1967, Omar Bongo continued his predecessor's consolidation of power by officially outlawing the opposition. Twenty-three years later, under pressure from protesters and a deteriorating economy, Bongo called a national conference to establish an inclusive political organization and granted legal status to all participating parties. The opposition rejected two attempts to form "inclusive" governments as covert maintenance of imperial rule. Ostensibly running as an independent in 1993, Bongo retained his position in fraudulent elections leading to violent social protests and repressive security measures. In 1994 the government and opposition leaders signed an agreement, known as the Paris Accords, aimed at instituting true democratic reforms.

A July referendum resulted in a call for reforms including nonpartisan election monitoring, limiting presidential powers and restructuring the notoriously brutal presidential guard as prescribed by the Paris Accords. Opposition parties hope reforms will provide a transparent framework for free and fair legislative elections scheduled for May 1996.

International rights organizations voiced concern over the government's stated intention to repatriate all illegal foreigners on 31 January 1995. Under the African Human Rights Charter, ratified by Gabon, the collective expulsion of foreigners is illegal. Prior to the extension of the original deadline, a leaflet threatening foreigners with death circulating around the capital, Libreville, caused considerable panic among legal and illegal aliens alike. The Gabonese defense minister called upon the population to remain calm and allow the "humanitarian" repatriation exercise to proceed in an orderly manner.

Political Rights and Civil Liberties:

Gabonese citizens cannot change their government democratically. Reforms drafted in the Paris Accords and adopted by referendum in July may alter that situation after 1996 legislative elections. Bongo has retained power through manipulating the election process for twenty-eight years.

Courts exercise considerable autonomy; however, lacking procedural safeguards, the judiciary remains vulnerable to government manipulation. Constitutionally guaranteed rights to legal counsel and public criminal trials are generally respected. However, the law presumes one is guilty as charged; therefore, judges may deliver a verdict at an initial hearing if sufficient evidence is presented.

Torture remains a routine means for extracting confessions. Prison conditions are poor, with insufficient food and water, inadequate medical facilities and frequent beatings. The government often detains illegal and legal refugees without charge, and there have been reports of forced labor.

Free speech and press freedom are increasingly respected, with the exception of broadcast media. There are over a dozen independent weeklies, primarily controlled by opposition parties, in addition to a government daily. Military destruction of private radio stations has punctuated severe restrictions on electronic media. Foreign newspapers, magazines and broadcasts are widely available.

The constitution does not restrict the rights of assembly and association, but permits are required for public gatherings. Freedom to form and join political parties is generally respected, although civil servants may face harassment because of their associations. Members of the Gabonese League of Human Rights have reported being threatened, censured and intimidated.

Although workers have the right to unionize and strike, unions must register with the government in order to be officially recognized. Despite legal protections the government has taken action against numerous strikers and unions, and used force to suppress illegal demonstrations.

Although there are no legal restrictions on travel, authorities routinely stop individuals to check their identification documents. Extortion is common, particularly when the traveler is not Gabonese. Soldiers have physically prevented opposition leaders from leaving the country, and ordinary citizens have charged ethnic discrimination and year-long delays in issuance of passports.

Religious freedom is constitutionally guaranteed and respected. Although the government maintains its ban on Jehovah's Witnesses, the law is rarely enforced and permits are routinely issued to the group for large gatherings.

In June several thousand women staged a peaceful march in Libreville protesting an amendment to the existing polygamy law. Currently, both partners must consent to marriage under traditional law, which permits polygamy, or to a monogamous arrangement. The current amendment, proposed by Bongo, dispenses with the obligatory consent of the woman.

Other legal protections exist for women, including equal-access laws for education, business and investment. In addition to owning property and businesses, women constitute over 50 percent of the salaried workforce in the health and trading sectors. They continue to face legal and cultural discrimination, however, particularly in rural areas and in regard to domestic violence, which persists at an extremely high level.

The Gambia

Polity: Military
Economy: Capitalist
Population: 1,090,000
PPP: $1,260
Life Expectancy: 45.0
Ethnic Groups: Mandinka (42 percent), Fulani (18 percent), Wolof (16 percent), Jola, Serahuli
Capital: Banjul

Political Rights: 7
Civil Liberties: 6
Status: Not Free

Overview:
In November, the Gambia's ruling Armed Forces Provisional Ruling Council (AFPRC) unveiled a constitution pledging elections for July 1996. Western donors have pressured the young officers who seized power in July 1994 to return civilian government to what had been one of Africa's most enduring democracies. But their commitment to free elections became increasingly suspect through 1995 as the junta increased its repressive powers. Critics of the regime were arrested and several suspicious deaths recorded.

The Gambia was a democracy until 1994, ruled by President Sir Dawda K. Jawara and his People's Progressive Party for nearly three decades after independence from Britain in 1965. The tiny, poor country relied on foreign aid for over three-quarters of its national budget, and on European tourists for most foreign exchange. A 1981 leftist military coup was reversed by armed intervention from Senegal, which surrounds the Gambia on three sides. In 1982 the countries created a Confederation of Senegambia, which lasted seven years. The Gambia dissolved the arrangement amid differences caused by the countries' colonial heritages (Senegal was a French colony) and Gambians' fear of total absorption by Senegal.

Senegal did not intercede during the 1994 coup, led by Captain Yahya Jammeh. Roundly condemned internationally, the AFPRC received a mixed reception at home, denouncing alleged corruption in the Jawara government and promising transparency, accountability and early elections after cleaning up the administration. However, the junta quickly imposed several decrees curtailing civil and political rights and began a sustained, if episodic, campaign against independent media.

A November 1994 counter-coup was crushed and several alleged plotters executed. In June 1995, seven soldiers convicted of participating in the plot received nine-year sentences. The regime had announced earlier that alleged plot leader and former interior minister Captain Sadibou Haidara, who had helped overthrow Jawara, had died in prison of "natural causes." On 24 June, Finance Minister Ousman Koro Ceesay's body was discovered in a burned car just outside the capital, Banjul, following a meeting with Jammeh. In October soldiers arrested at least seventy former officials and suspected opponents of Jammeh, who reportedly were planning demonstrations.

Broadly worded decrees adopted in July and November greatly expanded the National Intelligence Agency's search and seizure powers and the interior ministry's arrest powers, respectively.

The Gambia's international ties grew increasingly precarious in 1995. Renewed ties with Libya, announced in January, raised fears of regional destabilization. Some observers fear a Gambian connection to an ongoing guerrilla war by ethnic Jola people in the southern Senegal province of Casamance. Their traditional lands—to which Jammeh is native—straddle the two countries' frontier.

Political Rights and Civil Liberties: Gambians cannot change their government democratically. A 22 July 1994 coup by junior officers of the Gambia National Army deposed the elected government and dissolved parliament. A series of AFPRC decrees have banned all political activity and restricted fundamental rights.

The junta has promised July 1996 elections under a new constitution adopted late in 1995. Apparently considering a presidential bid, Jammeh presided over weekly rallies but simultaneously denounced "western-style democracy" as unsuitable, warning, "If the [external] pressure continues the Council will continue to rule for the next thousand years."

Free expression has been severely limited since the coup. AFPRC decrees three and four allow arbitrary detention and prohibit possession and distribution of literature deemed "political." Security agents have harassed, intimidated and beaten journalists, and arrested several. Independent newspapers continue publishing, but practice extensive self-censorship. Journalists who report openly face serious consequences. Several from the newspaper *The Point* were arrested in April but acquitted in September by a Nigerian magistrate serving on secondment in the Gambia, who was uncowed by military pressure. Closely controlled news reporting by state-run Radio Gambia also is broadcast by the country's two private radio stations. There is no television, but Senegalese broadcasts are received throughout the country.

The Gambia's legal system has mostly been eviscerated since the coup. Arbitrary detention and a lack of due process are now standard. There have been several extrajudicial killings, and torture in jails and barracks is reported. Public assembly is severely limited and meetings of any kind without permission forbidden, except for religious observances.

Women suffer *de facto* discrimination in many areas despite legal protections. Women's education and wage employment opportunities are far fewer than men's, especially in rural areas. Islamic shari'a law provisions applied in family law and inheritance restrict women's rights.

The junta has maintained prevailing labor laws, though restrictions on civil liberties apply to all trade union activities as well. The 1990 Labor Act allows all workers but civil servants and security forces to form unions, and provides for the right to strike. Two umbrella groups, the Gambian Worker's Confederation and the Gambian Workers' Union, remain in existence but their ability to act under the military regime is unclear.

Georgia

Polity: Presidential-par-
liamentary democracy
(foreign military-influenced)
Economy: Statist transitional
Population: 5,427,000
PPP: $2,300
Life Expectancy: 72.8

Political Rights: 4*
Civil Liberties: 5
Status: Partly Free

Ethnic Groups: Georgians (70 percent), Armenian (8 percent) Russian
(6 percent), Abkhazian, Azeri, Ossetian, others
Capital: Tbilisi
Ratings Change: *Georgia's political rights rating changed from 5 to 4 because
of greater political stability, a new constitution and the direct election of
President Shevardnadze.

Overview:

Eduard Shevardnadze survived an assassination attempt
and was overwhelmingly elected president in 5 November
elections that also saw his Centrist Union win 150 of 235
seats in parliament. In consolidating power, Shevardnadze pushed through a new
constitution and disbanded the 3,000-strong paramilitary *Mkhedrioni*, which had
supported him in the 1992-93 civil war, arresting its leader, Jaba Ioseliani. An
austerity program improved the country's economic outlook.

Absorbed by Russia in the early nineteenth century, Georgia proclaimed
independence in 1918, gaining Soviet recognition two years later. In 1921, it was
overrun by the Red Army. In 1922, it entered the USSR as a component of the
Transcaucasian Federated Soviet Republic, becoming a separate union republic in
1936. Georgia declared independence from a crumbling Soviet Union after a
referendum in April 1991. Nationalist leader and former dissident Zviad
Gamsakhurdia was elected president, but his authoritarian and erratic behavior led
to his violent ouster by opposition units that included the Mkhedrioni. In early
1992, former Soviet Foreign Minister Shevardnadze was asked by a temporary
State Council to head a new government, and he was subsequently elected speaker
of the parliament, making him acting head of state. In 1993, Georgia experienced
the violent secession of the long-simmering Abkhazia region and armed insurrection by Gamsakhurdia loyalists. Although Shevardnadze blamed Russia for arming
and encouraging Abkhazian separatists, he legalized the presence of 19,000
Russian troops in five Georgian bases in exchange for Russian support against
Gamsakhurdia, who was defeated and reportedly committed suicide. In early 1994,
Georgians and Abkhazians signed an agreement in Moscow that called for a ceasefire,
stationing Commonwealth of Independent States troops under Russian command along
the Abkhazian border, and the return of refugees under United Nations supervision.

In November elections, Shevardnadze won nearly 75 percent of the vote. His
main rival, former Communist boss Dzumber Patiashvili, got 19.3 percent. In the
parliamentary vote, only three of the fifty-two political groups running managed to
clear the 5 percent threshold, with Shevardnadze's Centrist Union garnering the

lion's share, and the moderate opposition National Democratic Party running second. In August, parliament had adopted a new constitution that restored Georgia as a presidential, federal republic with a strong executive.

In September, Georgia's switch to a permanent currency marked the culmination of an austerity campaign that wiped out hyperinflation in less than a year. Prices were freed, state spending was frozen and large-scale privatization was launched. Oil reserves were discovered in eastern and western regions and, after much wrangling, Russia agreed to a pipeline carrying oil from neighboring Azerbaijan through Georgia.

In 1995, Abkhazian leaders' calls for independence and reunification with Russia were rejected by Moscow, which signed protocols protecting Georgia's borders. Abkhaz-Georgian negotiations were suspended through much of the year.

Political Rights and Civil Liberties: Georgians have the means to change their government democratically, but the government's loss of control over Abkhazia and South Ossetia affected the scope of the government's power and representation. The November elections were judged generally free and fair by international observers. However, voting in ten of eighty-five districts (in Abkhazia and South Ossetia) was postponed indefinitely. The new constitution creates a federal state and gives the president the power to appoint and dismiss the prime minister, to dismiss the cabinet, and to appoint governors, heads of district administrations and city mayors.

There are over sixty political parties registered. Fifty-two contested the November elections, but only three groupings met the 5 percent threshold for representation in parliament.

The ongoing political crisis has led to repression of the independent press. In addition to censoring news from Abkhazia, the government has closed newspapers and detained journalists. Under a 1991 press law, journalists are obliged to "respect the dignity and honor" of the president and not impugn the honor and dignity of citizens or undermine the regime. Publications could face legal action for "malevolently using freedom of the press, [and] spreading facts not corresponding to reality..." The government controls newsprint and the distribution network, as well as radio and television, which reflect official views and have denied access to the opposition. Ibervision, the putatively independent television station, has faced government pressure, and self-censorship is a problem in all media.

There are restrictions, often arbitrary, on freedom of assembly. Freedom of religion is generally respected in this predominantly Christian Orthodox country. Ethnic and minority rights remain under stress. While some Georgian refugees have returned to Abkhazia, repatriation plans were halted in the face of violence against ethnic Georgians and stalled negotiations.

The legal system remains a hybrid of laws from Georgia's brief period of pre-Soviet independence, the Soviet era, the Gamsakhurdia presidency and the State Council period. Many "political" crimes remain on the books as a means to prosecute and deter opponents, and the system is plagued by documented cases of illegal arrests, arbitrary dismissal of defense attorneys and related problems. Members of the judiciary have engaged in corrupt practices, including bribery and bending to the influences of political leaders and gangsters. Nongovernmental

Georgian human rights groups report that political prisoners are subjected to poor prison conditions, torture, beatings and other abuses, as well as to violations of due process.

The Georgian Confederation of Trade Unions, the successor to the official Communist-era structure, includes about thirty different sectoral unions. There is a legal right to strike. Government concern about the status of and discrimination against women is minimal. Women are found mostly in traditional, low-paying occupations.

Germany

Polity: Federal par-
liamentary democracy
Economy: Mixed
capitalist
Population: 81,704,000
PPP: $21,120
Life Expectancy: 76.0
Ethnic Groups: German (95 percent), numerous immigrant groups
Capital: Berlin

Political Rights: 1
Civil Liberties: 2
Status: Free

Overview:	**G**ermany's parliament sidestepped a post-War taboo after months of national debate, voting to dispatch troops to support U.N. peacekeepers in Bosnia. In April, an article in *Der Spiegel* accusing German intelligence agents of setting up last summer's spectacular plutonium-smuggling arrests prompted calls for the resignation of Bernd Schmidbauer, Chancellor Helmut Kohl's chief intelligence coordinator. Another controversy involved unresolved investigations of thousands of former East German officials charged with abuses of power, espionage, falsifying election results and manslaughter for sanctioning border shootings at the Berlin Wall prior to reunification. Two high-court decisions were handed down barring the prosecution under German law of spies who acted against West Germany exclusively from the East's territory, and of judges who jailed critics of the East German regime, unless their actions were deemed autocratic and excessive.

Germany was divided into Soviet, U.S., British and French occupation zones following the Allies' 1945 defeat of Hitler's Third Reich. Four years later the Allies helped establish a democratic Federal Republic of Germany, while the Soviets oversaw the formation of the Communist-dominated German Democratic Republic (GDR). Berlin remained divided, a status reinforced by the 1961 construction of the Berlin Wall. After the collapse of Erich Honecker's hardline GDR regime in 1989 and the destruction of the wall in March of 1990, citizens voted in the country's first free parliamentary election, backing parties that supported rapid reunification.

Germans continue to adjust five years after reunification, and despite growing unemployment the economy continues to prosper. Growing social unification is apparent in the increasing numbers of former East Germans who now identify themselves simply as Germans and in the rising eastern birth rate, interpreted by many as a sign of hope for the future.

Political Rights and Civil Liberties: Citizens can change their government democratically. The federal system allows a considerable amount of self-government among the sixteen states. Individuals are free to form political parties and receive federal funding, provided the parties are democratic in nature.

In 1995, foreign residents organized for the first time, forming the Democratic Party of Germany (DPD). Although party membership has not attained the 51 percent citizenship threshold required to field candidates, the DPD campaigns for changes in the electoral system and the 1913 citizenship law. Currently, non-nationals aged sixteen to twenty-three are eligible for citizenship provided they have lived in Germany for eight years. All others may apply after fifteen years of residency, but dual citizenship is prohibited.

In February, two extremist parties were declared unconstitutional on the grounds that they resembled the Nazi party. Earlier in the year, the National Party of Germany's leader and documentary filmmaker Bela Ewald Athens were prosecuted for publicly denying the Holocaust. Authorities also jailed fifty-five skinheads for a week after they planned a rally commemorating the death of Rudolf Hess. Restrictions on expression, assembly and association have been criticized as overly broad and carrying the potential for abuse against minorities.

The press and broadcast media are free and independent, offering pluralistic viewpoints with the exception of neo-Nazi sentiment. Broadcast networks are required to provide equal opportunities for expression of opinion. Recent letterbomb attacks on outspoken critics of extremist groups may curtail freedom of speech to some extent.

An emotional controversy over the barring of crucifixes from classrooms in Bavaria brought religious freedom to the fore in 1995. The introduction of a conciliation process for cases when parents or children demand the removal of religious symbols resolved the conflict in the overwhelmingly Roman Catholic state. Religious freedom is generally respected throughout Germany, although Scientologists are banned from public proselytizing and members of certain fringe groups may be banned from civil service.

Women's rights have also topped the agenda this year, with Chancellor Kohl backing an ultimately unsuccessful bill requiring that women constitute one-third of candidates for parliamentary seats and party offices. A resolution designed to reconcile the opposing abortion policies of East and West was passed, making abortion illegal except in cases of rape or danger to the mother's life but providing no penalty for women and doctors involved in illegal procedures. In addition, stiffer penalties for marital rape were approved by the lower house.

Labor, business and farming groups are free, highly organized and influential. In its first strike in eleven years, IG Metall won pay increases this year without granting any concessions to employers. Trade union federation membership has dropped sharply since 1991 due to the collapse of industry in the East and layoffs in the West. Debate persisted throughout the year concerning whether traditionally limited shopping hours are out of touch with market demands and stifle job growth, or whether they provide a vital protection for small German businesses.

Ghana

Polity: Dominant party
Economy: Capitalist-statist
Population: 17,453,000
PPP: $2,110
Life Expectancy: 56.0
Ethnic Groups: Akan (including Fanti) (44 percent), Mossi-Dagomba (16 percent), Ewe (13 percent), Ga (8 percent), Ashanti, some fifty others
Capital: Accra

Political Rights: 4*
Civil Liberties: 4
Status: Partly Free

Ratings Change: *Ghana's political rights rating changed from 5 to 4 because of increased openness in the political arena, including proper by-elections and voter registration.

Overview: Ghana's measured liberalization continued through 1995, bringing increased media openness and economic reform.
Progress was tempered by lingering authoritarian tendencies in President Jerry Rawlings's government, as opposition parties sought to forge a united front heading toward late-1996 elections.

Long known as the Gold Coast and once a major slaving center, Ghana in 1957 became the first sub-Saharan country to gain independence from Britain. The 1966 overthrow of Ghana's charismatic independence leader, Kwame Nkrumah, led to a fifteen-year series of military coups. Alternating military and civilian governments were nearly interchangeable in terms of incompetence and mendacity. In 1979, then-Flight-Lieutenant Rawlings led a coup against the ruling military junta, returning power to a civilian government as promised after performing "house-cleaning" of corrupt senior army officers. The civilian administration did not live up to Rawlings's expectations, however, and he seized power again in December 1981 and set up the Provisional National Defense Council (PNDC). The PNDC junta, initially radically socialist and populist, brutally suppressed any dissent, banning political parties and free expression. A crumbling economy worsened by severe drought in the early 1980s convinced Rawlings that only massive international aid could help Ghana revive its fortunes. Rejecting socialism, Rawlings transformed Ghana into an experimental model for structural adjustment programs urged by international lenders.

Political liberalization has lagged behind economic reform. Political parties were legalized after a new constitution was adopted in April 1992. Rawlings was declared president after November 1992 elections. Extensive irregularities convinced opposition parties to boycott legislative elections a month later, and the PNDC successor, the National Democratic Congress (NDC), swept into parliament unopposed, effectively continuing one-party rule.

Anti-government opposition heightened during 1995 as serious inflation eroded living standards and reports of government corruption by a reinvigorated media incensed the public. In May the opposition coalition Alliance for Change called a mass march in Accra, the capital. Its slogan, *Kumi Preko* ("Kill Me Now"), an allusion to deteriorating living conditions, was taken literally as armed government supporters opened fire to crush the demonstration, killing five.

Throughout 1995 opposition forces debated how to choose a single challenger to Rawlings in next year's presidential contest. Yet opposition unity is not assured as a decades-old political rivalry between supporters of socialist and free-market economics continues in a modified form. International voter registration and education assistance may help ensure free and fair elections. However, lack of access to state media and the NDC's use of state resources for campaigning will seriously hamper the opposition, whose continued disunity would also help Rawlings extend his rule. Rawlings took a leading role in seeking to end Liberia's civil war, and also sought to patch frayed relations with neighboring Togo. He also attempted to bolster his international support through extensive travels, including trips to the U.S. that featured a White House visit and a Hollywood reception at which he received an award from Michael Jackson.

Political Rights and Civil Liberties: Ghanaians cannot change their government democratically. Multiparty elections in 1992 in which Rawlings took 53 percent of the vote were neither free nor fair. The 1996 elections present another opportunity for a genuine democratic transition. Ghana's 140-member Parliament is elected on a single-member district system and is almost entirely dominated by the ruling party coalition.

The constitution guarantees freedom of expression, and there is vigorous and sometimes vociferous political debate. About twenty opposition newspapers of varying quality and political persuasion are published regularly. But financial constraints and government pressure limit private media. Criminal libel laws that make reporting false information a felony have been used to intimidate the media. The power of state media also creates serious imbalances. The government controls most broadcasting and the two daily newspapers, and allows little expression of opposition views. In July, Ghanaian authorities agreed to open the airwaves and allow competition to the Ghana Broadcasting Corporation. Authorities issued a total of thirty-six provisional television and radio licenses, but demanded "commitment fees" of 40 million cedis ($40,000) for television and 20 million cedis ($20,000) for radio licensees, a move that could seriously restrict the number of stations that actually begin broadcasting. Media openness and accessibility will be a barometer of government intentions as elections near.

Permits are not required for meetings or demonstrations, and the rights to peaceful assembly and association are constitutionally guaranteed. Many nongovernmental organizations operate openly and freely, including human rights groups. Religious freedom is respected, although tensions between Christian and Muslim communities and within the Muslim community itself occasionally turned violent in 1995.

Ghanaian courts have acted with increased autonomy under the 1992 constitution, but remain subject to considerable governmental influence. Traditional courts in rural areas often handle minor cases according to local customs that do not meet constitutional standards. Lack of resources also means that large numbers of people are held in pretrial detention for long periods under harsh conditions.

Ghanaian women enjoy equal rights under the law but suffer societal discrimination that is particularly serious in rural areas, where opportunities for education and wage employment are limited. Domestic violence against women is reportedly common, but is often unreported. The *tro-kosi* system of young girls being forced into indefinite servitude to traditional priests is still practiced in parts of northern Ghana.

Civil servants may not join unions. Other unions must officially register under the Trades Union Ordinance, but this requirement is not currently used to block union formation. The Industrial Relations Act requires mediation and arbitration before strikes are deemed legal. The umbrella Trade Union Congress is the only labor confederation. Long closely aligned with the ruling party, it has recently demonstrated some autonomy.

Ghana's vigorous privatization program proceeded in 1995, but corruption continues to hinder growth. Investigative reports forced an investigation of high-level malfeasance, and seven senior officials remained under scrutiny at year's end.

Greece

Polity: Parliamentary democracy
Economy: Mixed capitalist
Population: 10,456,000
PPP: $8,310
Life Expectancy: 77.6
Ethnic Groups: Greek (98 percent), Macedonian, Turk
Capital: Athens

Political Rights: 1
Civil Liberties: 3
Status: Free

Overview: Nineteen-ninety-five was a year of rebuilding bridges for Greece, which found itself increasingly isolated from its European partners on Balkan issues. Meanwhile, internal politics focused on Prime Minister Andreas Papandreou's failing health and imminent resignation.

Greece became a monarchy following independence from the Ottoman Empire in 1830. The ensuing century brought continued struggle between republicans and royalists, occupation by the Axis powers in April 1941, and civil war between royalist forces and communists until 1949. Following a 1967 coup that brought a military junta to power, a failed attempt by members of the Greek navy to restore the king led to the formal deposition of the monarch and establishment of a republic. The country returned to civilian rule under a parliamentary democracy in July, 1974 and a year later the current constitution went into effect.

The Pan-Hellenic Socialist Movement (PASOK) defeated the New Democracy Party in October 1993 and returned former premier Papandreou to power. In recent years the party has splintered into a pro-European faction seeking participation in European monetary union to combat economic and foreign-policy problems, and the more traditional, populist Socialists. In March, PASOK narrowly avoided the dissolution of parliament and an election by securing the election of popular conservative Costis Stefanopoulos to the presidency. PASOK's latest challenge has been maintaining party unity while potential candidates line up to succeed the ailing prime minister.

Several major changes in foreign policy have added to the party's instability of late. Alongside the planning of a friendship treaty aimed at ending tensions over ethnic Greeks in southern Albania, Greek-Albanian relations improved with the arrests of North Epirus Liberation Front members believed to be responsible for a 1994 raid on an Albanian military post during which two soldiers were killed. In March, the Socialists lifted a veto of the European Union (EU) customs union agreement with Turkey, in return for securing entry into the EU for both parts of Cyprus by the turn of the century. Finally, in September, the foreign ministry ended a nineteen-month economic blockade against Macedonia in return for a promise that the former Yugoslav republic will redesign its flag and alter the language of its constitution to remove any hint of a claim on the Greek province of the same name.

Political Rights and Civil Liberties: Citizens of Greece can change their government democratically. Although voting is compulsory for those aged eighteen to seventy, an enormous bureaucracy does not permit changes of voting address, forcing nearly 650,000 people to travel to former residences in order to vote. The International Helsinki Federation for Human Rights (IHF) reported that during the first direct elections for local prefects and prefecture councils in 1994, two primarily Turkish districts were joined to adjacent districts to avoid the election of ethnic Turks.

Apart from politically related restrictions, the media possess substantial freedom. The public prosecutor may press charges against publishers and seize publications deemed offensive to the president or religious beliefs. "Unwarranted" publicity for terrorists is banned from the media. In many instances, television and newspapers have exercised strict self-censorship in regard to the prime minister's health and retirement.

With the exception of the military and the police, Greeks enjoy freedom of association and the right to organize unions. This year witnessed a series of strikes and protests prompted by the introduction of new taxes and enforced collection of those already in existence. Previously less than half the country's taxes had been collected, and consumers generally bargained their way out of sales tax.

The IHF reported severe limitations on freedoms of expression, assembly and political participation for minorities, as well as religious persecution and police brutality against Greek nationals and foreigners. Greek authorities do not acknowledge a Macedonian minority and have refused to issue birth certificates for ethnic Macedonian citizens. According to the IHF, some Pomak villages lie in "restricted areas" and require official authorization for entry by nonresidents and exit by residents. Article 19 of the citizenship law stipulates that persons of non-Greek origin leaving Greece "without the intention of returning" may be stripped of their Greek nationality. Article 20 has been used to revoke the citizenship of Macedonian activists living abroad for putting themselves in the "service of foreign powers."

Religious freedom remains restricted as Greek Orthodox bishops must approve the building of all houses of worship, and other religious groups are prohibited from proselytizing. According to the IHF, members of non-Greek Orthodox communities have been barred from entering certain occupations such as primary school teaching, police and the military. Jehovah's Witnesses are particularly targeted with persecution including imprisonment for conscientious objection, forced participation in Orthodox services and celebrations for schoolchildren and prosecution for unauthorized use of lecture halls the government considers temples.

Grenada

Polity: Parliamentary democracy
Economy: Capitalist-statist
Population: 94,000
PPP: $3,822
Life Expectancy: 70.0
Ethnic Groups: Mostly black
Capital: St. George's

Political Rights: 1
Civil Liberties: 2
Status: Free

Overview:

The opposition New National Party (NNP) won a single-seat majority in June elections and NNP leader Keith Mitchell became prime minister. Mitchell was subsequently accused of carrying out political vendettas against civil servants.

Grenada, a member of the British Commonwealth, is a parliamentary democracy. The British monarchy is represented by a governor-general. The nation gained independence in 1974 and includes the islands of Carriacou and Petit Martinique. The bicameral parliament consists of a fifteen-seat House of Representatives and an appointed Senate, with ten senators appointed by the prime minister and three by the leader of the opposition.

Former prime minister Eric Gairy was overthrown in a 1979 coup by Maurice Bishop's Marxist New Jewel Movement. In 1983 Bishop was murdered by New Jewel hard-liners Bernard Coard and Hudson Austin, who took control of the country. A joint U.S.-Caribbean military intervention removed Coard and Austin, and Governor-General Paul Scoon formed an advisory council to act as an interim administration.

In elections held in 1984 the NNP, a coalition of three parties led by Herbert Blaize, overwhelmed Gairy's rightist Grenada United Labour Party (GULP). Blaize died in 1989 and was replaced by Deputy Prime Minister Ben Jones.

By that time the NNP coalition had unraveled and there were five principal contenders in the 1990 election: The National Party (TNP) headed by Jones; the centrist National Democratic Congress (NDC) led by Nicholas Braithwaite, former head of the 1983-84 interim government; the rump of the New National Party (NNP) headed by Keith Mitchell; the leftist Maurice Bishop Patriotic Movement (MBPM) led by Terry Marryshow; and Gairy's GULP. The NDC won seven seats, took in a defector from the GULP, and Braithwaite became prime minister with a one-seat majority.

After implementing an unpopular IMF-style adjustment program, the aging Braithwaite stepped down in early 1995 in favor of agricultural minister George Brizan.

The 1995 campaign was a raucous seven-party steeplechase. Brizan sought to retain power by pointing to favorable reports about Grenada by the IMF and the World Bank and promised an improved economy. The other candidates accused the ruling NDC of corruption and harped on high unemployment.

The NNP startled local observers by coming out of the pack to win eight of fifteen seats. The NDC won five seats, and the GULP, two. Mitchell became prime minister. Afterward, NDC deputy leader Francis Alexis split off to form the Democratic Labour Party (DLP), underscoring the fractious nature of Grenadian politics.

In his first months in office Mitchell was accused by opposition leader Brizan and others of censoring news unfavorable to the government in state-run television and radio broadcasts, and of purging civil servants appointed during the NDC administration. Mitchell denied the allegations.

Political Rights and Civil Liberties:

Citizens are able to change their government through democratic elections. But there has been a decline in turnout as youth in particular appear to have lost confidence in the system because of fragmented politics and allegations of corruption in successive governments.

Constitutional guarantees regarding the right to organize political, labor or civic groups are generally respected.

There are numerous independent labor unions but labor rights have come into question since 1993. A law passed in 1993 gives the government the right to set up a tribunal empowered to make "binding and final" rulings when a labor dispute is considered of vital interest to the state. The national trade union federation claimed the law was an infringement of the right to strike.

The exercise of religion and the right of free expression are generally respected. Newspapers, including a number of weekly political party organs, are independent. Television is both private and public, and radio is operated by the government. In 1995 there were allegations that the Mitchell administration was censoring news broadcasts in the state-run media.

There is an independent, nondiscriminatory judiciary whose authority is generally respected by the police. In 1991 Grenada rejoined the Organization of Eastern Caribbean States court system, with right of appeal to the Privy Council in London. Like many Caribbean island nations, Grenada has suffered from a rise in violent drug-related crime, particularly among increasingly disaffected youth. Prison conditions are poor.

In 1986, after a two-year trial, thirteen men and one woman, including Bernard Coard and Hudson Austin, were found guilty of the 1983 murder of Maurice Bishop and sentenced to death. In 1991 the Grenada Court of Appeals turned aside the last of the defendants' appeals. The former Braithwaite government commuted the death sentences to life imprisonment for all fourteen defendants.

Guatemala

Polity: Presidential-leg-
islative democracy
(military-dominated)
(insurgencies)
Economy: Capitalist-statist
Population: 10,621,000
PPP: $3,330
Life Expectancy: 64.8
Ethnic Groups: Mayan and other Indian (over 60 percent), mestizo
Capital: Guatemala City

Political Rights: 4
Civil Liberties: 5
Status: Partly Free

Overview: **A**lvaro Arzu, a moderate conservative, came in first in the 12 November presidential election and was the favorite to win a January 1996 runoff. Meanwhile, there was no improvement in human rights and the military remained the country's most powerful institution.

Eighteen years after independence from Spain, the Republic of Guatemala was established in 1839. The nation has endured a history of dictatorship, coups d'etat and guerrilla insurgency, with only intermittent democratic government. It has had elected civilian rule since 1985. Amended in 1994, the 1985 constitution provides for a four-year presidential term and prohibits re-election. An eighty-member unicameral Congress is elected for four years.

Right-wing businessman Jorge Serrano became president in 1991 after winning a runoff election. In 1993 Serrano attempted an *autogolpe,* or self-coup, by dissolving the legislature. After initially supporting him, the military changed its mind amid mass protests and international pressure and sent Serrano packing to Panama. The Congress, under pressure from an alliance of unions, business-sector moderates and civic groups, chose as president Ramiro de Leon Carpio, the government human rights ombudsman.

De Leon Carpio, however, was practically powerless to halt human rights violations by the military or curb its power as final arbiter in national affairs. United Nations-mediated talks between the government and the Guatemalan National Revolutionary Unity (URNG) left-wing guerrillas inched forward but no pact had been signed by the end of 1995.

The URNG called a unilateral truce for the 1995 election and backed the left-wing New Guatemala Democratic Front (FDNG). The top presidential contenders were former Guatemala City mayor Arzu of the National Advancement Party (PAN) and Alfonso Portillo Cabrera of the hard-right Guatemalan Republican Front (FRG). FRG founder and former dictator Efrain Rios Montt was constitution-ally barred from running but remained a power in the party.

Arzu won 36.55 percent of the vote and Portillo Cabrera 22.04 percent. A handful of candidates split the rest. The runoff was scheduled for 7 January. The PAN won forty-three seats in Congress, the FRG twenty-one, the centrist National Alliance nine and the URNG-backed FDNG six.

Political Rights and Civil Liberties: Citizens can change governments through elections. But people are increasingly disillusioned with the process, and turnout in 1995 was only 46.8 percent. Guatemala's dominant institution, the armed forces, greatly restrict constitutional powers granted to civilian administrations. The rule of law is undermined further by the endemic corruption that afflicts all public institutions, particularly the legislature and the courts.

The constitution guarantees religious freedom and the right to organize political parties, civic organizations and labor unions. However, political and civic expression are severely restricted by a climate of violence, lawlessness and military repression. Political and criminal violence, including murder, disappearances, bombings and death threats, continue unabated. Politicians, student organizations, street children, peasant groups, labor unions, Indian organizations, refugees returning from Mexico, human rights groups, and the media are all targeted.

The principal human rights offenders are the 40,000-member military, especially its intelligence unit; the rural network of paramilitary Self-Defense Patrols (PACs), an extension of the army; the police (under military authority); a network of killers-for-hire linked to the armed forces and right-wing political groups; and vigilante "social-cleansing" groups. There is evidence that the military runs a network of clandestine jails in which people suspected of ties to the URNG guerrillas are tortured during interrogation.

In the last two years there has been an increase in rights violations and a reversion to systematic brutality—killings, abductions and torture. The main targets were members of rights organizations and civic groups calling for political reform and the reining in of the army. Guatemala remains among the most dangerous places in Latin America for human rights activists.

In 1992 President de Leon Carpio, then the official human rights ombudsman, characterized the situation as "a government without the power to stop impunity." Unfortunately, there has been only minimal improvement since then. Those few judges who have brought the first successful prosecutions against members of the security forces for rights violations—usually cases where great international pressure was applied—have received death threats.

Despite penal code reforms in 1994 the judicial system remains little more than a black hole for most legal or human rights complaints. Reforms included trying soldiers accused of common crimes in civilian rather than military courts, but most civil courts remained corrupted.

The Runejel Junam Council of Ethnic Communities (CERJ) advocates for the country's Indians, a majority of the population and probably the most segregated and oppressed indigenous community in the Western hemisphere. CERJ is a principal advocate of dismantling the PACs, which violate a constitutional article stating that no individual can be forced to join any civil-defense organization.

Workers are frequently denied the right to organize and subjected to mass firings and blacklisting, particularly in export-processing zones where a majority of workers are women. Existing unions are targets of systematic intimidation, physical attacks and assassination, particularly in rural areas during land disputes. Guatemala is among the most dangerous countries in the world for trade unionists. Child labor is a growing problem in the agricultural industry.

The press and most of the broadcast media are privately owned, with several independent newspapers and dozens of radio stations, most of them commercial. Five of six television stations are commercially operated. However, journalists are at great risk. In 1994 at least two were murdered, numerous others suffered physical attacks and a number of media outlets were subjected to various attacks including bombings. Numerous others received threats. In recent years over a dozen Guatemalan journalists have been forced into exile. The 1993 murder of newspaper publisher Jorge Carpio Nicolle remains unresolved.

↑ Guinea

Polity: Dominant party (military-influenced) **Political Rights:** 6
Economy: Capitalist **Civil Liberties:** 5
Population: 6,549,000 **Status:** Not Free
PPP: $592
Life Expectancy: 44.5
Ethnic Groups: Fulani (40 percent), Malinké (30 percent), Susu (20 percent), others
Capital: Conakry
Trend Arrow: Guinea's up trend arrow is due to increased political representation.

Overview:

The political process in Guinea opened marginally as June 1995 elections for the country's national assembly gave the opposition significant representation, while producing a large victory for President Lasana Conte's ruling Progress and Unity Party (PUP). International observers described the results as generally free and fair, even in the face of opposition complaints of serious irregularities. A threatened opposition boycott of the new parliament's first meeting in August did not materialize after it evoked little popular support, but the country clearly remains far from what President Conte (declared victor in highly dubious December 1993 elections) claims is a complete transition to democracy.

Alone among France's many African colonies in rejecting continued close ties with France, Guinea declared independence in 1958 under Ahmed Sekou Touré and his Guinea Democratic Party. France responded by removing or destroying all "colonial property" and imposing an unofficial economic boycott. Despite an early effort to introduce egalitarian laws, Sekou Toure's one-party rule became increasingly repressive, and his disastrous Soviet-style economic policies increasingly impoverished the country. Today Guinea ranks last or near last on all social development indicators. When Sekou Toure died in 1984, Lasana Conté led a military coup and promoted rapprochement with France.

A new constitution adopted in 1990 reflected the African trend toward multipartyism. However, Guinea's politics and parties are largely ethnic-based. The PUP is strongly Susu, the Rally of the Guinean People (RPG) party mostly Malinke, and both the Party for Renewal and Progress (PRP) and the Union for the New Republic (UNR) are Fulani-dominated. Ethnicity and patronage are the subtext to almost every political debate.

The convening of the National Assembly ended the transitional role of a legislature appointed by President Conte. The opposition's strength denied Conté's PUP the two-thirds majority required to enact several types of legislation, but the president retains decree power that could cripple the parliamentary process. The specter of war and near-anarchy in neighboring Liberia and Sierra Leone could temper political passions somewhat, as could even marginal economic improvements. Privatization and economic liberalization are drawing new investment, especially from France, which is further reestablishing its influence in its former colony by providing military training and assistance.

Political Rights and Civil Liberties: Guineans were denied the right to choose their executive democratically, as mandated by the constitution, when Conte was declared victor in fraudulent, manipulated elections in 1993. June 1995 legislative elections were far more open, but irregularities and government influence over state institutions affected the campaign. Guinea's political system is more open today than at any time in its independent history, but the right of the people to change their government is not yet respected.

The legislative elections passed calmly, especially compared to the violence-wracked 1993 presidential contest. The polls were contested by twenty-one parties, nine of which won at least one seat in the new parliament under an electoral system that allocated two-thirds of seats according to proportional representation. This has produced a strong platform for opposition voices, but has not offered any real role in national decision-making. Municipal elections on 29 June followed a similar pattern, and a few violent clashes followed posting of results.

Vigorous and sometimes strongly partisan private publications operate in the capital, Conakry, but are little noted in largely illiterate, poor rural areas. Constitutional guarantees of freedom of expression are contradicted by a restrictive press law allowing the government to censor or close publications arbitrarily. The Ministry of Communications controls broadcast media and the country's largest newspaper, and allows little coverage of the opposition.

Freedom of association guaranteed by the constitution is restricted in practice. Prior notice for any public meetings is required, and the government has banned many demonstrations and occasionally arrested organizers of unlicensed opposition meetings. Political parties must register with the government, but may apparently be formed freely, as at least forty-six were recognized. Many nongovernmental groups operate openly, including rights groups such as the Guinean Organization for the Defense of Human Rights (OGDH). Religious rights are protected by the constitution and respected in practice.

The judicial system remains underdeveloped and weak, despite its legally independent status. Corruption, nepotism, ethnicity and political interference, as well as a lack of resources and training, can individually or severally affect the course of justice. Security forces continue to act with impunity. Arbitrary arrests and detention are common, and occasional serious maltreatment and torture of detainees is reported. Traditional courts formed along ethnic lines often handle minor civil cases.

Women's rights protected by the constitution are often not respected in practice, and women have far fewer educational and employment opportunities than men. Many societal customs discriminate against women. Female genital mutilation as a traditional rite is widely practiced. Spousal abuse and other violence against women are said to be prevalent.

Although the constitution enshrines the right to form and join unions, the country's preponderantly subsistence-farming economy leaves a very small formal sector, and only about 5 percent of the workforce is unionized. Several labor confederations compete in this small market and have the right to bargain collectively. A labor court in the capital and civil courts elsewhere regularly hear labor grievances.

Guinea had undertaken privatization plans and some civil service reforms—thousands of "phantom employees" were struck from payrolls in 1995—under pressure from the World Bank and other international lenders and donors. French private investors are increasingly involved and are helping to revive French influence in the country. However, corruption and harassment remain serious obstacles to business growth and the exploitation of rich gold and bauxite deposits.

Guinea-Bissau

Polity: Presidential-parliamentary democracy
Economy: Mixed statist transitional
Population: 1,073,000
PPP: $820
Life Expectancy: 43.5

Political Rights: 3
Civil Liberties: 4
Status: Partly Free

Ethnic Groups: Balanta (30 percent), Fulani (20 percent), Mandjague (14 percent), Mandinka (13 percent), mulatto, Moor, Lebanese and Portuguese minorities
Capital: Bissau

Overview:
One year after the country's first democratic multiparty elections, President Joao Bernardo Vieira and Prime Minister Manuel Saturnino da Costa have turned the government's attention to pressing economic and social conditions. The country has embarked on an IMF-supported program of economic reform with the aim of reducing public expenditure, increasing revenue, and achieving food self-sufficiency to help alleviate widespread poverty.

Guinea-Bissau has been independent from Portugal since 1973. In revising the constitution in May 1991, the National Assembly struck down the status of the African Party for the Independence of Guinea-Bissau and Cape Verde (PAIGC) as the "leading force in society," legalized political parties and established direct elections for both the president and the legislators. By 1993, more than two dozen parties had been formed, thirteen of which registered for national elections in 1994. The PAIGC won a majority in parliament and President Vieira retained his post in a runoff vote, in elections accepted as free and fair by both the opposition and the U.N. observer mission.

The country remains among the poorest in the world, with an extremely low life expectancy, high infant mortality and a falling standard of living. The government's economic reform package will require raising the price of fuel, transportation and electricity as well as continued cutbacks in civil service jobs. According to U.N. statistics, significantly more than half of all civil servants have no qualifications and very few prospects for employment in the private sector. Adding to the hardship is the insufficiency of even private-sector salaries in covering basic necessities.

Political Rights and Civil Liberties: Citizens of Guinea-Bissau held their first democratic elections in 1994. The fifteen-year reign of President Vieira's PAIGC persists, but the opposition is gaining political strength. In his traditional New Year message, Vieira thanked the opposition parties for contributing to successful multiparty elections, and encouraged critical but constructive scrutiny of the government by the population at large.

The judiciary remains a part of the executive branch, and the regime retains the power to detain individuals suspected of antigovernment activities. Political trials are held in secret by military tribunals. Due to executive interference and a lack of qualified judges, arrests and the conduct of trials in civil and criminal cases are often arbitrary. Customary law prevails in rural areas.

Freedoms of assembly and expression have recently become more open. In the 1994 election campaign, political parties were allowed to hold rallies and in some instances openly denounce the PAIGC without any government interference. Journalists, however, rarely criticize the president or high government officials directly, unless the latter lose the former's favor. The government attempted to prevent a march by the Human Rights League observing the organization's national day against torture in September; after an official ban failed to stop the marchers, the Ministry of the Interior relented and instead ordered security forces to be present.

Despite the establishment of two independent newspapers in recent years, freedoms of speech and of the press remain curtailed. Due to the sparse distribution of newspapers and illiteracy over 60 percent, the population relies more heavily on the radio for information. As part of its pledge to implement the Platform for Action, a nonbinding U.N. document on strengthening the rights of women, the government plans to significantly reduce illiteracy by the year 2000. Recently, the broadcast media have become more bold in criticizing specific government policies and in giving coverage to the opposition. This year *Radio Galaxia de Pindjiguity* officially became the first private radio station in operation.

Although religious groups must register with the government, freedom of worship is respected. Proselytizing is permitted and no religious group has been denied registration since 1982. The majority of the population practice animism; however, there are also a significant Muslim population and a small Christian minority.

Despite the existence of informal police checkpoints on major roads to monitor the movement of people and goods, citizens may travel freely within the country. There are no legal restrictions on foreign travel, but in 1994 there were reports of opposition leaders who were prevented from leaving the country. The government has announced its intention to restructure its police force "for service in a democratic society" with the assistance of the French.

Labor unions exist but the government limits citizens' right to strike. In 1994 a five-day teachers' strike brought condemnation and threats of violence from the government. The National Union of Teachers leader, Luis Nacassa, was arrested without legal notice and charged with initiating an "illegal strike."

Guyana

Polity: Parliamentary democracy
Economy: Mixed statist
Population: 835,000
PPP: $1,800
Life Expectancy: 65.2
Ethnic Groups: East Indian (51 percent), black (36 percent), mixed (5 percent), Indian (4 percent), European
Capital: Georgetown

Political Rights: 2
Civil Liberties: 2
Status: Free

Overview: The government of Prime Minister Cheddi Jagan moved forward on constitutional reform, but the effort was overshadowed by a disastrous cyanide spill at the huge Omai gold mine.

Guyana is a member of the British Commonwealth. From independence in 1966 until 1992 it was ruled by the autocratic Forbes Burnham and the black-based People's National Congress (PNC). In 1980 Burnham installed a constitution providing for a strong president and a sixty-five-seat National Assembly elected every five years. Twelve seats are occupied by elected local officials.

Desmond Hoyte became president after Burnham died in 1985 and was re-elected to a full term in a fraudulent election. In 1990 the U.S. tied economic assistance to political reform and Canada and Great Britain also applied pressure.

Jagan's East Indian-based, Marxist People's Progressive Party (PPP), the social democratic Working People's Alliance (WPA) and three smaller parties joined in the Patriotic Coalition for Democracy (PCD).

Hoyte finally conceded to electoral reforms—a new voter registry and a revamped election commission—and international election monitors.

The election was finally held in 1992. Hoyte touted economic improvements and promised better living conditions, but the social costs of the PNC's austerity program in this already very poor country had been severe.

The PPP believed it could win on its own and the PCD unraveled. Jagan, who had moderated his Marxism since the collapse of communism, presented himself as a democrat and formed an alliance, PPP-Civic, with noted civic figures. The WPA, the only mixed-race party in the country, campaigned on a platform of multiracial cooperation.

East Indians, who outnumber blacks by about 52 percent to 36 percent, turned out as expected for the PPP-Civic. Jagan was elected president with 52 percent of the vote, as Hoyte took 41 percent. The WPA candidate, economist Clive Thomas, won less than 2 percent. In the legislature, the PPP won thirty-six of sixty-five seats, the PNC twenty-six, the WPA two, and the centrist United Force (UF) one.

Despite fears among Afro-Guyanese, Jagan has governed in a relatively evenhanded manner. He was slow to move on promised constitutional and electoral reforms, but in 1995 got to work with an eye toward the next elections, due in 1997. The economy strengthened, with growth of over 8 percent in 1994.

But disaster struck in August 1995 with a major cyanide spill at the Omai gold mine. Gold is Guyana's largest export earner. An official Commission of Inquiry was opened, with the aim of reporting in time for the mine to reopen at the beginning of 1996. But the PNC, the WPA and civic groups criticized the composition of the commission amid concerns of a cover-up on behalf of the Canadian companies that own the mine.

Political Rights and Civil Liberties: Citizens can change their government through elections, but the 1980 constitution gives the president inordinate powers. Work on promised constitutional reform did not begin until 1995.

The rights of free expression, freedom of religion and freedom to organize political parties, civic organizations and labor unions are generally respected. However, without more explicit constitutional guarantees, political rights and civil liberties rest more on government tolerance than institutional protection.

The judicial system is independent but remains understaffed and underfunded. Prisons are overcrowded and conditions are deplorable.

The police force has improved but still needs better training. It remains vulnerable to corruption, particularly given the penetration of the hemispheric drug trade in Guyana. In 1995 there were a number of reports of police using unnecessary force.

The Guyana Human Rights Association (GHRA) is independent, effective and backed by independent civic and religious groups.

Domestic violence against women is a concern, as is the government's reluctance to address the issue.

Racial clashes have diminished since the 1992 election, but long-standing animosity between blacks and Indo-Guyanese remains a concern. The government has taken steps to form a multiparty race relations committee to promote tolerance.

Labor unions are well-organized. In 1995 the government sought to dilute the right to strike among some public sector unions, and companies are not obligated to recognize unions in former state enterprises sold off by the government.

Several independent newspapers operate freely, including the *Stabroek News* and the *Catholic Standard*, a Church weekly. Most television and radio stations are controlled by the government, but present differing points of view.

There is a cabinet ministry of indigenous affairs, and the government has moved on a development plan to address the social concerns of 40,000 Amerindians living in the interior. But the three main Amerindian organizations continued to demand more land and local control.

Haiti

Polity: Presidential-par-
liamentary democracy
Economy: Capitalist-
statist
Population: 7,180,000
PPP: $1,046
Life Expectancy: 56.6
Ethnic Groups: Black (95 percent), mulatto
Capital: Port-au-Prince

Political Rights: 5
Civil Liberties: 5
Status: Partly Free

Overview: In an election boycotted by major opposition parties, Rene
Preval was elected to succeed President Jean-Bertrand
Aristide. But Haiti has no democratic traditions to draw on
and extremely weak institutions, and the prospect of renewed upheaval remained.

Since gaining independence from France in 1804 following a slave revolt, the
Republic of Haiti has endured a history of poverty, violence, instability and
dictatorship. A 1986 military coup ended twenty-nine years of rule by the Duvalier
family, and the army ruled for most of the next eight years.

Under international pressure, the military permitted the implementation of a
French-style constitution in 1987. It provides for a president elected for five years,
an elected parliament composed of a twenty-seven-member Senate and an eighty-
three-member House of Representatives, and a presidentially appointed prime minister.

In the 1990 elections Aristide, a charismatic left-wing priest, won in a landslide
over conservative Marc Bazin. Aristide moved to establish civilian authority over
the military and end corruption. Haiti's mostly mulatto elites and the military then
conspired against him, prompting him to overstep the constitution and call on
supporters to defend the government through violent means.

Aristide was overthrown in September 1991 and barely escaped the country.
Haiti came under the ruthless control of the military triumvirate of Gen. Raoul
Cedras, Gen. Philippe Biamby and Lt. Col. Michel Francois.

When the U.S. and U.N. imposed a trade and oil embargo, the military agreed
to negotiate with Aristide, but reneged on an accord for his return by unleashing a
network of tens of thousands of armed civilian thugs. The military then built a
political base by creating an armed political group, the Front for the Advancement
and Progress of Haiti (FRAPH).

In September 1994, facing an imminent U.S. invasion, Cedras and Biamby
agreed to step down. U.S. troops took control of the country in a "soft" invasion.
Francois left for the Dominican Republic, Cedras and Biamby for Panama.

Aristide was reinstated soon after, his security and that of average Haitians
dependent on a combined U.S. and U.N. force. A $550 million international aid
package was promised.

Before the June 1995 parliamentary elections Aristide dismantled the military.
The June vote's legitimacy was questioned by international observers and led to a
split among Aristide supporters. The more militant Lavalas movement remained

firmly behind him. But the National Front for Change and Democracy (FNCD), a leftist coalition that had backed him in 1990, believed they had been victimized by fraud and boycotted the parliamentary runoff elections. In the end, Lavalas won an overwhelming majority in the parliament.

In the fall Lavalas demanded that Aristide be allowed to stay in power to make up for the three years he was in exile. Aristide seemed to consider the option himself. Under pressure from Washington, he reaffirmed that he would hand power to an elected successor.

Lavalas nominated Preval, Aristide's prime minister in 1991. With Aristide backing him and the FNCD and most other major opposition parties boycotting, the outcome was a foregone conclusion. Less than one-third of the electorate turned out on 17 December. About 89 percent voted for Preval, who was scheduled to take office 7 February 1996.

The year ended amid uncertainty as to whether the still overwhelmingly popular Aristide would continue to exercise power through Preval; whether the new government would move on a privatization program delayed by Aristide, and upon which further international aid hinged; and what Michel Francois, just across the border in the Dominican Republic, and former FRAPH members and military backers might do once the U.S. and U.N. forces began leaving Haiti in February 1996.

Political Rights and Civil Liberties: There were serious irregularities and fraud charges in the 1995 parliamentary elections. This led most major opposition parties to boycott the 1995 presidential vote, which, along with a very low turnout (less than one-third), called into question the legitimacy of the presidential transition.

The constitution guarantees a full range of political rights and civil liberties. But political and civic expression remained restricted in 1995 because of an almost nonexistent rule of law and a security vacuum only partially filled by thousands of U.S. and U.N. peacekeepers. The international force, despite Aristide's repeated requests, was under orders not to disarm the population despite evidence that thousands of former military personnel and backers had stowed away caches of weaponry.

An interim police force, composed of former soldiers following the disbanding of the army, often used unnecessary deadly force, but no member was ever disciplined. The government began phasing out the interim force in favor of a new National Police, which, with limited international training, appeared to be falling into traditional patterns of repressive behavior in the second half of 1995. There were dozens of allegations of use of excessive force and at least two shooting deaths, but no disciplinary measures were taken. The police shooting of a child in November led to rioting in which a police station was ransacked and burned.

Neither police force was able to deal with a sharp increase in violent crime, some of it linked to disgruntled former soldiers. The crime wave prompted dozens, possibly hundreds, of vigilante killings by crowds who attacked suspected criminals as well as alleged former military collaborators.

The government took no action to curb these killings. In fact, President Aristide, in an incendiary speech in November at the funeral of a murdered Lavalas congressman, urged followers to go to wealthy neighborhoods "where there are big houses and heavy weapons" to help police confront armed opponents of the regime.

That set off five days of nationwide mob violence in which houses were burned and at least a dozen people were killed.

The killing of the Lavalas congressman was only one of about two dozen execution-style, apparently political killings that occurred in 1995. However, most victims were linked either to current opposition groups or to the former military regime. None of these cases, at least one of which may have involved agents of the Aristide government, had been resolved by the end of the year.

The judicial system remains a fundamental problem. It was purged of Aristide appointees under military rule and totally corrupted. Record-keeping was poor when records were kept at all. The reinstated Aristide government, with some international assistance, took steps to establish a working judiciary.

But the system remained essentially dysfunctional, particularly in rural areas, while Aristide himself was prone to fire judges and replace them with loyalists unconstitutionally. The government pressed the judiciary on a few high-profile human rights cases dating back to military rule, and convictions were achieved with the help of foreign lawyers. But the government appeared unwilling or unable to address rights violations under its own tenure.

Prisons under military rule were death traps. In 1995 they became merely hellish. A majority of prisoners remained unsentenced and there were many reported beatings, including of minors.

There are a number of independent newspapers and radio stations. However, outlets critical of the government were frequent targets of intimidation including violent mob attacks. Television is state-run and strongly biased toward the government.

Labor unions were able to preserve some of their organization under military rule by establishing an underground network with international assistance. In 1995 they began rebuilding. But labor guarantees, as with all other legally endowed rights, remained weak and ultimately unenforced.

Honduras

Polity: Presidential-legislative democracy (military-influenced)
Economy: Capitalist-statist
Population: 5,460,000
PPP: $2,000
Life Expectancy: 67.7
Ethnic Groups: Mestizo (90 percent), Indian (7 percent)
Capital: Tegucigalpa

Political Rights: 3
Civil Liberties: 3
Status: Partly Free

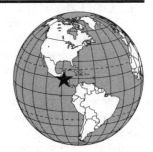

Overview: President Carlos Roberto Reina took some steps toward strengthening civilian rule, but the military continued using threats and violence to preserve its status as the country's most powerful institution.

The Republic of Honduras was established in 1839, eighteen years after independence from Spain. It has endured decades of military rule and intermittent elected government. The last military regime gave way to elected civilian rule in 1982. The constitution provides for a president and a 130-member, unicameral Congress elected for four years.

The two main political parties are the center-left Liberal Party (PL) and the conservative National Party (PN). In the 1993 election the PN nominated Oswaldo Ramos Soto, a table-pounding right-winger. The PL, which had held power during most of the 1980s, nominated Reina, a sixty-seven-year-old progressive and former president of the Inter-American Court of Human Rights. The campaign was marked by vicious personal attacks. Reina won with 52 percent of the vote. The PL won seventy seats in the congress, the PN fifty-six. Two small left-wing parties took the remaining four.

Reina promised a "moral revolution" and greater civilian control over the military. In his first two years results were mixed. Government corruption remains entrenched, but Reina's foreign minister was jailed on a charge of selling passports. Obligatory military service was abolished and steps taken to separate the police from the military.

But the military under Gen. Luis Alonso Discua sent tanks into the streets for a day in August 1995 when the government moved to try ten officers for rights violations. There were also indications that hardline military elements were behind a grenade attack against Reina in January and systematic vandalism of the presidential phone system late in the year.

In October the military imposed on Congress its choice—Col. Mario Hung Pacheco—to succeed Gen. Discua as armed forces commander. Hung Pacheco, a hardliner like Discua, mixed promises to abide by the constitution with veiled threats of action should the military's autonomy be threatened. Tensions rose at year's end after Reina recommended that the post of armed forces commander be abolished someday in favor of a civilian defense minister.

Political Rights and Civil Liberties:

Citizens are able to change their government through elections, but in 1993 elections 100,000 registered voters were incorrectly listed and unable to vote.

Constitutional guarantees regarding free expression, freedom of religion and the right to form political parties and civic organizations are generally respected. But political rights and civil liberties are restricted by repressive measures taken against peaceful protests and mounting crime.

The military exerts inordinate influence over elected governments. By law, legislators elect the armed forces commander for a three-year term from a list of nominees provided by the military. Inevitably, the military imposes its favored candidate. A constellation of military-owned businesses makes the armed forces one of Honduras's ten largest corporations.

The military remains the principal human rights violator. In 1993 a government human rights office was established, but the military has generally refused to cooperate with it. In late 1995 the government challenged military impunity, taking the unprecedented step of indicting eight officers for kidnappings in 1982. But the military defied arrest warrants, prosecutors were threatened and it was unclear whether a trial could go forward.

Many violent attacks now stem as much from greed as from politics, as economic interests, including the military and drug traffickers, compete for profit and leverage. Targets include businessmen, trade unionists and peasant leaders. Arbitrary detention and torture by police continue despite steps to put the police under civilian authority. Rights groups have held vigilante groups responsible for dozens of extrajudicial killings of alleged criminals.

The judicial system, headed by a Supreme Court, is weak and rife with corruption. Some judges have asserted themselves in human rights cases, but face death threats and violent attacks. Most criminal cases against the military remain in the purview of military courts and usually result in dismissal of charges. Prison conditions are deplorable and over 90 percent of those jailed have not been convicted of a crime.

Labor unions are well organized and can strike. Strikes frequently lead to violent clashes with security forces. Labor leaders, religious groups and indigenous-based peasant unions pressing for land rights remain subject to repression. Unions have achieved collective bargaining agreements in some export processing zones. But management abuses remain widespread, including firings for union activities. Women workers, a majority in the zones, are subject to sexual harassment, forced overtime without pay and physical abuse.

Most press and broadcast media are private. There are several newspapers representing various political viewpoints, but a licensing law restricts the practice of journalism. Some media have become targets of intimidation as they have become bolder in covering human rights cases and corruption.

Hungary

Polity: Parliamentary democracy
Economy: Mixed capitalist
Population: 10,238,000
PPP: $6,580
Life Expectancy: 69.0
Ethnic Groups: Hungarian (90 percent), Roma (4 percent), German (3 percent), Slovak, Romanian
Capital: Budapest

Political Rights: 1
Civil Liberties: 2
Status: Free

Overview: The ruling coalition led by Socialist Prime Minister Gyula Horn, facing declining foreign investment, mounting inflation and soaring budget and current accounts deficits, launched an unpopular austerity program in March 1995 that led to a decline of the government's popularity and dissension within the Socialist Party. The program shored up confidence among international lending institutions and investors as the economy picked up toward year's end.

With the collapse of the Austro-Hungarian empire after World War I, Hungary lost two-thirds of its territory under the 1920 Trianon Treaty, leaving 3.5 million

Hungarians as minorities in neighboring Romania, Slovakia, Serbia, Croatia and Ukraine. After World War II, Soviet forces helped install a Communist regime. In 1956, Soviet tanks quashed an armed uprising by Hungarians. Under the politically repressive regime of Janos Kadar Hungary enjoyed relative economic well-being under "goulash communism," which had aspects of a market economy. By the late 1980s, with the economy deteriorating, the ruling Hungarian Socialist Workers Party (MSzMP) lost its sense of legitimacy. The ouster of Kadar in 1988 led the way to political reform and the eventual introduction of a multiparty system in 1989.

In 1994 parliamentary elections, the Hungarian Socialist Party (MSzDP), a successor to the MSzMP made up largely of "reform" communists, unseated the conservative Hungarian Democratic Forum (MDF), which had won control of the 386-member parliament in 1990. The MSzDP won 209 seats, the pro-market Alliance of Free Democrats (SzDSz) captured 70; the MDF, 37; the pre-war rightist Smallholders Party, 26; the Christian Democrats, 22, and the Young Democrats (FiDeSz), 20. The Socialists agreed to share power with the SzDSz, and former foreign minister Gyula Horn was named prime minister.

In early 1995, the government's commitment to economic reform came into question after it canceled an important privatization deal, removed the privatization chief, delayed naming a central bank governor, backtracked on mass privatization and saw the resignation of Finance Minister Laszlo Bekesi, the architect of the Socialist Party's reform program. These factors led to tensions within the governing coalition between MSzDP pro-reform moderates and the liberal SzDSz on one side, and the leftist-populist wing of the Socialists on the other. Foreign investors were angered after the government canceled a deal to sell a state-owned hotel chain to an American investor.

In March, the government moved to rectify a gloomy economic picture. Lajos Bokros, a pro-reform banker, was named finance minister, and Gyorgy Suranyi, an advocate of an independent central bank, was named governor on the Central Bank. To restore confidence in its commitment to market reform, the government announced radical spending cuts and devalued the forint by 9 percent. The economic reform package met strong opposition from unions, and led to the resignations of the welfare and national security affairs ministers. The government announced it would dismiss 19,000 civil servants as part of the plan to slash state spending. A poll found two-thirds of Hungarians "outraged" at the reform package, which included cuts in welfare, child care benefits, maternity pay and free higher education. More than thirty laws faced amendment.

The government also moved to step up privatization, including the partial sell-off of Matav, the Hungarian telecommunications company. The state holding company launched a program to speed up the sale of some 1,000 state companies, which would increase the private sector's share of the economy to over 80 percent. Laszlo Pal, the trade and industry minister long seen as an obstacle to the rapid sale of state-owned utilities, was sacked. While the Constitutional Court overruled some of the planned budget cuts, the program had a positive impact on the economy. Balance of payments and public finances improved, and a recovery was spurred by exports—made competitive by higher productivity and the devalued forint—and investment. Parliament passed legislation to make the forint fully convertible by 1 January 1996.

In other issues, parliament reelected Arpad Goncz, a political prisoner under the Communists, to a second five-year term as president. Relations with Slovakia soured after it passed anti-Hungarian language laws. Romania and Hungary remained at loggerheads over the Hungarian minority in Transylvania. High-level talks were called off in September.

Political Rights and Civil Liberties: Hungarians can change their government democratically under a multiparty system enshrined in a much-amended Communist-era constitution. Close to 200 parties have been registered since 1989, but most are small or inactive. The 1994 elections were free and fair.

Hungary has a broad range of independent newspapers and magazines. After yearsof bitter political wrangling, parliament passed a media bill on 21 December that will allow substantial public broadcasting. Under the law, two state-owned TV stations will be privatized. There is free public discussion.

Freedoms of assembly and association are respected. Freedoms of conscience and religion are viewed as fundamental liberties not granted by the state. The country's estimated 500,000 Roma (Gypsies) continue to suffer de facto discrimination in employment and housing.

The judiciary is independent and the Constitutional Court has ruled against the government on several occasions, notably nullifying aspects of the economic austerity program. In 1993, the Court lifted the statute of limitations on the persecution of former Communist officials who suppressed the 1956 uprising. In February, four men accused of shooting at civilians during the revolt were cleared of charges. A month earlier, two men were sentenced to five years in prison for shooting into an unarmed crowd. The convictions evoked criticism from President Goncz, who said knowledge of the shootings was too murky to justify the rulings.

An estimated 2.5 million Hungarian workers belong to independent trade unions. The largest is the Confederation of Hungarian Trade Unions. In 1995, a national railway strike was called to protest the government's austerity program. Women enjoy the same legal rights as men and are represented in government and business.

Iceland

Polity: Parliamentary democracy
Economy: Capitalist
Population: 268,000
PPP: $17,660
Life Expectancy: 78.2
Ethnic Groups: Icelander
Capital: Reykjavik

Political Rights: 1
Civil Liberties: 1
Status: Free

Overview: After campaigning that largely avoided the topic of European integration, April 1995 elections produced a new center-right ruling coalition with an equally divided cabinet and a comfortable majority in the *Althing* (parliament). With strong historical, cultural and economic ties to Europe, Iceland will not find it easy to ignore continued integration. The prospect of agreeing to the European Union (EU) common fisheries policy, however, has so far been too great a sacrifice for Iceland, which relies on the fish industry for 80 percent of its export goods and half its total export revenues.

Iceland's first 300 years as an independent republic ended with the imposition of Norwegian rule in 1262. Denmark controlled Iceland from the next century until 1874, when it received limited autonomy. It achieved full independence in 1944 after U.S. and British occupation of Denmark. Multiparty coalitions have dominated government since then. The center-left coalition formed in 1991 and including Prime Minister Davio Oddson's Independence Party and the Social Democratic Party (SDP) succeeded last year in stabilizing the faltering economy to a degree. After attempting to appeal to younger voters and non-fish industries by formally advocating application for EU membership, the SDP lost three seats and more than 4 percent of the popular vote. The Independence Party opted to join forces with the anti-EU Progressive Party, pledging to continue economic stabilization efforts and eliminate the country's budget deficit. Toward those ends, the government is likely to concentrate on rebuilding depleted fish stocks and bolstering manufacturing industries—based on Iceland's hydroelectric and geothermal power—and tourism, which are seen as likely sources of future economic growth.

Political Rights and Civil Liberties:

Icelanders have the means to change their government democratically. The constitution, adopted by referendum in 1944, provides for a popularly elected, primarily ceremonial president responsible for appointing a prime minister from the largest party in parliament. In elections every four years, sixty-three representatives are chosen for the Althing in a mixed system of proportional and direct representation. There are currently six political parties representing the electorate, of which one, Awakening of the Nation, broke away from the SDP just four months before the election and managed to secure four Althing seats.

The independent judiciary is headed by a Supreme Court and includes town and magistrates' courts at the lower level. Two special courts handle cases of impeachment of government officials and disputes between employers and workers. Over 95 percent of eligible workers belong to free labor unions and all enjoy the right to strike as well as freedom of assembly and association.

Constitutional bans on censorship are respected, and the media exercise complete freedom of expression. A wide range of publications includes both independent and party-affiliated newspapers. An autonomous board of directors oversees the Icelandic State Broadcasting Service, which operates a number of transmitting and relay stations. The U.S. Navy also broadcasts from the NATO base at Keflavik.

Iceland's population is highly homogeneous not only in Icelandic descent but also in religious affiliation, with virtually the entire country holding at least nominal membership in the state-supported Lutheran Church. Despite the uniformity, legal protections against discrimination are respected. Included among these are the right to freedom of worship and the outlawing of discrimination on the basis of race, language, social class and gender. Legal barriers have been insufficient to eradicate all discrimination, and many female workers charge they are still paid less than their male counterparts for equal work.

↑ India

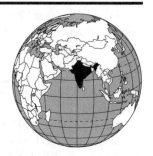

Polity: Parliamentary democracy (insurgencies)
Economy: Capitalist-statist
Population: 922,312,000
PPP: $1,230
Life Expectancy: 60.4

Political Rights: 4
Civil Liberties: 4
Status: Partly Free

Ethnic Groups: Indo-Aryan (72 percent), Dravidian (25 percent), others
Capital: New Delhi
Trend Arrow: India recieved an upward trend arrow due to improvements in the electoral process at the state level.

Overview: In 1995 Indian Premier P.V. Narasimha Rao, after weathering a string of state election losses and a leadership challenge, prepared to lead his ruling Congress Party into national elections due by May 1996.

India achieved independence from Britain in February 1947. Faced with escalating political and religious tension, in July 1947 the country was partitioned into largely Hindu India, under Prime Minister Jawaharlal Nehru of the center-left Congress Party, and Muslim Pakistan. Nehru's daughter, Indira Gandhi, led India from 1966-77 and from 1980 until October 1984, when her Sikh bodyguards killed her to avenge the army's storming of a Sikh temple. Her son, Rajiv Gandhi, immediately took over as prime minister.

In the November 1989 elections V.P. Singh led the centrist National Front Coalition to victory, sending the Congress Party into opposition for only the second time since independence. The Singh government's August 1990 proposal to increase the reservation of university slots and government jobs for members of lower castes led to widespread rioting across northern India. In November the government lost a vote of confidence, and in March 1991 a subsequent minority government collapsed. On 21 May, with balloting underway for a new parliament, Tamil separatists assassinated Rajiv Gandhi as he campaigned for the Congress Party near Madras.

When voting concluded in June, the Congress Party (226 seats) and its smaller allies took 243 of the 511 contested seats, and the National Front 131. The right-wing Hindu fundamentalist Bharatiya Janata Party (BJP) and its allies took 123 seats. Veteran Congress politician Rao became prime minister of what many predicted would be a short-lived minority government.

In December 1992 a mob of 200,000 Hindu fundamentalists, encouraged by BJP activists, destroyed a sixteenth-century mosque allegedly sitting on a holy Hindu site in the northern town of Ayodhya. This touched off a week of violence across the country during which 1,200 were killed.

In January 1993 communal violence in Bombay and Ahmedabad left 600 dead. Most of the victims were Muslim, and thousands of Muslim businesses and homes were looted and burned. The Bombay police avoided aiding Muslim victims and in some cases participated in the violence.

In the November 1993 elections in Uttar Pradesh, India's most populous state, two parties representing lower-caste Hindus and backed by poor Muslims formed a governing coalition. This marked the first time that lower caste-based regional parties took power at the state level. In the fall of 1994 sporadic violence rocked Uttar Pradesh after the state government increased to 50 percent the proportion of civil service jobs and university spots reserved for lower castes and *dalits* (untouchables).

Since the fall of 1993 the Congress Party has lost eleven of sixteen state elections, mostly to Hindu nationalist and regional parties. The biggest beneficiary has been the BJP, which in March 1995 took power in Gujarat and entered into a coalition in Maharashtra with the militant Shiv Sena party. The BJP already shared power in Rajasthan and Delhi.

Heading into national elections due by May 1996, Rao is also facing a revolt within his party. Congress Party dissidents accuse his government of corruption, claim that economic reforms introduced since 1991 have hurt the poor, and accuse Rao of abandoning the Party's commitment to secularism in failing to prevent the destruction of the Ayodhya mosque and protect Muslims during the Bombay riots. Arjun Singh, Rao's chief rival, resigned from the cabinet in protest in December 1994, and in February 1995 Rao expelled him from the Party. In May, following state election defeats, Congress Party rebels staged a rear-guard rally in New Delhi and named N.D. Tiwari to replace Rao as party leader. Rao rejected the move and expelled Tiwari from the party.

Political Rights and Civil Liberties:

Indian citizens can change their government democratically. However, the rule of law is weak and security forces commit human rights abuses with virtual impunity. Corruption is widespread at all levels of government. Politics in several states, particularly Bihar, is increasingly dominated by criminal gangs. During the 1995 state election campaign in Bihar, fighting between rival political groups killed over eighty people, including four politicians.

Chief Election Commissioner T.N. Seshan has ordered a photo identity card to be issued to voters to help prevent fraud. During the recent state elections the Election Commission enforced laws on campaign spending limits fairly strictly.

Police, army and paramilitary forces are accused of extrajudicial executions, rape, torture, arbitrary detentions, "disappearances" and destruction of homes, particularly in Kashmir and Punjab, and in Assam and other northeastern states. *(See the report on Kashmir in the Related Territories section).* An official National Human Rights Commission established in October 1993 is not authorized to investigate alleged abuses by army or paramilitary units, but occasionally does so.

In Punjab, terrorist violence has sharply decreased since police began a massive crackdown in July 1992. However, on 31 August 1995 a car bomb killed Beant Singh, the chief minister of Punjab state, along with a dozen security officers. The Babbar Khalsa, a Sikh militant group, took credit for the killing. The 1983 Armed Forces (Punjab and Chandigarh) Special Powers Act grants security forces wide latitude in using lethal force in the state. Police killings of alleged terrorists has continued, although at a reduced rate. Local rights groups charge police with staging "encounter killings," essentially killing suspects after capture and claiming death occurred during the chase. The police are also accused in dozens of unresolved "disappearances," and of harassment of human rights activists.

Large numbers of Hindus from other parts of the country and Muslims from northern Bangladesh have moved into the seven states of northeast India since independence, largely in violation of the 1873 Innerline Regulations protecting indigenous tribal areas. Some eighteen tribal-based insurgent groups in the region are fighting for greater autonomy and more secure land rights. The 1958 Armed Forces Special Powers Act grants security forces wide latitude in using lethal force in Assam and four nearby states. In 1995 the army and police continued to carry out "encounter killings" and harassment of rights activists, particularly in Assam.

Northeastern militant groups are accused of atrocities leading to hundreds of deaths each year of security personnel, Muslim and Hindu settlers, and members of other indigenous tribes and ethnic groups. The most powerful of these groups, the Nationalist Socialist Council of Nagaland, is suspected in a 25 February attack on a train near the town of Diphu in Assam, which killed twenty-seven soldiers. Fighting between Naga and Kuki tribesmen in Manipur has killed several hundred people in recent years.

Elsewhere, in the eastern states of Bihar, Andhra Pradesh and Orissa, the Maoist People's War Group and other Naxalite guerrillas frequently target politicians and wealthy landlords. Police in Bihar are accused of killing Naxalite rebels in staged "encounter killings."

The broadly drawn 1980 National Security Act (NSA) allows police to detain security suspects for up to one year (two in Punjab) without charge or trial. In May 1995 the government allowed the controversial 1985 Terrorist and Disruptive Activities Prevention Act (TADA) to expire. TADA had allowed authorities to detain individuals for speech or action violating the "integrity of India," and in practice had been misused to arbitrarily detain thousands of political dissidents, rights activists and journalists.

The judiciary is independent of the government in ordinary cases, although the system is severely backlogged and is often inaccessible to poor people. Some suspects are held awaiting trial longer than they would have been if convicted and sentenced. Non-security trials are generally conducted with adequate procedural safeguards, although bribery of judges is common. In Punjab some courts remain closed due to threats by militants against judges.

Police use of torture against suspects is widespread throughout India. Police frequently abuse ordinary prisoners, particularly those belonging to lower castes, and there are occasional deaths in police custody. In West Bengal state a magisterial inquiry has been ordered in only one custodial death out of the 197 reported between 1977-94. Female prisoners are often raped by guards and male convicts. Conditions are most brutal in the lowly Class "C" cells.

In Bihar the Naxalite Maoist Communist Center has instituted extrajudicial "people's courts" that hand down harsh punishments for crimes, including amputation of hands and facial parts, and have carried out summary executions against alleged "class enemies." In other areas tribal customs often supersede the law and punishments occasionally defy accepted norms of decency.

India has a vigorous private press. The Official Secrets Act allows the government to ban publication of articles dealing with sensitive security issues; journalists say in practice this is occasionally used to limit criticism of government actions, particularly in Punjab. Sikh militants in Punjab and right-wing Hindus in Gujarat and Maharashtra frequently harass journalists. Government radio and television monopolies ensure coverage favorable to the ruling Congress Party.

Numerous human rights organizations operate relatively freely, although activists are frequently harassed by police and occasionally tortured or killed. The right to peaceful assembly is generally respected, but state authorities can ban outdoor assemblies and impose curfews under Section 144 of the Criminal Procedure Code. In May 1995 police arbitrarily detained nearly 35,000 opposition party activists across Tamil Nadu state who were striking to demand the resignation of the chief minister on corruption charges.

Several thousand women are killed in disputes over dowries each year. Hindu women are often denied their proper inheritances, and Muslim females generally get one-half the inheritance of males. Forced prostitution is widespread. Over 150,000 Nepalese women, many under the age of sixteen, have been trafficked to brothels in large Indian cities, and many are held in conditions of servitude. Due to a preference for male offspring, by some estimates over 10,000 female babies are killed yearly.

Most Indian cities have large numbers of street children. Child prostitution is a severe problem, and child marriage, although banned, is fairly common.

Although discrimination based on caste status is illegal, in practice caste frequently determines an individual's occupation and marriage options. Members of lower castes are often subjected to random beatings, rape and arson, and hundreds die annually in caste-based violence.

Religious freedom is respected in this secular country, although communal violence has characterized India since independence. After entering into a coalition government in Maharashtra in March, the militant Shiv Sena ordered officials to begin rounding up illegal Muslim immigrants, raising fears of a larger crackdown against Muslims. In September the distributor of Salman Rushdie's latest book, *The Moor's Last Sigh*, announced it would not distribute the novel in Maharashtra, most likely because of the book's unflattering portrayal of a character resembling Shiv Sena leader Bal Thackeray.

In northeastern Arunachal Pradesh state, student groups have campaigned for the expulsion of 70,000 Buddhist Chakmas, who since the 1960s have fled conflict with Muslims in what is now Bangladesh. Some 50,000 Chakma refugees also live in six camps in Tripura state. Human rights groups charge the Rao government with reducing rations in order to speed their repatriation. There are 80,000 Tamil refugees from Sri Lanka in Tamil Nadu.

Workers can join independent unions. The central government can ban strikes in certain "essential" industries, and occasionally uses this power. Bonded labor is illegal but exists in rural areas. The International Labor Organization estimates there are up to 44 million child laborers, many of them working in conditions of servitude.

Indonesia

Polity: Dominant party (military-dominated)
Economy: Capitalist-statist
Population: 195,924,000
PPP: $2,950
Life Expectancy: 62.7
Ethnic Groups: Javanese (45 percent), Sundanese (14 percent), Madurese (8 percent), Coastal Malay (8 percent), others
Capital: Jakarta

Political Rights: 7
Civil Liberties: 6
Status: Not Free

Overview: In 1995 a court overturned a ban on Indonesia's leading independent newspaper, but crackdowns against the press and dissidents continued.

In August 1945 President Sukarno unilaterally proclaimed Indonesia's independence from the Dutch. In September 1965 the Army Strategic Reserve, led by General Suharto, thwarted a left-wing coup attempt. The army subsequently slaughtered over 300,000 suspected Communists, including many ethnic Chinese. In March 1966 Suharto assumed key political and military powers, formally becoming president in March 1968.

Highly authoritarian and corrupt rule have characterized Suharto's administration. Besides the ruling Golkar Party, the government permits the Indonesian Democratic Party (PDI), which favors some political liberalization, and the United Development Party (PPP), a coalition of Islamic groups.

The 500-member parliament has 400 elected seats and 100 (75 after 1997) reserved for the military. The 1,000-member People's Consultative Assembly, including the parliament plus 500 members appointed by Suharto and provincial governors, meets once every five years to elect the president and vice-president. Suharto has never faced any opposition.

At June 1992 parliamentary elections Golkar received 67.5 percent of votes—down from 73 percent in 1987—but still took 282 of 400 contested seats; the PPP won sixty-two and the PDI, fifty-six.

In March 1993 the Assembly formally gave Suharto a sixth five-year term, and elected armed forces commander General Try Sutrisno, who similarly ran unopposed, vice-president.

A mid-April 1994 strike in Medan, a northwestern city, sparked anti-Chinese riots. By some accounts authorities covertly instigated the riots to discredit Indonesia's independent labor movement, which had organized the strike.

In June 1994 the Information Ministry closed *Tempo*, Indonesia's premier newsmagazine, and two other outspoken weeklies. In a surprising 3 May 1995 ruling a court overturned the ban on *Tempo*, calling the closure arbitrary.

Political Rights and Civil Liberties: Citizens cannot change their government democratically due to institutional barriers, the military's prominent political role and Suharto's dominance. Military personnel hold 20 percent of national, provincial and district legislative seats, and officers hold many key administrative posts. The army and police violate civilians' rights with impunity. Official corruption is rampant.

All parties must embrace the consensus-oriented Pancasila philosophy, effectively limiting political discussion. In March 1995 the ruling Golkar expelled an outspoken member from parliament, and in May the PPP expelled another for questioning Pancasila. The government frequently tries to label political and social activists as Communists.

In August authorities removed compulsory "ET" (ex-political prisoner) marks from identity cards of the over one million Indonesians arrested following the 1965 coup attempt. However, they and their families still face official harassment.

The gravest violations occur in Aceh, East Timor and West Papua (*See East Timor and West Papua reports in the Related Territories section*). In Aceh province, on the northern tip of Sumatra, the army has killed some 2,000 civilians and *Aceh Merdeka* (Free Aceh) guerrillas since 1989. Security forces in Aceh often arbitrarily detain suspects for lengthy periods, and torture is routine.

The judiciary is not independent. The executive appoints and dismisses judges, and the government frequently pressures them. The chief judge in the Tempo case (*see Overview above*) was "promoted" to a new position following the verdict.

Police frequently use excessive force in routine situations, and torture suspects and prisoners. Hundreds are serving sentences under the 1963 Antisubversion Law. Scores or even hundreds of others, including many dissidents, are imprisoned under felony-sedition or hate-sowing statutes. The Agency for Coordination of Assistance for the Consolidation of National Security has wide latitude in dealing with suspected national security threats.

The government often pressures editors not to print particular stories. Journalists practice self-censorship. The state-sponsored Indonesian Journalists Association (PWI) must license all journalists. In March 1995 the PWI expelled thirteen members belonging to the unofficial Alliance of Independent Journalists (AJI), effectively blacklisting them, and pressured editors of several papers to dismiss AJI journalists. On 1 September a court sentenced two leading AJI members to thirty-two months' imprisonment for "sowing hatred" against the government and publishing an unlicensed newspaper, *Independen.* A week earlier an eighteen-year-old had received a twenty-month sentence for helping to distribute *Independen.* The government operates the national television and radio networks, and smaller private stations face restrictions on news coverage.

Nongovernmental organization (NGO) activists face official harassment and are frequently barred from speaking at public forums. In September a court sentenced a journalist who edited a newsletter of the *Pijar Foundation,* an outspoken NGO, to two years. An official human rights commission formed in January 1994 has been surprisingly outspoken against official abuses.

Police must be notified of all political meetings. Public assemblies require permits, which are often denied, and police often forcibly disband peaceful demonstrations for lack of permits.

Religious freedom is generally respected in this predominantly Muslim country. Chinese citizens face restrictions on operating Chinese-language schools and on publicly displaying Chinese-language characters.

Domestic violence, rape and female genital mutilation are relatively widespread throughout Indonesia. There are thousands of street children in Jakarta and other cities.

The government's strict numerical requirements for trade union registration have resulted in a de facto single union system. The government controls the All Indonesian Workers' Union, the sole recognized union, and considers the independent Indonesian Welfare Labor Union (SBSI) illegal. Civil servants and most state enterprise workers may not join unions.

Factory owners frequently pay workers below the minimum wage. Military intervention in labor disputes and union affairs under Manpower Decree No. 342 continues, despite the law's January 1994 revision. Workers may strike, although organizers often lose their jobs. Since May 1993 at least three labor activists have died mysteriously. In October 1995 the Supreme Court overturned a three-year sentence against SBSI leader Mochtar Pakpahan for inciting the Medan riots (*see Overview above*). Other SBSI leaders were also released.

Iran

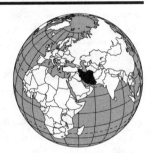

Polity: Presidential-parliamentary (clergy-dominated)
Political Rights: 6
Civil Liberties: 7
Status: Not Free
Economy: Capitalist-statist
Population: 61,280,000
PPP: $4,420
Life Expectancy: 67.5
Ethnic Groups: Persian (51 percent), Azeri (24 percent), Kurd (7 percent), Turkic, Arab, others
Capital: Teheran

Overview:

In 1995 Iranian President Ali Akbar Hashemi Rafsanjani faced deepening unrest as the economy deteriorated and hardline clerics continued to resist political and economic reforms.

British and Soviet forces occupied Iran during World War II, installing Mohammad Reza Pahlavi as hereditary monarch in 1941. Except for a brief period out of power following a left-wing coup in 1953, the shah ruled in a corrupt, authoritarian manner until fleeing Iran in January 1979 amid widespread unrest. In February fundamentalists led by Ayatollah Ruhollah Khomeini established the world's only Islamic republic.

The December 1979 constitution provides for a directly-elected president and a twelve-member Council of Guardians. The Council of Guardians must certify that all bills passed by the directly-elected 270-member *majlis* (parliament) accord with Islamic law, and must approve all presidential and parliamentary candidates, effectively maintaining the political dominance of a core of Shiite Muslim clerics and their allies. In early 1981 Khomeini usurped power from elected officials and unleashed a period of mass executions of political opponents.

The 1980-88 war with Iraq devastated the economy. Following Khomeini's June 1989 death, Ayatollah Ali Khamenei assumed the role of supreme religious leader. In July a constitutional referendum approved a stronger presidency, and in

August Rafsanjani, a cleric, took office after winning 94.5 percent of votes. During his first term Rafsanjani introduced limited free-market reforms, overcoming opposition from more radical clerics favoring statist economic policies.

Pro-Rafsanjani candidates won roughly three-quarters of seats in nonparty April and May 1992 majlis elections. In May and June, demonstrations against several municipalities' efforts to destroy squatter settlements cost Rafsanjani the support of many MPs. Blaming economic reforms for causing hardship, they shifted their allegiance to Khamenei, who opposed the liberalizations.

In June 1993 Rafsanjani won a second four-year term, capturing a relatively low 63.2 percent of votes despite running against three weak contenders. The results reflected widespread disillusionment with the revolution's failure to improve living standards. In 1994 Rafsanjani's power continued to wane as a series of bombings, riots and anti-government rallies underscored the country's economic difficulties and the regime's lack of legitimacy.

On 4 April 1995 economic riots broke out in the Teheran suburb of Akbar Abad and in a nearby town, Islamshar, after food prices doubled and the value of the currency, the *rial*, dropped sharply. Security forces responded by shooting at least ten people to death.

Political Rights and Civil Liberties:

Iranians cannot change their government democratically. The Council of Guardians must formally approve all presidential and legislative candidates. The narrow criteria, which include being "pro-revolution," effectively prevent opposition candidates from running. In practice, the country is run mainly by a Shiite clerical elite and there is no separation of religion and state. Political parties are strongly discouraged, and the few that exist are barred from participating in elections.

State control is maintained through arbitrary detention, torture and summary trials and executions. Several hundred people are executed annually for political reasons, often on false drug or other criminal charges. There are no avenues of appeal or legal limits on the length of detention, so suspects can be held indefinitely. In February 1994 the United Nations Special Rapporteur estimated that Iran held 19,000 political prisoners.

The Intelligence and Interior Ministries operate informant networks and monitor correspondence. In 1994 the Islamic Revolutionary Councils, which monitor government employees' religious fervor, purged dozens of civil servants.

Women face discrimination in legal, educational and employment matters, as well as severe harassment. The government encourages fundamentalist gangs known as *Komiteh*, and the even more radical *Bassij* ("those who are mobilized"), to enforce strict Islamic dress guidelines for women regardless of their faith. The penal code permits flogging or stoning of women for alleged moral offenses. Homes are frequently raided under the pretext of searching for alcohol, which is illegal.

The judiciary is not independent. Judges, as with any officials, must meet strict political and religious qualifications, and bribery is common. Civil courts feature some procedural safeguards, although a law in effect since May 1995 allows judges to serve simultaneously as prosecutors during trials. Revolutionary Courts try political and religious cases, but are often arbitrarily assigned cases normally falling under civil courts' jurisdiction. Defendants are often charged with vague crimes, and there are no due process rights in the Revolutionary Courts, with some trials lasting less than five minutes.

Some public criticism of government policy is allowed, and several relatively outspoken newspapers and cultural journals exist. However, this tolerance is arbitrary and crackdowns occur frequently. In 1995 authorities closed at least four outspoken publications.

All radio and television is state-owned, and broadcasts promote government views. A ban against satellite dishes took effect on 21 April, and the government authorized certain police units to raid homes to remove dishes.

The government has weakened or eliminated most independent civic institutions. Demonstrations not sponsored by the government are rare but occasionally tolerated.

Religious freedom is limited. In 1994 three Protestant leaders whom authorities accused of proselytizing were found murdered. Authorities rarely grant the necessary approval for publication of Christian texts, and church services are routinely monitored. Christians and Jews face restrictions on operating schools and discrimination in education, employment, property ownership and other areas. Knowledge of Islam is required for university admission and civil service jobs, constraining non-Muslims. Entire Jewish families cannot travel abroad together.

The 300,000-strong Baha'i minority is not officially recognized and faces significant official discrimination, including confiscation of property; arbitrary detention; a ban on university admission; heavy employment restrictions; and prohibitions on teaching their faith. Authorities have also placed cultural restrictions on the Kurdish community, and in Kurdish regions security forces have razed villages and frequently clash with opposition groups. The government has announced that the estimated 1.6 million Afghan refugees remaining in Iran must leave by March 1997. Some Afghans apparently have been forcibly repatriated.

There are no independent labor unions. The government-controlled Worker's House is the only authorized federation, and there is no collective bargaining. Private-sector strikes occur infrequently and are sometimes disbanded by the militant Revolutionary Guards.

Iraq

Polity: One-party   **Political Rights:** 7
Economy: Statist   **Civil Liberties**: 7
Population: 16,664,000 **Status:** Not Free
PPP: $3,413
Life Expectancy: 66.0
Ethnic Groups: Arab (75 percent), Kurd (15 percent),
Turk, others
Capital: Baghdad

Overview: Iraqi strongman Saddam Hussein staged a sham presiden-
                      tial election in October 1995 aimed at demonstrating his
                      absolute authority in the wake of civil unrest and the
defections of two senior members of his regime.

Iraq achieved independence from the British in 1932. Since then the minority Sunni Muslims have ruled under successive governments. A July 1958 military coup overthrew the Hashemite monarchy, establishing a left-wing republic. A 1968 coup brought the Arab *Ba'ath* (Renaissance) Socialist Party to power. The frequently amended 1968 provisional constitution establishes a Revolutionary Command Council (RCC) with virtually unlimited and unchecked authority. In 1979 Saddam Hussein, considered the strongman of the regime since 1973, formally assumed the titles of State President and RCC Chairman.

In September 1980 Iraq attacked Iran, touching off a fierce eight-year war. In August 1990 Iraq invaded Kuwait. A twenty-two-nation coalition liberated Kuwait in February 1991. Immediately following its defeat, the army ruthlessly crushed a nascent Shiite uprising in the south. In April the U.N. Security Council passed Resolution 687, providing that in order to sell oil internationally Iraq must destroy its weapons of mass destruction, accept long-range monitoring of its weapons facilities and recognize Kuwait's sovereignty.

In May 1994 Hussein sacked Prime Minister Ahmed Hussein Khudayir al-Samarral and assumed the post himself after the continuing effects of the oil embargo pushed the Iraqi dinar to new lows against the dollar. In May 1995 Doulaymi tribesmen in Anbar Province staged bloody anti-government riots, and in June predominantly Doulaymi army units launched a failed rebellion. In the aftermath the army reportedly executed at least 120-150 Doulaymi soldiers and officers.

In August Lieut. Gen. Hussein Kamel, a son-in-law of the president and a key figure in the regime, defected to Jordan along with his brother, also a presidential son-in-law. Seeking to demonstrate that his absolute authority remained intact, on 16 October Hussein staged Iraq's first presidential election. Hussein stood as the sole candidate in the sham affair, winning 99.96 percent of the vote.

During the year the army continued its four-year-old campaign against Shiite rebels in the southern marshlands. The army has indiscriminately targeted civilian Shiite Marsh Arab villagers, razed homes and drained the southern Amara and Hammar marshes in order to flush out Shiite guerrillas. Tens of thousands of Shiite civilians have been forcibly relocated, driven out of the country, or killed and the 6,000-year-old civilization of the Marsh Arabs has been destroyed.

Political Rights and Civil Liberties:

Iraqi citizens cannot democratically change their government. Saddam Hussein holds supreme power in one of the most repressive regimes in the world, and relatives and close friends from his birthplace, Tikrit, hold most important positions. A 1991 law outlaws opposition parties, and the rubber-stamp, 250-seat National Assembly holds no independent power. All media are state-run and promote government views.

Citizens are denied all basic freedoms. The rule of law is nonexistent and state control is maintained through widespread arbitrary detentions—primarily of Shiites—routine torture of detainees and summary executions. The U.N. has documented the disappearance of over 16,000 Iraqi citizens in recent years, many of them in northern Iraq *(see Kurdistan report in the Related Territories section)* as well as in the southern marshlands. The security services routinely search homes without warrants, monitor personal communications, and maintain a large network of informers.

Defendants in ordinary cases receive some judicial safeguards. Political and "economic" cases are tried in separate security courts where confessions extracted through torture are admissible as evidence and there are no procedural safeguards. In both regular and security courts, punishments are generally out of proportion to the crime committed.

The death penalty is frequently used for any expression of dissent, as well as for economic offenses including price control violations and currency speculation.

In the summer of 1994 the government announced severe penalties for theft, corruption and currency speculation including amputation, branding and execution. The government also announced that desertion from the army would be punished by amputation of the ear and branding of the forehead. The authorities have reportedly executed several doctors for refusing to carry out these punishments.

The Shiite Muslim majority faces particularly severe persecution. The worst abuses occur in the southern marshlands, where in addition to the ground campaign (*see Overview above*) the army has arrested thousands of Shiites and brought them to detention centers in and around Baghdad. The government has executed an undetermined number of these detainees. Throughout the country authorities have arrested Shiite clergy, and the government directly administers many Shiite holy sites. Bans on some Shiite public ceremonies and on the publication of Shiite books remain in effect.

Other restrictions on religion apply to both the Shiite and Sunni communities. A 1981 law gives the government control over mosques, the appointment of clergy, and the publication of religious literature. The government harasses the tiny Turcoman and Christian Assyrian communities, and Jewish citizens face restrictions in traveling abroad and in contacting Jewish groups outside the country.

Resources are frequently diverted to the army and other privileged groups. As a result, food shortages, exacerbated by the oil embargo, have caused particular hardship for children. The U.N. has authorized Iraq to sell a limited quantity of oil in order to purchase food and medicine, but the regime has refused.

Numerous areas are off-limits for travel inside the country, and foreign travel is tightly restricted. The state-backed General Federation of Trade Unions is the only legal labor federation, and independent unions do not exist. The right to collective bargaining is not recognized by law and is not practiced. The right to strike is limited by law and strikes do not occur.

Ireland

Polity: Parliamentary democracy
Economy: Capitalist
Population: 3,588,000
PPP: $12,830
Life Expectancy: 75.3
Ethnic Groups: Irish (Celtic), English
Capital: Dublin

Political Rights: 1
Civil Liberties: 1*
Status: Free

Ratings Change: *Ireland's civil liberties rating changed from 2 to 1 because the government ended the formal state of emergency and peace was sustained.

Overview: **U**pon assuming leadership of the new ruling coalition, conservative *Fine Gael* (Family of the Gaels) leader and *Taoiseach* (prime minister) John Bruton faced the daunting task of nurturing a stalling Northern Ireland peace process. Two major referendums were undertaken in 1995, one calling for the legal right to information concerning abortion and the other seeking to overturn a constitutional ban on divorce.

Bruton succeeded *Fianna Fail* (Soldiers of Destiny) leader Albert Reynolds, who resigned in 1994 following accusations of mismanagement in the delayed extradition of a pedophilic priest to Northern Ireland. Reynolds was instrumental in orchestrating the Provisional Irish Republican Army (IRA) and loyalist paramilitary ceasefires, which began last year following the historic Downing Street Declaration. By the time Taoiseach Bruton took office, the peace process had stalled over the British and Northern Unionist demand that the IRA begin disarming before all-party talks could begin.

All but six counties in the North won home rule from the British Commonwealth in 1921 and became a self-proclaimed republic twenty-seven years later. The six counties of Northern Ireland remained within the United Kingdom at the insistence of their Protestant majorities [see *Northern Ireland* under United Kingdom, Related Territories]. Despite Articles 2 and 3 of the Irish constitution, which lay claim to the territory, the republic plays only a consultative role in Northern affairs as set out by the 1985 Anglo-Irish Accord. The predominantly Protestant Unionists of the North oppose the degree of influence afforded Ireland by the Accord, and vehemently object to a cross-border council proposed in the framework document for continued negotiations released by the British and Irish government in February 1995.

Highly emotional debates surrounded the issues of divorce and abortion. A 1992 referendum approved the right to travel and to obtain information concerning abortion following the controversial case of a fourteen-year-old rape victim whom the attorney general prevented from going to Britain to obtain an abortion. A bill proposed by the government in March was attacked by anti-abortion groups, who charged that providing the names and addresses of clinics in Britain would equal advocating abortion. The bill passed in both houses of parliament and was signed into law by president Robinson after affirmation by the Supreme Court in May. At the end of November, 50.3 percent of the electorate voted in favor of legalizing divorce.

Political Rights and Civil Liberties: Irish citizens can change their government democratically. Residents of Northern Ireland are considered citizens and may run for office in the South. At present, only diplomatic families and security forces living abroad have the right to absentee ballots. The government has pledged to grant emigrants the right to elect three Senate members, but emigrant voting rights advocates argue that the gesture hardly constitutes true representation.

The Irish press is comparatively free, with the exception of broadcasting anything likely to undermine state authority or promote violence. Despite censorship of sexually explicit materials, satellite broadcasts make pornography available. In addition to international cable broadcasts, international newspapers, particularly from Britain, are gaining a growing share of the Irish market. The government has been accused of placing Irish newspapers at a disadvantage by levying on them the highest value-added tax in the European Union. Fierce competition along with concentrated ownership and harsh libel laws result in de facto restrictions on free speech.

In February the government ended the formal state of emergency instated in 1939 at the outbreak of World War II, but stopped short of revoking all special powers associated with emergency provisions. Among these provisions are special search, arrest and detention powers given to the police and a non-jury, three-judge Special Criminal Court for alleged terrorists. The regular judiciary is independent; however, many judges appear prejudiced regarding crimes against women, giving light sentences to or releasing alleged rapists. The Council for the Status of Women has accused the ruling party leaders of failing to support women in politics, and claims that women are underrepresented on virtually all parliamentary committees. Although women occupy two of fourteen cabinet positions along with the presidency, no woman has been appointed to the body working on developing the relationship between Britain and Ireland. The percentage of women in the paid labor force has grown significantly in the last two decades, but remains among the lowest in the European Union.

The Roman Catholic Church is strong, yet religious freedom for other faiths remains intact. Several issues in recent years have brought the Church into conflict with the state, including the liberalization of condom sales in response to the spread of AIDS, the 1993 legalization of homosexual acts, and this year's referenda on abortion and divorce.

Israel

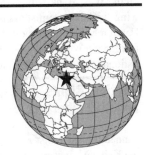

Polity: Parliamentary democracy
Economy: Mixed capitalist
Population: 5,530,000
PPP: $14,700
Life Expectancy: 76.5
Ethnic Groups: Jewish (83 percent), Arab (17 percent)
Capital: Jerusalem (most countries maintain their embassies in Tel Aviv)

Political Rights: 1
Civil Liberties: 3
Status: Free

Overview: The November 1995 assassination of premier Yitzhak Rabin by a Jewish extremist underscored the deep divisions among Israelis over the ongoing transfer of much of the West Bank to Palestinian administration.

Israel was formed in May 1948 out of less than one-fifth of the original British Palestine Mandate. Its Arab neighbors, having previously rejected a United Nations partition plan that would have also created an Arab state, attacked Israel immediately following independence. Israel fought Egypt in 1956 and in June 1967 routed several Arab armies after Egypt closed the Gulf of Aqaba to its ships, taking the Gaza Strip, the Sinai Peninsula, the West Bank, the Golan Heights and East Jerusalem. In 1979 Israel signed a peace treaty with Egypt that led to the return of the Sinai in 1982.

Israel has been a parliamentary democracy since independence. Arabs and other minorities freely elect representatives to the 120-seat *Knesset* (parliament). The conservative Likud party formed a governing coalition after 1977 parliamentary elections, ending twenty-nine years of center-left rule. Likud and the Labor Party shared power following 1984 and 1988 elections, until Labor withdrew in March 1990.

At the June 1992 elections, former prime minister Yitzhak Rabin led Labor to victory with forty-four seats, with Likud taking thirty-two; the leftist *Meretz*, twelve; the right-wing *Tzomet*, eight; the National Religious Party, six; the Sephardic, ultrareligous *Shas*, six; the United Torah Jewry, four; the leftist Democratic Front, three; the right-wing *Moledet*, three; and the Arab Democratic Party, two. Rabin formed a sixty-two-seat coalition with Meretz and Shas.

Through a series of secret negotiations Israel and the Palestine Liberation Organization (PLO) reached an August 1993 breakthrough agreement providing for gradual Palestinian autonomy in the Occupied Territories (*See Occupied Territories and Palestinian Autonomous Areas report in the Related Territories section*). In July 1994 Israel and Jordan formally declared an end to their forty-six-year state of war, signing a formal peace treaty in October.

Since the Israeli-PLO accord a series of suicide bombings by Palestinian militants has turned many Israelis against the peace process. Meanwhile, a core of religious Jews opposes any steps that could lead to an independent Palestinian state on the West Bank, which they consider sacred land. On 4 November 1995 a right-wing Jewish extremist assassinated Rabin as he left a peace rally in Tel Aviv. Foreign Minister Shimon Peres became acting prime minister and subsequently formed a government. The Israeli-Arab peace process figures to be the key issue in national elections due by November 1996.

Political Rights and Civil Liberties: Israeli citizens can change their government democratically. Arab-based parties and far-right Jewish groups hold seats in parliament. In March 1994 the Israeli cabinet banned the extremist *Kach* party of the late Rabbi Meir Kahane, and an offshoot, the Kahane Lives party, neither of which held seats. Since the September 1993 Israeli-PLO peace accord, suicide bombings by Islamic militants have killed over eighty-five Israelis and wounded over 270 others.

The *Shin Bet* (General Security Service), responsible for internal security, is accused of torturing Palestinian detainees. Internal security regulations from 1987 allow security forces to apply "moderate physical pressure" to suspects during interrogation. In November 1994, following a series of suicide bombings, the government further eased restrictions on the use of physical force against suspects who might have knowledge of imminent terrorist attacks. The April 1995 death in custody of a suspected Palestinian militant highlighted the practice of violently "shaking" some detainees to obtain evidence.

The judiciary is independent of the government, and procedural safeguards are respected. Security trials can be closed to the public only on limited grounds. Access to some sensitive evidence in such cases can be withheld from defense attorneys, although such evidence cannot be used for a conviction. Ordinary prisons and police detention facilities are overcrowded. Detention facilities run by the Israeli Defense Forces to hold security prisoners do not meet international norms.

A 1979 law provides for administrative detention without charge for renewable six-month periods, subject to automatic review every three months. Although most administrative detainees are Palestinians, several Israeli Jews have been detained under the law.

Newspaper and magazine articles dealing with security matters must be submitted to a military censor. Editors can appeal censorship decisions to a three-man tribunal that includes two civilians. Arabic-language publications are censored more frequently than Hebrew-language ones. All newspapers are privately owned, and vigorously critique government policies. Freedoms of assembly and association are respected.

Women frequently do not receive equal pay for equal work, and face discrimination in employment opportunities. Domestic violence is a problem, and in Druze and Bedouin communities women are sometimes victims of traditional "family honor" killings. All religions worship freely. Each community has jurisdiction over its members in questions of marriage and divorce. Orthodox Jewish authorities have jurisdiction over marriage, divorce and burial affairs for the entire Jewish community.

Druze citizens serve in the army, but frequently face social ostracism and discrimination in employment opportunities and government services. Arab citizens similarly do not receive the same quality of government services as Jewish citizens. Israeli Arabs are at a disadvantage by not being subject to the draft (although they may serve voluntarily), since veterans receive preferential access to housing subsidies and some other economic benefits.

Workers can join unions of their choice and enjoy the right to strike and bargain collectively. Three-quarters of the workforce either belong to unions affiliated with *Histadrut* (General Federation of Labor in Israel) or are covered under its social programs and collective bargaining agreements. The Global Manpower company has brought Chinese laborers to Israel with promises of high salaries that have not been honored, and strike leaders have been sent home.

Italy

Polity: Parliamentary democracy
Economy: Capitalist-statist
Population: 57,675,000
PPP: $18,090
Life Expectancy: 77.5
Ethnic Groups: Italian, small German, Slovene, Albanian and Roma minorities
Capital: Rome

Political Rights: 1
Civil Liberties: 2
Status: Free

Overview:

After the Populist Northern League's defection brought down Silvio Berlusconi's government, President Oscar Luigi Scalfaro appointed a technocratic government under

Lamberto Dini to overcome political deadlock and tackle Italy's deteriorating public finances. Although Berlusconi and his allies originally nominated Dini, Berlusconi's former treasury minister, they spent 1995 blocking him from achieving his limited mandate of passing a supplementary budget, changing regional electoral laws, guaranteeing free access to the media during political campaigns and reforming Italy's troubled pension system.

Modern Italian history dates from nineteenth-century unification as a parliamentary monarchy under the House of Savoy. After a twenty-one-year period under fascist dictator Benito Mussolini beginning in 1922, the monarchy was abolished by popular referendum and a provisional government was established to oversee the transformation to a republic under a new constitution effective January 1948. The ensuing four decades saw over fifty governments, most dominated by the Christian Democratic Party.

A massive anticorruption campaign over the last four years has led to the arrests of thousands of high-level politicians and business figures, including former Socialist leader and current fugitive Bettino Craxi and ex-Christian Democratic premier Arnaldo Forlani. Seven-time Christian Democratic Prime Minister Giulio Andreotti now faces a lengthy trial on charges of consorting with the Sicilian Mafia.

As the traditional postwar political system collapsed under the weight of rampant corruption, billionaire media tycoon Silvio Berlusconi launched his *Forza Italia* movement, forged a rightist coalition with the Northern League and the fascist-oriented MSI/National Alliance party, and captured a parliamentary majority in March 1994. The Northern League withdrew its support less than a year later, however, and Berlusconi's government fell.

In spite of persistent center-right efforts to topple his government and force early elections, Dini survived 1995 while methodically holding to his self-declared mandate. With the precarious support of various parties of the center and left, occasionally joined by right-wing defectors, Dini survived two confidence votes called by Berlusconi, two others he gambled on himself in order to push legislation through parliament, and one vote of no confidence specifically in his justice minister (currently under appeal). At year's end, Dini tendered his resignation as promised to President Scalfaro, who refused to accept it and instead invited him to remain with a new and broader mandate. Berlusconi, now under investigation for corruption in his media empire, has recently ceased his persistent calls for elections, advocating instead a new government of "the best minds" from all political parties.

Political Rights and Civil Liberties: Italians can change their government democratically. Electoral reforms in 1993—which allowed voters to choose individual candidates rather than party lists and converted 75 percent of parliamentary seats to a "first-past-the-post" system—have helped move Italian politics toward a bipolar structure with broad alliances on the right and left. The trend was particularly apparent in April's regional elections, when 90 percent of the electorate turned out to support parties on both sides almost equally.

Italian citizens are free to form political organizations with the exception of reorganizing the prewar fascist party, which is constitutionally forbidden. Attempting to guarantee the end of authoritarian rule, the postwar constitution established an elaborate system of checks and balances in which the Senate and the Chamber of Deputies wield equal powers. The result has been a heavy reliance on the popular referendum as a tool for breaking political deadlock, which many argue diminishes the power of parliament to efficiently legislate.

The independent judiciary is notoriously slow. Authorities may detain without trial defendants deemed capable of tampering with evidence or fleeing Italy, sometimes for years. Italy's prisons are so overcrowded and lacking in proper health care facilities that deaths by illness and suicides are common, often among inmates awaiting trial. A threatened lawyers' strike in June highlighted the backlog of some 2.8 million unheard cases, causing delays of up to a decade between arrest and sentencing.

The press in Italy is generally free and competitive, with minor restrictions in the areas of obscenity and defamation. Although most of the eighty dailies are independently owned, editorial opinion is highly influenced by the church and tends to lean to the right. In a June referendum, voters rejected three proposals directly aimed at breaking up Berlusconi's broadcasting empire, while calling for the privatization of state-owned channels. Prior to the referendum, a presidential decree banned all propaganda spots on television thirty days prior to elections.

Freedom of speech is constitutionally guaranteed, as are freedoms of assembly and association with the exception of overtly fascist and racist groups. Unions were particularly visible in 1995, both as participants in the pension-reform negotiations and in support of striking state airline workers at Alitalia and journalists across the country. Referendum voters supported weakening the power of labor unions in contract negotiations, and the government announced new legislation to tighten controls over the right to strike in public-sector services.

Religious freedom is guaranteed in this overwhelmingly Roman Catholic country. Italy's first grand Mosque opened in 1995. Many of the estimated 650,000 Muslims currently residing have migrated from Northern Africa. Anti-immigrant violence has increased in recent years, bolstered by calls from the National Alliance and other extreme-right groups to crack down on illegal workers and immigrants. After an ultimatum from the Northern League, Dini's government agreed to tighten control on immigration in order to secure narrow passage of the 1996 budget.

Women continue to face obstacles to economic advancement and female participation in government remains an estimated 10 percent. A major victory for women's rights advocates came in September with the doubling of prison sentences for rapists from five to ten years; also, the crime's legal categorization changed from a "moral offense" to a "crime against the person," thus receiving the same legal treatment as murder and assault.

Jamaica

Polity: Parliamentary democracy
Economy: Capitalist
Population: 2,447,000
PPP: $3,200
Life Expectancy: 73.6
Ethnic Groups: Black (76 percent), Creole (15 percent), European, Chinese, East Indian
Capital: Kingston

Political Rights: 2
Civil Liberties: 3
Status: Free

Overview: The formation of the National Democratic Movement (NDM) by Bruce Golding, former chairman of the opposition Jamaica Labour Party (JLP), indicated a possible end to Jamaica's traditional two-party polity.

Jamaica, a member of the British Commonwealth, achieved independence in 1962. It is a parliamentary democracy, with the British monarchy represented by a governor-general. The bicameral parliament consists of a sixty-member House of Representatives elected for five years, and a twenty-one-member Senate, with thirteen senators appointed by the prime minister and eight by the leader of the parliamentary opposition. Executive authority is invested in the prime minister, who is the leader of the political party commanding a majority in the House.

Since independence, power has alternated between the currently ruling, social-democratic People's National Party (PNP) and the conservative JLP. The PNP's Michael Manley was prime minister from 1972 to 1980, and again from 1989 until his resignation for health reasons in 1992. JLP leader Edward Seaga held the post from 1980 until 1989.

In 1992 the PNP elected P.J. Patterson to replace Manley as party leader and prime minister. In early elections called in 1993 the PNP won fifty-two parliamentary seats and the JLP eight. Both parties differed little on continuing the structural adjustment begun in the 1980s, but the JLP was hurt by longstanding internal rifts.

Irregularities and violence marred the vote. The PNP agreed to address subsequent JLP demands for electoral reform. But the contentious process dragged on through 1995. Meanwhile, the Patterson government continued to confront labor unrest and an unrelenting crime wave.

In October, Golding, a well-respected economist and businessman, left the JLP to launch the NDM, one of the most significant political developments since independence. Golding brought with him a number of key JLP figures, including one other member of parliament, cutting the JLP's seats to six.

Seaga charged that the NDM was made up of the "Mercedes and BMW crowd" while Patterson held his fire. The first opinion polls showed the NDM running just behind the PNP and just ahead of the JLP, indicating that the next elections, due by February 1998, could be the country's first three-horse race.

Political Rights and Civil Liberties: Citizens are able to change their government through elections. However, the 1993 elections were marked by thuggery on both sides in urban areas, police intimidation, large-scale confusion, scattered fraud and voter turnout of 59 percent, the lowest since the pre-independence 1962 elections.

Progress on electoral reform has been slow, causing local elections to be postponed for two straight years. Opinion polls show that nearly half the population is not inclined to vote in the next elections, indicating a high level of disillusionment with politics.

Constitutional guarantees regarding the right to free expression, freedom of religion and the right to organize political parties, civic organizations and labor unions are generally respected.

Labor unions are politically influential and have the right to strike. An Industrial Disputes Tribunal mediates labor conflicts.

Criminal violence, fueled by poverty and drugs, and human rights violations by police are a major concern. Violence is now the major cause of death in Jamaica, and the murder rate continues to rise. Much of the violence is due to warfare between drug gangs known as posses. But domestic violence, particularly against women, common criminal activity and vigilante actions in rural areas are major factors.

The police have been responsible for over 2,000 deaths in the past eight years, as well as numerous cases of physical abuse of detainees. The work of the Jamaica Council for Human Rights has led to successful prosecution in a number of cases, with victims receiving court-ordered, monetary reparations. But officers found guilty of abuses usually go unpunished and many cases remained unresolved.

The judicial system is headed by a Supreme Court and includes several magistrate's courts and a Court of Appeal, with final recourse to the Privy Council in London. The system is slow and inefficient, particularly in addressing police abuses and the deplorable, violent conditions in prisons and police lock-ups. There is a mounting backlog of cases, a shortage of court staff at all levels, and a lack of resources.

To stem the crime wave the government has taken the controversial steps of restoring capital punishment, which had been suspended in 1988, and flogging. Rights groups protested both measures. Critics charged that flogging was unconstitutional because it could be characterized as "inhuman or degrading punishment."

Newspapers are independent and free of government control. Journalists occasionally are the targets of intimidation during election campaigns. Broadcast media are largely public but open to pluralistic points of view. Public opinion polls play a key role in the political process and election campaigns feature televised debates on state-run television.

Japan

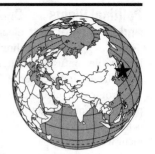

Polity: Parliamentary democracy
Economy: Capitalist
Population: 125,236,000
PPP: $20,520
Life Expectancy: 79.5
Ethnic Groups: Japanese (98 percent), Korean, Ainu
Capital: Tokyo

Political Rights: 1*
Civil Liberties: 2
Status: Free

Ratings Change: *Japan's political rights rating changed from 2 to 1 because the July elections were the first to be held under a new, fairer electoral law.

Overview: Two years after reform-oriented parties swept the conservative Liberal Democratic Party (LDP) out of office after thirty-eight years of continuous rule, Japanese voters sensed little had changed. With the LDP back as the dominant partner in a year-old coalition government, the opposition New Frontier Party (NFP) tapped into this disillusionment with a strong showing in the July 1995 upper house elections.

Following its defeat in World War II, Japan adopted an American-drafted constitution in 1947 that invested legislative authority in the two-house *Diet* (parliament) and ended the emperor's divine status. In October 1955 the two wings of the opposition Japan Socialist Party (JSP) united, and in November the two main conservative parties merged to form the ruling LDP. This "1955 system" remained in place throughout the Cold War as the LDP won successive elections and the leftist JSP served as an institutional opposition.

By the early 1990s the LDP's involvement in a series of corruption scandals had led to calls for political reform. Ordinary Japanese increasingly began to question the LDP's favoritism towards big business, farmers and other special interests, as well as the burdensome regulations imposed by the country's powerful bureaucracy.

In the July 1993 elections, the LDP lost its lower-house majority for the first time in thirty-eight years, taking a 223-seat plurality. The JSP, renamed the Social Democratic Party (SDP), saw its share plunge from 136 seats to 70; the newly formed Japan Renewal Party (JRP) took 55; the Buddhist Komeito party, 51; the Japan New Party, the original pro-reform party founded in May 1992, 35; the Democratic Socialist Party, 15; the Japan Communist Party, 15; the newly-formed New Harbinger Party (NHP), 13; and minor parties or independents, 34. In August the SDP and six smaller conservative and centrist parties formed a governing coalition, throwing the LDP into the opposition for the first time ever.

In June 1994 the LDP returned to power in coalition with the SDP, its longtime rival, and the smaller NHP. The SDP's Tomiichi Murayama took office as prime minister, allowing the faction-riven LDP to avoid the internally divisive process of choosing one of its own for the post. Voter disillusionment quickly increased over this opportunistic left-right alliance. In early December nine conservative opposition parties joined to form the NFP. Its platform included economic deregulation and a more assertive Japanese foreign policy.

In the 23 July 1995 elections for 126 of the 252 seats in the upper house of parliament, the governing coalition lost 10 seats to finish with 65, while the NFP, in its first national poll test, scored well with 39 seats. Smaller parties and independents split the remainder. International trade and industry minister Ryutaro Hashimoto was elected LDP president in September, and Ichiro Ozawa, a onetime LDP backroom fixer-turned-reformer, won the top NFP spot in December. Hashimoto and Ozawa will lead their respective parties to lower-house elections due by July 1997.

Political Rights and Civil Liberties: Japanese citizens can change their government democratically. The current lower house of parliament was elected in 1993 under an electoral system heavily weighted in favor of rural areas. Reform legislation passed in 1994 reduced the permissible disparity in population between urban and rural districts; tightened campaign finance laws; and scrapped the multiple-seat constituencies in favor of a 500-seat lower house with 300 single-seat districts and 200 seats chosen on a proportional basis, and an upper house with 152 single districts and 100 seats chosen in proportional balloting. The July 1995 upper-house elections were the first to be held under the new laws.

A continuing civil liberties concern involves the 700,000 Korean permanent residents, many of whom can trace their ancestry in Japan for two or three generations. Koreans regularly face discrimination in housing, education and employment opportunities, are not granted automatic Japanese citizenship at birth, and must submit to an official background check and adopt Japanese names to become naturalized. Both the Burakumin, who are descendants of feudal-era outcasts, and the indigenous Ainu minority also face unofficial discrimination and social ostracism.

The judiciary is independent. The Criminal Procedure Code allows authorities to restrict a suspect's right to counsel during an investigation, and counsel may not be present during an interrogation. Local human rights groups have criticized the frequent practice of using police cells to hold the accused between arrest and sentencing, and report that police sometimes physically abuse suspects to extract confessions. Local groups have also criticized prison conditions for their rigid emphasis on discipline. In addition, immigration officers are accused of regularly beating detainees.

Civic institutions are strong and freedoms of expression, assembly and association are respected in practice. Exclusive private press clubs provide journalists with access to top politicians and major ministries, and in return journalists often practice self-censorship of sensitive stories. Foreign news services must negotiate with each club directly, and entry is occasionally denied.

For decades the Education Ministry has censored passages in history textbooks describing Japan's military aggression in the 1930s and 1940s. In March 1993 the Supreme Court ruled that the Ministry has the right to censor textbooks on "reasonable grounds."

Women face significant discrimination in employment opportunities and are frequently steered into clerical careers. The 1986 Equal Employment Opportunity Law discourages discrimination in the workplace but does not make it illegal. Thousands of women from the Philippines and Thailand have been trafficked to Japan for prostitution. There is full freedom of religion; Buddhism and Shintoism predominate. Workers, with exception of police and firefighters, are free to join independent unions of their choice and hold strikes.

Jordan

Polity: Monarchy and elected parliament
Economy: Capitalist
Population: 4,101,000
PPP: $4,270
Life Expectancy: 67.9
Ethnic Groups: Palestinian and Bedouin Arab (98 percent), Circassian, Armenian, Kurd
Capital: Amman

Political Rights: 4
Civil Liberties: 4
Status: Partly Free

Overview: Pro-government candidates swept Jordan's municipal elections in July 1995, defeating Islamic fundamentalists opposed to the normalization of relations with Israel.

The British installed the Hashemite monarchy in 1921, and granted Jordan full independence in 1946. King Hussein came to the throne in 1952 and formally assumed constitutional powers in May 1953. The 1952 constitution vests executive power in the king, who appoints the prime minister and can dissolve the bicameral National Assembly. The Assembly consists of a forty-member Senate appointed by the king, and an eighty-member, directly elected Chamber of Deputies.

In 1957, following a coup attempt by pan-Arab leftists, the king banned political parties. In the 1967 war with Israel Jordan lost the West Bank, which it had seized in 1948 after the British Mandate ended.

In April 1989 rioting erupted in several southern cities over price increases. King Hussein responded by lifting restrictions on freedom of expression and ending the ban on party activity. The country held nonparty elections in November 1989, the first elections in thirty-three years.

Jordan's first multiparty elections since 1956 followed on 8 November 1993. The key issue was the Israeli-Palestine Liberation Organization accord signed two months earlier. With Palestinians assuming greater control in the West Bank, and forming 60 percent of Jordan's population, many non-Palestinian Jordanians worry about Palestinian instability spilling into their country. Final results gave pro-government independents and Bedouin tribal leaders fifty-four seats, while the Palestinian-based Islamic Action Front (IAF), the fundamentalist Muslim Brotherhood's political party, took sixteen. Smaller parties split the remainder.

In October 1994 Jordan and Israel signed a formal peace treaty. At the 11-12 July 1995 municipal elections government supporters scored heavy victories over IAF candidates campaigning against the accord with Israel.

In another development, on 5 January Prime Minister Abdul-Salam Majali resigned and was replaced three days later by a former premier, Sharif Zaid Bin Shaker.

Political Rights and Civil Liberties: Although the country held multiparty elections in November 1993, Jordanians cannot change their government democratically. King Hussein holds broad executive powers and must approve all laws. Prior to the 1993 vote the government amended the electoral law to favor tribal leaders over the Islamic opposition.

The authorities frequently arbitrarily arrest suspected Islamic fundamentalists during sweeps. Police often abuse detainees to extract confessions. The judiciary is generally independent of the government, but can be influenced in sensitive cases. Defendants in civil court trials receive adequate safeguards, although bribery of judges is relatively common. Defendants in state security cases often lack sufficient pretrial access to lawyers.

Jordanians freely criticize government policies, although direct criticism of King Hussein is rare. The Penal Code permits the government to take legal action against individuals for inciting violence or defaming heads of state or public officials. Since 1994 the government has taken measures to limit opposition to Jordan's normalization of relations with Israel. The authorities have suspended clergy from sermonizing, purged some teachers from public schools, and in May 1995 banned a conference organized by an eleven-party coalition opposed to the peace deal.

The 1993 Press and Publications Law restricts coverage of subjects including the royal family, the armed forces, and monetary policy. Several journalists have been tried and fined under the law, and journalists generally practice self-censorship. The press law also requires licensing of journalists and editors. The government occasionally pressures editors not to run certain stories. Broadcast media are state-owned but provide some criticism of government policies.

Since 1989 the government has granted permits for peaceful public demonstrations. Civil society is relatively underdeveloped but local human rights groups operate freely. However, since the press law restricts publication of information about the security forces, it is nearly impossible to report on the abuse of detainees.

Islam is the state religion. The government does not permit the Baha'i faith to run schools, and Baha'i family legal matters are handled in the Islamic *shari'a* courts.

On average there are thirty to sixty "honor killings" each year, in which males kill a female relative for alleged moral offenses. The penal code sharply limits the sentences for such killings compared with regular murder sentences. Women must receive permission from a male guardian to travel abroad, cannot pass nationality on to their children and are discriminated against in inheritance and divorce matters. There is a growing population of street children.

Private-sector workers can join independent unions. The government can legally prohibit private-sector strikes by referring disputes to an arbitration committee. Some government employees can form unions but none may strike. The International Confederation of Free Trade Unions has criticized the government for not adequately protecting workers from anti-union discrimination.

Kazakhstan

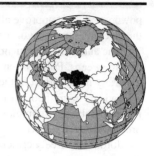

Polity: Dominant party
(presidential-dominated)
Economy: Statist
transitional
Population: 16,876,000
PPP: $4,270
Life Expectancy: 69.6
Ethnic Groups: Kazakh (43 percent), Russian (35 percent),
Ukrainian (6 percent), others
Capital: Almaty

Political Rights: 6
Civil Liberties: 5
Status: Not Free

Overview: **D**ecember's parliamentary elections failed to fill a quorum
in the 135-member lower house (*Majlis*) and were marred
by irregularities. A new constitution, adopted by referendum, gave President Nursultan Nazarbayev broad new powers. The popular but
authoritarian Nazarbayev sought to maintain stability while attracting investment in
the country's potential oil and agricultural wealth.

From 1730 to 1840 Russia controlled this sparsely populated, multi-ethnic land
the size of India stretching from the Caspian Sea to the Chinese border. After a
brief period of independence in 1917, it became an autonomous Soviet republic in
1929 and a union republic in 1936. Kazakhstan declared independence from a
crumbling Soviet Union in December 1991.

Nazarbayev, former first-secretary of Kazakhstan's Communist Party, was directly
elected in 1991. A 1993 constitution established a strong presidency. Nazarbayev appoints
the prime minister, deputy prime minister, and defense and interior ministers. Nazarbayev
heads the ruling National Unity Party.

The 1994 parliamentary elections to the 177-member, unicameral Supreme
Council (*Kenges*) were rife with fraud and irregularities. Even though pro-
Nazarbayev forces controlled over 60 percent of the seats, elected from state lists
and constituencies, parliament resisted Nazarbayev's reform legislation, including
measures dealing with price liberalization and private property.

In March 1995, faced with continuing opposition charges that parliament was
illegitimate because of irregularities and a challenge from the Constitutional Court,
Nazarbayev dissolved parliament and ruled by decree, scheduling elections for a
new bicameral parliament—a forty-seven-member Senate and a 135-member
Majlis—for December. Forty senators were to be directly elected, and seven
chosen by the president. About 100 members threatened to form an alternative
assembly, but the effort never materialized. Nazarbayev ordered a referendum
extending his term—which was to end in 1996—to 2000, and on 29 April a
reported 95 percent supported the measure.

The 5 December Senate elections were largely uncontested, with Nazarbayev
supporters taking all seats. Four days later, only forty-three deputies were elected
to the Majlis, two short of the required quorum. Runoffs were to be scheduled for
twenty-three seats where candidates received under 50 percent. International

observers cited irregularities including family voting. The Communist Party complained that only nine of twenty-eight candidates received registration, while thirty-eight National Unity Party candidates were registered. The other parties elected, such as the Democratic Party, were created by incumbent deputies and members of Nazarbayev's government. Most opposition parties boycotted, although some candidates ran as independents.

Nazarbayev showed his attitude toward parliament when he told European observers that his administration had passed seventy decrees, including laws on taxation and land ownership that "for years were being debated by the deputies."

On 30 August, voters overwhelmingly approved a new constitution, allowing Nazarbayev to dissolve parliament if it approves a no-confidence vote in the government or twice rejects his nominee for prime minister. It also codified periods of presidential rule by decree. Voter turnout was reportedly 85 percent.

In other issues, Russia and Kazakhstan moved closer to creating a "Euro-Asian Union," signing agreements on military cooperation, a customs union and currency convertibility. The countries also agreed to build the first stage of a pipeline linking Kazakhstan's vast oil and gas reserves with Western markets.

Political Rights and Civil Liberties: Citizens cannot change their government democratically. A new constitution only enshrined de facto power in the hands of President Nazarbayev, whose regime has cracked down on the opposition and controls the media. December's parliamentary elections failed to meet international standards.

Opposition parties include the Socialists (former Communists), the nationalist Azat (Freedom) Party, the ethnic-Russian Unity Party, the Rightist Republican Party, and smaller groups. Opposition parties have complained of harassment, surveillance, denial of access to state-run media, and arbitrarily being banned from registering candidates. These problems marred the March 1994 parliamentary vote, and the Constitutional Court upheld candidates' complaints, a factor leading to new elections in December 1995.

Obstacles to press freedom include economic factors as well as government interference. Provisions in the criminal code proscribe insulting the honor of the president. Over 1,200 "means of mass information" are registered. Independent local radio stations must petition the Ministry of Communications because broadcast towers remain state-owned. The main cities have at least one local independent or quasi-independent television station. The only national stations are state-controlled. Independent newspapers face financial difficulties, as do party and union publications, particularly outside the capital, Almaty. The most financially successful independent newspaper, *Karavan*, saw its warehouse destroyed by fire, which editors believe was government-sponsored arson.

The constitution guarantees religious freedom, but religious associations may not pursue political goals. Christians, Muslims and Jews worship freely. Minority and ethnic rights remained an issue. Russians, Germans and others have charged discrimination in state-run businesses, government, housing and education. Many Russians have left, particularly from northern industrial cities like Karaganda. There are Russian-, German- and Korean-language newspapers. The government has sought to stanch the Russian "brain drain" by making Russian the language of interethnic communication and simplifying citizenship procedures.

The judiciary is not wholly free of government interference. Judges are subject to bribery and political bias. Judges are appointed by the Ministry of Justice with little or no parliamentary oversight.

The largest trade union remains the successor to the Soviet-era General Council of Trade Unions, and is practically a government organ. The Independent Trade Union Center, with twelve unions, includes the important coal miners' union in Karaganda. Although business and other professional associations have been formed, the government dealt a blow to nongovernmental organizations by approving a law prohibiting foreign financing of public associations. Several independent women's groups exist to address such issues as discrimination in hiring and education, and domestic violence.

Kenya

Polity: Dominant-party **Political Rights:** 7*
Economy: Capitalist **Civil Liberties:** 6
Population: 28,261,000 **Status:** Not Free
PPP: $1,400
Life Expectancy: 55.7
Ethnic Groups: Kikuyu (21 percent), Luhya (14 percent), Luo (13 percent), Kalenjin (12 percent), Kamba (11 percent), Somali (2 percent), others
Capital: Nairobi
Ratings Change: *Kenya's political rights rating changed from 6 to 7 because of increased repression of the opposition and ethnic violence.

Overview: Ethnic violence, increasing attacks on opposition politicians and rising media repression marked further consolidation of President Daniel arap Moi's autocratic rule and Kenya's continued march away from prospects for multiparty democracy and respect for human rights in 1995.

Seized by British imperial forces in the late 1700s, Kenya remained under British control until achieving independence in 1963 under President Jomo Kenyatta's Kenya African National Union (KANU). Kenyatta led the Mau-Mau rebellion of 1952-58, an armed struggle dominated by people of his Kikuyu ethnicity. The Kikuyu remained pre-eminent in Kenyan politics until Kenyatta's death in 1978. The accession to power of Vice-President Daniel arap Moi kept KANU in power but eventually led to a reduction of Kikuyu influence. Opposition parties were banned in 1982, and ethnic tensions between Moi's Kalenjin ethnic group and others—widely believed to have been provoked by the government—flared by the end of the decade.

Under pressure from international aid donors, Moi lifted the ban on opposition parties and permitted multiparty elections in December 1992. Amid opposition discord and highly suspect electoral conduct, Moi was proclaimed victor with 36 percent of the vote.

A microcosm of the ethnic tensions and political repression that today wrack Kenya was on view in October when a leading opposition figure, Koigi wa Wamwere, was sentenced to four years' imprisonment and six lashes on armed robbery charges. Independent observers described the court proceedings as a show trial. Wamwere's lawyers and journalists seeking information on the case have been harassed and detained. Ethnic tensions were exacerbated by the fact that Wamwere is a Kikuyu, while the trial judge was from Moi's ethnic group. Relations among Kenya's other ethnic groups are also fraying, with western Luo-speaking people and coastal Muslims feeling increasingly marginalized.

Several donor nations have withheld portions of their aid to Kenya in an effort to press for domestic economic and political reform. International condemnation of the regime's human rights record, coupled with broad domestic criticism of abuses and corruption, so far have served only to reinforce Moi's intention to cling to power.

Political Rights and Civil Liberties: The right of Kenyans to choose their government freely is severely restricted. In the three years since Moi's tainted re-election, the regime has used police powers and executive decrees to muzzle opposition, relying on a generally compliant judiciary to back repressive actions. The regime has ruled out constitutional changes, including an independent election commission, which opposition and nonpartisan groups have demanded to create a level playing field for presidential and parliamentary elections scheduled for 1997. Without significant constitutional and legal reform, the existence of a multiparty system in Kenya remains little more than window dressing for KANU's tight grip on power.

The government has refused to register Safina (Swahili for "Noah's Ark"), a new opposition party that is campaigning on a non-ethnic and anti-corruption platform. In August, Safina leaders and journalists were beaten with whips and clubs by KANU activists while police stood by. The highly-visible role played by white Kenyan Richard Leaky in Safina has evoked racist responses from the Moi regime, including charges that Leaky and American and British businessmen are conspiring with the Ku Klux Klan, and that Italians in Kenya are seeking to undermine the regime.

New legislation introduced in the KANU-controlled parliament in July that increases restrictions on political parties is likely to be more effective than crude propaganda in undercutting Safina and other peaceful opposition. This is one of many examples of the regime's continued use of the law as a tool of repression rather than a means for justice. Another example came in October as a lawyer, seeking to file charges against a government minister over alleged involvement in ethnic violence that took over 1,500 lives from 1990-94, was instead himself arrested on charges of sedition. Kenyan human rights groups have documented numerous killings and instances of torture by police.

An October 1995 report from within the government itself said some $270 million in official funds had simply disappeared without trace. The government responded to a Roman Catholic bishops' statement that Kenya's political leaders face a crisis of credibility because of corruption and lawlessness only by denouncing the Catholic and Anglican churches for allegedly supporting the political opposition.

Freedom of expression is severely limited. The regime and its ruling party,

KANU, retain complete control over broadcast media. The state-run Kenya
Broadcasting Corporation censors news about Kenya received from BBC World
Television. Independent media are also under growing pressure. The government
has threatened to expel foreign correspondents for their reporting on increasing
crime, corruption and the ongoing political crisis. Local print journalists have been
assaulted, independent magazines are subject to harassment in their business
operations and President Moi has decreed it a crime to "insult" him. Sedition laws
are being used in efforts to silence any criticism.

Human rights advocates and environmentalists also reported attacks and
threats. The Law Society of Kenya, Legal Advice Center and Kenya Human Rights
Commission said they face a campaign of intimidation because of their demands
for respect for basic human rights. Another move to stifle free discussion was the
banning in February of a private legal research group, Clarion, the Center for Law
Research International, that issued reports on governmental corruption and the need
for judicial reform.

These factors are serious constraints on Kenya's economic as well as political
development. New investment is scarce as overseas investors remain wary of the
chances of serious instability. While unions are active, the legal right to strike has
been superseded by a 1993 Ministry of Labor decree forbidding all strikes. Central
government civil servants and university academic staff may join only government-
designated unions.

Kiribati

Polity: Parliamentary
democracy
Economy: Capitalist-
statist
Population: 79,000
PPP: na
Life Expectancy: 54.0
Ethnic Groups: Micronesian (84 percent),
Polynesian (14 percent), others
Capital: Tarawa

Political Rights: 1
Civil Liberties: 1
Status: Free

Overview:
The Republic of Kiribati consists of thirty-three islands of
the Gilbert, Line and Phoenix groups scattered over two
million square miles of the Pacific Ocean. The country,
with a Micronesian majority and a Polynesian minority, became an independent
member of the British Commonwealth on 12 July 1979.

The 1979 constitution established a unicameral *Maneaba ni Maungatabu*
(House of Assembly) with thirty-nine directly elected members who serve four-
year terms, one representative from Banaba Island elected by the Banaban Rabi
Council of Leaders, and the attorney general, if he is not already an elected
member. The president is directly elected from a list of three to four candidates

nominated by the parliament from among its members, and is limited to three four-year terms. In July 1991 founding President Ieremia Tabai served out his third term and threw his support in the presidential election behind Teatao Teannaki, who beat his main competitor, Roniti Teiwaki.

In May 1994 parliament voted to set up a select committee to investigate misuse of public funds by a cabinet minister. Reading this as a vote of no-confidence in the administration, the speaker dissolved parliament and President Teannaki resigned. Acting according to the constitution, a three-man caretaker administration took power consisting of the speaker, the chief justice and the chairman of the Public Service Commission (PSC). A bizarre but ultimately inconsequential constitutional crisis emerged on 1 June, when police forcibly removed acting head of state Tekire Tameura on the grounds that his tenure as PSC chairman had expired three days earlier.

On 21-22 July the country held early elections for a new parliament, with 206 candidates competing. Following runoff balloting on 29-30 July, the newly formed opposition Maneaban Te Mauri Party (MTM) won nineteen seats, with the remainder split among the ruling National Progressive Party and smaller, less formal groupings. In September voters elected the MTM's Teburoro Tito as president.

A five-person select committee, established in late 1994, is reviewing the 1979 constitution in advance of a planned constitutional convention in 1996. The 1994 constitutional crisis, albeit minor, highlighted the fact that many clauses are vague and ill-defined.

Political Rights and Civil Liberties:

Citizens of Kiribati can change their government democratically. In addition to the directly elected parliament, local Island Councils serve all inhabited islands. Politics are generally conducted on a personal and issue-oriented basis rather than on a partisan level. Several parties nominally exist but in reality lack true platforms and even headquarters.

Fundamental freedoms of speech, press, assembly, religion and association are respected in theory and practice. The independent judiciary is modeled on English common law, and provides adequate due process rights. In July 1993 the parliament amended the Broadcasting Act to lift the government monopoly on radio and television (although no television service of any kind currently exists). The government-run Kiribati Broadcasting Service's radio station and the country's sole newspaper, a state-owned weekly, offer pluralistic viewpoints. Church newsletters are also an important source of information.

Women are entering the workforce in increasing numbers but still face social discrimination in this male-dominated society. Citizens are free to travel internally and abroad. Workers are free to organize and join unions, bargain collectively and stage strikes. Although over 90 percent of the workforce is in subsistence agriculture and fishing and operates outside of the wage structure, the well organized Kiribati Trade Union Congress includes seven trade unions with approximately 2,500 members.

Korea, North

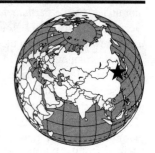

Polity: Communist one-party
Economy: Statist
Population: 23,487,000
PPP: $3.026
Life Expectancy: 71.1
Ethnic Groups: Korean
Capital: Pyongyang

Political Rights: 7
Civil Liberties: 7
Status: Not Free

Overview:
In 1995, a year after the death of Stalinist ruler Kim Il Sung, North Korea remained the most tightly controlled country in the world.

The Democratic People's Republic of Korea was formally established in September 1948, three years after the partition of the Korean Peninsula. Marshall Kim Il Sung, installed with Soviet backing, created a Stalinist personality cult based largely on his supposed leading role in fighting the Japanese in the 1930s. For decades Kim used an all-encompassing "ideology," *Juche* (I Myself), stressing national self-reliance and independence, to justify the country's isolation from the rest of the world. Meanwhile the government nurtured a slavish devotion to the "Great Leader" Kim and his son, "Dear Leader" Kim Jong Il, by indoctrinating citizens through the media, the workplace, the military, mass spectacles and cultural events.

In December 1991 the younger Kim replaced his father as Supreme Commander of the armed forces in what appeared to herald the world's first Communist dynastic succession. Kim Il Sung died suddenly of a heart attack on 8 July 1994. The February 1995 death of defense minister Marshall Oh Jin-u left Kim Jong Il as the sole surviving member of the three-man politburo of the ruling Workers' Party. However, by year's end Kim, who is known to be unpopular with the military, had still not assumed the two top positions held by his father—state president and general secretary of the Workers' Party. Nevertheless, South Korean intelligence analysts say Kim is firmly in charge of the country.

The perilous state of the economy, which has contracted since 1990, has forced North Korea to open up somewhat to the outside world. In October 1994 the United States and North Korea signed a complex, three-stage deal under which North Korea agreed to a ten-year timetable for dismantling its clandestine nuclear program. In exchange the U.S., South Korea and Japan are providing emergency oil supplies and will build two light-water reactors. Although the economic situation appears to be marginally improving, in recent years defectors have reported severe food shortages, which were exacerbated by widespread flooding in late 1995. During the year North Korea accepted emergency rice donations from South Korea and Japan.

Political Rights and Civil Liberties:
North Koreans live in the most tightly controlled country in the world and cannot change their government democratically. The Supreme People's Assembly holds no independent power.
Elections are held on a regular basis but all candidates are state-sponsored, either by the ruling Workers' Party or by smaller, state-organized parties. Opposition

parties are illegal, and owing to the regime's repressive, isolationist policies and the effects of severe economic hardship, there appears to be little organized dissent of any sort. The government denies citizens all fundamental freedoms and rights. The rule of law is nonexistent and there are no elements of civil society.

Under the Criminal Law citizens are subject to arbitrary arrest, detention and execution for "counterrevolutionary crimes" and other broadly defined political offenses. In practice these offenses can include nonviolent acts such as attempted defection, criticism of the Kim family or the government and listening to BBC or other foreign broadcasts.

The judiciary is government-controlled. Defense lawyers attempt to persuade defendants to plead guilty rather than advocate for them. Prison conditions are brutal. Prisoners are severely mistreated, and according to some reports summary executions occur frequently. Entire families are sometimes imprisoned together. The regime operates "re-education through labor" camps where forced labor is practiced. Tens of thousands of political prisoners and their family members are reportedly held in these remote camps. Defectors say some political prisoners are "re-educated" and released after a few years, while others are held indefinitely.

Authorities conduct monthly checks of residences, and electronic surveillance of homes is common. Children are encouraged at school to report on their parents' activities. The government assigns a security rating to each individual that, to a somewhat lesser extent than in the past, still plays a role in determining access to education, employment and health services. North Koreans face a steady onslaught of propaganda from radios and televisions pre-tuned to government stations.

Religious practice is restricted to state-sponsored Buddhist and Christian services. Permission to travel outside one's town is generally granted only for state business, weddings or funerals. The government reportedly forcibly resettles politically suspect citizens, and access to the capital, Pyongyang, is tightly controlled. Few citizens are permitted to travel abroad. All jobs are assigned by the state. The General Federation of Trade Unions of Korea is the sole legal trade union federation, and its affiliates function as tools of state control. There is no right to strike, and strikes do not occur.

Korea, South

Polity: Presidential-parliamentary democracy
Economy: Capitalist-statist
Population: 44,851,000
PPP: $9,250
Life Expectancy: 71.1
Ethnic Groups: Korean
Capital: Seoul

Political Rights: 2
Civil Liberties: 2
Status: Free

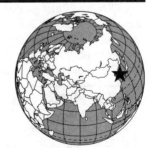

Overview: **S**outh Korean President Kim Young Sam's administration initiated criminal proceedings in late 1995 against two former presidents, offering the possibility of reforming a governing system characterized by corrupt links between business and politics.

The Republic of Korea was established in August 1948. General Park Chung Hee led the country under military rule from 1961 until his assassination in 1979, with General Chun Doo Hwan seizing power in another coup. In May 1980 the army killed several hundred antigovernment protesters in the southern city of Kwangju. In June 1987, violent student-led protests rocked the country after Chun picked another army general, Roh Tae Woo, as his successor. Roh responded by submitting to direct presidential elections in December 1987, in which he beat the country's best known dissidents, Kim Young Sam and Kim Dae Jung.

The February 1988 constitution limits the president to a single five-year term, and revoked his power to dissolve the 299-seat National Assembly. In January 1990 Kim Young Sam and another opposition leader, Kim Jong Pil, merged their parties with the ruling party to form the governing Democratic Liberal Party (DLP).

At the March 1992 parliamentary elections the DLP won 149 seats; Kim Dae Jung's opposition Democratic Party, 97; the conservative United National Party, 31; the Party for New Political Reform, 1; independents (mostly progovernment), 21. In the 18 December presidential vote, the cleanest in the country's history, the DLP's Kim Young Sam took 42 percent of the vote to beat Kim Dae Jung and billionaire businessman Chung Ju Yung.

Kim took office in February 1993 as the first civilian president since 1961. In its first two years in office the Kim administration reduced the security services' internal surveillance powers, sacked several top generals, and ended the practice of allowing individuals to maintain bank accounts under false names.

Nevertheless, Kim's popularity has been eroded by a string of industrial and construction accidents and a perception that his reforms have not gone deep enough. In the 27 July 1995 local elections, the country's first regional polls since 1960, opposition parties won ten of the fifteen mayoralties and governorships contested.

In September Kim Dae Jung founded a new opposition party, the National Congress for New Policies, in advance of national elections due by April 1996. In late October former president Roh stunned the country by admitting that he had accumulated $654 million in corporate donations while in office. Amid public outrage, in December the government took the unprecedented acts of charging Roh with corruption, and of charging Roh and Chun Doo Hwan with treason over the 1979 coup and criminal liability in the Kwangju massacre.

Political Rights and Civil Liberties: South Koreans can change their government democratically. The judiciary is independent. Corruption investigations carried out by the executive branch frequently appear to be politically motivated.

The continued application of the broadly-drawn National Security Law (NSL) remains the country's key human rights issue. Since President Kim took office scores of people have been arrested under the NSL for allegedly pro-North Korean, nonviolent expression. NSL and ordinary detainees are frequently beaten to extract confessions, and suspects are generally not allowed access to attorneys during interrogation.

The broadcast media are state-supported but generally offer pluralistic views, while the largely private print media practice some self-censorship. Civic institutions are strong and local human rights groups operate openly.

Under the Kim administration the authorities have been generally lenient in granting permits for peaceful demonstrations. Women face social and workplace discrimination, and domestic violence is fairly widespread. Religious freedom is respected. Travel to North Korea is tightly restricted.

The Trade Union Law prevents the establishment of alternative unions or confederations in industries or fields where a union already exists. In practice this maintains the dominance of the Federation of Korean Trade Unions (FKTU), formed during military rule, and its affiliated unions. Civil servants and public and private school teachers may not form unions or bargain collectively. Strikes are not permitted in government agencies, state-run industries and defense industries. Laws against "third-party" intervention prevent outside experts and unrecognized unions from helping workers.

In May some 1,000 riot police stormed the Hyundai car factory in Ulsan to arrest scores of workers who had organized an allegedly illegal strike. In early June police raided Seoul's main temple and Catholic cathedral to arrest thirteen Korea Telecom union activists for alleged links to an unrecognized labor group. In another labor issue, many "Foreign Vocational Trainees" are forced to work longer hours and for less pay than they were initially promised, are not allowed to leave factory compounds and are often beaten and otherwise abused.

Kuwait

Polity: Traditional monarchy and limited parliament
Economy: Mixed capitalist-statist
Population: 1,506,000
PPP: $8,326
Life Expectancy: 74.9
Ethnic Groups: Kuwaiti (45 percent), other Arab (35 percent), Iranian, various foreign workers
Capital: Kuwait City

Political Rights: 5
Civil Liberties: 5
Status: Partly Free

Overview: In 1995 Kuwait's increasingly outspoken National Assembly overcame a government challenge to its right to review decrees issued by the emir during periods when parliament is dissolved.

The 1962 constitution vests broad executive powers in an emir from the al-Sabah family, which has ruled this Persian Gulf state since 1756. The emir appoints the prime minister and Council of Ministers.

In 1976 the emir suspended the National Assembly. The current emir, Sheik Jabir al-Ahmad al-Sabah, reopened the Assembly in 1981 but suspended it again in 1986. In October 1990, while in exile in Saudi Arabia following the Iraqi invasion two months earlier, the emir agreed to hold elections in 1992. In February 1991 a thirty-two-member, United States-led coalition liberated the country.

At the October 1992 elections opposition candidates, including several from the radical Islamic Popular Grouping, took thirty-one of the fifty seats. The emir reappointed Crown Prince Sheik Saad as prime minister, who in turn minimized the opposition's gains by giving key cabinet posts to the al-Sabah family.

Since the election the National Assembly has increased its supervisory powers over the state budget and has investigated huge losses in the country's financial holdings. In 1995 the government brought a challenge to the Constitutional Court seeking to overturn the Assembly's right to review decrees passed by the emir during the 1986-92 parliamentary dissolution. MPs feared that without this right the emir would be encouraged in the future to dissolve parliament temporarily to pass decrees that could not be reviewed. In May the government dropped its challenge after parliament blocked passage of its economic reform proposals.

Political Rights and Civil Liberties: Kuwaiti citizens cannot change their government democratically. The hereditary emir holds executive powers and under the constitution can suspend parliament, declare martial law and suspend articles of the constitution. The government limited suffrage in the October 1992 parliamentary elections to "first-class" males—based on ancestry—who form only 15 percent of the population. Political parties are banned under a 1986 decree but operate informally. National Assembly elections are due in 1996.

Following Kuwait's liberation in February 1991 numerous extrajudicial executions were carried out against suspected Iraqi collaborators and sympathizers. Nearly all of the killings, as well as dozens of disappearances in 1991, remain unresolved.

Police often abuse detainees to extract confessions. The judiciary is not independent; the executive branch controls its finances and foreign judges serve one-year renewable contracts. In the State Security Courts cases have been decided on the basis of confessions obtained through torture. There have been no military court trials since 1991, but most of the individuals being held as Iraqi collaborators were convicted in these courts in trials that did not meet international norms. Several hundred Palestinians, Iraqis and *bidoon* (stateless persons of Bedouin origin) are detained under administrative deportation orders not subject to review.

Citizens freely criticize the government but refrain from directly criticizing the al-Sabah family. The press law prevents publication of articles critical of the royal family, as well as articles that might "create hatred, or spread dissension among the people." This broad definition leads to some self-censorship. On 16 March 1995 the government used a 1986 decree to suspend the daily *al-Anba* for five days. Broadcast media are state-owned and coverage favors the government.

The government occasionally denies permits for political gatherings. Since 1985 the government has only licensed new nongovernmental organizations (NGOs) with ties to the royal family. In 1993 the government ordered all unlicensed NGOs to shut down, and in practice this has curtailed the activities of several human rights NGOs formed since 1991.

Since the mid-1980s the government has purged the bidoon from the census rolls, denying the 150,000 bidoon remaining in Kuwait access to social services and the right to legally hold jobs or travel abroad. Some 100,000 foreign-born domestic servants are not covered by the labor law and are subject to rape, beatings and other abuse. Kuwaiti women, in addition to being denied suffrage, face discrimination in employment opportunities and must receive permission from their husbands or close male relatives to travel abroad. Under Islamic law, Muslim women receive less inheritance than men. Domestic violence occurs frequently. Islam is the state religion, and Hindus, Sikhs and Buddhists may not build places of worship.

The government maintains financial control over unions through subsidies that in practice account for 90 percent of union budgets. Only one union is allowed per industry or profession, and only one labor federation, the pro-government Kuwaiti Trade Union Federation, is permitted. Strikes are legal, but the labor law mandates arbitration if a settlement cannot be reached. There are legal restrictions on the right of association for foreign workers.

Kyrgyz Republic

Polity: Presidential-parliamentary democracy
Economy: Statist (transitional)
Population: 4,405,000
PPP: $2,850
Life Expectancy: 69.0
Ethnic Groups: Kirghiz (52 percent), Russian (22 percent), Uzbek (13 percent), German, others
Capital: Bishkek
Ratings Change: *The Kyrgyz Republic's civil liberties rating changed from 3 to 4 because of harassment of the press and journalists.

Political Rights: 4
Civil Liberties: 4*
Status: Partly Free

Overview: Pledging continued economic reform, President Askar Akayev won a second five-year term in December.

February's elections to a new, streamlined 105-member parliament (*Jogorku Kenesh*), though marred by irregularities, weakened Communist dominance with the election of independents.

In 1991, this small, impoverished Central Asian country between China and Uzbekistan declared independence from the Soviet Union. Akayev, a respected physicist, committed the country to democratic and market reforms in what was called the "Silk Revolution." But resistance from a Communist-dominated, 350-member parliament elected in 1990 led Akayev to dissolve it in 1994 (after the government resigned to strengthen his hand) and decree a constitutional referendum to create a bicameral body with a thirty-five-seat lower chamber as a permanent legislature and a seventy-member upper chamber to meet only occasionally to approve the budget and confirm presidential appointees. Nearly 75 percent of voters approved the proposal.

The 5 February 1995 first round of parliamentary elections filled only sixteen seats. Among electees were two former Communist Party leaders, raising fears of a

Communist resurgence. However, the 19 February second round, in which candidates did not have to clear 50 percent to win seats, saw only four Communist former deputies elected, with eighty-two seats going to a mix of governing officials, businessmen, intellectuals such as author Chingis Aitmatov and clan leaders. Party affiliation was not a major concern since more than one organization could nominate a single candidate.

In August, Akayev proposed a referendum to extend his presidency, due to expire in 1995, to 2001. A parliamentary group collected 1.2 million signatures supporting the proposal, but in September the upper chamber voted it down amid public demonstrations against any extension. Elections were called for December.

Presidential elections on 24 December pitted thirteen challengers against Akayev, who won over 60 percent of votes. Runners-up were former Communist Party secretary Absamat Masaliyev and former parliamentary speaker Medetkan Sherimkulov. Neither offered any alternative to Akayev's economic reforms. Some nominees complained about being ignored by state-run media.

Key issues included the economy. In June, the country was promised over $680 million in foreign aid after international financial institutions approved its reform program, which included price liberalization, privatization and currency stabilization. Cameco, the Canadian mining company, has invested over $360 million and employs 1,800 people. It formed a joint venture with the state-owned Kyrgyzaltyn to exploit the Kumtor gold mine. Yet unemployment approached 20 percent and workers remained underpaid, with monthly salaries equivalent to $20-$30, or were not paid at all for weeks on end.

Political Rights and Civil Liberties: Citizens can change their government democratically. Parliamentary and presidential elections included such violations as ballot-stuffing, inflation of voter turnout, media restrictions and intimidation. Akayev has been accused of high-handed rule.

Political parties run the gamut from the Communists to the nationalist Asaba on the right. Others include the Social Democrats, the Republican Party, the Agrarians and Erk (Freedom). The largest group is the pro-government Democratic Movement of Kyrgyzstan. Most parties are small and weak, with vague platforms and little financial support.

Press laws restrict publication of state secrets and advocating war, violence or ethnic intolerance. In July, two journalists from *Res Publica*, a business-supported independent paper, were sentenced to eighteen months' imprisonment (with a year suspended) for insulting the president's honor and dignity. Akayev had sued the Russian-language paper for claiming he had a villa in Switzerland. Authorities closed *Politika* and the former parliament's newspaper, *Svobodnyi Gori*, both of which had criticized Akayev and his government. No private local broadcasters exist. Only one private radio station, Radio Almaz, and one private television station, Pyramid, operate nationally.

Freedoms of assembly and movement are generally respected. Religious freedom is guaranteed in this predominantly Islamic country.

Although the constitution guarantees minority rights and the government has shown sensitivity to the Russian minority (in 1995, Russian was elevated to a state language), there has been an exodus of educated and skilled Russians and Germans. In December 1994 the Kyrgyz Folksrat (People's Council of Germans) and government began implementing a program to support Germans and stem their migration. Akayev is committed to women's rights, and many women occupy government posts. The Democratic Women's Party was registered in October 1994.

In 1995, constitutional revisions allowed greater executive oversight of the judiciary. Judges' lack of experience and low salaries created an environment for corruption. The government stated that it hoped presidential nomination of all judges would increase the consistency with which laws are applied and enforced.

Although a 1992 law permits the formation of independent unions, nearly all workers belong to the Federation of Independent Trade Unions of Kyrgyzstan, successor to the Soviet-era federation. Over 450 nongovernmental organizations exist, including business, sports and charitable associations.

Laos

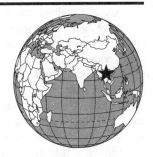

Polity: Communist one-party
Economy: Mixed-statist
Population: 4,837,000
PPP: $1,760
Life Expectancy: 51.0
Ethnic Groups: Lao (50 percent), Thai (20 percent), Phoutheung (15 percent), Miao (Hmong), Yao, others
Capital: Vientiane

Political Rights: 7
Civil Liberties: 6
Status: Not Free

Overview: The January 1995 death of Prince Souphanouvong, a stalwart of the ruling Lao People's Revolutionary Party (LPRP) known as the "Red Prince," left Laotian President Nouhak Phoumsavan as one of the last influential members of the country's older generation of pro-Vietnam Marxists. A younger crop of technocrats continues to restructure Laos as a market-oriented authoritarian regime.

This landlocked Southeast Asian country became a French protectorate in 1893. Following the World War II Japanese occupation, the Communist *Pathet Lao* (Land of Lao) won independence from the French in October 1953. Royalist, Communist, and conservative factions turned on each other in 1964. In May 1975 the Pathet Lao took the capital, Vientiane, from a royalist government and seven months later established a one-party state under Prime Minister Kaysone Phomvihane's LPRP.

The LPRP introduced market reforms in 1986 to revive an economy decimated by a decade of central planning. The authorities have privatized farms and some state-owned enterprises, removed price controls, and encouraged foreign investment.

In August 1991 the rubber-stamp National Assembly approved the country's first constitution, which codifies the LPRP's leading political role. The constitution also expanded the powers of the president, who serves as head of the armed forces and can remove the prime minister. Kaysone subsequently took over as president, while veteran revolutionary Khamtay Siphandone succeeded him as prime minister.

Kaysone, the undisputed head of the "Iron Troika" that had led the Laotian Communist movement since the mid-1950s, died in November 1992. The National Assembly named the surviving Troika members, Assembly Speaker Nouhak Phoumsavan and Prime Minister Khamtay, to succeed Kaysone as state president and LPRP chairman, respectively. The government permitted pre-approved independents to compete for the first time in the December 1992 elections for the eighty-five seat National Assembly. Several independents are believed to have won seats, although the government has not provided a breakdown.

Political Rights and Civil Liberties: Laos is a one-party state controlled by the Lao People's Revolutionary Party (LPRP), and citizens cannot change their government democratically. Opposition parties are not expressly banned, but in practice are not tolerated by the government.

Some elements of state control, including the widespread monitoring of civilians by police, have been relaxed in recent years. However, the security services still search homes without warrants, monitor some personal communications, and maintain neighborhood and workplace committees that inform on the population.

The Hmong, the largest of several hill tribes that collectively comprise half the population, have conducted a small-scale insurgency since the Communist takeover. Both the Hmong guerrillas and the government are accused of occasional human rights violations relating to the insurgency, including extrajudicial killings. The Hmong accuse the government of carrying out chemical warfare operations, but these charges have not been confirmed.

The rule of law is nonexistent. The judiciary is subservient to the government and trials lack adequate procedural safeguards. The government suspended the bar in late 1992 pending the introduction of a new set of rules regarding private lawyers, although lawyers can still assist defendants. Mistreatment of detainees and prisoners is apparently rare, although prison conditions are harsh.

The government has released nearly all of the tens of thousands of people who were sent to "re-education camps" following the 1975 Communist victory. However, the regime is holding at least three members of the former royalist government, and may be holding several hundred political prisoners overall, including three LPRP officials who have been held since 1990 for denouncing official corruption and calling for a multiparty system. In 1992 the three received fourteen-year prison sentences.

Freedoms of speech and press are nonexistent. Newspapers and electronic media are controlled by the government and promote its views. All associations are controlled by the LPRP and there are no independent elements of civil society. Political assemblies, except for those organized by the government, are illegal. The government's record on religious freedom is mixed. Buddhists can generally worship freely, but the Catholic Church is unable to operate in the north, and in recent years some Christian clergy members have reportedly been detained. Christian seminaries have been closed since the Communist takeover.

Members of minority groups are underrepresented in the government, and these hill tribes are largely unable to influence official policy regarding their lands.

Thousands of Laotians who fled after the Communist takeover have been voluntarily repatriated, and the government has apparently not targeted them for specific harassment. Since 1994 the government has eased restrictions on internal travel, and Laotians are also increasingly freer to travel abroad.

Under the 1990 Labor Code all unions must belong to the LPRP-dominated Federation of Lao Trade Unions. There is no legal right to bargain collectively or strike, and in practice such activity does not occur.

Latvia

Polity: Presidential-parliamentary democracy (ethnic limits)

Political Rights: 2*
Civil Liberties: 2
Status: Free

Economy: Mixed capitalist transitional
Population: 2,527,000
PPP: $6,060
Life Expectancy: 69.1
Ethnic Groups: Latvian (52 percent), Russian (34 percent), Ukrainian, Pole, Belarusian, Lithuanian
Capital: Riga
Ratings Change: *Latvia's political rights rating changed from 3 to 2 because of an overall improvement in the political climate and compliance with international standards that led to its February admission to the Council of Europe.

Overview: Parliamentary elections in October 1995 left Latvia without a government until late December, as parties failed to agree on a prime minister. Other issues included the failure of several banks and changes in pension laws.

An independent republic from 1918 to 1940, Latvia was forcibly incorporated into the Soviet Union after the Hitler-Stalin pact. More than fifty years of Soviet occupation saw a massive influx of Russians accompanied by the deportation of ethnic Latvians; the proportion of Latvians fell from 77 percent in 1940 to 52 percent in 1991, the year the country declared independence from a crumbling Soviet Union.

In the October 1995 vote for the 100-member parliament (*Saeima*), Latvia's Way, the moderate party made up of pro-market ex-Communists that had taken 30 percent of the vote in the 1993 election and ruled in coalition with the Farmer's Union, saw its percentage halved. The biggest surprise was the showing (over 15 percent) of the Movement for Latvia, formed in November 1994 and led by Joachim Siegerist, a German-Latvian aristocrat who does not speak Latvian but whose consistently anti-Communist (and allegedly anti-Semitic) positions appealed to pensioners and rural voters. Also running strongly was Saimneks (roughly, Masters in Your Own Home) led by Ziedonis Cevers, a former leader of Latvia's

Komsomol and interior minister in the first post-Communist government. The party is run by smooth young ex-Communist functionaries and businessmen who emerged from the old nomenklatura. Cevers's message was a hybrid mixture of free-market rhetoric peppered with left-wing welfare assurances.

On 7 December, the *Saeima* voted fifty to forty-five with five abstentions to approve a government proposed by Cevers, one vote short of the fifty-one required for approval. After much wrangling, the Saeima on 21 December voted 74 to 24 to approve the government of thirty-seven-year-old businessman Andris Skele, who has no party affiliation. Six of the nine parties in parliament, five of which have a deputy prime minister in the Cabinet, approved his nomination

Despite Latvia's populist surge the economy was among the most robust in the former Soviet Union. But the collapse of one-third of the country's sixty-seven commercial banks unnerved depositors and investors, as did proposed changes in pension laws. With a quarter of Latvians already on pensions—the highest proportion in the world—the government proposed that future benefits be linked to contributions, leaving current workers to pay for two sets of pensions, their own and their parents'.

A persistent issue was the status of Russian-speakers, nearly half the population. Only 40 percent had managed to pass Latvian language and history tests and prove the five-year minimum length of residence needed for citizenship. As a result, nearly one-third of Latvia's adult population could not vote.

Political Rights and Civil Liberties: Citizens of Latvia can change their government democratically, but a substantial number of non-Latvian, mostly Slavic residents are excluded from citizenship and voting rights.

Latvia has a multiparty system and there are about twenty-five parties registered. October parliamentary elections were free and fair.

There is an independent press in both Latvian and Russian, but newspapers and other publications face economic difficulties. The state-controlled Latvian radio broadcasts nationally on three channels in Russian and Latvian. There are ten to twenty private radio and television stations, with two cable companies. Media are editorially independent. While there is freedom of expression, in May police confiscated nearly 1,000 copies of a Latvian translation of Hitler's *Mein Kampf* and charged the publisher with offenses under anti-racism laws.

The rights of association and assembly are respected. Business, cultural and other nongovernmental institutions are allowed to exist, among them the League of Non-Citizens. Religious rights are respected in this largely Lutheran country.

The judiciary is generally free from government interference, and reforms continue. Latvia was admitted to the Council of Europe in February 1995, but the president of the Council condemned ongoing discrimination against ethnic Russians by Latvian officials, particularly in the Department of Citizenship and Immigration. There were documented cases of wrongful denial of citizenship registration in violation of Latvian law.

The Free Trade Union Federation of Latvia, founded after independence, is the only significant labor confederation. Russian-dominated, Communist-era unions are not truly independent because of their known affiliation with the Russian army and the KGB. Women enjoy the same legal rights as men, but face discrimination in hiring and pay.

⬇ Lebanon

Polity: Presidential-parliamentary (military- and foreign-influenced, partly foreign-occupied)
Economy: Mixed statist
Population: 3,696,000
PPP: $2,500
Life Expectancy: 68.5
Ethnic Groups: Arab (90 percent), Armenian (4 percent) Greek, Syro-Lebanese
Capital: Beirut

Political Rights: 6
Civil Liberties: 5
Status: Not Free

Trend Arrow: Lebanon received a downward trend arrow, and moved into the Not Free category, because parliament arbitrarily amended the constitution to extend the president's term and the government is increasingly marginalizing the Christian community.

Overview: The Lebanese parliament, acting at Syria's behest, arbitrarily amended the constitution in October 1995 to extend pro-Syrian president Elias Hrawi's term for at least three years. With 40,000 troops in Lebanon, Syria continues to dominate the country politically.

Lebanon won full sovereignty from France in 1946. The genesis of the country's 1975-90 civil war lay in the unwritten 1943 National Pact, which gave Christians political dominance over the Muslim population through a perpetual 6:5 ratio of parliamentary seats.

Following three decades in which non-Christian groups tried unsuccessfully to end this religious-based political system, in 1975 civil war broke out among Muslim, Christian and Druze militias. The country's reconciliation began at Taif, Saudi Arabia in November 1989, with an accord that resulted in a new power-sharing constitution in 1990. The Taif accord continued the tradition of a Christian president chosen by the parliament for a single six-year term, but transferred many executive powers to the prime minister, by agreement a Sunni Muslim. A Shiite Muslim serves as speaker of parliament. The accord also split parliament evenly among Muslims and Christians.

In May 1991 the government signed a treaty allowing Syria to maintain troops in Lebanon and linking the countries' economic and security policies. The deal effectively ceded control of Lebanon to its more powerful neighbor.

The country held its first elections in twenty years in August and September 1992. Most Christians and some Muslims boycotted the vote to protest the continuing Syrian army presence in major cities, and three-fourths of the seats were won by nominally pro-Syrian candidates. In October President Elias Hrawi named businessman Rafik al-Hariri as prime minister.

In late February 1994 a bomb in a Maronite Christian church north of Beirut killed eleven people. The government blamed the bombing on the Maronite Christian-based Lebanese Forces (LF), a former militia turned political party. The authorities banned the party in March and subsequently arrested LF head Samir Geagea and other leadership figures. Many viewed the crackdown as an attempt to silence the country's most powerful Christian group.

In mid-October 1995 the parliament arbitrarily amended the constitution to extend Hrawi's term by three years. The move scrapped a parliamentary vote for a new president due in November and particularly angered the increasingly marginalized Christian community, who view Hrawi as a Syrian lackey.

Political Rights and Civil Liberties: Lebanese citizens cannot change their government democratically. The 1992 elections were neither free nor fair, owing to the Syrian army presence in major cities, the gerrymandering of electoral districts to favor pro-Syrian candidates, and vote rigging and other irregularities. Syria, which has 40,000 troops in Lebanon, makes all major political decisions. The arbitrary extension of President Hrawi's term in October 1995 revealed constitutional guarantees to be virtually meaningless. Parliamentary elections are due in 1996.

Israel maintains a "security zone" in southern Lebanon, established in 1985 to prevent Palestinian guerrillas from launching rocket attacks into northern Israel. The zone is manned by troops from Israel and the Christian-based South Lebanon Army (SLA). The Iranian-backed, Shiite Hezbollah militia controls many southern towns, and sporadic fighting continues between Israeli troops and Hezbollah guerrillas. Palestinian factions administer several refugee camps. All of these extra-governmental groups arbitrarily detain suspects and administer justice in areas under their control. Extrajudicial killings and other abuses continue, mainly among some seventeen Palestinian factions.

Security forces arbitrarily arrest suspects and use excessive force against detainees, particularly members of the former Lebanese Forces militia. The judiciary is not independent and corruption is common.

The state-owned Lebanon Television has a legal monopoly on television until 2012, although private stations are tolerated. Between March and July 1994 the government barred the country's private electronic media from broadcasting news. Criticism of the president and foreign leaders is legally restricted, and the 1991 Syria-Lebanon security agreement broadly prohibits publication of security-related information. In this environment, journalists practice considerable self-censorship. Police must approve all leaflets and other nonperiodical materials, and citizens have been imprisoned for unauthorized pamphleteering.

Public assemblies require government permits, which are frequently denied to Christian groups. The authorities often use force to break up unsanctioned demonstrations. Several human rights groups operate openly.

Women suffer legal and social discrimination, and rape is relatively widespread. The country has a growing population of street children. Freedom of religion is respected. Internal travel is restricted in areas of southern Lebanon under Israeli or Hezbollah control. Government workers may not join trade unions or hold strikes, although in practice they have staged brief strikes to press their demands.

Lesotho

Polity: Parliamentary democracy (military- and royal-influenced)
Economy: Capitalist
Population: 2,050,000
PPP: $1,060
Life Expectancy: 60.5
Ethnic Groups: Sotho
Capital: Maseru

Political Rights: 4
Civil Liberties: 4
Status: Partly Free

Overview: A tenuous balancing act among competing political parties, divided security forces and the influence of the royal family and traditional chiefs continued to put Lesotho's nascent democracy at risk in 1995. Spurred by South Africa, however, the various factions began serious negotiations aimed at producing long-term stability, and local elections were conducted for the first time.

A landlocked country entirely surrounded by South Africa, Lesotho escaped incorporation into the apartheid system by virtue of its status as a British protectorate, and achieved independence in 1966. King Moshoeshoe II ruled for thirty years until being deposed in a 1990 military coup that installed his son as King Letsie III. Under a new constitution, the first democratic elections since annulled 1970 polls produced a government under the Basotho Congress Party (BCP), led by Prime Minister Ntsu Mokhehele. But after serious military infighting and a suspension of constitutional rule in 1994, the king voluntarily stepped aside to allow his father's reinstatement in January 1995. The return of Moshoeshoe II has encouraged national reconciliation, but rivalries within the security forces and a weak democratic tradition still pose challenges to the rule of law. Security forces remain controlled by the Defense Commission, which operates outside parliamentary control, and the civil service is considered generally antagonistic to the elected BCP government.

Constitutionally-mandated elections for village, ward and district development councils occurred in August 1995. It remains unclear how much power the councils will exercise, particularly because their relationship with traditional chiefs remains ambiguous. The dueling power structures could provide another arena for factional rivalry.

Moshoeshoe II's reinstatement was followed by South African President Nelson Mandela's July 1995 visit, which signaled closer cooperation between the two countries, especially in economic matters. South Africa's interest has also underscored the need to maintain stability or face the possibility of its external imposition. Representatives of thirteen parties, including the main opposition figure, Basotho National Party (BNP) leader Evaristus Sekhonyana, met late in 1995 to seek consensus on improved consultation with the government, and on the professionalization and depoliticization of the military and civil service.

Political Rights and Civil Liberties: Lesotho's citizens freely chose their government in open 1993 elections under a democratic constitution. But the democratic transition's fragility was demonstrated by the brief military/royal usurpation of power in 1994 and the continued strong role played by both institutions. The BCP government, which won a landslide victory in 1993, remains severely constrained in exercising its constitutional authority. August 1995 local elections broadened the scope of political participation, although whether councils will complement or compete with traditional clan and chieftaincy structures remains unclear.

All broadcasting remains government-controlled. There is a lively independent press, although journalists practice self-censorship, especially on sensitive issues or in times of tension. A wide range of South African radio and television programming is available.

Constitutional rights to assembly and religious freedom are generally respected. Yet ongoing instability and general unaccountability within the security forces leave many feeling insecure. Lesotho Human Rights Alert Group (LHRAG) members fear persecution for aiding victims of security force abuses, but have nonetheless conducted human rights education campaigns.

Local courts operate independently, although higher courts remain subject to outside influence. Some laws inconsistent with the 1993 constitution remain in force, including the 1984 Internal Security Act, which provides for up to forty-two days' detention without charges in political cases.

Labor rights are guaranteed by the constitution but meet a mixed reaction in practice. After teachers struck in August, the National Assembly enacted legislation barring such strikes in the future. The legally recognized right to collective bargaining is sometimes rejected by government negotiators. Legal requirements for union registration exist, but have not been used to prevent unregistered unions from operating. Only about 10 percent of the labor force in the largely mountainous and agricultural country is unionized.

The International Labor Organization has complained of substandard conditions for Lesotho's 12,000 clothing and textile industry workers, 90 percent of whom are women. Women's rights in other areas are not fully respected. The Lesotho government has signed but not ratified the United Nations Convention on Discrimination Against Women. The 1993 constitution prohibits discrimination based on sex, but customary practice and law still restrict women's rights in several areas, including contracts, property rights and inheritance. Legally, a woman is considered a minor as long as her husband is alive. Domestic violence is considered to be widespread, although statistical evidence is lacking.

Business opportunities are limited in Lesotho, which relies almost entirely on South Africa for its economic viability. Most modern-sector economic activity is either controlled by the state or concentrated among an elite with high-level political connections or access to foreign capital. Land is property of the kingdom, and its distribution is generally controlled by local chiefs.

Liberia

Polity: Monrovia: interim **Political Rights:** 7
civilian goverment   **Civil Liberties:** 6
(foreign military- and   **Status:** Not Free
foreign-influenced); else-
where: rival ethnic-based militias
Economy: Capitalist
Population: 3,039,000
PPP: $1,045
Life Expectancy: 55.4
Ethnic Groups: Krahn, Mandinka, Gio, Mano, other indigenous groups
(95 percent), Americo-Liberian (5 percent)
Capital: Monrovia

Overview: **A**fter nearly six years of traumatic civil war and over 150,000 deaths, Liberians signed a thirteenth peace accord in the Nigerian capital of Abuja in August. The agreement has so far proved the most durable of the many efforts and is likely the last, best chance for any early return of calm to the ravaged nation. The pact provides for August 1996 elections, but the process of returning 800,000 refugees from neighboring countries and disarming a welter of at least eight competing ethnic militias and subfactions makes its implementation problematic.

Settled by freed American slaves in 1847, Liberia was dominated by their "Americo-Liberian" descendants for more than a century. In 1980, army Sergeant Samuel Doe effected a bloody coup, and consolidated his hold by concentrating power among members of his Kranh ethnicity and suppressing others in increasingly brutal fashion. At the end of 1989, the National Patriotic Front of Liberia (NPFL), led by ex-government minister Charles Taylor and backed by the Gia and Mano ethnic groups, launched a guerrilla struggle against the Doe regime. A joint armed intervention by several West African countries (ECOMOG) prevented Taylor from consummating his 1990 victory against the Armed Forces of Liberia (AFL), and set up an interim government. In 1991, the United Liberation Movement (ULIMO), another rebel group dominated by Kranh and Mandingo people, entered the increasingly chaotic fray. ULIMO has since split, but remains a major force, along with the Liberia Peace Council (LPC). Today, the rule of law in any consistent form is almost entirely absent, and reports of killings and other abuses, especially from the countryside, continue.

Several abortive peace plans brokered by West African leaders have been negotiated and abandoned in a cycle of mistrust and revenge. Ugandan and Tanzanian troops have come and gone as part of the peacekeeping force. U.N. observers and aid workers have been able to work only fitfully amid near-anarchy in the countryside, occasionally suspending operations despite the desperate need for assistance to the civilian population. Yet the August 1995 "Abuja Accord" appears to be taking hold, particularly since it was preceded by an understanding between Taylor and the Nigerian authorities, which for five years had been adamantly opposed to his taking power.

The pact led to the creation of a seven-member Council of State headed by an obscure university lecturer, Wilton Sankawulo, and including the three most powerful faction leaders: Taylor, Alhaji Kromah of ULIMO-K, and George Boley of the LPC. A cabinet that forms the Liberian National Transitional Government (LNTG) and reports to the Council of State was appointed after negotiations among the factions. With a plan for elections and pledges for demobilization of over 50,000 fighters in hand, the U.N. Security Council agreed to extend the U.N. observer mission in Liberia through early 1996 and increase its size to over 150 people. But if the current plan fails to clear its formidable obstacles—including a lack of cash for implementation as well as the dubious good will of the several factions—the U.N. will likely withdraw permanently, perhaps followed by ECOMOG, and leave Liberia to resolve its own problems.

Political Rights and Civil Liberties:

Liberians do not enjoy the right to change their government through democratic means. Elections were last held in 1986 under the Doe dictatorship and could not be considered free and fair. Presidential and legislative elections are now set for August 1996 under the terms of the current peace accord. Meeting this timetable will prove highly difficult. Most Liberians have been displaced from their homes over five years of war, and one-third of the country's 2.5 million people have fled the country. Their repatriation, compilation of voter lists and creation of an electoral infrastructure represent an enormous task which Liberia cannot afford and the international community seems loath to fund. The next year's bill for peacekeeping and election administration alone would tally over $220 million. Even if these challenges are successfully overcome, they will be meaningless unless there is large-scale disarmament of the more than 50,000 fighters—among them perhaps as many as 10,000 children—distributed among at least eight factions.

The current Council of State reflects the armed might of the various factions, with the leaders of the three strongest groups holding co-equal seats. Negotiations with other armed groups have continued in an effort to make the peace process comprehensive, but entry is still determined by leaders' control of guns, not votes.

While chaotic conditions prevail across the countryside, the situation improved somewhat in the capital, Monrovia, largely due to the presence of West African troops. A number of independent newspapers operate and publish articles critical of various leaders. However, a large degree of self-censorship prevails, some due to increasing pressures by interim government authorities and some to many threats made against journalists by people claiming to represent one or another faction. Both the interim government and the Taylor NPFL faction operate radio stations, each of which is biased in favor of its political masters.

Little media freedom exists outside Monrovia, save for journalists' occasional and often risky reporting forays. Similarly, a number of religious groups, relief organizations and human rights groups, including the Center for Law and Human Rights Education, are able to operate openly in the capital but cannot safely or effectively work in the countryside, where the patchwork of factional control makes travel difficult and dangerous. Relief operations resumed as the new peace pact allowed mine clearance and opening of a few major roads, but relief workers remain cautious after the breakdown of several earlier agreements.

Aid workers have warned of acute danger of famine in several parts of Liberia. Normal economic life does not exist, and food production is at record lows. Little official trade is reported, though black-marketeering under the control of various armed factions is reportedly rampant.

Libya

Polity: Military
Economy: Mixed statist
Population: 5,248,000
PPP: $9,782
Life Expectancy: 63.1
Ethnic Groups: Arab and Berber (97 percent), Tuareg
Capital: Tripoli

Political Rights: 7
Civil Liberties: 7
Status: Not Free

Overview:

Libya faced greater internal tensions in 1995 than at any time since Colonel Mu'ammar al-Qadhafi seized power in a 1969 coup, as armed Islamist groups clashed with security forces in a growing challenge to Qadhafi's dictatorial but secular regime. Common concern with its neighbors over the Islamist challenge helped reinforce relations frayed during the year as Qadhafi ordered the expulsion of thousands of Egyptian, Palestinian and Sudanese workers. European concern over the security situation in several Maghreb states could also lead to softer support for United Nations sanctions imposed in April 1992 due to Libya's refusal to extradite two suspects in the December 1988 bombing of Pan American Flight 103 over Scotland. The sanctions' effects are serious but ultimately limited by their exclusion of oil exports, which earn Libya 90 percent of its foreign exchange.

Long support for radical revolutionary and terrorist groups has earned Libya its status as a near-pariah state. Colonized by Italy in 1912 and the site of fierce World War II battles, Libya achieved independence in 1952 after a short period of joint Anglo-French administration. The country remained a firm Western ally under King Idriss, hosting a large American military presence, until Qadhafi took over in 1969. Qadhafi's personalized, highly idiosyncratic rule has led Libya to clashes with its neighbors (with Egypt in 1977, and running territorial disputes with Chad) and to adventures farther afield, such as the ill-fated expeditionary force that vainly sought to bolster Ugandan Idi Amin's crumbling army in 1979. Qadhafi rules by decree, with a nearly total absence of accountability and transparency.

Qadhafi appeared increasingly isolated domestically during 1995, and relied more on family members, including his sons, to fill his circle of closest advisors. Ethnic-based rivalries among senior junta officials remained a potential threat to his twenty-seven-year rule, but it was unclear whether the growing armed Islamist presence in Libya would exacerbate or at least temporarily heal the junta's internal divisions. Security forces fought gun battles with Islamist groups during April and September, and rumors of other clashes occasionally surfaced through the year. In 1994, Qadhafi broadened *shari'a* law provisions in an effort to mollify fundamentalist sentiment. Yet domestic problems include increasing unemployment and economic dislocation brought on by both low world oil prices and sanctions. This has led in turn to higher inflation and a serious rise in corruption that could further erode support for the regime.

But Qadhafi's weakness at home may evoke greater foreign support, especially as he discovers commonalities with conservative authoritarian rulers in neighboring Algeria, Egypt and Tunisia in a region-wide struggle against radical Islamic fundamentalists. A security cooperation agreement was signed with Algeria that includes provisions for exchange of intelligence and training. There are also signs that Qadhafi's regional rehabilitation could draw Libya back into the international fold, although American opposition to any easing of sanctions will at least slow the process.

Political Rights and Civil Liberties: Libyans cannot change their government democratically. There is no formal constitution, and principles and structures of governance are either drawn from Qadhafi's *Green Book*—a melange of Islamic belief and socialist theory—or created on an ad hoc basis. Libya is officially known as a *jamahiriya* (state of the masses), a form of governance propounded by the *Green Book*'s "Third Universal Theory." While there is the formal conduct of elections, including mandatory voting, real power remains in the hands of Qadhafi and a small group of top leaders who appoint civil and military officials at every level and rule by decree. An elaborate structure of Revolutionary Committees and People's Committees serves as a tool of repression more than consultation.

Neither free expression nor free media exist in Libya. There is very limited public debate within the nominally elected bodies. The rare criticisms of the government or its actions that are allowed are usually harbingers of impending policy changes or political purges. State-controlled broadcasting and print media offer a highly propagandistic view of events both in Libya and abroad. Official controls are so rigid that little formal censorship is required, except over foreign programming rebroadcast in Libya.

The state prohibits political parties or any other type of association not sanctioned by the regime. There are regular but usually sketchy reports of torture and mistreatment of detainees, and brutality is said to be increasing in response to Islamist guerrilla activities. But it is notoriously difficult to garner accurate information regarding events within Libya. The regime's security apparatus is pervasive, and contact with foreigners are closely monitored.

Marginalized Berber and Tuareg peoples have suffered discrimination under policies intended to "Arabize" them. Women's access to education and employment has improved under the regime, yet cultural norms that relegate women to an inferior role still prevail, and may regain strength as Qadhafi seeks to placate fundamentalist opinion by stricter imposition of shari'a law, which among other matters addresses marriage, divorce and inheritance rights.

Religion, like every other aspect of life in Libya, is subject to the state. Islamic practice is tailored to Qadhafi's interpretations, and mosques are closely monitored for incipient political opposition. A small Christian community is permitted to worship quietly in two churches.

All unions are state-run. There is no freedom to form or join unions, nor are there rights to strike or to collective bargaining. The economy is similarly statist, although large-scale foreign investment is welcomed in extractive industries.

Liechtenstein

Polity: Prince and parliamentary democracy
Economy: Capitalist-statist
Population: 31,000
PPP: na
Life Expectancy: 69.5
Ethnic Groups: Alemannic German (95 percent), Italian, other European
Capital: Vaduz

Political Rights: 1
Civil Liberties: 1
Status: Free

Overview:

Liechtenstein continued in 1995 to face the difficult task of preserving its state in the face of increasing European integration and domestic economic expansion. Under the guidance of business-minded "manager-Prince" Hans Adam, the principality has sought membership in several international organizations including the U.N, the European Free Trade Association, the General Agreement on Tariffs and Trade, and the European Economic Area in an effort to maintain future independence through avoiding isolationism. The principality remains wary of European Union membership as requirements of population mobility could boost the number of foreign workers, who already comprise three-fifth's of the country's workforce. Low unemployment, liberal tax policies and a GNP among the highest in the world make Liechtenstein attractive to both foreign workers and businesses, as well as a growing body of trustee-lawyers and bankers.

The Principality was created in its current form in 1719, having been purchased by the Austrian Liechtenstein family. The royal family lived for the most part in Moravia (once part of the Austro-Hungarian Empire, now a Czech land) until 1938, when the spread of Nazism forced them to flee to Liechtenstein. Native residents of the state are primarily descended from the Germanic Alemanni tribe and the official language remains a German dialect.

The prince exercises legislative powers jointly with the twenty-five member *Landtag* (legislature). He appoints the prime minister from the majority party or coalition and the Deputy Chief of Government from the minority in the Landtag. Prince Hans Adam has effectively ruled Liechtenstein since 1984 although he did not assume his father's title until the elder sovereign's death in 1989. In response to debate concerning the balance of power between the prince and the people, Hans Adam announced his intention to call a referendum aimed at clarifying the structure and future of the principality's government.

Political Rights and Civil Liberties:

Liechtensteiners have the means to change their government democratically. Parties with at least 8 percent of the vote receive representation in the Landtag, which is directly elected every four years. The sovereign possesses the power to veto legislation and dissolve the Landtag. Prime Minister Mario Frick of the liberal Fatherland Union (VU) has headed a coalition with the Progressive Citizens' Party (FBP) since 1993. The Free List environmentalist party holds one seat.

The independent judiciary is headed by a Supreme Court and includes both civil and criminal courts, as well as an administrative Court of Appeal and a state court for questions of constitutionality. Due to the principality's minuscule size, regional disparities are minimal and modern social problems are comparatively few. An unusual policy, however, keeps significant numbers of second- and third-generation residents from acquiring citizenship. The native population decides whether to grant citizenship to those who have five years' residence by local vote. Prime Minister Frick wants to liberalize the citizenship law and thereby reduce the "immigrant" population to about half its present size.

The enfranchisement of women at the national level was unanimously approved in the legislature but only narrowly endorsed by male voters in 1984 after defeat in referenda in both 1971 and 1973. By 1986, universal adult suffrage at the local level had passed in all eleven communes. General elections in 1989 awarded a seat in the Landtag to a woman for the first time. Three years later, a constitutional amendment finally guaranteed legal equality. Although laws exist addressing spousal abuse and the government actively prosecutes abusers, domestic violence against women persists on a large scale.

The country is too small to have numerous organizations, but association is free and a small trade union exists. Workers have the right to strike but have not done so in over twenty-five years. The prosperous economy includes private and state enterprises. An ongoing labor shortage coupled with high wage rates is beginning to drive some companies to set up factories in neighboring Switzerland and Austria.

Liechtenstein has one, state-owned television station, but no radio services of its own. Residents receive radio and television freely from neighboring countries. Both major parties publish newspapers five times each week. Although Roman Catholicism is the state religion, other faiths are free to practice. Roman Catholic or Protestant religious education is compulsory in all schools, but exemptions are routinely granted.

Lithuania

Polity: Presidential-parliamentary democracy
Economy: Statist transitional
Population: 3,705,000
PPP: $3,700
Life Expectancy: 70.4
Ethnic Groups: Lithuanian (80 percent), Russian (9 percent), Polish (8 percent), Ukrainian, Belarusian, others
Capital: Vilnius

Political Rights: 1
Civil Liberties: 2*
Status: Free

Ratings Change: *Lithuania's civil liberties rating changed from 3 to 2 because of improvements in the court system.

Overview: Responding to political and public pressure, the Lithuanian parliament passed a budget for 1996 that substantially increased government expenditures for social programs.

The government of Prime Minister Adolfas Slezevicius faced demonstrations by pensioners protesting the social pains of market reforms and by bank depositors angry at the collapse of several banks. At the end of the year, Lithuania formally submitted an application for membership in the European Union.

An independent state from 1918 to 1940, Lithuania was forcibly annexed by the Soviet Union under provisions of the Hitler-Stalin Pact. It regained independence from a disintegrating Soviet Union in 1991.

In 1992 parliamentary elections, the (former Communist) Lithuanian Democratic Labor Party (LDDP), retook political control from the anti-Communist Lithuanian Reform Movement (Sajudis), capturing 79 of 141 seats. Sajudis chairman and President Vytautas Landsbergis was replaced as head of state by LDDP Chairman Algirdas Brazauskas, who was directly elected the following year.

In October 1995, some 7,000 demonstrators marched through Vilnius to protest cuts in social spending brought on by economic reforms. In response, parliament adopted a draft budget that was 30 percent larger than 1995, with increased expenditures for social welfare (79 percent), health care (42 percent), education (37 percent) and culture (34 percent). Doctors' salaries would be raised 24 percent and teachers' by 28 percent. The budget deficit would still remain about 2 percent, within International Monetary Fund (IMF) guidelines.

July's failure of Aurabankas, one of the country's largest banks, as well as several smaller financial institutions, raised public anxiety. Yet, the overall economic picture looked promising. The government pushed for a constitutional amendment to allow foreigners to own land, thus paving the way for EU membership.

Political Rights and Civil Liberties:

Citizens have the means to change their government democratically. There are sixteen political parties and associations. The 1992 parliamentary and 1993 presidential elections were deemed free and fair by observers.

The constitution and statutes protect press freedom, though slander and libel laws tend to favor claimants. There are several independent newspapers. Both national radio stations are state-owned, but offer diverse views. There are over 100 local radio stations. Over 50 percent of local television stations are private; all medium and large cities have their own private stations and studios. There are four national TV stations in all. The state controls one; two are privately owned but one of them broadcasts mainly in Polish. The fourth broadcasts programming from Ostankino in Moscow, and is privately owned. Journalists have been victimized by organized criminal gangs.

Free speech and the rights of assembly and association are respected. Freedom of religion is guaranteed and respected in this predominantly Roman Catholic country. Polish and Russian minorities have complained that the government pays little attention to their cultural needs and has cut funding to Russian schools. A treaty with Poland pledges the government to respect the rights of the Polish minority.

The judiciary is independent of government influence, and a nine-member Constitutional Court reviews laws or decrees that might conflict with the constitution. In 1995, a new system of courts went into effect, instituting a Supreme Court, a Court of Appeals and regional courts. In 1993, several tough laws were passed to combat rapidly spreading organized crime activities.

Various independent trade unions established the Lithuanian Trade Union Association in 1992, and workers in most sectors have the right to strike. There are nearly 800 nongovernmental organizations such as charitable funds and professional associations. Women are represented in certain professions and in managerial sectors. There are several women's organizations working to increase government and public awareness of spousal abuse and other women's issues.

Luxembourg

Polity: Parliamentary democracy
Economy: Capitalist
Population: 408,000
PPP: $21,520
Life Expectancy: 75.7
Ethnic Groups: Luxembourger (70 percent), other European (30 percent)
Capital: Luxembourg

Political Rights: 1
Civil Liberties: 1
Status: Free

Overview:

In January Jean-Claude Juncker succeeded Prime Minister Jacques Santer after the latter was unexpectedly named to fill the European Commission presidency shortly after last year's national elections. Juncker, a former finance and labor minister and chairman of Santer's Christian Social Party, pledged continuity with the government set up by his predecessor.

In 1867, the Grand Duchy of Luxembourg became an internationally recognized, independent and neutral country. Although an economic union was formed with Belgium in 1922, the country maintains its own political institutions. The 1868 constitution has been revised several times to allow for democratic reforms and eliminate the status of "perpetual neutrality." Since World War II, when Germany occupied the country for the second time, Luxembourg has been deeply committed to European integration. Despite Luxembourg's status as a founding member of the European Community, fears persist that larger countries will eventually downgrade the role of smaller nations in expanding international bodies.

After three decades of prosperity, Luxembourg is one of just three countries judged by their peers to have met the Maastricht Treaty convergence criteria for European Monetary Union. Wary of the treaty's provision that EC citizens can vote or stand for election in states other than their own, the government called for and won an exception requiring five years in residence to vote and ten years for election eligibility. The exception calmed fears that the interests of non-nationals composing over one-third of the population would overwhelm those of Luxembourgers, thereby largely depriving any xenophobic political voice of its potential audience.

Even in the face of economic recession among its three primary trading partners, Luxembourg maintained a positive growth rate and the lowest unemployment in the European Union. Some concern exists that high salaries, generous social benefits and strict employee protection regulations will result in Luxembourg pricing itself out of most markets.

Political Rights and Civil Liberties: Luxembourgers have the means to change their government democratically. Voting is compulsory for citizens, and foreigners may register after five years in residence. Executive authority is primarily exercised by the prime minister and cabinet on behalf of the grand duke. As head of state, Grand Duke Jean appoints the prime minister from the party or coalition commanding a majority in the sixty-member, directly elected and proportionately representative Chamber of Deputies. Some legislative activity occurs in the appointed Council of State, but its decisions are subject to veto by the Chamber.

Since World War II, a series of coalition governments has been dominated traditionally by the Christian Social Party. The current center-left ruling coalition includes the Socialist Workers' Party of Luxembourg. In addition to the liberal Democratic People's party and the two coalition partners, several smaller parties and interest groups exist. A Superior Court of Justice heads up an independent judiciary including criminal, district, administrative and social courts. The grand duke appoints judges for life.

A vibrant free press exists in Luxembourg. The only restrictions on print journalism focus on pornography. While there is no domestic news agency, a number of foreign bureaus operate. The small nation is home to the oldest European commercial broadcaster, *Compagnie Luxembourgeoise de Telediffusion,* as well as the first privately owned television satellite system in Europe. In an effort to encourage media diversification, the government has been offering tax incentives to film makers and film production companies it hopes will set up shop within its borders.

Religious freedom is respected in this predominantly Roman Catholic country. Some discussion has evolved concerning measures to protect the distinct ethnic and cultural blend of French and German heritage, primarily through language. French is employed for administrative purposes, while German is the language of commerce. The local language, a Frankish dialect called Letzeburgesch, is used in conversation and some media, but is not an officially recognized European language.

Two competing labor federations affiliated with the Socialist and Christian Social parties organize workers. With the prospect of increased freedom of movement in Europe and a labor force already relying on 25 percent cross-border commuters, unions are feeling the pressure on their relations with government. Prime Minister Juncker took office with a reputation as both a tough pragmatist and defender of labor interests; however, he has already proven himself adept at tackling touchy issues including Sunday work hours and automatic pay increases for seniority. In ensuring that social and economic questions are addressed in a timely fashion, Juncker aims to facilitate Luxembourg's incorporation into an integrated Europe.

Macedonia

Polity: Presidential-   **Political Rights:** 4
parliamentary democracy **Civil Liberties:** 3
Economy: Mixed statist **Status:** Partly Free
Population: 2,127,000
PPP: na
Life Expectancy: 70.0
Ethnic Groups: Macedonian (65 percent), Albanian
(22 percent), Turk (5 percent), Macedonian Muslim (3 percent),
Roma (2 percent), Serb (2 percent)
Capital: Skopje

Overview: **O**n 3 October 1995, an assassin's bomb seriously injured seventy-eight-year-old President Kiro Gligorov, who has kept this former Yugoslav republic largely free of ethnic violence despite tensions with a large Albanian minority and simmering historical rivalries with neighboring Serbia, Albania, Greece and Bulgaria. After U.S. mediation, Greece lifted a crippling nineteen-month trade embargo imposed when Macedonia took the name of a Greek region and used a cherished Greek symbol—a sixteen-point star—in its flag.

Ruled by Ottoman Turks for 500 years until the 1912-13 Balkan Wars, Macedonia was then divided among Greece, Serbia and Bulgaria. In 1941, Macedonians fought Nazi and Bulgarian occupiers. Communist partisan and subsequent Yugoslav leader Josip Broz (Tito) battled to unite Greece's Macedonian territories with Yugoslavia during Greece's Communist-incited 1946 civil war, fueling Greek distrust of Macedonian motives. Several neighboring states deny that a distinct Macedonian ethnicity exists.

Gligorov, a former Communist leader and head of the Social-Democratic Alliance for Macedonia (SDLM), was appointed interim president in 1992 and directly elected in 1994. October 1994 parliamentary elections, Macedonia's first since independence from Yugoslavia, witnessed fraud and irregularities, and runoffs were boycotted by the opposition nationalist Internal Macedonian Revolutionary Organization-Democratic Party of Macedonia (VMRO-DPMNE), the free-market nationalist Democratic Party, and others. The SDLM won 95 of 120 seats.

Ethnic tensions escalated after the rector of a new university for ethnic Albanians, Fadil Sulejmani, was arrested following February 1995 demonstrations outside university offices in Tetovo. Authorities claimed the university, funded privately by ethnic Albanians, was illegal and could not hold classes. Sentenced to two-and-a-half years, Sulejmani was released four months later on bail. To defuse the situation, the university held classes in private homes. Authorities agreed to upgrade the training college for Albanian high-school teachers to university level. Gligorov continued working closely with the moderate, Albanian-based Party for Democratic Prosperity-National Democratic Party.

Greece's embargo and the U.N. embargo on the former Yugoslavia continued damaging the economy even as authorities tried to implement privatization and other reforms with backing from international financial institutions. The government's economic team restored macroeconomic stability; inflation, 2,500 percent in 1993, was 1 percent by mid-1995. However, unemployment hovered at 30 percent, and many workers went unpaid. Remittances from Macedonians and Albanians abroad helped offset a drop in standard of living.

Gligorov's negotiations to end the Greek embargo angered nationalists. On 13 September, the U.N. announced Greece would lift sanctions after Macedonia agreed to change its flag and renounce any constitutional claims on Greek territory.

On 3 October a bomb severely wounded Gligorov, killed his driver and injured several others. The VMRO was suspected, but the investigation turned up no direct links. Determined to show unity after the attempt, parliament overwhelmingly approved the compromise with Greece, subsequently ratifying the entire treaty.

On 22 December Gligorov announced he would resume his duties in early 1996, rejecting speculation about a successor and ending months of tension and political uncertainty.

Political Rights and Civil Liberties: Macedonians can change their government democratically, though October 1994 election irregularities led several leading opposition groups to boycott the runoff. Albanian groups allege undercounting in the 1994 census. Albanians—particularly emigres from the repressed Yugoslavian enclave of Kosovo—are denied full citizenship and voting rights.

Several political parties, including those representing Albanian and Serb interests, run the gamut from leftist to extreme nationalist.

National television facilities and channels, and major newspaper publication and distribution facilities, remain government-controlled and -supervised. Albanian-language television is limited to one hour daily, and the Albanian-language newspaper is distributed only three days weekly. State media have denied opposition groups access. Though independent newspapers and local electronic media exist, most operate on shoestring budgets.

Freedoms of assembly and association are restricted if deemed detrimental to "public safety and order." Religious freedom is respected; the dominant faiths are Macedonian Orthodox and Muslim (Albanians and Turks). However, Albanian dervishes remain at odds with authorities over the return of a monastery.

The judiciary remains somewhat subject to political and government interference. The constitution specifically mentions Macedonian, Albanian, Turk, Roma (Gypsy) and Vlach minorities, but not Serbs. Albanians have consistently criticized discrimination in citizenship, government employment and education; underrepresentation in the military and police; and police brutality and due process violations. An estimated 100,000 Bosnian refugees face discrimination and public resentment. Organized crime, which grew out of smuggling groups formed during the embargoes, is a problem, and corruption is widespread.

The Union of Independent and Autonomous Trade Unions confederation was formed in 1992. The Council of Trade Unions of Macedonia is the Communist federation's successor. Gender equality is legally and constitutionally guaranteed, but women face discrimination in employment and education, particularly in rural and Albanian areas.

Madagascar

Polity: Presidential-par-
liamentary democracy
Economy: Mixed statist
Population: 14,763,000
PPP: $710
Life Expectancy: 56.5
Ethnic Groups: Malayan-Indonesian highlanders,
black and mixed coastal peoples, European, Asian
and Creole minorities
Capital: Antananarivo

Political Rights: 2
Civil Liberties: 4
Status: Partly Free

Overview:

After nearly three years of tension between President Albert Zafy and Prime Minister Francisque Ravony, a September 1995 constitutional referendum gave Zafy the authority to appoint a new premier. Ravony's government resigned the following month and Zafy appointed his close associate, former minister of agriculture and rural development, Emmanuel Rakotovahiny, to the position. Even Zafy's political allies criticized the move as part of an autocratic trend.

Madagascar, consisting of the world's fourth largest island and five small isles off the southeastern coast of Africa, won independence from France in 1960. After seventeen years in power, Admiral Didier Ratsiraka's leftist authoritarian regime bowed to social unrest and nonviolent mass demonstrations in 1991 and formed a new unity government including the opposition. A High Constitutional Court decree had legalized independent political parties the previous year, and several opposition parties were campaigning for a new constitution, a sovereign national conference and Ratsiraka's resignation.

Voters approved a new constitution in 1992 and elected Zafy, leader of the Active Forces opposition coalition, to the presidency with over 65 percent of the vote in a February 1993 runoff election. The opposition consolidated this victory four months later, taking seventy of 138 seats in the National Assembly. Their majority was weakened following the defeat of Roger Ralison, the Active Forces candidate for premier, by Ravony, who was supported by a coalition of representatives from coastal regions.

Zafy called a referendum after charging that his relationship with the prime minister—whom he dubbed a liar, a hypocrite and a corrupt holdover from Ratsiraka's administration—was making it impossible for him to rule. Their differences centered primarily around a "parallel financing" scheme that aimed to procure private financing for development projects to fuel the national growth rate, but which ended up costing Madagascar's ailing economy several million dollars. With 63 percent of the vote, Zafy won the power to appoint a new premier, prompting the opposition charge that he was coming close to reinstating the system tossed out with Ratsiraka's Marxist dictatorship. Indeed, Zafy's own party urged him to reconsider nominating Rakotovahiny and take into account the true strengths of each party in forming his new government.

Political Rights and Civil Liberties: Malagasy voters can change their government by democratic means. Turnout in the September 1995 referendum was below 50 percent, one of the weakest showings in the country's history. The bicameral parliament consists of a Senate and a National Assembly of directly elected and proportionally representative deputies. Each house has a four-year mandate and is subject to dissolution. In May the High Constitutional Court and National Assembly both approved laws establishing a new three-tiered local government structure, with only communal elections being held this year due to funding shortages.

Independent political parties have been legal since 1990, although this year sixteen opposition party members were arrested as a "threat to security." A group calling itself AMF-3FM had held open weekly meetings in Antananarivo, the capital, and its leaders had begun a forty-day hunger strike to draw attention to poverty and economic crisis in the country. They were arrested following their decision to set up a "phantom" government, which the authorities said would disturb and confuse the general population.

An independent judiciary functions without government interference. Upon his inauguration, Zafy granted general amnesty to political prisoners and reduced sentences for certain crimes, thus undoing many abuses of the previous government.

Several free labor organizations exist, many with political affiliations. Workers have the right to join unions and to strike. This year began with widespread strikes protesting falling incomes and rising basic commodity prices exacerbated by rapid population growth, persistent unemployment and widespread malnutrition. More than 80 percent of the labor force is employed in agriculture, fishing and forestry making subsistence level wages. Overwhelming poverty and regional differences limit the equality of opportunity.

Women account for over 40 percent of the labor force and perform the bulk of subsistence activities. They are significantly better represented in government and urban managerial occupations than women in mainland African countries. This and the matrilineal nature of citizenship may be due to matriarchal elements in the precolonial culture.

Religious groups are free to practice. Over half the population adheres to traditional Malagasy religions and coexists with Christians as well as Muslims. There is a vibrant free press including several dailies and one weekly newspaper published in Antananarivo. A year after the government abolished censorship, Ratsiraka attempted to reimpose it under the 1991 state of emergency, but the private press refused to cooperate. However, some self-censorship does exist. Television is government-controlled and under some pressure to slant news coverage, but private radio stations now exist.

Malawi

Polity: Presidential-par-
liamentary democracy
Economy: Capitalist
Population: 9,727,000
PPP: $820
Life Expectancy: 45.6
Ethnic Groups: Chewa, Nyanja, Tumbuku, other Bantu
Capital: Lilongwe

Political Rights: 2
Civil Liberties: 3
Status: Free

Overview:

Malawi's year-old democracy was seriously tested as military and labor unrest, rising crime and economic difficulties tarnished the government's image. Opposition-ists and rights activists criticized a new constitution adopted in May, but soldiers' participation in an anti-crime drive proved popular with both the public and the army. President Bakili Muluzi's United Democratic Front and its parliamentary partner, the Alliance for Democracy (AFORD), signed a coalition agreement that should enhance government stability, especially given opposition disarray.

President (later President-for-Life) Hastings Kamuzu Banda ruled autocrati-cally through the Malawi Congress Party (MCP) and its paramilitary youth wing, the Malawi Young Pioneers, for three decades following independence from Britain in 1964. Facing an economic crisis and international pressure, Banda accepted a June 1993 referendum on multiparty rule that was approved overwhelmingly.

Banda eventually agreed to May 1994 presidential and legislative elections, and both he and the MCP were soundly defeated. Muluzi won with 42 percent in voting reflecting potentially destabilizing ethnic and regional divisions. The army's bloody December 1993 destruction of the Young Pioneers made free elections more possible. Approximately 2,000 Banda loyalists fled to neighboring Mozambique, from where they threatened attacks.

In December, a jury acquitted Banda and his closest adviser, John Tembo, of plotting the 1983 murders of several senior politicians. Other charges may still be brought against the two men.

**Political Rights
and Civil Liberties:**

Citizens changed their government in Malawi's first multiparty elections on 17 May 1994, electing a president and 177 National Assembly members to five-year terms. Citizens over eighteen of age may vote; however, military personnel were barred from 1994 balloting for fear of politicizing the army.

The formalized government coalition gave it a comfortable legislative majority. AFORD leader Chakufwa Chihana became Second Vice President after legislators created the post via constitutional amendment. The government has sought to balance cabinet and other appointments to prevent perceptions of regional bias. The MCP's fifty-five seats make it the only parliamentary opposition, though other parties exist. Kalempo Kalua, head of the Malawi Democratic Party, the fourth largest, was arrested in September on charges of threatening the president, but released on bail.

The government has worked through the courts in several high-profile cases, most notably the trial of Banda and John Tembo. An allegedly pro-MCP army officer suspected of fomenting mutiny in April remained under arrest, but the government has also brought more dubious cases against political and media opponents.

Charges of government interference with state broadcasting and intimidation of independent journalists tarnished Malawi's reputation as having among Africa's freest media. Legislation passed in early November requires journalists to reveal sources under certain circumstances or face up to two years' imprisonment and $1,300 in fines. Within two weeks, the owner of the weekly *The Tribune* was arrested after publishing an article alleging an assassination plot against Muluzi.

The state-owned Malawi Broadcasting Corporation (MBC) first introduced television to Malawi in 1994, but its radio service is particularly influential in largely illiterate rural areas. Journalists report that at least one MBC journalist was fired and others removed from news positions after broadcasting opposition criticisms of the government, and that MBC was discouraged from reporting labor unrest. Although Malawi's free press remains vibrant, government tendencies toward interference and outright censorship are worrisome.

Rights to free expression and assembly are otherwise generally respected. The May 1995 constitution includes strong protections, although critics argued it allows excessive presidential power and inadequately addresses women's and children's rights. Many nongovernmental organizations operate openly and unhindered, including human rights and civil liberties groups. Religious practice is free, and the country's roughly 12 percent Muslim minority suffers no discrimination.

There are no reported political prisoners or detainees, but police brutality reportedly remains common. Internationally assisted efforts to retrain the 5,000-member police force are underway, but unlearning ingrained antidemocratic behaviors is difficult, especially as violent crime increases.

Although the new constitution addresses women's rights, societal practices preserve discrimination in educational, employment and business opportunities. The situation is worst in rural areas, where women are denied inheritance and property rights. Violence against women is reportedly commonplace, and the Society for the Advancement of Women plans to provide shelters and counseling for battered women. Ten of 177 legislators are women.

The right to form unions is guaranteed. Unions must register with the labor ministry, but this has not hindered union formation since the elections. Strikes are permitted, with requirements for notice and mediation imposed on workers in essential services. Collective bargaining is common though not specifically codified. Malawi's labor movement has been testing its strength under the democratic system. The Civil Servants' Trade Union has called four strikes since late 1994, which have attracted public support. The union's image was boosted in October after authorities confirmed union charges that thousands of "ghost-workers" were padding civil service payrolls, costing the nation some $2.5 million monthly.

Malaysia

Polity: Dominant party
Economy: Capitalist
Population: 19,944,000
PPP: $7,790
Life Expectancy: 70.8
Ethnic Groups: Malay (46 percent), other indigenous
(9 percent), Chinese (32 percent), Indian (13 percent)
Capital: Kuala Lumpur

Political Rights: 4
Civil Liberties: 5
Status: Partly Free

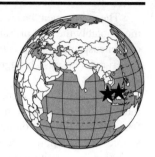

Overview:
Malaysia's ruling National Front coalition, enjoying control over the media and the institutions of state power, rolled over the opposition in the April 1995 parliamentary elections.

Malaysia was established in 1963 through a merger of the ex-British, independent Federation of Malaya with the British colonies of Sarawak, Sabah and Singapore (Singapore withdrew two years later). The king, as ceremonial head of state, can delay federal legislation for thirty days. Executive power is vested in a prime minister. The parliament consists of a fifty-eight-member Senate and a 192-member, directly-elected House of Representatives.

The economic success of the ethnic-Chinese minority triggered race riots in 1969. In 1971 the government introduced the New Economic Policy (NEP), which discriminated in favor of Malays through racial quotas in education, civil service opportunities and business affairs. The 1991 National Development Policy has the same goals as the NEP.

The fourteen-party, ruling National Front coalition has captured at least a two-thirds majority in the lower house in nine straight general elections since 1957. The coalition is dominated by the United Malays National Organization (UMNO), a secular, conservative, ethnic-Malay-based party. In 1981 Dr. Mahathir Mohamad won the UMNO presidency and became prime minister.

In 1988, following a party row over alleged mismanagement and corruption, former Trade Minister Razaleigh Hamzah led disgruntled UMNO members in forming *Semangat* '46 (Spirit of '46, the year UMNO was founded in Malaya). In 1989 Semangat '46 joined with the Islamic fundamentalist Pan-Malaysian Islamic Party (Pas) and two smaller parties in a Malay-based opposition coalition, but failed to topple the National Front in the October 1990 national elections.

In the 24-25 April 1995 parliamentary elections the National Front took 162 seats, while for the opposition the Democratic Action Party took nine; the United Sabah Party, eight; Pas, seven; Semangat '46, six.

Political Rights and Civil Liberties:
Malaysians have a limited ability to change their government democratically. The government exercises significant control over the media, bans outdoor campaign rallies and wields numerous security laws against dissidents, creating a chilling effect on political activity. The federal government strongly influences state politics by dissuading foreign investment and reducing development funds to opposition-held states.

The government continues to detain former Communists, religious extremists, and others under the broadly drawn 1960 Internal Security Act (ISA) and the 1969 Emergency (Public Order and Prevention of Crime) Ordinance (EO), both of which permit detention of suspects for up to two years. As of mid-1995 the authorities held some sixty people under the ISA.

Police occasionally abuse suspects to extract confessions. The judiciary is independent in civil and criminal cases, but less so in political cases and in cases involving corporate interests. Premier Mahathir controls all important judicial appointments.

Freedom of speech is restricted by the 1970 Sedition Act Amendments, which prohibit discussion of sensitive issues including the privileges granted to ethnic Malays. In March the authorities arrested opposition politician Lin Guan Eng on two separate occasions, once under the Sedition Act and again for press law violations, over comments at a January political rally.

The 1984 Printing Presses and Publications Act requires all publications to renew their permits annually. A 1987 amendment to this Act bars the publication of "malicious" news, expands the government's power to ban or restrict publications and prohibits publications from challenging such actions in court. The government occasionally uses these powers to shut down newspapers, and journalists practice self-censorship. In March two journalists were arrested under the 1972 Official Secrets Act for using "classified information" in an article three months earlier. All major newspapers and all radio and television stations are owned by individuals or companies close to the ruling National Front.

During the 1995 election campaign the opposition received virtually no coverage in either the broadcast media or the major dailies. In February the government warned three Chinese-language dailies against being too outspoken. In Kelantan, the only opposition-held state, the federal government reportedly restricts the circulation of pro-opposition newspapers, and has delayed granting a license for the state to establish its own television and radio broadcasting.

The 1967 Police Act requires permits for all public assemblies. Political rallies have been banned since the 1969 riots, although indoor "discussion sessions" are permitted. Under the 1966 Societies Act any association (including political parties) of more than six members must register with the government, and the authorities have revoked some opposition organizations' registration. The independent National Human Rights Association and several smaller groups function without harassment.

In June police forcibly dispersed some 1,000 Vietnamese refugees protesting plans for involuntary repatriation. In another issue, in July *Tenaganita*, a local nongovernmental organization, reported that several illegal immigrant detainees had died from physical abuse, disease and malnutrition. In August the government admitted that forty illegal immigrants had died in the previous eighteen months in a detention center near the capital, Kuala Lumpur.

The government is responsive to reports of domestic violence and the trafficking of girls for prostitution. Official policy discriminates against Chinese, Indians and other non-Malays in education, employment and business affairs. Islam is the official religion in this secular country, but non-Muslims worship freely. In summer 1994 the authorities banned the messianic Islamic al-Arqam movement under the Societies Act.

Each trade union and each labor federation may cover only one particular trade or occupation, and the government must approve all unions and can revoke their registration. In the 120,000-worker electronics industry the government permits only "in-house" unions rather than a nationwide union. There are legal restrictions on the right to strike. Unions must provide advance notice in several "essential services," some of which are not considered essential by the International Labor Organization, and the government can avert strikes by referring disputes to arbitration.

Maldives

Polity: Nonparty, presi-
dential-legislative (elite-
clan dominated)
Economy: Capitalist
Population: 261,000
PPP: $1,200
Life Expectancy: 62.1
Ethnic Groups: Mixed Sinhalese, Dravidian, Arab, and black
Capital: Male

Political Rights: 6
Civil Liberties: 6
Status: Not Free

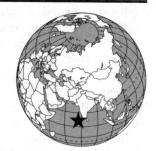

Overview: The Republic of Maldives is a 500-mile-long string of twenty-six mostly uninhabited atolls in the Indian Ocean. The British granted independence in July 1965. In 1968 a referendum ended the ad-Din sultanate's 815-year rule, and a new constitution gave the president extensive powers including the right to dismiss the prime minister and appoint top officials.

The *majlis* (parliament), which must approve all legislation, has forty seats directly elected every five years and eight seats reserved for presidential appointees. Every five years the majlis elects a single presidential candidate, and forwards this choice to the electorate for a yes-or-no referendum. Political parties are not banned but until recently were strongly discouraged by the government. To date no parties exist, although parliamentary groupings are becoming increasingly outspoken.

Successive governments have faced several coup attempts. Most recently, in 1988 President Maumoon Abdul Gayoom called in Indian troops to crush a coup attempt by Sri Lankan mercenaries allegedly hired by a disgruntled Maldivian businessman. In the aftermath, the president strengthened the National Security Service (NSS) and named several relatives to top government posts. The February 1990 majlis elections brought in a crop of activists who sought to enact democratic reforms. In the ensuing months journalists began to report on official corruption and nepotism. By June the government had banned most independent media, and late in the year it arrested several journalists.

In August 1993 Gayoom again won the parliamentary nomination for the presidential referendum, beating out Illyas Ibrahim—a minister who had fled the country after Gayoom accused him of using witchcraft to win the nomination—and another minister. In October Gayoom, South Asia's longest-serving head of state, won a fifth term with 92 percent approval in the yes-or-no referendum. The president pledged to change the constitution to allow multiple candidates in the next referendum, scheduled for 1998.

Following the election a court convicted Ibrahim in absentia on treason charges for having actively campaigned for the presidential nomination, which is illegal under Maldivian law. The government also sentenced eight of his supporters to seven years' banishment on remote atolls, subsequently reduced to one year on appeal. In December 1994 citizens elected a new majlis in elections that were judged generally fair.

Political Rights and Civil Liberties:

Maldivians cannot change their government democratically. The president, who under the constitution must be a male Sunni Muslim, holds broad executive powers but is indirectly elected. Individuals may not campaign for the parliamentary nomination for president. Political parties are not expressly banned, but none exists.

The Penal Code prohibits speech or actions that could "arouse people against the government," although a 1990 amendment decriminalized factual newspaper reports about government errors. A 1968 law prohibits statements considered inimical to Islam or threatening to national security, and in September 1994 a citizen received a six-month sentence under this law.

The government can shut down newspapers and sanction journalists for articles allegedly containing unfounded criticism. In 1990 the government revoked the licenses of two publications, *Sangu* and *Hukuru*, and both remain closed. Journalists practice some self-censorship, but the mainly private press carries some criticism of the government. The sole television and radio stations are state-owned but increasingly carry pluralistic views.

In December 1990 the majlis passed a strict Prevention of Terrorism Act that could be applied retroactively. In November and December 1990 police arrested several journalists, who were later charged under the Act. By October 1993 all of the arrested journalists appeared to have been released.

The president exercises control over the judiciary through his power to appoint and remove judges. The legal system is based on both Islamic law and civil law, and does not always afford adequate procedural protection to the accused. Persons suspected of terrorism, conspiring to overthrow the government or drug offenses can be detained without trial indefinitely. Criminals have been banished to remote atolls as punishment. The NSS occasionally monitors personal communications and searches homes without warrants.

The constitution guarantees freedom of assembly, but the government restricts political gatherings to private premises during campaigns. Clubs and civic associations are permitted, but there are no local human rights groups and civil society is underdeveloped. Women face social discrimination, and under Islamic law women receive half the inheritance accorded to men.

The constitution defines all citizens as Muslims, and conversion to other religions can lead to loss of citizenship. It is illegal to practice any religion except Islam, although private worship by non-Muslims is tolerated. The government neither encourages nor expressly denies workers the right to form unions, stage strikes and bargain collectively, and in practice such activity does not occur.

Mali

Polity: Presidential-par- **Political Rights:** 2
liamentary democracy **Civil Liberties:** 3*
Economy: Mixed statist **Status:** Free
Population: 9,375,000
PPP: $550
Life Expectancy: 46.0
Ethnic Groups: Mande (Bambara, Malinke, Sara Kole)
(50 percent), Peul (17 percent), Voltaic (12 percent),
Songhai (6 percent), Tuareg and Moor (10 percent), others
Capital: Bamako
Ratings Change: *Mali's civil liberties rating changed from 4 to 3, moving it to the
Free category, because a negotiated end to the Tuareg rebellion helped end insur-
gency-related human rights abuses.

Overview: The negotiated resolution of a five-year conflict among
Arab Tuareg guerrillas, ethnic black militias and government forces has brought quiet to a vast swath of northern
Mali wracked by sporadic, bloody conflict. Plans for reconstruction in the north
and the return of over 160,000 Tuareg refugees in neighboring countries are
underway. Local government was returned to northern areas in July, but longer-
term efforts to accommodate Tuaregs in the increasingly open and democratic
system dominated by the country's black African majority may prove difficult.

For over three decades after achieving independence from France in 1960, Mali
was ruled by military or one-party dictators. President Moussa Traoré was overthrown by his own military in March 1991, after over 100 protesters were killed as
demonstrations demanding a multiparty system were brutally crushed. Traoré was
sentenced to death in 1993 for having ordered the suppression.

A national conference followed the coup, and one-person-one-vote elections
that most observers judged free and fair brought Alpha Oumar Konaré to the
presidency in April 1992. A period of democratic consolidation has followed, with
increasing respect for fundamental freedoms.

The end of armed conflict in the north has seen a sharp drop in human rights
abuses carried out by various factions. The flood of modern weaponry along the
fringes of the Sahara could lead to new security problems, however, and simple
banditry is likely to remain a problem.

Political Rights Mali's current government was elected by universal suffrage in
and Civil Liberties: free and fair elections. Domestic debate is open and extensive.
Konare's Alliance for Democracy in Mali (ADEMA) party
controls 76 of 116 seats in the National Assembly, but political deliberations are often
spirited, even within ADEMA. About fifty registered political parties offer regular,
sometimes scathing criticism of government policies. The next presidential and legislative elections are scheduled for 1997, and Konare is expected to seek re-election against
what is today a fractured opposition. A variety of independent newspapers and radio and
television stations operate freely. The media are among the most open in Africa.

Mali's human rights record has been marred mostly by atrocities committed by different parties to the Tuareg rebellion in the north. After agreement was reached with several armed factions during the first half of 1995, on 11 June the last active rebel force, the Azaouad (Arab) Islamic Front, announced a unilateral end to hostilities. A major component of the new peace agreement is the integration of about 1,600 Tuareg guerrilla fighters into the armed forces. Three languages spoken by Tuareg people have received recognition as national languages and will be used in schools in Tuareg areas.

Although an earlier agreement, the 1992 "National Pact," foundered amidst renewed violence, a new desire for peace among neighboring countries who had helped supply rival combatants improves the new pact's prospects. Foreign ministers of Algeria, Burkina Faso, Chad, Libya, Mali, Mauritania, Niger and Senegal met in Algiers in late August, and agreed to support the peace process throughout the Sahelian region. Donor countries agreed to help fund renewed health and education projects in the war-scarred region, but disputes over land tenure and water rights must be handled delicately to avoid a revival of conflict.

President Konaré must resolve other problems also. Mali is exceedingly poor, and decades of one-party rule left an entrenched and corrupt bureaucracy that still stifles economic development and opportunity. There are fears that unemployment and economic hardship could help fuel local variants of Islamic fundamentalism. World Bank and International Monetary Fund experts, whose structural adjustment programs have caused at least a temporary decline in living standards, are praising Mali's economic development. Foreign investment is increasing.

Labor unions remain a strong force after having played a leading role in the pro-democracy movement. Minority and religious rights are protected by law, and although predominantly Muslim, Mali is a secular state. Legal advances in protection of women's rights are yet to be matched in practice, especially in rural areas. The government has undertaken an educational campaign to reduce the prevalence of female genital mutilation, though it is not illegal.

Malta

Polity: Parliamentary democracy
Economy: Mixed capitalist-statist
Population: 372,000
PPP: $8,281
Life Expectancy: 76.1
Ethnic Groups: Maltese (mixed Arab, Sicilian, Norman, Spanish, Italian, and English)
Capital: Valletta

Political Rights: 1
Civil Liberties: 1
Status: Free

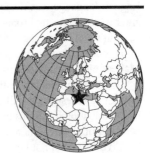

Overview: **D**ue to Malta's dearth of natural resources and terrain ill-suited for agricultural pursuits, the small island nation's government has sought to encourage economic diversification while pursuing external budgetary support.

After a long history of domination by foreign powers, Malta became a formal possession of Britain in 1814 with the Treaty of Paris. It gained independence in 1964, and the prime minister assumed governing power from the British monarch.

Five years after a constitutional amendment established republican status in 1974, the strategically located Mediterranean islands lost their British military installations and accompanying expenditures at the expiration of an Anglo-Maltese defense agreement. At that time, the Labor Party government turned to Libya's Colonel Mu'ammar al-Qadhafi, who promised financial support, after which Italy pledged to protect Malta's neutrality and provide loans and subsidies. When Dr. Edward Fenech Adami of the National Party was sworn in as prime minister in 1987, the defense and aid agreements with Italy had lapsed along with military arrangements with Libya, but political and economic cooperation with Libya were reaffirmed the following year.

Parliamentary leadership has alternated between the two main parties, the Malta Labor Party and the Nationalist Party. The constitution was amended in 1987 to allow the awarding of extra seats, such that the party winning a majority of the popular vote might secure a legislative majority in the House of Representatives. After sixteen years of Labor Party rule, the Nationalists began dismantling their left-of-center economic and religious policies, including deregulating the church and initiating privatization in the public sector.

Political Rights and Civil Liberties: Maltese are able to change their government democratically. Normally, sixty-five members are elected by proportional representation to the House of Representatives. Additional seats are added to allow the party winning a majority of the popular vote to command a parliamentary majority. Parliament elects a president to a five-year term. Although the role is largely ceremonial, the president is charged with appointing a prime minister and the cabinet from the parliament.

Since 1992, the government has sponsored media diversification. There are two English-language weeklies in addition to several Maltese newspapers. Both public and private domestic broadcasting are available, as are international radio broadcasts in several languages and Italian television programming. The only exception to freedom of speech and press is a 1987 law prohibiting foreign involvement in Maltese election campaigns.

Roman Catholicism is the state religion, but freedom of worship for religious minorities is respected. All groups possess freedom of association. There are independent labor unions as well as a federation, the General Union of Workers. A constitutional amendment banning gender discrimination took effect in July 1993, but divorce is still not legal.

Marshall Islands

Polity: Parliamentary democracy
Economy: Capitalist-statist
Population: 56,000
PPP: na
Life Expectancy: 72.5
Ethnic Groups: Marshallese (Micronesian)
Capital: Majuro

Political Rights: 1
Civil Liberties: 1
Status: Free

Overview: The Marshalls, consisting of thirty-three Micronesian islands in the Pacific Ocean, came under German control in 1885. Japan seized the islands in 1920, governing them under a League of Nations mandate until the United States Navy occupied them in 1945. The U.S. administered the islands under a United Nations trusteeship after 1947.

The 1979 constitution provides for a bicameral parliament with a directly-elected, thirty-three seat *Nitijela* (House of Representatives) that serves a four-year term. The lower house chooses a president, who holds executive powers as head of state and of government, from among its members. The upper *Iroji* (Council of Chiefs) is made up of twelve traditional leaders who offer advice on customary law.

In 1979 parliament elected Amata Kabua as the country's first president. In 1983 the Marshall Islands signed a Compact of Free Association with the United States, which entered into force in October 1986. The country is fully sovereign but defense remains the responsibility of the United States until at least 2001. In 1990 the U.N. recognized the dissolution of the trusteeship, and in 1991 the country received full membership in the world body.

Parliament re-elected Kabua in 1984, 1988 and 1991. At the 1991 parliamentary balloting, an informal Our Islands party chaired by Kabua emerged to defeat a Democratic Party headed by Tony DeBrum, a former Kabua associate. On 20 November 1995 the country again held parliamentary elections, but by year's end no breakdowns on party or individual loyalties among the winning candidates had been released.

A key issue facing the country is the Kabua government's controversial August 1994 proposal to rent remote, uninhabited islands as nuclear waste dumps. The issue is particularly sensitive in light of the sixty-seven atmospheric nuclear tests the United States conducted over the islands in the 1940s and 1950s. Data released in 1994 indicated that the extent of the radioactive fallout from the tests was greater than previously disclosed. The 1994 nuclear waste proposal is on hold pending an environmental impact study, which could take eight or more years to complete. Meanwhile some Marshallese leaders are pressing for a review of the Compact of Free Association, claiming that a trust fund to rehabilitate several contaminated islands, which was negotiated as part of the Compact, is insufficient to meet the country's needs.

Political Rights and Civil Liberties: Citizens of the Marshall Islands can change their government democratically. Political orientation is based mainly on personal loyalties rather than party affiliations.

The Constitution contains a bill of rights, and these civil liberties guarantees are respected in practice. The rule of law is well established. The judiciary is independent of the government, and trials are conducted with adequate due process safeguards. The sole newspaper, the weekly *Marshall Islands Journal*, is privately owned. The paper carries diverse views and criticizes the government, although journalists occasionally practice self-censorship on sensitive political issues. The official monthly *Marshall Islands Gazette* contains general notices and avoids political coverage. Three of the four radio stations are privately owned, and all stations offer pluralistic views. Opposition members own the local cable television station.

Freedom of assembly is respected in practice. Civil society is underdeveloped, although several women's advocacy groups have formed, including the umbrella organization Women United Together for the Marshall Islands. Women are underrepresented in government positions. However, inheritance of property and traditional rank is matrilineal, and in most matters of social status women are equal to men. Most incidents of domestic violence go unreported.

There are no restrictions on religious observance in this predominantly Christian country. Freedom of internal movement is unrestricted except on Kwajalein Atoll, the site of a major U.S. military installation. All citizens can travel abroad.

The government broadly interprets the constitution's guarantee of free association to extend to trade unions, although none has formed. There is no formal right to strike or to engage in collective bargaining, although the government does not discourage such activity.

Mauritania

Polity: Dominant party (military-dominated)
Economy: Capitalist-statist
Population: 2,274,000
PPP: $1,650
Life Expectancy: 51.5
Ethnic Groups: Black Maur (40 percent), white Maur (30 percent), Tuculor, Hal-Pulaar, Soninke, Wolof, others
Capital: Nouakchott

Political Rights: 6*
Civil Liberties: 6*
Status: Not Free

Ratings Change: *Mauritania's political rights rating changed from 7 to 6, as did its civil liberties rating, because of a slow liberalization that includes more open discussion in an expanded civil society.

Overview: Mauritania continued slow liberalization in 1995, but political divisions still reflected its long history of slavery, and the parliamentary system did little more than mask continued one-party rule. The government increasingly tolerated criticism, however, and opposition parties sought to guarantee free and fair 1997 legislative and 1998 presidential elections.

Mauritania's borders were formalized at independence in 1960 after nearly six decades as a French colony. Its 2.2 million people include the dominant white Maurs of Arab extraction, Arabic-speaking, Muslim black Maurs, and other black Africans (about one-third of the population) mainly inhabiting the southern frontiers along the Senegal River valley. The mix has been a major political factor. For centuries both white and black Maurs subjugated and enslaved black Africans. Although slavery has been outlawed—several times—servitude lingers, and allegations of continuing slavery persist.

Mauritania was a one-party state until a 1978 coup installed a military junta. The coup stemmed from economic disintegration, partly resulting from Mauritania's disastrous decision to join Morocco in seizing Spanish Sahara (now Western Sahara). The new junta left Western Sahara, renouncing Mauritania's claim. A 1984 internal purge made Colonel Maaouya Ould Sid Ahmed Taya the junta's chairman.

In 1989-90, tens of thousands of black Mauritanians fled to Senegal and Mali as Arab militants and soldiers dispossessed them. Several thousand were detained, and as many as 600 executed. Many remain as refugees.

Slow liberalization has not yet resulted in democratization. In January 1992 Ould Taya won a six-year term in the country's first multiparty elections, which were so riddled with irregularities that major opposition parties boycotted General Assembly elections in March 1992. The ruling Social Democratic Republican Party (PRDS) won, continuing de facto one-party rule. Eighteen registered parties exist, the strongest opposition force being the Union of Democratic Force-New Era (UFD-EN). In December, eight people were jailed for illegally forming a party allegedly sympathetic to Iraqi leader Saddam Hussein. An Islamist party, Oumma, is also banned.

The opposition is currently committed to contesting 1997 legislative elections, and maneuvering continued through 1995 as various coalitions formed and floundered. The opposition has exhibited more disarray than unity, and Ould Taya is exploiting this. While Senegal-based banned black resistance groups—including the Mauritanian Forces of African Liberation and the United Front for Armed Resistance in Mauritania—still advocate armed struggle, the PRDS has apparently gained some support among black Wolof and Peul peoples, the main victims of 1989-90 ethnic cleansing.

Economic problems include an enormous foreign debt. In February, rioters in the capital, Nouakchott, protested a 25 percent rise in bread prices. And in late 1995, massive flocks of birds threatened to halt planting in Mauritania's only rich agricultural lands, along the Senegalese border.

Political Rights and Civil Liberties:

Mauritanians cannot change their government democratically. A 1991 constitution has not been respected. The 1992 presidential polls were fraudulent, and 1992 legislative polls less so only because an opposition boycott made fraud unnecessary. The PRDS retains strong military support.

Censorship and state ownership of broadcast media and two daily newspapers curtail media freedom. Government media seldom present opposition viewpoints or taboo subjects including allegations of continued slavery or criticism of Islam. "Promoting national disharmony" and "insulting the president" are crimes. Yet private newspapers, many party-affiliated, often criticize the government. All publications must register, and authorities have suspended several for short periods and seized individual issues of others.

Parties and nongovernmental organizations must also register officially, although this is only a formality for most. Some Islamist and black African groups are banned. Several unregistered rights groups function, including the Mauritanian Human Rights Association. There are reports that black Africans are barred from assembling or harassed when they attempt to do so without permission. The El Hor (Free Man) Movement which advocates black rights may become a political party. Widespread discrimination against blacks continues and despite the slavery ban, approximately 30,000 remain in servitude with little means of escape.

Religious freedom does not exist. All Mauritanians are Sunni Muslims by statute, and may neither possess other religious texts nor enter non-Muslim households. Non-Mauritanian Shi'a Muslims and Christians may worship privately.

The legal system is government-influenced and *shari'a* law shapes many decisions, especially family and civil matters. A woman's testimony carries half the weight of a man's. Legal protections regarding property and pay equality are often respected only among the urban elite.

Although only about one-fourth of workers are in the formal sector, nearly all wage-earners are unionized. The 1993 Labor Code ended the Union of Mauritanian Workers' (UTM) monopoly. The government-aligned UTM remains dominant, but authorities have officially recognized the independent General Confederation of Mauritanian Workers. The right to strike is exercised occasionally, and collective bargaining is protected, but the government negotiates all labor agreements and can impose binding, tripartite arbitration.

Mauritius

Polity: Parliamentary democracy
Economy: Capitalist
Population: 1,117,000
PPP: $11,700
Life Expectancy: 70.2
Ethnic Groups: Indo-Mauritian (68 percent), Creole (27 percent), Sino-Mauritian, and Franco-Mauritian
Capital: Port Louis

Political Rights: 1
Civil Liberties: 2
Status: Free

Overview: In December's elections, an opposition alliance swept Prime Minister Aneerood Jugnath from the office he has held since 1982. Led by Dr. Navin Ramgoolam, son of the island's revered first premier, along with Jugnath's former Finance Minister, Paul Berenger, the opposition secured all sixty parliamentary seats in the largest election upset since Jugnath came to power thirteen years ago.

Mauritius is often cited as one of postcolonial Africa's few success stories. The flourishing economy has enjoyed average real growth rates of about 6 percent per annum over the last twenty-five years, with a rapidly increasing per capita income and virtually no unemployment. Among the country's assets are a well integrated multinational population, political stability, and preferential access to markets in Europe and the U.S. for its principle exports, sugar and garments. Over the past decade, the Mauritian standard of living has improved markedly and the island's infrastructure has been overhauled. The economy currently faces the challenge of stimulating productivity which has thus far been unable to keep pace with rising wages. The cost of rapid growth and economic prosperity has been the destruction of all but 1 percent of the country's native forest and much rare wildlife as well as the significant loss of its Creole culture.

As Mauritius has no indigenous people, an ethnically mixed population has grown with the progeny of immigrants. Since gaining independence from Britain in 1968, Mauritius has maintained one of the most successful democracies in Africa. In 1993, the island became a republic within the British Commonwealth with a largely ceremonial president as head of state. The National Assembly consists of a speaker, sixty-two directly elected members and the attorney general, if he is not already an elected member. Additionally, as many as eight "best loser" seats are awarded according to party or ethnic underrepresentation.

The new parliament as represented by Ramgoolam has stated its intention to pass legislation aimed at ensuring equal opportunity and ending gender discrimination, give higher priority to social welfare, and continue the free trade and economic liberalization policies of the previous administration.

Political Rights and Civil Liberties:

Citizens of Mauritius are able to change their government in free, fair and competitive elections. Separate administrative structures govern its island dependencies—the largest of which, Rodrigues Island, has a central government and local councils as well as two elected deputies in the National Assembly. Ethnic and religious minorities are assured of legislative representation through the "best loser" system. The independent judiciary is headed by a Supreme Court and based upon both French and British precedents.

There are no known political prisoners and no reports of political or extrajudicial killings. Civil rights are generally respected, but criminal suspects have reported the use of excessive force by police. Despite accusations that former prime minister Jugnath favored his own Hindi community, freedom of religion is respected and both domestic and international travel are unrestricted.

While press freedom is generally upheld, journalists are prohibited from criticizing the government under a 1984 law. There are numerous private daily and weekly publications. The government-owned Mauritius Broadcasting Corporation operates both radio and television facilities. Broadcasts are in English, French, Hindi, and Chinese and have increasingly included independent news reporting.

Freedoms of assembly and association are respected. There are nine labor federations comprising 300 unions. No laws exist mandating equal pay for equal work or prohibiting sexual harassment in the workplace. The government has attempted to improve the status of women by removing legal barriers to advancement; however, women still occupy a subordinate role in society and make up just over 20 percent of the paid labor force. In addition, they represent only about one-third of the student population at the University of Mauritius.

Although domestic violence against women is prevalent, there are no laws addressing family violence. Both governmental and nongovernmental agencies have begun initiatives to educate the public on domestic violence issues and to provide assistance to victims of abuse.

Mexico

Polity: Dominant party (insurgency)
Economy: Capitalist-statist
Population: 91,840,000
PPP: $7,170
Life Expectancy: 69.9
Ethnic Groups: Mestizo (70 percent), Indian (20 percent), European (9 percent), others
Capital: Mexico City

Political Rights: 4
Civil Liberties: 4
Status: Partly Free

Overview: Economic crisis, corruption scandals, unsolved high-profile political assassinations and the unresolved Zapatista Indian rebellion made authoritarian Mexico one of the most volatile Latin American states.

Mexico achieved independence from Spain in 1810 and established a republic in 1822. Seven years after the Revolution of 1910 a new constitution was promulgated, under which the United Mexican States is a federal republic consisting of thirty-one states and a Federal District (Mexico City). Each state has elected governors and legislatures. The president is elected for a six-year term. A bicameral Congress consists of a 128-member Senate elected for six years with at least one minority senator from each state, and a 500-member Chamber of Deputies elected for three years—300 directly and 200 through proportional representation. Municipal governments are elected, except the mayor of Mexico City whom the president appoints.

The nature and dynamics of power in Mexico do not correspond to the constitution. Since its founding in 1929, the Institutional Revolutionary Party (PRI) has dominated the state through a top-down, corporatist, authoritarian structure maintained through co-optation, patronage, corruption and repression. The formal business of government takes place mostly in secret and with little legal foundation.

Carlos Salinas won the 1988 presidential election through massive and systematic fraud. Most Mexicans believe Salinas actually lost to Cuauhtemoc Cardenas, who headed a coalition of leftist parties that later became the Party of the Democratic Revolution (PRD).

Wielding the enormous power of the presidency, Salinas overhauled the economy and joined the North American Free Trade Agreement with the U.S. and

Canada. Political reforms were minimal and the basic structures of the state-party system remained.

Salinas conceded a few gubernatorial election victories to the right-wing National Action Party (PAN), which supported his economic policies, to temper PAN demands for political reform and to prevent the PAN and the PRD from forming a pro-democracy coalition.

Until the outbreak of the Zapatista rebellion in the southern state of Chiapas on New Year's Day 1994, it was assumed that Salinas's hand-picked successor, Luis Donaldo Colosio, would defeat Cardenas and PAN congressman Diego Fernandez de Cevallos in the 1994 presidential election.

But the Zapatistas rocked the political system. Their demands for democracy and clean elections resonated throughout Mexico. Colosio infuriated PRI hardliners when he, too, began to advocate democratization.

Colosio was assassinated on 23 March 1994. As theories abounded about whether PRI hardliners or drug traffickers were responsible, Salinas substituted Ernesto Zedillo, a forty-two-year-old U.S.-trained economist with little political experience.

PRI hardliners put aside their animosity for PRI technocrats, putting the state-party machinery firmly behind Zedillo. The PRI used the enormous resources of the state, its control of broadcast media and the support of the wealthy business caste.

On 21 August 1994 Zedillo won with nearly 50 percent of the valid vote. The PRI won ninety-five Senate seats, the PAN twenty-five and the PRD eight. In the Chamber the PRI won 300 seats, the PAN 118 and the PRD 70. Both opposition parties disputed the elections' legitimacy. Only PRI legislators in the Chamber voted to sanction the results.

The PRI then went back to war. Reform proponent Francisco Ruiz Massieu, the PRI secretary general, was assassinated on 28 September 1994, his murder evidently ordered from somewhere within the PRI.

Weeks after Zedillo took office on 1 December 1994, the Mexican peso collapsed. Despite a massive U.S. bailout, the economy fell into a deep, year-long recession. Zedillo's promises to reform politics and establish the rule of law were lost on most Mexicans, who struggled to survive amid massive job losses and a currency worth less than half its previous value.

In early 1995 the now-reviled Salinas went into self-imposed exile and his brother Raul was implicated in the Ruiz Massieu murder and a major corruption scandal. By year's end, however, and despite Zedillo's appointment of an attorney general from the PAN, none of the assassinations had been cleared up and no PRI boss had been held accountable for corruption.

Zedillo generally appeared weak amid renewed public sniping between PRI factions and an IMF-directed austerity program that left most Mexicans gasping. Negotiations with the Zapatistas dragged on, with allegations at year's end that the military was planning an offensive against them. Meanwhile, Mexicans wondered if the PRI dynasty might finally have begun to unravel. But there was complete uncertainty and much anxiety about what might take its place—democratization, chaos or outright dictatorship.

Political Rights and Civil Liberties: The 1994 elections were freer than in the past, but decidedly unfair because of the ruling party's domination of state resources and broadcast media, and its still substantial control over the electoral system despite some reforms in 1994. The PRI relied less on traditional fraud like ballot-stuffing and more on the enormous power and resources at its disposal as the state-party. The grossly unlevel playing field gave the PRI a decisive advantage.

Mexican observer groups exposed numerous irregularities—voter intimidation, lack of secrecy, and the "shaving" of credentialled voters from registration lists. Although these irregularities did not affect the outcome of the presidential race, they were prevalent in poor southern states where the left-wing opposition was strongest and may have affected the composition of the Congress.

Since the second half of 1994, the PAN has won a few gubernatorial races in elections much freer than in the past. But local PRI machines held fast by hook and crook in others. Moreover, negotiations for fundamental political reform between the PRI and the two major opposition parties remained inconclusive by the end of 1995.

Constitutional guarantees regarding political and civic organization are generally respected in the urban north and central parts of the country. However, political and civic expression is restricted throughout rural Mexico, in poor urban areas and in poor southern states where the government frequently takes repressive measures against the left-wing PRD and peasant and indigenous groups. The nearly feudal conditions in southern states were at the root of the New Year's Indian rebellion in Chiapas.

Civil society has grown in recent years, including human rights, pro-democracy, women's and environmental groups. However, groups critical of the government remain subject to numerous forms of sophisticated intimidation that rights activists refer to as "cloaked repression"—from gentle warnings by government officials and anonymous death threats, to unwarranted detention and jailings on dubious charges.

An official human rights commission was created in 1990. But only minimal progress has been made in curtailing the widespread violation of human rights—including false arrest, torture, disappearances, murder and extortion—by the Federal Judicial Police under the attorney general, now a member of the right-wing opposition appointed by Zedillo, and by the national and state police forces. The rights commission is barred from examining political and labor rights violations, and is unable to enforce its recommendations.

Targets of rights violations include political and labor figures, journalists, human rights activists, criminal detainees and, with regard to extortion, the general public. Corruption and rights violations remain institutionalized within the Federal Judicial Police, which often makes political arrests under the pretext of drug enforcement, and Mexico's other law enforcement agencies. Many police dismissed for poor conduct have subsequently been implicated in kidnappings for ransom, which take place at a rate of about one per week.

During the outbreak of the Chiapas rebellion the military was responsible for widespread human rights violations, including sweeps of towns and villages that led to the deaths of dozens of civilians, mass arbitrary arrests, torture of detainees and summary executions of at least five Zapatista fighters. The government, with the complicity of the official human rights commission, engaged in cover-ups of many of these violations and the military has never been held accountable.

During a military crackdown against the Zapatistas in early 1995, there were numerous reports of arbitrary detentions, torture and coerced confessions. Ranchers and landowners, sometimes aided by police, stepped up attacks by their own private police against indigenous and left-wing groups.

Supreme Court judges are appointed by the executive and rubber-stamped by the Senate. The court is prohibited from enforcing political and labor rights, and from reviewing the constitutionality of laws. Overall, the judicial system is weak, politicized and riddled with the corruption infecting all official bodies. In most rural areas, respect for laws by official agencies is nearly nonexistent. Lower courts and law enforcement in general are undermined by widespread bribery. The exposure of endemic government corruption rarely results in legal proceedings. Drug-related corruption is evident in the military, police, security forces, and increasingly in government at both the local and national levels.

Zedillo's efforts to overhaul the judiciary and proposals to reform the police have done little to establish even a semblance of the rule of law. Mexico remains far from ending the impunity that exists for nearly every class of crime, from high-profile political assassination and corruption to drug-trafficking and kidnapping.

Officially recognized labor unions operate as political instruments of the PRI. The government does not recognize independent unions, denying them collective-bargaining rights and the right to strike. Independent unions and peasant organizations are subject to intimidation, blacklisting and violent crackdowns. Dozens of labor and peasant leaders have been killed in recent years in ongoing land disputes, particularly in southern states where Indians comprise close to half the population. There is also increasing exploitation of teenage women in the manufacturing-for-export sector, as the government consistently fails to enforce child-labor laws.

The media, while mostly private and nominally independent, are still to a great extent controlled or influenced by the government through regulatory bodies, dependency on the government for advertising revenue and operating costs, cronyism and intimidation. A handful of daily newspapers and weeklies are the exceptions.

More than twenty-five journalists have been killed or disappeared in the last five years, with most cases still unresolved. Another was killed in 1995 and numerous others were threatened, many of them while investigating drug-related corruption in the government.

The ruling party's domination of television, by far the country's most influential medium, was evident in the blanket, uncritical coverage of the PRI during the 1994 election campaign. Opposition parties were given limited time on Televisa, the dominant PRI-allied network, while it systematically supported PRI candidates. Televisa news-anchor Jacobo Zabludovsky remains a virtual mouthpiece for the government. Two newly privatized stations have shown little inclination to buck the government line.

In 1992 the constitution was amended to restore the legal status of the Catholic Church and other religious institutions. Priests and nuns were allowed to vote for the first time in nearly eighty years. Nonetheless, activist priests promoting the rights of Indians and the poor, particularly in southern states, remain subject to threats and intimidation by conservative landowners and local PRI bosses. Three foreign priests working in Chiapas were detained and expelled from Mexico in June 1995.

Micronesia

Polity: Federal par-
liamentary democracy
Economy: Capitalist
Population: 123,000
PPP: na
Life Expectancy: 70.5
Ethnic Groups: Micronesian majority, Polynesian minority
Capital: Palikir

Political Rights: 1
Civil Liberties: 1
Status: Free

Overview:
The Federated States of Micronesia occupy the Caroline Islands archipelago in the Pacific Ocean. The 607 islands have a Micronesian majority and Polynesian minority population. In 1899, Germany purchased the Carolines from Spain, and in 1914 Japan seized the islands, ruling them from 1920 under a League of Nations mandate. The United States Navy occupied the islands during World War II, and in 1947 the Caroline Islands became a part of the U.S. Trust Territory of the Pacific.

In July 1978, four districts of the Trust Territory—Yap, Chuuk, Pohnpei and Kosrae—approved a constitution grouping themselves into the Federated States of Micronesia. The constitution, which went into effect in May 1979, provides for a unicameral, fourteen-Senator Congress. One Senator is elected at-large from each of the four states for a four-year term, with the remaining ten Senators elected for two-year terms from single-member districts. The president and vice-president are selected by the Congress from among its four at-large members.

In 1982, the territory concluded a Compact of Free Association with the United States, which entered into effect in November 1986. The country is fully sovereign, although the U.S. is responsible for its defense until at least 2001. In December 1990 the U.N. formally recognized the end of the trusteeship, and in September 1991 admitted the country to the world body.

At the March 1991 parliamentary elections John Haglelgam, the country's second president, failed to keep his seat and thus could not stand for a second presidential term. In May the Congress elected Bailey Olter of Pohnpei state, a former vice-president, to succeed Haglelgam. At the 3 March 1995 parliamentary elections Olter retained his seat in balloting which, as in the past, was conducted on an individual rather than party basis. In the subsequent parliamentary balloting for the presidency Olter defeated Senator Jacob Nena of Kosrae state, the vice president, to hold on to the top office.

The economy is heavily dependent on fishing, subsistence agriculture, tourism and U.S. aid. In early 1995 the Micronesian Maritime Authority reported that excessive commercial fishing by fleets from Japan, Korea and other nations may be depleting the country's stock.

**Political Rights
and Civil Liberties:**
Citizens of the Federated States of Micronesia can change their government democratically. There are freely elected governments at the federal, state and municipal levels. Politics tend to be based on individual and clan loyalties, and while parties are permitted none has formed.

The rule of law is strong and basic freedoms are respected in practice. The judiciary is independent of the government, and trials are open and fair. There are no private newspapers, although the federal government publishes a twice-monthly information bulletin, *The National Union*, and the four state governments publish their own newsletters. The four state governments each operate a radio station, and religious groups also own stations. Some states also operate television services.

Freedom of association is respected but few civic associations have formed. There are no restrictions on freedom of assembly, and during the 1995 parliamentary campaign candidates frequently held public question-and-answer sessions. Citizens enjoy full freedom of religion.

The country's main human rights issue is the condition of women. Domestic violence, often alcohol-influenced, is a serious problem. Although assault of women by spouses or male relatives is a criminal offense, the authorities, influenced by traditional norms, often view domestic violence as a family issue. The government formed a National Women's Advisory Council in 1992 to educate women as to their rights, although so far its activities have been limited. Women also face social discrimination that has kept most of them in entry-level jobs.

There are no formal restrictions on labor rights, although owing to the small size of the wage economy workers generally have not exercised their right of association. Workers have the right to form trade "associations," although so far none has been formed. There is no legislation regarding collective bargaining, and its practice appears to be limited.

Moldova

Polity: Presidential-parliamentary democracy
Economy: Statist (transitional)
Population: 4,344,000
PPP: $3,670
Life Expectancy: 67.6
Ethnic Groups: Romanian (65 percent), Ukrainian (14 percent), Russian (13 percent), others
Capital: Chisinau

Political Rights: 4
Civil Liberties: 4
Status: Partly Free

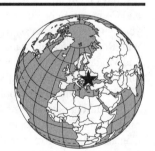

Overview: In 1995, Moldova, under the leadership of President Mircea Snegur, continued to consolidate economic gains resulting from market reforms and made headway in peacefully addressing separatist pressures in the mostly Slavic Transdniester region and the self-styled Gagauz Republic.

Moldova, a predominantly Romanian-speaking former Soviet republic bordering Ukraine and Romania, declared independence from the Soviet Union in 1991. Snegur, running unopposed and with the backing of the nationalist Moldovan Popular Front (MPF), was elected president by an overwhelming majority. In 1990,

Slavs in the Transdniester region, a sliver of land that was part of Ukraine until 1940 and joined to Moldova after Soviet annexation, proclaimed the Dniester Moldovan Republic (DMR). The 150,000-member Gagauz, a Turkic Christian people, did the same. Fighting in the Transdniester, where local Slavs were supported by Russian Cossacks, mercenaries and elements of Russia's 14th Army, ended with a ceasefire in mid-1992. In 1994, Russia and Moldova agreed to a three-year timetable for withdrawing the 14th Army, and in December of that year parliament voted to grant the Gagauz limited autonomy. In February 1994 parliamentary elections, the Democratic-Agrarian Party—a coalition of former Communists and moderate supporters of Moldovan statehood and closer economic ties with Russia—won fifty-six of 104 seats. The MPF and Christian Democrats, who supported re-unification with Romania, won just nine.

In 1995, Snegur resigned from the Democratic-Agrarian Party, rejecting its pro-Russian leanings and resistance to speedy reforms. He instead favored greater economic cooperation with Europe. In June, Moldova became the first Commonwealth of Independent States country to receive membership in the Council of Europe. Under Snegur, Moldova's old-guard politicians have overseen a painful economic stabilization program that since 1993 reduced inflation from 230 percent to 1 percent; included a "fast and clean" privatization program and the creation of well-regulated capital markets; and attracted foreign investment. GDP is expected to grow 6 percent in 1996.

Snegur also hoped that prosperity, rather than politics, would eventually pull the Transdniester's 700,000 residents back into the fold. In DMR local elections, 91 percent approved a referendum calling for the 14th Army to stay in Moldova. A few days later, however, the Russian ambassador to the Organization on Security and Cooperation in Europe said Russia planned to honor its commitment to a three-year withdrawal process, regardless of the referendum. With fears of reunification with Romania fading, flagging Russian support, a lack of international recognition and Moldova's economic revival, the DMR made several concessions, including allowing the leu, Moldova's stable currency, to be used alongside its own coupon. Moldovan leaders have spoken of giving Transdniester broad local autonomy.

In March, voters in the Gagauz republic voted for limited autonomy in a referendum aimed at easing tensions with Moldova's government. By summer, all Gagauz militias surrendered their weapons and local leaders hosted Moldovan Prime Minister Andrei Sangheli.

Political Rights and Civil Liberties: Moldovan citizens can change their government democratically. The 1994 constitution enshrines a multiparty system. International observers deemed Moldova's first post-Soviet parliamentary elections in February 1994 "free and fair," though local authorities forbade elections in Transdniester and there were some irregularities during the campaign.

There are several independent political parties and blocs; twenty-six parties participated in the 1994 parliamentary elections.

Political parties and independent groups publish newspapers that frequently criticize government policies. No more than 20 percent of newspapers can be considered private. A 1994 press law sets out criminal sanctions against "contesting or defaming the state and people." Several independent local radio stations exist, but there is no private national radio. There is one independent local television station (covering the town of Balti), together with several small cable networks whose programs do not compete with the only national television broadcaster, the state-owned Teleradio-Moldova.

There are restrictions on freedom of assembly. In June, the legislature adopted a bill banning rallies seen as slandering the state or subverting the constitutional system. Religious freedom is accepted, though the Orthodox Church has used its influence to discourage proselytizing.

The judiciary is not fully independent, though Western institutions have worked with Moldovan officials to design judicial and legal institutions and strengthen the rule of law. While inter-ethnic relations have improved, Romanians in the DMR have protested Russification policies, including the use of the Cyrillic alphabet.

The Federation of Independent Trade Unions of Moldova has replaced the Soviet-era federation. Government workers cannot strike, nor can those in essential services such as health care. However, in the spring teachers and students struck over changing the official language from Romanian to Moldovan. While women enjoy equal rights under the law, they are underrepresented in government and leadership positions, and face job discrimination. Over 300 nongovernmental organizations are registered, but most are poorly funded and small.

Monaco

Polity: Prince and legislative democracy
Economy: Capitalist-statist
Population: 31,000
PPP: na
Life Expectancy: na
Ethnic Groups: French (47 percent), Italian (16 percent), Monegasque (16 percent), others
Capital: Monaco

Political Rights: 2
Civil Liberties: 1
Status: Free

Overview:

Despite two decades of land reclamation efforts that increased total area by over 20 percent, the Principality of Monaco covers less than one square mile. Bordering the Mediterranean coast and surrounded on three sides by France, the Principality is a full member of the United Nations and is internationally recognized as independent and sovereign. During the first six centuries of rule under the Grimaldi family, Monaco was intermittently controlled by European powers until independence was gained from France in 1861. Under a treaty ratified in 1919, France undertook to protect the territorial integrity, sovereignty and independence of the principality in return for a guarantee that the exercise of Monegasque policy would conform to French interests.

The head of state—currently Prince Rainier III—appoints both a Minister of State and a three-member Council of Government, which assists him in exercising executive authority. Legislative power is the joint responsibility of the prince and an eighteen-member National Council. Laws are initiated by the prince and then drafted in his name by the Council of Government and debated for passage in the National Council. The prince holds veto power over the National Council and he alone promulgates new laws, which are then published in *Journal de Monaco*, the official weekly.

Recent political activity has focused primarily on lowering the level of economic dependence on tourism and foreign business enterprises, as well as anticipating the effects of increasing European integration. Despite Monaco's reputation, revenue from the gambling casinos of Monte Carlo accounts for less than 5 percent of its income. Major revenue sources include tourism, financial services, turnover taxes, and light industrial and commercial activities.

Political Rights and Civil Liberties: Citizens of Monaco can change the National Council and their municipal Communal Councils through democratic means. The sovereign and his government must exercise their powers within the framework of the 1962 constitution, the provisions of which take precedence over all institutions with the exception of international treaties.

Members of the National Council are directly elected through universal suffrage. Although electoral lists persist in place of political parties, recent years have witnessed a trend toward more competitive politics, with two new lists successfully competing in the 1993 National Council elections. The Communal Council is also a directly elected body under the leadership of the Mayor of Monaco-ville.

The prince delegates judicial authority to the Courts and Tribunals, which dispense justice independently but in his name. The principality does not have a Minister of Justice. It does, however, have a Supreme Court to deal with constitutional claims and jurisdictional conflicts.

Freedoms of both expression and association are constitutionally guaranteed. However, denunciations of the Grimaldi family are prohibited by an official Monegasque Penal Code. Two years ago, police arrested four pro-Tibetan activists for wearing T-shirts that read "Olympics 2000—Not in China" while protesting near the International Olympic Community meeting. Additionally, various pro-Tibet banners were confiscated on the grounds that the Tibetan flag is banned in Monaco.

Press freedom is generally respected. Aside from the weekly government journal and the monthly *Gazette Monaco-Cote d'Azur,* French newspapers publish widely available Monaco additions. Radio and television are government-operated, and sell time to commercial sponsors. All French broadcasts are freely transmitted to the principality. France maintains a controlling interest in Radio Monte Carlo, which broadcasts in several languages.

The constitution differentiates between rights of nationals and of residents. For example, although Monaco experiences chronic labor shortages and relies heavily on migrant and cross-border labor, nationals are given legal preference in employment. Citizenship laws and preservation of culture often figure into debate as indigenous Monegasques constitute only about 15 percent of the population. Among the remedies adopted was the reintroduction of the local Monegasque dialect into educational usage, along with a 1992 law stipulating that foreign women marrying male Monegasque citizens would no longer be accorded automatic citizenship. Instead, a provision was introduced requiring the women to remain with their spouses for five years to acquire eligibility. In the same year, women citizens were granted the right to pass their nationality on to their children.

Freedom of association exists, including the right of workers to organize. Trade unions are independent of the government. The state religion is Roman Catholicism, and religious freedom is constitutionally guaranteed.

Mongolia

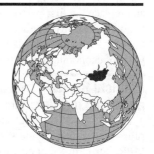

Polity: Presidential-par-
liamentary democracy
Economy: Statist
transitional
Population: 2,287,000
PPP: $2,389
Life Expectancy: 63.7
Ethnic Groups: Khalkha Mongol (75 percent), other
Mongol (8 percent), Kazakh (5 percent), others
Capital: Ulaanbaatar

Political Rights: 2
Civil Liberties: 3
Status: Free

Overview: China controlled this vast Central Asian region for two centuries until 1911, and again in 1919 until Soviet-backed Marxists revolted in 1921. The Mongolian People's Revolutionary Party (MPRP) formed a Communist state in 1924 following three years of nominal rule by aging Buddhist lamas. For the next sixty-five years the country existed as a virtual republic of the Soviet Union.

The country's one-party system began to crack in December 1989 with the formation of the opposition Mongolian Democratic Union. In May 1990 the government scrapped the MPRP's monopoly on power, and in July the country held its first multiparty elections. The MPRP took 357 of 430 seats in the Great Hural (parliament) against an unprepared opposition. In September the Hural named the MPRP's Punsalmaagiyn Ochirbat as president.

In January 1992, parliament approved a new constitution providing for an executive president directly elected for a four-year term. The president names the prime minister and can veto legislation, subject to a two-thirds parliamentary override. The constitution also created a smaller, seventy-six seat Great Hural, and provided for private land ownership.

At the June 1992 Great Hural elections the MPRP, split into factions ranging from orthodox Communists to free-market reformers, took seventy-one seats. Two opposition parties, the Mongolian United Party (MUP) and the Social Democratic Party (SDP) took four seats and one seat, respectively. Many voters blamed the country's economic hardship on the market reforms introduced since 1990, which they associated with the opposition. The MPRP formed a new government under Prime Minister Jasrai.

In April 1993, MPRP hardliners combined forces to dump Ochirbat as the party's candidate for the June presidential election, choosing instead Lodongiyn

Tudev, editor of the party paper *Unen* (Truth). Two days later the opposition Mongolian National Democratic Party, formed in October 1992 through a merger of the MUP and three other opposition parties, and the SDP jointly named Ochirbat as their candidate. Ochirbat won the 7 June election with 57.8 percent of the vote, compared to Tudev's 38.7 percent.

In April 1994 opposition activists held a brief hunger strike to protest official corruption. The activists also called on the government to fully privatize the media and replace the first-past-the-post electoral system with proportional representation balloting. The strike ended with a government promise to review the demands. For the year Mongolia recorded its first GDP growth, at 2.1 percent, after four straight years of economic contraction.

Political Rights and Civil Liberties: Mongolians changed their government in June 1992 through free although not entirely fair parliamentary elections. Electoral districts favor rural areas, where the ruling Mongolian People's Revolutionary Party (MPRP) has the most support. The MPRP also limited opposition access to the state-run media, and unlike the opposition had ample supplies of printing equipment and newsprint and sufficient stocks of gasoline to campaign in the countryside. By contrast, the June 1993 presidential elections were reasonably free and fair. Elections for the Great Hural are due to take place in 1996.

A key concern is that many of the civil liberties guarantees in the constitution have yet to be codified into law. The judiciary is independent of the government. The law does not provide the accused the right to see an attorney, and in practice defense attorneys are frequently denied access to their clients. A significant human rights issue involves the mistreatment of detainees and convicts. Police and prison officials often beat or otherwise abuse detainees and prisoners. Mongolian law requires prisoners to work for food, clothing, electricity and heat. In April 1995 Amnesty International reported that between autumn 1993 and autumn 1994 more than ninety prisoners had died, many from starvation and related illnesses. The group also reported that prisoners had been deliberately starved prior to trial.

The key constraint on the press is a lack of resources. Most newspapers are printed on a single, aging, government-owned printing press. The government no longer controls the allocation of newsprint, but newsprint is still sometimes in short supply. There are several radio stations and one television station, all owned by the government but offering pluralistic views. Freedom of assembly is respected.

A local human rights group functions freely and freedom of association is respected, although civil society is still rudimentary. The government has established several shelters to assist a growing population of street children. Domestic violence is a problem. Freedom of religion is respected in practice, and since the 1990 revolution Buddhist activity has blossomed throughout the country.

All workers can join independent unions. However, civil servants and "essential workers" cannot strike, and the law allows the government to sanction union leaders for calling a strike in an essential industry or where there is "insufficient cause."

Morocco

Polity: Monarchy and limited parliament
Economy: Capitalist-statist
Population: 29,169,000
PPP: $3,370
Life Expectancy: 63.3
Ethnic Groups: Arab and Berber (99 percent), black
Capital: Rabat

Political Rights: 5
Civil Liberties: 5
Status: Partly Free

Overview: **K**ing Hassan II's long-term program of controlled democratization proceeded through 1995 with a continued mix of greater openness and occasional repression. Amnesty International was invited to the country as the government acknowledged human rights problems, but serious abuses reportedly continued. Morocco claimed cooperation with the United Nations over Western Sahara, but appeared to be obstructing a referendum on nationhood there. As expanded privatization aimed to spur growth, union strike leaders were arrested. And a severe drought hurt the economy, evoking fears that social dislocation may increase support for Islamist radicals.

Controlled by France for forty-four years, Morocco regained its independence in 1956 under King Hassan's father, Muhammed V. Since assuming the throne upon his father's death in 1961, Hassan II has survived several assassination attempts and abortive military coups. Several serious, often economically motivated urban uprisings, the latest in December 1990, were brutally suppressed. Over three decades, Hassan II has slowly allowed more open institutions to evolve. A 1992 constitution increased parliamentary powers. Two-thirds of the Chamber of Representatives' 333 deputies are directly elected by universal suffrage, and the remainder by an electoral college of trade union, employer, professional groups and local council representatives.

Real power remains with the king, who appoints the prime minister and may at his discretion dissolve the legislature, which has very limited authority. But the strong opposition showing in 1993 parliamentary elections—the Democratic Bloc took 119 seats despite many credible reports of irregularities—has convinced King Hassan to seek their participation in the government. Opposition parties refused Hassan's invitation to join a national unity cabinet, demanding that a number of reforms be enacted first, including redrawing of the electoral code. The new government formed in February 1995 made a significant concession, creating a Ministry of Information independent of hardline Interior Minister Driss Barsi.

Hassan II claims direct lineage from the prophet Mohammed and carries the title "Commander of the Faithful." Islamist radicals, however, are as serious a concern in Morocco as elsewhere across the Maghreb. Civil war in neighboring Algeria raises fears of its spread westward. Morocco's Islamic activists are closely monitored, and sixty or more are detained. Increasing consultation and democratization could reduce their appeal, as could economic improvements including more and better jobs. Unemployment is already high, and widespread labor unrest could raise the political costs of privatization programs that may eliminate rather than create jobs in the short term.

Political Rights and Civil Liberties: Moroccans are unable to change their government by democratic means. The king is head of state and must approve any constitutional changes. The 1992 constitution created a parliament of proscribed powers. While it is a useful forum for political debate, with sixteen political parties represented and oppositionists holding over one-third of the seats, it does not govern. Provincial and local officials are appointed, and only less-powerful municipal councils are elected. While there is a greater tendency toward openness, governance is neither transparent nor accountable.

Constitutional guarantees of free expression appear subject to infinite interpretation. The current period of liberalization has permitted growth of a significant and pluralistic independent press. Hundreds of titles are available, but serious constraints remain. Broadcast media remain mostly in government hands. Publication licensing requirements are used as a means of political control. The press code allows seizure and pre-publication censorship by the Interior Ministry. Criticizing the king, his family or the institution of the monarchy could bring five to twenty years' imprisonment. Other taboo issues include the validity of Morocco's claim to Western Sahara and the sanctity of Islam. Over the last decade, a total of at least sixteen books, magazines and newspapers have been banned, and numerous issues of foreign publications seized. The Interior Ministry also blocked a number of performances by a popular satirist, Ahmed Sanoussi, who often lampooned government censorship.

Freedom of assembly is constitutionally protected but limited by several decrees allowing the government to restrict or prohibit public gatherings by requiring permits from the Interior Ministry. In mid-1995, rallies planned by youth organizations were banned. Religious freedom is limited to Islam, Christianity and Judaism, and proselytizing is banned. Many nongovernmental organizations operate, and three officially recognized human rights groups have released reports detailing alleged abuses. In 1995, they issued reports condemning torture and harsh prison conditions, harassment of former political prisoners, denial of passports to them and others, and lack of investigation into the disappearance of at least 300 Western Saharan activists over the last decade. They also urged an end to Marxist leader Abraham Serfaty's exile and restoration of his citizenship. Another opposition leader, Abdessalem Yassine of the banned Islamist organization Justice and Charity, remained under house arrest without charge for a fifth year.

Yassine's detention is officially illegal but cannot be effectively challenged in the courts, which are highly subject to political control. Many family law cases are handled by special judges trained in *shari'a* law, which does not offer women equal treatment. Other civil code provisions also discriminate against women, and societal discrimination can be acute. Much domestic violence goes unreported and unpunished since there is no requirement for women to receive property or support after a divorce. An active women's lobby, led by the Moroccan Association for Human Rights for Women, is campaigning for legal reforms to protect women's rights.

Morocco's formal labor sector is strongly unionized. About five million workers belong to seventeen umbrella federations, some of which are aligned with various political parties. The government generally respects labor rights, including the right to bargain collectively and to strike. However, in another sign of Hassan's ambivalence toward democratization, a number of unionists were jailed after a wave of strikes by phosphate, railway and dock workers, and teachers between April and June 1995.

Mozambique

Polity: Presidential-legislative democracy
Economy: Mixed statist
Population: 17,423,000
PPP: $380
Life Expectancy: 46.5
Ethnic Groups: Lomwe, Makonde, Makua, Ndau, Shangaan, Thonga, Yao, others
Capital: Maputo

Political Rights: 3
Civil Liberties: 4*
Status: Partly Free

Ratings Change: *Mozambique's civil liberties rating changed from 5 to 4 because of improvements in rural security and gradual opening of the domestic political process and civil society.

Overview: Mozambique continued to enjoy tenuous stability and a slow economic recovery under its elected government, after over two decades of war and repressive rule. Peace prevailed, but rising lawlessness, corruption and lingering rivalry between the ruling National Front for the Liberation of Mozambique (FRELIMO) and its longtime guerrilla foe, the Mozambique National Resistance (RENAMO), threatened even limited progress in what the U.N. classifies as the world's poorest country.

Years of bitter guerrilla war preceded independence from Portugal in 1975 under one-party rule by the then-Marxist FRELIMO. RENAMO rebels were organized and armed first by the white-minority Rhodesian regime, and then by South Africa's secret services. The bush war was among Africa's most deadly. Peace became possible only with the end of the Cold War and majority rule in South Africa, which cut the warring sides' supporters' desire to finance a proxy war. Coupled with a general war-weariness, this led to a negotiated peace in the 1992 Rome Accords.

Both sides largely disarmed and accepted multiparty elections, and FRELIMO jettisoned its socialist economic polices along with one-party rule. Joaquim Chissano won a clear victory in October 1994 elections that also gave FRELIMO 129 of 250 legislative seats. RENAMO took the balance, save for nine seats won by the Democratic Union. The U.N. had paid for the elections, and despite initial protests RENAMO accepted the results along with promises of further international funding. It has requested funding to continue until the next polls in 1999.

A five-year economic development program was adopted in April 1995 with broad parliamentary backing, but other tensions remained. RENAMO leader Afonso Dhlakama has demanded greater influence in government appointments, particularly in the central provinces that are RENAMO's stronghold, and where it continues to run a parallel administration. Lack of cooperation will hinder chances of even limited small-scale rural development, despite economic liberalization and extensive mine-clearing efforts under U.N. supervision. Nearly all infrastructure, from the educational and judicial systems to roads and port facilities, is badly deteriorated.

Political Rights and Civil Liberties: In October 1994, citizens freely chose their government in Mozambique's first open elections, with a massive turnout. The U.N., which spent over $60 million to run the polls, declared them free and fair, and the victorious FRELIMO formed a new government. However, democratic consolidation remains uncertain, and funding may not be available to conduct the 1999 presidential and legislative elections. Already, local polls set for 1996 have been postponed until May 1997 for lack of international aid. The opposition RENAMO won a significant 38 percent of the vote that is not reflected in its scant influence in the new parliament, where FRELIMO enjoys an absolute majority. Failure to include RENAMO more closely in decision-making could produce dangerous disillusionment with the democratic process among former guerrillas.

Media freedom is guaranteed by both the constitution and the peace pact. However, the state maintains direct control over most media and owns or influences several of the most important newspapers. Self-censorship is widely practiced, with little direct criticism of the president or reporting on widespread corruption. Criminal libel laws are an important deterrent to open expression. Government media offer little coverage of the opposition. Independent newspapers and fax newsletters are published, but their reach hardly extends beyond the capital, Maputo.

Eighteen political parties contested the 1994 legislative elections, and some suffered intermittent harassment. Nongovernmental organizations are increasingly able to work openly, and some like the Mozambican Human Rights League issue reports critical of official conduct.

Persistent reports of police brutality are particularly worrisome and are compounded by a weak judiciary and a lack of government accountability. Prison conditions are described as grim.

Religious freedom is reportedly respected. Women suffer both legal and societal discrimination. Mozambique's legal structures are relics of the Portuguese colonial era, and often conflict with new statutes or the constitution. Inheritance laws limit widows' rights, and women have less access to education and formal sector jobs, particularly in rural areas where 80 percent of the population lives. Wife-beating is reportedly common.

Mozambique's labor movement was long under FRELIMO control. The major trade confederation, the Organization of Mozambican Workers, is now nominally independent and has elected leaders for the first time. A second and independent group, the Organization of Free and Independent Unions, was formed in 1994. Other than employees of essential services, workers have the right to strike and to bargain collectively. However, the weakness of the union movement and the economy in general has allowed the government to effectively set wages. Minimum monthly pay for a factory worker is U.S. $22.

The government is committed to a broad privatization program, and has attracted some major Western investors. Inflation is still running near 40 percent, however, and endemic corruption remains a severe constraint on growth.

Namibia

Polity: Presidential-legislative democracy
Economy: Capitalist-statist
Population: 1,540,000
PPP: $4,020
Life Expectancy: 58.8
Ethnic Groups: Ovambo (47 percent), Kavango (9 percent), Herero (7 percent), Damara (7 percent), Baster and Colored (7 percent), European (7 percent), Nama/Hottentot (5 percent), Bushman (3 percent), others
Capital: Windhoek

Political Rights: 2
Civil Liberties: 3
Status: Free

Overview: **N**amibia remained one of Africa's most democratic societies in 1995, although unfulfilled economic expectations sparked demonstrations leading to the first serious violence since its 1990 independence from South Africa. The government, dominated by President Sam Nujoma's South West Africa People's Organization (SWAPO), faced increasing claims on limited resources from ethnic minorities and a large number of unemployed.

Conquered by German colonialists in the late 1800s, Namibia became a South African protectorate after Germany's expulsion during World War I. It was administered under the apartheid system from 1948 until achieving independence under a U.N.-supervised transition, including free and fair elections, following thirteen years of guerrilla war. In November 1994, Namibia's first post-independence elections resulted in a sweeping SWAPO victory and Nujoma's re-election with over 70 percent of the vote. Rule of law has been consolidated since independence, and legislation expanding constitutional guarantees was enacted. Through 1994 there was broad support for national reconciliation and a willingness by all groups to defer expectations of quick economic progress.

New militancy emerged among several groups in 1995. Former guerrillas demonstrated, demanding jobs and land. Workers also took to the streets voicing economic grievances. Both protests sparked violence and the first deployment of riot police since independence. Ethnic minorities also protested, claiming disproportionate channeling of government development funds to the Ovambo ethnic group, which makes up about half the population and is a bedrock of SWAPO support.

Political Rights and Civil Liberties: Namibians can change their government democratically. Citizens went to the polls for the second time in November 1994. Nujoma's landslide re-election was matched in legislative contests, where SWAPO captured fifty-three of seventy-two National Assembly seats. SWAPO's dominance raises fears among some that it may use its two-thirds legislative majority to make constitutional changes inimical to multiparty democracy. SWAPO dominance may also raise ethnic tensions in this diverse country, as its main support comes from the dominant Ovambo group.

Nevertheless, Namibia's rights record is considered among Africa's best. Political discussion is open and uninhibited. Political parties organize and operate freely. The greatest constraint to party development is lack of finances, especially given Namibia's minimal population density. Opposition parties accuse SWAPO of using government transport and employees for party activities.

The media are free. Although the state dominates electronic media, it has generally respected the editorial independence of the Namibia Broadcasting Corporation, which regularly presents views critical of the government. Private radio stations operate, and independent newspapers, some unabashedly partisan, operate unhindered and apparently without self-censorship on political issues.

Local rights groups indicate some areas in need of improvement. The Legal Assistance Centre and the National Society for Human Rights have complained of improper arrests and police mistreatment of suspects, and fear that a major crackdown on violent crime may lead to further excesses. Especially in rural areas, local chiefs with power over traditional courts sometimes disregard constitutional procedures in arresting and trying suspects, although usually regarding only minor matters.

Namibia's smaller ethnic groups, including the Herero and Damara, are demanding larger government allocations for development in their home areas. There is also increasingly vocal criticism of the large income disparity between Namibia's elite, made up of the 6 percent white minority and a small but burgeoning number of blacks, and the vast majority of Namibians, who earn an average monthly wage of about U.S. $21.

The right to form and join trade unions is constitutionally guaranteed, as is the right to strike for all but essential public sector workers. The 1992 Labor Act extended these rights to government employees and farm and domestic workers. Union registration is required but routine, and the government has not interfered with union formation or operation. Several 1995 strikes were at least partially motivated by union claims that the new Labor Court created under the 1992 law is pro-employer. Some domestic and farm workers remain heavily exploited, union organizers say, because many are illiterate and do not understand their rights. The National Union of Namibian Workers and the Namibia People's Social Movement are the two main union federations.

Women continue to face serious discrimination despite constitutional guarantees. Obstacles in customary law and formal legislation persist, such as unequal property rights, and the legal definition of married women as minors without economic rights. But traditional societal practices remain the greatest problem. In some areas, widows can be divested of all property by their late spouse's family.

Most economic development has centered around capital-intensive extractive industries. Medium-size business remains dominated by the white minority. The state has encouraged private investment, but the small domestic market has limited economic opportunity for small-scale entrepreneurs. The government's greatest challenge in 1996 will be to maintain its generally exemplary rights record while confronting possibly increasingly vociferous criticism of its economic performance.

Nauru

Polity: Parliamentary democracy
Economy: Mixed capitalist-statist
Population: 10,000
PPP: na
Life Expectancy: 66.0

Political Rights: 1
Civil Liberties: 3
Status: Free

Ethnic Groups: Nauruan (58 percent), other Pacific islander (26 percent), Chinese (8 percent), European (8 percent)
Capital: Yaren

Overview: Nauru, a tiny island located 1,600 miles northeast of New Zealand, became a German protectorate in 1888. Following World War I, Australia administered the island under mandates from the League of Nations and later from the United Nations. The country achieved independence on 31 January 1968. The 1968 constitution provides for an eighteen-member parliament, representing fourteen constituencies, that is popularly elected for a three-year term. Parliament elects the president, who serves as head of state and of government, from among its members. Political parties are legal but none has formed. The elected Nauru Local Government Council provides public services. Following the November 1995 general elections parliament elected Lagumot Harris president. Harris replaced three-term incumbent Bernard Dowiyogo.

Phosphate mining has given the islanders one of the highest per capita incomes in the world, although decades of mining have left 80 percent of the island uninhabitable. Following independence, the Nauruan government began seeking greater compensation from Australia for mining done during the trusteeship period. Nauru claimed that the royalties it received at the time were inadequate since Australia had sold the phosphates domestically at below world-market prices.

In May 1989, Nauru sued Australia in the International Court of Justice for additional royalties as well as for compensation for the physical damages done to the eight-square-mile island. In July 1993, the two sides reached an out-of-court settlement under which Australia agreed to pay $70.4 million in compensation over twenty years.

The government's $700 million Nauru Phosphate Royalties Trust (NPRT) will provide income for future generations after the phosphate supply is depleted.

However, in recent years several government agencies have borrowed from the fund, leaving it dangerously overloaded with high-risk property investments. Moreover, the NPRT has made numerous unsound investments, including providing financing in 1993 for a failed London musical, and has also been duped into committing money to scams. In January 1994, *Pacnews* reported that $8.5 million is still missing from the NPRT as a result of questionable investment schemes in 1992.

Political Rights and Civil Liberties: Citizens of Nauru can change their government democratically. Political parties are legal although none has formed. Instead, parliamentary blocs coalesce according to specific ideas or issues.

The judiciary is independent of the government, and defendants enjoy full procedural safeguards. The government-owned Radio Nauru carries Radio Australia and BBC broadcasts but not local news. There is a private fortnightly newspaper, the *Central Star News,* and a weekly government information bulletin. A private television service broadcasts from New Zealand. News and ideas are easily transmitted via word of mouth on the tiny island. Several foreign publications are available, although in 1993 the Dowiyogo government banned the July issue of *Pacific Islands Monthly*, which carried a cover article on the NPRT (*see Overview*). The issue reportedly remained on sale despite the ban.

Freedom of assembly is generally respected. In a rare exception, in July 1993 the Dowiyogo government reportedly threatened to dismiss civil servants belonging to the People's Movement, a female-based organization formed to protest the NPRT's mismanagement, if the group demonstrated during a South Pacific Forum meeting. The group staged protests with banners and placards, and no dismissals were reported.

A key problem is the treatment of women in this male-dominated society. The Dowiyogo government emphasized the child-bearing role of women, and reportedly revoked the scholarships of some Nauruan women studying abroad in order to discourage them from joining the workforce. The Dowiyogo government also failed to address the problem of domestic violence.

There are no restrictions on freedom of association, although in practice there are few formal elements of civil society. Freedom of religion is respected. There are no restrictions on foreign travel, and all inhabited areas on the island can be reached by foot.

The constitution guarantees workers the right of association, but the Dowiyogo government and its predecessors generally discouraged such activity, and no trade unions have formed. There are few labor laws and no formal right to bargain collectively or hold strikes. Foreign workers are generally housed in inadequate facilities and claim that they do not receive the same level of police protection as Nauruan citizens. By law, any foreign worker who is fired must leave the country within sixty days.

Nepal

Polity: Parliamentary democracy
Economy: Capitalist
Population: 22,579,000
PPP: $1,170
Life Expectancy: 53.5
Ethnic Groups: Newar, Indian, Tibetan, Gurung, Magar, Tamang, Bhotia, others
Capital: Kathmandu

Political Rights: 3
Civil Liberties: 4
Status: Partly Free

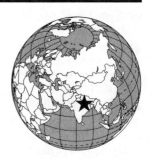

Overview: The Nepali Congress Party (NPC) returned to power in a tripartite coalition in September 1995 after passing a no-confidence motion against the nine-month-old Communist Party of Nepal (United Marxist-Leninist) (CPN-UML) government.

Prithvi Narayan Shah unified this Himalayan kingdom in 1769. Britain handled Nepal's foreign affairs between 1860-1923. The country's first elections in 1959 brought the leftist NPC to power. The next year the king dissolved parliament, banned political parties and began ruling by decree. The current monarch, King Birendra, came to power in 1972.

Mass pro-democracy demonstrations beginning in early 1990 climaxed violently in April when police fired on demonstrators in Kathmandu, killing more than fifty people. The king subsequently legalized political parties and in November approved a new constitution granting executive powers to a government headed by a prime minister. The constitution also established a bicameral parliament consisting of an elected 205-seat House of Representatives, and an appointed sixty-member National Council. The king can wield emergency powers under certain situations with the assent of two-thirds of parliament.

In May 1991, Nepal's first multiparty elections in thirty-two years brought the NPC to power under Prime Minister Giraja Prasid Koirala. In 1993, Communist parties organized a series of general strikes protesting electricity price hikes and a 1991 agreement allowing India to build a power plant straddling Nepalese soil. Koirala also came under increasingly strident attacks from within his party following a February 1994 by-election defeat. In July Koirala resigned, clearing the way for early elections in November.

Key issues during the election campaign included rising prices and criticism of the Congress Party's factionalism and corruption. Results of the 15 November elections gave the CPN-UML eighty-eight seats; NPC, eighty-three; the pro-monarchist National Democratic Party (RPP), twenty; and minor parties and independents, fourteen. On 30 November, King Birendra swore in Man Mohan Adhikari as the head of Asia's first freely elected Communist government.

The minority Adhikari government began instituting populist measures, including redistributing land to poor families and providing $16,000 block grants to 4,033 villages around the country. On 9 June, facing a no-confidence motion called by the NPC, Adhikari advised the king to dissolve parliament and call fresh elections. On 28 August the Supreme Court ruled the request unconstitutional, and on 10 September the NPC, joined by the RPP and the tiny Nepal Goodwill Party, passed a no-confidence vote to bring down the government. The three parties formed a coalition government under the NPC's Sher Bahadur Deuba.

Political Rights and Civil Liberties: Nepalese changed their government democratically in November 1994, in elections marred by vote-selling, ballot-box tampering and other irregularities. At least six people died in politically related violence during the campaign and on election day.

In the past two years, the police have shown greater tolerance in dealing with public demonstrations. However, police frequently use excessive force in routine situations, beat suspects to extract confessions and abuse prisoners. Several people have died in custody in recent years. The government has largely failed to prosecute offending officers.

Authorities frequently ignore a legal requirement to bring detainees before a court within twenty-four hours of arrest. The Public Security Act (PSA), as amended in 1991, allows authorities to detain suspects for up to twelve months without charges. Both the Koirala and the Adhikari governments used the PSA to detain leftist activists in advance of and during demonstrations, generally for less than two days. The 1970 Public Offenses Act grants Chief District Officers broad powers to detain suspects.

The Supreme Court is independent, as evidenced most recently in its August 1995 decision canceling early elections (*see Overview above*), although lower courts are sometimes influenced by the government. Adequate procedural safeguards are observed during ordinary trials.

The Constitution restricts expression that could jeopardize national security or do harm in other broadly defined areas. The Press and Publications Act prevents publication of articles on a variety of grounds, including showing disrespect toward the monarchy, and also requires licensing of journalists. Despite these restrictions, private newspapers and magazines vigorously criticize government policies. Under the Koirala government thugs assaulted several journalists who wrote articles critical of the government. The sole television and radio stations, which are state-owned, do not cover opposition viewpoints adequately.

Nepal's nascent civil society includes several active human rights and social welfare organizations. The Adhikari government barred an April conference on Kashmir from being held in Kathmandu. In September, police briefly detained some thirty Tibetans who had presented a protest letter at the Chinese embassy. During the year, police forcibly dispersed several demonstrations by radical left-wing groups, which have in turn attacked small entrepreneurs for not honoring nationwide strikes. Religious freedom is respected.

Caste discrimination is prevalent in rural areas. More than 100,000 ethnic Thaurus, a lower-caste group, are bonded laborers in southwestern Nepal. Women face legal discrimination in property rights and divorce matters, and rarely receive the same educational opportunities as men. Domestic violence is common. According to Women Acting Together for Change, up to 200,000 Nepalese women have been trafficked to Indian brothels. Authorities have taken measures to reduce the number of children working in the carpet industry. There are several hundred street children in Kathmandu and other cities.

Nepal hosts some 87,000 Bhutanese refugees (*see Bhutan report*) and has assimilated over 18,000 Tibetan asylum-seekers. However, police occasionally use excessive force against Tibetans crossing the border, and in spring 1995 the Adhikari government deported over 100 Tibetans who had entered Nepal.

Workers are free to join independent unions. Strikes are prohibited in certain "essential services," and the government can suspend a strike or the operation of a trade union if it considers this to be in the national interest.

Netherlands

Polity: Parliamentary democracy
Economy: Mixed capitalist
Population: 15,459,000
PPP: $17,780
Life Expectancy: 77.4
Ethnic Groups: Dutch (97 percent), Indonesian, others
Capital: Amsterdam

Political Rights: 1
Civil Liberties: 1
Status: Free

Overview:

Floods in early February brought the most devastating natural disaster to hit the Netherlands in over forty years. The following month, the right-wing Liberals became the country's largest party, surpassing their senior coalition partner, the Labor Party, by over 10 percent of the vote.

The Dutch won independence from Spain in the sixteenth century, whereupon the governors of the House of Orange assumed rule of the United Provinces of the Netherlands. A constitutional monarchy based on representative government emerged at the close of the Napoleonic period. The present monarch, Queen Beatrix, appoints the arbiters of executive authority, the Council of Ministers, as well as the governor of each province. The bicameral States General (parliament) consists of an indirectly elected First Chamber and a larger and more powerful directly elected Second Chamber.

In the May 1994 general election, the Christian Democratic Appeal (CDA) was relegated to the opposition for the first time in modern Dutch politics. March 1995 provincial elections brought only 22.9 percent of the vote to the CDA, down from 32.6 percent in 1991. The Liberals captured 27.2 percent. The other two partners in the ruling right-left coalition, Labor and Democrats 66, took 17.1 and 15.6 percent respectively.

As postwar prosperity has devolved into economic stagnation, the country has felt pressured by international competition to shed some of the excesses of a social welfare system that favors inactivity over labor. For every 100 workers, there are eighty-five people living on some form of public assistance. Much recent political upheaval stems from the debate over austerity measures and controversial CDA proposals to freeze pensions and benefits.

Two weeks of downpours across northern Europe and melting Alpine snow drove over 200,000 people from their homes and caused hundreds of millions of dollars in damage. With two-fifths of the Netherlands lying below sea level, residents depend on the strength of a 1,500-mile network of dikes to protect their lives and property from swelling rivers.

Political Rights and Civil Liberties: The Dutch are able to change their government democratically. A series of amendments to the original constitution has incorporated welfare-state provisions and democratic reform. Local voting rights are accorded to foreigners after five years in residence. Despite the existence of the Women's Party, only about 15 percent of those participating in government are female, with a lower percentage at the local level.

A Supreme Court heads an independent judiciary including five courts of appeal, nineteen district courts and sixty-two lower courts. Prosecutors sometimes bring cases to trial for the express purpose of establishing legal precedent; last year, in an effort to create policy regarding infant euthanasia, two doctors were brought to trial for the "mercy killing" of newborns in their care.

Although generally self-censoring in regard to the royal family, the press is free and independent. All Dutch newspapers cooperate in administrating the independent Netherlands News Agency. Radio and television broadcasting, offering pluralistic viewpoints, operate autonomously under the supervision and regulations of the state. Free speech is observed with the exception of the promulgation of racist ideas and incitements to racism.

Recent years have seen a rise in anti-immigrant sentiment and some discrimination in housing and employment, directed especially against foreigners from developing nations. As the economic reality of a generous welfare system becomes increasingly difficult to manage, concern has grown about sharing diminishing public funds with asylum-seekers and foreigners. The extreme right-wing Center Democrats gained three seats in the lower house in May 1994, taking 2.5 percent of the popular vote. Although charges were brought against party leader Hans Janmaat and others for racist remarks, the Justice Ministry ultimately decided the group did not pose a significant enough threat to justify banning it.

The state continues to subsidize church-affiliated schools based on the number of registered students. The population is over 50 percent Protestant and roughly 35 percent Catholic. Freedom for other religious faiths and freedom of association are respected. This year, KLM Airlines pilots went on strike for the first time since 1958, over disputes concerning productivity and cost reductions. With the exception of civil servants, workers have the right to organize and the right to strike.

New Zealand

Polity: Parliamentary
democracy
Economy: Capitalist
Population: 3,546,000
PPP: $14,990
Life Expectancy: 75.5
Ethnic Groups: European (79 percent), Maori (12 percent),
Pacific islander (3 percent), others
Capital: Wellington

Political Rights: 1
Civil Liberties: 1
Status: Free

Overview: In 1995 New Zealand premier Jim Bolger's National Party
government continued to grapple with the land claims of an
increasingly restive Maori minority.

New Zealand achieved full self-government prior to World War II, and gained
formal independence from Great Britain in 1947. Since 1935, political power in
this parliamentary democracy has alternated between the mildly conservative
National Party and the center-left Labor Party, both of which helped develop one of
the world's most progressive welfare states. In response to an increasingly competitive global trade regime, in 1984 the incoming Labor government began an
economic deregulation program that included cutting farm subsidies, slashing
tariffs and privatizing many industries.

The harsh effects of the economic reforms and a deep recession contributed to
a National Party landslide at the October 1990 parliamentary elections. However,
rather than slow the reforms new Prime Minister Jim Bolger's government
continued them by slashing welfare payments, restructuring the labor law to
discourage collective bargaining, and ending universal free hospital care.

With the economy showing signs of an upswing, at the November 1993
parliamentary elections the National Party took fifty seats; Labor, forty-five; the
Alliance, a five-party, center-left coalition headed by Jim Anderton, two; and the
populist New Zealand First, two. In a concurrent referendum, voters chose to
replace the current first-past-the-post electoral system with a mixed-member
proportional system (MMP), designed to increase the representation of smaller
parties. At the next election the MMP will give each citizen two votes for an
expanded parliament. The first will be for one of sixty-five geographical constituency seats, and the second will go toward filling fifty-five seats through party-
preference proportional representation.

A key issue facing the Bolger government is the resolution of land claims by
the Maori minority. Under the 1840 Treaty of Waitangi, the Maori ceded sovereignty to the British in return for guarantees on land rights. However, by 1890 the
Maori had lost all but 4.4 million hectares of the country's 26.8 million total, and that
figure has since shrunk to 1.2 million hectares. In late 1994, the government
established a $633 million fund to settle all outstanding Maori land claims
within ten years. In December 1994, the government reached a settlement with the
Waikato tribe that included a $41.6 million cash payment and public land valued at

$66.5 million. However, many Maori leaders rejected the fund as being too small and refused to negotiate.

In 1995 Maori activists waged a civil disobedience campaign that included symbolic occupations of parks and other tracts they claimed as ancestral lands. In May the Tainui tribe signed a cash and land package worth $112 million, putting pressure on other Maori groups to either negotiate or be left out of the action.

Political Rights and Civil Liberties: New Zealanders can change their government democratically. Four parliamentary seats are reserved for representatives of the Maori minority. An MMP electoral system (*see Overview above*) will be implemented for the first time at national elections due by November 1996. Several new parties have formed to contest the vote.

New Zealand has no written constitution, but all fundamental freedoms are respected in practice. The judiciary is independent and trials are free and open. The country has a vigorous private press. The broadcast media are both privately and publicly held and express pluralistic views. In January 1995, Maori activists disrupted a news broadcast at the central studio of the TVNZ television network to protest what it called insufficient Maori-language programming. The network promised to review the grievances. Civil society is well developed. Freedom of religion is respected. The authorities are responsive to complaints of rape and domestic violence.

The indigenous Maori minority and the tiny Pacific Islander population face unofficial discrimination in employment and education opportunities. The 1983 Equal Employment Opportunities Policy, designed to bring more minorities into the public sector, has been only marginally successful. Maori leaders are also pressing for more equitable returns on their so-called reserved land. An agreement reached in the nineteenth century, and codified in 1955, leases Maori land in perpetuity to the "settlers." Today, the rents received by the Maori on some 2,500 leases average far lower than those received by commercial landowners.

Workers can join independent trade unions and collective bargaining is legal. However, the 1991 Employment Contracts Act (ECA) has weakened the power of unions by banning compulsory membership and other practices that had made unions the sole, mandatory negotiators on behalf of employees. Contracts are now generally drawn up at the factory or even at the individual level, and wages and union membership rolls have fallen. In 1994, the ILO criticized a provision of the ECA that prohibits strikes designed to force an employer to sign on to a multicompany contract.

Nicaragua

Polity: Presidential-leg- **Political Rights:** 4
islative democracy **Civil Liberties:** 4*
(military-influenced) **Status:** Partly Free
Economy: Capitalist-statist
Population: 4,433,000
PPP: $2,790
Life Expectancy: 66.7
Ethnic Groups: Mestizo (69 percent), European (17 percent),
black (9 percent), Indian (5 percent)
Capital: Managua
Ratings Change: *Nicaragua's civil liberties rating changed from 5 to 4 because of
a more professional police performance.

Overview: Nicaragua overcame a paralyzing constitutional crisis, but
mounting social unrest and a fractured political landscape
were the panorama as the country moved toward presidential elections in October 1996.

The Republic of Nicaragua was established in 1838, seventeen years after independence from Spain. Its history has been one of internal strife and dictatorship. The
decades-long Somoza dynasty succumbed to the 1979 Sandinista Revolution. The
Sandinista National Liberation Front (FSLN) attempted to impose a Marxist dictatorship, which led to civil war and indirect U.S. intervention on behalf of the Contras. The
FSLN finally conceded in 1987 to a new constitution that provides for a president and
ninety-six member National Assembly elected every six years.

In 1990 newspaper publisher Violeta Chamorro easily defeated incumbent
president Daniel Ortega of the FSLN. Her fourteen-party National Opposition
Union (UNO) won a legislative majority.

Chamorro gave enormous authority to her son-in-law and presidency minister,
Antonio Lacayo. Lacayo reached an accommodation with Ortega's brother
Humberto, allowing Humberto to remain head of the military, leading to allega-
tions within UNO of a co-governing set-up. UNO soon unraveled into a number of
factions. Later the FSLN split, with moderates following former vice-president
Sergio Ramirez to found the social-democratic Sandinista Renewal Movement
(MRS), and hardliners remaining with Daniel in the rump FSLN.

In 1994, the MRS and anti-Lacayo UNO factions proposed constitutional
reforms to limit presidential powers and ban close relatives of a sitting president
from running for the office. Lacayo and Daniel Ortega opposed the measures and
the battle, manifested through efforts to control the Supreme Court, paralyzed the
government until a compromise resolution was reached in mid-1995.

In February 1995, after passage of a law ensuring the military's autonomy,
Humberto Ortega turned over command of the military to his number two, Gen.
Joaquin Cuadra.

In the second half of 1995, politics focused on the 1996 election. An array of
potential presidential candidates are jockeying for position, including Daniel

Ortega, Sergio Ramirez, former Contra Eden Pastora, Antonio Lacayo and Arnoldo Aleman, the feisty conservative mayor of Managua, who led in some polls. Many wondered whether the Machiavellian Humberto Ortega would reemerge to enter the race. Meanwhile, increasingly violent labor strikes and student demonstrations mounted against the government's market reforms.

Political Rights and Civil Liberties: Nicaraguans can change governments through elections. However, the Chamorro government's authority has been undermined by continued Sandinista control of the military. The 1994 military law legalized the separation of the military from civilian authority, and allows it to act as a tax-free enterprise with substantial holdings and with full control of the national customs system. As an armed corporation accountable mostly to itself, the military is practically a state within a state.

The constitution permits the organization of political parties, civic groups and labor unions. But political and civic activity are restricted by intermittent political violence, official corruption and a mounting crime wave, much of it drug-related, all in a climate of general impunity.

Numerous bands of former Contras continue to operate in the north, competing in their criminal activities with groups of former Sandinista soldiers. The cash-strapped government has been unable to guarantee land grants or credits to former Contras, the core of the 1990 Contra demobilization agreement.

In response to about 5,000 claims involving property confiscated by the Sandinista regime, the government passed a 1995 law providing some compensation in the most egregious cases. But as with any law in Nicaragua, implementation and enforcement remained uncertain at best.

In 1995, Nicaragua's independent rights groups reported continuing intimidation, extrajudicial killings, kidnappings, false arrest, and torture during interrogation. Military and police abuses are directed frequently against demobilized Contras and UNO supporters, particularly in rural areas. In January 1995, the military was implicated in the "La Marinosa" massacre of thirteen alleged rural bandits. In December, police fired on student demonstrators, leaving two dead and dozens wounded.

A number of high-profile murder cases remained unresolved, including those of at least nine former Contra leaders murdered since 1990, and Arges Sequira, the murdered leader of a group demanding the return of property confiscated by the Sandinistas. The military has stonewalled the investigation of the 1990 murder of Jean Paul Genie, a young man who according to a group of Venezuelan jurists, was killed by members of Humberto Ortega's armed escort in a highway incident. In 1995, the Inter-American Human Rights Court agreed to try the case.

The surging crime wave has overwhelmed the police and civil courts. Prisons are overcrowded and conditions deplorable, with most detainees held for months and in some cases years before being brought to court.

Labor rights are complicated by the fact that the Sandinistas wield their public unions as violent instruments to influence government economic policy. Through the public sector unions they control, the Sandinistas have managed to gain ownership of over three dozen privatized state enterprises. The legal rights of non-

Sandinista unions are not fully guaranteed because they have no effective recourse when labor laws are violated by either government or violent Sandinista actions.

Print media are partisan, representing hardline and moderate Sandinista, and pro- and anti-government positions. Before leaving office, the Sandinistas dismantled the seventeen-station state radio network and "privatized" it, mostly to Sandinista loyalists. They also retained possession of one of the three television stations. The government has pressured the conservative daily *La Tribuna* by denying it government advertising and placing obstacles against importing machinery. Physical attacks against journalists, usually by police, are not uncommon.

The Catholic Church has been outspoken in its criticism of the judicial system and Nicaragua's general social erosion. In 1995, Church property was the target of a mysterious campaign, as sixteen small bombs designed to damage only property were set off around the country.

Niger

Polity: Presidential parliamentary democracy
Economy: Capitalist
Population: 9,151,000
PPP: $820
Life Expectancy: 46.5
Ethnic Groups: Hausa (56 percent), Djerma (22 percent), Fulani (9 percent), Tuareg (8 percent), Arab, Dhaza, others
Capital: Niamey

Political Rights: 3
Civil Liberties: 5
Status: Partly Free

Overview: Political squabbling and ethnic violence threatened Niger's transitional democracy, but by year's end a renewed truce with Tuareg rebels was holding, and strong union pressure forced compromise between Niger's two most powerful politicians.

Niger experienced three decades of one-party and military rule by Hausa and Djerma ethnic leaders following independence from France in 1960. A one-party, nominally civilian state replaced thirteen years of military rule in 1987, when General Ali Seibou became head of state and leader of the National Movement of Society for Development (MNSD). In 1990, Niger joined Africa's trend toward democratization. The umbrella Niger Union of Trade Union Workers (USTN) organized massive demonstrations, and international pressure complemented internal demands for reform. A 1991 all-party conference agreed on a transitional High Council of State to prepare a constitution which was overwhelmingly approved by national referendum late in 1992. February 1993 legislative elections deemed free and fair by international observers returned a majority for Ousmane Mahamane's Alliance of Forces for Change (AFC). Ousmane won a five-year presidential term a month later.

Democratization faltered in 1994 amid political infighting and open rebellion. Defections cost the AFC its majority, and new elections were called for January

1995. The elections, judged credible, gave the MNSD forty-three of eighty National Assembly seats. MNSD leader Hama Amadou was named prime minister. By mid-1995, the rivalry between the president and the premier threatened to paralyze the government as each issued contradictory decrees, raising the specter of confrontation between the presidential guard and the army. In August, USTN leaders threatened mass strikes to oust both if there was no compromise, and the two quickly reached agreement.

Threats of renewed rebellion by Tuareg nomads diminished in December after clashes in the north almost pushed Niger to renewed war. Violence over four years had killed hundreds amid serious rights abuses. Negotiators reaffirmed a general amnesty and 24 April peace pact between the government and the Armed Resistance Organization, granting Tuareg demands for autonomy and development of their desert homelands. But while Tuareg areas settled down, new violence flared in the extreme southeast. Democratic Renewal Front (FDR) guerrillas, composed of Kanuri and Toubou people, engaged in sporadic actions to protest alleged discrimination. Also, student marches protesting economic difficulties and nonpayment of grants became riots. In a hopeful sign, the army has not intervened in Niger's democratic, if messy, political process.

Political Rights and Civil Liberties: Nigeriens elected their government freely for the first time in 1993. January 1995 elections were generally free and fair, and resulted in a new legislative majority and prime minister. The 1992 constitution provides for universal suffrage by secret ballot for all citizens over eighteen. The new system distributes power among the presidency, parliament and an independent judiciary, and the legislature includes special districts to represent ethnic minorities.

Freedom of expression is generally respected and reflected in a vigorous independent press. Under the 1992 constitution, a Superior Council of Communication (CSC) is charged with protecting the media. Private radio stations have been licensed, but the government dominates broadcasting and publishes a daily newspaper. Over a dozen private newspapers, some strongly partisan, publish regularly and carry a range of opinions. However, the Paris-based *Reporters sans Frontieres* warns that a bill before parliament requiring state media to report important "public declarations or demonstrations" could threaten media autonomy and restrict the CSC's role by giving the government a direct hand in editorial decisions.

Freedoms of assembly and association are largely respected, although authorities can prohibit gatherings they deem could provoke violence. Religious freedom is respected, but parties based on religion, ethnicity or region are barred. Many nongovernmental organizations function, including the National League for Defense of Human Rights and the Nigerien Association for the Defense of Human Rights, Democracy, Liberty and Development.

The judiciary is by law independent. The Supreme Court has demonstrated some real autonomy, but lower courts remain subject to local influences and constrained by lack of training and resources. Traditional courts handle some civil matters.

Women suffer extensive societal discrimination, and some laws apparently contradict constitutional guarantees. Women have inferior status in inheritance rights and divorce. Islamic fundamentalists have opposed revisions of the most discriminatory provisions. Domestic violence against women is reportedly widespread. Ethnic minorities have long asserted bias in development, education and employment; some have turned to armed rebellion.

The 1992 constitution formalized labor rights. Although the formal sector workforce is only about 5 percent, unionized civil servants and others exercise formidable power. A 1993 law requires advance notice and negotiations before a strike, and workers can be required to provide essential services. All collective bargaining agreements are negotiated under an agreement among government, employers and unions that defines work categories and wage guidelines. Labor issues could become increasingly contentious as the government applies structural adjustment programs, cutting the civil service and privatizing state enterprises.

Nigeria

Polity: Military   **Political Rights:** 7
Economy: Capitalist   **Civil Liberties:** 7*
Population: 101,232,000 **Status:** Not Free
PPP: $1,560
Life Expectancy: 50.4
Ethnic Groups: Hausa (21 percent), Yoruba (20 percent), Ibo (17 percent), Fulani (9 percent), Kanuri, others
Capital: Abuja
Ratings Change: *Nigeria's civil liberties rating changed from 6 to 7 because of increased repression against media and minority activists and no sign of early return to civilian rule.

Overview: **A** year of increasing desperation and repression in Nigeria seemingly reached its nadir on 1 October, when dictator General Sani Abacha used an independence day address to state that a return to civilian rule remained still at least three years away. That news was leavened by Abacha's announcement that death sentences pronounced by a secret military tribunal against alleged coup plotters had been commuted—under intense international pressure—to long prison terms, though other, secret executions were reported.

But in November a new low was struck with the execution of environmentalist and indigenous rights activist Ken Saro-Wiwa after his conviction on spurious murder charges. Nigerians' hopes for a return of the rule of law, and for an end to rampant lawlessness, corruption and drug trafficking, appeared increasingly distant as the military junta entrenched itself more firmly.

Since independence from British rule in 1960, Nigeria has known only ten years under elected governments. A succession of military dictatorships dominated by officers from the mainly Muslim north of the country has ruled the country for the past eleven years, and retained firm control over the far wealthier southern regions. June 1993 presidential polls were meant to mark Nigeria's full and final transition to civilian rule.

But the military regime of General Ibrahim Babangida quickly annulled the 1993 elections, won by southerner Chief Moshood K.O. Abiola. The military named an interim government charged with holding new elections, which even the least cynical observers did not expect to see anytime soon.

As strikes against a worsening economic situation wracked the country, the high court returned a surprise ruling declaring the interim government illegal. In November 1993, General Sani Abacha, a principal architect of previous coups, moved this time to take power for himself. All democratic structures were dissolved and political parties banned. A predominantly military Provisional Ruling Council was appointed.

In June 1994, Chief Abiola was arrested after declaring himself Nigeria's rightful president. General Abacha's 1 October 1995 speech promised a rotating presidency to assure that people from each region of Nigeria would have an opportunity to hold power. But it was an empty pledge; a compliant "constitutional convention" earlier in the year effectively had confirmed Abacha's open-ended term of office, and reshuffling within the ruling clique apparently has cemented his power for now. Further, the blatant rejection of the will of the people evidenced by the discarding of the June 1993 poll results offers little assurance that the military will honor any genuine future election.

The threat of political instability is also hindering Nigeria's economic prospects, as rampant corruption and widespread lawlessness in some areas discourage investment. The corruption is fed in part by large-scale drug trafficking. Some observers believe there is official participation in the trade, which includes massive transshipments of heroin from Asia, and the United States government says that at minimum Nigeria is not acting in good faith to curb trafficking. As a result, the U.S. has "decertified" Nigeria, a status that makes the country ineligible for foreign assistance beyond basic humanitarian aid. Decertification also requires that the U.S. vote against any loans to Nigeria from major multilateral development banks. Development prospects are also hindered by pervasive government involvement in the economy through parastatals and a plethora of other regulatory disincentives.

Despite nearly global condemnation, General Abacha appears intent on clinging to power. He is bolstered by his army, and also has money. Revenues from oil and gas extracted by European companies such as Shell (Anglo-Dutch), Elf (French) and Agip (Italian), which are expected to begin a $4 billion project soon, and American companies like Chevron, which signed a $320 million investment deal with the Abacha regime in March, help keep the dictatorship solvent.

Political Rights and Civil Liberties: Nigerians are denied their right to choose their government freely. Political activity outside state structures is banned. As repression continues, ethnic tensions remain high, and Nigeria's 100 million people are closer to serious internal conflict than at any time since the horrific civil war of 1967-70. Sporadic acts of anti-regime terrorism have occurred, including a sports stadium bombing that killed three people in Kwara State in May.

Treason trials by closed military tribunals (created by a previous military regime in 1976) of army officers and civilians accused of plotting a coup against Abacha dominated Nigeria's internal politics for much of 1995. Arrests were made at the end of December 1994 and in March 1995 after allegations of coup attempts. Whether any such plot was set into motion or even existed is far from certain. In July, the tribunal handed down fourteen death sentences and several life terms. International media reports claim that dozens of other lower-ranking military men were summarily executed shortly after the purported 1 March coup attempt.

Most notable among those convicted were senior politicians and ex-generals Olusegun Obasanjo and Shehu Musa Yar'Adua. Obasanjo had led a previous military regime from 1976-79, but handed power to a civilian government, and was pressing General Abacha to do the same. Yar'Adua was the number two in the same military regime, and was seen in some quarters as a compromise civilian successor to Abacha. Several prominent journalists were found guilty of allegedly concealing information about the plot. Charles Obi, editor of *Weekend Classique,* Chris Anyanwu, editor-in chief-of the *Sunday Magazine*, George Mba, assistant editor of *Tell* magazine, and reporter Kunle Ajibade were given life sentences by a secret military tribunal.

While the fourteen death sentences have been commuted, the military dictatorship has kept a tight rein on all opposition. Ken Saro-Wiwa's case is instructive. Saro-Wiwa provoked the army's wrath through writings and advocacy exposing military brutality against the southeastern Ogoni people, whose traditional land has been usurped and despoiled by oil drilling operations. The regime's response to Saro-Wiwa's campaign was his arrest on what most observers believe are trumped-up murder charges and conviction by a special court that could not be appealed. Neither he nor eight others received the same "clemency" shown the alleged coup plotters.

Freedom of expression was dealt several other blows during the year as journalists were arrested and newspapers forced to suspend publication. As part of his 1 October speech, Abacha announced that bans would be lifted on some publications. The threat of renewed closure is creating greater self-censorship, however, as the threat of draconian action hangs over every Nigerian journalist.

Union activities remain tightly controlled. Four oil workers' union leaders have been detained incommunicado without charge since the army quashed industrial unrest in August and September 1994. The regime continues to interfere grossly in union affairs.

Religious strife has also flared, and June saw severe rioting in the northern city of Kano that was directed mainly at the area's Christian minority.

Norway

Polity: Parliamentary democracy
Economy: Mixed capitalist
Population: 4,344,000
PPP: $18,580
Life Expectancy: 76.9
Ethnic Groups: Norwegian, indigenous Finnish and Lappic (Saami) minorities, immigrant groups
Capital: Oslo

Political Rights: 1
Civil Liberties: 1
Status: Free

Overview: Remarkable political stability has emerged in the aftermath of last year's heated battle and referendum over European Union (EU) membership. After forming a coalition to defeat Prime Minister Gro Harlem Brundtland in her support of EU membership, environmentalists, leftists, nationalists, and rural and fishing lobbies have been hard-pressed to agree on much since. Consequently, deep divisions in the opposition have worked heavily in favor of the minority Labor government. In lieu of EU membership, Brundtland has been courting Asian countries and pursuing as close a relationship as possible with the EU short of full membership.

The Eisvold Convention, Norway's present constitution, was drawn up under a period of de facto independence just prior to the acceptance of the Swedish monarch as king of Norway in 1814. After the peaceful dissolution of its relationship with the Swedish crown, Norway chose a sovereign from the Danish royal house and began functioning as a constitutional monarchy with a multiparty parliamentary structure. A 165-member legislature, the *Storting*, is directly elected by universal suffrage and proportional representation for a four-year term. Once elected, the Storting selects one-quarter of its own members to serve as the upper chamber or *Lagting*. Neither body is subject to dissolution, although a vote of no confidence will result in the resignation of the cabinet. In such a case, the chairman of the party holding the most seats, exclusive of the party stepping down, will be asked to form a new government.

The present minority Labor government was formed following the 1993 general election in which Labor carried only 37 percent of the vote. Further disadvantaging Brundtland's government was the strong showing of the anti-EU Center Party at the expense of the pro-European Conservatives. Despite the EU referendum, which initially split the party, Brundtland's new approach to relations with the EU has met with considerable backing domestically as well as from Norway's European neighbors. The EU is expected to allow Norway into the Schengen accord on open borders, largely due to fellow Nordic nations' reluctance to break up their decades-old Nordic passport union. The country also enjoys virtually full access to the EU's single market through membership in the European Economic Area. Despite warnings of economic isolation outside the EU, the economy grew by almost 4.5 percent this year, unemployment continues to fall from its current 5 percent, and the government is set to invest its first surplus revenues in its Petroleum Fund next year.

Political Rights and Civil Liberties: Norwegians at home and abroad have the means to change their government democratically. Since 1989, the approximately 20,000 strong Lappic (Saamic) minority has elected an autonomous assembly that functions as an advisory body on matters including regional control of natural resources and preservation of Saami culture.

An independent judicial system headed by a Supreme Court, operates at the local and national levels. Judges are appointed by the king with advice from the ministry of justice. A special labor relations court handles all matters concerning relations between both public and private sector employers and workers, a majority of whom belong to labor unions.

Women constitute roughly 45 percent of the paid labor force, although half that number are employed part-time. Women workers are concentrated in lower-pay employment, primarily in sales, clerical and human services jobs. With more than one-third of the national legislature seats, and eight out of nineteen cabinet positions awarded to women in 1993, the Storting has the highest percentage of female representation of any national assembly.

The state finances the Evangelical Lutheran Church, in which more than 90 percent of the population holds at least nominal membership. While other churches receive public funding if they register with the government, there are some minor restrictions on religious freedom. For example, the law requires that the sovereign and at least half the cabinet must be Lutherans. Under certain circumstances, potential employers are permitted to inquire as to the religious convictions of job applicants. Discrimination on the basis of race, gender, language and class, however, are prohibited by law.

Freedom of the press is constitutionally guaranteed, and many newspapers are state-subsidized in order to support political pluralism. The majority of newspapers are privately owned and openly partisan. Broadcasting is also state-funded, but the government does not interfere with editorial content on radio and television. Private radio stations were authorized in 1982, followed by the first licensed commercial television channel in 1991. The Film Control Board has the right to censor blasphemous, overly violent and pornographic films. The power to censor alleged blasphemy, however, has not been exercised in over twenty years.

Oman

Polity: Traditional monarchy
Economy: Capitalist-statist
Population: 2,170,000
PPP: $11,710
Life Expectancy: 69.6
Ethnic Groups: Arab (74 percent), Baluchi, Zanzibari, Indian
Capital: Muscat

Political Rights: 6
Civil Liberties: 6
Status: Not Free

Overview:

Oman, an absolute sultanate located on the southeastern Arabian peninsula and several offshore islands, received independence from the British in 1951. In July 1970 the current sultan, Qabus ibn Sa'id al Sa'id, overthrew his father in a palace coup and began modernizing what had been a severely underdeveloped country. In 1971 the left-wing Popular Front for the Liberation of Oman began an insurrection in the southern Dhofar Province, which the government finally suppressed in 1975. Since then the sultan, who rules by decree with the assistance of a Council of Ministers, has faced little opposition.

In the spring of 1991, the sultan organized caucuses of prominent citizens in each of the country's fifty-nine provinces to nominate three citizens per province for a new *majlis al-shura* (consultative council). The sultan selected one nominee per province to sit in this majlis, which first convened in December 1991. The majlis comments on legislation and voices citizens' concerns but has no legislative powers. In 1994 the sultan named an expanded, eighty-seat majlis that will sit through 1997.

In early 1994, diplomats and visitors to Oman reported a spate of Islamic fundamentalist activism, possibly related to the rising unemployment rate among youths. In May, June and September police arrested at least 200 alleged fundamentalists and questioned dozens of others. The government ultimately tried 131 suspects before a State Security Court on charges of subverting national unity and using Islam for political purposes. In verdicts handed down on 12 November 1994, the court sentenced two defendants to death and the others to prison terms ranging from three to fifteen years. The sultan subsequently commuted the death sentences.

Political Rights and Civil Liberties:

Citizens of Oman lack the democratic means to change their government. The sultan holds absolute power and rules by decree, and there are no elections at any level. Political parties are strongly discouraged and none exists. The sultan limited the right to participate in the nominating process for the unelected majlis to prominent citizens. The sultan appoints provincial governors, and tribal leaders wield significant authority over local matters in rural areas. The only redress for ordinary citizens is through petitions to local governors, and through direct appeals to the sultan during his annual three-week tour of the country.

There are sporadic calls for autonomy from Shihayeen tribesmen in Rous al-Jibal Province on the Musandam Peninsula. The province is geographically separate from the rest of Oman, fronting the Straight of Hormuz and bordering the United Arab Emirates on three sides, and has been administered by Oman since 1970.

The sultan heavily influences the rudimentary judicial system, which operates mainly according to tradition. Police occasionally detain suspects without charge beyond the permitted twenty-four-hour period, and do not always permit attorneys to visit detainees. The criminal code does not outline the rights of the accused. In practice, defendants are presumed innocent and generally enjoy some procedural rights. However, the trials of suspected Islamic fundamentalists in 1994 (*see Overview above*) were held in secret in a special State Security Court and did not meet international standards.

All criticism of the sultan is prohibited, although citizens do criticize government policies. The 1984 Press and Publication Law permits the government to censor all publications. Omani journalists exercise significant self-censorship. Two of the four daily papers are owned by the government, and the other two rely heavily on government subsidies. Coverage in all four dailies supports government policies. The state-controlled television and radio broadcasts carry only official views, and the government does not permit private broadcast media.

By law, all public gatherings must be approved by the government, although this is not always strictly enforced. All associations must be registered, and the government permits only strictly nonpolitical groups. Islam is the official religion, and the majority of the population are Sunni Muslims. The authorities monitor mosque sermons. Christians and Hindus can worship freely, but non-Muslims may not publish religious books.

Despite some gains in career opportunities, women face discrimination in the job market. Women must receive permission from their husbands or male relatives to travel abroad, and under Islamic law receive half the inheritance that men do. Foreign women hired as domestic workers are sometimes harassed by their employers. Female genital mutilation is practiced in some rural areas.

The labor law makes no provision for trade unions, and none exists. Employers of more than fifty workers must form a body of labor and management representatives to discuss working conditions. However, these committees cannot negotiate over wages. Strikes are illegal, although brief strikes occasionally occur. Employers exercise significant leverage over foreign workers due to a requirement that employers provide them with letters of release before they can change jobs.

Pakistan

Polity: Presidential-par- **Political Rights:** 3
liamentary democracy **Civil Liberties:** 5
(military influenced) **Status:** Partly Free
Economy: Capitalist-statist
Population: 129,700,000
PPP: $2,890
Life Expectancy: 61.5
Ethnic Groups: Pujabi, Sindhi, Pathan, Urdu, Baluchi, Afghan, Mohajir, others
Capital: Islamabad
Trend Arrow: Pakistan's downward trend arrow reflects pressures from Islamic
fundamentalism as well as increasing civil strife in Karachi.

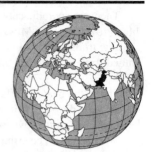

Overview: Prime Minister Benazir Bhutto faced an upsurge of Islamic
fundamentalist militancy in 1995 as well as continuing factional,
ethnic and sectarian violence in the commercial capital, Karachi.

Pakistan was formed in 1947 through the partition of India. In 1971, East
Pakistan separated to form Bangladesh. The 1973 constitution provides for a
National Assembly, which currently has 207 directly-elected seats and ten reserved
for non-Muslims, and an eighty-seven-seat Senate appointed by the four provincial
assemblies. The president is chosen for a five-year term by an electoral college
consisting of the national and provincial assemblies and the Senate.

In 1977, General Zia ul-Haq overthrew populist premier Ali Bhutto. In 1985,
with the country still under martial law, parliament approved the Eighth Amendment, which allows the president to dismiss the prime minister and dissolve
parliament. Zia and his successor, Ghulam Ishaq Khan, used the Eighth Amendment to sack three successive elected governments, most recently those headed by
Bhutto's daughter, Benazir Bhutto, in 1990, and Nawaz Sharif in 1993. In May
1993, the Supreme Court ruled the latter move unconstitutional as Khan had made
no effort at mediation. A deal brokered in July called for fresh elections in October.

At the 6 October elections Bhutto's Pakistan People's Party took eighty-six
seats; Sharif's conservative Pakistan Muslim League (PML) seventy-two; twelve
minor parties and fifteen independents took forty-three seats. Bhutto secured the
support of several independents to be named prime minister, and in November the
parliament elected Farooq Leghari, a Bhutto ally, as president.

Bhutto has faced an upsurge in Islamic fundamentalism and a series of law and
order crises. In response to the former, in early 1995 the government moved to regulate
foreign funding to the thousands of *madrassas* (Islamic schools) in Pakistan, many of
which are suspected of training militants. In September police arrested at least thirty-six
army officers for allegedly plotting a coup to establish an Islamic republic.

In Karachi, escalating factional, ethnic and sectarian violence killed over 1,500
people in 1995. In the Northwest Frontier Province (NWFP), in November 1994,
the army quelled a full-blown insurrection by tribesmen demanding the imposition
of Islamic law. In 1995, violence continued as tribesmen temporarily laid siege to
the province's Swat district.

Political Rights   **P**akistanis can change their government through reasonably
and Civil Liberties: free elections. However, democratic institutions are severely
  undermined by a weak rule of law and by the concentration of
political and economic power in the hands of a corrupt, nepotistic landowning elite. In
addition, there are several million bonded laborers and nomads who are ineligible to vote;
the over one million citizens of the Northern Areas are not represented in parliament; and
in the NWFP's Federally Administered Tribal Areas (FATA), parliamentary representatives are elected by tribal leaders, disenfranchising most of the two million Pashtun
tribesmen living there. The Bhutto government suspended provincial legislatures in the
NWFP in 1994, and in Punjab in 1995, to install more compliant chief ministers.

Police and soldiers kill scores of suspects annually in extrajudicial, staged
"encounters." Police routinely torture detainees to extract confessions, and
frequently rape female detainees and prisoners. Several prisoners die each year due
to mistreatment. In Karachi security forces have arbitrarily detained, tortured and in
some cases summarily executed hundreds of activists of the Mohajir Quami
Movement (MQM). Security forces are rarely punished for such offenses.

The Sunni-based *Sipah-e-Sahaba* and other Sunni and Shiite extremist groups
committed violent attacks during the year against civilians and against mosques of
rival groups. Several political parties, most notably the MQM, reportedly torture
opponents, and the MQM has killed hundreds of civilians in terrorist attacks.

The Bhutto government has resorted to widespread detention of opposition
activists before and during planned demonstrations, and has arbitrarily arrested and
detained political opponents. The judiciary is not independent. The president can transfer
judges and block tenure, and powerful individuals and Islamic fundamentalists exert
pressure on judges. The court system is severely backlogged. Special courts established
to try certain violent crimes do not afford defendants adequate due-process rights. In
the FATA, local leaders administer justice according to tribal customs.

Freedom of peaceful assembly is generally respected, although the government has
used excessive force during demonstrations in Karachi. Laws and constitutional provisions restrict freedom of expression regarding the army, Islam and other broad subjects.

Media freedom deteriorated in 1995, as authorities took numerous journalists
and editors to court on defamation and other charges. In March, the Supreme Court
formed a committee to investigate criticism of the judiciary in the media. In June,
the government banned six Karachi-based newspapers for sixty days but, faced
with a nationwide newspaper strike, lifted the ban within a week. Journalists are
frequently harassed by police and attacked by extremist groups. The government
controls nearly all electronic media, regulating content.

The 1979 Hadood Ordinances, which authorize strict punishment for violating Islamic
behavioral codes, have never been implemented but remain on the books. The 1986
blasphemy law and a 1992 law mandating the death penalty for blasphemy convictions
also remain unenforced. In February, a high court in Lahore overturned a lower-court death
sentence on two Christians accused of blasphemy. Nevertheless, in recent years Islamic
fundamentalists have arbitrarily killed several Christians accused of blasphemy.

Hindus, Ahmadis and other minority groups are often attacked and face
discrimination in education and other areas. Women face social discrimination, and
rape and domestic violence are serious problems. Under the Hadood Ordinances,
women must provide four male witnesses to prove they were raped. The accused

can file a countercharge of adultery, which carries the death penalty and thus deters many women from reporting rape. Several women are killed each year by male relatives in dowry disputes or for suspected adultery. Police rarely vigorously investigate cases involving violence against women.

Human rights activists are frequently harassed. Asma Jahangir, chairperson of the independent Human Rights Commission of Pakistan, has received death threats for criticizing the blasphemy law. The government has arrested and taken legal action against several activists working to end bonded labor. On 18 April, a gunman killed Iqbal Masih, a twelve-year-old who had publicized the severe problem of child labor.

Workers in agriculture, hospitals, radio and television and export-processing zones cannot form unions. The 1952 Essential Services Maintenance Act restricts union activity and strikes in numerous sectors. Due to legally mandated cooling-off periods and other restrictions, strikes rarely occur.

Palau

Polity: Presidential-leg- **Political Rights:** 1
islative democracy   **Civil Liberties:** 2
Economy: Capitalist   **Status:** Free
Population: 17,000
PPP: na
Life Expectancy: na
Ethnic Groups: Palauan (Micronesian, Malayan
and Melanesian), mixed Palauan-European-Asian, Filipino
Capital: Koror

Overview: These 200-odd Micronesian islands of the Carolines chain in the western Pacific were transferred from Spanish to German control in 1899. The Japanese seized the islands in 1914, and began a formal administration under a League of Nations mandate in 1920. The United States Navy took the islands in 1944, and in 1947 the possessions became part of the U.S. Trust Territory of the Pacific under a United Nations mandate.

A constitution adopted by referendum in 1979 vests executive powers in a directly elected president who serves a four-year term, with a vice-president elected on a separate ticket. The constitution also provides for a bicameral parliament with an eighteen-member Senate, and a sixteen-seat House of Representatives, with one member coming from each of the states.

Between 1983 and February 1990, the territory held seven plebiscites on a Compact of Free Association with the United States. Each plebiscite secured at least 60 percent support for the Compact, but none failed to cross the three-fourths threshold required for formal approval. The three-fourths threshold was legally necessitated due to the fact that while the Compact theoretically allows the U.S. to store or base conventional and nuclear forces on the islands, the constitution bans any weapons of mass destruction from Palau. Thus, approval of the Compact would require the three-fourths majority needed to concurrently amend the constitution. In November 1992, voters circumvented this by amending the constitution to require a simple majority for passage of the Compact. In concurrent balloting, Vice President Kuniwo Nakamura defeated challenger Johnson Toribiong in the presidential race.

Meanwhile, the changing geopolitical situation enhanced the credibility of the U.S. promise not to store, test or dispose of any nuclear or other nonconventional weapons on the islands. In November 1993, voters finally approved the Compact with a 68 percent majority. Under the Compact, Palau is a sovereign country but the U.S. remains responsible for defense. The U.S. is providing $442 million in aid over fifteen years in exchange for the right to maintain military facilities. In December 1994, Palau became the 185th member of the U.N.

Political Rights and Civil Liberties: Citizens of Palau can change their government democratically. Elections are competitive and tend to revolve around personalities and issues rather than party affiliations. The judiciary is independent of the government. The rule of law is strong. President Haruo Remelik was assassinated in 1985 in an act that did not appear to be politically motivated. His successor, President Lazarus Salii, killed himself in 1988 while facing allegations of fiscal mismanagement and official corruption. In another concern, Palau is increasingly being used as a transshipment point for illegal drugs going from Southeast Asia to the U.S.

Some sixteen clans wield fairly strong traditional authority, and there are often tensions between the chiefs and political leaders. The clans control land and sea rights, and have placed some property restrictions on foreigners. Noncitizens may not own land but may hold leases.

Palau is a matrilineal society, and each of the two traditional high chiefs is chosen by one of the two Councils of Women Chiefs. While women thus have a fairly high social status, domestic violence is nevertheless a problem. Freedom of association is respected, although there are few functional elements of civil society.

Panama

Polity: Presidential-legislative democracy
Economy: Capitalist-statist
Population: 2,631,000
PPP: $5,600
Life Expectancy: 72.8
Ethnic Groups: Mestizo (70 percent), West Indian (14 percent), European (10 percent), Indian (6 percent)
Capital: Panama City
Trend Arrow: The down trend arrow reflects concerns about authoritarian tendencies within the executive branch.

Political Rights: 2
Civil Liberties: 3
Status: Free

Overview: Bullying of the media and labor unions led to widespread protests and allegations of authoritarian government against President Ernesto Perez Balladares.

Panama was part of Colombia until 1903, when a U.S.-supported revolt resulted in the proclamation of an independent Republic of Panama. A period of weak civilian rule ended when a 1968 military coup brought Gen. Omar Torrijos to power

After the signing of the 1977 canal treaties with the U.S., Torrijos promised democratization. The 1972 constitution was revised, providing for the direct election of a president and a legislative assembly for five years. After Torrijos's death in 1981, Gen. Manuel Noriega emerged as Panamanian Defense Force (PDF) chief and rigged the 1984 election that brought to power the Democratic Revolutionary Party (PRD), then the political arm of the PDF.

The Democratic Alliance of Civic Opposition (ADOC) won the 1989 election, but Noriega annulled the vote and declared himself head of state. He was removed during a U.S. military invasion and ADOC's Guillermo Endara became president.

Endara's prestige plummeted and ADOC unraveled amid charges of corruption and poverty-fueled social unrest. In the 1994 election, the three main presidential candidates were the PRD's Perez Balladares, singer-actor Ruben Blades and Ruben Carles, a former official in the Endara government. Perez Balladares, a forty-seven-year-old millionaire and former banker, removed some of the Noriega taint by re-identifying the PRD with its late founder, Torrijos.

Perez Balladares won with 33.3 percent of the vote. The PRD won thirty-two of seventy-one seats in the Legislative Assembly and, with the support of allied parties that won six seats, achieved an effective majority.

Perez Balladares kept a campaign promise by choosing for his cabinet technocrats and politicians from across the ideological spectrum. In 1995, however, economic reforms, rising unemployment and a doubling of ministerial salaries led to widespread protests by labor unions and students. The president's popularity declined further when the government met protests with harsh crackdowns.

Political Rights and Civil Liberties: Citizens can change their government through democratic elections, and the constitution guarantees freedom of political and civic organization and freedom of religion. More than a dozen political parties from across the political spectrum participated in the 1994 elections.

However, political expression and civil liberties are undermined by the government's increasing tendency to bully the media and to use repressive measures against peaceful protests.

Labor unions are well organized. But labor rights were diluted in 1995 when Perez Balladares pushed labor-code revisions through Congress. When forty-nine unions initiated peaceful protests, the government cracked down in a series of violent clashes that resulted in four deaths and hundreds of arrests. According to UNICEF, the workforce includes over 60,000 children making less than the monthly minimum wage of $150.

The media are a raucous assortment of radio and television stations, daily newspapers and weekly publications. The 1994 election featured a televised presidential debate. However, restrictive media laws dating back to the Noriega regime remain on the books. Rather than eliminate them as he had promised, in 1995, Perez Balladares began to apply them against media critical of his government. The government also withheld government advertising from the daily *La Estrella de Panama* when it dropped Tomas Altimirano Duque, the nation's vice-president, as director of the newspaper. There is also a restrictive journalist-licensing law.

The Panamanian Defense Forces (PDF) were dismantled after 1989, and the military was formally abolished in 1994. But the civilian-run Public Force (national police) that replaced the PDF is poorly disciplined and prone to corruption and physical abuse. It includes former lower-ranking military officers whose loyalty to democracy remains in question. It has been ineffectual against the drug trade, as Panama remains a major transshipment point for both cocaine and illicit arms, and a money-laundering hub.

The judicial system, headed by a Supreme Court, was revamped in 1990. But it remains overwhelmed and its administration is inefficient, politicized, and undermined by the corruption endemic to all public and governmental bodies. The disarray is compounded by an unwieldy criminal code and a surge in cases, many involving grievances against former soldiers and officials which have accumulated over two decades of military rule.

In 1995, there were nearly 18,000 court cases pending, with the numbers climbing due to a drug-fueled crime wave. Less than 15 percent of the nation's prison inmates had been tried and convicted. The penal system is marked by violent disturbances in decrepit facilities packed with up to eight times their intended capacity. The country has barely more than twenty public defenders.

Since 1993, indigenous groups have protested the encroachment by illegal settlers onto Indian lands, and delays by the government in formally demarcating the boundaries of those lands.

Papua New Guinea

Polity: Parliamentary democracy (insurgency)
Economy: Capitalist
Population: 4,107,000
PPP: $2,410
Life Expectancy: 55.8
Ethnic Groups: Papuan, Melanesian, some 1,000 indigenous tribes
Capital: Port Moresby

Political Rights: 2
Civil Liberties: 4
Status: Partly Free

Overview: In 1995, Papua New Guinea Premier Sir Julius Chan took measures to reform the country's corruption-ridden provincial governments and to end the six-year-old secessionist insurgency on Bougainville Island.

This South Pacific country, consisting of the eastern part of New Guinea and some 600 smaller islands, won independence from Australia in September 1975. The 1975 constitution vests executive power in a National Executive Council consisting of a largely ceremonial governor-general, a prime minister and other ministers appointed by the premier. The unicameral parliament, which sits for a five-year term, has eighty-nine nationally elected seats, and twenty seats elected one apiece from the nineteen provinces plus the capital district of Port Moresby.

At the country's fifth post-independence elections in June 1992, the ruling, urban-based Papua New Guinea United Party (Pangu Pati), which had held thirty seats, took twenty-two. The People's Democratic Movement (PDM) took fifteen; People's Action Party, thirteen; People's Progress Party, ten; the Bougainville-based Melanesian Alliance, nine; three smaller parties, eight; and independents, thirty-one, with one seat vacant. In July, the new parliament elected PDM leader Paias Wingti, a former premier, to the top spot again over the incumbent, the Pangu Pati's Rabbie Namaliu.

In September 1993, Wingti pulled a "political coup" by resigning and immediately getting himself re-elected, thus winning, under a 1991 constitutional amendment, a fresh eighteen months of immunity from no-confidence motions granted to an incoming premier. In August 1994, the Supreme Court invalidated Wingti's election and ordered a new leadership poll. Parliament elected PPP leader Sir Julius Chan, the deputy premier and a former premier.

Chan immediately took steps toward ending the low-grade insurgency on the island of Bougainville, 560 miles northeast of the capital, that has been the country's most severe crisis since independence. In December 1988, miners and local landowners organized guerrilla attacks on the Australian-owned mine at Panguna to demand compensation and a 50 percent share of the profits. The mine closed in May 1989, but the newly styled Bougainville Revolutionary Army (BRA) then declared an independent Republic of Bougainville. In September 1994, Chan signed a preliminary peace pact with BRA leaders, and a ceasefire subsequently went into effect. On 10 April 1995, the government swore in a thirty-two member Bougainville Transitional Government, although the BRA refused to take the five seats allotted to it. Instead, in September the government entered into another round of inconclusive talks with the BRA's unofficial Bougainville Interim Government.

During the year, the government reformed the system of corruption-ridden provincial governments by naming an MP as governor of each province, while the former provincial premiers are now deputy premiers. However, the move will consolidate central power and risks inflaming secessionist tensions.

Political Rights and Civil Liberties:

Citizens of Papua New Guinea can change their government democratically, although national and provincial elections are generally marred by some violence and irregularities. Official corruption is rampant.

The judiciary is independent of the government. The press is vigorous, although the government restricts journalists' access to Bougainville. The state-run National Broadcasting Commission (NBC) exercises full independence in its news coverage. Police approval for public demonstrations is occasionally refused on public safety grounds. There is an increasingly active nongovernmental organization community.

The Defense Forces, army-backed militias and the BRA have carried out torture, disappearances, arbitrary detentions and extrajudicial executions against combatants and civilians on Bougainville island, although such incidents, as well as armed conflict, have decreased following the September 1994 ceasefire. Civilian administration is slowly being restored, but some areas are still under BRA control. There are reports of rape and harassment at army-run "care centers" on the island.

On the mainland, the police force continues to abuse detainees and prisoners. In the highlands, police occasionally burn homes to punish communities suspected of harboring criminals or of participating in tribal warfare, or as collective punishment for individual crimes. Tribal fighting in the highlands has killed dozens of people in recent years. Bands of criminals known as "rascals" have created a severe urban law-and-order crisis. In May 1993 parliament tightened the system of bail and passed an Internal Security Act (ISA), which allows police to operate without obtaining warrants in certain circumstances.

Women face significant social discrimination, and rape and domestic violence are serious problems. Foreign logging interests continue to swindle villagers and largely renege on promises to build local schools and hospitals, and are most likely behind the occasional attacks and death threats against forestry officials. There is full freedom of religion.

Workers are free to join independent unions and strike. The International Labor Organization has criticized a law allowing the government to invalidate arbitration agreements or wage awards not considered in the national interest.

Paraguay

Polity: Presidential-legislative democracy (military-influenced)
Economy: Capitalist-statist
Population: 4,960,000
PPP: $9,850
Life Expectancy: 74.6
Ethnic Groups: Mestizo (95 percent), Indian, European, black
Capital: Asuncion

Political Rights: 4
Civil Liberties: 3
Status: Partly Free

Overview: President Juan Carlos Wasmosy lost popularity amid corruption scandals and rising crime, while army commander Gen. Lino Oviedo, possibly the most powerful man in the country, continued to maneuver politically in defiance of the constitution.

After the 1989 coup that ended the thirty-five-year dictatorship of Gen. Alfredo Stroessner, Gen. Andres Rodriguez took over Stroessner's Colorado party and engineered his own election to finish Stroessner's last presidential term.

The Colorados won a majority in a vote for a constituent assembly, which produced the 1992 constitution. It provides for a president, a vice-president and a bicameral Congress consisting of a forty-five-member Senate and an eighty-member Chamber of Deputies elected for five-year terms. The president is elected by a simple majority and reelection is prohibited. The constitution bars the military from engaging in politics.

In the 1992 Colorado primary election Luis Maria Argana, an old-style machine politician, defeated construction tycoon Wasmosy. Rodriguez and Oviedo engineered a highly dubious re-count that made Wasmosy the winner.

The 1993 candidates were Wasmosy, Domingo Laino of the center-left

Authentic Radical Liberal Party (PLRA), and Guillermo Caballero Vargas, a wealthy businessman. Wasmosy promised to modernize the economy. Laino played on his decades of resistance to Stroessner. Caballero Vargas campaigned as a centrist free of the politics of the past.

Every poll showed Wasmosy trailing until three weeks before the election, when Oviedo threatened a coup if the Colorado Party lost, and stated the military "would govern together with the glorious Colorado party forever and ever." Fear of a coup proved decisive, as Wasmosy won with 40.3 percent of the vote. Laino took 32 percent and Caballero Vargas 23.5. The Colorados won a plurality of seats in each house of Congress.

Oviedo was then promoted to army commander, becoming the most powerful officer in the armed forces. Wasmosy has since allowed Oviedo to eliminate rivals from within the military by retiring them. Oviedo, backed by a hardline Colorado faction, appears to have been using Wasmosy as a stepping stone for achieving the presidency himself.

In August 1995, Oviedo held a political meeting with Colorado leaders, yet again flouting the prohibition against military interference in politics. A Colorado-linked judge turned aside opposition objections and Wasmosy, the nominal commander-in-chief, ruled that Oviedo did not have to go before Congress on the matter.

Meanwhile, the government took increasingly repressive measures to quell the labor strikes and demonstrations by peasants demanding land reform that have marked Wasmosy's entire term.

Political Rights and Civil Liberties: The 1992 constitution provides for regular elections. But elections are neither free nor fair because of military interference, and because of serious irregularities and incidents of fraud. Overall, the inordinate and illegal influence of the military greatly weakens the authority of the civilian government.

The constitution guarantees free political and civic organization and religious expression. However, political rights and civil liberties are undermined by the government's resort to repressive tactics during demonstrations and protests and the lack of rule of law.

Peasant and Indian organizations demanding land often meet with police crackdowns, detentions, and forced evictions by vigilante groups in the employ of large landowners. Over a dozen peasants have been killed in the ongoing disputes. Activist priests who support land reform are frequently targets of intimidation. The government's promise of land reform has been largely unfulfilled, as nearly 80 percent of agricultural land remains in the hands of foreign companies and a few hundred Paraguayan families.

There are numerous trade unions and two major union federations. Labor actions are often broken up violently by the police and military, with labor activists detained. The 1992 constitution gives public-sector workers the rights to organize, bargain collectively and strike, but these rights are often not respected in practice. A new labor code designed to protect worker rights was passed in October 1993, but enforcement has been weak.

The judiciary remains under the influence of the ruling party and the military, susceptible to the corruption pervading all public and governmental institutions, and mostly unresponsive to human rights groups presenting cases of rights violations committed either before or after the overthrow of Stroessner. Allegations include illegal detention by police and torture during incarceration, particularly in rural areas. Colombian narcotraffickers continue to expand operations in Paraguay, and accusations of high official involvement in drugs date back to the 1980s.

The media are both public and private. State-run broadcast media present pluralistic points of view and there are a number of independent newspapers. However, journalists investigating corruption or covering strikes and protests remain subject to intimidation and violent attacks by security forces. Free expression is also threatened by vague, potentially restrictive laws that mandate "responsible" behavior by journalists and media owners.

Peru

Polity: Presidential-military (insurgencies)
Economy: Capitalist-statist
Population: 23,981,000
PPP: $3,300
Life Expectancy: 66.0
Ethnic Groups: Indian (45 percent), mestizo (37 percent), European (15 percent), black, Asian
Capital: Lima

Political Rights: 5
Civil Liberties: 4
Status: Partly Free

Overview: President Alberto Fujimori was re-elected in April in what can best be described as a state-controlled plebiscite. Having consolidated his presidential-military regime, he suggested he might want to stay in power indefinitely.

Since independence in 1821, Peru has seen alternating periods of civilian and military rule. Civilian rule was restored in 1980 after twelve years of dictatorship.

Fujimori, a university rector and engineer, defeated novelist Mario Vargas Llosa in the 1990 election. In 1992 Fujimori, backed by the military, suspended the constitution and dissolved Congress. The self-coup was orchestrated by Vladimiro Montesinos, the de facto head of the National Intelligence Service (SIN), who engineered the support of the military. The move was popular because of people's disdain for Peru's corrupt, elitist political establishment and fear of the Shining Path guerrillas.

Fujimori held a state-controlled election for an eighty-member constituent assembly to replace the Congress. The assembly drafted a constitution effectively ratifying Fujimori's authoritarian rule, which was approved in a state-controlled referendum following Shining Path leader Abimael Guzman's capture.

Fujimori's principal opponent in the 1995 elections was former U.N. Secretary General Javier Perez de Cuellar, who vowed to end Fujimori's "dictatorship" and initially looked strong in opinion polls. Fujimori countered with a massive public-spending and propaganda campaign that utilized state resources, and was supported by the military. The SIN was employed to spy on and discredit Perez de Cuellar and other opposition candidates.

On 9 April Fujimori steamrolled to victory, outpolling Perez de Cuellar by about three to one, while his loose coalition of technocrats and sycophants won a majority in the new 120-seat Congress. Fujimori called it a victory for "direct government," stating, "This is a democracy in which the intermediaries, the political parties, are eliminated." In November, Fujimori suggested he might run again when his term ends in 2000.

Political Rights and Civil Liberties: The Fujimori government is a presidential-military regime with the trappings of formal democracy. Fujimori frequently voices his disdain for representative democracy and his own self-identification with the state.

The 1995 election was essentially a state-controlled plebiscite. While Fujimori was not unpopular, the massive use of state resources and the military and state intelligence during the campaign amounted to overkill. The Fujimori-controlled Congress later amended the electoral law to require 500,000 signatures to form a political party, yet another step toward eliminating political competition.

The military is virtually the president's political party. Gen. Nicolas Hermoza has remained military commander for over four years though he has surpassed the age limit for active duty. The SIN, unofficially headed by top Fujimori aide Vladimiro Montesinos, manages the political landscape.

Under the December 1993 constitution, the president can rule virtually by decree. Fujimori can dissolve Congress in the event of a "grave conflict" between executive and legislature, as he did in 1992. The constitution overturned Peru's tradition of no re-election. Fujimori's legal aides say he can remain president until 2005 because his 1995 election would mark his first term under the new constitution.

In 1994 a new, nominally independent election commission was named. But the regime-controlled Congress blocked the commission's attempts to limit the regime's overwhelming advantages in the 1994-95 campaign.

Fujimori shut down the judicial system in 1992, overhauled it and effectively made it an arm of the executive. Files on military corruption and involvement in drug-trafficking were removed from the courts. In 1994, judicial reforms were made and a new Supreme Court named. But judicial independence remains suspect as the regime has unhesitatingly overridden legal and constitutional norms when its interests have been at stake.

A draconian 1992 antiterrorist decree practically eliminates judicial guarantees in a system of military tribunals with anonymous judges installed to try alleged subversives. Defense lawyers may not call witnesses, government witnesses are unidentified and sentences are pronounced within hours. Amnesty International said there were at least 200 prisoners of conscience in 1995, in addition to nearly 4,000 imprisoned under the antiterrorism law. Despite government declarations that the Shining Path terrorist threat is virtually over, the faceless court system was extended in October 1995 for another year and nearly half the population remained under a militarized state of emergency.

In June 1995, the regime implemented an amnesty law absolving everyone implicated in human rights violations during the counterinsurgency against the Shining Path, thus reprieving hundreds of police and soldiers responsible for extrajudicial killings, rapes, disappearances and torture. The regime imposed a law dictating that the judiciary could not dispute the amnesty's constitutionality.

Human rights activists who protested the amnesty were subjected to anonymous death threats and occasionally violent intimidation by security forces.

Torture remains routine in police detention centers and conditions remain deplorable in prisons for common criminals, where up to 80 percent of those jailed have not been sentenced.

The new labor code restricts collective-bargaining rights and authorizes the government to disband any strike it deems to be endangering a company, an industry, or the public sector. Labor leaders who oppose privatization are subject to jail sentences of up to six years. Those who go abroad to criticize the government's failure to comply with international labor standards are called "traitors" and threatened with imprisonment. Forced labor, including child labor, is prevalent in the gold-mining regions of the Amazon.

The press is largely private. Radio and television are both private and public. State-owned media are blatantly pro-government. Since 1992, many media, especially television and print journalists have been pressured into self-censorship or exile by a broad government campaign of intimidation—death threats, libel suits, withholding of advertising, police harassment, arbitrary detentions and physical mistreatment. Since 1993, between ten and thirty journalists have been in jail at any one time. Most were charged with "apology for terrorism" and several were convicted in the faceless courts.

Philippines

Polity: Presidential-legislative democracy (insurgencies)
Economy: Capitalist-statist
Population: 68,424,000
PPP: $2,550
Life Expectancy: 66.3
Ethnic Groups: Christian Malay (92 percent), Muslim Malay (4 percent), Chinese (2 percent)
Ratings Change: *The Philippines's political rights rating changed from 3 to 2, reflecting a more transparent political system and a peace pact with a right-wing army group.
Capital: Manila

Political Rights: 2*
Civil Liberties: 4
Status: Partly Free

Overview: **P**hilippines President Fidel Ramos hit the halfway mark in his six-year term in May 1995 with a strong showing by his ruling coalition in congressional elections.

The Philippines, a 7,100-island archipelago in Southeast Asia, achieved independence in 1946 after forty-three years of United States rule and subsequent World War II Japanese occupation. Strongman Ferdinand Marcos ruled for twenty-one years until he was deposed in the February 1986 "people power" revolution, in which thousands protested his alleged victory over Corazon Aquino in massively rigged elections. After several top military officials declared their support for Aquino, including acting army chief of staff Fidel Ramos, Marcos fled the country and Aquino took office. The February 1987 constitution provides for a directly elected president (the vice-president is elected separately) limited to a single six-year term, and a bicameral Congress consisting of a twenty-four-member Senate and a House of Representatives with 201 directly elected members and up to fifty more appointed by the president.

Ramos won the May 1992 presidential election with just 23.5 percent of the vote. One-time actor Jaime Estrada won the vice-presidential race. In concurrent lower-house balloting, the centrist Democratic Filipino Struggle (LDP) coalition won eighty-seven seats. Ramos' Lakas-NUCD took fifty-one; the conservative National People's Coalition, forty-eight; and the centrist Liberal Party, fifteen. In June Ramos took office in the first peaceful transfer of power since 1965.

Midway through his term, Ramos has successfully pushed through an economic deregulation program, although few of the benefits of the country's recent GDP growth have filtered down to the masses. Nevertheless, at the 8 May 1995 congressional elections, a pro-Ramos coalition of the Lakas-NUCD party and the LDP took nine of twelve Senate seats contested, and over half of the 201 House seats. Even as he consolidated power, Ramos continued to deny charges that congressional allies are seeking to amend the constitution to keep him in power past 1998, either by scrapping the single-term limit or by installing a parliamentary system that would allow him to remain in power as premier.

In 1995, Ramos also reached a peace pact with the right-wing Reform the Armed Forces Movement, which had launched several coup attempts against Aquino. During the year talks resumed with the Communist Party of the Philippines, which since 1969 has waged an insurgency through its New People's Army (NPA), and with the Moro National Liberation Front (MNLF), which is seeking autonomy for predominantly Muslim provinces on southern Mindanao Island.

Political Rights and Civil Liberties: Filipinos can change their government democratically, although violence and irregularities continue to mar elections. The rule of law is weak, and political power is disproportionately held by economic oligarchies, wealthy landowners and political elites. Official corruption is rampant.

Security forces continue to commit human rights violations, although the number of such incidents has declined in the past two years along with decreased insurgency action. The army and the 65,000-strong Citizens Armed Forces Geographical Units (CAFGU), a poorly trained paramilitary force used to maintain security in formerly Communist-controlled areas, carry out arbitrary arrests, disappearances and extrajudicial killings. Police reportedly torture suspects, particularly during interrogations. Police and soldiers are also frequently involved in bank robberies, kidnappings (particularly of ethnic Chinese) and other illicit activities.

The NPA is responsible for extrajudicial executions, torture and kidnappings, as well as bombing attacks, assassinations and other forms of urban terrorism. Although a ceasefire with the MNLF and a breakaway faction, the Moro Islamic Liberation Front, has largely held, the Muslim-extremist Abu Sayyaf group has continued a string of kidnappings, extrajudicial executions and other rights violations. A 4 April attack by the extremist group on the town of Ipil on Mindanao killed at least fifty-three people. Politicians and wealthy landowners maintain several hundred private armies, many of which include police and army personnel and are responsible for extrajudicial killings.

The judiciary is independent of the government, although the judicial process favors politically connected and wealthy individuals, and the system is heavily backlogged. The private press is vigorous, although journalists face intimidation outside Manila from illegal logging outfits, drug smugglers and others. Freedom of assembly is generally respected, although in May 1994 the Ramos Administration tried to ban a private meeting regarding East Timor. The Supreme Court overruled the government, but authorities barred foreign participants from attending. During political demonstrations, police generally follow a policy of "maximum tolerance," giving nonviolent protesters substantial leeway. There are numerous nongovernmental organizations and civil society is well developed. However, security forces frequently accuse human rights activists of having links with the Communist insurgency, thus creating a climate that leads to abuses including arbitrary detentions, torture and occasional extrajudicial killings of activists.

Freedom of religion is respected. Trafficking of Filipino women abroad is a serious problem, and domestic prostitution, including child prostitution, is rampant. Rape and domestic violence are widespread. Cities have large numbers of street children. The government has forcibly resettled tenant farmers and urban squatters to make way for development projects.

Workers are free to join independent unions. The International Labor Organization has criticized several labor code provisions restricting the right to strike, including a 1989 law allowing the government to order compulsory arbitration of disputes in industries deemed essential to the national interest. Police continue to harass strikers, and several labor activists have been extrajudicially executed in recent years. Anti-union discrimination has prevented workers from organizing in all but one of the country's export processing zones (EPZ). Most egregiously, in the Rosario EPZ south of Manila, the provincial government has colluded with businesses to suppress trade union activity, and workers frequently receive less than the minimum wage.

Poland

Polity: Presidential-parliamentary democracy
Economy: Mixed capitalist
Population: 38,613,000
PPP: $4,380
Life Expectancy: 71.1
Ethnic Groups: Polish (8 percent), German, Ukrainian, Belarusian
Capital: Warsaw

Political Rights: 1*
Civil Liberties: 2
Status: Free

Ratings Change: *Poland's political rights rating changed from 2 to 1 because of further democratic consolidation.

Overview: Lech Walesa, founder of the Solidarity trade union movement that helped topple Poland's Communist regime, was defeated for re-election as president in November by

Alexander Kwasniewski, leader of the post-Communist Democratic Left Alliance (SLD), which won control of parliament in 1993. A political crisis loomed at year's end following Walesa's allegations that Prime Minister Josef Oleksy, named to his post in March, had had close, longtime contacts with Soviet and Russian intelligence.

Partitioned by Prussia, Russia, and Austria in the eighteenth century, Poland re-emerged as an independent republic after World War I. In 1939, it was invaded and divided between Nazi Germany and Stalinist Russia, coming under Germany's full control after its 1941 invasion of Russia. After the war, its eastern territories stayed part of Ukraine but it acquired large tracts of eastern Prussia. The Communists gained control after fraudulent elections in 1947.

In 1980, striking workers in the Gdansk shipyards established the Solidarity free trade union. In December 1981, after Solidarity threatened a national referendum on the Communist government, Gen. Wojciech Jaruzelski declared martial law, banned Solidarity and detained most senior activists.

In 1989, roundtable discussions between the opposition and the Communists ended Communist dominance. In 1992, a "Little Constitution" gave considerable power to Walesa, who was directly elected in 1990. The combination of a fragmented parliament, with some thirty parties, and a powerful president led to a series of failed governments, while radical market reforms steadily improved economic conditions.

In 1993, Poles swept former Communists back into power under a new electoral law designed to reduce the number of parties in parliament. The SLD won 171 seats in the 460-seat *Sejm* (lower house), followed by the Peasant Party (PSL), a descendant of the Communist-era party, with 131 seats. The Democratic Union, the mainstream Solidarity party, captured 74 seats; the leftist Union of Labor, 41; Walesa's Non-Party Bloc to Support Reform, 20; and the nationalist Confederation for an Independent Poland, 24. The PSL's Waldemar Pawlak was named prime minister.

In early 1995, Walesa and the Pawlak government battled over issues, including taxes and the appointment of defense, internal and foreign ministers, which under law must be approved by the president. A rift also developed in the ruling SLD-PSL coalition over Pawlak's political style, the sluggish pace of economic reform and his confrontations with Walesa. With the president threatening to dissolve parliament, opposition groups called for a caretaker nonparty government of national unity.

In March, after a three-month crisis, Walesa agreed to the appointment of parliamentary speaker Josef Oleksy of the SLD as prime minister of a new coalition government, the sixth in post-Communist Poland. Oleksy had headed the 1989 roundtable negotiations.

The key political event in 1995 was November's presidential election. By late summer, Walesa—whose poll ratings had fallen to single digits—had nearly caught up with frontrunner Kwasniewski by emphasizing his anti-Communist credentials. But many Poles continued to see Walesa as a meddler who had split Solidarity, undermined past democratic governments and waged a personal war against the ex-Communist-dominated parliament. As expected, Kwasniewski led in the 5 November first round by 35.1 percent to Walesa's 33.1 percent. Kwasniewski won the 19 November runoff with 51.7 percent, with strong support among younger voters, the unemployed and pensioners. At his 22 December swearing-in, Kwasniewski vowed to continue market reforms and press for Poland's entry into the European Community and NATO.

Kwasniewski was almost immediately embroiled in controversy when Walesa and the outgoing interior minister claimed to have documentary proof that Oleksy had held regular meetings with Soviet and Russian intelligence since at least 1983. Oleksy denied the charges in a 27 December radio interview, rejecting calls for his resignation or a temporary leave of absence. A parliamentary commission was preparing to investigate the matter at year's end.

Political Rights and Civil Liberties:

Poles can change their government democratically. In 1992 Walesa signed into law a "Little Constitution" giving the president considerable power, including approval of defense, interior, and foreign ministers.

Most of Poland's estimated 200 political parties are small or exist mainly on paper. The 1993 parliamentary and 1995 presidential elections were free and fair. Five teams of judges examined some 593,000 complaints stemming from the presidential elections. Two teams concluded that while Kwasniewski had lied about his college education, this did not influence the outcome of the vote. The results were ultimately confirmed.

There is a bustling free and independent press, and 85 percent of the media is private. Article 270 of the Penal Code states that anyone who "publicly insults, ridicules, or derides the Polish nation, Polish People's Republic, its political system, or its principal organs may be punished by between six months' and eight years' imprisonment." Article 273 imposes a prison term of up to ten years for violating Article 270 in print or through the mass media. The law has been enforced on several occasions. Foreign ownership of newspapers and magazines is limited to 45 percent.

Freedoms of discussion, assembly and association are respected. Religious freedom is respected, although critics have charged that the Roman Catholic Church exercises undue influence on public life, particularly regarding the drafting of a new constitution. Anti-Semitism is a problem confronting Poland's 10,000-15,000 Jews, and a sermon by Walesa's priest in Gdansk included anti-Semitic references. But Jewish cemeteries and synagogues have been restored, and there are cultural centers and schools, many supported by U.S.-based foundations.

The judiciary is not wholly free of government interference, and financial and personnel woes continue to plague the justice ministry, the prosecutor's office and the courts. Most judges are Communist-era holdovers. Political parties, parliamentary commissions, the State Security Office (under interior ministry jurisdiction), the government and the president's office continue to exert political pressure on the justice minister and prosecutors.

Four national interbranch industrial unions are registered, along with seventeen other major independent industrial branch unions and three agricultural unions. The Independent Self-Governing Trade Union Solidarity claims 2 million members. Spinoffs from mainstream Solidarity include the Christian Trade Union Solidarity (16,200 members) and Solidarity '80 (156,000 members). The National Alliance of Trade Unions, the successor to its Communist-era namesake, has about 3 million members and sixty-one parliamentary deputies. Other unions include the Free Miners' Union, which claims over 300,000 members, and the National Teachers' Union. There were several strikes in 1995, including railway and health-service workers.

While the extant constitution guarantees gender equality, women face discrimination in the job market. Anecdotal evidence suggests a significant level of domestic violence, particularly in rural areas, often involving alcoholism and spousal abuse. As many as 20,000 nongovernmental organizations of various types operate in Poland.

Portugal

Polity: Presidential-parliamentary democracy
Economy: Mixed capitalist
Population: 9,424,000
PPP: $9,850
Life Expectancy: 74.6
Ethnic Groups: Portuguese, African minority
Capital: Lisbon

Political Rights: 1
Civil Liberties: 1
Status: Free

Overview: After leading his Social Democratic Party to two absolute majorities in 1987 and 1991, Prime Minister Anibal Cavaco Silva stepped down as party leader, opting to enter the presidential race rather than face the possibility of heading an unstable minority or coalition government. His successor, former defense minister Fernando Nogueira, was defeated by Antonio Guterres whose Socialist Party (PS) won over 43 percent of the vote and fell just short of a parliamentary majority. The new prime minister faces the task of bringing Portugal into closer integration with the European Union (EU) and preparing a 1997 budget that will qualify the small, vulnerable economy for the European single currency by 1999.

After amassing a vast colonial empire, Portugal's monarchy ended in a bloodless revolution in 1910. The subsequent republic, plagued by chronic instability and violence, ended in a military revolt in 1926, followed by Antonio Salazar's fascist dictatorship from 1932 to 1968. After intermittently liberalizing and suppressing political opposition, Salazar's successor, Marcello Caetano, was overthrown by the Armed Forces Movement in the "Carnation Revolution," a bloodless coup in 1974. The transition to democracy began the following year with the election of a constitutional assembly that adopted a democratic socialist constitution.

Cavaco Silva's ascension to power marked the end of a period of political and economic instability following the revolution. He oversaw the country's entry into the European Community (EC) in 1986 and a subsequent influx of EC funds largely responsible for an era of modernization and economic stabilization. His popularity waned in mid-1992 with the onset of an economic recession, and more recently with allegations of government and PSD corruption and inefficiency. In October, Cavaco Silva joined another prominent candidate, Socialist mayor of Lisbon Jorge Sampaio, in the race for a five-year term as president. The president serves as military chief of staff and chairs the sixteen-member Council of State, a consultative body with powers of absolute veto in regard to defense and military policy. He plays an additional, limited role as political arbiter and constitutional guardian.

The platforms upheld by both Social Democrats and Socialists in the latest parliamentary elections were virtually identical, with the focus mainly on free-market policies and closer integration into the EU. In a close race until the end, Guterres and Nogueira campaigned to mobilize a weary electorate on their twenty-seventh call to the polls in just twenty-one years. A year from now, Guterres's government will have to hit a deficit target of 3 percent of GDP in the 1997 budget if Portugal is to qualify for the European single currency and avoid isolation on the periphery of an expanding EU.

Political Rights and Civil Liberties: **P**ortuguese have the right to change their government democratically. In direct, competitive elections, both the president and parliament are chosen by voters including a large number of Portuguese living abroad. Political association is unrestricted with the exception of fascist organizations. In some instances, members of small extreme-right groups have run candidates for public office without interference.

Freedoms of assembly and speech are respected with few exceptions. Although the law forbids insults directed at the government or the armed forces with the intention of undermining the rule of law, the state has not exercised its right to prosecute under this provision,

The print media are owned by political parties and private publishers. They are generally free and competitive. Until 1990, television and radio stations were state-owned with the exception of the Catholic radio station *Radio Renascenca*. Substantial legislation aimed at reprivatizing state-run stations controlled by *Radiodifusao Portuguesa* resulted in the launching of three private stations in 1994. Although television broadcasting remains dominated by the state-owned *Radiotelevisao Portuguesa,* by mid-1994 two independent stations had begun operation.

Workers have the right to strike and are represented by competing Communist and non-Communist organizations. In recent years the two principal labor federations, the General Union of Workers and the General Confederation of Portuguese Workers Intersindical, have charged "clandestine" companies with exploiting child labor in the impoverished north. The minimum employment age will be raised from fifteen to sixteen in January of 1997, when the period of compulsory schooling is due to be extended.

The status of women has improved with economic modernization. Concentrated in agriculture and domestic service, women workers now comprise 37 percent of the official labor force. Despite a few prominent exceptions, female representation in government and politics remains minimal, averaging less than 10 percent.

Qatar

Polity: Traditional monarchy
Economy: Capitalist-statist
Population: 525,000
PPP: $22,380
Life Expectancy: 70.5
Ethnic Groups: Arab (40 percent), Pakistani (18 percent), Indian (18 percent), Iranian
Capital: Doha

Political Rights: 7
Civil Liberties: 6
Status: Not Free

Overview:

Located on the northern coast of the Arabian Peninsula, Qatar became a British protectorate in 1916. Under the 1970 Basic Law, adult males of the Al Thani family choose an emir from among their number. The Basic Law also provides for a Council of Ministers and a partially elected *Majlis al-Shura* (Advisory Council). However, no elections have ever been held, and the majlis is appointed.

The country achieved independence from Britain in 1971. In 1972 Sheik Khalifa ibn Hamad Al Thani deposed his cousin, Emir Ahmad ibn 'Ali ibn 'Abdallah Al Thani, in a palace coup. Following two decades of autocratic rule under the Sheik Khalifa, in December 1991 fifty prominent citizens signed a petition calling for democratic reforms. The government interrogated several signers and prevented three from leaving Qatar to attend a pro-democracy conference in Kuwait. In September 1992, Saudi troops attacked a Qatari border post and killed two guards. Relations between the two countries remain tense.

On 27 June 1995, Crown Prince Hamad—long recognized as the real power in the country—deposed his father in a palace coup while the emir was in Switzerland. Diplomats suggested that Hamad wanted Qatar to take a stronger stance in the border dispute with Saudi Arabia. In November, the new emir told the Advisory Council that he was considering allowing municipal elections in the future, although he did not offer a date.

Political Rights and Civil Liberties:

Citizens of Qatar lack the democratic means to change their government. Political parties are illegal, and there are no elected political institutions at any level. The emir holds absolute power, serves as prime minister and appoints the cabinet. While the emir consults with leading members of society on policy issues and works to reach a consensus with the appointed majlis, the only recourse for ordinary citizens is to submit appeals to the emir.

The security apparatus includes the Interior Ministry's *Mubahathat* (Investigatory Police), which handles sedition and espionage cases, and the military's *Mukhabarat* (Intelligence Service), which monitors political dissidents. Both services can detain suspects indefinitely without charge while conducting an investigation, although long-term detention occurs infrequently.

These two units, together with the Interior Ministry's regular police and General Administration of Public Security unit, mostly monitor foreigners, who outnumber Qataris four to one.

The judiciary is not independent. Most judges are foreign nationals and the government can revoke their residence permits at any time. Civil courts have jurisdiction in civil and commercial disputes, while Islamic *Shari'a* courts handle criminal and family cases. In the Shari'a courts trials are not open to the general public, although family members are permitted, and lawyers only help the participants prepare cases and are not permitted in the courtroom. Non-Muslims cannot bring suits as plaintiffs in the Shari'a courts, limiting their ability to obtain legal redress.

Freedoms of speech, expression and press are severely restricted. Public criticism of the ruling family or of Islam is not permitted. The privately owned press exercises significant self-censorship. In mid-October Sheik Hamad nominally ended official censorship of newspapers, although it is too early to judge the practical effects of this action. The electronic media are state-owned and promote official views. A government censorship board screens all locally published books and cultural items. Academic freedom is not protected and university professors reportedly practice self-censorship. Civil society is limited to sports clubs, professional associations and other strictly nonpolitical organizations, which are monitored by the government.

Foreign nationals employed as domestic workers face sexual harassment and physical abuse. Although the authorities have investigated and punished several employers, most women apparently do not report abuse for fear of losing their residence permits.

Islam, as interpreted by the Wahabbi branch of the Sunni tradition, is the official religion. Non-Muslims may not worship publicly, and face discrimination in employment opportunities. Women face social as well as legal discrimination in divorce and inheritance matters. Men may prevent wives and other female relatives from traveling abroad, and women must get permission from male relatives to apply for driver's licenses. Children trafficked from South Asia and Africa are occasionally used as jockeys in camel races and face the threat of serious injury or death.

Workers cannot form labor unions or bargain collectively. Workers can belong to "joint consultative committees" composed of worker and management representatives that discuss issues including working conditions and work schedules, but not wages. If a dispute arises, the government's Labor Conciliation Board attempts to mediate. Most workers, with the exception of government employees and domestic workers, can hold strikes if mediation fails. Strikes rarely occur in practice, in part because employers may dismiss employees after the Board has heard a case. Employers sometimes exercise leverage over foreign workers by refusing to grant mandatory exit permits.

Romania

Polity: Presidential-par- **Political Rights:** 4
liamentary democracy **Civil Liberties:** 3
Economy: Mixed statist **Status:** Partly Free
transitional
Population: 22,687,000
PPP: $2,840
Life Expectancy: 69.9
Ethnic Groups: Romanian (88 percent), Hungarian (9 percent),
German, Roma (Gypsy)
Capital: Bucharest

Overview: In 1995, Romania under Prime Minister Nicolae Vacaroiu
showed increased economic stabilization and growth. But
ongoing tensions with the large Hungarian minority and
ultranationalist parties' continuing political influence complicated reform and
tarnished Romania's international image as it sought integration into European
structures.

Overrun by Ottoman Turks in the 1400s, Romania became independent
following the 1878 Berlin Congress. Romania gained territory after World War I,
but lost some to the Soviet Union and Bulgaria in 1940. King Michael took over in
1944, dismissed the pro-German regime and backed the Allies. In 1945, he was
forced to accept a Communist-led coalition government.

Nicole Ceausescu's autarkic economics and bizarre personality devastated
Romania during his 1965-89 rule. A popular uprising and palace coup by disgruntled Communists toppled Ceausescu, who was tried and executed on Christmas 1989. Anti-Ceausescu elements had secretly established the National Salvation
Front (NSF) and announced a provisional government under President Ion Iliescu,
a high-ranking Communist.

The 1992 local and national elections saw the NSF split between neo-Commu-
nist and more reformist members. Iliescu's new Democratic National Salvation
Front (DNSF) won a combined 163 of 484 seats in the bicameral legislature, and
the opposition coalition, the Democratic Convention (DC), won 116. The rump-
NSF under former Prime Minister Petre Roman held 61 seats; the ultranationalist
Romanian National Unity Party (PRNU), 44; the Democratic Union of Magyars in
Romania (UMDR), 39; the ultranationalist Greater Romania Party (PRM), 22; the
pro-Communist Socialist Labor Party (SLP), 18; the Agrarian Democrats, 5.
Minority representatives held the remainder. Parliament named Vacaroiu, a
nonparty financial expert, prime minister in November. In 1993, the DNSF and
several extra-parliamentary parties formed the Party of Social Democracy of
Romania (PSDR).

In early 1995, the PSDR signed a pact with the PRM, formalizing a tacit
agreement reached after the 1992 vote. The ultranationalist presence in junior
ministerial posts and in top-level government jobs in media, culture and education
exacerbated tensions with the Hungarian minority, foreign investors and diplomats.

In February leaders from the government, the PRNU and UDMR met in the U.S. with international mediators to try settling ethnic disputes blocking a treaty between Hungary and Romania—a condition for European Union (EU) and NATO membership. In June, Romania refused to include clear commitments to minority rights in the planned treaty, dampening chances for an agreement.

The opposition Democratic Convention fragmented in 1995, as the Liberal Party, Civic Alliance and UDMR departed. The opposition was further hurt in November by the death of staunch anti-Communist and National Peasant Party leader Coreliu Coposu. The ruling coalition also appeared strained. PRM Chairman Corneliu Tudor called Iliescu a "brash dictator" who had "delivered the country to the Jews." PRNU leader Gheorghe Funar also weighed in after Iliescu character-ized both men as "Romanian Zhirinovskys" during a U.S. visit. The PSDR severed ties with the PRM, which subsequently withdrew its support for the Cabinet, though the PSDR maintained its hold on parliament.

A new education law sparked student protests in October and rallies by Hungarians in December. Romanian students were protesting financial aid cuts, while the Hungarians said the law discriminated against their language.

Romania's economy grew in 1994-95 as conditions improved in Western Europe, Romania's main export market, and as a dynamic private sector produced 35-40 percent of GDP. Improved macroeconomic indicators encouraged foreign investors. Authorities launched a mass privatization program in April under which Romanians would receive shares in some 2,500 state companies. But lack of laws on competition, procurement and intellectual property, combined with widespread corruption and incompetence among civil servants, hindered Romania's EU membership efforts.

Political Rights and Civil Liberties: Citizens can change governments democratically. The opposition claimed irregularities in 1992 elections, citing the high number of invalid ballots in particular.

Though over 300 legal parties exist, the PSDR and central government have purged many opposition local and regional officials elected in 1992. The govern-ment suspended 133 mayors for "breaking the law" and another 264 resigned. The EU claimed the central government was seeking to rebuild the undemocratic pre-1989 administrative system. Analysts say the dismissals are PSDR attempts to consolidate power before 1996 general elections.

In September, journalists from both private and state media protested legisla-tion stipulating long prison sentences on reporters convicted of libeling or insulting officials. The legislation was amended so as not to single journalists out, but prison sentences for libel and slander were maintained. The government controls the only nationwide television channel, although at year's end the private PRO-TV and Romania TV-International announced plans to expand programming. Government control of newsprint production and distribution has affected independent newspa-pers, many of which face financial difficulties. Private FM stations reach small audiences, and private television stations in the capital are restricted to local penetration.

Penal code amendments dealing with "spreading of false information that undermines state security" hinder free expression. Hungarians may not sing

Hungary's national anthem or raise its flag. Religious freedom is respected; clergy of some fifteen recognized denominations may receive financial support, and another 120 are entitled to juridical status and tax exemptions. Restitution of religious property remains unresolved.

Under a 1992 judiciary reorganization, the justice ministry controls judges' selection and advancement. Constitutional Court decisions may be overruled by a two-thirds vote in parliament, an infringement of judicial independence. Hungarians, Roma (Gypsies), and homosexuals face discrimination and arbitrary application of due process.

A labor superstructure, the NCRFTU-Fratia National Trade Union Confederation, was created in 1993. Workers frequently strike, and unions representing teachers, actors, health-care workers, energy and factory workers staged strikes in 1995.

Some 8,000 nongovernmental organizations range from business to political interest groups. Women are guaranteed equal protection and rights under law, but have faced discrimination in hiring and advancement. Corruption is a problem plaguing government agencies and business.

Russia

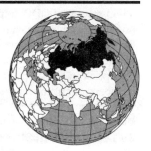

Polity: Presidential-parliamentary democracy
Economy: Mixed statist transitional
Population: 147,480,000
PPP: $6,140
Life Expectancy: 67.6
Ethnic Groups: Russian (82 percent), over 100 ethnic groups
Capital: Moscow

Political Rights: 3
Civil Liberties: 4
Status: Partly Free

Overview:
Communists and nationalists took firm control of Russia's parliament in December elections while an ailing, increasingly unpopular President Boris Yeltsin pushed liberal reformers out of government, raising doubts about economic reforms, foreign policy and Yeltsin's chances in elections scheduled for 1996. The ongoing rebellion in Chechnya further undermined the government's credibility and effectiveness.

Relations with the West were strained over Russian plans to sell reactors to Iran; opposition to NATO's eastward expansion; sparring over the war in Bosnia; support of lifting sanctions against Iraq; and deployment of troops in many former Soviet republics.

With the USSR's collapse in December 1991, Russia—the only constituent republic not to declare sovereignty—gained de facto independence under Yeltsin, elected Russian president in June. In 1992, Yeltsin was repeatedly challenged by a hostile, antireform legislature. Parliament replaced acting-Prime Minister Yegor

Gaidar, a principal architect of reforms, with Viktor Chernomyrdin, a Soviet-era manager.

In 1993, the Yeltsin-parliament struggle intensified over presidential powers and a new constitution. In September, Yeltsin suspended hardline Vice President Aleksandr Rutskoi, dissolved parliament and set parliamentary elections for December. Opposition deputies barricaded themselves in the parliamentary complex. In early October, after riots by extremists supporting the protesters, troops crushed the uprising, arresting Rutskoi and legislative speaker Ruslan Khasbulatov.

In November, Yeltsin approved a new constitution giving the president considerable power to appoint senior members of the executive and judicial branches and dissolve the lower house of parliament if it repeatedly declined his choice of prime minister or repeatedly voted a lack of confidence in the president. The draft proclaimed Russia "a democratic, federative, law-governed state," and guaranteed the full spectrum of human rights. It established a bicameral Federal Assembly: a Federation Council (Upper House) consisting of two representatives from the country's eighty-nine regions and territories, and a 450-member State Duma. In December, voters approved the constitution but elected ultranationalists, including Vladimir Zhirinovsky's Liberal-Democratic Party, and Communists. The Liberal-Democrats got 22.79 percent of the vote and fifty-nine seats; Russia's Choice, 15.38 percent and forty seats; the Communist Party, 12.35 percent and thirty-two seats. The centrist Women of Russia won twenty-one seats; the Agrarian Party, twenty-one; the Yavlinsky-Boldyrev-Lukin Bloc, twenty; Russian Party of Unity and Accord, eighteen; and the Democratic Party, fourteen.

Throughout much of 1994, Yeltsin sent mixed signals on the future of reforms. Deputy Prime Minister Gaidar, in charge of the economy, and Finance Minister Boris Fyodorov resigned charging irresponsible economic policies. Chernomyrdin declared the era of "shock reforms" over. The new government consisted mainly of industrialists and farm lobbyists. In June, Yeltsin reasserted his role in economic policymaking, announcing a series of decrees to loosen government export controls, reduce taxes, and define procedures for liquidating bankrupt state industries. A second wave of mass privatization was launched, but the government also renewed credits to state enterprises, weakening the ruble, which crashed in October. The following month, Yeltsin unnerved reformers and Western creditors with a rush of new appointments that promoted conservatives and reformers in roughly equal measure.

In December, Yeltsin ordered 40,000 troops to invade Chechnya, a Muslim-dominant region that had declared independence in 1991. The protracted, bloody campaign drew sharp criticism from democrats and Communists.

Chechnya, the parliamentary elections and Yeltsin's health problems colored his actions in 1995. The Chechnya debacle, in which tens of thousands of civilians were killed and the Chechen capital, Grozny, virtually razed, was dramatically brought home in June, when a Chechen separatist commander stormed the southern Russian town of Budyonnovsk and seized a hospital and over 1,000 hostages. At least 121 died in subsequent clashes with Russian forces. Although a partial accord was signed in July, sporadic firefights and bombings went on all year, eventually prompting a renewed Russian offensive.

The hostage situation sparked a political crisis when parliament moved for a no-confidence measure that would have forced Yeltsin to either fire his cabinet or dissolve parliament. In an eleventh-hour gesture of conciliation, Yeltsin fired three of the leading hawks in his government, including the national police chief and head of the renamed KGB security service, for their part in the hostage crisis. Opposition lawmakers mustered only 193 votes in favor of the motion, 33 short of the number required for passage.

The failure of the no-confidence motion emboldened Chernomyrdin, who vowed to continue tough economic reforms worked out with international lenders in the spring in the face of powerful vested interests in Russia's industrial establishment. But widening disparities between the small economic elite and those left out of the process, growing poverty, a dramatic rise in organized and violent crime, and business corruption combined to sour many Russians on the reforms. In August, the new centrist party created by Yeltsin and Chernomyrdin, Our Home is Russia, suffered a humiliating defeat in Yeltsin's home province of Sverdlovsk when its gubernatorial candidate lost by a two-to-one margin. The vote highlighted Yeltsin's declining popularity. Reformist parties such as Gaidar's Russia's Choice and Grigory Yavlinsky's Yabloko bloc attracted widespread resentment at the social costs of economic restructuring, though Yavlinsky himself remained popular.

Polls indicated that Communists led by Gennady Zyuganov and nationalists were poised to do well in December's elections. Though Russia's president wields much more constitutional power than its parliament, the vote was seen as a referendum on Yeltsin and his programs six months before scheduled presidential elections. Yeltsin's health problems complicated matters, as he was hospitalized for mild heart attacks in July and October.

In all, forty-three parties registered for the 17 December vote. Zyuganov, an uncharismatic apparatchik, portrayed himself to Western business leaders as amenable to economic reforms, though in the past he had called for the renationalization of industries and restoration of the Soviet Union. Other parties included Zhirinovsky's Liberal Democrats; the nationalist Congress of Russian Communities, spearheaded by popular Afghan war hero Gen. Alexander Lebed; Derzhava, led by the right-wing Aleksandr Rutskoi; the Agrarian Party; and Women of Russia.

In late October, the Central Electoral Commission created a furor when it banned Yabloko from competing in the elections. Russia's Supreme Court overturned the ruling on 4 November. Later that month, the Constitutional Court refused to hear a challenge to the electoral law by about 100 Duma deputies, who questioned a controversial requirement that parties win 5 percent of the popular vote to claim seats in parliament.

As expected, Communists and nationalists scored impressive victories. Nearly 70 million of 107 million eligible voters went to the polls. Each voter cast two votes—one for a single candidate and one for a party. Half the 450 members were elected in single-seat constituencies, and the rest according to party lists. The Communists took 157 seats; Our Home is Russia, 55; Liberal Democrats, 51; Yabloko, 45; Agrarians, 20; Democratic Choice, 9; Power to the People, 9; the Russian Communities, 5; and Women of Russia, 3. Independents won 77 seats, and the rest went to smaller parties. Some 1.3 million ballots were declared invalid.

Some experts estimated that the Communists, their allies and sympathizers among the independents controlled some 212 seats, just short of the 226 needed for a majority.

In his New Year's Eve address, Yeltsin reiterated his commitment to economic reforms and democracy, but with the likely ouster of moderate Foreign Minister Andrei Kozyrev and other reformers, as well as the removal of Tatiana Paramova as acting head of Russia's central bank, it appeared Yeltsin would jettison reformers in his bid for re-election in 1996.

The government continued to send mixed signals on the economy. In the first half of 1995, international lending institutions praised macroeconomic stabilization and the fiscal and monetary austerity outlined in a tough budget. But in mid-October, both Yeltsin and Chernomyrdin called for higher social spending and questioned the 1996 budget. The statements raised concerns in the IMF and suggested that government commitments to tough economic reforms were wavering prior to the elections. The second stage of privatization was also watered down, and other structural changes including tax reform remained unimplemented.

In foreign affairs, the Clinton-Yeltsin summit in May did not settle such central disputes as Russia's nuclear technology sales to Iran, and while Russia reiterated its commitment to NATO's Partnership for Peace, it remained staunchly opposed to NATO expansion into East-Central Europe. Russia maintained troops and "peace-keeping forces" in nine former republics, and tensions remained between Russia and Ukraine despite a deal on the Black Sea fleet.

Political Rights and Civil Liberties: Russians can change their government democratically. The 1993 constitution established a strong presidency, but decentralization and institutional checks limit executive authority. The 1995 parliamentary elections were generally free and fair, though over one million votes were invalidated.

Over 200 political parties exist, but most are small or inactive. With few exceptions, most political associations and groups lack a broad popular base and are built around parliamentary leaders and factions.

Although press freedom is legally guaranteed, in 1995 the media came under increased government pressure, particularly after the Chechnya crisis. Criminal gangs threatened, attacked and killed journalists to discourage reporting on criminal activity. Over 150 independent television and radio companies operate in Russia, and foreign cable and satellite broadcasts are available in large cities. In mid-1995, the State Press Committee announced that there were 10,500 newspapers in Russia, most with print runs of under 10,000 copies. In March, the popular executive director of Ostankino television, which went public in 1994, was murdered in a mafia-style hit. In August, the Glasnost Fund for the Protection of Journalists announced that not one month had gone by without the killing of a journalist on the territory of the former Soviet Union since 1993. Criminal proceedings were also launched against journalists: a writer for *Noviy Zglyad* was charged with "inflaming national, social and religious divisions" for reportage on Chechnya. Steve LeVine, a U.S. journalist who reported on Russian atrocities against Chechens, was denied entry into the country. Several newspapers faced financial pressures, including the influential *Nezavisimaya Gazeta*, a leading democratic publication, which claimed bankruptcy. State-controlled Public Russian Television was accused of censorship when it dropped a hard-hitting public affairs broadcast and former dissident Aleksandr Solzhenitsyn's weekly 15-minute slot.

Freedoms of assembly and religion are generally respected in this primarily Russian Orthodox country. There were reports of violence and intimidation directed at Evangelical Christians, especially in Muslim regions and southern Russia. Incidents of anti-Semitism were also reported. On 14 April, legislators passed an amendment to the 1990 law on religious freedom banning "creation and activities of religious associations which violate public safety and order."

Legal reforms are incomplete. A July 1993 law allows for the choice of a trial by jury for crimes such as treason, rape and murder in five oblasts. A controversial presidential crime decree allowed detention of suspects for thirty days without charge, the search of premises and company accounts without a warrant, and the use of evidence obtained by phone-tapping and infiltration of criminal gangs. In August, the Duma passed a law giving judges and jurors theoretical protections from illegal influence. But there is a shortage of lawyers and legal professionals— 28,000 public prosecutors and 20,000 independent lawyers for a population of 148 million. Russian prosecutors continue to have much broader powers than those in the West.

The Federal Security Service, a successor to the KGB, still enjoys extrajudicial powers, including the right to search premises without a court order. Pretrial detention centers are generally deplorable, and prisoners often languish for months in filthy, overcrowded cells before coming to trial. Police in the capital, Moscow, have been accused of racist attacks against ethnic minorities, particularly from the Caucasus, including arbitrary detention and searches, extortion and assault.

An independent commission report claimed serious, widespread human rights violations, citing ethnic and religious discrimination, labor exploitation, attacks on the media and violations of prisoners' rights. Abuses by Russian forces were rampant in Chechnya.

The Federation of Independent Unions of Russia, a successor to the Soviet-era federation, claims 60 million members (independent estimates put the figure at 39 million). Newer, independent unions represent between 500,000 and one million workers, including seafarers, dockworkers, air traffic controllers, pilots and some coal miners. There were several strikes, including a one-day walkout by coal miners in February. A multitude of nongovernmental organizations operate freely, including human rights organizations. Some extremist groups were banned after the October 1993 crisis.

Women are entitled to the same legal rights as men, and are well represented at many levels of the economy. However, women face discrimination in such areas as equal pay and promotions. Women's groups have raised such issues as domestic violence and women's role in society.

Rwanda

Polity: Dominant party
(military-dominated)
Economy: Mixed statist
Population: 7,794,000
PPP: $710
Life Expectancy: 47.3
Ethnic Groups: Hutu (90 percent), Tutsi (9 percent), Twa (1 percent)
Capital: Kigali
Ratings Change: *Rwanda's civil liberties rating changed from 7 to 6
because of improved security in most areas and a small but
significant revival of civil society.

Political Rights: 7
Civil Liberties: 6*
Status: Not Free

Overview:

Rwanda's new Tutsi-dominated government faced a year of continuing instability as Hutu extremists, with foreign cash, training and weapons, kept a firm hold over more than a million refugees along the country's frontiers and threatened to throw the country back into full-scale war. Sporadic killings and indiscipline by government forces, as well as rebel terror attacks, helped increase fear and uncertainty and thwarted efforts to encourage the refugees' return. A U.N. military observer presence will likely last only into early 1996, further raising uncertainty.

The rivalry between dominant Hutus and minority Tutsis is rooted in Belgian colonization, which created a country that forced the groups to vie for power in a modern state. Traditional Tutsi dominance ended with a Hutu rebellion in 1959 and independence in 1962. Hundreds of thousands of Tutsi were killed or fled the country over the next decades in recurring paroxysms of violence. In October 1990, the Tutsi-led Rwanda Patriotic Front (RPF) launched a guerrilla war to force the Hutu regime, then led by General Juvenal Habyarimana, to accept power-sharing and allow the resettlement of Tutsi refugees.

A half million people or more, mostly ethnic Tutsi but also including many politically-moderate Hutu, were massacred in 1994 in one of the swiftest acts of genocide ever recorded. The genocide was planned and encouraged by Hutu chauvinists intent on ending any claim to land and power by the Tutsi minority (roughly 15 percent of the 8 million pre-genocide population).

The immediate spark for the slaughter was the suspicious crash that killed Habyarimana, along with Burundian President Cyprien Ntaryamira, as their plane approached the airport at Rwanda's capital, Kigali. But the massacres had already been well planned; piles of machetes had been imported and death lists were read out over the radio. As the killings spread, a small U.N. force in Rwanda withdrew, and Tutsi rebels advanced. The only intervention came in late 1994, when French troops arrived in a futile effort to preserve some territory for the crumbling government army.

A huge international relief effort helped ease the suffering of over 2 million Hutu refugees along Rwanda's frontiers. But among refugees in Zaire were large numbers of ex-government troops. Credible reports claim French advisors and weapons, with the cooperation of Zairian authorities, have aided in rearming and retraining the defeated force, which is still commanded by the architects of the genocide.

In September, the U.N. Security Council voted to investigate arms shipments to these troops. An international tribunal that has struggled to collect evidence against the main actors in the genocide returned its first indictments in mid-December. But its work is hampered by scant funding, the near total breakdown of Rwanda's judicial system and a lack of access to suspects who have found safe haven in France and several African countries. An agreement to expedite return of refugees was brokered at a Cairo summit conference hosted by Jimmy Carter in December, but its implementation is uncertain and Rwanda could explode again into violence at any time.

Political Rights and Civil Liberties: Rwandans cannot change their government democratically. Elections were last held in 1988 under one-party rule. A 1992 power-sharing pact negotiated between the then-government and rebel RPF never came into force. The current government is self-appointed and dominated by the RPF, which took power after its capture of Kigali in July 1994, but includes representatives of other parties. A seventy-member, multiparty legislature was appointed in November 1994. No date for elections has been set, and the RPF is highly unlikely to allow voting on a one-person, one-vote basis, which would inevitably return power to the Hutu majority.

Several political parties exist, although a 1990 law prohibits parties based on ethnicity or religion. The new government also banned two parties closely identified with the 1994 massacres, but has made well-publicized efforts to include Hutu representatives in the government, including the appointment of President Pasteur Bizimungu. A Cabinet shakeup in September brought four new moderate Hutu ministers into the government.

Broadcast media are still controlled by the state, and a number of independent newspapers publishing in Kigali reportedly exercise considerable self-censorship. The role of the media in Rwanda has become a contentious test case for media freedom and responsibility. During the genocide, fifty journalists were among those murdered, while some of their colleagues, in particular radio journalists, played a major role in inciting the killings. Some journalists may be charged as accomplices to genocide. Suggestions of how best to combat such "hate media" range from bombing, to jamming radio stations, to setting up rival media outlets.

Freedom of religion is generally respected, although many clerics were numbered among both the victims and perpetrators of the genocide. A number of local nongovernmental organizations, including the Collective Rwandan Leagues and Associations for the Defense of Human Rights (CLADHO), operate freely. International human rights groups and relief organizations have been very active, although in December the government suspended operations of a number of these groups.

A high state of insecurity still prevails in some areas, especially in the west where Hutu extremists are launching incursions from Zaire. Massacres by government soldiers in May and September left at least hundreds of Hutu dead, but appeared to be the results of indiscipline and revenge rather than official policy. The killings did have a chilling effect on efforts to encourage the return of refugees from Zaire and Tanzania, however, as did the continuing arrests of genocide suspects within Rwanda.

At year's end over 60,000 people—many surely involved in the genocide but others likely arrested on false accusations—were held under poor conditions in prisons meant for only about one-third that number, and arrests were continuing. The virtual paralysis of the Rwandan justice system means little effective investigation is underway, and there is little likelihood that fair trials can be held anytime soon. A new five-member supreme court was appointed in October. Three of the four previous justices were genocide victims, and all but one-fourth of the country's 800 pre-April 1994 magistrates are dead or in exile. Meanwhile, constitutional and legal safeguards regarding arrest procedures and detention are largely ignored.

Women also receive legal protection, but there is serious de facto discrimination. In 1994, rape by government forces and Hutu militias was widespread. Other constitutional provisions provide for labor rights, including the right to form trade unions, to engage in collective bargaining and to strike. Yet the genuine exercise of any rights is now at best problematic, as Rwanda struggles to reestablish a ravaged economy and society and faces the continued specter of renewed war.

St. Kitts-Nevis

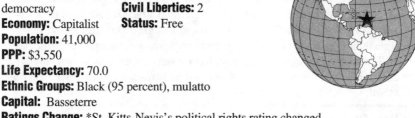

Polity: Parliamentary democracy
Economy: Capitalist
Population: 41,000
PPP: $3,550
Life Expectancy: 70.0
Ethnic Groups: Black (95 percent), mulatto
Capital: Basseterre
Ratings Change: *St. Kitts-Nevis's political rights rating changed from 2 to 1 because it held a free and fair election in which an opposition party came to power.

Political Rights: 1*
Civil Liberties: 2
Status: Free

Overview: In July, the opposition St. Kitts Labour Party (SKLP) led by Denzil Douglas won a resounding election victory over the People's Action Movement (PAM) of Kennedy Simmonds, which had been in power for fifteen years.

The nation consists of the islands of St. Kitts (St. Christopher) and Nevis. The British monarch is represented by a governor-general, who appoints as prime minister the leader of the party or coalition with at least a plurality of seats in the legislature.

The constitution provides for a National Assembly, with members elected for five years from single-member constituencies, eight on St. Kitts and three on Nevis. Senators, not to exceed two-thirds of the elected members, are appointed, one by the leader of the parliamentary opposition for every two by the prime minister.

Simmonds came to power in 1980 with the support of the Nevis Reformation Party (NRP) and led the country to independence in 1983. The center-right PAM-NRP coalition won majorities in the 1984 and 1989 elections.

Nevis has its own Assembly consisting of five elected and three appointed members. Nevis is accorded the right to secession if approved by two-thirds of the elected legislators and endorsed by two-thirds of voters in an island-wide referendum. In the 1992 Nevis Assembly elections, the newly founded Concerned Citizens Movement (CCM) won three of five seats.

In the 1993 vote, the SKLP and the PAM each won four seats. On Nevis the CCM took two seats and the NRP one. The CCM opted to support neither the PAM nor the SKLP, leaving the PAM-NRP coalition with a plurality of five seats. In accordance with the constitution, Governor General Clement Arindell asked Simmonds to form a new government.

An outraged Douglas and the SKLP, which had actually won the popular vote, called for a shutdown of the country to protest the new government. That led to violent disturbances and Arindell declared a two-week state of emergency. The SKLP boycotted parliament in 1994.

In fall 1994, the Simmonds government was shaken by a drugs-and-murder scandal that involved the deputy prime minister and two of his sons, and the killing of a police official who had been investigating a third son's murder.

The weakened government agreed to new elections by November 1995 during a "forum for national unity" chaired by the Chamber of Commerce and attended by the main political parties and civic organizations.

The 1995 election, held on 3 July, again featured a face-off between the fifty-seven-year-old Simmonds and the forty-year-old Douglas. This time voters overcame their fear of the fiery Douglas and opted overwhelmingly for change as the SKLP won seven of eight seats on St. Kitts, even defeating Simmonds in his own constituency. On Nevis, the CCM retained its two seats and the NRP held on to the third.

Political Rights and Civil Liberties: Citizens are able to change their government through elections. Constitutional guarantees regarding free expression, the free exercise of religion and the right to organize political parties, labor unions and civic organizations are generally respected.

However, civil liberties were undermined in 1995 by provocative political demonstrations that resulted in violent clashes with police, and by an upsurge in violent drug-related crime.

Moreover, the hemispheric drug and money-laundering trade has penetrated political parties and the economy to some degree, as evidenced by the 1995 scandal involving the PAM (*described above*) and by the business relations between leaders of the now ruling SKLP and Noel "Zambo" Heath, a known drug trafficker.

The judiciary is independent and the highest court is the West Indies Supreme Court (based in St. Lucia), which includes a Court of Appeal and a High Court. In certain circumstances, there is right of appeal to the Privy Council in London.

The rule of law, traditionally strong, has been tested by increasing drug-related crime and corruption. In 1995, it appeared that the police had become divided along political lines between the two main political parties. The national prison is overcrowded and conditions are poor.

The main labor union, the St. Kitts Trades and Labour Union, is associated with the ruling SKLP. The right to strike, while not specified by law, is recognized and generally respected in practice.

Television and radio on St. Kitts are owned by the government and opposition parties habitually claim the ruling party takes unfair advantage. Each of the major political parties publishes a weekly or fortnightly newspaper. Opposition publications freely criticize the government. There is a religious television station and a privately owned radio station on Nevis.

St. Lucia

Polity: Parliamentary democracy
Economy: Capitalist
Population: 144,000
PPP: $3,026
Life Expectancy: 72.0
Ethnic Groups: Black (90 percent), mulatto
Capital: Castries

Political Rights: 1
Civil Liberties: 2
Status: Free

Overview: The government of Prime Minister John Compton was buffeted by a major corruption scandal and had to contend, too, with strikes in the banana industry and public sector job actions.

St. Lucia, a member of the British Commonwealth, achieved independence in 1979. The British monarchy is represented by a governor-general.

Under the 1979 constitution, there is a bicameral parliament consisting of a seventeen-member House of Assembly elected for five years, and an eleven-member Senate, with six senators appointed by the prime minister, three by the leader of the parliamentary opposition, and two by consultation with civic and religious organizations. The prime minister is the leader of the majority party in the House. The island is divided into eight regions, each with its own elected council and administrative services.

The leftist St. Lucia Labour Party (SLP) won the 1979 elections, but factional disputes within the SLP led to new elections in 1982. The radical faction led by George Odlum broke off to form the Progressive Labour Party (PLP). The 1982 elections saw the return to power of Compton and the center-right United Workers Party (UWP).

The UWP won again in the 1987 and 1992 elections against the SLP, which had declared a social democratic orientation under the leadership of Julian Hunte. The PLP won no seats in either contest.

The 1992 campaign was bitter, marked by a few violent incidents, a dispute over boundaries between electoral districts, and an exchange of personal accusations, including one by *The Star*, an anti-Compton weekly, that alleged the sixty-five-year-old prime minister had had an affair with a teenage student. But the electorate was not distracted from the core issue, the economy.

St. Lucia has experienced economic growth in recent years, at a time when many of its Caribbean neighbors have been struggling. Despite the need for improved social services—one of the SLP's main campaign planks—voters in 1992 returned the UWP to power, increasing its parliamentary majority to 11-6 over the SLP.

In 1995, the Compton government continued to grapple with strikes and disruptions in the banana industry, which employs about 30 percent of the work force. Farmers remained disgruntled over low prices set by the government because of increased competition from Latin America. At mid-year there was a six-week public strike over salary demands. Despite subsequent negotiations, the issue remained unresolved by late fall.

Also in 1995, an official Commission of Inquiry concluded that St. Lucia's ambassador to the United Nations, Charles Flemming, had misappropriated more than U.S.$100,000 in U.N. funds. It dismissed Flemming's claim that he had sought and disbursed the funds with the approval of Compton. But the scandal hurt Compton as it came amid a swirl of other allegations about wrongdoing in his government.

Political Rights and Civil Liberties:

Citizens are able to change their government through democratic elections. Constitutional guarantees regarding the right to organize political parties, labor unions and civic groups are generally respected, as is the free exercise of religion.

The competition among political parties and allied civic organizations is heated, particularly during election campaigns when there are mutual charges of harassment and occasional violence. Opposition parties have complained intermittently of difficulties in getting police permission for demonstrations and charged the government with interference.

Newspapers are mostly private or sponsored by political parties. The government has been charged with trying to influence the press by withholding government advertising. Television is privately owned. Radio is both public and private. In late 1995, the government refused to reissue a license for Radyo Koulibwi, a small FM station critical of the ruling party.

Civic groups are well organized and politically active, as are labor unions, which represent a majority of wage earners. However, legislation passed in 1995 restricts the right to strike. The measure provides for a fine of about U.S. $2,000 or two years' imprisonment for inciting any person to "desist from performing...any lawful activity on his property or on the property of another person." The government said the measure was aimed at curtailing strikes in the banana industry.

The judicial system is independent and includes a High Court under the West Indies Supreme Court (based in St. Lucia), with ultimate appeal under certain circumstances to the Privy Council in London. Traditionally, citizens have enjoyed a high degree of personal security. However, an escalating crime wave, much of it drug-related, violent clashes during banana farmer strikes and increased violence in schools have produced great concern among citizens. Prisons are greatly overcrowded.

St. Vincent and the Grenadines

Polity: Parliamentary democracy
Economy: Capitalist
Population: 116,000
PPP: $3,322
Life Expectancy: 71.0
Ethnic Groups: Black, mulatto
Capital: Kingstown

Political Rights: 2
Civil Liberties: 1
Status: Free

Overview: **D**eputy Prime Minister Parnel Campbell resigned amid a scandal involving an offshore bank loan, prompting Prime Minister James Mitchell to postpone plans to retire at the end of his term.

St. Vincent and the Grenadines is a member of the British Commonwealth, with the British monarchy represented by a governor-general. St. Vincent achieved independence in 1979, with jurisdiction over the northern Grenadine islets of Beguia, Canouan, Mayreau, Mustique, Prune Island, Petit St. Vincent and Union Island.

The constitution provides for a fifteen-member unicameral House of Assembly elected for five years. Six senators are appointed, four by the government and two by the opposition. The prime minister is the leader of the party or coalition commanding a majority in the House.

In 1994, Mitchell won a third term when his center-right New Democratic Party (NDP) won twelve seats. The other three seats were won by the SVLP-MNU, an alliance between two center-left parties—the St. Vincent Labour Party, which had held power in 1979-84, and the Movement for National Unity.

In the campaign the SVLP-MNU charged Mitchell with abuse of power during his previous term when the NDP held all fifteen seats. The NDP emphasized its record on economic growth.

The SVLP-MNU charged that there were voter registration irregularities and that the government had failed to comply with a constitutional provision that calls for an electoral boundaries commission to review constituency lines prior to elections after a national census. The SVLP-MNU presented a series of motions to invalidate all or part of the elections. By fall 1995, many had been struck down by the High Court, but some appeals were pending.

Meanwhile, the SVLP-MNU united to form the Unity Labour Party (ULP). Former SVLP leader Vincent Beache was elected ULP leader. MNU leader Ralph Gonsalves was elected deputy leader.

In mid-1995, Deputy Prime Minister Campbell faced charges of financial impropriety because he had disregarded government regulations by taking a loan from an offshore bank. With the ULP pressing for a no-confidence vote in parliament, Campbell resigned. Mitchell, prime minister since 1984, then stated he would postpone plans to retire at the next general election.

Political Rights and Civil Liberties: Citizens can change their government through elections. However, the legitimacy of the 1994 elections was tainted by apparent registration irregularities and the government's failure to comply with a constitutional provision requiring an electoral boundaries review after a national census.

It remained unclear to what extent irregularities caused some eligible voters to be disenfranchised, but they were not so extensive as to alter the overall outcome of the vote. But the lack of a boundaries review meant that voters may have been disproportionately distributed in some existing constituencies, which could have affected the result in those constituencies.

Constitutional guarantees regarding free expression, freedom of religion and the right to organize political parties, labor unions and civic organizations are generally respected.

Political campaigns are hotly contested, with occasional charges from all quarters of harassment and violence, including police brutality, as well as allegations of funding from drug traffickers. The 1994 campaign saw an ugly rock-throwing clash between supporters of the main parties that left one NDP supporter dead.

Labor unions are active and permitted to strike. Nearly 40 percent of all households are headed by women, but the trend has yet to have an impact in the political or civic arenas.

The press is independent, with two privately owned independent weeklies, the *Vincentian* and the *News*, and a few fortnightlies run by political parties. The opposition has charged the *Vincentian* with government favoritism. Radio and television are government-owned. Television offers differing points of view. Equal access to radio is mandated during electoral campaigns, but the ruling party takes inordinate advantage of state control over programming.

The judicial system is independent. The highest court is the West Indies Supreme Court (based in neighboring St. Lucia), which includes a Court of Appeal and a High Court, one of whose judges is resident on St. Vincent. There is a right of ultimate appeal in certain circumstances to the Privy Council in London.

The independent St. Vincent Human Rights Association has criticized long judicial delays and the large backlog of cases caused by a shortage of personnel in the local judiciary, and has charged that the executive at times exerts inordinate influence over the courts. Prison conditions remain poor and there are allegations of mistreatment.

Penetration by the hemispheric drug trade is increasingly a cause for concern and there are allegations of drug-related corruption within the government and police force, and of money-laundering in St. Vincent banks. The drug trade has also caused an increase in street crime.

San Marino

Polity: Parliamentary democracy
Economy: Capitalist
Population: 25,000
PPP: na
Life Expectancy: 76.0
Ethnic Groups: Sammarinese (78 percent), Italian (21 percent)
Capital: San Marino

Political Rights: 1
Civil Liberties: 1
Status: Free

Overview:

The oldest and second smallest republic in the world, San Marino was reputedly founded by a stonemason in the fourth century. Although the Sammarinese are ethnically and culturally Italian, their long history of independence dates from Papal recognition in 1631. An 1862 customs union with Italy began an enduring relationship of economic, political, foreign affairs and security cooperation. Despite substantial reliance on Italian assistance ranging from budget subsidies to news media, San Marino has maintained its own political institutions and became a full member of the United Nations in 1992.

Legislative power rests with a unicameral, sixty-member Grand and General Council directly elected by proportional representation every five years. Directly elected Auxiliary Councils serving two-year terms and led by an elective Captain are the arbiters of local government in each of the country's nine "castles." The legislature appoints two captains-regent—one representing the city of San Marino and one the countryside—to exercise executive authority for six-month terms. The legislature also appoints a ten-member Congress of State, consisting of the heads of government administrative departments, to assist the captains-regent.

The government extends official recognition to seventeen communities of the more than 10,000 Sammarinese living abroad. Official recognition carries the possibility of government subsidies for office space and travel. The state also funds summer education and travel programs to bring Sammarinese students living abroad to the republic.

Political Rights and Civil Liberties:

Sammarinese are able to change their government democratically. In 1993, the foreign ministry covered 75 percent of travel costs for emigrants to return to the republic and vote. Adult suffrage has been universal since 1960. The 1974 elections were the first in which women were permitted to stand as candidates for seats in the Grand and General Council.

San Marino carries on a long tradition of multiparty politics, with six parties represented in the current Council. Although the ruling center-left coalition maintained a substantial majority in the 1993 elections, three smaller parties emerged including a hard-line splinter group from the recently reconstituted Communist party. Free association is permitted in all social, religious and political groups as well as trade unions.

An independent judiciary based on Italian law encompasses justices of the peace, a law commissioner and assistant law commissioner, the criminal judge of the Primary Court of Claims and two Appeals Court judges. A Supreme Court of Appeal, the *Consiglio de XII*, acts as a final court of appeal in civil cases.

The press in San Marino is free, and Italian newspapers and broadcasts are readily available. Although no dailies exist, the government, some political parties, and the trade unions publish periodicals, bulletins and newspapers. *Radio Titano* is privately operated and remains the country's only broadcasting service. An information bulletin called *Notizie di San Marino* is broadcast daily over *Radio Televisione Italiano*.

The republic has a vibrant, primarily private-enterprise economy. In addition to agriculture, principal economic activities include livestock raising, light manufacturing and tourism, which is the leading source of foreign exchange. Trade is dominated by Italy in accordance with a customs union agreement stipulating that the larger country will contribute to its small partner's budget in exchange for a monopoly of its markets.

Although immigrants and refugees are eligible for citizenship only after thirty years' residence, San Marino claims never to have refused asylum to people in need. Another citizenship law prohibits the foreign spouses and children of female Sammarinese, but not those of their male counterparts, from automatically gaining citizenship.

Sao Tome and Príncipe

Polity: Presidential-parliamentary democracy
Economy: Mixed statist (transitional)
Population: 140,000
PPP: $600
Life Expectancy: 67.0
Ethnic Groups: Mulatto majority; Portuguese minority
Capital: Sao Tome

Political Rights: 1
Civil Liberties: 2
Status: Free

Overview: An abortive, bloodless coup disrupted this tiny island nation's democratic government for eight days in August 1995. About forty of the army's junior officers stormed the presidential palace before dawn on 15 August, arrested President Miguel dos Anjos Trovoada, dissolved parliament, suspended the four-year-old constitution and placed the prime minister under house arrest. Facing international condemnation and threats by the U.S. and Europe to cut off aid, coup leaders freed the president and entered into mediated talks with political leaders and Angolan negotiators. The soldiers were granted amnesty and the democratic government returned to power.

Sao Tome and Principe, two islands about 125 miles off the coast of Gabon in the Gulf of Guinea, became Portuguese territories in 1522 and 1523, and a collective Portuguese Overseas Province in 1951. In 1973, the Portuguese government granted local autonomy and the following year began negotiating independence with the Movement for the Liberation of Sao Tome and Principe (MLSTP). A nationalist group originally formed in 1960 as the Committee for the Liberation of Sao Tome and Principe, the MLSTP oversaw a transitional government established after independence was declared on 12 July 1975. Until an August 1990 referendum established multiparty democracy, the MLSTP remained the only legal party and its leader, Manuel Pinto da Costa, served as president. In March of 1991 Trovoada, an independent candidate backed by the opposition Democratic Convergence Party, became the first democratically elected president.

Although the August coup ended with the peaceful restoration of the democratic government, coup leaders publicly claimed success. The objective was never to seize power, they said, but simply to draw attention to the grave problems that the country faces. The action was at least partially motivated by economic frustrations, as army wages had not been paid for six months and the president had scaled back the military early in his administration. Coup leaders reportedly gained widespread support from frustrated residents of the poverty-stricken island. Trovoada's government made promises of jobs and money before coming to power, but has been unable to stop the cocoa-based economy from declining. The island has a $260 million foreign debt and nearly 40 percent unemployment.

Political Rights and Civil Liberties: Citizens of Sao Tome and Principe can change their government democratically. Free and fair legislative elections in October 1994 marked the first time in Africa that a former ruling party was able to regain its majority through peaceful, democratic elections.

The August 1990 referendum established an independent judiciary headed by a Supreme Court whose members are designated by and responsible to the Assembly. The system, however, remains overburdened, understaffed and underfunded.

The constitution provides for freedom of the press and freedom of expression. The government controls most print and broadcast media, including newspapers, a radio and a television station, and STP-Press, a cooperative effort between the Angola News Agency and Sao Tome's national radio station. Pamphlets criticizing the government circulate freely. A 1994 law allows the opposition to take part in controlling the state-owned media and requires the ruling party to consult with the opposition on "major issues of political interest."

Citizens have the constitutional right to assemble and demonstrate with forty-eight hours' advance notice to the authorities. They may also travel freely within the country; however, exit permits are required to travel abroad. Roman Catholicism is the dominant religion, but freedom of religion is respected. Women hold a limited number of leadership positions, although most occupy domestic roles. Most islanders live in poverty due to an ailing economy that relies on cocoa for three-quarters of all export earnings.

Saudi Arabia

Polity: Traditional monarchy
Economy: Capitalist-statist
Population: 18,486,000
PPP: $9,880
Life Expectancy: 69.7
Ethnic Groups: Arab (90 percent), Afro-Asian (10 percent)
Capital: Riyadh

Political Rights: 7
Civil Liberties: 7
Status: Not Free

Overview: In 1995, Saudi Arabia's King Fahd continued to crack down on a largely nonviolent but radical Islamic fundamentalist opposition.

King Ibn Saud consolidated the Nejd and Hejaz regions of the Arabian Peninsula into the Kingdom of Saudi Arabia in 1932, and incorporated Asir a year later. Since the king's death in 1953, successive members of the Saud family have ruled this absolute monarchy. The king rules by decree and serves as prime minister, appointing all other ministers. The current ruler, King Fahd, assumed the throne in 1982. Crown Prince Abdallah serves as deputy prime minister, while the king's brother, Prince Sultan, is the defense minister.

During the 1990-91 Gulf crisis, the kingdom allowed some 500,000 Western soldiers to be stationed on its soil. This widened a rift between conservatives, including the ruling family and business interests, and an increasingly vocal core of Islamic fundamentalists.

In May 1993, several Islamic fundamentalists announced the creation of the Committee for the Defense of Legitimate Rights (CDLR), headed by Muhammad al-Masaari, a radical cleric, to press for a more rigorous application of Islamic laws. The highest government-appointed religious body, the *Ulemas* (Muslim Scholars) Council, promptly banned the CDLR, and Masaari subsequently fled the country.

In September and October 1994, the government detained 157 Islamic fundamentalists who were protesting the recent arrests of two prominent clerics. Although authorities released most of the detainees by mid-October, several remained imprisoned by year's end.

In August 1995, the government beheaded Abdalla al-Hudaif, a CDLR supporter, following secret trials in which nine other activists received lengthy sentences. On 13 November a car-bomb attack at a military communications center in Riyadh, believed to be the work of fundamentalists, killed several people. By late 1995, there were serious concerns over the health of the beleaguered King Fahd. Adding to the king's woes is a fiscal austerity program, introduced in 1994 to cope with shrinking oil revenues, that has shredded a social compact in which the public had largely tolerated the corrupt and authoritarian regime in exchange for lavish social spending.

Political Rights and Civil Liberties: Saudi citizens cannot democratically change their government. Political parties are illegal, the king rules by decree, and there are no elections at any level. In December 1993 King Fahd inaugurated an appointed *Majlis al-Shura* (Consultative Council), consisting of sixty pro-regime businessmen, technocrats and tribal leaders. The body lacks real authority and is not broadly representative of the population.

The judiciary is not independent of the government. The legal system is based on a strict interpretation of *Shari'a* (Islamic law). Police routinely torture detainees, particularly Islamic fundamentalists and non-Western foreigners, to obtain confessions. Defense lawyers are not permitted in the courtroom, and trials are generally closed and are conducted without procedural safeguards. In some cases non-Arabic foreigners are not provided with translators. Beheadings are carried out for rape, murder, drug trafficking and other offenses, and the large majority of those executed are foreigners.

Suspects arrested by the Interior Ministry's General Directorate of Intelligence, also known as the *Mubahith*, are often held, incommunicado, for weeks or months without being charged. Since 1993, the authorities have arbitrarily detained several hundred nonviolent Islamic fundamentalist activists. In recent years, hundreds of Shiites and Christians have also been arbitrarily detained.

Criticism of the royal family, the government or Islam is not permitted. The government has imposed gag orders on several radical clerics, and in September 1994 arrested two CDLR members for refusing to comply. A 1965 national security law prohibits newspapers from reporting on any public criticism of the government, while a 1982 media policy statement restricts coverage on several broad topics. The government frequently provides newspapers with official views on sensitive issues. The Interior Minister must approve and can remove all editors-in-chief, and the government has fired or transferred editors-in-chief on numerous occasions. The privately-held press practices substantial self-censorship. The government owns all radio and television stations, and news coverage reflects its views. Since March 1994, the government has barred Saudis from owning satellite dishes.

The government must grant permission to form associations, and only strictly nonpolitical groups are permitted. Political assemblies are prohibited.

Islam is the official religion and all citizens must be Muslims. The Shiite minority, which is concentrated in the Eastern Province, faces significant official discrimination in employment opportunities and religious affairs, including restrictions on the private construction of Shiite mosques. Worship by non-Muslims is prohibited.

Women are segregated in workplaces, schools and restaurants, and must wear the *abaya*, a black garment covering the entire head, body and face. The official Committee for the Promotion of Virtue and the Prevention of Vice's *Mutawwa'in*, essentially religious police, harass women for violating conservative dress codes or appearing in public with an unrelated male, and occasionally enter homes without obtaining a warrant. Informal Islamic vigilante groups also patrol neighborhoods.

Women must obtain permission from close male relatives to travel internally or abroad, cannot drive cars, and are informally prevented from working in certain fields. Women also face legal discrimination in divorce and inheritance matters, and domestic violence is reportedly common. African nationals reportedly practice female genital mutilation in some areas.

Foreign-born domestic workers face physical and sexual abuse, are forced to work long hours and are sometimes denied their wages. The court system discriminates against African and Asian workers, and this inability to obtain redress through the courts allows their employers to take advantage of them. Employers generally hold the passports of foreign employees and must obtain exit visas for them, and in practice use this as leverage in resolving business disputes, or as a means of forcing employees to do extra work. The government prohibits trade unions, and collective bargaining and strikes are illegal.

Senegal

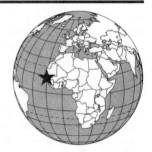

Polity: Dominant party
Economy: Mixed
capitalist
Population: 8,312,000
PPP: $1,750
Life Expectancy: 49.3
Ethnic Groups: Wolof (36 percent), Mende (30 percent),
Fulani (17 percent), Serer (16 percent), others
Capital: Dakar

Political Rights: 4
Civil Liberties: 5
Status: Partly Free

Overview: President Abdou Diouf reestablished a national unity government in March, quieting opposition concerns that dated from his February 1993 re-election and that mounted when economic dislocation followed the CFA franc's January 1994 devaluation. It remained unclear whether the Socialist Party (PS)-dominated coalition government would hold. Meanwhile, increased rebel activity in the southern Casamance region produced new security and human rights concerns.

Since independence from France in 1960, Senegal has escaped the extreme repression experienced by its neighbors. President Leopold Senghor exercised de facto one-party rule under the PS for over a decade, but Senegal slowly liberalized. Three additional parties were permitted between 1974-81, after which most restrictions were lifted, but the PS remained dominant through patronage and electoral manipulation. Diouf succeeded Senghor in 1981, winning 1988 and 1993 contests marked by confusion and irregularities that oppositionists deemed fraudulent. Diouf has faced strong domestic dissent as he has sought to revive a badly flagging economy by imposing austerity budgets proposed by international lenders. Unemployment and diminished earning power have brought followers to both mainstream opposition politicians and Islamist groups. The government banned the Islamist youth movement Moustarchidina wal-Moustarchidati (MwM) after security forces harshly repressed February 1994 protests in the capital, Dakar. Iran's ambassador, charged with funding Islamist groups, was expelled in 1994.

Diouf's success in drawing into the government the main opposition, the

Senegal Democratic Party (PDS), has subdued his principal critics. PDS leader Abdoulaye Wade was jailed on allegations of involvement in a ranking electoral official's murder following Diouf's 1993 victory, but authorities dropped the charges after several months, lacking evidence. Although Wade and other senior PDS officials have received cabinet-level appointments, real power remains with Diouf and the PS. In September, two ministers from the small, opposition Independence and Labor Party were dismissed from the government, and there were signs of increased factionalism within the PS.

Armed opposition renewed early in the year in the southern Casamance Province, where a July 1993 ceasefire had largely held. Almost entirely cut off from the rest of Senegal by the Gambia, Casamance produces almost all Senegal's rice, has most of its remaining forests and boasts popular tourist beaches. But little of the money earned from the region's resources has gone to local development. Accusing the Diouf government of neglecting Casamance, the Movement of Democratic Forces of Casamance (MFDC), led by ex-Catholic priest Diamacoune Senghor, launched a separatist campaign in 1982. Senghor is now under house arrest in Casamance's regional capital, Ziguinchor, and control of the MFDC's armed wing has apparently passed to younger, more radical leaders.

Late in November, reports indicated the army was preparing a major offensive against the rebels. There is concern that some aid for the rebels is coming through the Gambia, which this year renewed relations with Libya. Increased Senegalese military cooperation with Guinea-Bissau—resulting from talks Diouf conducted there after Senegalese bombing of border villages severely strained relations— could reduce the MFDC's use of Guinea-Bissau for sanctuary. Senegalese military personnel are accused of using force indiscriminately against Casamance villages, and the MFDC has reportedly attacked civilian transport as well as military targets.

Long-term military operations in Casamance could deter tourism, disrupt rice production and deflate hopes for steady economic improvement.

Political Rights and Civil Liberties: Senegalese cannot change their government democratically, because the dominant Socialist Party has prevented the rise of a genuine opposition. For three decades after independence, voting regulations strongly favored the PS. The 1992 Electoral Code lowered the voting age to eighteen and introduced the secret ballot, creating a fairer framework, but election administration remains largely controlled by the government, which also uses patronage and control over state media to maintain power. In May 1993, the PS won eighty-four of 120 National Assembly seats, while the opposition PDS took twenty-seven. Four smaller opposition parties shared the other nine. The current national unity government has reduced serious political debate.

Freedom of expression is generally respected, although broadly-defined laws against "discrediting the state" and disseminating "false news" may produce self-censorship. Independent media operate freely despite the potential legal threat, often criticizing the government and political parties. Registration of publications is required, but this is now routine; the government does not practice censorship and allows unrestricted circulation of foreign periodicals. In August a bomb exploded outside the home of the editor of the weekly *Le Temoin,* a day after he had published a strong attack on the rebel MFDC.

Freedom of assembly is restricted by permit requirements, and all MwM activities and most public marches have been banned since the February 1994 riots. Religious freedom is respected. Many nongovernmental organizations exist, including several local and regional human rights groups.

Although independent, the judiciary remains subject to outside interference because of poor pay and lack of long-term tenure. Scarce resources also hinder the administration of justice. Police often overstep already-broad powers of detention, and prisoners are kept for long periods without charge or access to counsel.

Constitutionally guaranteed women's rights are often unrealized in practice, especially in the countryside. Some Islamic and local customary laws discriminate against women, particularly regarding inheritance and marital relations. Women's opportunities for education and formal-sector employment are much less than men's. Spousal abuse and other domestic violence against women are reportedly common.

Unions are politically powerful, and workers' rights to organize and strike are legally protected. The ruling party controls the main union group, the National Confederation of Senegalese Workers, but the smaller National Union of Autonomous Labor Unions of Senegal is more independent.

Privatization, implemented under international loan and debt-rescheduling packages, is slowly dismantling the extensive network of state corporations. Political connections remain very important to business opportunity, and obstruct independent business development.

Seychelles

Polity: Presidential-leg- **Political Rights:** 3
islative democracy   **Civil Liberties:** 3*
Economy: Mixed-statist **Status:** Partly Free
Population: 73,000
PPP: $3,683
Life Expectancy: 71.0
Ethnic Groups: Seychellois (mixed African, South Asian, European)
Capital: Victoria
Ratings Change: *Seychelles's civil liberties rating changed from 4 to 3 because of increased democratic consolidation.

Overview: Marking its second year as a multiparty legislature, the National Assembly of Seychelles took on legislation aimed at combating rising crime in addition to continuing debate concerning cuts in public spending and reducing fiscal deficits. The crime rate in this Indian Ocean Archipelago, while minor in comparison to those of many mainland African cities, has been rising, particularly in regard to assault and burglary. In response, three amendment bills were entered into the debate, which would introduce stiffer penalties for a range of crimes and increase protection for witnesses. Ironically, a 1995 constitutional amendment, the "Economic Development Bill," provides any international "businessmen" willing to deposit at least $10 million in a Seychellois bank with legal immunity against criminal proceedings, except for drug-related crimes and acts of violence committed in the Seychelles. According to the National Assembly, the amendment supersedes all international extradition orders and cannot be further amended without a referendum and a two-thirds parliamentary majority.

The passage of the controversial amendment reflects the government's urgent need to address the persistently depressed economy, which has contributed to the emigration of nearly one-third of the population and the development of a thriving informal economy. The small island economy has little industry and few natural resources, but enjoys a flourishing tourism industry—seaside vacationers provide about one-third of the islands' income. The private sector has been pressing for economic liberalization and loosening of restrictions on foreign exchange transactions. Relaxation of currency regulations could lead to considerable political fallout for the government, as factory closures and layoffs would likely result.

In the multiparty 1993 general election, President France Albert Rene was elected to a fourth consecutive term after having won single-party balloting in 1979, 1984 and 1989. Rene, designated prime minister at independence in 1976, became president the following year after a near-bloodless coup ousted Sir James Richard Mancham. After Rene declared his Seychelles People's Progressive Front (SPPF) the only legal party, Mancham and other opposition leaders operated parties and human rights groups in exile. By 1992, the SPPF had passed a constitutional amendment legalizing opposition parties, and many exiled leaders returned to participate in a constitutional commission and multiparty elections.

Political Rights and Civil Liberties: Despite some residual authoritarian elements, Seychellois can change their government democratically. Both the president and the National Assembly are elected by universal adult suffrage. The 1993 constitution provides for a thirty-three-seat National Assembly, with twenty-two members directly elected and eleven allocated on a proportional basis to parties with at least 9 percent of the vote. Local governments comprised of district councils, which had been abolished in 1971, were reinstated as of 1991.

Although they are largely engaged in subsistence agriculture, almost 98 percent of all adult women are classified as "economically active." They are also more likely than men to be literate. Four ministers in the present cabinet are women.

Media freedom has improved in recent years. The press includes a government-owned daily, a pro-SPPF Catholic weekly and an SPPF monthly. During the last general election campaign, the government-controlled Seychelles Broadcasting Corporation provided substantial coverage to both government and opposition candidates. Opposition parties have been allowed to set up several weeklies to balance print coverage. Freedom of speech has improved since 1993, although some self-censorship remains.

The judiciary includes a Supreme Court, a Court of Appeal, an Industrial Court and magistrates' courts. Judges generally decide cases fairly, but still face some government pressure.

Workers formally possess the right to strike, but regulations inhibit its free exercise. The National Workers' Union is associated with the SPPF. The government may deny passports for reasons of "national interest," but does not restrict domestic travel. Religious freedom is respected in this overwhelmingly Roman Catholic country.

Sierra Leone

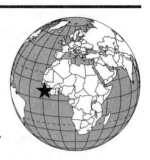

Polity: Military (insurgency)   **Political Rights:** 7
Economy: Capitalist   **Civil Liberties:** 6
Population: 4,509,000   **Status:** Not Free
PPP: $880
Life Expectancy: 39.0
Ethnic Groups: Temme (30 percent), Mende (30 percent), Krio (2 percent), others
Capital: Freetown

Overview: Sierra Leone suffered another tumultuous year of guerrilla fighting, internal intrigue and external interference as the ruling military junta pledged free elections for February 1996 and massive civilian suffering remained unabated in the war-ravaged countryside.

About one in five of Sierra Leone's nearly 5 million people have fled fighting to seek safety in the capital Freetown, or in neighboring countries. Starvation and disease are claiming hundreds of lives each day, while both government and rebel forces are accused of massive human rights violations. As many as 100,000 people may have died in five years of fighting.

Internal strife has swept Sierra Leone since early 1991 when the rebel Revolutionary United Front (RUF), began a guerrilla campaign from neighboring Liberia aimed at ending twenty-three years of increasingly corrupt one-party rule by the All Peoples Congress (APC) party. Protests against poor pay and conditions by junior army officers sent to confront the rebels turned into a military coup in April 1992. Captain Valentine Strasser seized power and heads a military junta, the National Provisional Ruling Council (NPRC). Political parties were banned, and sporadic harassment of the media and other independent voices ensued. Widespread disorder and distrust of the military regime leave few observers optimistic that 1996's scheduled election can or will be conducted freely and fairly. Order has all but disappeared from the countryside and maintains only a tenuous hold even in the main cities.

After fighting see-sawed at the outskirts of Freetown early in 1995, government forces appeared to gain the upper hand, but only with considerable foreign assistance. Combat ground troops from Guinea, artillery and air support from Nigeria, and finally mercenaries hired privately from South Africa all bolstered the regime's rag-tag army. The RUF reportedly is receiving assistance from factions in the Liberian civil war and from Libya. With external sponsors apparently willing to continue supporting their proxies, early resolution of the conflict seems unlikely.

Political Rights   The people of Sierra Leone do not have the right to choose
and Civil Liberties: their government freely. The military's pledges to restore
civilian rule in multiparty elections, now set for 26
February, has received reactions ranging from skepticism to cynical rejection. An
initial hurdle will be the estimated $17 million cost to conduct the polls, which
chairman of the Interim National Electoral Commission James Jonah, a widely-
respected former senior United Nations diplomat, says donor countries have
pledged but not delivered. The ban on political parties was lifted in June, and
fifteen are now officially registered. However, the RUF's pledge to block the
elections could mean that voting would be restricted to the capital, Freetown, and a
few other secure areas.

Concern over the military's sincerity in promising to step down was fueled by
the announcement on state radio of yet another alleged coup plot against the junta.
Six officers were arrested for "plotting to overthrow the government of the NPRC
and stop the ongoing democratization process." Analysts question whether this
coup plot represented a genuine threat by some elements of the military to block a
return to civilian rule. Others dismissed it as another example of the junta's
paranoia. Four Vietnamese hotel waiters holding British passports, arrested in an
alleged coup plot in 1994, were released when the only evidence introduced at their
trial was a widely-available road map of the capital. Further doubt was raised when
the regime announced the formation of its own political party, the National Unity
Party, which says it will contest the scheduled February poll.

The junta and the rebel RUF continue to battle for control of the countryside,
including diamond-rich areas that are the country's major source of hard-currency.
Fighting has severely wracked the east and south, Sierra Leone's largest grain-
producing regions. With tens of thousands of farms abandoned, the risk of famine
is rising.

Although most of the country remains in turmoil, a semblance of normal life
went on in Freetown. Political parties are re-organizing in anticipation of
February's election. Independent newspapers continued to publish, despite arrests
and harassment of several editors and reporters over reporting on the war and
corruption.

As the war went on, civilians continued to bear the brunt of the violence. The
RUF, led by former army corporal Foday Sankoh, has exhibited savagery nearly
matched by ill-disciplined government forces. In a September 1995 report,
Amnesty International charged that civilians are targeted deliberately both by
soldiers loyal to the regime and by rebels, and that blatant human rights violations
are committed routinely by both parties. "The conflict has developed into a
campaign of terror aimed primarily at civilians. Unarmed civilians have been
captured and held hostage, ill-treated and tortured, deliberately and arbitrarily
killed," the report said, citing hostage-taking, torture and summary executions.

Singapore

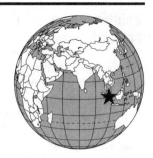

Polity: Dominant party
Economy: Mixed
capitalist
Population: 2,988,000
PPP: $18,330
Life Expectancy: 74.8
Ethnic Groups: Chinese (77 percent), Malay
(15 percent), Pakistani and Indian (7 percent)
Capital: Singapore

Political Rights: 5
Civil Liberties: 5
Status: Partly Free

Overview:　　In 1995, Singaporean Premier Goh Chok Tong's government continued to use the judiciary to stifle the media in a pair of high-profile rulings against the *International Herald Tribune*.

Singapore came under British control in 1867. The colony became self-governing in 1959, entered the Malaysian Federation in 1963 and in 1965 became fully independent under Prime Minister Lee Kuan Yew. The authoritarian People's Action Party (PAP) swept all elections from 1968 to 1980 before losing a by-election in 1981.

In October 1990, Lee stepped down in favor of his handpicked successor, Goh Chok Tong, although the former premier still exerts considerable influence as senior minister. At snap elections in August 1991, the PAP had its worst showing ever, but still won seventy-seven seats; two opposition parties, the Singapore Democratic Party and the center-left Worker's Party, took three and one seats, respectively.

In August 1993 Singapore held elections for a new, expanded presidency with the power to approve budgets, oversee the country's assets and approve political appointments. The strict requirements—candidates must have held one of several senior public offices, or have run a company with paid-up capital of over $62.5 million—left only about 400 citizens eligible. A three-member Presidential Election Committee rejected two Worker's Party candidates, J.B. Jeyaretnam and Tan Soo Phan, for lack of proper character and financial experience. In a clear rebuff to the PAP, deputy prime minister Ong Teng Cheong won with only 58.7 percent of the vote against a retired civil servant who barely campaigned. Parliamentary elections are due by the fall of 1996.

In January 1995, a court fined the *International Herald Tribune* and four defendants over an October 1994 article charging that judiciaries in unnamed regional countries "bankrupt opposition politicians." In July, a court awarded libel damages over an August 1994 *International Herald Tribune* article that allegedly suggested nepotism in the appointment of Lee's son, Lee Hsien Loong, as deputy premier.

**Political Rights
and Civil Liberties:**　　Citizens of Singapore nominally can change their government through free elections, although the ruling PAP maintains its political dominance through various institu-

tional advantages, partisan use of security laws and media regulations, and use of the judiciary to weaken and intimidate opposition politicians.

The Internal Security Act (ISA) permits the authorities to detain suspects without trial for an unlimited number of two-year periods. Currently there are no ISA detainees, although the government is using the ISA to restrict the travel, residence, speech and publishing rights of two former detainees, both political dissidents. Under the Criminal Law (Temporary Provisions) Act, which also authorizes detention without trial, the government is holding several hundred people for narcotics offenses or alleged involvement in secret societies. A 1989 constitutional amendment limits judicial review of detentions under these two acts to procedural grounds, and bars the judiciary from reviewing the constitutionality of any antisubversion law.

The judiciary is not independent of the government. There is no right to public trial under the ISA and the Criminal Law (Temporary Provisions) Act. Police reportedly abuse detainees to extract confessions. In March the government executed a Filipina maid even after new evidence came to light suggesting that she may have been innocent in the murder of a colleague. The death penalty is mandatory for certain drug offenses. Caning, which was introduced under the 1966 Vandalism Act, is now carried out for other offenses as well, including rape and visa violations.

The government continues to harass opposition figures through dismissal from public-sector jobs, libel suits and the threat of such suits. The government brought Worker's Party leader J.B. Jeyaretnam close to financial ruin through a series of controversial court cases, including a 1986 fraud conviction that was criticized by the Privy Council in London. In March 1993 the National University dismissed Chee Juan Soon, a Singapore Democratic Party official, for petty alleged financial irregularities, and Dr. Chee later had to pay $200,000 in damages plus legal costs over a subsequent defamation suit.

The ISA contains broad restrictions on freedom of expression. The government tightly controls the media. By law, key "management shares" in the Singapore Press Holdings, which publishes all major newspapers, must be held by government-approved individuals. Editorials and domestic news coverage strongly favor the ruling party. An amendment to the Newspaper and Printing Presses Act allows the government to "gazette," or restrict circulation of, any foreign publication it feels has interfered with domestic politics. The *Far Eastern Economic Review*, *Asiaweek* and the *Asian Wall Street Journal* are currently gazetted. The government owns all or part of six television channels and ten of the fourteen radio stations.

The broadly drawn Official Secrets Act bars the unauthorized release of government data to the media. In March 1994 a court found the editor of the *Business Times*, a journalist and three economists guilty of breaching the Act in 1992 by publishing advance GDP figures.

The Societies Act requires organizations of more than ten people to register with the government, and restricts political activity to political parties. However, the PAP wields strong influence over ostensibly nonpolitical associations such as neighborhood groups, while the opposition is not permitted to form similar groups. Overall, there are few truly independent elements of civil society. Approval is required for individual speakers at public functions, and the authorities occasionally deny permits to opposition party members seeking to address dinners and banquets. The government must approve any public assembly of more than five people.

Freedom of religion is generally respected, although the Jehovah's Witnesses and the Unification Church are banned under the Societies Act. Ethnic Malays face unofficial employment discrimination. Workers can form independent unions, but most unions are affiliated with the pro-government National Trade Unions Congress. Workers, other than those in essential industries, are able to strike.

⬇ Slovakia

Polity: Parliamentary democracy
Economy: Mixed-capitalist transitional
Population: 5,370,000
PPP: $6,690
Life Expectancy: 70.9

Political Rights: 2
Civil Liberties: 3
Status: Free

Ethnic Groups: Slovak (82 percent), Hungarian (11 percent), Roma (5 percent), Czech (1 percent)
Capital: Bratislava
Trend Arrow: Prime Minister Meciar's feud with President Kovak, efforts to muzzle the press and a language law aimed at the large Hungarian minority raised fears of regression.

Overview:
In 1995, the acrimonious relationship between populist Prime Minister Vladimir Meciar and President Michal Kovac deteriorated as Meciar took measures to undermine presidential authority. The kidnapping of Kovac's son, allegedly by Slovak Intelligence Service (SIS) members; the beating of a prominent Christian Democrat; continued efforts to muzzle press criticism; and the treatment of 560,000 ethnic Hungarians unsettled the political atmosphere and, along with uncertainty over privatization, undermined foreign investors' confidence even as the economy improved.

Slovakia was established on 1 January 1993 following Czechoslovakia's formal dissolution, which ended a seventy-four-year-old federation. Hungarians controlled the region for 1,000 years prior to World War I, ruling repressively. Interwar Czechoslovak unity ended with Nazi Germany's dismemberment of Czechoslovakia, providing an opportunity for militant Slovak nationalists to seize power. The Nazi puppet state under Father Josef Tiso was tainted by its role in the deportation of Jews and Roma (Gypsies). Communists ruled a reunited Czechoslovakia from 1948-89.

Meciar and his Movement for a Democratic Slovakia (HZDS) won 1992 elections, but in 1994 his government was forced to resign amid political bickering and accusations by Kovac that it was undemocratic and manipulating privatization and state media. Former Foreign Minister Jozef Moravcik headed a caretaker government, accelerating economic reform and privatization. But the HZDS's popularity among pensioners, the unemployed and peasants, reinforced by Meciar's anti-reform and anti-Hungarian rhetoric, saw the party win 61 of 150 parliamentary seats in September-October 1994 elections. The leftist Common Cause coalition, led by the former Communist Party of the Democratic Left (SDL), won eighteen seats; a coalition of Hungarian parties, seventeen; the Democratic Union, fifteen; the left-wing Workers' Association (ZRS), thirteen; and the ultranationalist Slovak National party (SNS), nine. An HZDS, ZRS and SNS coalition government was announced in December.

Meciar arranged to replace the directors of state television, state radio and the government news agency with political allies. In March 1995 three satirical television programs were canceled, leading thousands to rally in the capital, Bratislava, against the changes.

Blaming Kovac for engineering his fall from power, Meciar pushed through a series of parliamentary measures to reduce Kovac's powers and slash the presidential budget and staff. The ruling coalition also passed a no-confidence vote against Kovac, a symbolic move without constitutional validity. Meciar tried in vain to secure the three-fifths majority needed to oust the president. In September, the government demanded that Kovac "abdicate" because he was "betraying our nation."

On 31 August, Kovac's son was kidnapped to Austria and released, only to be arrested in connection with a fraudulent business scheme in Germany. Police attempts to question SIS officials were squelched and two police officials dismissed, one after ordering the arrest of three SIS operatives. In late 1995, a former SIS agent verified the agency's complicity. A few days after the abduction, the deputy chairman of the Christian Democrats was beaten outside his home by allegedly SIS-recruited Russian and Yugoslav thugs. Also, the head of Slovakia's conference of bishops received anonymous bomb threats and was investigated by the police. He charged authorities with using Communist-era intimidation against the church for having declared "full trust" in Kovac.

In November, tensions increased after parliament passed a strict law curbing the use of languages other than Slovak and setting huge fines for violators. All seventeen Hungarian coalition members voted against the bill, which made Slovak the exclusive language for radio and television broadcasts, advertising and government information. The measure exacerbated relations between Slovakia and Hungary, and Slovakia's parliament delayed ratifying a Slovak-Hungarian treaty signed nine months earlier.

In 1995 Slovakia's GDP grew by 6 percent, hard currency reserves topped $4 billion, unemployment dipped to 13 percent and inflation hovered at 10 percent. But the battle over the scope, pace and form of privatization among Meciar, the Constitutional Court and Kovac prompted a sharp fall in foreign investment.

Political Rights and Civil Liberties:

Citizens can change their government democratically under a 1992 constitution; 1994 elections were deemed free and fair. Opposition parties have charged intimidation by government security forces. About fifty parties exist, and twenty registered for the 1994 elections. Several new parties were formed in 1995.

The media have come under government pressure. Government radio fired a Washington correspondent for reporting that a Slovak trade delegation was poorly prepared. A value-added tax and other measures sought to bankrupt independent newspapers, including foreign-supported publications. On 6 March, several dailies printed blank pages protesting the tax. Opposition calls for representation on state radio and television oversight boards have been ignored, and access has been denied. The penal code forbids the dissemination of "false" information and defamation of the president.

Freedom of expression has been eroded, and the language law curtails the use of foreign languages. Religious freedom in this overwhelmingly Roman Catholic country is respected, though the SNS and other nationalist parties are often openly anti-Semitic.

The judiciary is not wholly free from political interference, and the government has strained the constitution by eroding presidential power. But the Constitutional Court quashed two commissions investigating the "constitutional crisis" marking the fall of the first Meciar government and the death in an automobile accident of former Czechoslovak leader Alexander Dubcek. The former commission sought evidence to dismiss the president. The HZDS criticized the Court rulings. The Hungarian minority has faced legal and social discrimination, and Roma (Gypsies) have been targets of discrimination and violence, often ignored by the courts and police.

Workers can form unions and strike. The Slovak Confederation of Trade Unions is the main labor confederation. Women nominally have the same rights as men, but are underrepresented in managerial posts. In April 1995, the government stated that there were 9,800 registered nongovernmental organizations, including several human rights groups.

Slovenia

Polity: Presidential-par- **Political Rights:** 1
liamentary democracy **Civil Liberties:** 2
Economy: Mixed-statist **Status:** Free
(transitional)
Population: 1,982,000
PPP: na
Life Expectancy: 71.0
Ethnic Groups: Slovene (91 percent), Croat, Serb, Muslim,
Hungarian, Italian
Capital: Ljubljana

Overview: This small, Alpine former Yugoslav republic enjoyed both political stability and economic prosperity under Prime Minister Janez Drnovsek, leader of the ruling Liberal Democratic Party (LDS). But a bitter, longstanding dispute with Italy over the Croat- and Slovene-controlled Istria region led Rome to veto closer ties between the European Union (EU) and Slovenia, dampening Slovene enthusiasm for EU membership.

Controlled for centuries by the Hapsburg empire, Slovenia was incorporated into the newly created Yugoslavia after World War I. After declaring independence from Yugoslavia in June 1991, Slovenia's territorial defense forces secured its sovereignty by repelling the invading Yugoslav People's Army.

In the December 1992 presidential and parliamentary elections, popular incumbent Milan Kucan, leader of the (former Communist) Party of Democratic Renewal (LCS-PDR, later changed to LDS) was re-elected. The LDS captured the most seats in the newly created, bicameral 130-member parliament, which includes a 40-member National Council (upper house) and a 90-member National Assembly (lower house). After some realignment including the LDS's merger with three smaller left-of-center parties, the distribution in mid-1994, was: LDS, fifty; Christian Democrats, fifteen; Associated List of Social Democrats, fourteen; People's Party, ten; Slovene National Party Deputy Group, five; Social Democratic Party, four; Slovene National Right (SND), three; Democratic Party, two; and independents, two. By law, minority Italians and Hungarians are reserved one seat each.

With a per capita GDP of over $7,000, Slovenia is among Eastern Europe's most developed countries. Inflation has dropped to 11 percent and the economy grew by over 5 percent in 1995. In 1994, privatization was expanded.

A key issue in 1995 was Slovenia's efforts to join the EU, which already accounts for two-thirds of Slovenia's export market. In March, Prime Minister Drnovsek predicted it would win full membership in two or three years. But tensions continued with Italy over Istria, a peninsula divided between Croatia and Slovenia with a large Italian minority. After World War II Yugoslavia incorporated the area, minus the city of Trieste. At issue were the rights of Italians dispossessed after the war. Although Yugoslavia had agreed in 1975 and 1983 treaties to provide cash compensation, Italy's Berlusconi government declared this was no longer acceptable, calling for the actual property's return. Slovenes accused Italy of a revanchist desire to redraw postwar borders. To discourage Italy from blocking Slovenia's associate EU status, the European Commission bent its own state aid rules by offering tax breaks in Trieste. The dispute led many Slovenes to question the necessity of EU membership, and look instead to a Swiss model of free trade and neutrality. But 64 percent of Slovenes polled favored Slovenian inclusion in NATO.

Another key issue was the SND campaign to strip some 180,000 naturalized citizens of citizenship, mostly Serbs. The SND began collecting signatures demanding the government call a referendum on the issue, and the government asked the Constitutional Court to order a stop to the campaign.

On 30 November, Slovenia became the first former Yugoslav republic to lift sanctions against Yugoslavia.

Political Rights and Civil Liberties:

Slovenes can change their government democratically. Many parties and candidates contested the 1992 elections, which were judged free and fair.

At least thirty parties span the political spectrum, and over a dozen are represented in parliament. Twenty-two of forty upper-house members are directly elected, and eighteen designated by electoral colleges of professional and other interest groups. Forty of ninety lower-house members are elected by constituency-based majority voting, and fifty by proportional representation from party lists securing a minimum 3 percent of votes; Hungarian and Italian minorities are reserved one seat each.

Slovenia's newspapers, several party-affiliated, print diverse views. Though the state controls most radio and television, there are private stations including Kanal A television in Ljubljana, the capital. Journalists have faced limited suspension for commenting on government officials' statements, and self-censorship remains an issue.

Freedoms of assembly and religion are guaranteed and respected. Minority rights are guaranteed by law. However, SND attempts to strip naturalized citizens of citizenship suggest a growing intolerance of non-Slovenes in this largely homogeneous country. Violence against non-Slovenes—including 300,000 economic immigrants from other former Yugoslav republics and 25,000 Bosnian refugees—has been increasing. The judiciary is independent. Judges are elected by the National Assembly on the recommendation of an eleven-member Judicial Council, five of whose members are selected by parliament on the nomination of the president, and six of whom are sitting judges selected by their peers.

There are three main labor federations. Most workers may join unions, which are formally independent from government and political parties, though members may and do hold legislative positions. Women are guaranteed equality under the law. There are numerous nongovernmental business, charitable, cultural and professional associations.

Solomon Islands

Polity: Parliamentary democracy
Economy: Capitalist
Population: 399,000
PPP: $2,616
Life Expectancy: 70.4
Ethnic Groups: Melanesian (93 percent), Polynesian (4 percent), Micronesian, European minorities
Capital: Honiara

Political Rights: 1
Civil Liberties: 2
Status: Free

Overview:

In 1995, the government of Premier Solomon Mamaloni pushed ahead with new logging projects despite concerns over the environment, corruption in the industry and the needs of local landowners.

The Solomon Islands, a predominantly Melanesian country of ten large islands and four groups of smaller islands in the western Pacific Ocean, achieved independence from the British in 1978. The forty-seven-seat unicameral parliament is directly elected for a four-year term. Executive power is held by the prime minister and a cabinet. The largely ceremonial governor-general serves as head of state and represents the British crown in this constitutional monarchy.

In the 1989 parliamentary elections, the People's Alliance Party (PAP) won a plurality and named Solomon Mamaloni to head the country's first single-party government. In 1990, Mamaloni resigned from the PAP over charges that he was ruling in a nonconsultative fashion, but, with the support of several opposition MPs, remained as prime minister in a "national unity" government.

Key issues in the May 1993 elections, the country's fourth since independence, were the poor state of the economy, official corruption and the lack of adequate secondary schools. Mamaloni's new National Unity Group took twenty-one seats; PAP, seven; National Action Party, four; Labor Party, four; Christian Fellowship Group, three; United Party, two; Nationalist Front for Progress, one; and independents, five. In June a coalition of five parties and several independents elected Francis Billy Hilly, a business-man who ran as an independent, as prime minister over Mamaloni.

The Hilly government worked to ease tensions with neighboring Papua New Guinea, which had accused the Solomon Islands of supporting the secessionist Bougainville Revolutionary Army (BRA) on Bougainville Island. Since 1992, Papua New Guinean soldiers have launched several cross-border raids into the Solomon Islands, allegedly while in "hot pursuit" of BRA soldiers, and in a 1992 incident killed two civilians. The incursions have led to several shootouts with Solomon Islands forces. The Hilly government also declared a moratorium on logging, the country's main source of export earnings, citing rampant corruption in the awarding of contracts to foreign companies and concerns that trees were being felled at up to twice the environmentally sustainable rate.

The resignations of five cabinet members plus a government backbencher in September and early October 1994 convinced Governor-General Moses Pitakaka that the Hilly government lacked a parliamentary majority. Pitakaka sacked Hilly, who then claimed that the governor general lacked the authority to dismiss a prime minister and provoked a constitutional crisis by refusing to stand down. Pitakaka swore in Mamaloni as caretaker prime minister, temporarily giving the country two premiers. The High Court subsequently ruled in favor of Hilly. But Hilly resigned on 31 October, acknowledging that he did not command a parliamentary majority. In November, parliament elected Mamaloni as prime minister over Sir Baddeley Devesi, a former governor-general.

Mamaloni ended the logging moratorium, citing the country's bleak economic situation and the need to raise tax and foreign exchange revenues. In December the government slashed export duties on logs by 46 percent in an attempt to boost output.

In April 1995, the government granted the local Mavin Brothers company a $130 million timber concession on tiny Pavuvu Island under a contract that called for the company to resettle several thousand affected islanders and build new villages, roads and schools. Fifty-six landowners were subsequently arrested during a protest against the operation.

Political Rights and Civil Liberties:

Citizens of the Solomon Islands can change their government democratically. Party affiliations are weak and tend to be based on personal loyalties rather than ideology or policy goals. Power is decentralized through elected provincial and local councils.

The independent judiciary provides adequate procedural safeguards for the accused. Freedoms of speech and press are generally respected in practice. However, in May 1993 the Mamaloni government banned all media coverage of the border tensions with Papua New Guinea. The Hilly government lifted the restrictions after taking office one month later. The country's three private newspapers vigorously critique government policies. The state-owned Solomon Islands Broadcasting Corporation (SIBC) runs the sole radio service, which offers diverse viewpoints. SIBC plans to inaugurate television service in 1996.

Permits are required for demonstrations but have never been denied on political grounds. There are no restrictions on association, but civil society is underdeveloped. Freedom of religion is respected in this predominantly Christian country. Women face no official discrimination but have an inferior status in this traditionally male-dominated society. Domestic violence reportedly occurs frequently. Citizens may travel freely inside the country and abroad.

Workers are free to join independent unions and bargain collectively. The law recognizes only private-sector workers' right to strike, although a 1989 walkout by public school teachers established a *de facto* right to strike in the public sector.

Somalia

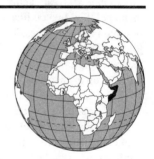

Polity: Rival ethnic-based militias; unrecognized de facto state in north
Economy: Mixed-statist
Population: 9,250,000
PPP: $1,001
Life Expectancy: 47.0
Ethnic Groups: Somali (Hawiye, Darod, Isaq, Isa, others), Gosha, Bajun
Capital: Mogadishu

Political Rights: 7
Civil Liberties: 7
Status: Not Free

Overview: Five years of intermittent warfare in Somalia continued to simmer and flare throughout 1995 as rival warlords pressed their claims, based in large part on control of clans and weapons, to rule the country. The $4 billion United Nations peacekeeping operation that cost the lives of dozens of U.N. and American troops and ended in March 1995 now appears little more than a pause on Somalia's road to disintegration.

The massive intervention already seems a faded memory on the ground, and the anarchy that spawned famine in 1992 threatens to return. The country also faces de facto division, as northern clans in what had been the colonial British Somaliland continued to consolidate their self-declared Somaliland Republic.

Civil war, starvation and lawlessness have wracked Somalia since the struggle to topple military dictator Siad Barre began in the late 1980s. Barre, who had seized power in 1969, increasingly relied on divisive clan politics to maintain his grip on power. By the time of his overthrow in January 1991, Somalia was awash with heavily-armed guerrilla movements and militias based on ethnic, clan or sub-clan loyalties. Fighting among the various factions—mostly over control of valuable assets like ports, airfields and banana plantations—led to near anarchy and helped precipitate widespread famine.

In December 1992, over 20,000 American troops landed amid a fanfare of publicity to pursue a mission of "humanitarian stabilization" in Somalia. They were eventually replaced by an 18,000-strong international force under United Nations command. The humanitarian mission, which succeeded in quelling clan combat long enough to end the famine, slowly deteriorated into battles with Somali militias.

Somalia became a prime example of what theorists describe as the "failed state." Absent a desire to effectively recolonize Somalia, the international community has largely withdrawn from the fray, and international aid agencies are able to operate only sporadically. There is no central authority, and many of the powers of the modern state, including administration of justice, are reverting to traditional clan authorities.

Political Rights and Civil Liberties: Somalians cannot change their government freely. In June, General Mohammed Farah Aideed, leader of the powerful Somali National Alliance, declared himself "interim president." His action was immediately rejected by his main rivals, Ali Madhi and Ali Hasan Osa, the former a second claimant to the title of interim president, and the latter the head of the United Somali Congress/Somalia National Alliance.

Factions regularly exchange accusations of external meddling in the form of financial support or arms shipments to their rivals. Libyan involvement is claimed, and Islamic fundamentalist militias are said to be receiving weapons and training from Afghanistan's Taleban movement.

Somalia has no functioning judicial system. No real political entities exist beyond the militias, and it is doubtful whether any autonomous civic or political group could organize safely. The lack of formal accountability for local clan or militia members and vacuum of central authority have created widespread lawlessness. Islamic courts have been formed in some areas in response, and these reportedly are imposing draconian sentences, including executions and amputations in keeping with Islamic *shari'a* law.

The few independent journalists in the country—reporting for international outlets—have been harassed and occasionally detained. There are no free domestic media.

Workers on banana plantations have complained of virtual slave labor conditions as poorly-paid men, women and children are forced to work long hours under guard by armed militiamen. Early this year, an Italian television cameraman was murdered near the port of Mogadishu—one of the most fiercely contested areas—because assassins mistook him for a Westerner involved in the banana trade.

Humanitarian operations were crippled in September when Aideed led some 500 militiamen to seize the town of Baidoa, the epicenter of 1992's famine, and the district in which international aid had continued to serve people most effectively despite the U.N. withdrawal. Aideed's forces held a score of foreign relief workers prisoner for several days and looted over $300,000 worth of vehicles and other equipment.

Relief agencies are able to operate more effectively and safely in the self-proclaimed Somaliland Republic, the only area with any semblance of coherent authority. The republic, with its capital in Hargeisa, lies on territory once ruled as

British Somaliland, which was joined to the larger Italian-controlled colony after Italy's defeat in World War II. The new republic's president, Mohammed Ibrahim Egal, expects a constitution to be completed by late 1996.

While the Somaliland Republic faces no current threat from the fractious forces to the south, it is also riven by clan-based internal divisions. Fighting around the town of Burao in March forced thousands to flee into Ethiopia, and treason charges have been brought against alleged "anti-Somaliland" individuals in Hargeisa. If Egal can consolidate his rule and achieve some accord among rival clans that respects fundamental rights, the international community may be hard-pressed not to accept a new country from the failed state of Somalia.

South Africa

Polity: Presidential-legis-   **Political Rights:** 1*
lative democracy (interim)   **Civil Liberties:** 2*
Economy: Capitalist-statist   **Status:** Free
Population: 43,474,000
PPP: $3,799
Life Expectancy: 62.9
Ethnic Groups: Black (Zulu, Xhosa, Swazi, Sotho,
others) (75 percent), European (Afrikaner, English) (14 percent),
Coloured (9 percent), Indian (3 percent)
Capital: Cape Town (legislative), Pretoria (executive), Bloemfontien (judicial)
Ratings Change: *South Africa's political rights rating changed from 2 to 1 and its civil liberties rating from 3 to 2 because of successful local elections and further consolidation of the rule of law.

Overview: President Nelson Mandela was dealt a rare political setback in September, when South Africa's Constitutional Court declared void decree powers granted him by the African National Congress (ANC)-controlled parliament.

But Mandela's reaction to the ruling, which disallowed the president's ability to set electoral districts, was enormously encouraging to the long-term process of implanting the rule of law in the country. "The judgment of the Constitutional Court confirms that our new democracy is taking firm root and that nobody is above the law," Mandela remarked. "This is something of which we should be proud and which the whole of our country must welcome."

Despite eruptions of serious ethnic violence in KwaZulu-Natal, South Africa's transition to a democratic and open society generally progressed smoothly in 1995 after the country's first-ever non-racial election in April 1994. The government of national unity installed after the ANC victory still includes the ANC's two main rivals, representing Afrikaners and Zulus, in a workable if occasionally uneasy alliance. Local elections produced large victories for the ANC. The last structural remnants of the apartheid regime that ruled the country for over four decades have been all but swept away, and a strongly independent judiciary is in place.

Political Rights and Civil Liberties: South Africans of all races now choose their national and local government representatives through free and fair elections. The process of extending electoral rights to the country's non-white majority on the basis of one person-one vote was completed with local elections in nearly all parts of the country in October.

Significant progress has also been made in drafting a new constitution, which is scheduled to be adopted by May 1996. Like the interim constitution, it includes extensive and strong provisions to protect human rights. Freedom of expression and assembly are guaranteed, as is the right to form and join trade unions. Explicit language bans detention without trial and any form of torture or "cruel, inhuman or degrading treatment or punishment."

Compliance with constitutional provisions is adjudicated by an eleven-member Constitutional Court. In its first case, the court ruled South Africa's death penalty unconstitutional on the basis of the interim constitution's provision stating that "every person shall have the right to life." The court's stature was immeasurably enhanced by President Mandela's September endorsement of its duty to decide even against his political priorities if the constitution so demanded.

A constitutionally-mandated Human Rights Commission has been appointed by parliament. The commission exists "to promote the observance of, respect for and the protection of fundamental rights...and develop an awareness of fundamental rights among all people of the republic." A gender commission, also constitutionally-mandated, has been formed "to promote gender equality and to advise and make recommendations to parliament [regarding] any laws or proposed legislation which affects gender equality and the status of women."

Putting the constitutional provisions into meaningful action in a country still divided by race and ethnicity will be a far greater challenge than negotiating the guiding principles. An important start was made when a tripartite forum comprising the government, business and unions reached agreement on a new Labour Relations Bill in July. The bill provides for new conciliation and bargaining frameworks that could help reduce industrial unrest that has plagued South Africa and encourage investment.

The Promotion of National Unity and Reconciliation Act was also passed in July. The legislation enables creation of a Truth Commission, which will deal with human rights violations, reparations, rehabilitation and amnesty. Amnesty for politically-motivated crimes applies to acts taken only up until 5 December 1993. Right-wing white extremists who staged an April 1994 bombing campaign in hopes of disrupting the elections are excluded. It is also unclear how the Act's provisions will affect former defense minister Magnus Malan and ten other former officials charged in October with responsibility for terrorist acts against ANC supporters in Natal Province in 1987.

White concerns over the Malan prosecution reflect greater concerns over the potential for "reverse discrimination." The demands of the mainly Zulu-backed Inkatha Freedom Party (IFP) represent another ethnic dimension. The IFP controls KwaZulu-Natal province after emerging as the strongest party there in the 1994 elections. IFP leader Mangosuthu Buthelezi is pushing hard for greater provincial autonomy, and has boycotted constitutional debates.

Other legacies of apartheid will make realization of both constitutional provisions and political promises difficult to achieve. Although every child has the constitutional right "not to be subject to neglect or abuse" and to "basic education and equal access to educational institutions," the government is far from able to meet these pledges. Vast disparities in income still translate to far superior facilities for most South African whites in terms of education and social services.

Eighteen million people, nearly half of the country's population, live in rural areas, where most eke out a subsistence living. The Restitution of Land Rights Act of November 1994 and new laws affecting tenant farmers are aimed at redressing hundreds of years of expropriation of small farmers' holdings. The scope and pace of the project are limited by a lack of funds to meet the laws' requirement to provide market-value compensation to white farmers now holding title to the land.

Other government programs are similarly constrained. The Reconstruction and Development Programme has been slow in getting its flagship project of home construction underway, but important progress has been made in child health and nutrition, electrification and water supply.

Rampant crime is another serious problem, one inextricably tied to the existence of an enormous, urban African underclass. Although President Mandela has promised massive "crime-busting" drives, success in energizing South Africa's economy will likely be the key to reducing criminality and making the dream of a single society for all South Africans a reality.

Spain

Polity: Parliamentary democracy
Economy: Capitalist
Population: 37,398,000
PPP: $13,400
Life Expectancy: 77.6
Ethnic Groups: Spanish (72 percent), Catalan (16 percent), Galician (8 percent), Basque (2 percent), others
Capital: Madrid

Political Rights: 1
Civil Liberties: 2
Status: Free

Overview: Allegations of corruption and scandal continued to plague the ruling Socialist Workers' Party, in power for thirteen years, and call into question the credibility of Prime Minister Felipe Gonzalez. The conservative Popular Party (PP) scored a clear victory over the ailing Socialists in local elections in May. Eleven of thirteen contested regional parliaments took a decisive turn to the right, as did thirty-two of the fifty-two provincial capitals. Bowing under the pressure of diminishing power, Gonzalez finally agreed to hold early general elections, now set for March 1996.

Spain has had a democratic government since 1977, following nearly forty years of dictatorship under Francisco Franco and a brief transitional government under Adolfo Suarez.

In recent years, thirty-nine people have been implicated in illegal financing of the Socialist Party; former governor of the Bank of Spain Mariano Rubio was accused of tax evasion, embezzlement and influence peddling; and the first civilian chief of the Civil Guard police, Luis Roldan, was arrested on the run in Laos and charged with corruption and fraud. By April, fourteen people including Rafael Vera, former second-in-command at the Interior Ministry, had been formally charged with connections to *Gal*, a network of anti-terrorist liberation groups alleged to have killed about twenty-six people in the 1980s' undercover war against ETA, the Basque Homeland and Freedom Group. Further scathing criticism from opposition parties in Parliament came with the disclosure in June of a list of prominent public figures—including the popular King Juan Carlos—whose private mobile telephone conversations had been taped by the Spanish intelligence service.

The deluge of allegations, combined with the Socialists' intention to relax restrictions on access to abortions, drove the Catalan Convergence and Union party (CiU) to end its support for Gonzalez's government. For two years, CiU leader Jordi Pujol has propped up Gonzalez since his party lost its eight-year absolute majority in Parliament, but severed ties for fear of offending the center-right of his own coalition, which is closely allied to other Roman-Catholic Christian Democratic Parties in Europe. A further blow to the Socialists came when an unsuccessful ETA assassination attempt against PP leader Jose Maria Aznar bolstered his popularity just weeks before the municipal elections.

Political Rights and Civil Liberties:

Spanish citizens have the right to change their government democratically. The country is divided into seventeen autonomous regions with a limited range of devolved powers, including control over such areas as health, tourism, local police agencies and instruction in regional languages. The bicameral federal legislature includes a territorially elected Senate and a Congress of Deputies elected on the basis of proportional representation and universal suffrage. Although the Socialist party has ruled that women must occupy 25 percent of senior party posts and a feminist party has been officially registered since 1981, female participation in government remains minimal.

A Supreme Tribunal heads the judiciary, which includes territorial, provincial, regional and municipal courts. The post-Franco constitution established the right to trial by jury, and seventeen years later Parliament passed corresponding legislation. Over 11,000 people were selected randomly to be on call for jury duty when the new law takes effect in 1996.

Freedom of speech and a free press are guaranteed. The press has been particularly influential in setting the political agenda in recent years, with national dailies such as *El Mundo* prompting the re-opening of the investigation into the Gal killings and an investigation instigated by *Diario-16* leading to the arrest of Luis Roldan. In addition to the state-controlled station, which has been accused of a pro-government bias, there are three independent commercial television stations.

Among the other constitutional provisions is the right to freedom of association and collective bargaining. However, Spain has one of the lowest levels of union membership in the European Union, and unions have failed to prevent passage of new labor laws facilitating dismissals and encouraging short-term contracting.

In 1978, the constitution disestablished Roman Catholicism as the state religion, while directing Spanish authorities to "keep in mind the religious beliefs of Spanish society." Freedom of worship and the separation of church and state are respected in practice.

Spain includes many cultural and linguistic groups, some with strong regional identities. Although popular support for the ETA separatist movement and its political wing, *Herri Batasuna*, have significantly declined, ETA remains the most active terrorist group in Western Europe, having claimed 800 lives in a twenty-five year span. Some of the roughly 500 incarcerated ETA activists report mistreatment by authorities while in detention.

Spain lacks antidiscrimination laws, and ethnic minorities, particularly immigrants, continue to report bias and ill-treatment.

Sri Lanka

Polity: Presidential-parliamentary democracy (insurgency)
Economy: Mixed capitalist-statist
Population: 18,171,000
PPP: $2,850
Life Expectancy: 71.9
Ethnic Groups: Sinhalese (74 percent), Tamil (18 percent), Moor (7 percent), others
Capital: Colombo

Political Rights: 4
Civil Liberties: 5
Status: Partly Free

Overview: Sri Lankan President Chandrika Kumaratunga attempted to end a twelve-year-old civil conflict that has killed some 50,000 people by offering a devolution package granting the Tamil minority greater autonomy, and ordering an offensive that captured the main Tamil guerrilla stronghold in November 1995.

Located off southeastern India, Sri Lanka achieved independence from the British in 1947. Political power has alternated between the centrist United National Party (UNP) and the leftist Sri Lanka Freedom Party (SLFP). The 1978 constitution vests broad executive powers in a president who can serve two six-year terms and can dissolve parliament. The 225-member parliament serves for up to six years.

Decades of Tamil resentment against alleged discrimination by the majority Sinhalese exploded in 1983 when Tamil guerrillas began attacking government troops. By 1985 the Liberation Tigers of Tamil Eelam (LTTE), which called for an independent Tamil homeland in the north and east, had emerged as the dominant guerrilla group. The presence of an Indian peacekeeping force from 1987-90 sparked a bloody antigovernment insurgency in the south by the leftist, Sinhalese-based People's Liberation Front (JVP). By 1990 the government had crushed the JVP, with help from military-backed death squads.

On 1 May 1993, a Tamil suicide bomber assassinated UNP President Ranasinghe Premadasa. Early parliamentary elections on 16 August gave the People's Alliance, an SLFP-dominated coalition, 105 seats. The UNP took 94; the pro-UNP Eelam People's Democratic Party, 9; the Sri Lanka Muslim Congress, 7; minor parties, 9, and independents, 1. The People's Alliance named Chandrika Kumaratunga prime minister after winning the support of the Muslim Congress plus the independent.

On 25 October, with a presidential campaign underway, a suicide bomber killed UNP candidate Gamini Dissanayake. In the 9 November presidential elections Kumaratunga won 62 percent of the vote, routing Dissanayake's widow, Srima Dissanayake, who took 35 percent. Kumaratunga appointed her mother, Sirima Bandaranaike, as prime minister—a post she had held in the 1960s and 1970s.

In April 1995 the LTTE sank two navy gunboats, breaking a three-month-old ceasefire. As fighting continued, in July the army launched an offensive to take the rebel stronghold of Jaffna on the northern Jaffna Peninsula. In August Kumaratunga floated a devolution package aimed at turning the country into a federated "union of regions," in which Tamils would receive significant autonomy in the northern and eastern regions. On 20 November, government troops took Jaffna after months of fighting that killed or wounded thousands and displaced some 400,000 civilians.

Political Rights and Civil Liberties: Sri Lankans can change their government democratically. However, only 19,000 of the 600,000-800,000 persons displaced by the civil war since 1983 were declared eligible to vote in 1994 parliamentary elections. There was no polling in LTTE-controlled areas. In May 1995 the government inexplicably postponed for one year local elections planned for June.

The LTTE's unilateral ending of the ceasefire in April and the renewed army offensive brought fresh human rights violations by both sides. The armed forces indiscriminately bombed and shelled populated areas of Jaffna Peninsula, killing hundreds of civilians, and reportedly used civilians as human minesweepers in the eastern city of Batticaloa. The army is suspected in a string of "disappearances" and extrajudicial killings of civilians and suspected LTTE sympathizers, including some thirty bodies found around Bolgoda Lake near Colombo. Police also arbitrarily arrested for questioning thousands of Tamils countrywide, releasing most within two days.

The LTTE massacred several dozen Sinhalese and Muslim villagers near Trincomalee and other eastern and northeastern towns, arbitrarily shelled civilian areas, took civilian hostages and was responsible for "disappearances" of civilians. As the army closed in on Jaffna city, the LTTE increasingly used child soldiers on the front lines. The LTTE, which had ruled its Jaffna Peninsula territory in a brutal and arbitrary manner, forcibly relocated Tamil civilians to areas still under its control.

A state of emergency, instituted in 1983 and partially withdrawn by the Kumaratunga government in 1994, remains in effect in Colombo, the north and east, and some central and western regions. Suspects can be detained indefinitely under the Emergency Regulations (ER), and for eighteen months under the Prevention of Terrorism Act.

The judiciary is independent. Security personnel routinely torture detainees, and under the ER confessions to police officers are admissible in court. Few police officers or soldiers have been charged with these and other abuses, creating a climate of impunity. In 1995 the government created three regional commissions to investigate "disappearances," although some witnesses complained of intimidation by security forces. In 1994, the Kumaratunga government established a Human Rights Task Force to monitor arrests and detentions.

The government controls the Lake House group, the largest media chain. Independent newspapers publish diverse opinions, but both authorities and opposition groups harass journalists. The army refused to grant independent journalists access to the war-torn north, and in September 1995 the government imposed censorship on reporting about the civil war. The government filed criminal defamation suits against editors of at least three newspapers for articles criticizing the president, and in September police raided the offices of four papers. The government owns the radio station and two of three television networks, and has a monopoly on domestic news broadcasts.

Freedom of peaceful assembly is generally respected. The country has vibrant civic institutions, and human rights groups are active.

Rape and domestic violence occur frequently. Domestic servants are often physically and sexually abused. There are several thousand child prostitutes, catering mainly to foreign tourists. Religious freedom is respected. Some 46,000 Muslims, forcibly expelled by the LTTE from northern towns in 1990, live in refugee camps.

Workers may join independent trade unions. State workers may not strike. The 1989 Essential Services Act allows the president to declare a strike in any industry illegal. Child labor remains a problem.

↓ Sudan

Polity: Military
Economy: Mixed capitalist
Population: 28,098,000
PPP: $1,620
Life Expectancy: 53.0
Ethnic Groups: Sudanese Arab (40 percent), Dinka (11 percent), Nuba (8 percent), Neur, Shilluk, Fur, some 600 other groups
Capital: Khartoum (executive), Omdurman (legislative)
Trend Arrow: Sudan's downward trend arrow is due to genocidal attacks against minority groups and increasing repression.

Political Rights: 7
Civil Liberties: 7
Status: Not Free

Overview: Africa's largest country remained torn by the continent's longest and bloodiest war, as the Arab-dominated, Islamic fundamentalist dictatorship sought to impose its will on the country's black minority and other secular and democratic forces. Massive rights abuses were reported, particularly against the western Nuba people, and repression of independent voices intensified. The regime's reputation as a supporter of international terrorism was reinforced by charges of official complicity in the 26 June assassination attempt against Egyptian President Hosni Mubarak in Addis Ababa.

Sudan has been embroiled in civil war for over half its forty years as a modern state, since regaining independence in 1956 after nearly eight decades of British rule. From 1956-72, Anya-Nya separatists representing mainly Christian and animist southern blacks battled government forces. A 1972 agreement gave the south extensive autonomy, and an uneasy peace prevailed for a decade.

In 1983, General Jafar Numeiri, who had toppled a parliamentary government in 1969, sought to dilute southern autonomy and introduce Muslim *shari'a* law. These moves—combined with pervasive racial and religious discrimination and fears of economic exploitation raised by government plans to pipe southern oil to the north—sparked new fighting. The war continued despite Numeiri's 1985 ouster and the restoration of civilian rule in 1986, and chances for peace dwindled after a 1989 coup deposed the elected government.

While the current Islamic regime seeks to maintain control, pressure against it is building. Riots flared in at least three cities in September, led first by students but then joined by many others. The protests were quashed amid reports of executions of students by government security agents.

Hopes for effective resistance to the regime were raised after an agreement was concluded in a June meeting of major opposition leaders in the Eritrean capital, Asmara. The resulting National Democratic Alliance (NDA) is a broad coalition of northern and southern secular and religious groups. Reconciliation among rival southern groups, considered crucial, has not yet occurred; only the SPLA has joined the grouping. The NDA has pledged to ban religious-based political parties and respect regional autonomy. It has also announced its intention to mount armed resistance in northern and eastern Sudan, which could pose a formidable threat to the regime. An NDA radio station has already begun broadcasts.

The NDA appears to have the backing of Eritrea, and perhaps of several other countries. Most important among these is Egypt, whose troops fought several border skirmishes with Sudanese forces following the assassination attempt against President Mubarak, which Egyptian and Ethiopian authorities have charged was planned by Sudanese officials. Uganda is also being drawn into fighting along Sudan's southern border, and has accused Sudan of supporting Christian millennialist rebels operating in northern Uganda. The entire frontier has become a patchwork of warring factions with different benefactors and sometimes indeterminate loyalties.

Political Rights and Civil Liberties: Sudanese cannot change their government democratically. General Omar Hassan Ahmad al-Bashir serves as president and prime minister, although Hasan Al-Turabi, head of the fundamentalist National Islamic Front (NIF), is considered a key figure and possibly the country's de facto leader. The regime declared an Islamic state and ushered in new repression. All political parties were banned and imposition of shari'a accelerated. The entire judicial and security apparatus is controlled by the NIF. Few independent voices are tolerated, and there is almost no accountability for official actions.

At least 500,000 people have died in the last decade of conflict. Devastation caused by the fighting has been followed by famine among the displaced populace. Fighting in southern Sudan has been exacerbated by ethnic divisions within southern ranks. The Sudan People's Liberation Army (SPLA), led by Colonel John Garang, split in 1991 when ethnic Nuer troops, protesting alleged Dinka domination, joined dissident Riak Machar in the Southern Sudan Independence Movement. The fissure seriously weakened the rebels' military position, but no group appears headed for a decisive victory.

Repression in the north continued in 1995 as several newspapers were closed and opposition figures arrested. The regime instituted a broad crackdown on access to information, including confiscation of fax and telex machines by which news and information deemed "politically sensitive" had been reaching the country. Typewriters and copiers have also reportedly been seized. The campaign was accompanied by numerous arrests and reports of harsh treatment of detainees. Former Prime Minister Sadiq al-Medhi, overthrown in the 1989 coup, was detained in May, but released in September along with several other political figures in a limited amnesty.

Widespread abuses have been reported by nearly every faction involved in the war. But particularly horrific excesses were detailed in the London-based Africa Rights' accounts of government atrocities against the western Nuba people. A possible motivation for what the group describes as a "war of annihilation" against 1.5 million Nuba people is the regime's desire to "Arabize" the Nuba Mountains, which include potentially oil-rich areas.

Rights groups have criticized massive relocation programs that are driving squatters—nearly all southern blacks—away from the capital, Khartoum. There have been many reports of seized children being forced into servitude while many others—perhaps 100,000 or more—were placed in Islamic schools. Many were taken from among 140 schools for displaced southern children that in 1992 were shut down or seized by officials, who described them as "havens for infidel Christian sympathizers" of the SPLA.

The regime's intent to impose fundamentalist values on Sudan's diverse society remains intact. After the Beijing Women's conference, Khartoum refused to honor any part of the resulting accord that conflicted with its fundamentalist interpretation of Islam. And in July, NIF leader al-Turabi offered an interviewer the last word on Sudan's Islamicization: "I prefer evolution and not revolution to implement shari'a. But of course if force is used then force should be countered by force. This is what all revolutions are about."

Suriname

Polity: Presidential-par-
liamentary democracy
Economy: Capitalist-
statist
Population: 423,000
PPP: $3,730
Life Expectancy: 70.3

Political Rights: 3
Civil Liberties: 3
Status: Partly Free

Ethnic Groups: East Indian (37 percent), Creole (31 percent),
Javanese (15 percent), Bush Negro, Indian, Chinese, European
Capital: Paramaribo

Overview: With the economy in shambles and the ruling coalition
losing popularity, ex-dictator Desi Bouterse looked to be a
front-runner in national elections scheduled for mid-1996.

The Republic of Suriname achieved independence from the Netherlands in
1975 and functioned as a parliamentary democracy until a 1980 military coup.
Bouterse emerged as the strongman of a regime that brutally suppressed civic and
political opposition.

In 1987 Bouterse gave way to civilian rule under a new constitution providing
for a parliamentary democracy, with a fifty-one-member National Assembly
elected for a five-year term and empowered to select the nation's president. The
Front for Democracy and Development, a three-party coalition, won the 1987
elections, taking forty of fifty-one legislative seats. The National Democratic Party
(NDP), the army's political front, won three seats. The Assembly elected
Ramsewak Shankar president.

In 1990, Shankar was ousted in a bloodless military coup and replaced by a
government controlled by Bouterse. Under international pressure, elections were
held in 1991. The winner was the New Front (NF), essentially the same coalition of
Hindustani, Creole and Javanese parties that had been ousted in 1990. The NF won
thirty seats and its presidential candidate, Ronald Venetiaan, took office. The NDP
won twelve seats and the newly formed Democratic Alternative 91 (DA 91), an
ethnically mixed coalition led by young professionals, nine.

Under Venetiaan a number of constitutional measures were adopted to limit the
power of the military, and in 1992 Bouterse resigned from the armed forces to
formally lead the NDP. But the economy continued to deteriorate, especially after
the Dutch cut off financial assistance in 1993 because of Venetiaan's refusal to sign
on to an International Monetary Fund structural adjustment program. The last two
years have been marked by increasing unemployment and poverty, food-price riots
and labor strikes.

In 1995, Bouterse capitalized on the economic malaise by leading demonstrations and making fiery speeches. Meanwhile, the wealth he and his former
military associates illicitly accumulated while in power has made the NDP one of
the richest organizations in the country. The fear of rising social tensions and
the real possibility that the NDP might win the 1996 elections were key factors

in the Dutch government's decision in late 1995 to renew aid to the Venetiaan government.

Political Rights and Civil Liberties: Citizens are able to choose their government in relatively free elections. The constitution guarantees the right to organize political parties, civic organizations and labor unions. Parties are organized mostly along ethnic lines, which promotes governmental gridlock in Suriname's ethnically complex society.

Labor unions are well-organized and legally permitted to strike, but other civic institutions remain weak. There were numerous labor stoppages in 1995.

The constitution guarantees the right of free expression. Radio is both public and private, with a number of small commercial radio stations competing with the government-owned radio and television broadcasting system. All broadcast in the various local languages and usually offer different points of view. There are a number of independent newspapers. Intimidation by the military has lessened, but anonymous threats continue and a number of outlets practice a degree of self-censorship.

A peace accord was signed in 1992 between the government and two rebel groups, the Bush Negro-based Jungle Commando and the indigenous-based, military-linked Tucuyana Amazonas. The guerrillas agreed to disarm, but the government has had difficulty complying with its commitment to economic and social programs in the country's interior, and tensions remain. Remnants of the insurgencies still roam the interior as bandits.

The constitution provides for an independent judiciary but the judicial system is weak and ineffective, particularly against corruption in the government and the military and in addressing human rights cases. The rule of law is especially weak in the thinly populated interior, where in 1995 there were allegations that private security police in the hire of foreign mining interests were intimidating Bush Negro villagers and encroaching on their land.

There are a number of respected human rights groups. With the return to civilian rule in 1991 and the lessening of rights violations, they have been seeking justice for violations committed under military rule. A primary obstacle is the terms of the 1992 accord granting amnesty to former rebels and the military for rights violations committed during the conflict.

Some rights cases have been brought before the Inter-American Court of Human Rights, whose authority has been recognized by the Venetiaan government. In 1991, the government accepted responsibility for the murder of seven Bush Negroes by the military in 1987 and agreed to pay damages to the victims' families.

Swaziland

Polity: Traditional
monarchy
Economy: Capitalist
Population: 967,000
PPP: $1,700
Life Expectancy: 57.5
Ethnic Groups: Swazi, Zulu, European
Capital: Mbabane

Political Rights: 6
Civil Liberties: 5
Status: Not Free

Overview:
Swazis live under southern Africa's last unelected government, a distinction that became more glaring in 1995 as democratic consolidation continued in South Africa and a tentative multiparty system took hold in Mozambique. Trade unionists and political activists are increasingly defiant in their calls for representative government, and King Mswati III has promised a new constitutional arrangement, but strong opposition from traditional chiefs will complicate reform.

Swaziland was a British protectorate that achieved independence with an elected parliament in 1968. Mswati III's predecessor, Sobhuza II, replaced the multiparty system with *tinkhundla* (regional councils) in 1973, and there have since been no genuine direct elections. A series of *vusela* (consultations) have been held among Swaziland's 900,000 people since 1991, ostensibly to determine what changes in political and economic structures the people desire. The king rejected a report suggesting multiparty elections, and in September-October 1993 local chiefs voted through the tinkhundla system for fifty-five of sixty-five members of the House of Assembly. The king appoints ten additional members, as well as twenty of thirty Senate members; the House of Assembly selects the remainder. Legislative power is highly restricted, and the king can issue decrees with the full force of law.

A 1973 ban on political activity is only sporadically enforced. In November, trade unionists and representatives from ten banned political groups agreed to form a united front to press for democratization. Increasingly vocal domestic demands for reform and pressure from international donors to open the system moved Mswati to promise a new constitution—replacing the suspended 1973 charter—that his advisors said would include a bill of rights. Such pledges are regarded with deep cynicism, however, and in October the parliament further curbed the media after criticisms of the king were published.

Political Rights and Civil Liberties:
Swaziland's citizens cannot change their government democratically. The bicameral legislature is indirectly elected and appointed, and does little more than rubber-stamp decisions by the king and his advisers.

While broad public contact through the vusela consultations produced sometimes surprisingly frank criticisms of the government, the institution appears more an effort to defuse public opinion than to heed it. Power remains closely held by the royal clan and other traditional chiefs.

Free expression is limited, particularly regarding political issues or the royal family. Self-censorship long prevailed in Swaziland, although the early 1990s produced increased openness. This trend may have been reversed in 1995, however, after the privately owned *Times of Swaziland* criticized Mswati for taking a thirty-person entourage to New York for the U.N. fiftieth anniversary celebration. The paper suggested the huge expense was especially inappropriate at a time when drought is threatening at least 90,000 Swazis with food shortages and perhaps famine. In response, late in October the legislature banned publication of any criticism of the monarchy. State-run television and radio, Swaziland's most important media, remain dominated by the government.

Religious freedom is respected, and a variety of Christian sects operate freely. Nonpolitical nongovernmental organizations are permitted. Political groupings, including the People's United Democratic Movement and the Swaziland Youth Congress, are illegal though somewhat tolerated, and security forces routinely harass and detain members, usually for brief periods.

In 1993, indefinite pretrial detention under the Non-Bailable Offences order was decreed for suspects of crimes including murder, robbery, rape, weapons offenses and poaching. The Swazi Law Society and international groups argue the decree serves effectively to convict people without trial and is a denial of the presumption of innocence.

Swazi women are discriminated against in both formal and customary law. A married woman is treated as a minor, and usually requires her husband's permission to undertake almost any economic activity, from borrowing money to opening a bank account. Employment regulations stipulate equal pay for equal work, but women still earn less than men doing the same jobs. Wife-beating and other violence against women is common, and traditional values still carry weight. In October, women wearing trousers were barred from all government offices.

The 1980 Industrial Relations Act recognized labor rights, and unions operate independently. Wage agreements are often reached by collective bargaining, and over three-quarters of the private workforce is unionized. Tripartite negotiations among trade unionists, the employers' federation and the government have produced agreement on new labor legislation geared to convince investors that there will be long-term labor peace.

Most Swazis engage in subsistence agriculture, but its free-market sector operates with little government interference. The government is considering plans to privatize some parastatal concerns, including the unprofitable national airline. But greater government transparency, and curbs on corruption and royal extravagance are also needed to attract foreign capital.

Sweden

Polity: Parliamentary democracy
Economy: Mixed capitalist
Population: 8,857,000
PPP: $18,320
Life Expectancy: 78.2
Ethnic Groups: Swede (88 percent), Finn (2 percent), Lappic (Saami), immigrant groups
Capital: Stockholm

Political Rights: 1
Civil Liberties: 1
Status: Free

Overview: Sweden's minority Social Democrats spent much of the year introducing austerity measures to curb a huge budget deficit inherited from their center-right predecessors. After ushering the party back into power following three years in opposition and persuading a reluctant electorate to vote for European Union membership, Prime Minister Ingvar Carlsson announced he would resign as both premier and party head in March 1996.

Sweden's long history of neutrality has allowed the government to concentrate on industrial development and create an extensive system of social welfare. For a century prior to 1970, Sweden enjoyed a growth rate unrivaled by any other industrialized nation and channeled its wealth into the generous benefit system. The early 1990s saw the worst economic recession in sixty years, with unemployment shooting up from virtually nothing in 1991 to 13 percent four years later. Amid plummeting popularity, the Social Democrats have introduced four austerity packages including both welfare cuts and higher taxes.

Months of unrest followed Carlsson's retirement announcement, and an embarrassing credit card scandal forced his apparent successor, Deputy Prime Minister Mona Sahlin, to resign from government, leaving the party with no obvious leadership. By December, however, the government's tough budget program had begun to produce positive results well above predictions and the party turned to Finance Minister Goran Persson, who accepted the challenge. In addition to stabilizing the fragile economic recovery, the government must also settle debates over plans to phase out the country's nuclear reactors by 2010 as well as disagreement over a future social welfare structure.

Political Rights and Civil Liberties: Swedes can change their government democratically. Every three years, 310 members are directly elected to the *Riksdag* (parliament) through universal suffrage. To ensure absolute proportionality to all parties securing over 4 percent of the vote, another thirty-nine representatives are selected from a national pool. Citizens living abroad are entitled to absentee votes in national elections, and non-nationals in residence for three years are permitted to vote in local elections. The 20,000 member Lappic (Saami) community elects its own local assembly with significant powers over education and culture.

The new constitution transformed the role of the sovereign, currently King Carl Gustaf XVI, making it a ceremonial one. Responsibility for appointing the prime minister transferred to the speaker of the house, with confirmation by the Riksdag as a whole. The independent judiciary includes six Courts of Appeal, 100 district courts, a Supreme Court and a parallel system of administrative courts.

Freedoms of assembly and association are guaranteed, as are the rights to unionize and strike. Strong and well organized trade union federations represent over 80 percent of the labor force. Despite historical ties with the Social Democrats, the labor movement has become increasingly independent in recent years.

Most Swedish newspapers are politically oriented if not party-owned. In 1977, the Mass Media Act extended the government's commitment to noninterference to all forms of information media. However, publications or videos containing excessive violence or national security information are subject to censorship.

Discussion arose this year concerning freedom of expression and incitements to racism. Several anti-immigrant attacks have occurred in recent years, including some by an underground racist group called the Aryan Resistance Front. Critics charge that the government has done very little to stop racist violence and right-wing extremism, and in isolated incidents may have even inadvertently subsidized extremist groups. Recently, however, the justice minister began a campaign to extend a 1930s law against political uniforms to include certain symbols such as the swastika, under the assumption that displaying such symbols constitutes agitation to racism.

Religious freedom is constitutionally guaranteed in this overwhelmingly Lutheran country. In 1995, the government and the Church agreed to disestablish the state religion. The change in status, which will not take effect in its entirety until 2000, will make baptism required for membership and do away with the mandatory 3 percent tax that members are currently required to pay. Muslims, Buddhists, Hindus and Jews are represented among the population, and compulsory religion classes in schools have expanded to include a variety of religious beliefs.

Sweden has attempted to foster gender equality through the social welfare system. In 1994, the Riksdag passed a law requiring fathers to take at least one of the twelve months' state-subsidized child-care leave or else lose a month's benefits. Women constitute roughly 45 percent of the labor force and average about 28 percent participation in local and national government. Largely due to the Social Democratic Labor Party policies, the current parliament is almost equally composed of men and women.

Switzerland

Polity: Federal par-
liamentary democracy
Economy: Capitalist
Population: 7,045,000
PPP: $22,580
Life Expectancy: 78.0
Ethnic Groups: German, French, Italian, Romansch
Capital: Bern (administrative), Lausanne (judicial)

Political Rights: 1
Civil Liberties: 1
Status: Free

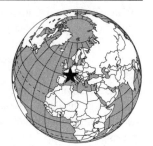

Overview:
With the electorate clearly polarized, voting in October significantly altered the dynamics of the thirty-six-year-old ruling coalition. Future relations with an integrated Europe remain a priority on the political agenda as the landlocked country becomes increasingly isolated among its EU neighbors.

With the exception of a brief period of centralized power under Napoleonic rule, Switzerland has remained a confederation of local communities as established in the Pact of 1291. The 1815 Congress of Vienna formalized the country's borders and recognized the state as one of perpetual neutrality. Despite the adoption of a new constitution in 1874 increasing the power of central government, a noncentralist tradition continues. An enormous degree of responsibility rests at the local and cantonal levels, and with the electorate itself.

Switzerland is often cited as a rare example of peaceful coexistence in a multi-ethnic state. Encompassing German, French, Romansch and Italian groups, the republic is divided into twenty cantons and six half cantons, with individual political systems, a dominant ethnic or linguistic group and distinct customs. Stable language borders clearly delineate the regions inhabited by linguistic groups, and adjustments are generally expected of migrants.

Growing concern over immigration played a large role in the 1992 referendum rejecting European Economic Area membership. With over 20 percent of the population currently comprised of foreigners, Swiss nationals feared a mass influx of EU immigrants. Current popular sentiment on future EU membership is approaching an even split. In October, the People's Party gained five seats, bringing them to just four seats behind the Christian Democrats, on a platform opposing EU membership and supporting substantial cuts in federal spending. Clearly the biggest victors in the elections, the pro-EU, pro-welfare Social Democrats emerged with fifty-four seats, up from forty-two in 1991, displacing the Radical Democratic Party as the coalition's strongest member. After largely avoiding the federal budget issue and EU membership since the 1992 referendum, the new parliament is expected to confront them head-on. A referendum calling for a new decision on European integration may soon be on the horizon.

Political Rights and Civil Liberties:
The Swiss can change their government democratically. Voters frequently use their power to call for a federal plebiscite with 100,000 signatures as well as their ability to

initiate constitutional amendments. The cantonal system allows considerable local autonomy, which helps to preserve localities' linguistic and cultural heritage.

At the national level, both houses of the Federal Assembly have equal authority. Once legislation has been passed in both the directly-elected, 200-member National Council and the Council of States, comprised of two members from each canton, it cannot be vetoed by the executive or reviewed by the judiciary. Seven members of the Federal Council, or *Bundesrat*—chosen from the Federal Assembly according to a "magic formula" ensuring representation for each party, region and language group—exercise executive authority. Each year, one member serves as president. The judicial system functions primarily at the cantonal level, with the exception of a federal Supreme Court that reviews cantonal court decisions involving federal law.

The government's postal ministry operates broadcasting services for the linguistically and politically pluralistic Swiss Radio and Television Society. As of 1993, about fifty private television and radio stations were in operation as well. Myriad privately owned daily, weekly and monthly publications are available in each of the most common languages and are free of government interference.

In addition to freedom of speech, freedoms of assembly, association and religion are observed. The only recent report of rights abuses was a 1994 Amnesty International report citing excessive force used by police against persons in custody, particularly foreigners. The report was issued shortly after the National Council increased police powers of search and detention of foreigners lacking identification, in an effort to curb the drug trade. In February 1995, federal laws aimed at dissuading drug traffickers from entering Switzerland authorized pretrial detention of illegal residents for as long as nine months. With 33,000 drug addicts in a population of 7 million, use of hard drugs has become one of the country's most pernicious social ailments.

Despite Switzerland's reputation as an egalitarian society, barriers to women's political and social advancement persist. Although women were granted federal suffrage in 1971, it was not until a 1990 Supreme Court order that the half canton, Appenzell-Innerrhoden, gave up its status as the last bastion of all-male suffrage in Europe. Until the mid-1980s, women were prohibited from participating in the Federal Council. Debates persist concerning the exclusion of women from the military. Some charge that the army creates networking opportunities for men, putting women at an economic disadvantage. In general, women's rights have improved over the last decade.

Syria

Polity: Dominant party
(military-dominated)
Economy: Mixed statist
Population: 14,661,000
PPP: $4,960
Life Expectancy: 67.1
Ethnic Groups: Arab (90 percent), Kurd, Armenian, others
Capital: Damascus

Political Rights: 7
Civil Liberties: 7
Status: Not Free

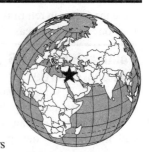

Overview: **S**yrian President Hafez al-Assad, seeking to preserve the Arab nationalist credentials on which his domestic legitimacy is based, coolly rebuffed Israeli peace overtures in 1995.

The French declared Syria a republic in 1941, and granted full independence in 1944. A 1963 military coup brought the pan-Arab, socialist Ba'ath Party to power. Leadership struggles within the Ba'ath Party continued until 1970 when the military wing, led by then-Lieut.-Gen. Hafez al-Assad, took power in a bloodless coup. Assad formally became president of this secular authoritarian regime in 1971. The 1973 constitution vests strong executive power in the president, who must be a Muslim and is nominated by the Ba'ath party and elected through a popular referendum. The directly elected People's Assembly, currently consisting of 250 members, serves a four-year term but holds little independent power.

In the late 1970s, the fundamentalist Muslim Brotherhood group, drawn from the Sunni majority, began a series of antigovernment attacks in several northern and central towns. In 1982 soldiers crushed an armed Muslim Brotherhood rebellion in Hama, killing approximately 15,000-20,000 militants and civilians. Since then the government has faced few overt threats from the Islamic fundamentalists.

Assad serves as head of government, commander-in-chief of the armed forces and secretary general of the Ba'ath Party. Members of his Alawite minority hold most key military and intelligence positions. In December 1991 Assad, running unopposed after being nominated by the Assembly, won a fourth seven-year term with a reported 99.982 percent of the popular vote. Government officials closely watched the voters, who had a "yes" or "no" choice.

The death of Major Basil al-Assad, the president's son and heir-apparent, in a January 1994 auto accident left the question of Assad's successor unclear. At the 24-25 August 1994 parliamentary elections the ruling National Progressive Front, dominated by the Ba'ath Party, took all of the 167 seats it contested, with pro-regime "independents" winning the remaining eighty-three seats.

In 1995, Assad appeared to be in no rush to sign a peace treaty with Israel leading to the return of the Israeli-controlled Golan Heights. Prior to losing the Golan in 1967, Syria had used the strategic territory to shell northern Israeli towns. With his domestic legitimacy based in part on his hard line against Israel, Assad preferred to wait to cut a deal on his terms—essentially a full Israeli withdrawal from the Golan in return for minimal Syrian concessions regarding diplomatic relations and other areas.

Political Rights and Civil Liberties: Syrians cannot change their government democratically. President Hafez al-Assad maintains absolute authority in this military-backed regime. Assad does not permit opposition groups, and political dissent is forcibly suppressed.

The Emergency Law, in effect since 1963 (except during 1973-74), allows the authorities to carry out "preventive" arrests and supersedes due-process safeguards during searches, arrests, detentions, interrogations and State Security Court trials. There are several internal security services, all of which operate independently of each other and without any judicial oversight. The authorities monitor personal communications and conduct surveillance of suspected security threats. Security forces are responsible for arbitrary arrests and "disappearances," and many of those arrested are held incommunicado without charge or trial for lengthy periods. Police routinely torture political and criminal detainees.

Since late 1991, the government has freed several thousand political prisoners, although many have faced harassment after their release. The regime reportedly still holds several thousand other dissidents, in many cases incommunicado. In January, the government released three political detainees who had been held without trial since 1970; observers believe at least three others arrested in 1970 are still being held. In 1993 the U.S. National Academy of Sciences reported that in the past decade some 287 scientists, engineers and health professionals had been imprisoned, most without charge, for criticizing the government and calling for political liberalization.

The judiciary is subservient to the government. Defendants in civil and criminal cases receive some due-process rights, although there are no jury trials. Security and political offenses are handled in military-controlled State Security Courts where there are no due process safeguards. Confessions obtained through torture are generally admissible as evidence. Trials in the Economic Security Court, which hears cases involving currency violations and other financial offenses, are also conducted without procedural safeguards.

Despite constitutional guarantees, the government sharply restricts freedom of expression. The government and the Ba'ath party own and operate all media, which are mouthpieces for the regime. By law citizens may not own satellite dishes. The government must grant permission for all assemblies, and in practice only state-sponsored gatherings take place. The government must also grant permission for private associations to form, and the few existing organizations are strictly nonpolitical.

Nearly two-thirds of the population is Sunni Muslim, but members of Assad's minority Alawite Shiite sect hold most key security and government positions. The state forbids both Jehovah's Witnesses and Seventh-Day Adventists from worshipping as a community or owning church property. The security apparatus closely monitors the Jewish community, bars Jews from most state jobs, and requires Jews to have their religion stamped on their passports and identity cards. Since 1992 the government has permitted Jews greater freedom to emigrate.

The government places linguistic and cultural restrictions on the Kurdish minority. The 360,000 Palestinian refugees, many of whom were born in the country, face some restrictions in traveling abroad. Traditional conservative practices place Syrian women in a subservient position in matters including marriage, divorce and inheritance.

All unions must belong to the government-controlled General Federation of Trade Unions. By law the government can nullify any private-sector collective bargaining agreement. Strikes are strongly discouraged and rarely occur.

Taiwan (Rep. of China)

Polity: Presidential-leg- **Political Rights:** 3
islative (transitional) **Civil Liberties:** 3
Economy: Capitalist- **Status:** Partly Free
statist
Population: 21,235,000
PPP: na
Life Expectancy: 74.5
Ethnic Groups: Taiwanese (84 percent), mainland Chinese
(14 percent), aboriginal (2 percent)
Capital: Taipei

Overview: President Lee Teng-hui saw his ruling Kuomintang Party
(KMT) lose seats in December 1995 legislative elections,
but remained favored to win the country's first direct
presidential elections, scheduled for March 1996.

The island, located 100 miles off the Chinese coast, came under control of China's Nationalist government after World War II. Following the Communist victory on the mainland in 1949, Nationalist leader Chiang Kai-shek established a government-in-exile on Taiwan. For the next four decades the KMT ruled Taiwan in an authoritarian manner. Both Taiwan and China still officially consider Taiwan to be a province of China. Today native Taiwanese make up 84 percent of the population, while aging mainlanders and their descendants comprise the minority.

The 1947 Nationalist constitution provides for a National Assembly that can amend the constitution and, until 1994, had the power to elect the president and vice-president. The president serves a six-year term (four years after 1996) and holds executive powers. The government has five specialized *yuan* (branches), including a Legislative Yuan that enacts laws.

The country's democratic transition began with the lifting of martial law in 1987. In 1988 Lee Teng-hui became the first native-born Taiwanese president, and a year later the government formally legalized opposition parties. In 1990 the Assembly elected Lee to a full term. Since then Lee has alienated the once-dominant mainlander faction of the KMT by asserting native Taiwanese control of the party, and by largely abandoning the party's formal commitment to eventual reunification with China.

In 1991 Taiwanese elected a new National Assembly. At the time the Assembly consisted mostly of aging mainlanders elected in 1947 or 1969. The KMT won 254 of 325 contested seats. The Democratic Progressive Party (DPP), which favors formal independence, took 66, and independents 5. In 1992 the country held its first full Legislative Yuan elections since the Nationalists fled the mainland, with the KMT taking 96 of the 161 seats.

In February 1993, the Legislative Yuan swore in Lien Chan as the first native Taiwanese prime minister. In August a group of disgruntled second-generation mainlanders led by Jaw Shau-kong bolted from the KMT to form the New Party. In July 1994, the National Assembly amended the constitution to clear the way for direct presidential elections in March 1996.

In August 1995, Lee formally announced his candidacy for the presidential elections. Key issues in the campaign for the 2 December Legislative Yuan elections included the increasing penetration of organized crime into politics and law enforcement, and criticism of the KMT's close links with big business. The KMT won only eighty-five seats; the DPP, fifty-four; the New Party, twenty-one; and independents, four (three seats were added to adjust for larger population).

Political Rights and Civil Liberties: Direct presidential elections scheduled for March 1996 should cap Taiwan's democratic transition. However, the ruling KMT maintains significant advantages over the opposition through its control of the media and the government apparatus, and through its huge financial holdings. Elections at all levels are marred by vote-buying and some campaign violence.

The judiciary is not fully independent in sensitive cases. Police abuse of suspects in custody is a continuing problem. The "Anti-Hoodlum Law" allows police to detain alleged hoodlums on the basis of testimony by secret informers, and suspects can be sent for reformatory education through administrative procedure rather than a trial.

In 1992, the government amended the Sedition Law to decriminalize advocacy of formal independence from China. However, the National Security Law and related statutes still place restrictions on such advocacy.

The Publications Law allows police to censor or ban publications considered seditious or treasonous. Journalists reportedly practice self-censorship on sensitive issues. The KMT, the Taiwan provincial government and the military maintain controlling shares in the country's three main television stations, and political coverage strongly favors the government. Private cable television provides diverse viewpoints. In 1993 and 1994 the government issued the first fully private radio licenses, but only for low-powered stations with limited ranges. Between August 1994 and January 1995 the government raided several pro-DPP pirate radio stations.

The Parade and Assembly Law (PAL) requires a permit for demonstrations. Although assemblies held without a permit are generally dispersed without charges being filed, some opposition leaders have been charged under a section of the PAL that holds organizers responsible for public order at demonstrations. Under the Civic Organizations Law all organizations must register with the government. Nongovernmental organizations are active and generally function without harassment.

Women face workplace discrimination, including lower salaries and fewer promotion opportunities than men. Incidents of rape and domestic violence are widespread. Child prostitution is also a serious problem, and over one-fifth of child prostitutes are from Taiwan's tiny aboriginal minority. The aboriginal population suffers from social and economic alienation; may not sell or develop land; has a limited say in policy decisions regarding its land and natural resources; and may not use non-Chinese names on legal documents. Conditions are harsh in detention camps holding illegal mainland Chinese immigrants and other foreign workers.

The authorities have refused to certify new trade unions on the grounds that competing unions in a given sector already existed. The law only permits one labor federation, and this grants a monopoly to the pro-KMT Chinese Federation of Labor. Civil servants, defense industry workers and teachers cannot unionize and may not bargain collectively. Several provisions of the labor code restrict the right to strike. The authorities can impose involuntary mediation of disputes; the majority of a union's members must approve a strike; and the authorities must approve the meetings to hold these strike votes. The lack of effective legislation against anti-union discrimination has facilitated the dismissal of scores of trade union activists in recent years.

Tajikistan

Polity: Dominant party (presidential-dominated)
Economy: Statist
Population: 5,839,000
PPP: $1,740
Life Expectancy: 70.2
Ethnic Groups: Tajik (65 percent), Uzbek (25 percent), Russian (4 percent), others
Capital: Dushanbe

Political Rights: 7
Civil Liberties: 7
Status: Not Free

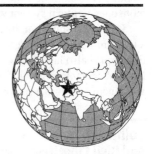

Overview: In 1995, this Central Asian republic remained in the repressive grip of President Emomali Rakhmonov as 25,000 Russian troops battled violent incursions by the Afghanistan-based opposition. February elections to the 181-member parliament were little more than a staged bid to reinforce presidential power, according to international observers who refused to send monitors.

Among the poorest former Soviet republics, Tajikistan was carved out of the Uzbek Soviet Republic on Stalin's orders in 1929. Leaving Samarkand and Bukhara, the two main centers of Tajik culture, inside Uzbekistan, angered Tajiks, who trace their origins to Persia. The four major regional clans are the Leninabad and Kulyab (the current ruling alliance), the Gharm and the Badakhshan.

In December 1992, after months of ethnic and political conflict, Russian-backed former Communist hardliners overthrew a governing coalition of Muslim activists from the Islamic Renaissance Party (IRP), secular democrats and national-ists. Rakhmonov, a Communist, was named head of state (he was directly elected in November 1994), and launched an ethnic war in the Gharm, Badakhshan and Pamiri regions that had supported the democratic-Islamic opposition. The terror drove some 60,000 people across the Armu Daray river into Afghanistan, from which the opposition launched violent raids.

The February 1995 parliamentary vote was boycotted by the opposition, including the Party of Popular Unity led by former presidential candidate Abdulmalik Abdulladjanov, who lost to Rakhmonov. Opponents blamed violations of election law and official pressure on their candidates. Of the handful of legal political parties, the Communists were the strongest, but even they fielded only 46 of 345 registered candidates; over 40 percent of seats were uncontested. Most new deputies were not formally affiliated with any party but were firmly pro-Rakhmonov.

The spring saw a renewal of heavy fighting along the Afghan-Tajik border, shattering a truce reached in the fall of 1994. Rebel leaders said that the Tajik Army and Russian border guards provoked the fighting by moving hundreds of troops into the mountains in violation of the ceasefire. On 24 April, opposition leaders at U.N.-sponsored negotiations in Moscow welcomed Rakhmonov's offer of face-to-face talks with IRP leader Said Abdulla Nuri, and agreed to a ceasefire until May. The two men met in Kabul and agreed to extend the ceasefire for three months. The return of Tajik refugees from Afghanistan, a new constitution and a more open political system were unresolved issues.

Fighting resumed in the fall after negotiations failed. In September, the head of a U.N. military observer group was killed along the Afghan-Tajik border. Opposition groups also launched a series of raids in the Pamir mountains in October and November, capturing Tajik soldiers and allegedly killing civilians. In December, amid increased border incidents, negotiations in the Turkmen capital, Ashgabat, remained deadlocked.

Political Rights and Civil Liberties: Citizens cannot change their government democratically in what is a de facto one-party Communist system controlled by President Rakhmonov. The constitution, adopted by referendum in 1994, provides for a strong executive, who serves as head of parliament and has broad powers to appoint and dismiss officials. Parliamentary elections were boycotted by the internal quasi-opposition parties, and were neither free nor fair.

While political parties are nominally permitted, there are only four officially recognized groups—the Communist Party, the Party of Political and Economic Revival, the Popular Party and the Party of Popular (People's) Unity. Party affiliation is weak, and all are pro-government. The IRP, the Democratic Party and the Lali Badakhshan are banned, and most of their top leaders reside outside the country.

The government has total control of the Tajik media. All opposition media are closed. Under the press law, there are legal penalties for libeling officials, and Soviet-era restrictions on criticism of government bureaucrats apply. In May, Mirzo Salimov, correspondent for the Moscow-based Tajik opposition newspaper *Charogi Ruz*, was arrested. The interior and security ministries refused to disclose his whereabouts or fate.

Islam was revived after many decades, though the regime has intruded into religious life to preclude fundamentalism and antigovernment activities.

Pervasive security forces and a Soviet-era judiciary subservient to the regime effectively curtail freedoms of expression, assembly and association. Killings and assassinations by both government forces and rebels are common. The government has been accused of ethnic cleansing in the southern Gharm and Pamir regions. External and internal refugees have returned to regions where the Kulyabis exercise less local authority and where the U.N. High Commission on Refugees is present; in other areas, returning refugees have faced harassment, intimidation and murder.

There are no independent trade unions. The rights of women are circumscribed in practice. The few nongovernmental organizations are monitored or repressed. Islamic groups are prevented from active participation in political life.

Tanzania

Polity: Dominant party **Political Rights:** 5*
Economy: Statist **Civil Liberties**: 5*
Population: 28,463,000 **Status:** Partly Free
PPP: $620
Life Expectancy: 52.1
Ethnic Groups: African, Asian and Arab minorities
Capital: Dar-es-Salaam
Ratings Change: *Tanzania's political rights rating changed from 6 to 5, as did its civil liberties rating, moving it into the Partly Free category, because of increased openess of the political system and more open media and public discussion.

Overview: Tanzania's opportunity to join the ranks of democratic states was squandered in October, as the country's first genuine multiparty legislative and presidential elections were marred countrywide by administrative chaos and irregularities, and in Zanzibar by outright fraud. But despite the many flaws, new President Benjamin Mkapa's strong showing offers the man dubbed "Mr. Clean" in a land riddled by corruption a chance to further open Tanzania's polity and economy. Yet it is unclear whether this would be done despite or with the participation of the long-ruling Chama Cha Mapinduzi (CCM, Party for the Revolution).

Under President Julius Nyerere the CCM dominated Tanzania's political life after independence from Britain in 1961. Following a bloody 1964 revolution that deposed its Arab sultans, Zanzibar and Pemba Islands merged with then-Tanganyika to become Tanzania, under a power-sharing arrangement that guaranteed the islanders limited autonomy. Islanders number 700,000 and are 90 percent Muslim, compared to 26 million mainly Christian and animist people on the mainland. Nyerere's socialist policies impoverished his country, and were accompanied by quiet repression little noticed amid far more flamboyant, brutal dictators and long anti-colonial and anti-white minority struggles in southern Africa.

Nyerere retired in 1985, but retained strong influence in the government of his successor, Ali Hassan Mwinyi. Opposition parties were legalized in 1992, but the one-party parliament was allowed to complete its five-year term in October 1995.

Preparation for elections was far from smooth. Amid generally open and spirited debate, authorities made extensive use of state resources for campaigning and imposed some media restrictions. Yet the lopsided results still surprised most observers. The CCM took four-fifths of the 232 parliamentary seats, and in the presidential contest challenger Augustine Mrema of the National Convention for Reconstruction and Reform reportedly won under 30 percent of votes. Local and international monitors denounced the election's conduct. The High Court summarily rejected opposition demands for fresh polls.

The administrative chaos observers said prevailed on the mainland made any real assessment of validity impossible. On Zanzibar and Pemba, 22 October balloting went smoothly with a massive turnout. The election was apparently stolen during the counting and reporting of votes. The official Zanzibar Election Commission (ZEC) took four days to announce that the ruling CCM's candidate for the islands' presidency had won by only about 1 percent of nearly 330,00 votes counted. Local legislative elections produced a similarly narrow CCM victory over the opposition Civic United Front. Independent observers found the ZEC miscounted or reversed results in several constituencies to keep the CCM in power.

Political Rights and Civil Liberties: The multiparty system introduced in 1992 failed it first serious test in October 1995 elections that were neither free nor fair. The presidential result may generally reflect the people's will, and President Mkapa's mandate appears legitimate, if tarnished. The CCM's landslide legislative victory is less credible. The ruling party's partisan use of state broadcasting and other government resources during the campaign tilted the electoral playing field even before the vote. And results in Zanzibar must be dismissed as little more than outright electoral theft.

With only about 20 percent of legislative seats going to the opposition, it remains unclear whether the legislature will provide a meaningful forum for debate, or whether the CCM will de facto continue its authoritarian—and largely incompetent and corrupt—one-party rule.

Media freedom has increased dramatically since political opposition was legalized in 1992, but government dominance over broadcast media still severely limits expression of pluralistic views. The few private radio stations broadcast only nonpolitical programming. The small independent press offered wide-ranging views, but circulation was limited mostly to the major cities. In 1995, several journalists who reported on extensive corruption were arrested or otherwise harassed, and publication of political cartoons was banned. In one of his first speeches as president, Mkapa, a former journalist, pledged to uphold press freedom, but criticized what he called a lack of professional ethics in reporting on the election.

Tanzania's judiciary has shown signs of increased independence, but remains subject to considerable political influence. Constitutional guarantees of free assembly are not always respected in practice. Laws allow rallies only by officially registered political parties, which may not be formed on religious, ethnic or regional bases and cannot oppose the union of Zanzibar and the mainland. Religious freedom is respected, although fundamentalist groups on Zanzibar are pressing for a stricter application of *shari'a* law there, and Muslims generally complain of discrimination. Numerous nongovernmental organizations are active, but some human rights groups have had difficulty in receiving required official registration. The distribution of Tanzania's population among many ethnic groups has diffused potential ethnic rivalries that have wracked its neighbors, but resentment against the small but economically advanced South Asian minority could become a serious flashpoint.

Women's rights often exist only on paper. Women's opportunities for formal-sector employment are restricted by both custom and statute. Especially in rural areas and in Zanzibar, traditional or Islamic customary law that is discriminatory toward women prevails in most family law matters. Domestic violence against women is common, and rarely prosecuted.

Workers cannot freely organize and join trade unions. The Organization of Tanzania Trade Unions is the official and only labor federation, and remains loosely linked to the ruling CCM. The right to strike is restricted by complex notification and conciliation requirements, and collective bargaining effectively exists only in the small private sector.

A large-scale privatization program is underway in hopes of reviving Tanzania's moribund economy. Lingering statist policies and pervasive corruption could hinder any early progress.

Thailand

Polity: Parliamentary democracy (military-influenced) **Political Rights:** 3
Civil Liberties: 4*
Status: Partly Free
Economy: Capitalist-statist
Population: 60,206,000
PPP: $5,950
Life Expectancy: 69.0
Ethnic Groups: Thai (75 percent), Chinese (14 percent), Malay, Indian, Khmer, Vietnamese
Capital: Bangkok

Ratings Change: *Thailand's civil liberties rating changed from 5 to 4 because of greater government efforts to deal with child prostitution and more vigorous media coverage of corruption and other sensitive issues.

Overview:
Early elections in July 1995 brought a seven-party coalition government to power under the Thai Nation party's Banharn Silpa-archa.

Thailand is the only Southeast Asian nation never colonized by a European country. In 1932 a bloodless coup, the first of seventeen coups or coup attempts this century, led to a new constitution limiting the power of the monarchy. Today King Bhumibol Alduyadej's only formal duty is to approve the prime minister, but he remains widely revered and exerts informal political influence.

A February 1991 coup deposed the elected government of Chatichai Choonhaven, who had attempted to limit the military's influence in politics. In

December, an interim National Assembly approved a controversial new constitution that allowed the military to appoint the entire 270-seat Senate, and permitted the prime minister to come from outside the ranks of elected MPs.

At the March 1992 Assembly elections, three pro-military parties won 190 seats to take a slim majority in the 360-seat House of Representatives. The Assembly named coup leader Suchinda Kraprayoon, who had not stood in the elections, as prime minister, leading to widespread street demonstrations in Bangkok in May. Soldiers killed over fifty protesters. King Bhumibol brokered Suchinda's resignation, and parliament subsequently amended the constitution to require that future premiers come from among the elected MPs. At fresh elections in September the Democratic Party took seventy-nine seats and formed a five-party, pro-democracy coalition under party leader Chuan Leekpai.

In May 1995, Chuan's coalition collapsed over a land-reform scandal. Chuan was not implicated, and after thirty-two months in office he earned the distinction of being Thailand's longest-serving elected premier. At the 2 July parliamentary elections the rural-based Thai Nation party won ninety-two seats; Democratic Party, eighty-six; New Aspiration Party, fifty-seven; National Development Party, fifty-three; Moral Force, twenty-three; Social Action Party, twenty-two; Dynamic Thai, eighteen; Thai Citizens, eighteen; and three smaller parties, twenty-two. Thai Nation's Banharn Silpa-archa formed a seven-party governing coalition and became premier. Skeptics questioned whether Silpa-archa, a patronage-oriented politician, would be able to deal with critical issues including a growing wealth disparity between Bangkok and the rural areas and an inadequate educational system.

In another development, in January the fall of the rebel Karen National Union headquarters in Burma sent 10,000 Karen refugees into Thailand, swelling the total to 90,000. Beginning in February, the Burmese army and the self-styled Democratic Karen Army of Burma carried out a series of attacks in Thai territory, killing or abducting several refugees and burning hundreds of homes.

Political Rights **T**hai citizens can change their government democratically,
and Civil Liberties: although the possibility of a future military coup cannot be discounted. Vote-buying is rampant in rural areas. Power is largely decentralized, although thousands of village headmen are not elected. Several high-level politicians have been implicated in drug-trafficking schemes and official corruption is widespread. An amnesty protects soldiers responsible for over fifty deaths in the May 1992 pro-democracy demonstrations.

The judiciary is independent of the government but highly corrupt. Police have been implicated in several summary executions, and frequently torture detainees and abuse prisoners. Conditions at the Suan Phlu immigration detention center are harsh, and female detainees are frequently raped.

Laws broadly restrict expression in several areas, including defaming the monarchy (*lese majeste*), advocating a Communist government, and speech that could potentially incite disturbances. In April, a Bangkok court dropped a two-year-old case of lese majeste against writer Sulak Sivaraksa.

The press freely criticizes government policies but exercises self-censorship regarding the military and other sensitive issues. In August package bombs were sent to the editor and publisher of *Thai Nation*, a major newspaper that had criticized promotions in the police ranks. In October, the government used the lese majeste law to temporarily deny visas to Australian journalists after an unflattering cartoon of the monarch appeared in a Melbourne daily. The government or military controls each of the five national television networks, and news coverage marginalizes the opposition. A government censorship committee occasionally deletes politically sensitive material from private radio broadcasts.

In July 1994, the government prevented foreign participation in a Bangkok conference on the Indonesian territory of East Timor. Rural officials occasionally falsely charge peaceful demonstrators with inciting unrest and intent to commit violence. Nongovernmental organizations (NGOs) operate openly, but are often monitored and sometimes harassed by police.

NGOs estimate that there are at least 250,000 prostitutes in Thailand, and up to one-fifth are under eighteen. Many are trafficked from hill tribes and from neighboring Burma. In some cases families sell girls into prostitution, where they essentially become bonded laborers. Efforts to crack down on prostitution are undermined by the complicity of police and local officials in prostitution schemes. Women also face domestic violence, and in the workplace are frequently paid below the minimum wage.

Muslims face societal and employment discrimination, and some say the school curriculum is biased toward the Buddhist majority. By some accounts there are several Muslim activists imprisoned on criminal charges for their political views. Roughly half of the 500,000-700,000 members of hill tribes are not registered as citizens, and thus cannot vote or own land and have difficulty in obtaining social services. In addition to the poor protection offered Karen refugees (*see Overview*), during the year the army pushed back or forcibly repatriated Shan and Lahu refugees from Burma.

The law grants only private-sector workers the right to join independent unions. State enterprise workers may only join "associations" that by law may not negotiate wages or hold strikes. Workers in the process of establishing a union are not protected from anti-union discrimination. Child labor is widespread. Safety regulations are flouted at many factories and enforcement is lax.

Togo

Polity: Military dominated
Economy: Mixed statist
Population: 4,410,000
PPP: $1,220
Life Expectancy: 55.0
Ethnic Groups: Aja, Ewe, Gurensi, Kabye, Krachi, Mina, Tem, others
Capital: Lome

Political Rights: 6
Civil Liberties: 5
Status: Not Free

Overview: **P**resident Gnassingbe Eyadema's manipulation of an elected parliament largely allowed him to continue the personalized rule he has exercised since seizing power in

1967. Security forces remain tightly controlled by members of Eyadema's Kabye ethnicity, which with other northerners dominate Togo's government. Togo's main foreign backer, France, sanctioned the democratic transition's subversion in the form of loans and high-level diplomatic visits. Chances of ethnic and political violence increased. Over 100,000 Togolese are refugees, and in May a car bomb rocked the capital, Lome, amid reports of nascent guerrilla activity.

Part of the Togoland colony seized from Germany in 1914, Togo remained French territory until its 1960 independence. Post-independence leader Sylvannus Olympio was assassinated in 1963, and Eyadéma deposed his successor in a January 1967 coup. With the constitution suspended, Eyadema extended his dictatorship through mock elections and a puppet party. As French policy in 1990 briefly pressured many African autocrats to democratize, Eyadema was simultaneously faced with mounting internal unrest that forced him to make concessions to opponents demanding democratization. In 1991, free parties were legalized and multiparty elections promised. The transition was not smooth, however, as soldiers and secret police harassed, attacked and killed oppositionists. Gilchrest Olympio, son of Togo's slain founding president and the strongest opposition candidate, was the victim of an assassination attempt before being banned from contesting the August 1993 election. Other candidates withdrew in protest against electoral conditions. American and German observers quit the country the day before polling, stating that conditions for a free and fair election no longer existed. Eyadema won a reported 96 percent of the vote.

February 1994 legislative elections saw diminished but considerable violence and intimidation. The opposition Action Committee for Renewal (CAR) won thirty-six of eighty-one seats and its ally, the Togolese Union for Democracy (UTD), took seven. Post-election bickering allowed Eyadéma to co-opt the smaller UTD, whose leader, Edem Kodjo, was named prime minister. CAR returned to the national assembly in August after a yearlong boycott , but can do little in a parliament dominated by Eyadéma's allies.

Political Rights and Civil Liberties: The Togolese people's right to choose their government has been only partially realized in form, and less so in fact. Eyadema's 1993 re-election was clearly fraudulent. Irregularities in 1994 legislative polls did not prevent an opposition victory—which might have been far larger in a genuinely open election—but several opposition deputies' defection to the government effectively abrogated the electorate's wishes. The degree of power wielded by Eyadema allows few constraints on his behavior, even if the opposition controlled the legislature.

The opposition has been allowed very limited access to official broadcast media. A variety of private newspapers publish in Lome, but independent journalists are subject to harassment and the perpetual threat of various criminal charges. In November, the editor of the opposition weekly *L'Eveil du Peuple*, Fulbert Atisso, was detained on charges of disseminating false information after reporting in September that soldiers had killed several villagers near the border with Ghana.

Togo's criminal courts generally respect legal procedures, and traditional courts handle many minor matters. But security forces remain above the law as an important tool of political repression. Amnesty International reported that arbitrary arrest, torture and killings continued despite Togo's new democratic facade. In July repression reached beyond Togo's frontiers, when a leading dissident was murdered in Accra, Ghana's capital.

Religious practice is constitutionally protected and generally respected, but the regime ignores similar protection of the right to assembly. Demonstrations are often banned or dispersed. Political parties, legal since 1991, operate openly but under constant menace. Nongovernmental organizations can organize, but government agents closely scrutinize and sometimes harass human rights groups, including the Togolese League for Human Rights and the Association for the Promotion of the Rule of Law.

Ethnic discrimination is prevalent, and most political power is held by members of a few northern ethnic groups. Southerners dominate commerce, and violence occasionally flares between the two groups. A constant potential flashpoint, the historical ethnic divide is exacerbated by the competition for state power within modern Togo's political boundaries.

Women's educational and employment opportunities are limited despite constitutional guarantees. Discriminatory laws allow a husband to receive his wife's earnings or bar her from working. Customary law denies women divorce and inheritance rights. Wife beating and other violence against women is widespread.

Essential workers are exempted from the constitutional right to form and join unions, and health care workers may not strike. The unionized 15 percent of the workforce is from the small formal sector; most people work in rural subsistence agriculture. Unions have the right to bargain collectively, but most labor agreements are actually brokered by the government in tripartite talks involving unions and management. Several labor federations are divided roughly along political lines.

Tonga

Polity: Monarchy and partly elected legislature
Economy: Capitalist
Population: 106,000
PPP: na
Life Expectancy: 74.5
Ethnic Groups: Tongan (98 percent), other Pacific islander, European
Capital: Nuku'alofa

Political Rights: 5
Civil Liberties: 3
Status: Partly Free

Overview: **D**emocratic activists continued to press their demands prior to elections to be held by February 1996.

This predominantly Polynesian, South Pacific kingdom of 169 islands became an independent member of the British Commonwealth in 1970. King Taufa' Ahau Tupou IV has reigned since 1965.

The 1875 constitution is the product of a time when chiefs held unlimited power over commoners, who were referred to as "eaters of the soil." Under the constitution the king holds broad executive powers, appoints the prime minister, and appoints and heads the Privy Council, which makes the major policy decisions. The thirty-seat, unicameral Legislative Assembly consists of nine nobles selected by and from among Tonga's thirty-three noble families, twelve ministers from the Privy Council, and only nine "People's Representatives" elected by universal suffrage. This arrangement grants the king and the nobility a perpetual supermajority.

In recent years there have been growing calls for a more broadly representative government within the framework of the existing monarchy. In August 1992 a group of reform-oriented People's Representatives, led by Akilisi Pohiva, formed the Pro-Democracy Movement (PDM). In November 1992 the PDM organized a seminal conference on amending Tonga's constitution. Pohiva called for universal elections for the entire Legislative Assembly, and for MPs rather than the king to select the cabinet. The influential Roman Catholic and Free Wesleyan churches supported the conference, and many of the nearly 1,000 attendees were members of the country's growing middle class.

At the February 1993 People's Representative elections, pro-democracy candidates including Pohiva won six seats, an increase of one over the outgoing Assembly. In August 1994 the PDM organized the kingdom's first political party, the Tonga Democratic Party, later renamed the People's Party (PP), which drew the support of five commoner MPs. The PP pledged to transform Tonga into a democracy, with direct elections for the entire Legislative Assembly and greater government accountability. The PP hopes to increase its support at the People's Representative elections due by February 1996.

Political Rights and Civil Liberties: Tongans cannot change their government democratically. The constitution grants the king and hereditary nobles a perpetual supermajority in the Legislative Assembly with twenty-one of thirty seats, allowing major policy decisions to be made without the assent of the popularly elected representatives. Roughly 95 percent of the population is represented by the nine seats reserved for commoners. The king and the nobility also hold a preeminent position in society through substantial land holdings.

The judiciary is not independent of the government in sensitive cases. Commoner leader and MP Akilisi Pohiva has faced three defamation suits over articles in his newspaper, *Kele'a* (Conch Shell), brought by the speaker of parliament, a business group and the crown prince, respectively. Pohiva claims that in two of the cases the Supreme Court failed to consider information that may have substantiated his published facts. Pohiva lost all three cases and was fined a total of nearly $80,000. The defamation suits suggest a concerted effort to weaken this leading pro-democracy activist. Citizens generally receive adequate due-process safeguards in ordinary cases.

Political coverage on the Tonga Broadcast Commission's Radio Tonga generally favors the government. The government refused to allow Radio Tonga to air paid messages advertising the November 1992 conference on constitutional reform (*see Overview*) or to cover the conference live. Heading into the 1993 People's Representative elections, Radio Tonga increasingly featured speakers opposed to the PDM, including the police minister, who warned that the penalty for treason is death or life imprisonment. Although the electoral law prohibits the media from publishing or broadcasting election-related material on the evening before a vote, on election eve Radio Tonga broadcast an antidemocracy statement by an MP. A private television service broadcasts for a few hours daily.

The four privately held newspapers, including the largest, *Kele'a*, and the country's two magazines freely criticize the government. The government-owned weekly carries some opposition news and views. In January 1994, the king signed legislation increasing penalties under the Defamation Act.

Freedom of assembly is generally respected. However, the government denied visas to foreign invitees to the November 1992 constitutional conference and intimidated participants in various ways, including sending police to monitor the proceedings. Freedom of association is respected, and several female-based nongovernmental organizations work on women's rights and development issues. However, traditional practices continue to relegate women to a subordinate role in society.

There are no restrictions on domestic or internal travel. Religious freedom is respected in this predominantly Christian society. The 1964 Trade Union Act recognizes the right of workers to form independent unions, although none has been formed.

Trinidad and Tobago

Polity: Parliamentary democracy
Economy: Capitalist-statist
Population: 1,306,000
PPP: $9,760
Life Expectancy: 71.6
Ethnic Groups: Black (43 percent), East Indian (40 percent), mixed (14 percent), European
Capital: Port-of-Spain

Political Rights: 1
Civil Liberties: 2
Status: Free

Overview: Following the closest election in Trinidad and Tobago's history, Basdeo Panday became the nation's first prime minister of East Indian descent.

Trinidad and Tobago, a member of the British Commonwealth, achieved independence in 1962. Under the 1976 constitution, the two-island nation became a republic with a president, elected by a majority of both houses in parliament, replacing the former governor-general. Executive authority remains invested in the prime minister.

The bicameral parliament consists of a thirty-six-member House of Representatives elected for five years, and a thirty-one-member Senate, with twenty-five senators appointed by the prime minister and six by the opposition. The prime minister is the leader of the party or coalition commanding a majority in the House.

In the 1986 elections the National Alliance for Reconstruction (NAR), an unprecedented coalition of black and East Indian elements led by A.N.R. Robinson, soundly defeated the black-based People's National Movement (PNM), which had ruled for thirty years. The coalition unraveled when Basdeo Panday, the country's most prominent East Indian politician, was expelled and went on to form the East Indian-based United National Congress (UNC).

In 1991, the PNM returned to power under new leader Patrick Manning by taking twenty-one of thirty-six parliamentary seats. Manning offered structural adjustment "with a human face." But the social costs of economic reform and divisions within the PNM sapped his popularity. By mid-1995 the PNM majority had been reduced to nineteen seats through a resignation and a by-election loss to the UNC. Hoping to renew his mandate, Manning called snap elections for 6 November.

Manning promised all citizens would benefit from recent macroeconomic improvements. Panday hammered the PNM on crime and unemployment and promised a government of national unity. In the end, *apan jhaat* (a Hindi phrase meaning "vote your race") prevailed. East Indians and blacks each constitute about 41 percent of the population, and the former voted overwhelmingly for the UNC and the latter for the PNM. Each party won seventeen seats on Trinidad.

On Tobago, the NAR retained its two seats and former prime minister Robinson became the power broker. In exchange for a high ministerial position for Robinson and a promise of greater autonomy for Tobago, the NAR joined the UNC to form a government with a narrow nineteen-seat majority. The sixty-two-year-old Panday became prime minister.

Political Rights and Civil Liberties: Citizens are able to change their government through democratic elections. Constitutional guarantees regarding the right to free expression and the right to organize political parties, civic organizations and labor unions are generally respected.

Civil liberties are increasingly threatened by a mounting wave of drug-related violence and common crime. The murder rate has risen steadily in recent years.

Drug-related and other types of corruption remain problems in the police force. The country is vulnerable to traffickers and money-launderers as it sits off Venezuela's coast along a prime drug-transshipment route.

An independent judicial system is headed by a Supreme Court consisting of a High Court and a Court of Appeal, with district courts at the local level. There is a right of ultimate appeal to the United Kingdom's Privy Council. The mounting crime wave has taxed the judiciary, and prisons are seriously overcrowded. Court cases are backlogged up to five years.

Local human rights organizations allege increasing police brutality including some extrajudicial killings. A 1994 law deprives certain repeat criminal offenders of release on bail. Rights groups challenged the law as unconstitutional. There are also scattered reports of police harassment against the Muslim community, which comprises 6 percent of the population, although religious freedom is generally respected.

In 1994 the government resumed capital punishment, a move condemned by rights groups. That year a convicted murderer was hanged while his lawyers argued in the Appeals Court and after the Privy Council in London had said it would stay the execution. The bar association president called the hanging "the most serious breach of the due process of law in this country."

Domestic violence remains a concern. However, a 1990 law allows men and women to obtain restraining orders against abusive spouses. The law also allows for children to be separated from abusive parents.

Labor unions are well organized, powerful and politically active. They are allowed to strike and have done so frequently in recent years. An independent industrial court plays a central role in labor arbitration.

Newspapers are privately owned, uncensored and influential. There are a number of independent dailies and weeklies. Radio and television are both public and private. Trinidad and Tobago's new media giant, Caribbean Communications Network (CCN), launched the country's second television station in 1991. The other station is state operated.

Tunisia

Polity: Dominant party
Economy: Mixed capitalist
Population: 8,896,000
PPP: $5,160
Life Expectancy: 67.8
Ethnic Groups: Arab-Berber (98 percent)
Capital: Tunis

Political Rights: 6
Civil Liberties: 5
Status: Not Free

Overview: Continued economic growth and secularism have won President Zine el-Abidine Ben Ali and his ruling Constitutional Democratic Rally (RCD) some genuine domestic and international support. But mounting repression prevents real political opposition and most criticism, and thousands of alleged Islamic fundamentalists and their suspected supporters remain in detention.

In a 1987 military coup General Ben Ali seized power from Habib Bourguiba, who had ruled since independence from France in 1956. Ben Ali introduced numerous reforms and promised a multiparty system, but soon began to renege on his pledges. Arrests and harassment crippled opposition parties, and the En-Nadha (Renaissance) party was banned in 1992. In May 1994, Ben Ali won a second five-year term with 99.9 percent of the vote in an election that barred all significant opposition. Legislative polls saw the president's RCD win all 144 seats contested in single-member districts. Although a pluralistic facade and a forum for protected debate were maintained by a proportional allotment of nineteen seats to other parties, the president and RCD dominate Tunisia's political life, including security forces and the courts.

Ben Ali's power grew in 1995, as local elections and parliamentary by-elections returned RCD candidates. The media came under increasing pressure. A sometimes brutal campaign against alleged Islamists also saw moderate opposition-ists jailed; Mohammed Moada, leader of the main legal opposition party, the Socialist Democratic Movement (MDS), was detained in October. The anti-Islamist effort affects all Tunisians' rights.

Political Rights and Civil Liberties:

Tunisians are unable to change their government demo-cratically. The RCD is a successor to parties that have controlled Tunisia since independence, and Ben Ali exercises sweeping decree powers. The 1992 presidential and legislative elections were neither open nor competitive. Legal obstacles blocked oppositionists from qualifying as candidates, and the RCD used state resources heavily in its campaign.

Repression is steadily attenuating the range of tolerated political activity. While two leading Communist Party figures received presidential pardons, the October arrest of MDS leader Moada and efforts to prosecute others could cause further radicalization of political debate. At least 2,000 suspected Islamists are in detention, some in dire conditions.

The government closely controls domestic broadcasting, and in September ended rebroadcast of Italian television. After a brief outright ban, authorities imposed severe regulations and a stiff tax on ownership of satellite dishes. Indepen-dent print media exercise considerable self-censorship, and the Press Code, as amended in 1993, includes vague prohibitions on defamation and subversion that authorities have used against critics. Official news guidelines are issued, and pre-distribution submission allows the government to seize without compensation any publication it wishes. All foreign publications are censored.

Legislation exacerbated conditions for nongovernmental organizations in 1992. Some continue to operate, including the Tunisian Human Rights League, which in late November issued a report criticizing restrictions on freedom of information. Political parties must be licensed, and none based on religion or region is permit-ted. Any party that could effectively challenge the RCD is unlikely to be allowed to register. Tunisians have little legal recourse, especially in political matters. The executive-controlled judiciary flouts legal limits on pretrial detention. According to Amnesty International, security forces use "arbitrary detention, imprisonment, torture, ill-treatment and... harassment" against opponents and dissidents with apparent impunity.

Islam is the state religion. Other religions may practice—except Bahai, who are occasionally harassed—but may not proselytize. Authorities tightly control the Muslim clergy, appointing prayer leaders and paying their salaries.

Women's rights have advanced further in Tunisia than anywhere in the Arab world. Employment rights are protected, and educational and employment opportu-nities have grown. Women's increasingly visible role represents a challenge to and bulwark against radical Islamists.

Though nominally independent, Tunisia's sole labor federation, the Tunisian General Federation of Labor, operates under severe restrictions. Rights to strike and bargain collectively are protected, though arbitration panels can impose labor settlements. If the regime introduces severe austerity as it privatizes state enter-prises, labor unrest could challenge the regime in 1996 and focus discontent.

Turkey

Polity: Presidential-par-
liamentary democracy
(military-influenced)
(insurgency)
Economy: Capitalist-statist
Population: 61,380,000
PPP: $5,230
Life Expectancy: 66.5
Ethnic Groups: Turk (80 percent), Kurd (20 percent), Armenian, Jewish
Capital: Ankara

Political Rights: 5
Civil Liberties: 5
Status: Partly Free

Overview: The pro-Islamic Welfare Party took a plurality of legislative seats in Turkey's December 1995 elections, called
after premier Tansu Ciller's governing coalition collapsed.

Mustafa Kemal Ataturk proclaimed Turkey a republic in 1923. Ataturk's
secular, nationalistic legacy remains a powerful influence. The military used the
doctrine of "Kemalism" to justify three coups between 1960 and 1980. The 1982
constitution provides for a unicameral Grand National Assembly (currently 550
seats) elected for a five-year term. The Assembly elects the president for a seven-
year term. The president can dismiss the prime minister, but the office is considered largely ceremonial.

The country returned to civilian rule in 1983. Elections in November gave the
conservative Motherland Party (Anap) a majority, and one month later Turgut Ozal
formed a government. In 1984 the Marxist Kurdistan Workers' Party (PKK) began
an insurgency in southeastern Turkey, demanding an independent Kurdish state. In
1989 parliament elected Ozal president.

The conservative True Path Party (DYP) won a plurality of 178 seats in 1991
parliamentary elections. DYP leader Suleyman Demirel formed a coalition
government. Following Ozal's death in 1993 parliament elected Demirel president,
and the DYP's Tansu Ciller became Turkey's first female prime minister.

In March 1994 parliament lifted the legal immunity of the thirteen pro-Kurdish
Democratic Party (DEP) MPs. In December a court sentenced six Kurdish MPs to
jail terms of up to fifteen years on charges of supporting the PKK and rebel leader
Abdullah Ocalan.

In September 1995 the governing coalition collapsed after the center-left
Republican People's Party (CHP) withdrew its support, citing Ciller's refusal to
increase public-sector wages and sack the hardline police chief of Istanbul. In mid-
October the CHP rejoined the coalition after Ciller called for early elections. At the
24 December elections the populist, pro-Islamic Welfare Party, taking advantage of
an 88 percent inflation rate and high unemployment, took 158 seats; DYP, 135;
Anap, 132; Democratic Left, 76; and CHP, 49. By year's end the parties were still
maneuvering to form a governing coalition, although the two main conservative
parties had ruled out an alliance with the Welfare Party.

Political Rights and Civil Liberties: Turks can change their government democratically, but the country is beset by widespread human rights abuses.

The judiciary is independent of the government. The criminal code permits political suspects to be held incommunicado for fifteen days—thirty in the ten southeastern provinces under a state of emergency declared in 1987. Those held under the state of emergency or the 1991 Anti-Terror Law (ATL) are not allowed access to lawyers during detention. Torture and sexual abuse against political detainees and common criminals are widespread. The independent Human Rights Foundation (HRF) documented thirty-four deaths in police custody in 1994, as well as numerous "disappearances" of suspects in custody. Trials under the ATL, held in state security courts, are often closed and confessions obtained through torture are admissible as evidence.

Over 19,000 people have died since the PKK insurgency began in 1984. Security forces carry out extrajudicial killings of suspected PKK terrorists and civilians, and are suspected in dozens of unsolved "mystery killings" of journalists, local politicians and other alleged PKK sympathizers, although the number of such killings appeared to decline in 1995. The army has forcibly depopulated over half of the 5,000 villages and hamlets in southeastern Turkey, frequently razing homes, while some villagers have fled to avoid fighting. Progovernment Kurdish "village guards" have garrisoned the remaining villages.

The PKK and smaller Kurdish groups such as *Dev Sol* (Revolutionary Left) have carried out scores of abductions and extrajudicial killings against village guards and civilians. The PKK has murdered dozens of teachers for teaching in Turkish rather than Kurdish.

In October 1995, parliament amended the ATL—under which some 170 journalists, writers, professors and activists had been imprisoned for free expression—to require prosecutors to show a harmful motive or intent. By year's end authorities had released over eighty persons convicted under the law. However, according to the HRF there are 154 articles affecting freedom of expression in various codes, and the government is still prosecuting free expression. In November, the HRF leadership was taken to court over a publication critical of government human rights violations, and in a separate action a columnist and editor went on trial.

In October, a court temporarily freed two jailed Kurdish MPs (*see Overview*) pending a retrial in state security court along with two other Kurdish MPs, and upheld fifteen-year sentences on four others. In 1995 the government also placed several members of the People's Democracy Party (HADEP), a successor to the banned DEP, on trial for allegedly supporting the PKK. At least a dozen HADEP members have been killed since the party's founding in May 1994. The government is also taking legal action against the Kurdish-based Democracy and Change party.

During the year authorities continued to raid and close publications. According to the independent Human Rights Association (HRA), the authorities seized 1,260 editions of publications in January and February 1995 alone. In February the authorities shut down the leading Kurdish paper, *Ozger Ulke* (Free Land), and in August shut down its successor, *Yeni Politika* (New Policy). Police often detain and occasionally torture journalists, and in recent years several journalists have died in custody.

Since the government eased restrictions on private broadcast media in the early 1990s, over 500 television and 2,000 radio stations have been launched. Coverage on the state-run broadcast media favors the government. A 1994 law established an official committee empowered to censor electronic media. In November 1995 the panel briefly suspended two private stations over their political coverage.

Kurdish may not be spoken at political gatherings, and Kurdish-language broadcasts are illegal. Under the ATL authorities frequently seize publications on Kurdish culture and history.

Security forces frequently forcibly disperse demonstrations even if the requisite permit for all assemblies is obtained. In March, after gunmen fired into several shops in an Istanbul shantytown, Shiite Alawites rioted for several days. Police responded by firing randomly into crowds, killing over thirty people. Authorities frequently detain and torture human rights activists, and in 1995 again raided and shut down several HRA branches.

Laws restrict religious worship to designated sites, and place some restrictions on building new sites. The authorities monitor Armenian and Greek Orthodox churches. Women face widespread domestic violence.

Private-sector workers and some civil servants can form trade unions. The government must approve union meetings, and can send police to monitor and record proceedings. Labor laws restrict the right to bargain collectively and hold strikes.

Turkmenistan

Polity: Dominant party (presidential-dominated)
Economy: Statist
Population: 4,471,000
PPP: $3,400
Life Expectancy: 65.0
Ethnic Groups: Turkmen (73 percent), Russian (10 percent), Uzbek (9 percent), Kazakh (3 percent), others
Capital: Ashgabat

Political Rights: 7
Civil Liberties: 7
Status: Not Free

Overview: The former Soviet Central Asian republic of Turkmenistan, bordering Iran and Afghanistan, remained in the iron grip of President Saparmurad Niyazov, former first secretary of the Turkmen Communist Party. Niyazov renamed himself Turkmenbashi, or Head of the Turkmen, while building a cult of personality. The one-party regime continued to curtail political and civil rights while seeking foreign investment to exploit the country's vast energy reserves and cotton-producing capacities.

Turkmenistan was ruled by various local leaders until the thirteenth century, when the Mongols conquered it. In the late nineteenth century, Tsarist Russia seized the country. In 1924, after the Bolsheviks ousted the Khan of Merv, the Turkmen Soviet Socialist Republic was declared.

Turkmenistan declared independence after a national referendum in October 1991; Niyazov won an uncontested election in December. In 1992, after the adoption of a new constitution, Niyazov was re-elected, claiming 99.5 percent of the vote. The main opposition group, Agzybirlik, formed in 1989 by leading intellectuals, was banned and its leaders harassed. The country has two parliamentary bodies, the fifty-member *Majlis* (Assembly) and the *Khalk Maslakhaty* (People's Council), which includes the members of the Assembly, fifty directly elected members and leading executive and judicial officials. Niyazov is president of the People's Council.

In December 1994 parliamentary elections, only Niyazov's Democratic Party of Turkmenistan (DPT) was permitted to field candidates. The president's extensive powers include the ability to prorogue the parliament if it passes two no-confidence motions within an eighteen-month period; issue edicts that have the force of law; appoint and remove all judges, and name the state prosecutor. He is also prime minister and commander-in-chief. Parliament extended his term to the year 2002.

Despite having an estimated 700 million barrels of oil and 280 trillion cubic feet of natural gas, in 1995 Niyazov had yet to fulfill his goal of transforming Turkmenistan into the Kuwait of Central Asia. Russia and Ukraine have restricted the use of their pipelines for Turkmeni gas and oil in an ongoing dispute over fees. Discussions on alternate routes through Afghanistan, Iran and Turkey have been inconclusive. Niyazov's failure to implement market reforms has led to shortages of milk, flour and cooking oil. He has spent much of the country's limited cash earnings on pet projects, including at $35 million mosque in French marble with 200-foot minarets.

Public anger spilled over in July 1995 when a small group of people in the capital, Ashgabat, marched on government offices and demanded new presidential elections. They were arrested, and two generals appeared on television claiming the protesters were drug addicts.

Political Rights and Civil Liberties: Citizens of Turkmenistan do not have the means to change their government democratically. Power is concentrated in the hands of the president. The one-party, single-candidate elections to a rubber-stamp parliament in 1994 were undemocratic. Candidates proposed as alternatives in some constituencies were all disqualified or withdrew on various pretexts.

The DPT is the only legal party. Opposition parties have been banned, and most leaders of Agzybirlik have fled, many to Moscow. Those still in the country face harassment and detention by the Committee on National Security (KNB), the successor to the Soviet-era KGB. Most telephones are bugged.

The judiciary is subservient to the regime; the president appoints all judges for a term of five years without legislative review.

The government controls and funds all electronic and print media. According to a prominent staff member of the state-owned newspaper *Turkmenskaya Iskra*, the paper exercises self-censorship. Newspapers mostly adhere to the old Communist style of publishing verbatim legislative texts, congratulatory speeches, letters flattering the president, and reports of successful harvests.

Local ordinances effectively ban freedom of assembly and public demonstrations. Although the population is overwhelmingly Sunni Muslim, the government has kept a rein on religion to avert the rise of Islamic fundamentalism. Religious congregations are required to register with the government. Muslims have a free hand if they do not interfere in politics, and the government has built several mosques.

There are no independent trade unions, and Turkmen law does not permit collective bargaining. Although women's rights are mentioned in the constitution, discrimination in education and other social-religious limitations restrict women's freedom. Married women are not allowed to be students. The government continued to discourage the formation of nongovernmental organizations in 1995. Attempts to register political or unsanctioned cultural groups have met with severe repression.

Tuvalu

Polity: Parliamentary democracy
Economy: Capitalist
Population: 10,000
PPP: na
Life Expectancy: 61.0
Ethnic Groups: Polynesian (96 percent)
Capital: Fongafale

Political Rights: 1
Civil Liberties: 1
Status: Free

Overview: This tiny, primarily Polynesian country, formerly the Ellice Islands, achieved independence in October 1978 as a "special member" of the British Commonwealth, participating in all Commonwealth affairs except for heads-of-government meetings. The 1978 constitution vests executive power in a prime minister who heads the cabinet and is elected by and from among the twelve-member *Fale I Fono* (parliament). The fono is directly elected for a four-year term in this parliamentary democracy. The governor-general, a Tuvalu citizen appointed by the prime minister, represents the Queen of England as head of state, can dissolve the fono if its members cannot agree on a premier, and appoints up to four cabinet members.

The country's fourth post-independence elections in September 1993 saw nine of twelve incumbent MPs re-elected. The new fono twice failed to elect a prime minister, with six votes each going to the incumbent, Bikenibeu Paeniu, and challenger Dr. Tomasi Puapua, the opposition leader and a former premier. Governor-General Sir Toalipi Lauti used his constitutional powers to dissolve this new fono, and the country held fresh elections in November. In December parliament elected Kamuta Latasi, a former general manager of BP Oil in Tuvalu, as prime minister. Latasi had been a backbencher in the Paeniu government but, supported by his wife, also an MP, crossed over and received the support of five former opposition MPs.

In January 1994 prime minister Latasi named Tulaga Manuella as governor-general, replacing Toomu Sione, who had served for only seven months, on the grounds that Sione had been a political appointee of the previous administration.

Tuvalu has a poor resource base and is dependent on food imports. Agricultural output consists mainly of the cocoa palm, taro and fishing. Much of the country's revenue comes from remittances by some 1,500 countrymen living abroad, as well as from the sale of stamps and coins. Interest from the Tuvalu Trust Fund, established in 1987 by major aid donors, covers one-fourth of the annual budget. There are serious concerns that a global warming trend could cause the sea level to rise and submerge the low-lying islands, and New Zealand has rejected Tuvalu's overtures to relocate its population there in that eventuality.

Political Rights and Civil Liberties: Citizens of Tuvalu can change their government democratically. Political parties are legal but only one loosely organized group has formed, former Prime Minister Bikenibeu Paeniu's Tuvalu United Party. Most elections hinge on village-based allegiances rather than issues. Power is decentralized on the eight permanently inhabited islands through six-person, directly elected island councils. These councils are generally influenced by hereditary elders who wield considerable authority.

The judiciary is independent of the government, and citizens receive fair public trials. Freedoms of speech and press are respected. State-run Radio Tuvalu and *Tuvalu Echoes*, a government-owned fortnightly, are the sole media and offer pluralistic viewpoints. A monthly religious newsletter is also published. There are no restrictions on the right to form associations or hold public assemblies or meetings.

Religious freedom is fully respected, and 70 percent of the population belongs to the Protestant Church of Tuvalu. The government promotes a voluntary family planning program out of concern that a rapidly growing population will overwhelm the country's limited resources. Women face traditional social discrimination but increasingly are securing positions in education and healthcare. The Paeniu government brought women into the cabinet and other senior positions, and in 1994 the International Center for Entrepreneurship and Career Development in Ahmedabad, India opened slots in its training programs for Tuvaluan women.

Citizens can travel freely internally and abroad. Workers are free to join independent unions, although only the Tuvalu Seamen's Union has been organized and registered. Strikes are legal but none has occurred, largely because much of the population is engaged outside the wage economy in subsistence agriculture.

Uganda

Polity: Dominant party (military-influenced)
Economy: Capitalist-statist
Population: 21,297,000
PPP: $860
Life Expectancy: 44.9
Ethnic Groups: Acholi, Baganda, Kakwa, Lango, Nkole, Soga, Teso, others
Capital: Kampala
Ratings Change: *Uganda's civil liberties rating changed from 5 to 4 because of increasingly open public discourse.

Political Rights: 5
Civil Liberties: 4*
Status: Partly Free

Overview: **A** constitution adopted in September advanced President Yoweri Museveni's vision of a nonparty democracy prior to April and May 1996 presidential and legislative elections. The new charter extended a formal ban on party activities for another five years, a policy heavily criticized by some Western nations, but de facto party organizing intensified. Oppositionists gathered in December to name Democratic Party leader Paul Ssemogerere as their joint candidate.

Idi Amin ousted President Milton Obote in a 1971 coup. Amin's buffoonery and brutality attracted world headlines, and hundreds of thousands were killed. After invading Tanzania in 1978, his troops were routed by Tanzanian forces assisted by Ugandan exiles, allowing Obote's return in fraudulent December 1980 elections. Obote and his backers from northern Uganda violently repressed his critics, mainly from southern ethnic groups. Opponents were tortured and murdered, and soldiers terrorized the countryside. An army coup ousted Obote again in July 1985, but conditions only worsened. Museveni took power in January 1986 after a five-year bush war.

Over 250,000 people were likely killed, most by government soldiers, before Museveni led his National Resistance Army (NRA) into the capital, Kampala. Museveni formed a broad-based government under the National Resistance Movement (NRM), with extensive local consultations with "Resistance Committees" first set up during the guerrilla war. The NRM government has been strongly influenced by the NRA (Museveni himself still carries the rank of Lieutenant-General and is defense minister) and faced a series of lingering guerrilla conflicts in the north and east. Remnants of the defeated government army were quelled by 1988 amid reports of NRA human rights abuses, but the millennialist Lord's Resistance Army still stages raids along the Sudanese frontier. That conflict has become increasingly entangled with Sudan's genocidal war against southern Sudanese rebels, and threatens to spark a major confrontation between Uganda and Sudan.

Although Uganda is currently safer and more stable than at any time since the mid-1960s, ethnic divisions remain the greatest threat to long term peace. Southern Baganda royalists demand more recognition of their traditional kingdom, and minorities in the northwestern West Nile region renewed guerrilla raids late in the year to press autonomy demands.

Sedition charges against several journalists raise concerns as the country readies for 1996 elections.

Political Rights and Civil Liberties: Ugandans cannot change their government democratically. Museveni's NRM has dominated the government since 1986. The National Resistance Council, an indirectly-elected body that advises but does not form the government, includes a broad spectrum of public representation. Local elections have been held at several levels.

In March 1994, a constituent assembly was elected in a vote observers judged free and fair, although candidates could not identify themselves as party members or representatives. NRM supporters won the most seats, and fashioned a new constitution providing for nonparty legislative and presidential elections. Despite this legal prohibition, both the Democratic Party and the Uganda People's Congress party, main rivals for power since independence in 1962, maintain offices and unofficially field candidates. A referendum on return to a multiparty system is expected in 1999.

There is broad public debate, and freedoms of expression and of the media are generally respected. A vigorous opposition press is highly critical of the government and offers a full range of opposition viewpoints. Two private radio stations report openly on local political developments. The largest newspapers and broadcasting facilities remain state-owned. While government corruption is reported and opposition positions are presented, coverage is often unbalanced.

Use of sedition laws to arrest or intimidate journalists poses a more serious threat to press freedom. In November the information minister threatened to punish "corrupt" journalists. The editor of *As-Salaam* weekly, Hussein Musa Njuki, died in custody on 28 August, apparently of natural causes although no inquest was performed.. Several other journalists have been charged, but so far the courts have usually quickly granted bail. In December a journalist was sentenced to prison for the first time since Museveni took power. Haruna Kanaabi, editor of the Islamic weekly *Shariat*, received a five-month sentence for sedition and publishing "false news" regarding Uganda's relations with Rwanda. The conviction could produce a chilling effect on Uganda's nascent free media.

Freedom of assembly is proscribed for banned political parties, though many meetings have been held without interference. Many nongovernmental organizations are active, and registration requirements are not used to block any particular group. At least a dozen are directly involved with human rights issues, including the Uganda Human Rights Activists, the Uganda Law Society, and the Foundation for Human Rights Initiatives. Religious freedom is constitutionally protected, and there is no state religion. Various Christian sects and Uganda's Muslim minority worship freely.

Uganda's judicial system has shown increasing autonomy, but remains hampered by inadequate resources and the army's uneven record of respect for civilian court authority. Prison conditions are harsh. Human rights violations by the NRA (in December the army's name was changed to Uganda People's Defense Forces) were reported in conflict zones, and far more egregious abuses were committed by Lord's Resistance Army guerrillas.

Discrimination against women based on traditional law is prevalent, particularly in the countryside. Inheritance, divorce and citizenship laws discriminate between men and women, who also must receive their husband's permission to obtain a passport. Domestic violence against women is widespread.

Uganda's largest labor federation, the National Organization of Trade Unions, is independent. A broadly defined array of "essential workers" is barred from forming unions. Strikes are permitted only after a lengthy reconciliation process, but several occurred in 1995.

Uganda has among Africa's most open economies. Liberalized exchange policies and broad privatization of state enterprises have helped encourage strong growth over the last five years.

Ukraine

Polity: Presidential-par-liamentary democracy
Economy: Statist-transitional
Population: 52,000,000
PPP: $5,010
Life Expectancy: 69.4
Ethnic Groups: Ukrainian (73 percent), Russian (22 percent), others
Capital: Kiev

Political Rights: 3
Civil Liberties: 4
Status: Partly Free

Overview: In 1995, President Leonid Kuchma wrested greater political power from parliament, but his attempts to push through a comprehensive economic reform program stalled in the face of bureaucratic and legislative resistance. By year's end mass privatization remained unimplemented, and a budget that included subsidies and social welfare programs threatened much-needed future assistance from Western lending institutions.

In other issues, Ukraine reached agreement with Russia on the Black Sea Fleet, avoided formal commitment to Commonwealth of Independent States (CIS) structures, and reiterated its neutrality while not opposing NATO's eastward expansion. Elections were also held for parliamentary seats not filled in a series of 1994 elections.

Ukraine, a major agricultural-industrial center, was the site of the medieval Kievan Rus' realm that reached its height in the tenth and eleventh centuries. Russia dominated the large eastern region for over 300 years, while Poland and Austria-Hungary ruled the west. Ukraine enjoyed a brief period of independent statehood between 1917 and 1920, after which Soviet rule was extended over most Ukrainian lands with the creation of the Ukrainian Soviet Socialist Republic. Western Ukraine was wrested from Poland in 1940 under the Hitler-Stalin Pact. Ukraine declared independence from a crum-bling Soviet Union in 1991, and Leonid Kravchuk was elected president by direct vote. Parliament was elected in 1990, and although dominated by former Commu-nists, the Democratic Bloc of over 100 deputies proved a formidable parliamentary faction that pressured hardliners to support sovereignty.

In 1994, political gridlock over the economy and presidential powers led to early elections for parliament (27 March) and president (26 June). The legislative elections were held under a flawed and complex electoral law passed in November 1993. The law was entirely majoritarian and clearly made it difficult for political parties to register candidates (only 11 percent of candidates had party affiliations), while any "group of electors" (minimum membership of ten) or "worker collectives" (no minimum membership) could easily nominate whomever they wanted.

The election law led to a series of runoffs (in some electoral districts in the capital, Kiev, voters went to the polls eight times), but by year's end some 10 percent of seats remained vacant and parliament suspended further balloting. While eighteen parties were represented in the new parliament, the deputies coalesced around nine major blocs, whose membership shifted during the year. After 7 August, the leftist Communist, Socialist, and Agrarian blocs accounted for 150 seats; Inter-Regional Bloc, 53; Centrists (many closely affiliated with Kravchuk), 38; Reform Bloc, 27; the democratic National Rukh Bloc, 29; Statehood Bloc, 27; and Independents, 49. Those who did not join any faction or were members of smaller parties made up the rest.

The economy was not a primary issue in the presidential race, which focused on the shape of the new constitution, the status of the Russian language, and the extent of cooperation with Russia. Kravchuk, who initially announced he would not run, offered a vague platform of "developing Ukraine's socially-oriented economy," and stressed his experienced helmsmanship in steering Ukraine toward independence, a theme that resonated in nationalist Western Ukraine. Kuchma, a former industrialist who served as premier in 1992-93, sprinkled promises of market reform with pledges of close economic ties with Russia, appealing to the largely Russian-speaking eastern Ukrainians, particularly Communists and factory bosses. In the first round, Kravchuk scored a narrow victory over Kuchma, 37.72 percent to 31.27 percent, but since neither polled over 50 percent, a runoff was needed. Turnout was 68 percent. Kuchma won the 10 July runoff by 52 percent to 45 percent, with over 71 percent of eligible voters taking part.

Kuchma moved quickly to assuage fears that he would strengthen ties with Russia at the expense of Ukrainian sovereignty, and he soon made it clear that he meant to pursue close economic, security and political relations with the U.S. and the West. Days after assuming the presidency, Kuchma met with the International Monetary Fund (IMF), which pledged to work with him on such problems as inflation, macroeconomic stabilization and price liberalization. In return for unifying the exchange rate, lifting export restrictions and raising energy prices, the IMF gave Ukraine half of a promised $730 million "systematic transformation facility" loan. The industrialized nations offered Ukraine $4.2 billion, including funds to shut down the Chernobyl nuclear plant and provide Ukraine with the opportunity to qualify for large IMF and World Bank loans. Promoted by President Clinton, the package was conditioned on the implementation of comprehensive market reforms. The European Union (EU) lent Ukraine $108 million to help with its balance of payments.

In 1995, parliament continued to drag its feet on reform. Kuchma replaced Prime Minister Vitaliy Masol, a Soviet-era holdover, with First Deputy Yevhen Marchuk, who had led the Ukrainian equivalent of the KGB for three years. In mid-May, Kuchma wrested new power from the legislature, which amended the constitution, giving up its power to name Ukraine's cabinet and its claim to authority over provincial and local governments. Kuchma facilitated his victory by threatening to take the matter to a nationwide referendum, which legislators knew they would almost certainly lose given his popularity and parliament's low rating in opinion polls. After a brief standoff Kuchma and parliament agreed to a "constitutional treaty" in June. In return for broader rights to issue decrees and appoint ministers, the president agreed to a one-year deadline for a new constitution.

Kuchma reshuffled his cabinet in July, partly in light of polls showing declining confidence in his economic policies. He removed several reformers to placate critics in parliament, including chief economic strategist Viktor Pynzenyk. Pynzenyk was widely disliked in parliament for opposing subsidies to Ukraine's bloated industrial sector, reeling from a payments crisis and raw material shortages. He was replaced by former economics minister Roman Shpek, another reformer, but was brought back as deputy prime minister for economic reform.

More recent moves suggest that Kuchma is surrounding himself with technocrats from his former base in Dnipropetrovsk. Longtime national Security Advisor Volodymyr Horbulin, former head of Ukraine's space agency, worked with Kuchma in Dnipropetrovsk, as did new First Deputy Prime Minister Pavlo Lazerenko and Valeriy Pustovaytenko, named administrative minister of the Cabinet of Ministers. Former dissident Serhiy Holowaty of the Reform faction became justice minister. In December, the president juggled his administration, naming Volodymyr Kuznetsov, also of Dnipropetrovsk, as first aide. Economic aide Anatoliy Halchinsky, a reform architect, resigned.

On 11 October 1995, parliament voted 234-61 to approve an IMF-driven program of macroeconomic stabilization emphasizing evolutionary, not revolutionary, measures. Eight previous programs since independence had largely failed. Eight factions voted with the government, attesting to Marchuk's growing political clout. While assuring political stability, the plan did not address Ukraine's critical economic problems. While Kuchma succeeded in instituting some reforms, including slashing taxes and liberalizing prices, the government program sent a mixed message by attempting to make a compromise between market and command policies. Reformist parliamentarians criticized a lack of emphasis on privatization.

A total of 380 candidates, seventy from party lists, ran to fill forty-five open parliamentary seats in 10 December elections. Results were valid (50 percent turnout) in only eighteen constituencies, and seven candidates were elected outright. Runoffs were held in eleven districts on 24 December, and five new deputies were elected, bringing the total number of legislators to 418.

Political Rights and Civil Liberties: Ukrainians can change their government democratically. International observers deemed the 1994 presidential and parliamentary elections generally free and fair, though irregularities were reported as well as pre-election intimidation and violence against democratic organizations and activists. Democrats claimed the November 1993 electoral law was designed to hinder a multiparty system by weakening political parties' role in the electoral process. In June, a new electoral law was drawn up to eliminate the 50 percent threshold.

Ukraine remains governed by the 1978 Constitution of the Ukrainian SSR, modified since independence by the introduction of a presidency and multiparty system. The president and parliament reached a constitutional accord on 7 June, giving the president a free hand in naming a new government. A new constitution is likely to be drafted by June 1996. Citizens are free to organize in political groupings and associations, and scores of political parties span the political spectrum.

A 1991 press law purporting to protect freedoms of speech and press covers only print media. Hundreds of independent Ukrainian- and Russian-language newspapers, periodicals and journals exist. Many receive some state subsidies, a form of indirect control. The price and availability of newsprint and print facilities, as well as an inadequate state-owned distribution system, have hampered publications. Some independent newspapers are mailed through the post office and distributed by vendors or privately-owned kiosks. The Ukrainian State Committee for Television and Radio broadcasts in Ukrainian and Russian, and Russian television is readily available. There are several private local television and radio stations throughout the country, which broadcast views and stories critical of the government. Satellite dishes are available. The state grants commercial channels air time and access to the state cable system, thereby creating the possibility of arbitrary restrictions on certain types of programs. Independent news agencies include the Ukrainian Press Agency, UNIAR and UNIAN, Vybir and Rukh Inform. In June 1995 there were over 3,000 publications in Ukraine, despite financial difficulties and declining circulation. There have been allegations that presidential advisors from Kuchma's Dnipropetrovsk circle have pressured a dozen publications to hire their hand-picked journalists.

Freedoms of discussion and assembly are recognized and generally respected, though police violently broke up a demonstration by people seeking to bury the late Orthodox Patriarch Volodymyr in Kiev's St. Sophia Cathedral. Although the previously outlawed Ukrainian (Uniate) Catholic and Ukrainian Autocephalous Orthodox churches are legal, conflicts between the two churches and the old Russian Orthodox Church continue over property and churches. There are three Ukrainian Orthodox churches, two with allegiances to patriarchs in Kiev and one with allegiance to Moscow. The Orthodox schism has sparked violent flare-ups. Ukraine's estimated 500,000 Jews are organized and maintain schools and synagogues.

An independent judiciary and the rule of law remain in formative stages. There have been modifications of Soviet-era laws that have enhanced defendants' rights in such areas as pretrial detention and appealing arrests. President Kuchma's tough crime bill, signed in July 1994, permits police to hold suspected criminals for up to thirty days; suspected criminal locations may be raided without search warrants. There are about 50,000 legal professionals in Ukraine, but most judges, especially on the regional level, were appointed during the Soviet era. In June 1995, Kuchma issued a decree dealing with legal reform that created a presidential committee on legislative initiatives and a committee to review Ukraine's legal and criminal codes.

Ukrainian workers are organized in several trade unions. The Federation of Trade Unions, a successor to the former official Soviet body, claims 21 million workers. In 1992, five independent unions united under the umbrella of the Consultative (Advisory) Council of Free Trade Unions, which interacts freely with international labor groups. Estimates of membership in independent unions range from 100,000-200,000; over 80 percent of the workforce is unionized. Women have educational opportunities, and are represented among the professional classes. Independent women's organizations exist and have raised such issues as spousal abuse and alcoholism. Nongovernmental organizations including human rights groups are free to organize and operate, although some have reported administrative interference.

United Arab Emirates

Polity: Federation of traditional monarchies
Economy: Capitalist-statist
Population: 1,904,000
PPP: $21,830
Life Expectancy: 73.8
Ethnic Groups: Native and other Arab, Persian, Pakistani, Indian
Capital: Abu Dhabi

Political Rights: 6
Civil Liberties: 5
Status: Not Free

Overview: Located on the Arabian Peninsula along the Persian Gulf, the emirates were originally known as the Trucial States because of defense agreements signed with Britain in the nineteenth century and lasting until 1968. Following several attempts at unification, the United Arab Emirates formally became a state in December 1971.

Each of the seven emirates is governed internally as an absolute monarchy. Under the 1971 constitution, the monarchs collectively form a Federal Supreme Council, which elects a state president and vice-president from among its members for a five-year term. The president appoints a prime minister and a cabinet. A forty-member consultative Federal National Council is composed of delegates appointed by the seven rulers, but holds no legislative powers. Separate consultative councils exist within several emirates. There are no political parties and no popular elections at any level. Sheik Zayed ibn Sultan al Nuhayyan of Abu Dhabi, the largest emirate, has been president since 1971.

In a key issue, in June 1994 a court sentenced twelve former top executives of the collapsed Bank of Credit and Commerce International (BCCI), two of them in absentia, to jail terms of up to fourteen years on charges of widespread fraud. The ruling family and government of Abu Dhabi had controlled 77 percent of BCCI. In May 1995 two of the emirs agreed to pay $10 million to settle claims against them in the United States over their involvement with BCCI.

The key foreign policy issue is an Iranian claim to three islands near the Straight of Hormuz. The islands had been jointly ruled for two decades by Iran and the emirate of Sharjah until 1992, when Iran expelled UAE citizens from them without explanation. In 1994 the United Arab Emirates announced it would refer the case to the International Court of Justice. In April 1995 Iran called instead for direct talks between the two countries.

Political Rights and Civil Liberties: Citizens of the United Arab Emirates cannot change their government democratically. Political parties are illegal, there are no popular elections, and all power is held by the seven emirs and their families.

The judiciary is generally independent of the government. The law permits incommunicado detention, which is sometimes practiced. On 16 January 1995, authorities arrested Sheik Abdel Mun'im al-Ali, an exiled Iraqi opposition leader.

By year's end Sheik al-Ali continued to be held, apparently without having been charged. There is a dual system of civil and shari'a (Islamic) courts, and the accused receive adequate procedural safeguards. The courts in most of the emirates are responsible to the Federal Supreme Court in Abu Dhabi, although the civil court systems in Dubai and Ras al-Khaimah are separate from the federal system.

The media are largely privately held, although journalists practice considerable self-censorship when reporting on government policy or other sensitive issues. In recent years the government has temporarily banned publications for exceeding its arbitrary guidelines on permissible news coverage. Television and radio stations are state-owned and offer only government views, although some stations augment their programming with CNN and other foreign services. All imported materials are reviewed by the Ministry of Information.

Permits are required for public assemblies, and some emirates allow conferences where government policies are discussed. All private associations must be strictly nonpolitical. Islam is the official religion, and most citizens are Sunni Muslims. Shiite mosques are not permitted in Ras al-Khaimah. Dubai reportedly placed private mosques under government control in 1993. Non-Muslims can generally practice freely. There are no restrictions on internal travel, except near defense and oil facilities. Members of the small, stateless Bedouin population, some of whom have lived in the country for more than one generation, cannot receive passports.

Women face societal discrimination, cannot hold majority shares in most businesses, and are legally disadvantaged in custody matters. Married women must receive written permission from their husbands to take jobs, and a husband can bar his wife from traveling abroad. The plight of Sarah Balabagan, a sixteen-year-old Filipina domestic servant accused of murdering her employer in July 1994 after he allegedly raped her, focused attention on the abuse such foreign nationals frequently suffer. In September 1995 a court sentenced Balabagan to death in a retrial after she had earlier received a seven-year sentence. In November an appeals court sentenced Balabagan to a year in jail and 100 lashes.

Workers lack the legal right to form trade unions, bargain collectively, or hold strikes, and such activity does not occur. Children, often from South Asian countries, continue to face dangerous conditions as jockeys in the sport of camel racing.

United Kingdom

Polity: Parliamentary
democracy
Economy: Mixed
capitalist
Population: 58,560,000
PPP: $17,160
Life Expectancy: 76.2

Political Rights: 1
Civil Liberties: 2
Status: Free

Ethnic Groups: English (82 percent), Scottish (10 percent),
Irish (2 percent), Welsh (2 percent), Asian, African and
Caribbean immigrants
Capital: London

Overview: After trailing the opposition Labour Party by thirty points
in polls for over a year and witnessing an embarrassing
defeat for his Conservative Party in May's local elections,
Prime Minister John Major resigned as Party leader in June, declaring to Conservative dissidents, "It is time to put up or shut up." Although Major survived this
gamble, the fact that one-third of Conservatives declined to support him exposed
deep divides, particularly regarding European integration.

The United Kingdom of Great Britain and Northern Ireland encompasses the
two formerly separate kingdoms of England and Scotland, the ancient Principality
of Wales, and six counties of the Irish Province of Ulster. *(See Northern Ireland
under Related Territories.)* Parliament has an elected House of Commons with
651 members chosen by plurality vote from single-member districts, and a
House of Lords with over 1,000 hereditary and appointed members. A cabinet
of ministers appointed from the majority party exercises executive power on
behalf of the mainly ceremonial sovereign. Queen Elizabeth II nominates the
party leader with the highest support in the House of Commons as prime
minister.

Conservatives have held power since 1979. After taking over party leadership
from Margaret Thatcher, Major abandoned her unpopular poll tax, continued to
privatize state industries, and attempted to balance pro-Europe forces against
specific national interests. However, by 1992 several major policy reversals and
scandals, coupled with gaping divides over Britain's role in the European Community, began to erode the Conservatives' support.

Labour has gained support particularly under Tony Blair, who persuaded the
party to abandon its longstanding commitment to a Marxist, nationalized industry
policy in favor of a more centrist endorsement of a "dynamic market economy." In
June, nationwide polls showed Blair was the most popular opposition leader since
such polls began fifty years ago.

Labour has also raised the specter of a movement to devolve power to new
Scottish and Welsh territorial parliaments. The proposed parliaments would control
services including health and education, with the larger Scottish parliament also
exercising limited lawmaking and taxation powers. Although both regions rejected

similar plans in referenda twenty years ago, a new decentralization movement has gained momentum.

Major's denunciation of the proposal may have contributed to Conservatives' dismal 11 percent showing in Scotland's April local elections, followed in May by the loss of fifty-nine of their sixty-seven council majorities in England. Labour took 48 percent of the local vote in England and the Liberal Democrats 23. Labour is expected to win the next general election, which the premier must call no later than 1997.

Political Rights and Civil Liberties:

Citizens can change their government democratically. Voters are registered by a government survey and include both Irish and Commonwealth (former British Empire) citizens resident in Britain. British subjects abroad retain voting rights for twenty years after emigration. Wales, Scotland and Northern Ireland currently have no regional legislatures, but elect members to the House of Commons.

The government follows a largely unwritten set of understandings and conventions with no codified mechanism for change. A 1995 nationwide survey found 79 percent favoring a written constitution and bill of rights, and 77 percent favoring a referendum system.

The lack of a bill of rights has facilitated passage of several laws widely criticized as endangering basic freedoms. The 1989 Prevention of Terrorism Act allowed suspects to be held for eight days of interrogation, and the new Criminal Justice and Public Order Act allows police to use a suspect's silence as evidence of guilt. The cost of Britain's civil justice system is so high that only the rich and the diminishing numbers of those eligible for legal aid can afford litigation. In addition, the government is attempting to award block grants to law firms providing legal aid services, effectively placing a monetary limit on the right to legal representation for the indigent.

Favoring press freedom and self-regulation, the government's "White Paper on the Press" rejected a proposal for civil and criminal legislation to establish a right of privacy. In a separate document issued in May, authorities proposed limiting the degree of control any single company could exert over print and broadcast media. Though primarily private and uncensored, the press is subject to strict libel laws. Although the British Broadcasting Corporation (BBC) is an autonomous public body, it responds to government pressure to censor controversial items. However, it offers pluralistic views and airs both government and opposition political broadcasts.

Freedom of movement is generally respected, but the Criminal Justice Act bars Roma (Gypsies) caravans from stopping at campsites. Significant numbers of exclusion orders, barring individuals from entering Britain or Northern Ireland under the Prevention of Terrorism Act, were lifted this year. However, several measures to limit immigration and asylum-seeking were introduced, including provisions to tighten visa requirements for all entrants and to criminalize employment of illegal immigrants.

The existence of two established churches, the Episcopalian Church of England and the Presbyterian Church of Scotland, does not restrict religious freedom. State-financed schools' mandatory daily worship sessions are meant to be "broadly Christian" by law.

Despite a weakened financial base resulting from legislation allowing workers to decide whether dues would be automatically deducted from their pay, labor groups remain powerful and active. In January, 15,000 mail delivery workers walked out over a dispute concerning working conditions in London.

Women represent nearly half of the paid labor force, but still earn only 75 percent of men's wages on average. Ten percent of current MPs are women. A controversial new Labour party rule mandates that promising Labour districts needing fresh candidates must pick from women-only short lists. Another continuing equal rights debate centered on a High Court decision in June to uphold Britain's ban on military service by gay men and lesbians. In September, the government said the policy was outdated and would be reviewed again in 1996.

United States of America

Polity: Federal presidential-legislative democracy
Economy: Capitalist
Population: 262,200,000
PPP: $23,760
Life Expectancy: 76.0

Political Rights: 1
Civil Liberties: 1
Status: Free

Ethnic Groups: European (73 percent), black (13 percent), Hispanic (10 percent), Asian-Pacific (3 percent), native American (Indian, Eskimo/Inuit, Aleut), (1 percent), others
Capital: Washington, D.C.

Overview:

President Bill Clinton, who began the year reeling from 1994 electoral setbacks to his Democratic Party, regained some ground and began campaigning for re-election in November 1996. The new Republican Party legislative majority, under Speaker of the House Newt Gingrich and Senate Majority Leader Bob Dole—the leading Republican presidential candidate—struggled to consolidate a self-styled revolution amid increasingly effective Democratic opposition. Budget disagreements between Clinton and Congress caused two government shutdowns late in 1995.

Since 1789, the United States has had elected civilian rule under a constitution providing for a president, bicameral legislature and independent judiciary headed by a Supreme Court. The 100-member Senate (upper house) consists of two members from each state, elected to staggered, six-year terms. Each state is guaranteed at least one member in the House of Representatives (lower house), with the remainder apportioned based on population. There are currently 435 representatives, who are elected biannually.

The president and vice-president are elected to four-year terms via an electoral college. Voters in each state and the federal district, Washington, D.C., vote for slates of electors, who usually unanimously support the candidate winning the popular vote in their jurisdiction. In the 1992 presidential elections, Clinton won

370 electoral votes to 168 for incumbent Republican George Bush, and 43 percent of the popular vote to Bush's 38 percent. Billionaire independent H. Ross Perot won no electoral votes but took 19 percent of the popular vote—the strongest third-party showing since 1912.

In 8 November 1994 midterm elections, Republicans captured control of the House for the first time in forty years, regained a Senate majority lost in 1986, and won a majority of governorships. The vote gave Republicans 230 House seats; Democrats, 204; and an independent socialist, one. Democrat Thomas Foley, the first House speaker to lose re-election since 1860, was replaced by Gingrich. With two Democratic defections and the fall 1995 resignation of Republican Bob Packwood, Republicans have a 53-46 Senate majority. Meanwhile, five House Democrats joined the Republicans during 1995.

In their 1994 campaign manifesto, the "Contract With America," Republican House candidates promised lower taxes; reforms to improve the efficiency and structure of Congress; increased defense spending; less regulation; and constitutional amendments mandating congressional term limits and balanced federal budgets. By April 1995, the House had acted on all points in the Contract, rejecting only term limits.

Clinton signed legislation obligating Congress to appropriate funds for any programs mandated to states, and requiring Congress to abide by civil rights and labor statutes from which it had exempted itself. But other legislation languished. A proposed balanced-budget constitutional amendment missed the necessary two-thirds majority by a single vote in the Senate, and Republican legislators opted to try balancing the budget through the legislative process.

Legislators resolved in June to balance the budget by 2002, while Clinton had outlined a ten-year plan. By late 1995 disagreement remained over the timetable, areas to be cut—with Clinton advocating smaller cuts in benefits for the poor and elderly—and whether to use executive or congressional economic projections.

The impasse sparked a six-day shutdown in mid-November, furloughing some 800,000 "nonessential" federal employees until Clinton reportedly accepted the Republican timetable. But disagreement remained regarding tax cuts and cuts in social programs, and the administration backed away from the timetable. A second shutdown affecting some 260,000 federal employees began 18 December amid increasing charges of politicking, with neither side willing to be perceived as weak in an election year.

Ethics questions dogged both Gingrich and Clinton in 1995. Gingrich was accused of a conflict of interest over a major book contract, which he subsequently abandoned, and in December the House Ethics Committee named a prosecutor to investigate alleged tax-law violations.

An independent prosecutor continued investigating Clinton and his wife, Hillary, regarding their investment in the failed Whitewater land venture during Clinton's tenure as Arkansas Governor. In June, close Clinton friend and former associate Attorney General Webster Hubbell was sentenced to twenty-one months in prison for tax evasion and mail fraud, and ordered to pay $135,000 in restitution in connection with Whitewater. Several others were indicted or entered pleas in 1995.

Republican lawmakers convened Whitewater-related hearings in July. Various documents and witnesses indicated the Clintons knew more than they had admitted about the Whitewater finances, and suggested Treasury and Justice Department obstruction of an investigation into connections between Whitewater and the failed Madison Guaranty savings and loan, operated by Whitewater partner James McDougal. Claiming attorney-client privilege, the Clintons late in 1995 disregarded a subpoena for notes from a 1993 meeting between their attorney and four presidential advisors. The Senate sought a court order to obtain the notes, deepening the constitutional confrontation.

Meanwhile, former Arkansas state employee Paula Jones pursued sexual harassment charges against Clinton. A late-1995 court ruling reversed a previous decision allowing him to avoid the suit during his presidency.

Charged with personal financial wrongdoing, Commerce Secretary Ronald Brown became the third Clinton Cabinet official to come under investigation.

Clinton fared better on the international front, where he could point to the restoration of civilian rule in Haiti and diplomatic ties with Vietnam. However, Clinton was criticized for disregarding overwhelming congressional and popular opposition in signing an executive order pledging a $50 billion bailout of Mexico's economy, following its currency's collapse late in 1994.

The U.S. brokered a tripartite peace plan among the Bosnian, Croat and Serbian governments, which on 8 September agreed to a two-state federation on Bosnian soil. A ceasefire took effect 12 October, and by year's end the U.S. had begun deploying some 20,000 troops under NATO command to enforce the agreement.

Armed antigovernment extremists were in the spotlight in 1995. On 19 April a 5,000-pound fertilizer bomb destroyed the Alfred P. Murrah Federal Building in Oklahoma City, killing 169 and wounding over 400. The attack came on the anniversary of the 1993 storming of the Branch Davidian cult compound in Waco, Texas by federal agents, which left some eighty dead, and officials deemed the bombing a reprisal. The bombing suspects' connection to an extreme Michigan militia group further raised concern over armed organizations, many with racist views, that see the federal government as a nefarious force infringing on personal liberties. Lawmakers eventually rejected antiterrorism legislation proposed by Clinton, fearing erosion of civil liberties.

Legislators began investigating the Waco events in July, and in September looked into Federal Bureau of Investigation (FBI) agents' August 1992 killing of extremist Randall Weaver's wife and son during a siege of his cabin near Ruby Ridge, Idaho. The Justice Department had previously determined that the FBI had withheld or destroyed documents regarding the incident. Four agents were suspended in August, and the Justice Department agreed to pay $3.1 million to the Weaver family, which had filed wrongful death claims of $200 million.

A group calling itself Sons of the Gestapo claimed responsibility for a 9 October train derailment near Phoenix, Arizona that left one dead and 100 injured, citing the Waco incident and other perceived crimes by the federal government as motives.

Political Rights and Civil Liberties:

Americans can change their government democratically. Voter turnout was a little over 50 percent in recent presidential elections. U.S. citizens abroad may vote, as may resident aliens in some localities. The party system is competitive. In recent years, until the 1994 Republican sweep, incumbent legislators won in overwhelming numbers. Legislators spend increasing amounts of time raising campaign funds from wealthy individuals and interest groups. Numerous states and localities have limited local, state and federal officials' terms, but in May 1995 the Supreme Court ruled states could not limit federal terms.

Minorities have gained increasing political representation since the 1960s, but controversy remains over the sometimes strangely shaped districts designed to guarantee minorities' election. Federal district courts and the Supreme Court have ruled inconsistently concerning redistricting requirements under the Voting Rights Act, but in April the Court ruled that "racially gerrymandered" districts in Louisiana and Georgia be redrawn.

In presidential election years, an ideologically unrepresentative minority chooses major-party nominees through a complicated, debilitating series of primary elections and local party caucuses. Early caucus and primary states play a disproportionate role in reducing the presidential field. Daunting petitioning hurdles in several states hamper small parties' or major-party insurgents' ability to get on ballots. In many states, rights of initiative and referendum allow citizens to place issues on the ballot and decide questions directly, sometimes overturning their elected representatives' decisions. California is noted for frequent referenda.

The media are generally free and competitive, but there are disturbing trends toward monopolization. In 1995, two of three television networks and the major cable news provider changed hands. On 31 July the Walt Disney Company announced plans to buy Capital Cities/ABC, Inc., expanding Disney's already vast media empire. The next day, the Westinghouse Corporation announced a buyout of CBS, another network, giving Westinghouse control of thirty-nine radio and fifteen television stations. And in September, Time Warner, Inc.—already a huge media presence—agreed to merge with Turner Broadcasting, owner of CNN and several other cable stations. This continuing consolidation is particularly worrisome because most Americans get their information from television news, which is increasingly difficult to distinguish from entertainment. A sweeping 1995 telecommunications bill threatened to accelerate media monopolization by eliminating many regulations.

Public and private discussions are very open, but the Oklahoma City bombing and other violence adversely affected public discourse. Some far-right talk-show hosts advocated shooting federal agents following the bombing, and the president and others exacerbated the problem by unfairly drawing links between merely conservative and violent, extremist programming. The "Unabomber," an antitechnology extremist responsible for twenty-two injuries and three deaths between 1978 and April 1995, sent a 35,000-word manifesto to two major dailies, the *New York Times* and the *Washington Post* in June, promising more bombings unless the full text and three annual follow-ups were printed. The papers' acquiescence in September was widely criticized as bowing to terrorism.

Several states and localities outlaw hateful expression. University and media efforts to ban allegedly racist and sexist language may constrain academic and press freedoms, as a tendency toward conformism among university faculties pressures independent thinkers to mouth "politically correct" views. Large corporations may discourage free speech among their activist opponents via lawsuits known as SLAPP suits (special litigation against public participation). Many deemed the *60 Minutes* television news program's November 1995 decision not to air an interview with a former tobacco company executive, for fear of being sued by the company, a surrender to powerful corporate interests.

Courts at all levels are severely backlogged, delaying the course of justice in countless criminal and civil cases. The high crime rate and growing public demand to punish criminals have led to severe prison overcrowding. Federal and state prisons and local jails hold well over one million people. The number of prisoners per 100,000 residents grew from 139 in 1980 to 373 in 1994. Police brutality against minorities and unequal sentencing based on race and class undermine the criminal justice system's foundations. Blacks accused of murdering whites receive death sentences more frequently than whites accused of similar crimes.

Freedom of association is guaranteed, but the labor movement continues to decline as its traditionally strong manufacturing base shrinks. The weak National Labor Relations Board and unenforced labor laws make it increasingly difficult for workers to organize. Strikes have become less effective due to management's increasing use of replacement workers, and the annual number of workers involved in lockouts and strikes declined from over 2.5 million in the early 1970s to under 500,000 during the 1990s. Legislation banning the use of replacement workers during strikes died in the Senate after a 1994 Republican filibuster. In 1995 members of the largest trade union confederation, the 13.3 million-member American Federation of Labor-Congress of Industrial Organizations, chose a new president through elections for the first time. Meanwhile, the country's three largest industrial unions, with 2 million members total, voted to merge within five years to bolster their influence.

Religious freedom is guaranteed. Supreme Court rulings in recent decades have limited religious displays on public property and prohibited organized prayer in public schools. After the 1994 election, Clinton appeared undecided regarding a proposed constitutional amendment allowing organized prayer in public schools, eventually supporting an officially approved moment of silence, as he had done as Arkansas governor.

Most poor Americans are white, but a large, disproportionately black underclass exists outside the economic mainstream. Affected by seemingly permanent unemployment, the underclass relies heavily on welfare payments. Heavy drug use, rampant crime, female-headed households, and large numbers of poorly fed, badly educated, illegitimate children characterize underclass neighborhoods. An October 1995 nationwide study showed that 32.2 percent of blacks in their twenties were behind bars, on probation or on parole, up from 23 percent in 1989. The figure tops 40 percent in Washington, D.C., where half of nonwhite children are on welfare. A growing black middle class has made significant gains in housing, education, and employment.

The black-white divide appeared to widen in 1995, as members of the two groups held seemingly irreconcilable views on subjects including the legal process and affirmative action programs. Congressional Republicans and several states advocated scrapping some or all such programs outright, while in June the Supreme Court ruled that federal efforts involving racial preferences were legal only where they directly addressed prior discrimination. In May 1995 the Court upheld a lower-court ruling deeming a blacks-only University of Maryland scholarship program unconstitutional. Clinton defended affirmative action in July, but issued an executive order mandating that federal agencies dismantle or alter programs containing quota-based preferences or leading to reverse discrimination.

Women have made significant socioeconomic gains in recent decades, but still lag behind men in income. Affirmative action has increased their representation in business and the professions, but women remain concentrated in lower-paying positions. Successful women and minorities often find "glass ceilings" limit their advancement in corporations that assign them to positions reserved for affirmative action.

Immigration remains controversial, especially in coastal and border states with the largest numbers of legal and illegal immigrants. In 1995 the U.S. allowed thousands of Cubans detained at its naval base in Guantanamo, Cuba and elsewhere to enter the U.S., but continued repatriating Haitian refugees, keeping Haitians who refused repatriation at Guantanamo. Critics charged the policy was racially motivated. In November 1994, California voters adopted Proposition 187, a referendum excluding illegal aliens from all but emergency public services. The referendum's passage sparked interest in other states, but legal challenges delayed its implementation.

The government restricts freedom of movement to a few countries, notably to Cuba. With certain exceptions, Americans wishing to visit Cuba must obtain a government license to spend money there, or face up to five years' imprisonment and a $100,000 fine.

Authorities seem largely indifferent to the plight of American Indians. One-third live in poverty, and unemployment on reservations exceeds 50 percent. Clinton pledged in April 1994 to "honor and respect tribal sovereignty." Tribes argue sovereignty is needed to reduce dependence on the federal government, though some are thriving on untaxed tobacco sales and casino gambling. Many Indian groups have cases in court, charging federal violation of treaty provisions regarding control over land and resources. Hawaiian natives postponed until 1996 a referendum on calling a constitutional convention to discuss options for sovereignty.

Uruguay

Polity: Presidential-
legislative democracy
Economy: Capitalist-
statist
Population: 3,186,000
PPP: $6,070
Life Expectancy: 72.5
Ethnic Groups: European (88 percent), mestizo (8 percent),
black and mulatto (4 percent)
Capital: Montevideo

Political Rights: 2
Civil Liberties: 2
Status: Free

Overview: In his first year in office, President Julio Sanguinetti saw his popularity plummet after implementing a severe economic adjustment package.

After gaining independence from Spain, the Republic of Uruguay was established in 1830. The Colorado Party dominated a relatively democratic political system through the 1960s. An economic crisis, social unrest and the activities of the Tupamaro guerrillas led to a right-wing military takeover in 1973. Civilian rule was restored through negotiations between the military regime and civilian politicians. Sanguinetti won the presidential election in 1984.

Under the 1967 constitution, the president and a bicameral Congress consisting of a ninety-nine-member Chamber of Deputies and a thirty-one-member Senate are elected for five years through a system of electoral lists that allows parties to run multiple candidates. The leading presidential candidate of the party receiving the most votes overall is the winner. In effect, party primaries are conducted simultaneously with the general election. Congressional seats are allocated on the basis of each party's share of the total vote.

Luis Alberto Lacalle of the centrist National Party narrowly won the 1989 presidential elections. The leftist Broad Front captured the mayoralty of Montevideo, the nation's capital. Lacalle's popularity fell as he tried to liberalize one of the most statist economies in Latin America.

In the 1994 campaign the fifty-eight-year-old Sanguinetti ran as a social democrat. The other main contenders were the Broad Front's Tabare Vasquez, the popular mayor of Montevideo, and the National Party's Alberto Volante.

The 1994 election was Uruguay's closest ever. The Colorados won 31.41 percent of the vote, the Nationals 30.23 percent and the Broad Front 30.02 percent. As the leading Colorado vote-getter, Sanguinetti was declared the winner. In the Chamber of Deputies the Colorados won thirty-two seats, the Nationals thirty-one and the Broad Front twenty-eight. In the Senate the Colorados won eleven seats, the Nationals ten and the Broad Front nine. The Broad Front held on to the mayoralty of Montevideo.

Sanguinetti handed out numerous cabinet positions to the Nationals, and took office in March 1995 at the head of what was in effect a ruling coalition with a congressional majority. Sanguinetti then stunned social democratic supporters by pushing through an austerity package that cut back Uruguay's legendary social security system. That led to a series of labor stoppages and a sharp decline for Sanguinetti in the opinion polls.

Political Rights and Civil Liberties:

Citizens are able to change their government through democratic elections. But factionalized, gridlocked politics in recent years have led to increasing apathy and disgust among citizens.

Constitutional guarantees regarding free expression, freedom of religion and the right to organize political parties, labor unions and civic organizations are generally respected. The former Tupamaro guerrillas now participate in the system as part of the Broad Front.

Political expression is occasionally restricted by violence associated with hotly contested political campaigns and labor disputes. In the 1994 electoral campaign there were a number of clashes between party supporters, a few legislative candidates were attacked and two Colorado Party offices were ransacked.

The judiciary is relatively independent, but has become increasingly inefficient in the face of escalating crime. It is headed by a Supreme Court appointed by the congress. The system includes courts of appeal, regional courts and justices of the peace.

Allegations of mistreatment in the penal system, particularly of youthful offenders, have increased. In recent years several police detainees alleged they had been tortured, and a number of police personnel have been prosecuted for ill-treatment or unlawful killings. New measures to prevent such practices have been implemented but there is a lack of effective investigation in some cases.

Human and legal rights organizations played a key role in a 1991 decision by the Inter-American Commission on Human Rights of the Organization of American States, which ruled that the 1986 law granting the military amnesty from rights violations during military rule violated key provisions of the American Convention on Human Rights.

Labor is well organized, politically powerful, and frequently uses its right to strike. The leading labor confederation is the left-wing PIT-CNT. Strikes are often marked by violent clashes and sabotage.

Civic organizations have proliferated since the return to civilian rule. Women's rights groups and groups representing the small black minority have organized against still deeply rooted discrimination.

The press is privately owned, and broadcasting is both commercial and public. There are numerous daily newspapers, many associated with political parties, and a number of weeklies. However, a number of publications have ceased publishing because of the government's suspension of tax exemptions for the import of newsprint. Television is an important part of the political landscape as campaigns feature debates and extensive coverage on the four channels that service the capital.

Uzbekistan

Polity: Dominant party (presidential-dominated)
Economy: Statist-transitional
Population: 22,694,000
PPP: $2,650
Life Expectancy: 69.2
Ethnic Groups: Uzbek (71 percent), Russian (8 percent), Tajik, Ukrainian, Turk, others
Capital: Tashkent

Political Rights: 7
Civil Liberties: 7
Status: Not Free

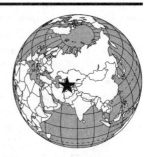

Overview: In 1995, President Islam Karimov consolidated his absolutist hold on power, orchestrating a national referendum to extend his term to the year 2000. The repressive regime sought foreign investment in abundant cotton, gold, oil and gas resources.

Among the world's oldest civilized regions, Uzbekistan became part of the Russian empire in the nineteenth century. In 1920, it became part of the Turkistan Soviet Socialist Republic within the RSFSR. Separated from Turkmenia in 1924, it entered the USSR as a constituent republic in 1925. In 1929 its eastern Tajik region was detached and also made a Soviet republic.

Karimov, former Communist Party first secretary, was elected president on 29 December 1991 as head of the People's Democratic Party (PDP), the former Communist Party. He received 86 percent of the vote, defeating well-known poet Mohammed Salih of the *Erk* (Freedom) Democratic Party, who got 12 percent. The largest opposition group, the nationalist *Birlik* (Unity), was barred from registering, and the Islamic Renaissance Party (IRP) and the Islamic *Adolat* group were banned entirely.

The 1992 constitution called for 1994 elections for a new, 250-member legislature, the *Ulu Majlis*, to replace the 500-member Supreme Soviet. Throughout 1993 the regime curtailed all opposition. Abdumannob Pulatov, a founder of Birlik, was tried for "insulting the honor and dignity of Uzbekistan's president" after being abducted while attending a human rights meeting in neighboring Kyrgyzstan. Seven Birlik members were already in custody, awaiting trial on trumped-up criminal charges. Pulatov was ultimately sentenced to three years' imprisonment, but the sentence was automatically commuted under a September 1992 amnesty still in force and he emigrated to the United States. The Erk Party was evicted from its headquarters. Six members of the *Melli Majlis* (alternative parliament) were tried and convicted, though all were subsequently amnestied.

December 1994 elections were marred by irregularities even with no real opposition participation. The PDP took 179 seats; progovernment, nonparty candidates, twenty; and *Vatan Taraqioti* (Fatherland Progress Party), nominally oppositionist but created by the government as a businesspersons' party, six. The PDP and its allies filled the remainder in 1995 by-elections.

A February 1995 national referendum Karimov ordered to extend his term to coincide with parliament's was allegedly approved by 99 percent of 11 million voters. Karimov personally controls everything from secret industrial production plans to garbage collection in Tashkent, the capital. He preaches stability and order at any price, often citing regional turbulence in neighboring Tajikistan and Afghanistan to justify his heavy-handed rule.

In economic matters, Uzbekistan sought $140 million from the International Monetary Fund to assist its market transition. On 1 July, the government planned to lift exchange controls on its national currency to attract foreign investors. With 200,000 ethnic Koreans, Uzbekistan has attracted substantial South Korean investment. The U.S. mining company, Newmont, signed a $225 million joint-venture deal, partly backed by the European Bank for Reconstruction and Development, to process gold.

Political Rights and Civil Liberties:

Uzbekistan is de facto a one-party state dominated by former Communists, who have severely restricted opposition political activity. The 1994 parliamentary elections were neither free nor fair, with only progovernment parties participating.

The constitution, while enshrining a multiparty system, undermines the right to organize parties. Article 62 forbids "organized activities leading...to participation in antigovernment organizations."

The press is censored, all nongovernment newspapers are banned, and government-owned television and radio offer little information. Only Russian-language television is offered, and authorities have restricted broadcasts to evenings. Foreign journalists have been harassed.

Freedoms of assembly, association and public discussion are seriously circumscribed. Religious freedom is nominally respected in this largely Sunni Muslim nation, but the government controls the Muslim Religious Board. Because Karimov fears Islamic fundamentalism, he has made concessions to Muslims. While Samarkand's 20,000 Jews faced little overt persecution, many have left for Israel. In 1995, two Jews were falsely accused of murder, launching a campaign by Western Jewish and human rights groups. German Lutherans, concentrated in Tashkent, have complained about the government's failure to return properties confiscated under Stalin.

The judiciary is subservient, with no mechanisms to ensure its independence. Karimov appoints all judges. Many penal code statutes limit free expression and association. Article 60 bans "anti-state activities," Article 191 criminalizes defamation of the president, and Article 204, aimed at "malicious delinquency," has been used to stifle opposition activity. A former premier told the *New York Times*: "We live in a police state that would have made the old Bolsheviks proud." The Interior Ministry and police are intrusive and arbitrary.

While trade unions are legal, their overall Soviet-era structure has been retained and there are no independent unions. Women are underrepresented in senior positions throughout society. Islamic traditions also undermine women's rights. With the ban on opposition activity, no nongovernmental organizations are registered.

Vanuatu

Polity: Parliamentary democracy
Economy: Capitalist-statist
Population: 174,000
PPP: $1,956
Life Expectancy: 65.2

Political Rights: 1
Civil Liberties: 3
Status: Free

Ethnic Groups: Indigenous Melanesian (90 percent), European, Vietnamese, Chinese, other Pacific islander
Capital: Vila

Overview:
Located in the Western Pacific Ocean, this predominantly Melanesian archipelago of some eighty islands, formerly called the New Hebrides, was an Anglo-French condominium until receiving independence in 1980. The condominium arrangement divided the islands into English- and French-speaking communities, creating rifts that continue today. The 1980 constitution vests executive power in a prime minister chosen by and from among a unicameral parliament, which is directly elected for a four-year term. A largely ceremonial president, currently Jean-Marie Leye, is elected for a five-year term by an electoral college consisting of the parliament and the provincial council presidents.

Francophones were largely excluded from key posts in the first post-independence government, led by Prime Minister Father Walter Lini's anglophone, center-left Party of Our Land (VP). A number of islands initially faced brief secessionist movements.

Lini's VP won subsequent elections in 1983 and 1987. In December 1988 President Ati George Sokomanu tried to dissolve parliament and replace it with an interim administration headed by his nephew, Barak Sope, and opposition leader Maxime Carlot. All three were later convicted on sedition charges, although in 1989 an appeals tribunal dismissed their sentences.

In August 1991 the VP dumped Lini as its leader. At the December elections, Carlot's francophone Union of Moderate Parties (UMP) won a plurality with nineteen seats. Carlot and Lini, whose new National United Party (NUP) took ten seats, shunted aside traditional Anglo-French animosities and formed a governing alliance. Carlot became the country's first francophone prime minister.

The coalition began unraveling in August 1993 when Carlot reshuffled the cabinet and refused to give Lini a post. Lini withdrew the NUP's support from the government, but four of his MPs broke ranks and backed Carlot. In June 1994 the four dissident MPs formed the People's Democratic Party (PDP), led by Deputy Prime Minister Sethy Regenvanu. In another development, in June the government placed restrictions on log exports in response to concerns that foreign logging companies were felling trees at an unsustainable rate.

At the 30 November 1995 elections for an expanded, fifty-seat parliament, the Unity Front, a four-party opposition coalition headed by Donald Kalpokas, took twenty seats; UMP, seventeen; NUP, nine; two minor parties, one each; and independents, two. In December parliament named the UMP's Serge Vohor as premier.

Political Rights and Civil Liberties: Citizens of Vanuatu can change their government democratically, although the former Carlot government's interference with the media placed the opposition at a disadvantage. Power is decentralized through six elected provincial councils.

The courts have a shown a pattern of siding with the government on cases involving the media and union activity. In June an Australian judge serving in Vanuatu resigned, questioning the independence of the chief justice.

The state-run Radio Vanuatu and the government-owned *Vanuatu Weekly* do not adequately cover opposition events and statements. On several occasions the Carlot government banned the government media from reporting on trade union views and other specific issues, including the Australian judge's June resignation. On several issues the Carlot government banned all media coverage. In 1993, the government threatened to revoke the publishing license of the now-defunct *Vanuascope* newspaper for defying a government ban on covering an opposition party, and in 1995 the government banned coverage of the French resumption of nuclear testing in the South Pacific. In early 1995, a government official threatened to deport the publisher of the country's only independent private newspaper, the *Vanuatu Post* (then known as the *Trading Post*) if the paper did not carry some French-language articles. In April, the finance minister threatened to revoke the *Trading Post's* publishing license after it criticized the licensing of a Taiwanese bank.

The independent Human Rights Forum, a nongovernmental organization, operates openly. Women generally occupy a subservient position in society, and domestic violence occurs frequently.

The Carlot government set a precedent by politicizing the civil service at the middle level. The country's five trade unions are all independent and belong to the Vanuatu National Council of Trade Unions (VCTU). Strikes are legal, but the Carlot government frequently interfered with labor actions. In 1993 and 1994 the government interfered with strikes by the National Teachers' Union and the Public Service Association, fired more than 1,200 striking civil servants, suspended more than 170 teachers, and fired two teachers for encouraging others to join a February 1994 general strike. Private employers meanwhile sacked at least twenty workers for joining the general strike. According to the VCTU, employers frequently use child labor under the guise of job "training."

Venezuela

Polity: Presidential-
legislative democracy
Economy: Capitalist-
statist
Population: 21,844,000
PPP: $8,520
Life Expectancy: 71.7

Political Rights: 3
Civil Liberties: 3
Status: Partly Free

Ethnic Groups: Mestizo (67 percent), European (21 percent), black
(10 percent), Indian (2 percent)
Capital: Caracas

Overview:

Disillusionment and cynicism deepened amid allegations of
official corruption, increasing social unrest and crime, and
military rumbling, placing Venezuela among the most
volatile states in Latin America.

The Republic of Venezuela was established in 1830, nine years after independence from Spain. Long periods of instability and military rule ended with the 1961 establishment of elected civilian rule. Under the 1961 constitution, the president and a bicameral Congress are elected for five years. The Senate has at least two members from each of the twenty-one states and the federal district of Caracas. The Chamber of Deputies has 189 seats.

Until 1993, the social-democratic Democratic Action (AD) party and the Christian Social Party (COPEI) dominated politics. Former AD president Carlos Andres Perez (1989-93) was nearly overthrown by nationalist military officers in two 1992 coup attempts. In 1993 he was charged with corruption and removed from office by Congress.

The aging Rafael Caldera, a former president (1969-74) and populist who had broken with COPEI and railed against Perez's market reforms, was elected president in late 1993 at the head of the sixteen-party National Convergence, which included Communists, other leftists and right-wing groups. Amid coup rumors, Caldera was first past the post with 31 percent of the vote in a field of seventeen candidates

The seventy-nine-year-old Caldera's term has been marked by a national banking collapse, the suspension of a number of civil liberties, mounting violent crime and social unrest and intermittent rumors of a military coup.

In 1995 Caldera's only high card, a reputation for honesty, was tarnished by allegations of corruption among his inner circle, including his sons and other relatives. With crime soaring, oil wealth drying up and the country in the worst economic crisis in fifty years, popular disillusionment with politics continued to deepen. In December state and local elections that saw pro-Caldera candidates crushed, 60 percent of voters stayed away from the polls, even though voting is mandatory.

In early 1995, the military presented Caldera with a plan for the full militarization of Caracas in the event of widespread disorder. The question was how much chaos the military, never comfortable with Caldera to begin with, would tolerate before taking stronger measures.

Political Rights and Civil Liberties: Citizens can change their government democratically. However, Venezuela's institutions have been severely eroded by decades of corruption and drug-trade penetration and badly damaged by two 1992 coup attempts. Trust in the political system has been in steep decline since the late 1980s. Voter abstention reached 60 percent in the 1995 state and local elections, the highest since the establishment of elected government. The elections themselves were marked by disorganization and allegations of fraud, which led to numerous rioting incidents.

The constitution guarantees freedom of religion and the right to organize political parties, civic organizations and labor unions. However, political expression and civil liberties are threatened by official antagonism toward the media and were undermined from mid-1994 to mid-1995 by the suspension of constitutional guarantees regarding arbitrary arrest, property rights and freedom of expression, movement and financial activity. The restoration of these guarantees, however, led to little change in security forces' repressive behavior against popular protests and labor strikes. Citizen security in general remains threatened by a drug-fueled crime wave that has resulted in hundreds of killings monthly in major cities and the advent of vigilante mob killings of alleged criminals.

In 1995, Venezuelan human rights organizations continued reporting widespread arbitrary detentions and torture of suspects, as well as dozens of extrajudicial killings by military security forces and the notoriously corrupt police. Criminal suspects, particularly in poor areas and near the tense border with Colombia, are subject to torture. Indigenous communities trying to defend their legal land rights are subject to abuses, including killings, by goldminers and corrupt rural police. Since the 1992 coup attempts, weakened civilian governments have had less authority over the military and the police, and rights abuses overall are committed with impunity. In 1995 rights activists remained targets of intimidation.

The judicial system is headed by a Supreme Court and is nominally independent. However, it is highly politicized and undermined by the chronic corruption that permeates the entire political system. It is slow, ineffective and generally unresponsive to charges of rights abuses by police and security forces. The judiciary is further undermined by drug-related corruption, with growing evidence of bribery and intimidation of judges.

Only about one-third of Venezuela's estimated 25,000 prisoners have been convicted of a crime. Prisons are severely overcrowded and rife with drugs. Prison violence, virtually out of control, leads to hundreds of deaths annually.

A separate system of military courts has jurisdiction over members of the military accused of rights violations and common criminal acts. Military court decisions cannot be appealed in civilian courts. As a consequence, the military is rarely held accountable and most citizens view it as above the law.

The press is privately owned. There are nearly a dozen daily newspapers. Radio and television are mostly private, supervised by an association of broadcasters under the government communications ministry. The practice of journalism is restricted by a licensing law and threatened by government control of foreign exchange required to purchase newsprint and other supplies.

Since 1994 the media in general have faced a pattern of intimidation. Government and military officials, including the president, frequently attack the media verbally and the Congress passed a series of restrictive laws involving the right of reply and journalistic conduct.

Labor unions are well-organized but highly politicized and prone to corruption. A new labor law in 1991 reduced the work week from forty-eight to forty-four hours and made it illegal for employers to dismiss workers without compensation. However, the law is often disregarded. Security forces frequently break up strikes and arrest trade unionists.

Vietnam

Polity: Communist one-party
Economy: Statist
Population: 75,029,000
PPP: $1,010
Life Expectancy: 65.2
Ethnic Groups: Vietnamese (85-90 percent), Chinese (3 percent), Muong, Thai, Meo, Khmer, Man, Cham
Capital: Hanoi

Political Rights: 7
Civil Liberties: 7
Status: Not Free

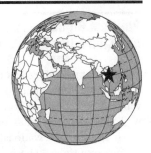

Overview:
Twenty years after the Communist reunification of the country, in 1995 the ruling Vietnam Communist Party (VCP) continued to crack down on peaceful political dissent and religious activity.

The French colonized Vietnam between 1862 and 1884. During World War II a resistance movement led by Ho Chi Minh fought the occupying Japanese and later battled the returning French. The country won independence in 1954, and was divided between a Communist government in the North and a French-installed one in the South. Planned elections to reunify the country were never held, and military forces and insurgent groups from the North eventually overtook the South and reunited the country in 1976 as the Socialist Republic of Vietnam.

The Sixth VCP Congress in 1986 launched a program of *doi moi* (renovation), which has decentralized economic decision-making, encouraged small-scale private enterprises and largely dismantled agricultural collectivization. In 1991 the VCP installed Do Moi as its party chairman.

In April 1992 the National Assembly approved a new constitution that codified many of the economic reforms. However, it formally established the VCP as the sole legal political party and retained the party-controlled "People's Committees," which supervise daily life at the local level. The document scrapped the collective state council in favor of a single presidency, to be elected by and from within the

National Assembly. July 1992 elections for the 395-seat National Assembly brought in a crop of young technocrats. The Assembly subsequently elected General Le Duc Anh as state president, and re-elected economic reformer Vo Van Kiet as premier.

In 1995 the government continued its long-running crackdown on religious freedom. Since 1981, when the authorities banned the independent Unified Buddhist Church of Vietnam (UBCV) in favor of the official Vietnam Buddhist Church, the government has arrested most of the UBCV's leadership. In December 1994 authorities formally arrested Thich Huyen Quang, the aging UBCV Patriarch, who had been under house arrest since February 1982.

In early January 1995 police arrested Thich Quang Do, the secretary-general of the UBCV. In a one-day trial on 14 August a court sentenced the Ven. Quang Do, along with five monks arrested in December 1994 for organizing flood relief on the Mekong River, to prison terms of up to five years for national security offenses.

Political Rights and Civil Liberties: Vietnamese citizens lack the democratic means to change their government. The ruling VCP is the only legal party and approves all political candidates. In recent years, the government has relaxed its monitoring of the population somewhat, although the authorities still maintain control through mandatory household registration, block wardens, selective monitoring of communications and a network of informants, as well as official peasant associations, religious bodies and other structures.

In October, the National Assembly approved an 834-article civil code delineating property rights, inheritance laws and other matters. While the government appears to be making some effort to establish a rule of law in commercial matters, basic civil liberties continue to be arbitrarily denied.

Police and security forces carry out arbitrary arrests. The authorities routinely ignore the legal safeguards in the 1989 Criminal Procedure Code regarding detention. The judiciary is not independent of the government, and the rudimentary court system does not always provide adequate safeguards even in ordinary trials. Prisoners face torture and brutal conditions.

Ordinary citizens increasingly have greater latitude in criticizing government corruption and inefficiency, but advocating political liberalization and other opposition to the government is illegal under Party Directive 135 and various provisions of the criminal code. In 1995, several prominent political prisoners remained in jail, including Dr. Nguyen Dan Que and Dr. Doan Viet Hoat. In June 1995, police arrested Hoang Minh Chinh, a prominent intellectual, after he circulated a petition questioning the VCP's legal monopoly, and Do Trung Hieu, a party official who detailed the authorities' efforts to crush the UBCV; both received prison sentences in November of twelve months and fifteen months, respectively. In August a court sentenced nine human rights advocates, including two Vietnamese-Americans, to prison terms of four to fifteen years after holding them since late 1993 for attempting to organize a prodemocracy conference. The two Americans were deported. Overall, several hundred political detainees and prisoners are believed to be held in "re-education camps."

The government controls all media, and there is no coverage of opposition views. In January the authorities shut down two publications, one merely for criticizing the government's efforts to ban firecrackers. All assemblies require permits, and while political protests are not permitted the authorities occasionally tolerate small demonstrations over routine issues. The government does not permit independent elements of civil society.

Since 1981, the government has driven the independent UBCV underground. According to Amnesty International, as of February the authorities were detaining thirty-six Buddhist monks, some since the late 1970s. Major Buddhist temples are kept under surveillance and are occasionally raided by police, and by law numerous religious activities require official permission, including holding meetings or training seminars, operating religious schools, or repairing places of worship.

The government has similarly placed Catholic religious affairs under the control of the state-organized Catholic Patriotic Association. The government maintains the right to approve Vatican appointments, and in April the authorities vetoed a slate of Vatican-nominated clerical candidates. The southern-based Cao Dai religious movement has not been allowed to open a seminary. In the central highlands, the government continued to arrest Protestant clergy and other members of the minority Montagnard ethnic group.

Members of ethnic minorities face restrictions regarding internal travel, education and employment. Women face informal social and workplace discrimination. Child prostitution is increasing.

All unions must belong to the state-controlled Vietnam General Confederation of labor. The 1994 Labor Code recognizes only a limited right to strike.

Western Samoa

Polity: Parliamentary democracy and family heads
Political Rights: 2
Civil Liberties: 2
Status: Free
Economy: Capitalist
Population: 179,000
PPP: $1,869
Life Expectancy: 67.6
Ethnic Groups: Samoan (93 percent), mixed (7 percent), European, other Pacific islander
Capital: Apia

Overview: Located 1,600 miles northeast of New Zealand, the western Samoan islands became a German protectorate in 1899. New Zealand claimed the islands during World War I and administered them until granting independence in 1962. The 1960 constitution provides for a head of state, ostensibly one of the four paramount island chiefs, who appoints the prime minister from among the members of an indirectly elected *Fono Aoao Faitulafono* (parliament). The head of state must approve all legislation passed by the parliament. Malietoa Tanumafali, one the paramount chiefs, is head of state for life, although his successors will be elected by parliament for five-year terms.

In a 1990 referendum voters narrowly approved direct elections for the parliament. Previously only the 25,000 *matai*, essentially family heads, could vote. However, forty-five of the forty-seven parliamentary seats are still reserved for matai, with the remaining two reserved for citizens of non-Samoan descent.

The country's first direct elections in April 1991 gave the ruling Human Rights Protection Party (HRPP) thirty seats; the opposition Samoan National Development Party, fourteen; and independents, three. The parliament re-elected Tofilau Eti Alesana as prime minister.

A pair of hurricanes in 1991 and 1992 wiped out the country's copra and coconut oil exports, sending foreign exchange reserves plummeting. In 1993 parliament approved a controversial 10 percent Goods and Services Tax (GST). The GST drew widespread criticism in this economically depressed country already suffering through a taro blight that devastated the staple food crop.

In December 1994, the chief auditor released a report alleging corruption against seven cabinet ministers. The cabinet subsequently named a commission of inquiry to investigate the charges against its own members, which predictably cleared the ministers.

In February 1995, the government charged two former MPs with sedition over antigovernment comments at a March 1994 rally against the GST. Coming just days before organizers planned another protest march against the GST, and with the government offering little proof of seditious intent, the charges appeared to be politically motivated. In June a magistrate threw out all seven sedition charges for lack of evidence. The GST and official corruption figure to be key issues in parliamentary elections due by mid-1996.

Political Rights and Civil Liberties: Western Samoans can change their government democratically, although only the matai can sit in parliament (with the exception of two seats reserved for non-Samoans) and in the village *fonos* (councils of matai). Several parties exist, although political affiliations are generally based more on individual loyalties than on policies or ideology.

The independent judiciary is modeled on the British system and defendants receive fair trials. However, many civil and criminal matters are handled at the local level by some 360 village fonos through traditional law. The 1990 Village Fono Law affirmed this authority but provided some right of appeal to the Lands and Titles Courts and to the Supreme Court. Fonos occasionally order harsh punishments, including the burning of houses and banishment from villages.

The 1993 Newspapers and Printers Act requires journalists to reveal their sources in libel cases or face a $2,000 fine and a three-month prison sentence. The 1993 Defamation Act forbids journalists from publishing defamatory statements made in court that refer to a person not involved in the proceedings. It also requires editors to publish an apology when a member of a group that has been criticized in print requests it. Neither law has yet been applied. There are several private newspapers, all of which reportedly practice some self-censorship on sensitive issues, and two private radio stations, including the outspoken Radio Polynesia.

There are no restrictions on freedoms of assembly and association. Although the government respects religious freedom in this predominantly Christian country, village leaders often choose the religion of their followers. The National Council of Churches and other religious groups freely comment on political matters and are highly influential. Domestic abuse and rape are serious problems, and traditional norms discourage women from seeking legal redress. Since 95 percent of the matai are men, and only the matai can sit in parliament and the village fonos, women are underrepresented in politics.

There are two independent trade unions, plus the Public Service Association which represents government workers, but in general the trade union movement is not well organized. Strikes and collective bargaining are legal but are practiced infrequently.

Yemen

Polity: Dominant coalition **Political Rights:** 5
(military-influenced) **Civil Liberties:** 6
Economy: Capitalist-statist **Status:** Not Free
Population: 13,215,000
PPP: $2,410
Life Expectancy: 50.2
Ethnic Groups: Arab majority, African, Asian
Capital: Sanaa

Overview: **T**wo years after Yemen held the first free elections on the Arabian Peninsula, President Ali Abdallah Salih continued to consolidate his power by cracking down on the media and arresting several opposition activists.

Located on the southern Arabian Peninsula, Yemen was formed in 1990 through the merger of the conservative, northern Yemen Arab Republic (YAR), and the Marxist, southern People's Democratic Republic of Yemen (PDRY). Upon unification, the YAR's Ali Abdallah Salih became president and the PDRY's Ali Salim al-Biedh vice-president. The 1991 constitution provided for a Presidential Council, composed of a president, vice president and three other officials, and a 301-seat House of Representatives, which elects the Presidential Council.

April 1993 parliamentary elections, held after a five-month delay due to civil unrest, gave the General People's Congress (GPC) of the former YAR 123 seats. The Islamic fundamentalist, tribal based *Islah* (Reform) Party (YIP), headed by Sheik Abdallah Hussein al-Ahmar, took sixty-two; the Yemeni Socialist Party (YSP) of the former PDRY, fifty-six; minor parties, twelve; and independents, forty-eight. The GPC, YIP and YSP formed a governing coalition. In October parliament formally elected Salih as president and al-Biedh as vice-president. However al-Biedh, who since August had refused to leave Aden, the former PDRY capital, boycotted the new government and called for demilitarization of the former north/south border, decentralization of authority and investigations into dozens of pre-election killings of YSP activists.

In late February 1994, Salih and al-Biedh signed an accord calling for political reforms and decentralization. However, tensions continued, and in late April a full-blown conflict broke out between the northern and southern armies. In May al-Biedh and other former PDRY leaders declared an independent state in the south. In July northern troops ended the war by capturing Aden, and al-Biedh and other secessionist leaders fled the country.

In September 1994, parliament revised the constitution, scrapping the Presidential Council in favor of a chief executive with broad powers. Parliament empowered itself to elect the next president, after which the position will be directly elected, and subsequently elected Salih to a fresh five-year term. In October the GPC and YIP formed a governing coalition.

In February 1995, thirteen opposition groups led by the YSP formed the Democratic Opposition Coalition. In March police arrested several dozen opposition members in the south, and in April police arrested three journalists linked to the YSP.

Political Rights and Civil Liberties: The 1993 Yemeni elections were reasonably free, although there were numerous irregularities and the ruling parties had significant advantages, including influence over the media. However, power is now concentrated in the hands President Salih and a small clique from his minority Shiite Zaydi sect. Tribal leaders wield considerable influence in some northern and eastern areas.

The 1994 civil war precipitated a deterioration in the human rights situation. Both sides indiscriminately shelled or otherwise conducted military operations around civilian areas, and arbitrarily detained hundreds of civilians. Following the war, YIP militants temporarily took over numerous police stations in southern cities, and in Aden flogged citizens for drinking alcohol and ransacked a Catholic church. Many observers feel the government now tacitly backs an "Islamization" of the south. Meanwhile, the clandestine Islamic Jihad organization has carried out several violent attacks in the south, including a raid on a wedding party in September 1995 that left ten people dead.

The judiciary is subject to interference by the government and other well connected interests, and procedural safeguards are inadequate. After the war the government merged the former northern and southern judiciaries into a system composed of shari'a (Islamic law) and commercial courts.

The authorities continue to carry out arbitrary arrests and detentions, particularly of YSP members, search homes and offices without warrants, and monitor personal communications. Security forces torture detainees to extract confessions and information. Prison conditions are generally abysmal. According to the U.S. State Department, over 4,000 persons are being held in prison without any documentation as to the reason for their incarceration. The government and other interests reportedly run extrajudicial prisons.

The government closed pro-YSP newspapers during the war, and after the war allowed some to reopen but under pro-GPC or YIP editors. In January 1995, the authorities shut down the Aden-based *Al-Ayyam* newspaper, which had published articles critical of the government. The government exercises considerable leverage over private newspapers through its ownership of the printing presses. The radio and television stations are state-owned and rarely offer pluralistic views.

The Ministry of Social Security and Social Affairs must register associations. The independent Yemeni Human Rights Organization operates openly. However, in 1994 the government dissolved a southern-based human rights group. Police and soldiers have violently dispersed protesters on several occasions. In February 1995, security forces broke up a demonstration in the capital, Sanaa, in support of freedom of expression. In March, police forcibly dispersed protests against price increases, killing several people.

Islam is the state religion. The tiny Jewish population in the north faces fewer official restrictions than in previous years, but Jewish citizens have limited employment opportunities.

Citizens with a non-Yemeni parent (known as *muwalladin*), as well as members of the tiny Akhdam minority, face discrimination in employment opportunities. Traditional norms discriminate against women, particularly in the north, and women face legal discrimination in marriage and divorce matters. Female genital mutilation is practiced in some areas, and domestic violence is reportedly common.

The labor law permits only one union per enterprise and only one trade union confederation, the progovernment Yemeni Confederation of Labor Unions. State employees are prohibited from joining unions. There is no explicit right to strike or bargain collectively, and such activity is rare. Child labor is prevalent.

Yugoslavia

Polity: Dominant party **Political Rights:** 6
Economy: Mixed statist **Civil Liberties:** 6
Population: 8,331,000 **Status:** Not Free
PPP: na
Life Expectancy: 72.6
Ethnic Groups: Serb (80 percent), Montenegrin (7 percent),
Sanjak Muslim (4 percent), Roma, Albanian, others
Capital: Belgrade

Overview: In 1995, Serbian President Slobodan Milosevic continued to dominate Yugoslavia, and on behalf of Bosnian Serbs signed the U.S-brokered Dayton Accords aimed at ending the war in Bosnia-Herzegovina.

The reconstituted Federal Republic of Yugoslavia (FRY) was formed in 1992 after Slovenia, Croatia, Macedonia and Bosnia seceded, leaving Serbia—which had seized control of the autonomous provinces of Kosovo and Vojvodina—and Montenegro as the only remaining republics. The Serbian and Montenegrin legislatures accepted a constitution declaring the FRY a "sovereign federal state based on the principles of equality of its citizens and member republics."

The bicameral Federal Assembly includes a 42-member Chamber of Republics (divided evenly between Serbia and Montenegro) and a 138-seat Chamber of Citizens. In December 1992 elections for the latter, Milosevic's Socialist Party of Serbia (SPS) won 47 seats; the ultranationalist Serbian Radical Party (SRS), under suspected war criminal and paramilitary commander Vojislav Seselj, 34; and the DEPOS opposition coalition, 20. Milosevic remained Serbian president, defeating U.S. businessman and FRY nonparty premier Milan Panic in a fraud-marred vote. Montenegrin President Momir Bulatovic defeated Milosevic ally Branko Kostic in a January 1993 runoff.

In 1993, Milosevic purged several leading Belgrade intellectuals from government institutions, harassed oppositionists, and moved against Seselj after the SRS-led ouster of FRY President Dobrica Cosic. The Federal Assembly elected former Communist official and Milosevic ally Zorin Lilac as president. The New Socialists' Radoje Kontic was appointed prime minister after Panic's ouster.

In October, Milosevic dissolved the 250-member Serbian parliament. Milosevic was strengthened after 19 December elections as the SPS won 123 seats, just shy of a majority. Seselj's SRS suffered huge losses, dropping from 73 to 39 seats. Another loser was Zeljko Raznatovic, alias "Arkan," an accused bank robber and militia leader from Kosovo. The charismatic Vuk Draskovic's Serbian Renewal Movement held 46 seats, down from 50.

Bosnia remained a dominant issue in 1995. In February, Milosevic rejected an American-backed proposal to lift trade sanctions on the FRY in exchange for recognition of Bosnia and Croatia. In 1994, he had imposed a porous blockade on Bosnian Serbs after they rejected the Vance-Owen peace plan, which would have given them almost half of Bosnia.

Though Milosevic rejected several proposals in the spring, Western sanctions damaged the Serb economy and increased public weariness with the Bosnian war. Smuggling and bribery allowed oil and other goods into the country, but low hard currency reserves and official reluctance to institute meaningful reforms crippled the economy. Industrial production declined sharply, and over one-third of Serbs lived in poverty compared to 6 percent in 1990. Milosevic began attacking ultranationalists, while the state-dominated media ran negative portrayals of Bosnian Serbs.

Added to the economic impetus for Milosevic's involvement in the U.S. effort to halt the Bosnian war were NATO air strikes, Croatian offensives that drove Serbs out of Western Slavonia and Krajina, and battlefield victories by Croat-Muslim forces in September. In November, Milosevic joined the Croatian and Bosnian presidents in signing the Dayton Accords (*see Bosnia-Herzegovina report*).

Shortly after signing the accords Milosevic reasserted political control at home. Three leading SPS members were purged in a clampdown on hardline nationalists opposed to the agreement: Former Yugoslav president Borislav Jovic, chief SPS ideologue Mihajlo Markovic, and Milorad Vucelic, chief of the powerful Television Serbia. The moves appeared to strengthen the position within the party of Milosevic's wife, Mirjana, an increasingly powerful political figure.

Political Rights and Civil Liberties: FRY citizens are constrained in changing their government. A parliament dominated by former Communists loyal to Milosevic appoints the president and prime minister.

Irregularities marred December 1993 elections to the Serbian republican parliament. Milosevic's control of the media, particularly state television, effectively excludes opposition views and access. Parliament violated the constitution and failed to consult the Constitutional Court in ousting President Cosic in 1993. Several well organized political parties exist, but face violence and intimidation.

Freedoms of assembly and expression are curtailed. Police routinely disband demonstrations violently. Milosevic strengthened the Serbian police by 20,000 in 1993, equipping special units with armored vehicles, helicopters, and rocket launchers.

State radio and television are subservient to Milosevic and the SPS, and staffed by Milosevic loyalists. With independent newspapers expensive or unavailable outside Belgrade, television is the main source of information. Authorities in 1994 sought to silence the independent press by buying controlling interests in leading publications, taking over *Borba*, the last newspaper critical of Milosevic. In 1995, ex-*Borba* journalists launched the independent *Nas* (Our) *Borba*, but the government denied access to newsprint, distribution and printing facilities. In May, Russia blocked U.N. efforts to allow newsprint delivery to the beleaguered paper. The independent television station Studio B and Radio B-92 have faced similar pressure, and the radio has muted its criticism of the regime since its launching in 1991. Police have threatened journalists in Kosovo.

Muslims in Kosovo and the Sandzak region between Serbia and Montenegro face repression and persecution. Serbs and Montenegrins are overwhelmingly Eastern Orthodox and practice their religion freely.

The federal judiciary, headed by constitutional and federal courts, is subordinate to Serbia. The government has openly ignored statutes barring the forced mobilization of refugees into military units. Serb refugees from Croatia and Bosnia were denied entry into Serbia, and males were ordered to join the Bosnian Serb army. Entry into Serbia was made extremely restrictive, in violation of international conventions.

Federal and republican laws prohibit discrimination against women, but women remain underrepresented in high-level government and business sectors.

The independent *Nezavisimost* trade union has faced harassment and persecution, and most unions are government- or SPS-controlled. Despite restrictions and intimidation, workers have gone on strike in several sectors over the last two years. Nongovernmental organizations such as professional and humanitarian groups exist, but political organizations face government harassment.

Zaire

Polity: Presidential-military and interim legislative
Economy: Capitalist-statist
Population: 44,060,000
PPP: $523
Life Expectancy: 52.0
Ethnic Groups: Bantu tribes (80 percent), over 200 other tribes
Capital: Kinshasa

Political Rights: 7
Civil Liberties: 6
Status: Not Free

Overview: President Mobutu Sese Seko managed to manipulate the Rwandan refugee crisis and return his dictatorship to international diplomatic respectability in 1995. But lawlessness and corruption continued to invite anarchy as the U.N. asked that permanent human rights observers be sent to monitor widespread abuses.

Colonized as the Belgian Congo in the nineteenth century, this vast area in central Africa was brutally exploited and left ill-prepared for independence in 1960. The country became a focus of Cold War competition until then-Colonel Joseph Mobutu seized power in 1964. A firm ally of the West, Mobutu was long forgiven not only his repressiveness but also his kleptocratic tendencies, which have left him among the world's richest men and Zaire among the world's poorest countries.

The Cold War's end left Mobutu with few friends, and domestic agitation for democratization and good governance forced him to open the political process in 1990. Mobutu's Popular Revolutionary Movement (MPR), the sole legal party since 1965, the Sacred Union of the Radical Opposition and Allied Civil Society (USORAS, a 200-group coalition), and scores of other groups attended a national conference that in December 1992 established a High Council of the Republic to oversee a democratic transition. The conference appointed USORAS leader Etienne Tshisekedi wa Mulumba as prime minister, but Mobutu dismissed Tshisekedi in 1993. Current Prime Minister Kengo wa Dondo has introduced limited economic reforms but holds little real power. Opposition disunity and Mobutu's manipulation delayed and derailed reforms. A January 1994 agreement called for multiparty elections under a Transition Act by July 1995. Voting has been postponed for at least two years, and the sixty-five-year old Mobutu has been reasserting political authority amid continued opposition bickering.

Rights abuses continued during the tenuous transition. Soldiers shot dead at least thirty protesters during a July march in the capital, Kinshasa, staged by the Unified Lumumbist Party. Security forces remained unchecked and near-anarchy prevailed in many rural areas. In November, a U.N. human rights observer recommended that permanent observers be dispatched to Zaire. The official also urged measures to control the army and open state media.

Mobutu used crises in Rwanda and Burundi to revive his international fortunes. Allowing Hutu extremists who had engineered the 1994 Rwanda genocide to regroup and re-arm in Zaire, Mobutu sought to destabilize the new Rwandan Patriotic Front government by allowing guerrilla raids and threatening mass expulsions of refugees. This won Mobutu much credit in France, a strong supporter of the ousted genocidal regime. His actions, since tempered, have brought grudging tolerance from other Western countries anxious to avoid further bloodshed.

Political Rights and Civil Liberties: Citizens cannot change their government democratically. There are no freely elected representatives, although the transitional parliament includes a broad range of opinions. Mobutu has been unopposed in presidential elections since 1970, and the three most recent legislative polls were neither free nor fair. In May, the transitional parliament created a forty-four-member, nominally autonomous election commission charged with preparing and overseeing elections. It remains uncertain whether the commission can accomplish its task.

Over 300 political parties have been registered since December 1990. Many attended the national conference or are in the transitional parliament. The delineation of real power remains fluid. Mobutu's control over most of the security forces is still a central factor.

Freedom of expression is guaranteed by both Zaire's constitution and the Transition Act. There is much open debate and an independent press exists. Newspapers normally reach only Kinshasa and some other large cities, however, and the state radio network is the major source of information throughout Zaire. Threats against independent journalists are reported, and often result in self-censorship. Political competition between Mobutu and Prime Minister Kengo was behind the November closing of a pro-Mobutu newspaper for printing "lying and defamatory articles."

Numerous nongovernmental organizations exist, including several human rights groups. Among the most active are the Zairian Association for the Defense of Human Rights, Zairian League of Human Rights and Voice of the Voiceless. These groups criticize security forces and government actions, but were subjected to threats and harassment. Church-based and grassroots groups have undertaken civic education projects. Freedom of assembly is restricted by decrees and permit requirements, and by the chance that security forces will violently break up any antigovernment demonstration. Religious freedom is respected, although religious groups must register with the government.

Zaire's judiciary is neither independent nor effective in protecting constitutional rights. Arbitrary detention is routinely used to harass and intimidate political activists. Lengthy pretrial detention is usual in prisons, where poor diet and lack of medical care can be life-threatening.

Women experience discrimination, especially in rural areas, despite an array of constitutional protections. Women have fewer employment and educational opportunities than do men, and are often paid less for equal work in the formal sector. Wives must receive husbands' permission to undertake many financial transactions.

The 1990 legalization of political parties also led to an opening of the union movement. Unions are no longer required to join the National Union of Zairian Workers (UNTZA), which was part of the ruling MPR. UNTZA has since shown some autonomy, and over 100 other unions exist. There have been numerous strikes protesting plummeting wages due to hyperinflation.

Zaire's formal economy is largely moribund. The state mining and railways corporations have declared bankruptcy, and all-pervasive corruption makes new business formation difficult.

⬇ Zambia

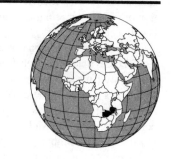

Polity: Presidential-par- **Political Rights:** 3
liamentary democracy **Civil Liberties:** 4
Economy: Mixed statist **Status:** Partly Free
Population: 9,072,000
PPP: $1,230
Life Expectancy: 48.9
Ethnic Groups: Bemba, Lozi, Lunda, Ngoni, others
Capital: Lusaka
Trend Arrow: Increased pressure against the media and reported
corruption are imperiling Zambia's democratic transition.

Overview:
Zambia's multiparty experiment was severely tested as
President Frederick Chiluba struggled to improve a
foundering economy hampered by drought and corruption,
and his Movement for Multiparty Democracy (MMD) failed to take steps to
consolidate the rule of law before 1996 elections.

For twenty-seven years after achieving independence from Britain in 1964,
Zambia was a one-party state under President Kenneth Kaunda's United National
Independence Party (UNIP). Kaunda's increasingly repressive regime faced
security and economic problems during long guerrilla wars against white rule in
neighboring Rhodesia and Mozambique. UNIP's socialist policies and plummeting
prices for Zambia's main export, copper, largely wrecked the economy.

Kaunda permitted 1991 free elections under international pressure. Former
unionist Chiluba won, and his MMD took 125 of 150 National Assembly seats.
Chiluba and the MMD have not yet acted on their popular mandate to reform
Zambia's economic and political life.

The new government is adhering to privatization plans under an International
Monetary Fund-imposed structural adjustment plan. Endemic corruption, drug trafficking and drought compound the resulting social dislocations. Malnutrition is increasing,
and famine is feared in some areas. Chiluba witnessed the desperate conditions when, at
a September rally in the southern town of Monze, the crowd grabbed all the food they
could and immediately disappeared into the bush before listening to his speech.

Seeking to deflect criticism, the MMD pressed, then abandoned, an effort to
declare former strongman Kaunda a noncitizen. Libel suits are used to discredit and
intimidate journalists. A vibrant press and growing civil society still operate with
few constraints, but amid increasing apprehension.

Political Rights
and Civil Liberties:
Zambians first elected their government freely in 1991. The
test for Zambia's democracy will be the October 1996
presidential and legislative elections.

The MMD dominates Zambia's political scene, but has been riven by internal
dissent, perhaps because it was initially held together only by opposition to one-
party rule. The main opposition, UNIP, remains weak, divided and weighted with
its authoritarian past, and smaller parties remain uninfluential.

Pressure on the independent press takes the form of physical assaults, surveillance, denial of printing facilities, and libel suits in response to stories on corruption. *Zambia Post* editor Fred M'membe, a particular target, faces 100 years in prison if convicted on all outstanding charges. The government increasingly controls state media, including all broadcasting except a few new radio stations. In November opposition leader Kaunda announced a boycott on interviews with state media, except live broadcasts which could not be censored. Authorities have introduced legislation restricting reporting on governmental corruption, and has sought to establish an official, mandatory press union to accredit all journalists.

Freedom of religion is respected. Many voluntary associations operate freely, and human rights groups include the Zambian Civic Education Association and the Law Association of Zambia. A governmental Human Rights Commission is also active.

There are regular complaints of police brutality, and severe prison conditions reportedly led to many deaths caused by shortages of food and health care. The Organization of African Unity criticized expulsions of foreigners, saying procedures and confiscation of property violated human rights standards.

Zambia's courts are overloaded, often taking years to hear cases. Many suspects have been detained awaiting trail for five years or longer. Government courts hear criminal cases, but many civil matters are decided by customary courts whose quality and consistency vary, and whose decisions often contradict legal and constitutional protections. Discrimination against women is especially prevalent in such courts.

In 1995, women's groups debated the need for special protections in the draft constitution. Other constitutional provisions would strengthen civil liberties, but its final form remains unclear. Women cannot participate fully in the economy and are disfavored in land allocation in rural areas. Wives must have their husband's permission to obtain contraceptives. Women's advocates have demanded government action to curb spousal abuse and other violence against women. Societal discrimination remains a serious obstacle to women's rights even when fair legislation exists.

The constitution guarantees the right to organize trade unions, and Zambia's union movement is among Africa's strongest. About two-thirds of the country's 300,000 formal-sector workforce is unionized. The Zambia Congress of Trade Unions, an umbrella for Zambia's nineteen largest unions, operates democratically without interference. The 1993 Industrial and Labor Relations Act protects collective bargaining rights, and unions negotiate directly with employers.

Zambia's largest, most important unions are found in the northern "copper belt." The miners' union supports government plans to privatize the Zambia Consolidated Copper Mines. Moves towards telecommunications privatization began late in 1995. Economic development is hindered by considerable corruption, inflation and distortions in the money supply caused, some economists believe, by drug money in the underground economy. Overall economic weakness limits Zambia's ability to create new businesses. Official statistics show nearly 80 percent of Zambians living below the official poverty line.

Zimbabwe

Polity: Dominant party
Economy: Capitalist-
statist
Population: 11,261,000
PPP: $1,970
Life Expectancy: 53.7
Ethnic Groups: Shona (71 percent), Ndebele (16 percent),
European, others
Capital: Harare

Political Rights: 5
Civil Liberties: 5
Status: Partly Free

Overview:
Increased authoritarianism threatened civil liberties, pushing Zimbabwe toward the one-party state envisioned by President Robert Mugabe and his African National Union-Patriotic Front (ZANU-PF). Economic distress and electioneering prior to 1996 presidential elections seemed to steer Mugabe toward more populist, intolerant positions as 1995 ended.

Zimbabwe achieved independence in 1980 after a guerrilla war against a white minority government that had declared independence from Britain in 1965 as Rhodesia. From 1983-87, a civil war suppressed resistance by Zimbabwe's largest minority group, the Ndebele, against the political dominance of Mugabe's Shona group. Severe rights abuses accompanied the struggle, which ended with an accord bringing Ndebele leaders into the government. Several senior Ndebele figures have since died suspiciously. ZANU-PF has dominated Zimbabwe since independence, tailoring laws and constitutional amendments to maintain power, including an exclusive state subsidy (in 1995-96 about $3.3 million) for party activities. Several laws restrict press freedom and are used to harass critics, but Zimbabwe's judiciary remains strongly independent and the government has respected its decisions.

After fifteen years in office, Mugabe appeared increasingly intolerant of dissent as he planned his campaign for another six-year term. In mid-December he threatened to ban all demonstrations, labeled local human rights groups "gangster organizations," and warned that they would "be ruthlessly dealt with," after a November demonstration against police brutality devolved into looting in the capital, Harare.

Also in mid-December, Mugabe proclaimed that white-owned farms should be seized without compensation if necessary for redistribution to black Zimbabweans. Currently, lands may be seized but not confiscated, and the government has lacked resources to make major purchases.

Senior opposition politician Reverend Ndabaningi Sithole was arrested, allegedly for plotting to assassinate Mugabe. The seventy-five-year old Sithole, president of ZANU-Ndonga party and Mugabe's political rival for over three decades, holds one of only three opposition seats in the 150-member National Assembly. In December, the alleged head of *Chimwenje*, a Mozambique-based guerrilla force reportedly aligned with Zanu-Ndonga, was sentenced to fifteen years' imprisonment as part of the Sithole plot.

Parliamentary elections in April and local polls in October entrenched ZANU-PF rule. Widespread voter apathy and limited opposition access to state-dominated or -influenced media allowed ZANU-PF to win nearly all seats contested.

In late November, outspoken Mugabe critic and former guerrilla Margaret Dongo won a parliamentary seat in a court-ordered repeat election, after her April defeat was found to be rigged. Voter apathy was evident, as only about 4,600 of 26,000 registered voters turned out. Deteriorating economic conditions and a widespread perception of official corruption have left voters disillusioned with politics.

Political Rights and Civil Liberties:

Citizens cannot change their government democratically, due to ZANU-PF domination. The party has significant influence over the electoral process and receives large state subsidies. Security forces have intimidated voters in opposition strongholds. Elections have been further marred by irregularities in voter registration and identification, and in vote counts. The president appoints twenty of 150 National Assembly members, and ten others are traditional chiefs beholden to the government. Only three oppositionists won seats in the 1995 parliament, and one has since been jailed.

Election media coverage has heavily favored the government, with opposition statements either absent or censored. State-run media thoroughly overshadow the small independent press. The government controls all broadcasting and several newspapers directly, and indirectly controls most others. Self-censorship is extensive, promoted by government control over editorial policy and appointments in most cases, and in the independent press by threat of anti-defamation statutes and a broad Official Secrets Act. The Parliamentary Privileges and Immunities Act has been used to force journalists to reveal sources in corruption stories before the courts and parliament.

In April two editors of the *Gazette* newspaper were detained on charges of criminal defamation after their newspaper reported that Mugabe had secretly married his former secretary. Although Mugabe later confirmed the marriage, the charges were not dropped.

Freedom of assembly is generally respected for groups deemed nonpolitical. There is no interference with religious practice. Civic organizations critical of the government operate but are closely scrutinized and sometimes harassed. Several human rights groups exist, including the Catholic Commission for Justice and Peace, the Zimbabwe Human Rights Organization (Zimrights), the Legal Relief Fund and the Southern African Human Rights Foundation. The last group has accused the government of confiscating its equipment and vehicles illegally.

The judiciary remains largely independent, but its decisions protecting basic rights have been subverted by successive constitutional amendments passed by the ZANU-PF-controlled legislature. Security forces, particularly the Central Intelligence Organization, often ignore basic rights regarding detention, search and seizure.

Women's rights receive strong protection under law, although married women still cannot hold property jointly with their husbands. Especially in rural areas, women's access to education and employment is limited, and few are either familiar with their rights or able to pursue them. Domestic violence against women is common. In July, Mugabe made international headlines by barring gay and lesbian groups from attending an international book fair in Harare.

The Labor Relations Act (LRA) broadly protects private-sector workers' rights, but public sector workers may not join unions. The Zimbabwe Congress of Trade Unions is independent and highly critical of government economic policies. The LRA also allows independent worker committees to exist outside union structures, which unionists see as a government ploy to weaken their influence.

Implementation of a structural adjustment program fashioned by international donors and creditors has been slow, and the government has yet to privatize numerous unprofitable enterprises. Corruption is also considered a serious obstacle to business development.

Armenia/Azerbaijan
Nagorno-Karabakh

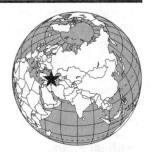

Polity: Armenian-occupied   **Political Rights:** 6*
Economy: Mixed statist   **Civil Liberties:** 6*
Population: 150,000   **Status:** Not Free
Ethnic Groups: Armenian (95 percent), Assyrian, Greek,
Kurd, others
Ratings Change: *Nagorno-Karabakh's political rights
rating changed from 7 to 6, as did its civil liberties
rating, because of a decline in violence.

Overview: Several attempts by the Organization for Security and
Cooperation in Europe (OSCE) Minsk Group to mediate
the crisis in this predominantly Armenian enclave within
Azerbaijan failed to find a permanent solution, despite a year-long series of
meetings in Bonn, Vienna, Moscow and other capitals. Sporadic fighting continued
despite a May 1994 ceasefire.

In 1921, Nagorno-Karabakh was transferred from Armenia and placed under
Soviet Azerbaijani jurisdiction by Joseph Stalin. Subsequently, the Nagorno-
Karabakh Autonomous Oblast (region) was created, with a narrow strip of land
bordering Armenia proper. In 1930, Moscow permitted Azerbaijan to establish and
resettle the border areas between Nagorno-Karabakh and Armenia.

In 1988, Azeri militia and special forces launched violent repression in
response to Karabakh Armenians' call for greater autonomy. In 1991, the legislatures of Nagorno-Karabakh and Shahumyan voted for secession. Multiparty
elections were held, and on 6 January 1992 parliament's inaugural session adopted
a declaration of independence and elected Artur Mkrtchian president. Following
Mkrtchian's assassination in April, Vice-President Georgi Petrossian became
president; he resigned in June 1993 and was replaced by Garen Baburian. Parliament did not meet during much of 1993 and 1994, as many parliamentarians were
fighting on the front lines. At the end of 1993, which saw military gains by the
Karabakh Armenians, Azeri forces launched offensives in the northern, southern
and eastern parts of the enclave.

In 1994, conflicts also arose between the Minsk Group and Russia over the
mediation process and the composition of peace-keeping forces, with Moscow
favoring Russian and Commonwealth of Independent States personnel and the
OSCE calling for a multinational contingent of 3,000 troops. On 22 December, the
Karabakh Supreme Council—the executive body of parliament—elected Robert
Kocharian, head of the state defense committee, to the post of president for a five-
year term. The president appointed parliamentarian Leonard Petrossian as prime
minister.

In January 1995, Kocharian created a governmental structure consisting of nine
ministries, seven state departments and five state enterprises. Elections to a thirty-
three-member parliament were held in April and May, with an 80 percent voter
turnout. Prior to the vote, a public organization, Democratia, was formed to assist

all political parties, unions and other groups in preparation for the elections, which were generally free and fair.

Throughout the year, there was virtually no progress in resolving the conflict, as Azeri, Armenian and Nagorno-Karabakh representatives disagreed on a range of issues. The most contentious was the fate of the Lachin corridor connecting Nagorno-Karabakh with Armenia and the city of Sushi. Azerbaijan has demanded that Lachin and Sushi be returned as a preliminary condition for further progress. The warring sides did agree on several prisoner exchanges.

Political Rights and Civil Liberties: Residents of Nagorno-Karabakh technically have the means to change their government democratically.

Parliamentary elections in summer 1995 were generally free and fair. Government structures and a cabinet have been established. There are several small political parties.

The undeclared state of war has impinged on rights and civil liberties. Border regions have been subjected to attacks that make governing difficult. The ethnic nature of the conflict has led to charges of "ethnic cleansing" and atrocities by both sides. Freedom of movement has been curtailed by war, and there are restrictions on assembly and association, as well as self-censorship in the press. Several Russian and Ukrainian mercenaries went on trial in 1995. With Armenians making up 95 percent of the territory's population, the Armenian Apostolic Church is the main religion, and the ethnic aspect of the war has constrained the religious rights of the few Muslims still left in the region.

China
Tibet

Polity: Communist one-party
Economy: Statist
Population: 4,590,000*
Ethnic Groups: Tibetan, Han Chinese

Political Rights: 7
Civil Liberties: 7
Status: Not Free

* This figure from China's 1990 census indicates Tibetans under Chinese control. It includes 2.096 million Tibetans living in the Tibet Autonomous Region (TAR), and 2.494 million Tibetans living in areas of eastern Tibet that beginning in 1950 were incorporated into four Chinese provinces.

Overview: Prior to the Chinese invasion in 1949, Tibet had been a sovereign state for the better part of 2,000 years, coming under modest foreign influence only during brief periods in the thirteenth and eighteenth centuries. In late 1949, China invaded Tibet with 100,000 troops, and in 1951 formally annexed the country.

Popular uprisings against Chinese rule culminated in mass pro-independence demonstrations in Lhasa, the capital, in March 1959. In the next several months

China crushed the uprisings, killing an estimated 87,000 Tibetans in the Lhasa region alone. The Tibetan spiritual and temporal leader, the fourteenth Dalai Lama, Tenzin Gyatso, fled to Dharamsala, India with 80,000 supporters.

In 1960 the International Commission of Jurists called the Chinese occupation genocidal, and ruled that prior to the 1949 invasion Tibet had possessed all the attributes of statehood as defined under international law. In 1965 China created the Tibet Autonomous Region out of an area containing only half the territory of pre-invasion Tibet. The rest of Tibet had, since 1950, been incorporated into four southwestern Chinese provinces. By the late 1970s more than one million Tibetans had died as a result of the occupation, and all but eleven of 6,200 monasteries had been destroyed.

Between 1987 and 1990 Chinese soldiers forcibly broke up peaceful demonstrations throughout Tibet, killing hundreds and arresting thousands more. In 1992 Beijing announced plans to expand Tibet's road and air links with China, a policy that will further facilitate the mass settlement of Han Chinese into Tibet.

In May 1995 the Dalai Lama identified six-year-old Gedhun Choekyi Nyima as the eleventh reincarnation of the Panchen Lama, Tibetan Buddhism's second most important religious figure. The Chinese authorities detained Abbot Chadrel Rimpoche, who had led a six-year search for the boy at Beijing's request, and an assistant for allegedly leaking the name to the Dalai Lama. Rejecting the Dalai Lama's authority in the matter, China organized a late-November ceremony in Lhasa and proclaimed Gyaincain Norbu, another six-year-old, as the Panchen Lama.

In another development, in April a Hong Kong newspaper published a secret Chinese document outlining a plan to settle ex-soldiers and paramilitary police officers from China in Tibet.

Political Rights and Civil Liberties:

Tibetans cannot change their government democratically. China appoints all officials and controls all major policy decisions.

The authorities continue forcibly to break up peaceful demonstrations and arbitrarily arrest Tibetans displaying symbols of Tibetan independence or cultural identity. In February and March police arrested at least 106 people during demonstrations at Lhasa and Phenpo, and expelled some 90 monks from their monasteries. There are several hundred Tibetan political prisoners, and security forces routinely torture prisoners and rape nuns. In 1994 Phuntsog Yangkyi, a nun, died in a police hospital after being beaten in prison, and in 1995 another nun, Gyaltsen Kelsang, died from injuries sustained in prison.

The Chinese government's Sinification policy includes sending top Tibetan students to study in China each year and granting economic incentives to lure ethnic Chinese into relocating to Tibet. By some estimates there are already 120,000 Chinese and only 40,000 Tibetans in Lhasa alone. Entrance to Lhasa is regulated through a strict permit system.

The Chinese government monitors monasteries, forbids religious figures from holding large public teachings, and generally bans possession of photographs of the Dalai Lama. Reports in early 1995 suggested that the government has recently closed numerous monasteries. In March authorities banned the building of new monasteries and nunneries, placed new limits on the number of monks and nuns permitted in any one monastery or nunnery, and capped the total number of clerics permitted in Tibet. Some politically active monks face severe internal travel restrictions. Following the Dalai Lama's naming of the eleventh Panchen Lama in May, the authorities purged numerous lamas from Tashi Lhunpo monastery in Shigatse, the traditional home of the Panchen Lama.

According to official Chinese statistics, Tibetans have a 25 percent literacy rate compared to 77 percent in China, reflecting Beijing's paltry spending on education in Tibet. In 1994 the government began a "patriotic education" campaign aimed at Tibetan primary and middle school students, which included daily ceremonies raising the Chinese flag and singing the Chinese national anthem. Although China's draconian family planning policy ostensibly does not extend to Tibetans and other minorities, sources say the one-child rule is enforced in Tibet.

India
Kashmir

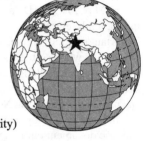

Polity: Indian-administered
Economy: Capitalist-statist
Population: 7,719,000
Ethnic Groups: Kashmiri (Muslim majority, Hindu minority)

Political Rights: 7
Civil Liberties: 7
Status: Not Free

Overview:

The destruction of a fifteenth-century shrine in May 1995 following a standoff between Indian police and Muslim militants, and the ensuing unrest, caused New Delhi to twice cancel planned elections.

Following the partition of India in 1947, Muslims from newly formed Pakistan backed a revolt in the predominantly Muslim, princely state of Kashmir. Hindu Maharajah Hari Singh ceded control of the territory to India in return for protection. Indian Premier Jawaharlal Nehru appointed Sheik Abdullah of the National Conference, a secular, left-wing party, as head of the territorial government. Nehru also promised a referendum on self-determination.

Following months of sectarian strife, a 1949 U.N.-brokered agreement recognized Pakistan's control of a portion of Kashmir, while India maintained most of Kashmir and predominantly Hindu Jammu, another ex-princely state. Article 370 of India's 1950 constitution granted Kashmir substantial autonomy, although in practice this has been gradually eroded. Similarly, a 1952 accord gave Kashmir power over all areas except defense, foreign affairs and communications. In 1953 Nehru dismissed Abdullah's government, and in 1957 India formerly annexed the territories as its state of Jammu and Kashmir.

In 1975, India returned Sheik Abdullah to power after he signed an agreement accepting Indian rule in return for the state's right to nullify any Indian law that encroached on the 1952 accord. In 1987, the Indian government rigged elections that brought a pro-Delhi coalition, led by the Sheik's son, Farooq Abdullah, to power.

In the summer of 1989, the Jammu and Kashmir Liberation Front began an insurgency seeking independence. Other groups seeking to incorporate Kashmir into Pakistan, including the powerful *Hizbul Mujahideen*, also launched insurgencies. In July 1990, amid rising violence, India placed the state under federal rule.

In March 1993, India replaced hardline governor Girish Chandra Saxena with a moderate, General K.V. Krishna Rao, in the hopes of drawing the militants into negotiations. Pro-Pakistani groups opposed to negotiations stepped up their attacks on security forces and moderate Kashmiri groups.

On 11 May 1995, a two-month standoff between several thousand Indian troops and 150 militants holed up in a fifteenth-century mausoleum in the town of Charar-i-Sharief ended after a fire destroyed the shrine and most of the local houses. Each side accused the other of starting the blaze, and the increasingly unstable situation caused India to cancel state elections planned for July.

In November, Indian premier P.V. Narasimha Rao announced that the government would hold the elections in December despite calls by the All Party Hurriyat Conference, an umbrella group of Kashmiri parties opposed to Indian rule, for a boycott of the vote. Late in the year, the Indian Election Commission, overriding Rao, canceled the polls due to the threat of violence.

In another matter, in July a militant group calling itself *al-Faran* abducted five Western tourists to demand release of twenty-one jailed militants. The group beheaded one of the tourists in August, and continued to hold the remaining four at year's end. In September, a Buddhist group demanding greater autonomy for the Ladakh region of Kashmir held seventeen tourists for four days.

Political Rights and Civil Liberties: India has never held a referendum on Kashmiri self-determination as called for in a 1948 United Nations resolution, and since 1990 Jammu and Kashmir have been under President's Rule (direct federal rule). Two-thirds of the estimated 20,000 people killed in the territory since 1989 have been civilians.

The 300,000 Indian soldiers and police in the territory routinely carry out arbitrary arrests, detentions and torture against civilians and suspected militants. Security forces have indiscriminately fired into crowds on numerous occasions, killing scores of civilians, routinely rape Kashmiri women, and have burned shops and homes. The army is also responsible for extrajudicial executions and "disappearances" of suspected militants.

The July 1990 Jammu and Kashmir Disturbed Areas Act and the Armed Forces (Jammu and Kashmir) Special Powers Act allows the authorities to search homes and arrest suspects without a warrant. Indian troops frequently cordon off entire neighborhoods and conduct house-to-house searches, and often detain hundreds of suspected militants in advance of Indian Republic Day and other holidays.

Kashmiri militants are responsible for the deaths of Indian security forces, public employees, suspected informers and members of rival factions, often through bomb attacks in Jammu, Srinagar and other towns. Separatists also frequently kidnap government officials, politicians and businesspeople.

The legal system is a shambles. Separatists routinely threaten judges, witnesses and the families of defendants. In June, the Indian government agreed to allow the International Committee of the Red Cross to visit some 3,000 Kashmiris held in detention centers.

Security forces and militants routinely harass local human rights activists, and have killed several since 1989. In separate incidents in April gunmen wounded the secretary of a local branch of the People's Union for Civil Liberties, a human rights group, and wounded Abdul Qayoom, president of the Jammu and Kashmir bar association, which frequently investigates human rights abuses. In early September, police released the head of a local branch of the bar association after detaining him for nearly three months. International human rights groups are routinely denied access to the territory.

India's 1971 Newspapers Incitements to Offenses Act, which is only in effect in Jammu and Kashmir, allows a district magistrate to censor articles that could allegedly provoke criminal acts or other disturbances. In recent years the authorities have detained several journalists for reporting on militant groups. In July, Muslim militants raided two newspaper offices and briefly abducted four journalists. In September, a parcel bomb killed BBC photojournalist Mushtaq Ali and wounded a correspondent.

Since 1990, more than 250,000 Hindu Kashmiris have fled the Vale of Kashmir, where the Muslim population is concentrated. Many reported that militants had robbed families and raped women.

Indonesia
East Timor

Polity: Dominant party (military-dominated)
Economy: Capitalist-statist
Population: 778,000
Ethnic Groups: Timorese, Javanese, others

Political Rights: 7
Civil Liberties: 7
Status: Not Free

Overview: In 1995, the Indonesian authorities continued to crack down on nonviolent dissent in East Timor, while tensions between the native population and migrants led to periodic social unrest.

The Portuguese arrived in Timor around 1520, and in the nineteenth and early twentieth centuries took formal control of the eastern half of the island. In 1974, Portugal agreed to hold a referendum on self-determination in East Timor in 1975. That year, the pro-independence, leftist Revolutionary Front for an Independent East Timor (FRETELIN) declared an independent republic. Indonesia invaded on 7 December, and formerly annexed East Timor in 1976 as the country's twenty-seventh province. By 1979 Indonesian soldiers had killed up to 200,000 Timorese. Skirmishes between Indonesian forces and FRETELIN continued throughout the 1980s. Today FRETELIN has fewer than 190 poorly-equipped fighters.

On 12 November 1991, Indonesian soldiers in the territorial capital of Dili fired on thousands of Timorese peacefully marching to the burial site of an independence supporter killed by security forces in October. Between 150 and 270 civilians were killed.

Four officers and six enlisted men, charged only with assault or disobeying orders during the Dili massacre, received light terms ranging from eight to eighteen months in a 1992 series of courts-martial. In separate proceedings, eighteen East

Timorese received terms ranging from six months to life imprisonment for alleged antigovernment activities. In November, Indonesian soldiers captured FRETELIN leader Jose "Xanana" Gusmao. In May 1993 a court sentenced Gusmao to life imprisonment, subsequently reduced to twenty years, in a sham trial.

In July 1994, police forcibly broke up a demonstration by more than 500 Timorese students. In November, police detained and beat some 135 demonstrators in Dili and conducted house-to-house searches.

In January 1995, observers reported the emergence of black-hooded gangs, believed to be linked to the military, that kidnapped and beat dozens of pro-independence Timorese. In mid-February, the intimidation campaign tapered off in Dili but spread to outlying towns and villages. The authorities arrested only sixteen youths in the attacks, with courts subsequently sentencing eight to five-year terms.

Political Rights and Civil Liberties: Since the 1976 Indonesian annexation of East Timor, which the United Nations does not recognize, the government and armed forces have committed widespread rights abuses against dissidents and ordinary citizens. Freedoms of speech, press, assembly and association are nonexistent.

Since late 1991, police have arbitrarily arrested thousands of civilians for periods of up to several months for nonviolent activities. Dissidents are frequently tortured and held incommunicado. On 9 January 1995 police arrested twenty-four Timorese youths for holding a prodemocracy demonstration in Dili. At least seven received prison terms of up to thirty months. In October, police arrested at least 150 youths following four days of clashes between pro-independence and pro-Indonesian Timorese.

The judiciary is not independent. Soldiers and police are rarely prosecuted for rights violations against civilians, and the few who have been tried and convicted received lenient sentences. On 12 January, Indonesian soldiers killed six unarmed civilians in Liquisa district. Two soldiers subsequently received terms of up to four-and-a-half years for violating an order from a superior. Trials of political dissidents lack procedural safeguards. The trial of Jose "Xanana" Gusmao (*see Overview*) fell short of international standards in several respects. The court refused to allow Gusmao to choose his own attorney, instead appointing a defense attorney close to police and prosecutors; several witnesses against Gusmao were themselves detainees, raising the possibility they had been coerced; and the court refused to allow Gusmao to read most of his defense statement.

The government has closed schools that refuse to use the official Bahasa Indonesia as their primary language. The majority Roman Catholic population faces frequent harassment on religious grounds.

The Indonesian government has used financial inducements to encourage an influx of some 25,000 predominantly Muslim settlers per year from Sulawesi and other islands to East Timor. The domination of the local economy by these migrants has been a frequent source of unrest. On 1 January 1995, Indonesian troops killed three people in Baucau, east of Dili, during civil disturbances after a Buginese trader killed a Timorese. Similar unrest broke out in Dili and other towns in September after a Muslim prison official made disparaging remarks about Roman Catholicism.

Foreign journalists are kept under constant surveillance and must obtain special passes to enter East Timor, which are granted infrequently. In November 1995, the authorities expelled sixteen foreign human rights activists within twenty-four hours after their arrival in the territory, and prevented a second group from flying from Bali to Dili. The activists reported an increase in riot police patrolling the streets, apparently to prevent attempts to commemorate the 1991 massacre.

West Papua (Irian Jaya)

Polity: Dominant party (military-dominated)
Economy: Capitalist-statist
Population: 1,700,000
Ethnic Groups: Mainly Papuan

Political Rights: 7
Civil Liberties: 7
Status: Not Free

Overview: The November 1994 killing of a mining company employee touched off an army crackdown leading to at least sixteen civilian deaths by mid-1995. Rights groups charged the New Orleans-based Freeport McMoRan Copper and Gold company with complicity in the killings.

By 1848, the Dutch controlled the entire western half of the island of New Guinea. In 1963, Indonesia assumed administrative responsibility for the territory under a United Nations agreement mandating that a referendum on self-determination be held by 1969.

In the mid-1960s, the guerrilla Free Papua Movement (OPM) began fighting for independence. Rather than hold a popular referendum, in the summer of 1969 Indonesia convened eight hand-picked regional councils for a sham "Act of Free Choice." The predominantly Melanesian population seemed to favor independence, but the councils voted unanimously for annexation by Indonesia. The Indonesian military had a heavy presence in the territory, and the U.N. special observer reported that "the administration exercised at all times a tight political control over the population." Nevertheless, the U.N. accepted the referendum. In 1973, Indonesia renamed the land known locally as West Papua as Irian Jaya.

In 1984, an army offensive against the OPM sent hundreds of villagers fleeing into neighboring Papua New Guinea, and security forces murdered prominent intellectual Arnold Ap. In 1989, the army conducted another series of anti-OPM offensives.

In recent years, there has been a series of rights violations linked to Freeport McMoRan's mining operations, which include the giant Grasberg Mine in the central highlands. In 1989, government teams in the Kurima district, in Freeport's mineral exploration zone, began offering villagers material incentives to relocate outside the district, and withdrew services in some villages.

In April 1995, the Australian Council for Overseas Aid (ACOA) reported that several civilians had been killed by soldiers or had disappeared since the November 1994 killing of a Freeport employee by suspected OPM guerrillas. The ACOA accused Freeport of having abetted several killings by allowing the military to use the company's vehicles and facilities. In August, the Roman Catholic Church of Jayapura made similar charges. In September, Indonesia's official National Commission on Human Rights confirmed that the army had killed sixteen civilians and caused four "disappearances" in the area since October 1994. The deaths included five persons killed inside Freeport's project area, along with the May killing of a minister and ten churchgoers. The army said several soldiers would be prosecuted. Through September the army had also killed some thirty-seven alleged OPM guerrillas.

In a related development, in October the U.S. Overseas Private Investment Corporation canceled Freeport's $100 million political insurance risk policy, citing environmental concerns at Grasberg including potentially toxic mining tailings polluting the Aiwa River system. The local population receives no direct compensation from the mining operations, and the few homes and schools Freeport has built for the villagers are shoddy.

Political Rights and Civil Liberties: Residents of West Papua cannot change their government democratically. Freedoms of speech, press, assembly and association are severely restricted. Several OPM guerrillas and suspected supporters are incarcerated under Indonesia's harsh antisubversion laws.

In September, Indonesia's official National Commission on Human Rights accused the Indonesian military of violations in the territory including extrajudicial killings, torture, arbitrary arrest and detentions, "disappearances," widespread surveillance of the local population and destruction of property. Many of the violations occurred in the Timika district, where Freeport's Grasberg Mine is located (*see Overview*). The ACOA and the Roman Catholic Church of Jayapura have made similar accusations, and the ACOA also reports that the army has burned numerous homes near Freeport's mines.

Since the 1970s, the Indonesian government has resettled more than 170,000 residents of Java and other overcrowded parts of the archipelago into West Papua under a controversial "transmigration" program. The government limits foreigners' access to the territory and restricts internal travel. Immigration officials have reduced the number of visas available to missionary workers, and missionaries and other foreign social workers are only able to receive two-year visas, extendible for only one year. There are several thousand Papuan refugees in neighboring Papua New Guinea's East Awin camp.

Iraq
Kurdistan

Polity: Dual leadership-elected parliament
Economy: Capitalist-statist
Population: 4,000,000
Ethnic Groups: Kurdish majority

Political Rights: 4
Civil Liberties: 4
Status: Partly Free

Overview: Iraqi Kurds have endured repression by successive Iraqi governments. In 1988 Iraq carried out mass murder, rape, torture, detention, forced deportation and chemical warfare against its Kurdish population. This *Anfal* (Spoils) campaign killed tens of thousands of Kurds.

Iraq suppressed a Kurdish uprising following the Gulf War. In April 1991, the United States, Britain, France and Turkey established, and continue to maintain, a secure region north of the thirty-sixth parallel.

In 1992, presidential elections, Massoud Barzani of the Kurdistan Democratic Party (KDP) and Jalal Talabani of the Patriotic Union of Kurdistan (PUK) virtually tied and cut a power-sharing deal. In concurrent balloting for a 105-seat Kurdish National Assembly, the KDP and PUK split the at-large seats, fifty-one to forty-nine. Two minor parties took the five seats reserved for Christian representatives. The KDP and PUK agreed to split the at-large seats evenly and formed a coalition government.

The KDP-PUK coalition began fraying in early 1994 due to power-sharing disputes and a personal rivalry between Barzani and Talabani. Fighting in the spring and summer between the two groups' *peshmerga* guerrillas (literally "those who face death") killed 2,000 people.

Fighting between the factions around Arbil, the regional capital, in December 1994 and January 1995 killed 500 people. At issue was the PUK's demand for a share of the customs duties levied by the KDP on trucks crossing in and out of Turkey. Sporadic fighting continued following ceasefire breakdowns in March and July.

In a major development, on 20 March Turkey launched a six-week offensive into northern Kurdistan aimed at destroying Turkish Kurdistan Worker's Party (PKK) bases, its third and largest offensive since 1992. Turkey carried out a second, smaller raid in July.

Political Rights and Civil Liberties: Iraqi laws passed prior to November 1991 remain in effect in Kurdistan, except for those judged by the National Assembly to be "against Kurdish interests."

In February 1995, Amnesty International accused the Kurdish administration, the PUK and KDP of arbitrary detentions, torture of prisoners and detainees, summary trials, and extrajudicial executions of unarmed POWs, political opponents and demonstrators. It accused the fundamentalist Islamic Movement of similar violations.

Turkish forces operating in Kurdistan in 1995 reportedly tortured PKK guerrillas and suspected sympathizers, forcibly evacuated and razed villages, and killed several civilians. Some 13,000 Kurds who fled southeastern Turkey in 1994 remain in Kurdistan.

Observers report a generally open climate for dialogue on political issues. Numerous newspapers are available. The two major parties run television stations, although news coverage is biased, and smaller parties operate radio stations. Traditional practices curtail the role of women in politics, education and the private sector. Religious groups practice relatively freely.

In February, PUK members assaulted and kidnapped Sadi Barzani, a university professor, and subsequently placed him under house arrest in Suleimaniya. The Kurdistan Human Rights Organization operates openly despite repeated harassment. Several of its members have fled Kurdistan following personal threats.

↑ Israel
Occupied Territories
& Palestinian Autonomous Areas

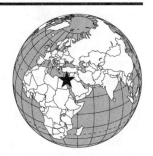

Polity: Military and PLO administered
Economy: Capitalist
Population: 2,184,000
Ethnic Groups: Palestinian, Jewish

Political Rights: 6
Civil Liberties: 5
Status: Not Free

Trend Arrow: The upward trend arrow reflects increased administrative autonomy for the majority Palestinian population.

Overview:　　　　**A** September 1995 agreement on the second stage of Palestinian autonomy extended self-rule to most Arab population centers in the West Bank.

The West Bank, Gaza Strip and East Jerusalem were part of the British Mandate between 1920-48. In 1948, Jordan seized East Jerusalem and the West Bank, while Egypt took control of Gaza. In 1967, Israel occupied the West Bank, Gaza Strip, East Jerusalem and the Golan Heights, which Syria had used to shell towns in northern Israel. The government annexed East Jerusalem in 1967 and the Golan Heights in 1981.

In December 1987, Palestinians living in the West Bank and Gaza began an *intifada* (uprising) against Israeli rule. A series of secret negotiations between Israel and the Palestine Liberation Organization (PLO) yielded an agreement in August 1993 for a five-year interim period of Palestinian autonomy in the territories.

In May 1994, Palestinian autonomy began in the Gaza Strip and Jericho. By year's end Israel had transferred authority over education, health and other local services in the West Bank to a new Palestinian Authority, headed by PLO chairman Yassir Arafat.

A September 1995 agreement on the second stage of autonomy provides for a phased withdrawal of Israeli troops and self-rule for most Palestinian population centers in the West Bank, to be completed by March 1996. The Israeli army will maintain a presence in Hebron, a predominantly Palestinian city home to 415 Israeli settlers. The remainder of the West Bank will stay under Israeli army control pending further negotiations, although the Palestinian authorities will run the civilian affairs of Palestinians living in these areas.

Political Rights　　**P**alestinians living in the West Bank and Gaza cannot
and Civil Liberties:　change their government democratically. A twenty-four-member interim Palestinian Authority (PA) holds legislative powers pending elections for a chief executive and Palestinian Council scheduled for January 1996. Palestinian authority does not cover the 130,000 Jewish settlers living in 140 West Bank settlements, some of whom are militantly opposed to the autonomy process.

The PA judiciary, consisting of criminal, civil and state security courts, is not independent, and due-process safeguards are often ignored. In April 1995, the PA inaugurated state security courts in which suspected Islamic militants are tried in secret, often in the middle of the night and without prior notice. The trials, conducted by security officials with no judicial background, sometimes last only a few minutes. Several militants were sentenced to terms of up to twenty-five years, and the PA reportedly arrested one judge who refused to continue serving.

The PA suspended newspapers on at least five occasions in 1995 for articles critical of Arafat and of the PA itself. In May, a Gaza state security court sentenced the editor of *al-Watan*, a newspaper sympathetic to the militant, fundamentalist Hamas group, to two years in jail for criticizing the PA. Palestinian police have questioned and detained several journalists, and the PA occasionally pressures newspapers into dropping certain stories. In July, the PA instituted a press law that broadly bars the publication of "secret information" on Palestinian security forces or of news that would harm "national unity" or incite violence. The press law empowers authorities to suspend publications and fine and jail journalists, and requires a license for publishing newspapers, magazines or pamphlets. The PA television and radio services rarely carry opposition or Israeli views.

Newspapers and magazines are still subject to Israeli military censors on security issues, although such controls have eased since 1993. In May, Israeli soldiers raided a Nablus-based Palestinian news outlet and sealed the premises under a six-month suspension order.

During the year the Palestinian authorities arrested hundreds of Islamic militants, many for their association with Hamas rather than for specific acts. The arrests frequently came after terrorist attacks against Jewish targets in Israel or the territories. Palestinian police also carried out arbitrary arrests, detention and torture of ordinary civilians, and routinely tortured detainees and prisoners, particularly those suspected of collaborating with Israeli intelligence. Two Palestinians died in detention in 1995, and two others died shortly after their release by Palestinian police.

Israeli soldiers continue to arrest, and in some cases torture, suspected Islamic militants. The April 1995 death of a suspected Islamic militant in Israeli custody highlighted the practice of violently shaking suspects to extract confessions. In February, the Israeli authorities lengthened the maximum period of administrative detention from six months to one year. Following the September accord the Israeli authorities began a three-phase release of up to 5,300 Palestinian prisoners. Killings of Palestinians by Israeli soldiers and by other Palestinians have declined.

Several Palestinian and Israeli human rights groups operate openly but face harassment. In February, Palestinian police detained a prominent human rights lawyer from the Gaza Center for Rights and Law (GCRL) for sixteen hours. The PA also banned a GCRL seminar on the state security courts.

The Israeli authorities frequently close the borders to the West Bank and Gaza in the wake of Palestinian terrorist actions, preventing tens of thousands of Palestinians from reaching their places of employment in Israel. In August, Israeli forces evicted several militant Jewish settlers from a disputed West Bank hilltop.

Morocco
Western Sahara

Polity: Appointed governors   **Political Rights:** 7
Economy: Capitalist   **Civil Liberties:** 6
Population: 212,000   **Status:** Not Free
Ethnic Groups: Arab, Sahrawi

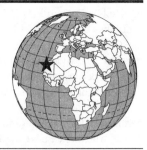

Overview:
A seven-year-old U.N.-backed plan to conduct a national referendum on the future of this disputed former Spanish colony seemed mired in Moroccan obstruction at the end of 1995. Observers feared that the U.N. monitoring force (MINURSO) would be pulled out when its mandate expires at the end of January 1996—a move that could spark a revival of the bloody guerrilla war that ravaged the territory from 1976 until a 1991 ceasefire.

The coastal strip of the Western Sahara was seized by Spain in 1888. The nomads who ranged over "Spanish Sahara's" vast desert interior were only gradually subdued over the next five decades. Both Morocco and Mauritania laid claim to parts of the region after achieving their own independence from France. When Spain withdrew from the colony in early 1976, both countries quickly moved in troops and announced the territory's partition. At the same time, however, local Sahrawis under the Polisario Front proclaimed formation of the Saharan Arab Democratic Republic and launched a guerrilla war with support and sanctuary provided by neighboring Algeria.

A 1975 opinion offered by the International Court of Justice found that Morocco was not entitled to sovereignty over the region. By 1979, Mauritania had tired of the costly war and withdrew, leaving Morocco its third of the disputed territory. Moroccan security forces responded harshly to Polisario's raids, and sought to quell political opposition through arbitrary detention, torture and extrajudicial killings. In 1984, the Organization of African Unity (OAU) recognized the Saharan Arab Democratic Republic, leading to Morocco's withdrawal from the OAU.

A senior U.N. official was set to visit the region early in 1996 to make a last effort to revive the U.N. peace plan. The referendum process ground to a halt in 1995 over the threshold question of who would be counted as a citizen of Western Sahara. Current voter registration procedures demand approval of two traditional sheiks for citizens to be recognized. New proposals, vehemently opposed by Polisario and Algeria, would allow a single sheik to grant approval. Polisario argued this would permit Morocco to import tens of thousands of non-Sahrawis to register and tip the balance in its favor. Moroccan forces are already accused of preventing people not known to support annexation from reaching registration centers, where U.N. observers are not present.

Polisario leaders have warned that abandonment of a free and fair referendum process will lead to a renewal of the Sahrawi war of independence that could include urban attacks in Morocco and also inflame regional tensions.

Political Rights and Civil Liberties:
Sahrawis cannot elect their own government. Since the end of Spanish rule, the territory has been under effective military occupation. Ten seats in the Moroccan parliament are reserved for Western Sahara residents, but any incorporation into Morocco is

rejected by Polisario. The U.N.-sponsored referendum to decide the territory's future has been repeatedly postponed and may not be held at all.

Civil liberties in the 85 percent of Western Sahara controlled by Morocco are restricted, and widespread human rights abuses have been reported. Several hundred Sahrawis detained by Moroccan security forces were released in 1994, but a similar number are unaccounted for and many may have been killed. There are also reports of torture and other abuses by Polisario forces, but lack of access to areas they control makes verification difficult. Polisario is reportedly still holding at least 1,000 Moroccan prisoners of war, whose release is complicated by Morocco's refusal to negotiate with Polisario.

Portugal
Macao

Polity: Appointed governor and partially elected legislature
Economy: Capitalist-statist
Population: 447,000
Ethnic Groups: Chinese, Mecanese, Portuguese

Political Rights: 6
Civil Liberties: 4
Status: Partly Free

Overview:

Portugal established the first European trading station on the Chinese coast in Macao in 1557. Consisting of a peninsula and two islands at the mouth of the Canton River, it is an entrepot for trade with China and a gambling mecca. The 1976 Organic Statute serves as the territory's constitution. It vests executive powers in a governor appointed by the Portuguese president, and grants legislative powers to both the Portuguese government and Macao's Legislative Assembly. The Assembly has eight directly elected members, eight named by businesses and other interest groups, and seven appointed by the governor.

The 1987 Sino-Portuguese Joint Declaration calls for China to assume sovereignty over Macao on 20 December 1999, with the enclave maintaining its legal system and capitalist economy for fifty years. In 1990 governor Carlos Melancia resigned over bribery charges. The current governor, General Vasco Rocha Viera, took office in 1991.

In 1992 legislative elections pro-Beijing candidates swept all eight of the directly elected seats. In 1993 China's National People's Congress approved the Basic Law, Macao's post-1999 constitution.

There is increasing concern over the slow pace of the "localization" of the civil service. Portuguese expatriates and Macanese of mixed Chinese-Portuguese descent hold all judicial positions and the majority of the government undersecretary and department head posts, and along with many of the 6,000 Macanese civil servants are expected to leave the territory or retire by 1999. Although Portuguese civil law, now being translated into Chinese, is to remain in effect after 1999, the expected exodus of these experienced judges and civil servants puts its application in doubt.

Political Rights and Civil Liberties:

Citizens of Macao lack the democratic means to change their government. The governor is appointed by Portugal and only one-third of the legislature is directly elected. The next election is due in 1996. Due to the dearth of legal and political experience among the MPs, and Portugal's practice of deferring to China on key policy decisions, the legislature holds little power. The colony had no voice in the 1987 Joint Declaration ceding control to China in 1999. China maintains a dominant influence in Macao through its business interests and control of two key entities: the General Association of Workers and the General Association of Residences, a civic group.

The legal system is based on Portuguese Metropolitan Law, and citizens are extended the rights granted by the Portuguese constitution. The judiciary is independent and defendants receive fair trials. The government is training Chinese-speaking judges in the expectation that the Portuguese and Macanese judges currently serving will retire before 1999.

The government owns a controlling interest in the television and radio stations, although opposition viewpoints are generally aired. In a notable exception, in 1992 the government suspended phone-ins to a radio talk show after callers repeatedly criticized the colonial administration. Newspapers are privately held and most are blatantly pro-Chinese. In July 1995 the publisher of *Gazeta Macaenese* inexplicably sacked the editor, a journalist and a photographer and temporarily shut down the paper, although it is unclear if this was politically motivated. Journalists practice self-censorship in reporting on China.

A ban on holding demonstrations within fifty yards of government buildings effectively bars protests from peninsular Macao, restricting them to the two islands. Workers can join independent unions and hold strikes. Nearly all 7,000 unionized private-sector workers belong to the pro-Beijing General Association of Workers, which is more of a political mouthpiece than an advocate of organized labor.

Turkey
Cyprus (T)

Polity: Presidential par- **Political Rights:** 4
liamentary democracy   **Civil Liberties:** 2
(Turkish-occupied)   **Status:** Partly Free
Economy: Mixed capitalist
Population: 178,000
Ethnic Groups: Turkish Cypriot, Turk, Greek Cypriot, Maronite

Note: See Cyprus (Greek) under country reports

Overview: **E**arly in 1995, President Rauf Denktash announced a fourteen-point plan to break the deadlock in relations with the island's Greek majority. Included among the proposals were the acceptance of confidence-building measures drawn up by U.N. negotiators, the eventual demilitarization of the island, and an exchange of territory to seal a solution based on a united yet bipartite federal state of Cyprus. The European Union (EU) and international observers have pressured all parties in the negotiations including Turkey, whose Prime Minister was told to help resolve the Cyprus problem or risk jeopardizing a hard-won EU customs agreement scheduled for January of 1996.

Turkish Cypriots are conscious of their economic situation in comparison to the prosperous South. Northern Cyprus, which suffers from constant shortages and high unemployment, is propped up by an estimated $200 million in annual assistance from Turkey. The island shares in Turkey's economic difficulties, including inflation as high as 200 percent. Due to nearly total reliance on its Greek Cypriot neighbors for a free but diminishing power supply, the North suffers frequent outages for twelve to fourteen hours per day. Turkish Cypriots are well aware that a settlement with the South would lift an embargo and ease shortages, while membership in the EU—now possible by the year 2000—could bring substantial regional aid.

Political Rights and Civil Liberties: Citizens of the Turkish Republic of Northern Cyprus (TRNC) can change their government democratically. The Turkish immigrants who settled in the wake of the 1974 Turkish invasion have the right to vote in TRNC elections. The 1,000-member Greek and Maronite communities are disenfranchised in the North but maintain the right to vote in Cypriot Republic elections.

The judiciary is independent and trials are fair. Civilians deemed to have violated military zones are subject to trial in military courts, which maintain all due process laws. In 1995, the TRNC allowed a team of experts from the United States to begin investigating the whereabouts of five American citizens of Greek Cypriot descent who disappeared during the 1974 invasion. The TRNC had refused to allow investigations previously, and it remains unclear whether the U.S. delegation will be permitted to inquire into the fate of more than 1,600 other Greek Cypriots missing since the invasion.

Advocates for Greek Cypriots living in Karpassia claim that these "enclaved" individuals are denied freedom of movement, speech, property and access to the Greek press. The authorities control the content of Greek Cypriot textbooks, and many titles are rejected on the grounds that they "violate the feelings" of Turkish Cypriots. Turkish Cypriots generally enjoy freedom of speech and press, with a variety of newspapers and periodicals in print. Broadcast media are government-owned.

The majority Sunni Muslims and the minority Greek and Maronite Orthodox Christians, as well as foreign residents, practice their religions freely. With the exception of travel to and from the Cypriot Republic, freedom of movement is generally respected. Workers possess the right to organize and join independent trade unions.

Hong Kong

Polity: Appointed governor and partly elected legislature
Economy: Capitalist
Population: 5,847,000
Ethnic Groups: Chinese (98 percent)
Ratings Change: *Hong Kong's political rights rating changed from 5 to 4 because of expanded democratic elections for the Legislative Council and local bodies.

Political Rights: 4*
Civil Liberties: 2
Status: Partly Free

Overview: Prodemocracy candidates took a majority of the directly elected seats in Hong Kong's September 1995 Legislative

Council elections, but China repeated its pledge to scrap all democratic institutions once the colony reverts to Chinese authority in 1997.

Located on the southern coast of China, the Crown Colony of Hong Kong consists of Hong Kong Island and Kowloon Peninsula, both ceded in perpetuity by China to Britain in the mid-1800s, and the mainland New Territories, leased for ninety-nine years in 1898. Executive power rests with a British-appointed governor who approves laws and presides over an advisory Executive Council. A sixty-seat Legislative Council (Legco) can propose, amend or reject legislation.

In 1984 Britain and China signed the Joint Declaration, which gives China sovereignty over Hong Kong on 1 July 1997. China agreed to maintain the colony's *laissez-faire* economy and judicial and political autonomy for fifty years. In 1990 Britain and China agreed that for the first time, eighteen Legco seats would be directly elected in 1991, twenty in 1995, twenty-four in 1999 and thirty in 2003. These plans were incorporated into the Basic Law, Hong Kong's post-1997 constitution. In 1991 the colony held its first-ever direct Legco elections for eighteen seats. Prodemocracy liberals won sixteen seats, led by Martin Lee's Democratic Party with twelve, with the remainder going to conservative and pro-China candidates.

In 1992 newly appointed colonial governor Christopher Patten outlined plans to broaden the franchise for the forty indirectly elected seats in the 1995 Legco elections. For thirty of these seats, elected by "functional constituencies" representing business and other interest groups, Patten proposed allowing more rank-and-file members of these constituencies to vote, and creating nine new broadly drawn constituencies. For the ten remaining indirectly elected seats, Patten proposed forming an electoral college drawn from the colony's district board seats. In December China announced that it would eliminate all existing elected bodies in 1997.

In June 1994 the Legco approved Patten's electoral plans. At local elections in September and in March 1995 prodemocracy candidates soundly defeated conservative and pro-Beijing candidates. In September 1995 Legco elections the Democratic Party won twelve directly elected seats and nineteen overall; prodemocracy candidates took a total of sixteen of the twenty directly elected seats. The main pro-China party, the Democratic Alliance for the Betterment of Hong Kong, won just two directly elected seats and five overall.

In October the Preliminary Working Committee (PWC), an advisory group appointed by Beijing, recommended that China water down or scrap Hong Kong's Bill of Rights after 1997. The PWC also recommended reversing six recent amendments to colonial laws that had given the governor sweeping, though rarely used, powers to declare martial law, impose censorship and restrict freedoms of assembly and association.

Political Rights and Civil Liberties: Hong Kong residents cannot change their government democratically. The British premier appoints the governor, and most Legislative Council seats are appointed or indirectly elected. Residents had no voice in the 1984 Sino-British agreement transferring sovereignty to China in July 1997. In 1991 London agreed to give British passports to some 220,000-250,000 heads of household and family members, but has refused to extend the right of abode to the 3.4 million residents who only have British Dependent Territory Citizen (BDTC) Status and not full British citizenship.

The colony has an independent judiciary, and defendants receive fair trials. In

June 1995 London and Beijing finalized arrangements for the colony's post-1997 Court of Final Appeal, which will replace the Privy Council in London as the court of last resort. No more than one foreign judge will sit on the five-member court, although liberals had pushed for greater flexibility; the court will be prohibited from hearing cases involving "acts of state such as defense and foreign affairs," and many fear China will use this vaguely worded clause to restrict the court's jurisdiction further; the post-1997, Beijing-appointed chief executive, and not the court, will define "acts of state;" and the court will not be set up until after 1997, preventing it from establishing precedents before the handover.

As 1997 approaches there has been chilling effect on the media and other institutions. The colony has a vigorous press but many journalists practice self-censorship to avoid antagonizing China. In January 1995 two television stations refused to run a BBC documentary about the sale of organs from executed prisoners in China. Chinese officials frequently warn Hong Kong journalists against being outspoken and claim they keep dossiers on journalists. Beijing also frequently advises civil servants to be loyal to China. In May rioting broke out as authorities prepared to repatriate some 1,500 refugees to Vietnam involuntarily. Police responded with tear gas and batons, injuring seventy-eight refugees, and in June similarly dispersed a smaller incident.

In the New Territories husbands or male relatives frequently cast electoral ballots for women according to local tradition. The lack of antidiscrimination legislation has contributed to discrimination against women in the workplace. Workers are free to join independent trade unions.

↑ Northern Ireland

Polity: British administration and elected local councils (military-occupied)
Economy: Mixed capitalist
Population: 1,630,000
Ethnic Groups: Protestant (mostly Scottish and English), (57 percent), Irish Catholic (43 percent)
Trend Arrow: Northern Ireland's up trend arrow is due to the continuation of the 1994 ceasefire.

Political Rights: 4
Civil Liberties: 3
Status: Partly Free

Overview:

The first anniversary of the Provisional Irish Republican Army (IRA) ceasefire in its campaign against British rule was marked on 1 September 1995. Negotiations to further the peace effort remained virtually deadlocked around British and Unionist insistence that paramilitaries begin disarming before all-party talks commence.

Northern Ireland consists of six of the nine counties of the Irish province of Ulster. At the insistence of the locally dominant Protestants, these counties remained within the United Kingdom after the other twenty-six predominantly Catholic counties gained home rule in 1921. Catholics now constitute a majority in four of the six counties and thirteen of the twenty-six local government bodies. The demographic trends have aroused deep anxieties among the Protestant population, which is largely descended from Scottish and English settlers of the seventeenth century. Britain's 1920 Government of Ireland Act set up the Northern Irish parliament, which functioned until the British imposed direct rule in 1972. Subsequent attempts at Catholic-Protestant power-sharing have failed.

Disorder resulting from a nonviolent Catholic civil rights movement in the 1960s prompted the deployment of British troops which have occupied Northern Ireland to date. Amid sectarian violence beginning in the 1970s, division grew within both the primarily Protestant "Unionist" and the Catholic "Nationalist" or "Republican" communities. In addition to numerous political factions including the conservative Ulster Unionist Party, the hardline Democratic Unionist Party, the interdenominational, unionist Alliance Party, the moderate pro-Nationalist Social Democratic and Labour Party (SDLP), and the pro-Nationalist political wing of the IRA, *Sinn Finn*, there are also paramilitary groups on both sides that engaged in acts of terrorism until 1994.

In February, the *London Times* printed a leaked draft of the government's "framework document" for a lasting political settlement, jeopardizing the peace process. Among the proposals of the draft were amendments to the Republic's constitution relinquishing any territorial claim on Northern Ireland; alteration of the Government of Ireland Act, which effectively sealed the partition; a new Ulster assembly with executive and legislative responsibilities; and a cross-border authority to coordinate the work of Irish Republic and Northern ministers in the areas of environment, transportation, tourism and agriculture.

Despite threats from the Ulster Unionist Party to withdraw the support of its nine MPs and possibly bring down British Prime Minister John Major's government, Major and his Irish counterpart, *Taoiseach* Bruton, published the proposals as a framework for further negotiations. The final outcome of peace talks will be put to the people of Northern Ireland in a referendum.

The most inclusive talks this year occurred at a U.S.-sponsored putative investment conference in Washington, DC attended by senior officials from the Unionists, Sinn Fein, the SDLP, loyalist paramilitaries, and the British, Irish, and American governments. The British government's refusal to invite Sinn Fein to all-party negotiations before the IRA begins to disarm has left the process at an impasse until a compromise can be reached.

Political Rights and Civil Liberties: The people of Northern Ireland are able to elect members to the British House of Commons and local government bodies. The regional parliament was suspended in 1972, when the British imposed direct rule. Unionists retain effective veto power over the six counties' unification with the Republic, prompting Nationalists to claim that they lack the right to self-determination.

Freedom of movement has improved markedly with the disappearance of British Troops in battle gear on the streets, the removal of check points and the revoking of exclusion orders by Northern Ireland Secretary Sir Patrick Mayhew. These orders, issued under Britain's Prevention of Terrorism Act, banned certain individuals from entering

Britain or the North. Despite improvements, on the Twelfth of July holiday celebrating Protestantism and the British crown, riot police barricaded Catholics into their neighborhood to prevent clashes with celebrating Protestants in Belfast, the capital.

Both Ireland and Britain granted early release to several IRA prisoners, and some Irish convicts were moved from prisons in Britain to Northern Ireland. In late March, however, Dr. Mary Allen was denied access to an IRA convict held in solitary confinement in Belmarsh jail near London.

Incidents between police and alleged Sinn Fein supporters continued. The most severe occurred in Londonderry during Major's visit, as a peaceful demonstration ended in at least twelve injured police officers and one arrest. "Punishment beatings" by paramilitary groups persist, according to a report in Ireland's *Sunday Tribune* citing seventy-nine vicious beatings in the North during the first six months of the ceasefire (thirty-three attributed to Loyalists, forty-six to Republicans). One such beating resulted in the suicide of the sixteen-year-old victim.

The Irish police claimed to have effectively "decapitated" the Irish National Liberation Army, the only paramilitary group refusing to accept the peace process publicly, by arresting four high-ranking members and seizing a large stash of weapons. Meanwhile, talks between Taoiseach Bruton and leaders of Loyalist paramilitary groups such as the Ulster Volunteer Force and the Ulster Defense Association have helped to calm fears of a return to violence. The province has enjoyed economic growth rates higher than the rest of the United Kingdom, with house prices rising and tourists and shoppers returning to the streets of Belfast. Hopes for a permanent ceasefire remain despite the slow pace of negotiations, as many believe that after over two decades of violence, peace in Northern Ireland has been its own best advertisement.

Puerto Rico

Polity: Elected governor and legislature
Economy: Capitalist
Population: 3,613,000
Ethnic Groups: Hispanic

Political Rights: 1
Civil Liberties: 2
Status: Free

Overview: Following approval by plebiscite, Puerto Rico acquired the status of a commonwealth in free association with the U.S. in 1952. Under its terms, Puerto Rico exercises approximately the same control over its internal affairs as do the fifty U.S. states. Residents, though U.S. citizens, cannot vote in presidential elections and are represented in the U.S. Congress by a delegate to the House of Representatives who can vote in committee but not on the floor.

The Commonwealth constitution, modeled on that of the U.S., provides for a governor and a bicameral Legislature, consisting of a twenty-seven-member Senate and a fifty-one-member House of Representatives, elected for four years. A Supreme Court heads an independent judiciary and the legal system is based on U.S. law.

Pedro Rosello of the pro-statehood New Progressive Party (PNP) was elected governor in 1992, defeating Victoria Munoz Mendoza of the incumbent Popular Democratic Party (PPD). Outgoing Gov. Rafael Hernandez Colon did not seek re-election after two terms in office.

With 83 percent of registered voters participating, Rosello took 49.9 percent of the vote, against 45.8 percent for Munoz, 3.8 percent for environmentalist Neftali Garcia and 3.3 percent for Fernando Martin of the Puerto Rican Independence Party (PIP). The PNP won thirty-six of fifty-one seats in the House and twenty of twenty-seven Senate seats. The PNP's Carlos Romero Barcelo, a former governor, won the race for the delegate to the U.S. Congress.

The election reflected anti-incumbency sentiment and immediate concerns over rising crime, high unemployment, government corruption and education. Still, the island's relationship with the U.S. remains a fundamental issue. In a nonbinding 1993 referendum, voters narrowly opted to retain commonwealth status. Any vote to change the island's status would have had to be approved by the U.S. Congress. Commonwealth status received 48.4 percent of the vote, statehood 46.2 percent, and independence 4.4 percent. The vote indicated significant gains for statehood, which in the last referendum in 1967 received only 39 percent of the vote.

In 1995, principal political issues were official corruption and the pending decision in Washington whether to retain Section 936 of the Internal Revenue Code, which gives major tax concessions to U.S. companies located on the island. Rosello backed phasing it out in favor of a tax-based job creation program. The PPD lobbied to retain Section 936.

The year's headline stealer, however, was an unidentified nocturnal creature that preyed on farm animals, dubbed the *chupacabras* (goat-sucker) by locals. Similar reports of inexplicable animal deaths date back to the 1970s, but the chupacabras became a national obsession.

Political Rights and Civil Liberties:

As U.S. citizens, Puerto Ricans are guaranteed all civil liberties granted in the U.S. The press and broadcast media are well developed, highly varied and critical. In recent years the Puerto Rican journalists association (ASPRO) has charged successive governments with denying complete access to official information. Labor unions are well organized and have the right to strike.

The greatest causes for concern are the steep rise in criminal violence in recent years, much of it drug-related, and the Rosello government's response to it. Puerto Rico is now the Caribbean's main drug transshipment point. Since mid-1993, about fifty public housing projects have been under the control of the National Guard, the first time that U.S. military units have been routinely deployed to fight crime.

The Rosello government claims the projects have been "liberated" from drug traffickers. Critics say the projects have been unconstitutionally "militarized" through "de facto martial law" and point to civil rights abuses including unlawful search and seizure and other transgressions. The policy seems to have reduced crime in some categories. The number of homicides, a harrowing 950 in 1994, dropped by about 10 percent in 1995. Corruption and criminal activity within the police force are continuing concerns.

Yugoslavia
Kosovo

Polity: Serbian
administration
Economy: Mixed-statist
Population: 2,018,000
Ethnic Groups: Albanian (90 percent), Serb, Montenegrin

Political Rights: 7
Civil Liberties: 7
Status: Not Free

Overview:

Kosovo, a largely ethnic-Albanian enclave within Serbia
that had been an autonomous region in Yugoslavia, saw
continued Serbian repression of Albanians in 1995.

For Serbs, Kosovo is the historical cradle of the Serbian medieval state and
culture. It was the site of the 1389 Battle of Kosovo Fields between Serbian Prince
Lazar and the Turks, which solidified Ottoman control over the Serbs for the next
500 years. Serbian President Slobodan Milosevic rose to power in 1987 over the
issue of Kosovo's status. Central to his platform was the subjugation of the then-
autonomous Yugoslav province (established by the 1974 constitution) to Serbian
authority. Persecution by ethnic Albanians caused some 50,000 Serb and
Montenegrin residents to flee Kosovo after the 1980 death of Yugoslav strongman
Josip Broz "Tito."

In 1989-1990, Milosevic moved to abolish the provincial government and
legislature and introduced a series of amendments to the Serbian constitution that
effectively removed the legal basis for Kosovo's autonomy. Albanians elected a
shadow president, Ibrahim Rugova, leader of the Democratic League of Kosovo
(LDK), and a 130-member parliament in 1992 to underscore the illegitimacy of
Serb rule. Bujar Bukoshi was named prime minister.

Serbian repression of Albanians is maintained by a 40,000-strong army and
militia force. Harassment, detention, intimidation and murder of Albanians are
endemic. Since the Serb takeover, Rugova's government has claimed that over
120,000 Albanians out of a total workforce of 250,000 have been fired, and over
200,000 Albanians have left for other parts of Europe and the United States. Serbs
were given control of hospitals, universities, businesses, schools and government.
While Albanian resistance has officially been nonviolent, several Serbian policemen and militiamen were murdered in the last five years.

In 1995, ethnic Albanians continued to suffer arbitrary detention, police raids
on shops and private homes, and the dragooning of young men into the Serbian
army. The Helsinki Committee on Human Rights, in a report issued in October,
cited numerous examples of murder and torture. As of late September, at least
eleven ethnic Albanians had died as a result of torture. In late November, Elizabeth
Rehn, a United Nations special envoy for human rights, visited Kosovo and
expressed concern over discrimination against Albanians, particularly in education
and medical care. Since 1989, about 150 Albanians have been killed and some
300,000 cases of torture and harassment have been reported. Since 1990, some 500
Albanians have been sentenced to prison for political reasons.

Throughout the year, Rugova and Prime Minister Bukoshi urged the U.S. to maintain sanctions against Yugoslavia. In a 7 December meeting in Washington with Secretary of State Warren Christopher, Rugova asked the U.S. to help mediate the crisis. The Kosovar government was reportedly dissatisfied with the Dayton Accords that ended the fighting in Bosnia because the Kosovo issue was not addressed, implying that it was an internal Serbian situation.

Political Rights and Civil Liberties: Kosovars cannot change the Serb-imposed government democratically. The Parliamentary Party and Social Democrats are technically outlawed, while the LDK and its leaders have been targets of harassment and detention. Kosovo's democratically elected legislature and government were forced underground after the 1992 elections, which Serbia did not recognize. In 1995, the Forum of Albanian Intellectuals of Kosovo complained that the LDK holds a monopoly on power and that the society is not truly pluralistic. Ultimate judicial authority lies with Belgrade.

Albanian television and radio have been abolished. A Belgrade-based conglomerate took over the newspaper, *Rilindja*, though the weekly *Zeri* continues to be published. Albanian judges, policemen and government officials have all been replaced over the last five years. Freedom of movement and other fundamental rights have been circumscribed by the Serbs. Corruption and drug smuggling by Kosovo Albanian criminal gangs are rampant.

Albanian cultural identity has been suppressed. Over the last five years, Albanian monuments have been destroyed, streets have received Serbian names, and signs in Cyrillic have replaced those in the Latin script. Serbian has supplanted Albanian as the official language. Since 1991, some 8,000 Albanian teachers have been dismissed. In 1993, Serb authorities shut down all Albanian-language secondary schools, denying schooling to an estimated 63,000 children. The crackdown shut all fifty-eight Albanian-language secondary schools and twenty-one of some 350 Albanian-language primary schools. A network of clandestine, underground schools has been set up in Albanian households.

The Independent Trade Unions of Kosovo (BSPK), an outlawed Albanian confederation, has been the subject of repression for refusing to affiliate with official Serbian unions and sign collective agreements approved by these unions. In 1995, scores of union leaders were arrested. From January to November 1995, seventeen Albanian party and union activists were sentenced to long prison terms in the town of Pec.

The Comparative Survey of Freedom—1995-1996 Survey Methodology

The purpose of the *Comparative Survey of Freedom* since its inception in the 1970s has been to provide an annual evaluation of political rights and civil liberties everywhere in the world.

The *Survey* attempts to judge all places by a single standard and to point out the importance of democracy and freedom. At a minimum, a democracy is a political system in which the people choose their authoritative leaders freely from among competing groups and individuals who were not chosen by the government. Putting it broadly, freedom is the chance to act spontaneously in a variety of fields outside the control of government and other centers of potential domination.

For a long time, Westerners have associated the adherence to political rights and civil liberties with the liberal democracies, such as those in North America and the European Union. However, there has been a proliferation of democracies in developing countries in recent years, and the *Survey* reflects their growing numbers.

Freedom House does not view democracy as a static concept, and the *Survey* recognizes that a democratic country does not necessarily belong in our category of "free" states. A democracy can lose freedom and become merely "partly free." Sri Lanka and Colombia are examples of such "partly free" democracies. In other cases, countries that replaced military regimes with elected governments can have less than complete transitions to liberal democracy. El Salvador and Guatemala fit the description of this kind of "partly free" democracy. (See the section below on the designations "free," "partly free," and "not free" for an explanation of those terms.) Readers should note that some scholars would use the term "semi-democracy" or "formal democracy," instead of "partly free" democracy, to refer to countries that are democratic in form but less than free in substance.

What the *Survey* is not

The *Survey* does not rate governments *per se* but rather the rights and freedoms individuals have in each country and territory. Freedom House does not score countries and territories based on governmental intentions or constitutions but on the real world situations caused by governmental and nongovernmental factors. The *Survey* does not quantify our sympathy for the situation a government finds itself in (e.g., war, terrorism, etc.) but rather what effect the situation itself has on freedom.

Definitions and categories of the *Survey*

The *Survey*'s understanding of freedom is broad and encompasses two sets of characteristics grouped under political rights and civil liberties. Political rights enable people to participate freely in the political process. By the political process, we mean the system by which the polity chooses the authoritative policy makers and attempts to make binding decisions affecting the national, regional or local community. In a free society this means the right of all adults to vote and compete for public office, and for elected representatives to have a decisive vote on public policies. A system is genuinely free or democratic to the extent that the people have a choice in determining the nature of the system and its leaders.

Civil liberties are the freedoms to develop views, institutions and personal autonomy apart from the state.

The *Survey* employs checklists for these rights and liberties to help determine the degree of freedom present in each country and related territory, and to help assign each entity to a comparative category.

Beginning with the 1995-96 edition of the *Survey*, we have reduced the number of questions on the political rights checklist from nine to eight. The deleted question, which involved decentralization of political power, was deemed deceptive because a lack of decentralization does not necessarily translate into a lack of freedom. The revised checklist also mandated changes in assignment of category numbers and freedom ratings (see below).

Political Rights checklist

1. Is the head of state and/or head of government or other chief authority elected through free and fair elections?
2. Are the legislative representatives elected through free and fair elections?
3. Are there fair electoral laws, equal campaigning opportunities, fair polling and honest tabulation of ballots?
4. Are the voters able to endow their freely elected representatives with real power?
5. Do the people have the right to organize in different political parties or other competitive political groupings of their choice, and is the system open to the rise and fall of these competing parties or groupings?
6. Is there a significant opposition vote, *de facto* opposition power, and a realistic possibility for the opposition to increase its support or gain power through elections?
7. Are the people free from domination by the military, foreign powers, totalitarian parties, religious hierarchies, economic oligarchies or any other powerful group?
8. Do cultural, ethnic, religious and other minority groups have reasonable self-determination, self-government, autonomy or participation through informal consensus in the decision-making process?

Additional discretionary Political Rights questions

A. For traditional monarchies that have no parties or electoral process, does the system provide for consultation with the people, encourage discussion of policy, and allow the right to petition the ruler?
B. Is the government or occupying power deliberately changing the ethnic composition of a country or territory so as to destroy a culture or tip the political balance in favor of another group?

When answering the political rights questions, Freedom House considers the extent to which the system offers the voter the chance to make a free choice among competing candidates, and to what extent the candidates are chosen independently of the state. We recognize that formal electoral procedures are not the only factors that determine the real distribution of power. In many Latin American countries, for example, the military retains a significant political role, and in Morocco the king maintains significant power over the elected politicians. The more people suffer under such domination by unelected forces, the less chance the country has of getting credit for self-determination in our *Survey*.

Freedom House does not have a culture-bound view of democracy. The *Survey* team rejects the notion that only Europeans and those of European descent qualify as democratic. The *Survey* demonstrates that, in addition to those in Europe and the Americas, there are free countries with varying kinds of democracy functioning among people of all races and religions in Africa, the Pacific and Asia. In some Pacific islands, free countries can have competitive political systems based on competing family groups and personalities rather than on European- or American-style parties.

Civil Liberties checklist

1. Are there free and independent media, literature and other cultural expressions? (Note: In cases where the media are state-controlled but offer pluralistic points of view, the *Survey* gives the system credit.)
2. Is there open public discussion and free private discussion?
3. Is there freedom of assembly and demonstration?
4. Is there freedom of political or quasi-political organization? (Note: This includes political parties, civic associations, ad hoc issue groups and so forth.)
5. Are citizens equal under the law, with access to an independent, nondiscriminatory judiciary, and are they respected by the security forces?
6. Is there protection from political terror, and from unjustified imprisonment, exile or torture, whether by groups that support or oppose the system, and freedom from war or insurgency situations? (Note: Freedom from war and insurgency situations enhances the liberties in a free society, but the absence of wars and insurgencies does not in itself make an unfree society free.)

7. Are there free trade unions and peasant organizations or equivalents, and is there effective collective bargaining?

8. Are there free professional and other private organizations?

9. Are there free businesses or cooperatives?

10. Are there free religious institutions and free private and public religious expressions?

11. Are there personal social freedoms, which include such aspects as gender equality, property rights, freedom of movement, choice of residence, and choice of marriage and size of family?

12. Is there equality of opportunity, which includes freedom from exploitation by or dependency on landlords, employers, union leaders, bureaucrats or any other type of denigrating obstacle to a share of legitimate economic gains?

13. Is there freedom from extreme government indifference and corruption?

When analyzing the civil liberties checklist, Freedom House does not mistake constitutional guarantees of human rights for those rights in practice. For tiny island countries and territories and other small entities with low populations, the absence of unions and other types of association does not necessarily count as a negative unless the government or other centers of domination are deliberately blocking association. In some cases, the small size of these entities may result in a lack of sufficient institutional complexity to make them fully comparable to larger countries. The question of equality of opportunity also implies a free choice of employment and education. Extreme inequality of opportunity prevents disadvantaged individuals from enjoying a full exercise of civil liberties. Typically, desperately poor countries and territories lack both opportunities for economic advancement and the

The Tabulated Ratings

The accompanying Table of Independent Countries (pages 536-537) and Table of Related Territories (page 538) rate each country or territory on seven-category scales for political rights and civil liberties, and then place each entity into a broad category of "free," "partly free" or "not free." On each scale, 1 represents the most free and 7 the least free.

Political rights

In political rights, generally speaking, places rated 1 come closest to the ideals suggested by the checklist questions, beginning with free and fair elections. Those elected rule. There are competitive parties or other competitive political groupings, and the opposition has an important role and power. These entities have self-determination or an extremely high degree of autonomy (in the case of related territories). Usually, those rated 1 have self-determination for minority groups or their participation in government through informal consensus. With the exception of such entities as tiny island countries, these countries and territories have decentralized political power and free sub-national elections. Entities in Category 1 are not perfect. They can and do lose credit for their deficiencies.

Countries and territories rated 2 in political rights are less free than those rated 1. Such factors as gross political corruption, violence, political discrimination against minorities, and foreign or military influence on politics may be present, and weaken the quality of democracy.

The same factors that weaken freedom in category 2 may also undermine political rights in categories 3, 4, and 5. Other damaging conditions may be at work as well, including civil war, very strong military involvement in politics, lingering royal power, unfair elections and one-party dominance. However, states and territories in these categories may still have some elements of political rights such as the freedom to organize nongovernmental parties and quasi-political groups, reasonably free referenda, or other significant means of popular influence on government.

Typically, states and territories with political rights rated 6 have systems ruled by military juntas, one-party dictatorships, religious hierarchies and autocrats. These regimes may allow only some minimal manifestation of political rights such as competitive local elections or some degree of representation or autonomy for minorities. Category 6 also contains some countries in the early or aborted stages of democratic transition. A few states in Category 6 are traditional monarchies that mitigate their relative lack of political rights through the use of consultation with their subjects, toleration of political discussion, and acceptance of petitions from the ruled.

other liberties on this checklist. We have a question on gross indifference and corruption, because when governments do not care about the social and economic welfare of large sectors of the population, the human rights of those people suffer. Government corruption can pervert the political process and hamper the development of a free economy.

How do we grade? Ratings, categories and raw points

The *Survey* rates political rights and civil liberties separately on a seven-category scale, 1 representing the most free and 7 the least free. A country is assigned to a particular category based on responses to the checklist and the judgments of the *Survey* team at Freedom House. The numbers are not purely mechanical; they also reflect judgment. Under the methodology, the team assigns initial ratings to countries by awarding from 0 to 4 raw points per checklist item, depending on the comparative rights or liberties present. (In the *Surveys* completed from 1989-90 through 1992-93, the methodology allowed for a less nuanced range of 0 to 2 raw points per question. Taking note of this modification, scholars should consider the 1993-94 scores the statistical benchmark.) The only exception to the addition of 0 to 4 raw points per checklist item is the discretionary question on cultural destruction and deliberate demographic change to tip the political balance. In that case, we subtract 1 to 4 raw points depending on the situation's severity. The highest possible score for political rights is 32 points, based on up to 4 points for each of eight questions. The highest possible score for civil liberties is 52 points, based on up to 4 points for each of thirteen questions. Under the methodology, raw points correspond to category numbers as follows:

The Tabulated Ratings

Category 7 includes places where political rights are absent or virtually nonexistent due to the extremely oppressive nature of the regime or extreme oppression in combination with civil war. A country or territory may also join this category when extreme violence and warlordism dominate the people in the absence of an authoritative, functioning central government. Places in Category 7 may get some minimal points for the checklist questions, but only a tiny fragment of available credit.

Civil liberties

Category 1 in civil liberties includes countries and territories that generally have the highest levels of freedoms and opportunities for the individual. Places in this category may still have problems in civil liberties, but they lose partial credit in only a limited number of areas.

The places in category 2 in civil liberties are not as free as those rated 1, but they are still relatively high on the scale. These countries and territories have deficiencies in several aspects of civil liberties, but still receive most available credit.

Independent countries and related territories with ratings of 3, 4 or 5 have progressively fewer civil liberties than those in category 2. Places in these categories range from ones that receive at least partial credit on virtually all checklist questions to those that have a mixture of good civil liberties scores in some areas and zero or partial credit in others. As one moves down the scale below category 2, the level of oppression increases, especially in the areas of censorship, political terror and the prevention of free association. There are also many cases in which groups opposed to the state carry out political terror that undermines other freedoms. That means that a poor rating for a country is not necessarily a comment on the intentions of the government. The rating may simply reflect the real restrictions on liberty which can be caused by non-governmental terror.

Typically, at category 6 in civil liberties, countries and territories have a few partial rights. For example, a country might have some religious freedom, some personal social freedoms, some highly restricted private business activity, and relatively free private discussion. In general, people in these states and territories experience severely restricted expression and association. There are almost always political prisoners and other manifestations of political terror.

At category 7, countries and territories have virtually no freedom. An overwhelming and justified fear of repression characterizes the society.

The accompanying Tables of Combined Average Ratings average the two seven-category scales of political rights and civil liberties into an overall freedom rating for each country and territory.

Political Rights

Category Number	Raw points
1	28-32
2	23-27
3	19-22
4	14-18
5	10-13
6	5-9
7	0-4

Civil Liberties

Category Number	Raw points
1	45-52
2	38-44
3	30-37
4	23-29
5	15-22
6	8-14
7	0-7

After placing countries in initial categories based on checklist points, the *Survey* team makes minor adjustments to account for factors such as extreme violence, whose intensity may not be reflected in answering the checklist questions. These exceptions aside, in the overwhelming number of cases, the checklist system reflects the real world situation and is adequate for placing countries and territories into the proper comparative categories.

At its discretion, Freedom House assigns up or down arrows to countries and territories to indicate positive or negative trends, whether qualitative or quantitative, that may not be apparent from the ratings. Such trends may or may not be reflected in raw points, depending on the circumstances of each country or territory. Only places without ratings changes since the previous year warrant trend arrows. The charts on pages 536-538 also show up and down triangles. Distinct from the trend arrows, the triangles indicate changes in political rights and civil liberties caused by real world events since the last *Survey*.

Free, Partly Free, Not Free

The accompanying map (pages 96-97) divides the world into three large categories: "free," "partly free," and "not free." The *Survey* places countries and territories into this tripartite division by averaging the category numbers they received for political rights and civil liberties. Those whose category numbers average 1-2.5 are considered "free," 3-5.5 "partly free," and 5.5-7 "not free." The dividing line between "partly free" and "not free" falls within the group whose category numbers average 5.5. For example, countries that receive a rating of 6 for political rights and 5 for civil liberties, or a 5 for political rights and a 6 for civil liberties, could be either "partly free" or "not free." The total number of raw points is the factor which makes the difference between the two. Countries and territories with combined raw scores of 0-28 points are "not free," and those with combined raw scores of 29-56 points are "partly free." "Free" countries and territories have combined raw scores of 57-84 points.

The differences in raw points between countries in the three broad categories represent distinctions in the real world. There are obstacles which "partly free" countries must overcome before they can be called "free," just as there are impediments which prevent "not free" countries from being called "partly free." Countries at the lowest rung of the "free" category (category 2 in political rights with category 3 in civil liberties or category 3 in political rights with category 2 in civil liberties) differ from those at the upper end of the "partly free" group (e.g., category 3 in both). Typically, there is more violence and/or military influence on politics at 3,3 than at 2,3 and the differences become more striking as one compares 2,3 with worse categories of the "partly free" countries.

The distinction between the least bad "not free" countries and the least free "partly free" may be less obvious than the gap between "partly free" and "free," but at "partly free" there is at least one extra factor that keeps a country from being assigned to the "not free" category. For example, Lebanon, which was rated 6,5 both last year and this year, but which was "partly free" last year, became "not free" this year after its legislature unilaterally extended the incumbent president's term indefinitely. Though not sufficient to drop the country's political rights rating to category 7, there was enough of a drop in raw points to change its category.

Freedom House wishes to point out that the designation "free" does not mean that a country has perfect freedom or lacks serious problems. As an institution that advocates human rights, Freedom House remains concerned about a variety of social problems and civil liberties questions in the U.S. and other countries that the *Survey* places in the "free" category. Similarly, in no way does an improvement in a country's rating mean that human rights campaigns should cease. On the contrary, we wish to use the *Survey* as a prod to improve the condition of all countries.

Readers should understand that the "free," "partly free," and "not free" labels are highly simplified terms that each cover a broad third of the available raw points. The labels do *not* imply that all countries in a category are the same any more than a bestseller list implies that all titles on it have sold the same number of books. Countries and territories can reach the same categories or even raw points by differing routes. We use the tripartite labels and tricolor maps to illustrate some broad comparisons. In theory, we could have eighty-five categories and colors to match the range of raw points, but this would be highly impractical. Anyone wishing to see the distinctions within each category should look at the category numbers and combined average ratings on pages 541-42.

The approach of the *Survey*

The *Survey* attempts to measure conditions as they really are around the world. This approach is distinct from relying on intense coverage by the American media as a guide to which countries are the least free. The publicity given problems in some countries does not necessarily mean that unpublicized problems of other countries are not more severe. For example, while U.S. television networks are allowed into Israel and El Salvador to cover abuses of human rights, they are not allowed to report freely in North Korea, which has far less freedom than the other two countries. To reach such comparative conclusions, Freedom House evaluates the development of democratic governmental institutions, or lack thereof, and also examines the quality of civil society, life outside the state structure.

Without a well-developed civil society, it is difficult, if not impossible, to have an atmosphere supportive of democracy. A society that does not have free individual and group expressions in nonpolitical matters is not likely to make an exception for political ones. As though to prove this, there is no country in the *Survey* that places in category 6 or 7 for civil liberties and, at the same time, in category 1 or 2 for political rights. Almost without exception in the *Survey*, countries and territories have ratings in political rights and civil liberties that are within two categories of each other.

The *Survey* rates both countries and related territories. For our purposes, countries are internationally recognized independent states whose governments are resident within their officially claimed territories. In the unusual case of Cyprus, we give two ratings, since there are two governments on that divided island. In no way does this imply that Freedom House endorses Cypriot division. We note only that neither the predominantly Greek Republic of Cyprus nor the Turkish-occupied, predominantly Turkish territory of the Republic of Northern Cyprus is the *de facto* government for the entire island. Related territories consist mostly of colonies, protectorates, occupied territories and island dependencies. However, the *Survey* also reserves the right to designate as related territories places within internationally recognized states that are disputed areas or that have a human rights problem or issue of self-determination deserving special attention. Northern Ireland, Tibet and Kashmir are examples falling within this category. The *Survey* excludes uninhabited related territories and such entities as the U.S.-owned Johnston Atoll, which has only a transient military population and no native inhabitants. Since most related territories have a broad range of civil liberties and some form of self-government, a higher proportion of them have the "free" designation than do independent countries.

This year for the first time we will provide only designations of "free," "partly free" and "not free" for the eight related territories with populations under 5,000, without corresponding category numbers. Notwithstanding, we will continue to score these territories according to the same methodology as the rest. They are: Cocos (Keeling) Islands, Rapanui (Easter Island), Falkland Islands, Niue, Norfolk Island, Pitcairn Islands, Svalbard and Tokelau. Also beginning this year, we will be providing essays only for territories designated "Partly Free," or "Not Free," nd for Puerto Rico, a U.S. territory with a civil liberties situation of particular concern.

No new countries or territories have been added to the *Survey* for 1995-96.

Tables and Ratings

Table of Independent Countries
Comparative Measures of Freedom

Country	PR	CL	Freedom Rating	Country	PR	CL	Freedom Rating
Afghanistan	7	7	Not Free	Finland	1	1	Free
⬩ Albania	3	4	Partly Free	France	1	2	Free
Algeria	6▲	6▲	Not Free	Gabon	5	4	Partly Free
Andorra	1	1	Free	The Gambia	7	6	Not Free
Angola	6▲	6▲	Not Free	Georgia	4▲	5	Partly Free
Antigua and Barbuda	4	3	Partly Free	Germany	1	2	Free
⬩ Argentina	2	3	Free	Ghana	4▲	4	Partly Free
Armenia	4▼	4	Partly Free	Greece	1	3	Free
Australia	1	1	Free	Grenada	1	2	Free
Austria	1	1	Free	Guatemala	4	5	Partly Free
Azerbaijan	6	6	Not Free	⬆ Guinea	6	5	Not Free
Bahamas	1	2	Free	Guinea-Bissau	3	4	Partly Free
Bahrain	6	6	Not Free	Guyana	2	2	Free
Bangladesh	3▼	4	Partly Free	Haiti	5	5	Partly Free
Barbados	1	1	Free	Honduras	3	3	Partly Free
Belarus	5▼	5▼	Partly Free	Hungary	1	2	Free
Belgium	1	1	Free	Iceland	1	1	Free
Belize	1	1	Free	⬆ India	4	4	Partly Free
Benin	2	2▲	Free	Indonesia	7	6	Not Free
Bhutan	7	7	Not Free	Iran	6	7	Not Free
Bolivia	2	4▼	Partly Free	Iraq	7	7	Not Free
⬆ Bosnia-Herzegovina	6	6	Not Free	Ireland	1	1▲	Free
Botswana	2	2▲	Free	Israel	1	3	Free
Brazil	2	4	Partly Free	Italy	1	2	Free
Brunei	7	5▲	Not Free	Jamaica	2	3	Free
Bulgaria	2	2	Free	Japan	1▲	2	Free
Burkina Faso	5	4	Partly Free	Jordan	4	4	Partly Free
Burma	7	7	Not Free	Kazakhstan	6	5	Not Free
⬩ Burundi	6	7	Not Free	Kenya	7▼	6	Not Free
Cambodia	6▼	6▼	Not Free	Kiribati	1	1	Free
Cameroon	7▼	5	Not Free	Korea, North	7	7	Not Free
Canada	1	1	Free	Korea, South	2	2	Free
Cape Verde	1	2	Free	Kuwait	5	5	Partly Free
⬆ Central African Republic	3	4	Partly Free	Kyrgyz Republic	4	4▼	Partly Free
				Laos	7	6	Not Free
⬩ Chad	6	5	Not Free	Latvia	2▲	2	Free
Chile	2	2	Free	⬩ Lebanon	6	5	Not Free
China (P.R.C.)	7	7	Not Free	Lesotho	4	4	Partly Free
Colombia	4▼	4	Partly Free	Liberia	7	6	Not Free
Comoros	4	4	Partly Free	Libya	7	7	Not Free
⬆ Congo	4	4	Partly Free	Liechtenstein	1	1	Free
Costa Rica	1	2	Free	Lithuania	1	2▲	Free
⬩ Côte d'Ivoire	6	5	Not Free	Luxembourg	1	1	Free
⬆ Croatia	4	4	Partly Free	Macedonia	4	3	Partly Free
Cuba	7	7	Not Free	Madagascar	2	4	Partly Free
Cyprus (G)	1	1	Free	Malawi	2	3	Free
Czech Republic	1	2	Free	Malaysia	4	5	Partly Free
Denmark	1	1	Free	Maldives	6	6	Not Free
Djibouti	5▲	6	Not Free	Mali	2	3▲	Free
Dominica	1▲	1	Free	Malta	1	1	Free
Dominican Republic	4	3	Partly Free	Marshall Islands	1	1	Free
				Mauritania	6▲	6▲	Not Free
⬩ Ecuador	2	3	Free	Mauritius	1	2	Free
Egypt	6	6	Not Free	Mexico	4	4	Partly Free
El Salvador	3	3	Partly Free	Micronesia	1	1	Free
Equatorial Guinea	7	7	Not Free	Moldova	4	4	Partly Free
Eritrea	6	4▲	Partly Free	Monaco	2	1	Free
Estonia	2▲	2	Free	Mongolia	2	3	Free
Ethiopia	4▲	5	Partly Free	Morocco	5	5	Partly Free
Fiji	4	3	Partly Free	Mozambique	3	4▲	Partly Free
				Namibia	2	3	Free

Table of Independent Countries Comparative Measures of Freedom

Country	PR	CL	Freedom Rating
Nauru	1	3	Free
Nepal	3	4	Partly Free
Netherlands	1	1	Free
New Zealand	1	1	Free
Nicaragua	4	4▲	Partly Free
Niger	3	5	Partly Free
Nigeria	7	7▼	Not Free
Norway	1	1	Free
Oman	6	6	Not Free
⬇ Pakistan	3	5	Partly Free
Palau	1	2	Free
⬇ Panama	2	3	Free
Papua New Guinea	2	4	Partly Free
Paraguay	4	3	Partly Free
Peru	5	4	Partly Free
Philippines	2▲	4	Partly Free
Poland	1▲	2	Free
Portugal	1	1	Free
Qatar	7	6	Not Free
Romania	4	3	Partly Free
Russia	3	4	Partly Free
Rwanda	7	6▲	Not Free
St. Kitts and Nevis	1▲	2	Free
St. Lucia	1	2	Free
St. Vincent and the Grenadines	2	1	Free
San Marino	1	1	Free
Sao Tome and Príncipe	1	2	Free
Saudi Arabia	7	7	Not Free
Senegal	4	5	Partly Free
Seychelles	3	3▲	Partly Free
Sierra Leone	7	6	Not Free
Singapore	5	5	Partly Free
⬇ Slovakia	2	3	Free
Slovenia	1	2	Free
Solomon Islands	1	2	Free
Somalia	7	7	Not Free
South Africa	1▲	2▲	Free

Country	PR	CL	Freedom Rating
Spain	1	2	Free
Sri Lanka	4	5	Partly Free
⬇ Sudan	7	7	Not Free
Suriname	3	3	Partly Free
Swaziland	6	5	Not Free
Sweden	1	1	Free
Switzerland	1	1	Free
Syria	7	7	Not Free
Taiwan (Rep. of China)	3	3	Partly Free
Tajikistan	7	7	Not Free
Tanzania	5▲	5▲	Partly Free
Thailand	3	4▲	Partly Free
Togo	6	5	Not Free
Tonga	5	3	Partly Free
Trinidad and Tobago	1	2	Free
Tunisia	6	5	Not Free
Turkey	5	5	Partly Free
Turkmenistan	7	7	Not Free
Tuvalu	1	1	Free
Uganda	5	4▲	Partly Free
Ukraine	3	4	Partly Free
United Arab Emirates	6	5	Not Free
United Kingdom*	1	2	Free
United States	1	1	Free
Uruguay	2	2	Free
Uzbekistan	7	7	Not Free
Vanuatu	1	3	Free
Venezuela	3	3	Partly Free
Vietnam	7	7	Not Free
Western Samoa	2	2	Free
Yemen	5	6	Not Free
Yugoslavia (Serbia and Montenegro)	6	6	Not Free
Zaire	7	6	Not Free
⬇ Zambia	3	4	Partly Free
Zimbabwe	5	5	Partly Free

PR and CL stand for Political Rights and Civil Liberties. 1 represents the most free and 7 the least free category.

⬆⬇ up or down indicates a general trend in freedom.

▲▼ up or down indicates a significant change in Political Rights or Civil Liberties since the last *Survey.*

The Freedom Rating is an overall judgment based on *Survey* results. See the "Methodological Essay" for more details.

* Excluding Northern Ireland.

Table of Related Territories
Comparative Measures of Freedom

Country & Territory	PR	CL	Freedom Rating
Armenia/Azerbaijan*			
Nagorno-Karabakh	6▲	6▲	Not Free
Australia			
Christmas Island	3	2	Free
Cocos (Keeling) Islands**			Free
Norfolk Island**			Free
Chile			
Rapanui (Easter Island)**			Free
China			
Tibet	7	7	Not Free
Denmark			
Faeroe Islands	1	1	Free
Greenland	1	1	Free
Finland			
Aland Islands	1	1	Free
France			
French Guiana	1	2	Free
French Polynesia	1	2	Free
Guadeloupe	1	2	Free
Martinique	1	2	Free
Mayotte (Mahore)	1	2	Free
New Caledonia	2	2	Free
Reunion	2	2	Free
St. Pierre and Miquelon	1	1	Free
Wallis and Futuna Islands	2	2	Free
India			
Kashmir	7	7	Not Free
Indonesia			
East Timor	7	7	Not Free
West Papua (Irian Jaya)	7	7	Not Free
Iraq			
Kurdistan	4	4	Partly Free
Israel			
⬆ Occupied Territories and Palestinian Autonomous Areas	6	5	Not Free
Morocco			
Western Sahara	7	6	Not Free
Netherlands			
Aruba	2	1	Free
Netherlands Antilles	1	2	Free

Country & Territory	PR	CL	Freedom Rating
New Zealand			
Cook Islands	1	2	Free
Niue**			Free
Tokelau**			Free
Norway			
Svalbard**			Free
Portugal			
Azores	1	1	Free
Macao	6	4	Partly Free
Madeira	1	1	Free
Spain			
Canary Islands	1	1	Free
Ceuta	1	2	Free
Melilla	1	2	Free
Turkey			
Cyprus (T)	4	2	Partly Free
United Kingdom			
Anguilla	2	1	Free
Bermuda	1	1	Free
British Virgin Islands	1	1	Free
Cayman Islands	1	1	Free
Channel Islands	2	1	Free
Falkland Islands**			Free
Gibraltar	1	1	Free
Hong Kong	4▲	2	Partly Free
Isle of Man	1	1	Free
Montserrat	1	1	Free
⬆ Northern Ireland	4	3	Partly Free
Pitcairn Island**			Free
St. Helena and Dependencies	2	1	Free
Turks and Caicos	1	1	Free
United States of America			
American Samoa	1	1	Free
Guam	1	1	Free
Northern Marianas	1	2	Free
Puerto Rico	1	2	Free
U.S. Virgin Islands	1	1	Free
Yugoslavia			
Kosovo	7	7	Not Free

* Nagorno-Karabakh is disputed territory, contested by Armenia and Azerbaijan.

** Micro-territories have populations of under 5,000. These areas are scored according to the same methodology used in the rest of the *Survey*, but are listed separately due to their very small populations.

Table of Social and Economic Comparisons

Country	Real GDP per capita (PPP$)	Life expectancy	Country	Real GDP per capita (PPP$)	Life expectancy
Afghanistan	819	43.5	Czech Republic	7,690	71.3
Albania	3,500	72.0	Denmark	19,080	75.3
Algeria	4,870	67.1	Djibouti	1,547	48.3
Andorra	na	na	Dominica	3,526	72.0
Angola	751	46.5	Dominican	3,280	69.6
Antigua and	4,436	74.0	Republic		
Barbuda			Ecuador	4,350	68.8
Argentina	8,860	72.1	Egypt	3,540	63.6
Armenia	2,420	72.6	El Salvador	2,250	66.4
Australia	18,220	77.6	Equatorial	700	48.0
Austria	18,710	76.2	Guinea		
Azerbaijan	2,550	70.6	Eritrea	na	na
Bahamas	17,360	73.1	Estonia	6,690	69.3
Bahrain	14,590	71.6	Ethiopia	330	47.5
Bangladesh	1,230	55.6	Fiji	5,410	71.5
Barbados	9,667	75.6	Finland	16,270	75.7
Belarus	6,440	69.8	France	19,510	76.9
Belgium	18,630	76.4	Gabon	3,913	53.5
Belize	5,619	73.6	The Gambia	1,260	45.0
Benin	1,630	47.6	Georgia	2,300	72.8
Bhutan	750	50.7	Germany	21,120	76.0
Bolivia	2,410	59.4	Ghana	2,110	56.0
Bosnia-	na	70.0	Greece	8,310	77.6
Herzegovina			Grenada	3,822	70.0
Botswana	5,120	64.9	Guatemala	3,330	64.8
Brazil	5,240	66.3	Guinea	592	44.5
Brunei	20,589	74.2	Guinea-Bissau	820	43.5
Bulgaria	4,250	71.2	Guyana	1,800	65.2
Burkina Faso	810	47.4	Haiti	1,046	56.6
Burma	751	57.6	Honduras	2,000	67.7
Burundi	720	50.2	Hungary	6,580	69.0
Cambodia	1,250	51.6	Iceland	17,660	78.2
Cameroon	2,390	56.0	India	1,230	60.4
Canada	20,520	77.4	Indonesia	2,950	62.7
Cape Verde	1,750	64.7	Iran	5,420	67.5
Central African	1,130	49.4	Iraq	3,413	66.0
Republic			Ireland	12,830	75.3
Chad	760	47.5	Israel	14,700	76.5
Chile	8,410	73.8	Italy	18,090	77.5
China (P.R.C.)	1,950	68.5	Jamaica	3,200	73.6
Colombia	5,480	69.3	Japan	20,520	79.5
Comoros	1,350	56.0	Jordan	4,270	67.9
Congo	2,870	51.3	Kazakhstan	4,270	69.6
Costa Rica	5,480	76.3	Kenya	1,400	55.7
Côte d'Ivoire	1,710	51.0	Kiribati	na	54.0
Croatia	na	70.0	Korea, North	3,026	71.1
Cuba	3,412	75.3	Korea, South	9,250	71.1
Cyprus (G)	15,050	77.0	Kuwait	8,326	74.9

Note: Freedom House obtained the figures for purchasing power parities (PPP) and life expectancy from the U.N.'s *Human Development Report 1995* (UNDP/Oxford University Press, 1995). PPPs are real GDP per capita figures which economists have adjusted to account for detailed price comparisons of individual items covering over 150 categories of expenditure. The U.N. life expectancy figures represent overall expectancy, not differentiated by sex. In some cases not covered by the U.N., the chart lists a combined average of male and female life expectancy obtained from Rand McNally. For several countries the chart lists these combined averages.

Table of Social and Economic Comparisons

Country	Real GDP per capita (PPP$)	Life expectancy	Country	Real GDP per capita (PPP$)	Life expectancy
Kyrgyz Republic	2,850	69.0	St. Lucia	3,026	72.0
Laos	1,760	51.0	St. Vincent and the Grenadines	3,322	71.0
Latvia	6,060	69.1	San Marino	na	76.0
Lebanon	2,500	68.5	Sao Tome and Principe	600	67.0
Lesotho	1,060	60.5	Saudi Arabia	9,880	69.7
Liberia	1,045	55.4	Senegal	1,750	49.3
Libya	9,782	63.1	Seychelles	5,619	71.0
Liechtenstein	na	69.5	Sierra Leone	880	39.0
Lithuania	3,700	70.4	Singapore	18,330	74.8
Luxembourg	21,520	75.7	Slovakia	6,690	70.9
Macedonia	na	70.0	Slovenia	na	71.0
Madagascar	710	56.5	Solomon Islands	2,616	70.4
Malawi	820	45.6	Somalia	1,001	47.0
Malaysia	7,790	70.8	South Africa	3,799	62.9
Maldives	1,200	62.1	Spain	13,400	77.6
Mali	550	46.0	Sri Lanka	2,850	71.9
Malta	8,281	76.1	Sudan	1,620	53.0
Marshall Islands	na	72.5	Suriname	3,730	70.3
Mauritania	1,650	51.5	Swaziland	1,700	57.5
Mauritius	11,700	70.2	Sweden	18,320	78.2
Mexico	7,300	70.8	Switzerland	22,580	78.0
Micronesia	na	70.5	Syria	4,960	67.1
Moldova	3,670	67.6	Taiwan (Rep. of China)	na	74.5
Monaco	na	na	Tajikistan	1,740	70.2
Mongolia	2,389	63.7	Tanzania	620	52.1
Morocco	3,370	63.3	Thailand	5,950	69.0
Mozambique	380	46.4	Togo	1,220	55.0
Namibia	4,020	58.8	Tonga	na	74.5
Nauru	na	66.0	Trinidad and Tobago	9,760	71.6
Nepal	1,170	53.5	Tunisia	5,160	67.8
Netherlands	17,780	77.4	Turkey	5,230	66.5
New Zealand	14,990	75.5	Turkmenistan	3,400	65.0
Nicaragua	2,790	66.7	Tuvalu	na	61.0
Niger	820	46.5	Uganda	860	44.9
Nigeria	1,560	50.4	Ukraine	5,010	69.4
Norway	18,580	76.9	United Arab Emirates	21,830	73.8
Oman	11,710	69.6	United Kingdom*	17,160	76.2
Pakistan	2,890	61.5	United States	23,760	76.0
Palau	na	na	Uruguay	6,070	72.5
Panama	5,600	72.8	Uzbekistan	2,650	69.2
Papua New Guinea	2,410	55.8	Vanuatu	1,956	65.2
Paraguay	3,390	70.0	Venezuela	8,520	71.7
Peru	3,300	66.0	Vietnam	1,010	65.2
Philippines	2,550	66.3	Western Samoa	1,869	67.6
Poland	4,380	71.1	Yemen	2,410	50.2
Portugal	9,850	74.6	Yugoslavia (Serbia and Montenegro)	na	72.6
Qatar	22,380	70.5			
Romania	2,840	69.9	Zaire	523	52.0
Russia	6,140	67.6	Zambia	1,230	48.9
Rwanda	710	47.3	Zimbabwe	1,970	53.7
St. Kitts and Nevis	5,938	70.0			

Combined Average Ratings— Independent Countries

FREE

1.0
Andorra
Australia
Austria
Barbados
Belgium
Belize
Canada
Cyprus
Denmark
Dominica
Finland
Iceland
Ireland
Kiribati
Liechtenstein
Luxembourg
Malta
Marshall Islands
Micronesia
Netherlands
New Zealand
Norway
Portugal
San Marino
Sweden
Switzerland
Tuvalu
United States

1.5
Bahamas
Cape Verde
Costa Rica
Czech Republic
France
Germany
Grenada
Hungary
Italy
Japan
Lithuania
Mauritius
Monaco
Palau
Poland
St. Kitts and Nevis
St. Lucia
St. Vincent & Grenadines
Sao Tome and Principe
Slovenia
Solomon Islands
South Africa
Spain

Trinidad and Tobago
United Kingdom

2.0
Benin
Botswana
Bulgaria
Chile
Estonia
Greece
Guyana
Israel
Korea, South
Latvia
Nauru
Uruguay
Vanuatu
Western Samoa

2.5
Argentina
Ecuador
Jamaica
Malawi
Mali
Mongolia
Namibia
Panama
Slovakia

PARTLY FREE

3.0
Bolivia
Brazil
El Salvador
Honduras
Madagascar
Papua New Guinea
Philippines
Seychelles
Suriname
Taiwan
Venezuela

3.5
Albania
Antigua and Barbuda
Bangladesh
Central African Republic
Dominican Republic
Fiji
Guinea-Bissau
Macedonia
Mozambique

Nepal
Paraguay
Romania
Russia
Thailand
Ukraine
Zambia

4.0
Armenia
Colombia
Comoros
Congo
Croatia
Ghana
India
Jordan
Kyrgyz Republic
Lesotho
Mexico
Moldova
Nicaragua
Niger
Pakistan
Tonga

4.5
Burkina-Faso
Ethiopia
Gabon
Georgia
Guatemala
Malaysia
Peru
Senegal
Sri Lanka
Uganda

5.0
Belarus
Eritrea
Haiti
Kuwait
Morocco
Singapore
Tanzania
Turkey
Zimbabwe

NOT FREE

5.5
Chad
Côte d'Ivoire
Djibouti

Guinea
Kazakhstan
Lebanon
Swaziland
Togo
Tunisia
United Arab Emirates
Yemen

6.0
Algeria
Angola
Azerbaijan
Bahrain
Bosnia-Herzegovina
Brunei
Cambodia
Cameroon
Egypt
Maldives
Mauritania
Oman
Yugoslavia

6.5
Burundi
The Gambia
Indonesia
Iran
Kenya
Laos
Liberia
Qatar
Rwanda
Sierra Leone
Zaire

7.0
Afghanistan
Bhutan
Burma
China
Cuba
Equatorial Guinea
Iraq
Korea, North
Libya
Nigeria
Saudi Arabia
Somalia
Sudan
Syria
Tajikistan
Turkmenistan
Uzbekistan
Vietnam

Combined Average Ratings— Related Territories

FREE

1.0

Aland Islands (Finland)
American Samoa (U.S.)
Azores (Portugal)
Bermuda (U.K.)
British Virgin Islands (U.K.)
Canary Islands (Spain)
Cayman Islands (U.K.)
Faeroe Islands (Denmark)
Gibraltar (U.K.)
Greenland (Denmark)
Guam (U.S.)
Isle of Man (U.K.)
Madeira (Portugal)
Montserrat (U.K.)
St. Pierre and Miquelon (France)
Turks and Caicos (U.K.)
U.S. Virgin Islands (U.S.)

1.5

Anguilla (U.K.)
Aruba (Netherlands)
Ceuta (Spain)
Channel Islands (U.K.)
Cook Islands (New Zealand)
French Guiana (France)
French Polynesia (France)
Guadeloupe (France)

Martinique (France)
Mayotte (Mahore) (France)
Melilla (Spain)
Netherlands Antilles (Netherlands)
Northern Marianas (U.S.)
Puerto Rico (U.S.)
St. Helena & Dependencies (U.K.)

2.0

New Caledonia (France)
Reunion (France)
Wallis & Futuna Islands (France)

2.5

Christmas Island (Australia)

PARTLY FREE

3.0

Cyprus (Turkey)
Hong Kong (U.K.)

3.5

Northern Ireland (U.K)

4.0

Kurdistan (Iraq)

5.0

Macao (Portugal)

NOT FREE

5.5

Occupied Territories & Palestinian
   Autonomous Areas (Israel)

6.0

Nagorno-Karabakh (Armenia/
Azerbaijan)

6.5

Western Sahara (Morocco)

7.0

East Timor (Indonesia)
Kashmir (India)
Kosovo (Yugoslavia)
Tibet (China)
West Papua (Irian Jaya) (Indonesia)

MICRO-TERRITORIES (ALL FREE)*

Cocos (Keeling) Islands (Australia)
Falkland Islands (U.K.)
Niue (New Zealand)
Norfolk Island (Australia)
Pitcairn Islands (U.K.)
Rapanui (Easter Island) (Chile)
Svalbard (Norway)
Tokelau (New Zealand)

* Micro-territories have populations of under 5,000. These areas are
scored according to the same methodology used in the rest of the
Survey, but are listed separately due to their very small populations.

Sources

Publications, organizations

AFL-CIO
Agence France Presse
American Institute for Free Labor Development
Amnesty International *Urgent Action Bulletins*
Amnesty International: *Report 1995*
Armenian Information Service
Asian Bulletin
Asian Survey
Associated Press
The *Atlantic Monthly*
Azerbaijan International (U.S.)
Balkan Medja (Bulgaria)
Caretas (Lima)
Carib News
Caribbean Insight
Caribbean Review
Catholic Standard (Guyana)
Center for Strategic and International Studies
Centers for Pluralism: Newsletters (Poland)
Central America Report
Central Statistical Office, Warsaw (Poland)
Christian Science Monitor
Columbia Journalism Review
Commission on Security and Cooperation in Europe (CSCE):
    Implementation of the Helsinki Accords (Reports)
Committee to Protect Journalists *Update*
Dawn News Bulletin (All Burma Students Democratic Front)
Democratic Initiatives (Ukraine)
Eastern European Constitutional Review
The *Economist*
EFE Spanish news agency
El Financiero (Mexico City)
El Nuevo Herald (Miami)
Elections Canada
EPOCA (Mexico)
Equal Access Committee (Ukraine)
Ethiopian Review
Ethnic Federation of Romani (Romania)
Far Eastern Economic Review
Foreign Broadcast Information Service (FBIS):
    FBIS Africa
    FBIS China
    FBIS East Europe
    FBIS Latin America
    FBIS Near East & South Asia
    FBIS East Asia
    FBIS Soviet Union/Central Eurasia
    FBIS Sub-Saharan Africa
The *Financial Times*
Free Labour World
Free Trade Union Institute
The *Globe & Mail* (Toronto)
The *Guardian*
Hemisfile
Hemisphere
Himal
Hong Kong Digest
Immigration and Refugee Board of Canada
Index on Censorship
Indian Law Resource Center
Inter-American Dialogue

Inter-American Press Association
International Commission of Jurists
International Foundation for Electoral Systems (IFES)
International Republican Institute
The *Irish Echo*
The *Irish Voice*
Jeune Afrique
Journal of Commerce
Journal of Democracy
La Jornada (Mexico)
Latin American Regional Reports
Latin American Weekly Report
Lawyer to Lawyer Network (Lawyers Committee for Human Rights)
Los Angeles *Times*
Miami *Herald*
Middle East International
Milan Simecka Foundation (Slovakia)
Miist (Ukraine)
Monthly Digest of News from Armenia (Armenian Assembly of
    America)
The *Nation*
National Bank of Hungary (Monthly Reports)
National Democratic Institute for International Affairs
National Endowment for Democracy (U.S.)
New African
The *New Republic*
New York *Newsday*
New York *Times*
New Yorker
North-South Magazine
North-South Center (Miami)
Organization of American States
The *Other Side of Mexico* (Equipo Pueblo)
Pacific Islands Monthly
Political Handbook of the World: 1994-95
Political Handbook of the World: 1995-96
Proceso (Mexico City)
Reforma (Mexico)
Sposterihach (Ukraine)
State Department *Country Reports on Human Rights Practices for 1995*
The *Statesman*
Statistical Handbook 1994: States of the Former Soviet Union
    (World Bank)
Swiss Press Review
The *Tico Times* (Costa Rica)
The *Week in Germany*
U.S. News and World Report
Ukrainian Center for Independent Political Research
Ukrainian Press Agency
Ukrainian Weekly
Uncaptive Minds (Institute for Democracy in Eastern Europe)
UNDP *Human Development Report*
UNICEF
U.S. Committee for Refugees (Special Reports)
Vuelta (Mexico)
Wall Street Journal
Washington *Post*
Washington *Times*
West Africa
World Population Data Sheet 1995 (Population Reference
    Bureau)

Human Rights Organizations

Amnesty International
Andean Commission of Jurists
Bangladesh National Women Lawyers Association
Caribbean Institute for the Promotion of Human Rights
Caribbean Rights
Child Workers in Nepal
Chilean Human Rights Commission
Civic Alliance (Mexico)
Committee of Churches for Emergency Help (Paraguay)
Council for Democracy (Mexico)
Croatian Democracy Project (Croatia)
Cuban Commission for Human Rights and National
   Reconciliation
Cuban Committee for Human Rights
Democracy After Communism Foundation (Hungary)
Fray Bartocomé de Las Casas Center for Human Rights
   (Mexico)
Free and Democratic Bulgaria Foundation
Group for Mutual Support (Guatemala)
Guyana Human Rights Association
Haitian Center for Human Rights
Honduran Committee for the Defense of Human Rights
Human Rights Commission (El Salvador)
Human Rights Organization of Bhutan
Human Rights Organization of Nepal
Human Rights Commission of Pakistan
Human Rights Watch:
   Africa Watch
   Americas Watch
   Asia Watch

Helsinki Watch
Middle East Watch
Inform (Sri Lanka)
Inter-American Commission on Human Rights
Inter-Hemispheric Resource Center
International Human Rights Law Group
International Human Rights Law Group (Romania)
Jamaica Council for Human Rights
Latin American Association for Human Rights
Latin American Commission for Human Rights and Freedoms of
   the Workers
Latin American Ombudsmen Institute
Lawyers Committee for Human Rights
Mexican Human Rights Academy
National Coalition for Haitian Refugees
National Coordinating Office for Human Rights (Peru)
Panamanian Committee for Human Rights
Permanent Commission on Human Rights (Nicaragua)
Permanent Committee for the Defense of Human Rights
   (Colombia)
Physicians for Human Rights
Runejel Junam Council of Ethnic Communities (Guatemala)
Tibet Information Network
Tutela Legal (El Salvador)
Venezuelan Human Rights Education Action Program
Vicaria de la Solidaridad (Chile)
Vietnam Committee on Human Rights
Washington Office on Latin America
Women Acting Together for Change (Nepal)

Delegations/visitors to Freedom House

Africa/Middle East	Asia/Pacific	Central Europe	Former USSR	Western Hemisphere
Algeria	Australia	Albania	Russia	Cuba
Ethiopia	Bhutan	Czech Republic	Ukraine	Dominican Republic
Iran	Burma	Estonia		Guatemala
Iraq (Kurds)	Cambodia	Hungary		Haiti
Israel	East Timor	Poland		Mexico
Mali	Hong Kong	Romania		Peru
Mauritania	India			
Nigeria	Kashmir			
Turkey	Korea (South)			
	Nepal			
	Pakistan			
	Tibet			

Delegations and On-Site Staff Investigations from Freedom House to:

Azerbaijan	Korea (South)
Burkina Faso	Mauritania
Burma	Mexico
Cameroon	Nepal
Cote d'Ivoire	Russia
Cuba	Senegal
Egypt	South Africa
Eritrea	Tanzania
Ghana	Trinidad & Tobago
Haiti	Uganda
Kenya	Ukraine